In Conflict and Order

Understanding Society

In Conflict and Order
Understanding Society

Third Edition

D. Stanley Eitzen
Colorado State University

Allyn and Bacon, Inc.
Boston • London • Sydney • Toronto

To my parents, David and Amanda

Library of Congress Cataloging in Publication Data

Eitzen, D. Stanley.
  In conflict and order.

  Includes index.
    1. Sociology.   2. Social structure.   3. Social
psychology.   I. Title.
HM51.E336 1985   301   84-20475
ISBN 0-205-08273-4 (pbk.)

Printed in the United States of America

10 9 8 7 6 5 4 3 2   90 89 88 87 86 85

Photo credits   Chapter 1: © 1984 Susan Lapides.   Chapter 2: State Historical Society of Wisconsin.   Chapter 3: © Eli Reed/Magnum Photos.   Chapter 4: © Eugene Richards/Magnum Photos.   Chapter 5: © Antonio Mendoza/The Picture Cube.   Chapter 6: © 1978 Thomas Hopker/Woodfin Camp and Associates.   Chapter 7: © Ellis Herwig/The Picture Cube. Chapter 8: © Eric Roth/The Picture Cube.   Chapter 9: © Robert V. Eckert/The Picture Cube. Chapter 10: © Carrie Boretz/Archive Pictures.   Chapter 11: © Myron A. Lofts/The Picture Cube. Chapter 12: © John P. Cavanagh/Archive Pictures.   Chapter 13: © Christian Delbert/The Picture Cube.   Chapter 14: © Gerald Thomas/The Picture Cube.   Chapter 15: © 1981 Susan Lapides. Chapter 16: Ken Robert Buck.   Chapter 17: Yoichi R. Okamoto/Picture Researchers, Inc.

Contents

PREFACE xi

PROLOGUE: FROM AUTHOR TO READER xiii

Part 1 The Sociological Approach 1

1 THE SOCIOLOGICAL PERSPECTIVE 2

Assumptions of the Sociological Perspective 4
Problems with the Sociological Perspective 7
Sociological Methods: The Craft of Sociology 8
PANEL 1–1 Minimizing Bias 14
Summary 15
Chapter Review 16
For Further Study 17
Notes and References 17

2 THE STRUCTURE OF SOCIAL GROUPS 18

The Micro Level 20
The Social Structure of Society 32
Summary 37
Chapter Review 38
For Further Study 39
Notes and References 39

3 THE DUALITY OF SOCIAL LIFE: ORDER AND CONFLICT 42

Social Systems: Order and Conflict 44
Social Problems from the Order and Conflict Perspectives 48
Synthesis of the Order and Conflict Models 49
PANEL 3–1 Los Angeles and the New Immigrants 54
Summary 65
Chapter Review 66
For Further Study 66
Notes and References 67

4 THE QUALITY OF SOCIAL LIFE: STABILITY AND CHANGE 70

Change in Social Systems 73
Forces for Stability 73
PANEL 4–1 The Bureaucracy as a Rational Tool: The Organization of
  Power 76

PANEL 4–2 The Bureaucracy as an Irrational Tool: "Laws" Governing the
  Behavior in Bureaucracies 78
Forces for Change 79
Summary 95
Chapter Review 96
For Further Study 97
Notes and References 98

Part 2 The Individual in Society; Society in the Individual 101

5 CULTURE 102

Culture: The Knowledge That People Share 105
PANEL 5–1 The Kiss as a Cultural Creation 112
PANEL 5–2 Cultural Time 115
American Values 117
PANEL 5–3 The Giant Plates of Culture 127
PANEL 5–4 Participant Observation 134
Summary 135
Chapter Review 136
For Further Study 137
Notes and References 137

6 SOCIALIZATION 140

The Personality as a Social Product 145
PANEL 6–1 The Teaching of Prejudice 150
PANEL 6–2 What Is the Purpose of Education? 152
Similarities and Differences Among Members of Society 153
PANEL 6–3 Socialization of Children for the Future 156
Summary 157
Chapter Review 158
For Further Study 159
Notes and References 160

7 SOCIAL CONTROL IN SOCIETY 162

Agents of Ideological Social Control 164
PANEL 7–1 The Amish 166
PANEL 7–2 The Politics of the "Non-Partisan" Advertising Council 172
Agents of Direct Social Control 174
PANEL 7–3 The Control of Illicit Sex Among the Arabs 176
PANEL 7–4 The Sterilization Solution 179
PANEL 7–5 Genetic Control of Future Generations 186
Summary 187
Chapter Review 188

For Further Study 189
Notes and References 189

8 DEVIANCE 194

What is Deviance? 196
Traditional Theories for the Causes of Deviance 199
PANEL 8–1 The Lower-Class Propensity to Criminal Activity 204
Society as the Source of Deviance 210
PANEL 8–2 The Politics of Pot 220
PANEL 8–3 The Collective Effort to Change Society:
   The Gay Rights Movement 222
Summary 224
Chapter Review 226
For Further Study 227
Notes and References 228

Part 3 Social Inequality 233

9 THE AMERICAN SYSTEM OF SOCIAL STRATIFICATION 234

Major Concepts, Assumptions, and Theories 236
Social Classes in the United States 239
PANEL 9–1 Status Seeking Among the Kwakiutl 240
PANEL 9–2 The Structural Conditions for Class Consciousness
   Among the Proletariat: The Potential for Social Change 250
PANEL 9–3 The Criteria for Upper-Class Membership 253
Social Mobility 258
PANEL 9–4 Baby Boomers and Social Mobility: A Cohort Analysis 259
The Consequence of Socioeconomic Status 263
PANEL 9–5 Political Ideologies and Inequality 269
Summary 269
Chapter Review 270
For Further Study 271
Notes and References 271

10 POVERTY IN THE UNITED STATES 276

The Extent of Poverty in the United States 279
The Costs of Poverty 280
The Causes of Poverty 282
PANEL 10–1 Blaming the Poor 286
PANEL 10–2 Who Benefits from Poverty? 290
The Elimination of Poverty 292
PANEL 10–3 Poverty: The Problem and a Proposal 299
Summary 301

Chapter Review 302
For Further Study 302
Notes and References 303

11 RACIAL AND ETHNIC MINORITIES 306

The Characteristics of Minority Groups 310
Racial and Ethnic Groups 312
Explanations of Racial and Ethnic Inequality 320
PANEL 11–1 Scientific Reasoning 324
PANEL 11–2 The English Languages Is My Enemy 330
Discrimination Against Blacks and Hispanics: Continuity and Change 333
PANEL 11–3 Reverse Discrimination 340
Summary 343
PANEL 11–4 "I Have a Dream," Martin Luther King, Jr. 344
Chapter Review 346
For Further Study 347
Notes and References 348

12 SEX ROLES AND SEX STRATIFICATION 352

The Roles and Ranking of Women and Men 354
Sex Stratification from the Order and Conflict Perspectives 357
PANEL 12–1 Second-Class Citizens? 358
The Learning of Traditional Sex Roles 360
The Reinforcement of Male Dominance 369
PANEL 12–2 Sampling 374
Structured Sex Inequality 376
PANEL 12–3 Hierarchy and Work Behavior 382
The Costs and Consequences of Sexism 383
PANEL 12–4 Masculinity and Self-Destructive Behaviors 387
Fighting the System 388
PANEL 12–5 The Goals and Tactics of the Women's Movement 389
Summary 390
Chapter Review 391
For Further Study 392
Notes and References 392

Part 4 Social Institutions 399

13 THE AMERICAN ECONOMY 400

Capitalism and Socialism 403
The Corporation-Dominated Economy 405
Capitalism and Inequality 410
The Structural Transformation of the Economy: American
  Capitalism Crisis 414

Other Economic Problems   421
PANEL 13–1 A Marxian Analysis of Economic Depressions   422
Summary   430
Chapter Review   430
For Further Study   432
Notes and References   432

14   FAMILIES IN AMERICA   438

The Mythical American Family   438
American Families of the Past   441
Families in Contemporary American Society   444
PANEL 14–2 What Happened to American Households During the
  1970–1980 Decade   446
Changing Family Roles   452
PANEL 14–3 I Want a Wife   454
PANEL 14–4 Whose Family Is This, Anyway?   458
PANEL 14–5 Happiness Is a Good Job   462
The Modern Family from the Order and Conflict Perspectives   472
Families of the Future   474
Summary   474
Chapter Review   475
For Further Study   477
Notes and References   477

15   EDUCATION IN AMERICA   482

The Characteristics of American Education   484
PANEL 15–1 "The Politics of the Classroom"   485
PANEL 15–2 Cooling Out the Failures   488
The Political Economy of Education in Corporate Society   491
Education and Inequality   493
Possible Ways to Promote Equality of Opportunity   502
Education from the Order and Conflict Perspectives   509
Chapter Review   510
For Further Study   511
Notes and References   511

16   RELIGION IN AMERICA   514

PANEL 16–1 The Cargo Cult of Melanesia   516
PANEL 16–2 Holy Tortilla   517
Religion from the Order Perspective of Emile Durkheim   519
Religion from the Conflict Perspective of Karl Marx   520
Some Distinctive Features of American Religion   520
Religious Trends   529
PANEL 16–3 The Freedom of Youth to Differ from Their Parents   533
The Role of the Church: Comfort or Challenge?   534

PANEL 16–4 The Church and the Establishment 538
Summary 539
Chapter Review 540
For Further Study 541
Notes and References 541

17 THE STRUCTURE OF POWER IN AMERICAN SOCIETY 544

Models of the National Power Structure 546
PANEL 17–1 The Antinuclear Movement 553
PANEL 17–2 Reagan's Ruling Class 565
The Consequences of the National Power Structure 571
PANEL 17–3 The Framers of the Constitution: Plotters or Patriots? 572
Conclusion 579
Chapter Review 582
For Further Study 583
Notes and References 583

EPILOGUE 587
GLOSSARY 588
INDEX 596

Preface

This is *not* a *traditional* textbook for the introductory course in sociology. Several foci separate it from most mainstream books. Foremost, the book examines social organizations from a critical perspective. Far from a dispassionate description of the way things are, this book enumerates the positive *and* negative consequences of social structure. The book will introduce sociology, then, by showing how structure is important and necessary while simultaneously leading to social problems. This view of social life provides an integrated framework that will aid the reader in developing a sociological perspective. The book is designed to provide a coherent, consistent, and critical view of society.

Many introductory students will only be exposed to sociology once. They should leave that course with a new and meaningful way of understanding themselves, others, and society. The most fundamental goal of this book is to assist the student in developing a sociological perspective—all else is secondary.

I have made the following major changes for this third edition.

1. The materials have been updated, using the latest census data.

2. One chapter has been added—"Education in America."

3. Two chapters—socialization and sex roles/sex stratification—have been combined into one—"Sex Roles and Sex Stratification." This act was not meant to minimize these crucial topics but was done in response to the suggestions of many instructors who felt that the original division was artificial.

4. The chapters on stratification, poverty, race, family, and the economy have been reworked substantially.

5. New topics that have been added include: the structural transformation of the economy, the politics of advertising, the public and private invasion of individual privacy, the gay rights movement, the contemporary structural conditions of class consciousness, the feminization of poverty, Reaganomics, the discrimination against native Americans, colonial theory, affirmative action, the segmented labor markets, the mechanisms that reinforce male dominance, capitalist patriarchy, the politics of the mainline churches, the political economy of education, the social class bias of the educational system, the funding of public education, the mechanisms to promote equality of opportunity in education, megamergers, interlocking directorates, the robotization of the workplace, the changing composition of the labor force, deindustrialization, the impact of Political Action Committees, the antinuclear movement, civil disobedience, and the class bias of the framers of the Constitution.

6. New boxed materials have been added to show that people can organize to counteract and change existing social arrangements. These make the point

that while there are strong social forces impinging on individuals, their behaviors are not totally controlled. People are not only the products of society but also its architects.

Although the final responsibility for this book is mine, it reflects the influence, work, and support of many persons. I am indebted to a number of scholars—Marvin Olsen, Peter Berger, William Ryan, Jerome Skolnick, Michael Parenti, Michael Harrington, Barry Bluestone, and Bennett Harrison—whose ideas I have incorporated. I am especially indebted to Maxine Baca Zinn, my co-author on another project, who has had a substantial impact on this new edition. In addition to her constructive criticisms and valuable suggestions, she wrote the chapter on the family and combined and revised the chapters on sex roles and sexism.

Prologue:
From Author to Reader

When I took my first course in sociology in 1953, the approach, typical of that day, emphasized the formal theoretical concepts of the discipline in a manner equivalent to premed courses. The result was that most students were left with the impression that sociology was composed of unrelated concepts, that it made simple events into abstract "principles," and that it had no meaning for their lives. By the time I had taught my first college course in sociology in 1967, a new approach was in ascendancy. In contrast to the tedious, concept-memorizing approach, the new mode was to make sociology relevant at all costs. The topics considered centered on such issues as racism, imperialism, gay rights, pornography, victimless crimes, welfare mothers, and alternative life-styles. While classes using this approach were interesting, the students were frequently left with little else than unrelated facts and titillating anecdotes. These students, as did the students of my day, had a serious failing—the inability to understand the importance of social factors in explaining the behavior of individuals and groups and to apply sociological explanations to new issues as they arise.[1]

This book will attempt to provide the student with the best of these two approaches while eliminating their weaknesses. The concepts of sociology are important to understand—but not as representing unrelated social phenomena. Social life coheres, and so should the concepts that identify its structure and processes. Sociology is inherently interesting, fascinating, relevant, and exciting, and any text that does not convey these qualities is misrepresenting and betraying the discipline.

The ultimate objectives of this book are to provide the reader with (1) an intuitive grasp of the sociological perspective; and (2) a consistent framework from which to view, understand, and interpret social life. The first goal, the adoption of the sociological perspective, will be emphasized explicitly in the first chapter and implicitly throughout the book. The sociological perspective focuses on the social sources of behavior. It requires the shedding of existing myths and ideologies by questioning all social arrangements. One of the most persistent questions of the sociologist is: Who benefits from the existing customs and social order and who does not? Since social groups are created by people, they are not sacred. Is there a better way? One editorial writer has posed a number of questions that illustrate the critical approach typical of the sociological perspective:

> Must we [Americans] try to perpetuate our global empire, maintaining far-flung military outposts, spending billions on the machinery of death, meddling in the affairs of other nations—or is there a better way? Must we con-

tinue to concentrate power and wealth in the hands of a few, preserving the income gaps that have remained virtually undisturbed through the New Deal, Fair Deal, New Frontier, and Great Society—or is there a better way? Must millions of our people be subjected to the cruel displacements of an irrational economy—or is there a better way? Must we stand by while our liberties are undermined, our resources squandered, our environment polluted—or is there a better way? Must private profit be the nation's driving force—or is there a better way?[2]

Although there will be disagreement on the answers to these questions, the answers are less important, sociologically, than the willingness to call into question existing social arrangements that many people consider sacred. This is the beginning of the sociological perspective. But being critical is not enough. The sociologist must have a coherent way to make sense of the social world, and this leads us to the second goal of this book—the elaboration of a consistent framework from which to understand and interpret social life.

This book is guided by the assumption that there is an inherent duality in all societies. The realistic analysis of any one society must include both the integrating and stabilizing forces, on the one hand, and the forces that are conducive to malintegration and change, on the other. American society is characterized by harmony *and* conflict; integration *and* division; stability *and* change. This synthesis is crucial if the intricacies of social structure, the mechanisms of social change, and the sources of social problems are to be understood fully.

This objective of achieving a balance between the order and conflict perspectives is not fully realized in this book, however. Although both perspectives are incorporated into each chapter, the scales tend to be tipped in favor of the conflict perspective. This slight imbalance is the conscious product of the way I, as author and teacher, view the structure and mechanisms of society. In addition to presenting what I think is a realistic analysis of society, it counters the prevailing view presented in contemporary sociology textbooks—the order perspective with its implicit sanctification of the status quo. Such a stance is untenable to me, given the spate of social problems that persist in American society. The emphasis of the conflict approach, on the other hand, questions the existing social arrangements, viewing them as sources of social problems, a position with which I agree. Implicit in such a position is the goal of restructuring society along more humane lines.

That I stress the conflict approach over the order model does not suggest that this book is a polemic. To the contrary, the social structure is also examined from a sympathetic view. The existing arrangements do provide for the stability and maintenance of the system. But the point is that by including a relatively large dose of the conflict perspective the discussion *is* a realistic appraisal of the system rather than a look through rose-colored glasses.

This duality theme will be shown primarily at the societal level in this book. But while the societal level is the focus of our inquiry, the small group and individual levels are not ignored. The principles that apply to societies are also appropriate for the small social organizations to which we belong, such as families, work groups, athletic teams, churches, and clubs. Just as important, the sociological perspective shows how the individual is affected by groups of all sizes. Moreover, it shows how the identity of the individual is shaped by social forces and how in many important ways the individual's thoughts and actions are determined by group memberships.

The linkage of the individual to social groups will be shown throughout the book. The relationship of the individual to the larger society will be illustrated by special panels. These will examine how societal changes and forces impinge on individuals and the choices available to us as we attempt to cope with these societal trends.

The book is divided into four parts. Part 1 introduces the reader to the sociological perspective, the fundamental concepts of the discipline, and the duality of social life. These chapters will set the stage for an analysis of the structure (organization) and process (change) of American society. The emphasis will be on the characteristics of societies in general and the United States in particular.

Part 2 describes the way human beings are shaped by society. The topics include the values that direct our choices, the social bases of social identity and personality, the mechanisms that control individual and group behavior, and the violation of social expectations—deviance. Throughout this section we examine the forces that, on the one hand, work to make all Americans similar and those that, on the other hand, make us different.

Part 3 examines in detail the various forms of social inequality present in American society. The opening chapter deals with how societies rank people in hierarchies. Also examined are the mechanisms that ensure that some people have a greater share of wealth, power, and prestige than others and the positive and negative consequences of such an arrangement. Other chapters focus on the specific aspects of stratification—poverty, racism, and sexism.

Part 4 discusses another characteristic of all societies—the presence of social institutions. Every society has developed historically a fairly consistent way of meeting its survival needs and those of its members. The family, for example, ensures the regular input of new members, provides for the stable care and protection of the young, and regulates sexual activity. In addition to the family, a separate chapter is devoted to religion, to education, to the economy, and to the polity. The understanding of institutions is vital to the understanding of society because these social arrangements are part of its structure, resist change, and have such a profound impact on the public and private lives of people.

The sociological analysis of American society is especially important and interesting now because of a unique combination of historical and structural factors. No American generation but the present has faced possible extinction from the effects of nuclear weapons and ecological disasters. No American generation but the present has faced the possibility of a future with severe energy and resource shortages that threaten the American values of progress, growth, and materialism. No generation but the present has grown up with the instant history and the constant violence of television. No generation has undergone such a rapid rate of change. The trend toward greater bureaucratization continues in business, religion, labor, school, sport, and government. All Americans are caught in its impersonal clutches. And, for the first time in American history young people face the prospect of being less successful than their parents.

While these and other changes have occurred with fantastic speed, American institutions have become afflicted with old age, unwilling to change. The intransigence of American institutions in the face of rapid social and technological change has caused a gap which, if not breached, will lead to increasing despair, discontent, alienation, and hostility by dislocated individuals and perhaps the ultimate demise of society.

The problems of American society are of great magnitude, and solutions must be found. But understanding must precede action—and that is one goal of this book.

The analysis of American society is a challenging task. It is frustrating because of the heterogeneity of the population and the complexity of the forces impinging upon American social life. It is frustrating because the diversity within the United States leads to many inconsistencies and paradoxes. Furthermore, it is difficult if not impossible for an American to be objective and consistently rational about his or her society. Nevertheless, the sociological study of American society is fascinating and rewarding. It becomes absorbing as one gains insights about his or her own actions and the behavior of others. Understanding the intricate complex of forces leading to a particular type of social structure or social problem can be liberating and lead toward collective efforts to bring about social change. This book attempts to give the reader just such a sociological perspective.

Finally, I am unabashedly proud of being a sociologist. My hope is that you will capture some of my enthusiasm for exploring and understanding the intricacies and mysteries of social life.

NOTES AND REFERENCES

1. For a critique of past approaches and a plea for one similar to that used in this volume, see Amitai Etzioni, "The Importance of Humanistic Sociology," *The Chronical of Higher Education* (Janury 19), 1976, p. 32.

2. "Voting for What We Want," *The Progressive* (November, 1976), p. 5.

Part 1

The Sociological Approach

1

The Sociological
Perspective

Life appears to be a series of choices for each of us. We decide how much schooling is important and what to major in. We choose a job, a mate, and a lifestyle. But how free are we? Have you ever felt trapped by events and conditions beyond your control? Your religious beliefs may make you feel guilty for some behaviors. Your patriotism may cost you your life—even willingly. These ideological traps are powerful, so powerful that we usually do not even see them as traps.

Have you ever felt trapped in a social relationship? Have you ever continued a relationship with a friend, group of friends, lover, or spouse when you were convinced that it was wrong for you? Have you ever participated in an act because others wanted you to that later seemed absolutely ridiculous, even immoral? Most likely your answers to these questions are in the affirmative because those closest to us effectively command our conformity.

At another level, have you ever felt that because of your race, gender, age, ethnicity, or social class certain opportunities were closed to you? For example, if you are a black football player certain positions on the team (usually quarterback, center, offensive guard, and kicker) will very likely be closed to you regardless of your abilities. If you are a white male, affirmative action legislation has reduced your advantage in the job market. As a female you may want to try certain sports or jobs but to do so is to call your "femininity" into question.

Even more remotely, each of us is controlled by decisions made in corporate boardrooms, in government bureaus, and in foreign capitals. Our tastes in style are decided on and manipulated by corporate giants through the media. High interest rates affect individual workers and their families in the housing and automobile industries by increasing unemployment. A war in the Middle East reduces the supply of oil and the price rises dramatically, restricting personal use here in the United States. That same war may mean that you will be called to action because you are the right age and sex. The weather in China and Russia affects grain prices in the United States, meaning bankruptcy or prosperity for individual farmers and high or low prices for individual consumers.

Finally, we are also trapped by our culture. We do not decide what is right or wrong, moral or immoral. These are decided for us and incorporated inside us. We do not decide what is beautiful and what is not. Even the decision on

what is important and what is not is a cultural bias embedded deep inside each of us.

Sociology is the science dealing with social forces—the forces outside us that shape our very lives, interests, and personalities. As the science of society and social behavior, sociology is interesting, insightful, and important. This is because sociology explores and analyzes the ultimate issues of our personal lives, of society, and of the world. At the personal level sociology investigates the causes and consequences of such phenomena as romantic love, violence, identity, conformity, deviance, personality, and interpersonal power. At the societal level sociology examines and explains poverty, crime rates, racism, sexism, pollution, and political power. At the global level sociology researches such phenomena as war, conflict resolution, and population growth. While other disciplines are also helpful in the understanding of these social phenomena, sociology makes a unique contribution.

The insights of sociology are important for the individual because they help us understand why we behave as we do. This understanding is not only liberating but is a necessary precondition for meaningful social action to bring social change. As a scholarly discipline, sociology is important because it complements and in some cases supersedes other disciplines concerned with understanding and explaining social behavior.

ASSUMPTIONS OF THE SOCIOLOGICAL PERSPECTIVE

To discover the underlying order of social life and the principles that explain human behavior, scientists have focused on different levels of phenomena. The result of this division of labor has been the creation of scholarly disciplines, each concentrating on a relatively narrow sphere of phenomena.

Biologists interested in social phenomena have focused on the organic bases for behavior. Psychological explanations assume the source of human behavior in the psyches of individuals.

The understanding of human behavior benefits from the emphases of the various disciplines. Each makes important contributions to knowledge. Of the three major disciplines focusing on human behavior, sociology is commonly the least understood. The explicit goal of this book is to remedy this fault by introducing the reader to the sociological ways of perceiving and interpreting the social world. Let us begin by considering the assumptions of the sociological approach that provide the foundation for this unique, exciting, and insightful way of viewing the world.

Individuals are, by their nature, social beings. There are two fundamental reasons for this assumption. First, children enter the world totally dependent on others for their survival. This initial period of dependence means, in effect, that each of us has been immersed in social groups from birth. A second basis for the social nature of human beings is that throughout history people have found it to their advantage to cooperate with others (for defense, for material comforts, to overcome the perils of nature, and to improve technology).

Individuals are, for the most part, socially determined. This essential assumption stems from the first, that people are social beings. Individuals are products of their social environments for several reasons. During infancy, the child is at the mercy of adults, especially parents. These persons can shape the infant in an infinite variety of ways, depending on their proclivities and those of their society. The parents will have a profound impact on that child's ways of thinking about himself/herself and about others. The parents will transmit religious views, political attitudes, and attitudes toward how other groups are to be rated. The child will be punished for certain behaviors and rewarded for others. Whether that child becomes a bigot or integrationist, traditionalist or innovator, saint or sinner, depends in large measure on the parents, peers, and others who interact with him or her.

The parents may transmit to their offspring some idiosyncratic beliefs and behaviors, but most significantly they act as cultural agents, transferring the ways of the society to their children. Thus, the child is born into a family but also into a society. This society into which the individuals are born shapes their personality and perceptions. Berger has summarized the impact of this in the following:

> Society not only controls our movements, but shapes our identity, our thoughts and our emotions. The structures of society become the structures of our own consciousness. Society does not stop at the surface of our skins. Society penetrates us as much as it envelops us.[1]

The individual's identity is socially bestowed. Who we are, how we feel about ourselves, and how others treat us are typically consequences of our location in society. Individuals' personalities are also shaped by the way we are accepted, rejected, and/or defined by others. Whether an individual is attractive or plain, witty or dull, worthy or unworthy, depends on the values of society and the groups in which the individual is immersed. Although genes determine one's physiology and potential, the social environment determines how those characteristics will be evaluated.

Suggesting that human beings are socially determined is another way of saying that they are similar to puppets. They are dependent on and manipulated by social forces. A major function of sociology is to identify the social forces that affect us so greatly. Freedom, as McGee has pointed out, can only come from a recognition of these unseen forces:

> Freedom consists in knowing what these forces are and how they work so that we have the option of saying no to the impact of their operation. For example, if we grow up in a racist society, we will be racists unless we learn what racism is and how it works and then choose to refuse its impact. In order to do so, however, we must recognize that it is there in the first place. People often are puppets, blindly danced by strings of which they are unaware and over which they are not free to exercise control. A major function of sociology is that it permits us to recognize the forces operative on us and to untie the puppet strings which bind us, thereby giving us the option to be free.[2]

So, one task of sociology is to learn, among other things, what racism is and to determine how it works. This is often difficult because we typically do not recognize its existence—because we have been puppets, socialized to believe and behave in particular ways.

To say that we are puppets is too strong. This assumption is not meant to imply a total **social determinism**.* The metaphor is used to convey the idea that much of who we are and what we do is a product of our social environment. But there are nonconformists, deviants, and innovators. Society is not a rigid, static entity composed of robots. While the members of society are shaped by their social environment, they also change that environment. Human beings are the *shapers* of society as well as the *shapees*. This is the third assumption of the sociological approach.

Individuals create, sustain, and change the social forms within which they conduct their lives. While individuals are largely puppets of society, they are also puppeteers. Chapter 2 will describe this process of how people in interaction are the architects of society. In brief, the argument is that social groups of all sizes and types (families, peer groups, work groups, corporations, communities, and societies) are made by people. What interacting persons create becomes a source of control over those individuals (that is, they become puppets of their own creation). But the continuous interaction of the group's members also changes the group.

There are three important implications of this assumption that groups are human-made. First, these social forms that are created have a certain momentum of their own that defies change. The ways of doing and thinking

---

*Advocates of social determinism are guilty of oversimplifying complex phenomena, just as are genetic determinists, psychological determinists, geographical determinists, and economic determinists.

common to the group are "natural" and "right." Although human-made, the group's expectations and structures take on a sacred quality—the sanctity of tradition—that constrains behavior in the socially prescribed ways.

A second implication is that social organizations, because they are created and sustained by people, are imperfect. Slavery benefited some segments of society by taking advantage of others. A competitive free enterprise system creates "winners" and "losers." The wonders of technology make worldwide transportation and communication easy and relatively inexpensive but create pollution and waste of natural resources. These examples show that there are positive and negative consequences of the way people have organized.

A final implication is that individuals through collective action are capable of changing the structure of society and even the course of history.[3]

PROBLEMS WITH THE SOCIOLOGICAL PERSPECTIVE

Sociology is not a comfortable discipline and therefore will not appeal to everyone. To look behind the "closed doors" of social life is fraught with danger. The astute observer of society must ask such questions as: How does it really work? Who really has the power? Who benefits under the existing social arrangements and who does not? To ask such questions means that the inquirer is interested in looking beyond the commonly accepted "official" definitions. As Berger has put it, "[the] sociological perspective involves a process of 'seeing through' the facades of social structures."[4] The underlying assumption of the sociologist is that things are *not* as they seem. Is the mayor of your town the most powerful person in the community? Is the system of justice truly just? Is professional sport free of racism? Is the United States a meritocratic society where talent and effort combine to stratify the people fairly? To make such queries is to call into question existing myths, stereotypes, and official dogma. The critical examination of society will demystify and demythologize. It sensitizes the individual to the inconsistencies present in society. Clearly that will result if you ask: Why does the United States, in the name of freedom, protect dictatorships around the world? Why do we encourage subsidies to the affluent but resent those directed to the poor? Why was Richard Nixon pardoned while his lackeys who followed orders in the Watergate situation were penalized? How powerful would Ted Kennedy be if his surname were Garcia? Why have over 50 percent of those killed by capital punishment in the United States been black? Why are many women opposed to the Equal Rights Amendment? Why in a democracy such as the United States are there so few truly democratic organizations?

The sociological assumption that provides the basis for this critical stance is that the social world is human-made—and therefore not sacred. The beliefs, the economic system, the law, the way power is distributed are created and sustained by people. They can, therefore, be changed by people. But if the change is to correct imperfections, then we must truly understand how social phenomena work. The central task of this book is to aid in such an understanding of American society.

The sociological perspective is also discomforting to many because the understanding of the constraints of society is liberating. Traditional sex roles, for example, are no longer "sacred" for many persons. But while this is liberating from the constraints of tradition, it is also freedom from the protection that custom provides. The robotlike acceptance of tradition is comfortable because it frees us from choice (and therefore blame) and from ambiguity. So the understanding of society is a two-edged sword, freeing us, but also increasing the probability of frustration, anger, and alienation.

Sociology is also uncomfortable because the behavior of the subjects is not always certain. Prediction is not always accurate, because people can choose between options or be persuaded by irrational factors. The result is that if sociologists know the social conditions, they can predict, but in terms of probabilities. In chemistry, on the other hand, scientists know exactly what will occur if a certain measure of sodium is mixed with a precise amount of chlorine in a test tube. Civil engineers armed with the knowledge of rock formations, type of soils, wind currents, and temperature extremes know exactly what specifications are needed in building a dam in a certain place. They could not, however, if the foundation and building materials kept shifting. That is the problem—and the source of excitement— for the sociologist. The political proclivities of Americans over the past few decades offer a good example of shifting attitudes. In 1964 the Republican candidate for President, Barry Goldwater, was soundly defeated and many observers predicted the demise of the Republican Party. But in 1968, Richard Nixon, the Republican, won. He won again in 1972 by a record-setting margin, leading to the prognostication that the Democratic Party would no longer be viable. Two years later, however, Nixon resigned in disgrace and in 1976 the Democratic candidate, Jimmy Carter, was the victor. In 1980 President Carter was defeated by Ronald Reagan and a number of liberal Senators were defeated by conservatives, leading many observers to predict the demise of liberalism. These dramatic political shifts illustrate that social life is highly complex and its study is beset by change and uncertainties. Although the goal is to reduce the margin of error, its complete elimination is impossible as long as human beings are not robots.

SOCIOLOGICAL METHODS: THE CRAFT OF SOCIOLOGY

Sociology is dependent on reliable data and logical reasoning. These necessities are possible, but there are problems that must be acknowledged. Before we describe the ways that sociologists use to gather reliable data and make valid conclusions, let's examine, in some detail, two major obstacles.

Problems in Collecting Data

A fundamental problem with the sociological perspective is that bane of the social sciences—objectivity. We are *all* guilty of harboring stereotyped conceptions of social categories such as blacks, hard hats, professors, homosexuals, fundamentalists, business tycoons, communists, jet-setters, and jocks. Moreover, we interpret people's behavior, events, and material objects

through the perceptual filter of our religious and political beliefs. When fundamentalists oppose the use of certain books in school, when abortion is approved by a legislature, when the President advocates cutting billions from the Federal budget by eliminating social services, or when the Supreme Court denies private schools the right to exclude certain racial groups, then most of us rather easily take a position in the ensuing debate.

Sociologists are caught in a dilemma. On the one hand, they are members of society with beliefs, feelings, and biases. At the same time, though, their professional task is to study society in a disciplined (scientific) way. This latter requirement is that scientist-scholars be dispassionate, objective observers. In short, if they take sides, they lose their status as scientists.

This ideal of **value neutrality** can be attacked from three positions. The first is that scientists should not be morally indifferent to the implications of their research. Gouldner has argued this in the following statement:

It would seem that social science's affinity for modeling itself after physical science might lead to instruction in matters other than research alone. Before Hiroshima, physicists also talked of a value-free science; they, too, vowed to make no value judgments. Today many of them are not so sure. If we today concern ourselves exclusively with the technical proficiency of our students and reject all responsibility for their moral sense, or lack of it, then we may someday be compelled to accept responsibility for having trained a generation willing to serve in a future Auschwitz. Granted that science always has inherent in it both constructive and destructive potentialities. It does not follow from this that we should encourage our students to be oblivious to the difference.[5]

The second argument against the purely neutral position is that such a stance is impossible. Becker, among others, has argued that there is no dilemma—because it is impossible to do research that is uncontaminated by personal and political sympathies.[6] This argument is based on several related assumptions. One is that the values of the scholar–researcher enter into the choice of what questions will be asked and how they will be answered. For example, in the study of poverty a critical decision involves the object of the study—the poor or the system that tends to perpetuate poverty among a certain segment of society. Or, in the study of the problems of youth, we can ask either: Why are some youth troublesome for adults, or, alternatively, why do adults make so much trouble for youth? In both illustrations there are quite different questions that will yield very different results.

Similarly, our values lead us to decide from which vantage point we will gain access to information about a particular social organization. If researchers want to understand how a prison operates, they must determine whether they want a description from the inmates, from the guards, from the prison administrators, or from the state board of corrections. Each view provides useful insights about a prison, but obviously a biased one. If the researchers obtain data from more than one of these levels, they are faced with making assessments as to which is the more accurate view, clearly another place in the research process where the values of the observers will have an impact.

Perhaps the most important reason why the study of social phenomena cannot be value-free is that the type of problems researched and the strategies employed tend either to support the existing societal arrangements or to undermine them. Seen in this way, social research of both types is political. Ironically, however, there is a strong tendency to label only the research aimed at changing the system as political. By the same token, whenever the research sides with the underdog, the implication is that the hierarchical system is being questioned—thus, the charge that this type of research is biased. Becker has provided us with the logic of this in the following:

When do we accuse ourselves and our fellow sociologists of bias? I think an inspection of representative instances would show that the accusation arises, in one important class of cases, when the research gives credence, in any serious way, to the perspective of the subordinate group in some hierarchical relationship. In the case of deviance, the hierarchical relationship is a moral one. The superordinate parties in the relationships are those who represent the forces of approved and official morality; the subordinate parties are those who, it is alleged, have violated that morality.[7]

It is odd that, when we perceive bias, we usually see it in these circumstances. It is odd because it is easily ascertained that a great many more studies are biased in the direction of the interests of responsible officials than the other way around.[8]

In summary, bias is inevitable in the study and analysis of social problems. The choice of a research problem, the perspective from which one analyzes the problems, and the solutions proposed all reflect a bias that is either supportive of the existing social arrangements or not. Moreover, unlike biologists, who can dispassionately observe the behavior of an amoeba under a microscope, sociologists are participants in the social life they seek to study and understand. As they study the busing riots in South Boston, children living in poverty, or urban blight, sociologists cannot escape from their own feelings and values. They must, however, not let their feelings and values render their analysis invalid. In other words, research and reports of research must "tell it like it is," not as the researcher might want it to be. Sociologists must display scientific integrity, which requires recognizing biases in such a way that they do not invalidate the findings.[9] Properly done in this spirit, an atheist can study a religious sect, a pacifist can study the military–industrial complex, a divorcee can study marriage, and a person who abhors the political stance of the Moral Majority can study that phenomenon in American politics.

In addition to bias, people gather data and make generalizations about social phenomena in a number of faulty ways. In a sense everyone is a "scientist" seeking to find valid generalizations to guide their behavior and make sense of their world. But most people are, in fact, very unscientific about the social world. The first problem, as we have noted, is the problem of bias. The second is that people tend to generalize from their experience. Not only is one's interpretation of things that happen to him or her subjective, but there is a basic problem of sampling. The chances are that one's experience will be too idiosyncratic to allow for an accurate generalization. For example, if you and your friends agree that abortion is appropriate, that does not mean that others in the society, even those of your age, will agree with you. Very likely, your friends are quite similar to you on such dimensions as socioeconomic status, race, religion, and geographic location. Another instance of faulty sampling leading to faulty generalizations is when we make assumptions from a single case. An individual may argue that blacks can make it economically in this country as easily as whites because he or she knows a wealthy black person. Similarly, one might argue that all Chicanos are dumb because the one you know is in the slowest track in high school. This type of reasoning is especially fallacious because it blames the victim.[10] The cause of poverty or crime or dropping out of school or scoring low on an IQ test is seen as a result of the flaw in the individual, ignoring the substantial impact of the economy or school.

Another typical way that we explain social behavior is to use some authority other than our senses. The Bible, for example, has been used by many persons to support or condemn certain activities, such as slavery, capital punishment, war, or monogamy. The Bible, however, is ambiguous on many subjects, offering contradictory statements. The media provide other sources of authority for individuals. The media, however, are not always reliable sources of facts either. Stories are often selected because they are unusually dramatic, giving the faulty impression of, for example, a crime wave or questionable air safety.

Finally, we use aphorisms to explain many social occurrences. The problem with this common tactic is that society supplies us with ready explanations that fit contradictory situations and are therefore useless. For instance, if we know a couple who are alike in religion, race, socioeconomic status, and political attitudes, that makes sense to us because "birds of a feather flock together." But the opposite situation also makes sense. If a couple are very different on a number of dimensions, we can explain this by the obvious explanation—"opposites attract." There are a number of other proverbs that we use to explain behavior. The only problem is that there is often a proverb or aphorism to explain either of two extremes:

Absence makes the heart grow fonder.
Out of sight, out of mind.

Look before you leap.
He who hesitates is lost.

Familiarity breeds contempt.
To know her is to love her.

Women are unpredictable.
Isn't that just like a woman.

You can't teach an old dog new tricks.
It's never too late to learn.

Above all, to thine own self be true.
When in Rome, do as the Romans do.

Variety is the spice of life.
Never change horses in the middle of the stream.

Two heads are better than one.
If you want something done right, do it yourself.

You can't tell a book by its cover.
Clothes make the man.

Many hands make light work.
Too many cooks spoil the broth.

Better safe than sorry.
Nothing ventured, nothing gained.

Haste makes waste.
Strike while the iron is hot.

Work for the night is coming.
Eat, drink and be merry for tomorrow you may die.

> There's no place like home.
> The grass is always greener on the other side of the fence.

These contradictory explanations are commonly used and, of course, explain nothing. The job of the sociologist is to specify under what conditions certain rates of social behaviors occur.

Sources of Data

Sociologists do not use aphorisms to explain behavior nor do they speculate based on faulty samples or authorities. Because we are part of the world that is to be explained, sociologists must get evidence that is beyond reproach. In addition to observing scrupulously the canons of science, there are four basic sources of data that yield valid results for sociologists: survey research, experiments, observation, and the use of existing documents. We shall describe these techniques only briefly here.*

Survey Research. Sociologists are interested in obtaining information about certain kinds of persons. They may want to know how political beliefs and behaviors are influenced by differences in sex, race, ethnicity, religion, and social class. Or sociologists may wish to know whether religious attitudes are related to racial antipathy. They may want to determine whether poor people have different values from others in society, the answer to which will have a tremendous impact on the ultimate solution to poverty.

To answer these and similar questions, the sociologist may use personal interviews or written questionnaires to gather the data. The researcher may obtain information from all the possible subjects or from a selected sample. Since the former is often impractical, a random sample of subjects is selected from the larger population. If the sample is selected scientifically, a relatively small proportion can yield satisfactory results—that is, the inferences made from the sample will be reliable about the entire population. For example, a probability sample of only 2000 from a total population of 1 million will provide data very close to what would be discovered if a survey were taken of the entire 1 million.[11]

Typically with survey research, sociologists use sophisticated statistical techniques to control the contaminating effects of confounding variables, to determine whether the findings could have occurred by chance or not, to determine whether variables are related, and whether such a relationship is a casual one.

Experiments. To understand the cause-and-effect relationship among a few variables, sociologists use controlled experiments. Let's assume, for example, that we want to test whether white students in interracial classrooms have more positive attitudes toward blacks than whites in segregated class-rooms. Using the experimental method, the researcher would take a number

---

*See the bibliography at the end of the chapter for references on the methods of sociology. Methodological footnotes and methods panels appear occasionally throughout this book to give insight into how sociologists obtain and analyze data.

Minimizing Bias

The essential problem for social scientists involves the credibility of their research. How is objectivity possible, though, when they cannot escape their personal values, biases, and opinions? The answer lies in the norms of science.

Sociologists share with other scientists norms for conducting research that minimize personal bias. Their research must reflect the standards of science before it is accepted in scholarly journals. These journals function as gate-keepers for a discipline. What they accept for publication is assumed by their readers to be scientific. The editors of scholarly journals send manuscripts to referees who are unaware of the identity of the authors. This system of anonymity allows the referees to make objective judgments about the credibility of the studies. They review, among other things, the methods used to assess validity and reliability. **Validity** is the degree to which a study actually measures what it purports to measure. **Reliability** is the degree to which another study repeating the same methods would yield the same results.

To guide sociologists, their professional association—the American Sociological Association—has a code of ethics, which includes a number of standards for objectivity and integrity in sociological research.*

1. Sociologists should be sensitive to the potential for damage to individuals or groups from public disclosure of research based on ungeneralizable samples or unsubstantiated interpretation. Especially where there is the potential to harm groups or individuals, sociological research should adhere to the highest methodological standards.

2. Sociologists must not misrepresent their own abilities, or the competence of their staff, to conduct a particular research project.

3. Sociologists—regardless of their work setting—must present their findings honestly and without distortion. There must be no omission of data from a research report which would significantly modify the interpretation of findings. And sociologists should indicate where and how their own theory, method and research design may bear upon or influence the interpretation.

4. Sociologists must report fully all sources of financial support in their research publications and must note any special relations to the sponsor that might affect the interpretation of findings.

5. Sociologists must not accept such grants, contracts or research assignments as appear likely to require violation of the principles above, and should dissociate themselves from the research if they discover a violation and are unable to achieve its correction.

6. The American Sociological Association may ask an investigator for clarification of any distortion by a sponsor or consumer of the findings of a research project in which he or she has participated.

*Excerpted from the "Revised ASA Code of Ethics," ASA *Footnotes* (August 1980), p. 12.

of white students previously unexposed to blacks in school and randomly assign a subset to an integrated classroom situation. Before actual contact with the blacks, however, all the white students would be given a test of their racial attitudes. This pretest establishes a bench mark from which to measure any changes in attitudes. One group, the **control group,** continues school in segregated classrooms while the other group, the **experimental**

group, now has blacks as classmates. Otherwise the two groups are the same. Following a suitable period of time, the whites in both groups are tested again (posttest) for their racial attitudes. If the experimental group is found to differ from the control group in racial attitudes (the **dependent variable**), then it is assumed that interracial contact (the **independent variable**) is the source of the change.

As an example of a less contrived experiment, a researcher could test the results of two different treatments on the subsequent behavior of juvenile delinquents. Delinquent boys who had been adjudicated by the courts could be randomly assigned to a boys' industrial school or a group home facility in the community. After release from incarceration, records would be kept on the boys' subsequent behavior in school (grades, truancy, formal reprimands) and in the community (police contacts, work behavior). If the boys from the two groups differ appreciably, then we can say with assurance, since the boys were randomly assigned to each group, that the difference in treatment (the independent variable) was the source of the difference in behavior (the dependent variable).[12]

Observation.   The researcher, without intervention, can observe as accurately as possible what occurs in a community, group, or social event. This type of procedure is especially helpful in understanding such social phenomena as the decision-making process, the stages of a riot, the attraction of cults for their members, and the depersonalization of patients in a mental hospital. Case studies of entire communities have been very instrumental in the understanding of power structures[13] and the intricacies of social stratification.[14] Long-time participant observation studies of slum neighborhoods and gangs have been very insightful in showing the social organization present in what the casual observer might think of as very disorganized activity.[15]

Existing Sources.   The sociologist can also make use of existing data to test theories. The most common sources of information are the various agencies of the government. Data are provided for the nation, regions, states, communities, and census tracts on births, deaths, income, education, unemployment, business activity, health delivery systems, prison populations, military spending, poverty, migration, and the like. Important information can also be obtained from such sources as business firms, athletic teams and leagues, unions, and professional associations. Statistical techniques can be used with these data to describe populations and the effects of social variables on various dependent variables.

SUMMARY

The sociological perspective allows us to understand ourselves, others, and social organizations. It requires of us the ability to stand back from social life to see the patterns, regularities, and constraints. This means not only a certain amount of detachment but also, and most fundamentally, the realization that the customs and existing forms of social organization are not sacred. This critical examination of social life will allow us to see the positive *and* negative consequences and, we hope, will lead us to work for more humane social arrangements. This critical analysis of social life is a two-edged sword, however. On the one hand, to know the forces constraining us is to be freed from their power. But while this is liberating, it also frees us from the protection that custom and tradition provide.

Sociology, because its subject matter is social life, has problems of separating fact from myth. There are the problems of bias and of generalizing from faulty samples. Sociologists, although they are part of the social reality under investigation, employ vigorous scientific methods to overcome these obstacles. Most important, they employ methods designed to get valid information that allows for accurate probability statements about social reality.

CHAPTER REVIEW

1. Sociology is the science dealing with social forces—the forces outside us that shape our very lives, interests, and personalities. Sociologists, then, work to discover the underlying order of social life and the principles regarding it that explain human behavior.

2. The assumptions of the sociological perspective are that: (a) individuals are, by their nature, social beings; (b) individuals are socially determined; and (c) individuals create, sustain, and change the social forms within which they conduct their lives.

3. Sociology is uncomfortable for many because it looks behind the facades of social life. This requires a critical examination of society that questions the existing myths, stereotypes, and official dogma.

4. The basis for the critical stance of sociologists is that the social world is not sacred because it is made by humans.

5. Sociology is dependent on reliable data and logical reasoning. Although value neutrality is impossible in the social sciences, bias is minimized by the norms of science.

6. Survey research is a systematic means of gathering data to obtain information about people's behaviors, attitudes, and opinions.

7. Sociologists may use experiments to assess the effects of social factors on human behavior. One of two similar groups—the experimental group—is exposed to an independent variable. If this group later differs from the control group, then the independent variable is known to have produced the effect.

8. Observation is another technique for obtaining reliable information. Various social organizations such as prisons, hospitals, schools, churches, cults, families, communities, and corporations can be studied and understood through systematic observation.

9. Sociologists also employ existing sources of data to test their theories.

10. Sociology is a science and the rules of scientific research guide the efforts of sociologists to discover the principles of social organization and the sources of social constraints on human behavior.

FOR FURTHER STUDY

The Sociological Perspective

Peter L. Berger, *Invitation to Sociology: A Humanistic Perspective* (Garden City, N.Y.: Doubleday (Anchor Books), 1963).

Peter Berger and Hansfried Kellner, *Sociology Reinterpreted* (Garden City, N.Y.: Doubleday (Anchor Books), 1981).

Randall Collins, *Sociological Insight* (New York: Oxford University Press, 1982).

Lewis A. Coser (ed.), *The Pleasures of Sociology* (New York: New American Library, 1980).

C. Wright Mills, *The Sociological Imagination* (New York: Oxford University Press, 1959).

Kenneth Westhues, *First Sociology* (New York: McGraw-Hill, 1982).

The Craft of Sociology

Earl R. Babbie, *The Practice of Social Research*, 2nd ed. (Belmont, Calif.: Wadsworth, 1979).

P. McC. Miller and M. J. Wilson, *A Dictionary of Social Science Methods* (New York: John Wiley & Sons, 1983).

Robert B. Smith, *An Introduction to Social Research: Volume I of Handbook of Social Science Methods* (Cambridge, Mass.: Ballinger, 1983).

Gideon Sjoberg (ed.), *Ethics, Politics, and Social Research* (Cambridge, Mass.: Schenkman, 1967).

NOTES AND REFERENCES

1. Peter L. Berger, *Invitation to Sociology: A Humanistic Perspective* (Garden City, N.Y.: Doubleday (Anchor Books), 1963), p. 121.
2. Reece McGee, *Points of Departure: Basic Concepts in Sociology*, 2nd ed. (Hinsdale, Ill.: Dryden Press, 1975), pp. x–xi.
3. See Charles H. Anderson, *Toward a New Sociology*, rev. ed. (Homewood, Ill.: Dorsey Press, 1974), p. 3.
4. Berger, *Invitation to Sociology*, p. 31.
5. Alvin W. Gouldner, "Anti-Minotaur: The Myth of Value-Free Sociology," *Social Problems* 9 (Winter, 1962), p. 212.
6. Howard S. Becker, "Whose Side Are We On?" *Social Problems* 14 (Winter, 1967), pp. 239–247.
7. *Ibid.*, p. 240.
8. *Ibid.*, p. 242.
9. Berger, *Invitation to Sociology*, p. 5.
10. See William Ryan, *Blaming the Victim*, rev. ed. (New York: Pantheon Books, 1976).
11. Bernard S. Phillips, *Social Research: Strategy and Tactics,* 2nd ed. (New York: Macmillan, 1971), pp. 307–313.
12. E. L. Phillips, E. A. Phillips, D. L. Fixsen, and M. M. Wolf, "Behavior Shaping Works for Delinquents," *Psychology Today* 7 (June, 1973), pp. 75–79.
13. See Floyd Hunter, *Community Power Structure* (Chapel Hill, N.C.: University of North Carolina Press, 1953); and Robert Dahl, *Who Governs?* (New Haven, Conn.: Yale University Press, 1961).
14. See W. Lloyd Warner and Paul S. Lunt, *The Social Life of a Modern Community* (New Haven, Conn.: Yale University Press, 1941); and Robert S. Lynd and Helen Merrill Lynd, *Middletown in Transition* (New York: Harcourt Brace Jovanovich, 1937).
15. See William Foote Whyte, *Street Corner Society: The Social Structure of an Italian Slum*, rev. ed. (Chicago: University of Chicago Press, 1955); Herbert J. Gans, *The Urban Villagers* (New York: Free Press, 1962); and Elliot Liebow, *Tally's Corner* (Boston: Little, Brown, 1967).

2

The Structure of
Social Groups

An experiment was conducted some years ago when 24 previously unacquainted boys, aged 12, were brought together at a summer camp.[1] For three days the boys, who were unaware that they were part of an experiment, participated in camp-wide activities. During this period the camp "counselors" observed the friendship patterns that emerged naturally. The boys were then divided into two groups of 12. The boys were deliberately separated in order to break up the previous friendship patterns. The groups were then totally separated for a period of five days. During this period the boys were left alone by the "counselors" so that what occurred was the spontaneous result of the boys' behavior. The experimenters found that in both groups, there developed (1) a division of labor; (2) a hierarchical structure of ranks—that is, differences among the boys in power, prestige, and rewards; (3) the creation of rules; (4) punishments for violations of the rules; (5) argot—that is, specialized language such as nicknames and group symbols that served as positive in-group identifications; and (6) member cooperation to achieve group goals.

This experiment illustrates the process of social organization. The "counselors" did not insist that these phenomena occur in each group. They seemed to occur "naturally." In fact, they happen universally.[2] The goals of this chapter are to understand this process, to understand the components of social structure that emerge, and how they operate to constrain behavior. Although the process is generally the same regardless of group size, we will examine it at two levels—the micro level and the societal level.

THE MICRO LEVEL

The Process of Social Organization[3]

"**Social organization** refers to the ways in which human conduct becomes socially organized, that is, the observed regularities in the behavior of people that are due to the social conditions in which they find themselves rather than to their physiological or psychological characteristics as individuals."[4] The social conditions that constrain behavior can be divided into two types: (1) **social structure**—the structure of behavior in groups and society; and (2) **culture**—the shared beliefs of group members that unite them and guide their behavior.

Social Structure. **Sociology** is the study of the patterns that emerge when people interact over time. The emphasis is on the linkages and network that emerges, which transforms an **aggregate** of individuals into a **group.** We start, then, with **social interaction.** When the actions of one person (or persons) affect another person, social interaction occurs. The most common method is communication through speech, the written word, or symbolic acts (for example, a wink, a wave of the hand, or the raising of a finger). Behavior can also be altered by the mere presence of others. The way we behave (from the way we eat to what we think) is affected by whether we are alone or with others. Even physical reactions such as crying, laughing, or passing gas are controlled by the individual because of the fear of embarrassment. It could even be argued that, except in the most extreme cases, people's actions are always oriented toward other human beings whether they are physically present or not. We, as individuals, are constantly concerned about the expected or actual reactions of others. Even when alone, an individual may not act in certain ways because of having been taught that such actions are wrong.

Social interaction may be either transitory or enduring. Sociologists are interested in the latter type because only then does patterned behavior occur. A case of enduring social interaction is a **social relationship.** Relationships occur for a number of reasons. It may be sexual attraction, familial ties, because the members have a common interest (for example, collecting coins or growing African violets), because they share a common political or religious ideology, because they cooperate to produce or distribute a product, or because of propinquity (neighbors). Regardless of the specific reasons, the members of a social relationship are united at least in some minimal way with the others. Most important, the members of a social relationship behave quite differently than they would as participants in a fleeting interaction. Once the interaction is perpetuated, the behavior of the participants is profoundly altered. An autonomous individual is similar to an element in chemistry. As soon as there is a chemical reaction between two elements, however, they become parts of a new entity, as Olsen has noted:

> The concepts of "elements" and "parts" are analogous to terms in chemistry. By themselves, chemical elements—sodium and chlorine, for instance—exhibit characteristics peculiarly their own, by which each can be separately identified. This condition holds true even if elements are mixed together, as long as there is no chemical reaction between them. Through a process of chemical interaction, however, the elements can join to form an entirely new substance—in this case, salt. The elements of sodium and chlorine have now both lost their individual identities and characteristics, and have instead become parts of a more inclusive chemical compound, which has properties not belonging to either of its component parts by themselves. In an emergent process such as this, the original elements are transformed into parts of a new entity.[5]

Olsen's description of a chemical reaction is also appropriate for what arises in a social relationship. Most sociologists assume that the whole is not identical to the sum of its parts—that is, through the process of enduring interaction something is created with properties different from the component parts.* The two groups artificially formed at the summer camp, for example, developed similar structural properties regardless of the unique personalities of the boys in each group.

Although groups may differ in size or purpose, they are similar in structure and the processes that create the structure. In other words, one group may exist to knit quilts for charity while another may do terrorist bombings, but they will be alike in many important ways. Their social structure involves the patterns of interaction that emerge, the division of labor, and the linking and hierarchy of positions. The social structure is an emergent phenomenon bringing order and predictability to social life within the group.

Culture.   The other component of social organization is culture—the shared beliefs of a group's members that serve to guide conduct. Through enduring social interaction common expectations emerge about how people

---

* This assumption—the **realist position**—is one side of a fundamental philosophical debate. The **nominalists,** on the other hand, argue that to know the parts is to know the whole. In sociology the realist position is dominant and found especially in the works of Emile Durkheim[6] and the contemporary classic by Charles Warriner.[7] The minority position in sociology is represented most prominently by George Homans.[8]

should act. These are called **norms.** Criteria for judging what is appropriate, correct, moral, and important also emerge. These criteria are the **values** of the group. Also part of the shared beliefs are the expectations group members have of individuals occupying the various positions within the group. These are **social roles.** The elements of culture will be described briefly below for the micro and macro levels and in detail in Chapter 5.

To summarize, social organization refers to both culture and social structure. Blau and Scott describe how they operate to constrain human behavior:

> The prevailing cultural standards and the structure of social relations serve to organize human conduct in the collectivity. As people conform more or less closely to the expectations of their fellows, and as the degree of their conformity in turn influences their relations with others and their social status, and as their status in further turn affects their inclinations to adhere to social norms and their chances to achieve valued objectives, their patterns of behavior become socially organized.[9]

Norms

All social organizations have rules (norms) that specify appropriate and inappropriate behaviors. In essence, norms are the behavioral expectations that members of a particular group collectively share. They ensure that action within social organizations is generally predictable.

Some norms are not considered as important as others and consequently are not severely punished if violated. These minor rules are called **folkways.** Folkways vary, of course, from group to group. A particular sorority may expect its members to wear formal dress on certain occasions and to never wear curlers to the library. In a church, wine may be consumed by the parishioners at the appropriate time—communion. To bring one's own bottle of wine to communion, however, would be a violation of the folkways of that church. Could you imagine an announcement in your church bulletin that communion will be next Sunday—B.Y.O.B.? These examples show that folkways involve etiquette, customs, and regulations which, if violated, do not threaten the fabric of the social organization.

The violation of the group's **mores,** on the other hand, is considered important enough so that it must be punished severely. This type of norm involves morality—in fact, mores can be thought of as moral imperatives. In a sorority, for instance, examples of the mores might be: disloyalty, stealing from a "sister," and conduct that brings shame to the organization, such as blatant sexual promiscuity.

Status and Role

One important aspect of social structure is comprised of the positions of a social organization. If one determines what positions are present in an organization and how they are interrelated (hierarchy, reciprocal pairs, etc.), then the analyst has a structural map of that social group. The existence of positions in organizations has an important consequence for individuals— the bestowing of a social identity. Each of us belongs to a number of organizations and in each we occupy a position (**status**). If you were asked— who are you?—chances are you would respond by listing your various statuses. An individual may at the same time be a student, sophomore, daughter, sister, friend, female, Baptist, Sunday School teacher, Democrat, waitress, American citizen, and Secretary-Treasurer of the local chapter of Weight Watchers.

The individual's social identity, then, is a product of the particular matrix of statuses that she or he occupies. Another characteristic of positions in organizations that has an important influence on social identity is that they tend to be differentially rewarded and esteemed. This hierarchical element of status reinforces the positive or negative image individuals have of themselves depending on placement in various organizations. Some individuals consistently hold prestigious positions (bank president, deacon, caucasian, male, chairman of United Fund), while others may hold only those statuses negatively esteemed (welfare recipient, aged, Chicano, janitor) and some occupy mixed statuses (bus driver, 32nd-degree Mason, union member, church trustee).

So group memberships are vital sources of our notion of our own identity. Similarly, when others know of our status in various organizations, they assign a social identity to us. When we determine a person's age, race, religion, and occupation, we tend to stereotype that person—that is, we assume that the individual is a certain "type." This has the effect of conferring a social identity on that person, raising expectations for certain behaviors which, very often, result in a self-fulfilling prophecy.

While the mapping of statuses provides important clues about the social structure of an organization, the most important aspect of status is the behavior expected of the occupant of a status. To determine that an individual occupies the status of father does not tell us much about what the group expects of a father. In some societies, for example, the biological father has no legal, monetary, or social responsibility for his children. His children are cared for by the mother and her brother. In American society, there are norms (legal and informal) that demand of the father that he be responsible for his children. Not only must he provide for them, but he must also, depending on the customs of the family, be a disciplinarian, buddy, teacher, Santa Claus, and tooth fairy.

The behavior expected of a person occupying a status in a group is the **role.*** The norms of the social organization constrain the incumbents in a status to behave in prescribed and therefore predictable ways, regardless of their particular personalities. Society insists that we play our roles correctly. To do otherwise is to risk being judged by others as abnormal, crazy, incompetent, and/or immature. These pressures to conform to role demands ensure that there is stability in social groups even though member turnover occurs. For example, ministers to a particular congregation come and go, but certain actions are predictable in particular incumbents because of the demands on their behavior. These demands come from the hierarchy of the denomination, from other ministers, and most assuredly from the members of the parish. The stability imposed by role is also seen with other statuses,

---

*This section will introduce the concept of role as it is appropriate to the context of social organization. We shall elaborate on it in Chapter 7.

such as professor, janitor, police officer, student, and even President of the United States.

The organizational demands on members in the various statuses do not make behavior totally predictable, however. Occupants of the statuses can vary within limits. There are at least three reasons for this. First, personality variables can account for variations in the behavior of persons holding identical status. People can be conformist or unconventional, manipulated or manipulators, passive or aggressive, followers or inspirational leaders, cautious or impetuous, ambitious or lackadaisical. The particular configuration of personality traits can make obvious differences in the behavior of individuals, even though they may face identical group pressures.

A second reason why role does not make social actors robots is that the occupants of a status may not receive a clear, consistent message as to what behavior is expected. A minister, for example, may find within his or her congregation individuals and cliques that make conflicting demands. One group may insist that the minister be a social activist. Another may demand that the pastor be apolitical and spend his or her time exclusively meeting the spiritual needs of the members.

Another circumstance leading to conflicting expectations—and unpredictability of action—results from multiple group memberships. The statuses we occupy may have conflicting demands on our behavior. As one example of this, the black Lieutenant Governor of Colorado, George Brown, when inaugurated was faced with the demands of his office, on the one hand, and the demands of his black constituency, on the other, who demanded that he do more for blacks. He opted to go slow on the latter, which resulted in a black walkout during his swearing-in ceremony. Other illustrations of conflicting demands because of occupying two quite different statuses are: daughter and lover, son and peer-group member, and businessman and church deacon. Being the recipient of incompatible demands results in hypocrisy, secrecy, guilt, and most important for our consideration—unpredictable behavior.

Although role performance may vary, stability within organizations remains. The stability is a consequence of the strong tendency of persons occupying statuses in the organization to conform. Let us look briefly at just how powerfully roles shape behavior. First, the power of role over personal behavior is seen very dramatically as one moves from one status to another. If you could observe your father's behavior, for example, at work, at parties, at church, and at a convention in a faraway city, chances are that the behavioral patterns would be inconsistent. Or, even closer to home, what about your own behavior at home, at church, at school, in the dorm, or in a parked car? In each of these instances the same individual occupies multiple statuses and faces conflicting role expectations, resulting in overall inconsistent behavior but very likely behavior that is expected for each separate role.

The power of role to shape behavior is also demonstrated as one changes status within an organization. The Amish, for instance, select their minister by lot from among the male adults of the group. The eligible members each select a Bible. The one choosing the Bible with the special mark in it is the new pastor. His selection is assumed to be ordained by God. Now this individual has a new status in the group—the leader with God's approval. Such an elevation in status will, doubtless, have a dramatic effect on that person's behavior. Without special training (the Amish rarely attend school beyond the eighth grade), the new minister will in all likelihood exhibit leadership, self-confidence, and wisdom. Less dramatically, but with similar results nonetheless, each of us undergoes shifts in status within the organizations to which we belong—from freshman to senior, bench warmer to first team, assembly-line worker to supervisor, and from adolescent to adult. These changes in status mean, of course, a concomitant shift in the expectations for behavior (role). Not only does our behavior change but so too our attitudes, perceptions, and perhaps even our personality.

A dramatic example of the power of role over behavior is provided by an experiment conducted by Philip Zimbardo. He wanted to study the impact of prison life on guards and prisoners. Using student volunteers, he randomly assigned some to be guards and others to be inmates. By utilizing subjects who were unassociated with a prison, the researcher could actually study the effects of social roles on behavior without the confounding variables of personality traits, character disorders, and the like.

Zimbardo constructed a mock prison in the basement of the psychology building at Stanford University. The students chosen as prisoners were "arrested" one night without warning, dressed in prison uniforms, and locked in the cells. The "guards" were instructed to maintain order. Zimbardo found that the college students assigned the roles of guard or inmate actually *became* guards and inmates in just a few days. The guards showed brutality and the prisoners became submissive, demonstrating that roles effectively shape behavior because they have the power to shape consciousness (thinking, feeling, and perceiving). Interestingly, Zimbardo, who is a psychologist, concluded that *social factors superseded individual ones:* "Individual behavior is largely under the control of social forces and environmental contingencies rather than personality traits, character, will power or other empirically unvalidated constructs."[10]

Finally, roles have the power to protect individuals. The constraints on behavior, implied in the role, provide a blueprint that relieves the individual from the responsibility for action. Thus, the certainty provided by role makes us comfortable. Gay liberation and women's liberation, to name two contemporary movements, are aimed at liberation from the constraints of narrowly prescribed sex roles. But to be free of these constraints brings not only freedom but also problems. So, too, when one is freed from the constraints of a particular community, job, or marriage, the newfound liberty, independence, and excitement are countered by the frustrations involving ambiguity, choice, loneliness, and responsibility.

Social Control

Although social groups vary in the degree of tolerance for alternative behaviors, they universally demand conformity to some norms. In the absence of such demands, groups would not exist because of the resulting anarchy. The mechanisms of social control are varied. They can occur subtly in the socialization process (see Chapter 6), so that persons feel guilty or proud, depending upon their actions. They can occur in the form of rewards (medals, prizes, merit badges, gold stars, trophies, praise) by family members, peers, neighbors, fellow workers, employers, and the community to reinforce certain behaviors. Also common are negative sanctions such as fines, demerits, imprisonment, and excommunication that are used to ensure conformity. More subtle techniques, such as gossip or ridicule, are also quite successful in securing conformity because of the common fear of humiliation before one's friends, classmates, coworkers, or neighbors.

An example of a particularly devastating and effective technique is the practice of "shunning" the sinner, used by some of the Amish and Mennonite religious sects. No one in the religious community, not even the guilty party's spouse and children, is to recognize his or her existence. In one celebrated case, Robert Bear was the victim of shunning. He took the case to court on the grounds that this practice was unconstitutional because it was too severe. Since the shun was invoked, Bear's wife had not slept with him, his six children were alienated from him, and his farm operation was in ruin because no one would work for him or buy his produce.[11] The courts ruled, however, that it was within the province of the church to punish its members for transgressions. The severity of the "shun" is an extremely effective social control device for the Amish community, guaranteeing, except in rare cases, conformity to the dictates of the group.

Whatever the mechanism used, social control efforts tend to be very effective, whether they be within a family, peer group, organization, community, or a society. Most of the people, most of the time, conform to the norms of their groups and society. Otherwise, the majority of the poor would riot, most of the starving would steal, and more young men would refuse to fight in wars. The pressure to conform comes from within us (internalization of the group's norms and values from the socialization process) and from outside us (sanctions or the threat of sanctions) and we obey. In fact, what we consider self-control is really the consequence of social control. These constraints are usually not oppressive to the individual. Indeed, we want to obey the rules.

Primary and Secondary Groups

A social **group** is a social organization created through enduring and patterned interaction. It consists of people who have a common identity, share a common culture, and define themselves as a distinct social unit. Groups may be classified in a number of ways, the most significant of which involves the kind and quality of relationships that members have with each other. Sociologists have delineated two types of groups according to the degree of intimacy and involvement among the members—primary and secondary.

Primary groups are those whose members are the most intimately involved with each other.[12] These groups are small and display face-to-face interaction. They are informal in organization and long lasting. The members have a strong identification, loyalty, and emotional attachment to the group and its members. Examples are the nuclear family, a child's play group, a teenage gang, and close friends. Primary groups are crucial to the individual because they provide members with a sense of belonging, identity, purpose, and security. Thus, they have the strongest influence on the attitudes and values of members.

Secondary groups, in contrast to primary groups, are much larger and more impersonal. They are formally organized, task oriented, and relatively nonpermanent. The individual member is relatively unimportant. The members may vary considerably in beliefs, attitudes, and values. Americans are greatly affected by this type of group. The government at all levels deals with us impersonally. So, too, does our school, where we are a number in a computer. We live in large dormitories or in neighborhoods where we are barely acquainted with those near us. We work in large organizations and belong to large churches.

One significant impact of the impersonal nature of secondary groups is that they spawn the formation of primary groups. Primary groups emerge at school, at work, in an apartment complex, in a neighborhood, in a church, or in an army. In other words, intensely personal groups develop and are sustained by their members in largely impersonal settings.

The existence of primary groups within secondary groups is an important phenomenon that has ramifications for the goals of the secondary group. Two examples from military experience make this point. In World War II the German army was organized to promote the formation of primary groups. The men were assigned to a unit for the duration of the war. They trained together, fought together, went on furloughs together, and were praised or punished as a group. This was a calculated organizational ploy to increase social solidarity in the small fighting units. This worked to increase morale, loyalty, and a willingness to die for the group. In fact, they often became more loyal to their fighting unit than to the nation.[13]

In contrast, the American army in Vietnam was organized in such a way as to minimize the possibility for forming primary groups. Instead of being assigned to a single combat unit until the war was over, soldiers were given a twelve-month tour of duty in Vietnam. This rotation system meant that in any fighting unit soldiers were continually entering and leaving. This prevented the development of a close relationship and a feeling of "all for one and one for all." Since each soldier had his own departure date his goal was not to win the war but to survive until he was eligible to go home. This individualism made morale difficult to maintain and loyalty to one's unit difficult if not impossible to achieve. It also made the goal of winning the war less attainable than would a system that fostered primary groups.[14]

Power of the Social Group

We have seen that primary and secondary groups structure the behavior of their members by providing rules, roles, and mechanisms of social control. The result is that most of us, most of the time, conform to the expectations of social groups. Let us examine some illustrations of the profound influence of social groups on individuals, beginning with the classic study of suicide by Emile Durkheim.

Group Affects Probability of Suicide.   One's attachment to social groups affects the probability of suicide. Suicide would appear on the surface to be one area that could strictly be left to psychological explanations. An individual is committing the ultimate individual act—ending one's own life—presumably because of excessive guilt, anxiety, and/or stress. Sociologists, however, are interested in this seemingly individual phenomenon because of the social factors that may produce the feelings of guilt or the undue psychological stress. Sociologists are not interested, however, in the individual suicide case as psychologists would be, but in a number of people in the same social situation. Let us look at how sociologists would study suicide by examining in some detail the classic study by the nineteenth-century French sociologist Emile Durkheim.[15]

Durkheim was the consummate sociologist. He reacted to what he considered the excessive psychologism of his day by examining suicide rates (the number of suicides per 100,000 people in a particular category) sociologically. Some of the interesting results of his study were that single people had higher rates than married people, childless married people had a higher rate than those with children, the rate of city dwellers exceeded that of rural people, and Protestants were more likely to be self-destructive than Catholics or Jews. Societal conditions were also correlated with suicide rates. As expected, rates were higher during economic depressions than in periods of economic stability, although surprisingly high rates were found during economic booms.

Durkheim went an important step beyond just noting that social factors were related to suicide rates. He developed a theory to explain these facts— a theory based on the individual's relationship to a social organization. Three types of suicide—the egoistic, altruistic, and anomic—were posited by Durkheim to illustrate the effect of one's attachment to a group (society, religion, family) on self-preservation. **Egoistic suicide** occurs when an individual has minimal ties to a social group. The person is alone, lacking group goals and group supports. This explains why married people are less likely to commit suicide than single people and why married people with children are not as likely to kill themselves as those who are childless. Being an important part of a group gives meaning and purpose to life. This lack of group supports also explains why Protestants during Durkheim's day had a higher suicide rate than Catholics. The Catholic religion provided believers with many group supports, including the belief in the authority of religious leaders to interpret the scriptures. Catholics also believed that through the confessional, sinners could be redeemed. Protestants, on the other hand, were expected to be their own priests, reading and interpreting God's word. When guilty of sin, Protestants again were alone. There was no confessional where a priest would assure one of forgiveness. The differences in theology left individual Protestants without religious authority and with a greater sense of uncertainty. This relatively greater isolation left Protestants without the group of believers and the authority of priests in times of stress.

Altruistic suicide occurs in a completely different type of group setting. When groups are highly cohesive, the individual member of such a collectivity tends to be group oriented. Such a group might expect its members to kill themselves for the good of the group under certain conditions. Soldiers may be expected to leave the relative safety of their foxholes and attack a strategic hill even though the odds are very much against them. The strong allegiance to one's group may force such an act, which would otherwise seem quite irrational. The kamikaze attacks by Japanese pilots during World War II were suicide missions where the pilot guided the ammunition-laden plane into a target. These pilots gave their lives because of their ultimate allegiance to a social group—clearly an example of altruistic suicide. Another example of obligatory suicide for the good of the group is found among Eskimos. Because life is so tenuous in their harsh environment, Eskimos are expected to carry their full burden in providing for the survival of the group. When individuals become too old and feeble to provide their share, they provide for the survival of the group by taking their own lives.

The third type of suicide—the **anomic**—is also related to the individual's attachment to a group. It differs from the other two types in that it refers especially to the condition where the expectations of a group are ambiguous or they conflict with other sets of expectations. Typically, behavior is regulated by a clear set of rules (norms). But there are times when these rules lose their clarity and certainty for individuals. This is a condition of anomie (normlessness). Anomie usually occurs in a situation of rapid change. Examples of anomic situations are: emigration from one society to another, movement from a rural area to an urban one, rapid loss of status, overnight wealth, widowhood, divorce, and drastic inflation or deflation. In all these cases, people are often not sure how to behave. They are not certain of their goals. Life may appear aimless. Whenever the constraints on behavior are suddenly lifted, the probability of suicide increases. The irony is that we tend to be comfortable under the tyranny of the group and that freedom from such constraints is often intolerable. The sexual freedom of married persons in American society, for example, is highly regulated. There is only one legitimate sex partner. The unmarried person is not limited. But while married persons might fantasize that such a life is "nirvana," the replacement of regulated sexual behavior with such freedom is a condition of normlessness conducive to higher suicide rates.[16]

Group Affects Perceptions.   The group may affect our perceptions. Apparently, our wish to conform is so great that we often give in to group pressure. Solomon Asch, a social psychologist, has tested this proposition by asking the subjects in an experiment to compare the length of lines on cards.[17] The subjects were asked one at a time to identify verbally the longest line. All the subjects but one were confederates of the experimenter, coached to give the same wrong answer, placing the lone subject in the awkward position of having the evidence of his senses unanimously contradicted. Each experiment consisted of 18 trials, with the confederates giving wrong responses on 12 and correct ones on six. For the 50 subjects going through this ordeal, the average number of times they went along with the majority with incorrect judgments was 3.84. While 13 of the 50 were independent and gave responses in accord with their perceptions, 37 (74 percent) gave in to the group pressure at least once (12 did eight or more times). In other experiments where the confederates were not unanimous in their responses, the subjects were freed from the overwhelming group pressure and generally had confidence enough in their perceptions to give the correct answer.

Muzafer Sherif also conducted a series of experiments to determine the extent of conformity among individuals.[18] An individual subject was placed in a dark room to observe a pinpoint of light. The subject was asked to describe how many inches the light moved (the light appears to move, even though it is stationary, because of what is called the "autokinetic effect"). In repeated experiments each of the subjects tended to be consistent as to how far they felt the light had moved. When placed in a group, however, individuals modified their observations to make them more consistent with those of the others in the room. After repeated exposures, the group arrived at a collective judgment. The important point about this experiment is that the group, unlike the one in the Asch experiment, was composed entirely of naive subjects. Therefore, the conclusion about group pressure on individual members is more valid, reflecting natural group processes.

Group Affects Convictions.   Sectarians with group support maintain their conviction despite contrary evidence. Leon Festinger and his associates at the University of Minnesota carefully studied a group which believed that a great flood would submerge the West Coast from Seattle to Chile on December 21 of that year.[19] On the eve of the predicted cataclysm the leader received a message that her group should be ready to leave at midnight in a flying saucer that had been dispatched to save them. The group of ten waited expectantly at midnight for the arrival of the saucer. It did not appear and finally at 4:45 A.M. the leader announced that she had received another communication. The message was that the world had been spared the disaster because of the force of good found among this small band of believers. Festinger was especially interested in how the group would handle this disconfirmation of prophecy. But this group, like other millennial groups of history, reacted to the disconfirmation by reaffirming their beliefs and doubling their efforts to win converts.

Group Affects Health and Life.   Membership in a group may have an effect on one's health and even life itself. Pakistan has a caste system. This means that children are destined to occupy the stratum of society that they are born into. Their occupation will be that of their parents with no questions asked. One of the lowest castes is that of beggar. Since the child of a beggar will be a beggar and the most successful beggars are deformed, the child will be deformed by his family (usually by an uncle). Often the method is to break the child's back because the resulting deformity is so wretched. All parents wish success for their children, and the beggar family wishing the same is forced by the constraints of the rigid social system to physically disable their child for life.

There is a religious sect in Cortez, Colorado, the "Church of the First Born," which does not believe in traditional medical care. Recently a three-year-old boy, whose mother belonged to this sect, died of diphtheria. The boy had never been immunized for this disease. Moreover, the mother refused medical treatment for her son after the illness had been diagnosed. The mother knew the consequences of her refusal of medical treatment because her nephew had died of diphtheria, but her faith and the faith of the other members kept her from saving her son's life. This is dramatic evidence for the power of the group to curb what we erroneously call "maternal instinct."

Another example of a group demanding hazardous behavior of its members is found among some religious sects of Appalachia that encourage the handling of poisonous snakes (rattlesnakes, water moccasins, and copperheads) as part of worship. Members pick up handfuls of poisonous snakes, throw them on the ground, pick them up again, thrust them under their shirts and blouses, and even cover their heads with clusters of snakes. The ideology of the group, thus, encourages members to literally put their faith to the ultimate test—death. The ideology is especially interesting because it justifies death by snakebite as well as being spared the bite or recovering if bitten.

> The serpent-handlers say the Lord causes a snake to strike in order to refute scoffers' claims that the snakes' fangs have been pulled. They see each recovery from snakebite as a miracle wrought by the Lord—and each death as a sign that the Lord "really had to show the scoffers how dangerous it is to obey His commandments." Since adherents believe that death brings one to the throne of God, some express an eagerness to die when He decides they are ready. Those who have been bitten and who have recovered seem to receive special deference from other members of the church.[20]

Group Affects Behavior.   The group can alter the behavior of members, even behaviors that involve basic human drives. Human beings are biologically programmed to eat, drink, sleep, and engage in sexual activity. But human groups significantly shape how these biological drives are met. How we eat, when we eat, and what we eat are all greatly influenced by social groups. Some groups have rigid rules that require periods of fasting. Others have festivals where huge quantities of food and drink are consumed. Sexual behavior is also controlled. Although there is a universal sex drive, mating is not a universal activity among adults. Some persons, because of their group membership, take vows of chastity. Some persons, because they have certain physical or mental traits, are often labeled by groups as undesirable and are therefore involuntarily chaste. Some societies are obsessed with sex while others are not. An example of the latter is the Dani tribe of New Guinea. Sexual intercourse is delayed between marriage partners until exactly two years after the ceremony. After the birth of a child there is a five-year period of abstinence.

These dramatic examples of the power of groups over individuals should not keep us from recognizing the everyday and continual constraints on behavior. Our everyday activities, our perceptions and interpretations, and our attitudes are the product of our group memberships. The constraints, however, are for the most part subtle and go unrecognized as such. In short, what we think of as autonomous behavior is generally not.

FIGURE 2–1   Process of Social Organization

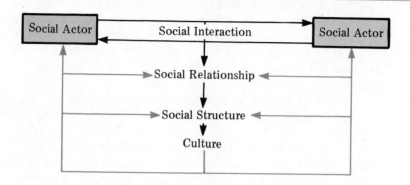

Source: This scheme is adapted from that developed by Marvin E. Olsen, *The Process of Social Organization*, 2nd ed. (New York: Holt, Rinehart and Winston, 1976).

In summary, social groups undergo a universal process—the process of social organization. Through enduring social interaction a matrix of social expectations emerges which guides behavior in prescribed channels, making social life patterned and therefore predictable. Thus, social organizations tend to be stable. But this is also a process, as Figure 2–1 indicates.

Interaction among the social actors in a social organization is constant and continuous, reinforcing stability but also bringing about change. Social organizations are never static. New ideas and new expectations emerge over time. Social change, however, is generally gradual. This is because, as shown in Figure 2–1, while social organizations are human-made, the creation, like Frankenstein's monster, to an important degree controls the creator. The culture that emerges takes on a sacred quality (the sanctity of tradition) that is difficult to question. This profoundly affects the attitudes and behaviors of the social actors in the social organization and the organization itself. As Wilbert Moore, the distinguished sociologist, has put it:

> Man is an inevitably social animal, and one whose social behavior is scarcely guided by instinct. He learns social behavior, well or poorly of one sort or another. [As a member of social groups] he invents values for himself and his collectivities, rules for his conduct, knowledge to aid him in predicting and controlling his environment, gods to reward and punish him, and other ingenious elements of the human condition. . . . Once [the products of this activity] are established in the human consciousness, they become, in turn, guides to behavior.[21]

THE SOCIAL STRUCTURE OF SOCIETY

We have focused on primary and secondary groups. These illustrate nicely the process and the components of social organization. But each of these groups exists in a larger social setting—a context that is also structured with norms, statuses, roles, and mechanisms of social control. These are the components of social structure through which society affects our attitudes and behaviors regardless of our other group memberships.

A **society** is the largest social organization to which persons owe their allegiance. It is an aggregate of people, united by a common culture, who are relatively autonomous and self-sufficient, and who live in a definite geographical location. It is difficult to imagine a society undergoing the same processes as other, smaller, social organizations because societies are typically composed of so many different persons and groups, none of whom were present at the beginning of the society. But the conceptual scheme for the process of social organization shown in Figure 2–1 is also applicable at the societal level. Continuing interaction among the members reinforces stability but also is a source of change. At any given time, the actors in the society are constrained by the norms, values, and roles that are the result of hundreds of years of evolution.

Society as a Social System

A society is a **social system,** composed of interdependent parts that are linked together into a boundary-maintaining whole. This concept of system implies that there is order and predictability within. Moreover, there are clear boundaries to a system in terms of membership and territory. Finally, the parts are interdependent. The economy illustrates this interdependence nicely. There is a division of labor in society that provides a wide range of products and services meeting the needs of society's members. The presence of economic booms and depressions illustrates further the interdependence in society. For example, a depression comes about (in overly simplistic terms) when the flow of money is restricted by high taxes, high interest rates, high unemployment, and restricted buying practices by individuals. When large numbers of persons delay buying items such as a new car or refrigerator because they are uncertain of the future, the sales of these decline dramatically. This decrease itself is a source of further pessimism, thereby further dampening sales. The price of stocks in these companies will, of course, plummet under these conditions, causing further alarm. Moreover, many workers in these industries will be laid off. These newly unemployed persons, in turn, will purchase only the necessities, thereby throwing other industries into panic as their sales decline. A depression, then, is the result of actions by individual consumers, boards of directors of corporations, banks, savings and loan associations, individual and institutional investors, and the government. Additionally, the actions of this nation and the actions of other nations greatly affect the economic conditions of each other because they, too, form an interdependent network.

Culture of Society

Culture explains much individual and group behavior, as well as the persistence of most aspects of social life. Social scientists studying a society foreign to them must spend months, perhaps years, learning the culture of that group. They must learn the meanings for the symbols (written and spoken language, gestures, and rituals) which are employed by the individuals

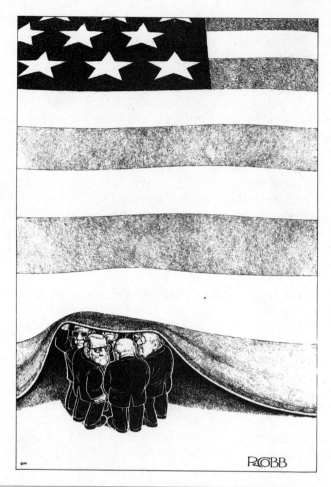

in that society. They must know the feelings people share as to what is appropriate or inappropriate behavior. Additionally, they need to know the rules of the society: which activities are considered important, the skills members have in making and using tools, as well as the knowledge members need to exist in that society. In short, analysts must discover all the knowledge that people share—that is, they must know the culture. A full discussion of culture and its transmission is found in Chapters 5–7.

Social Classes

A structural component of societies is the hierarchical arrangement of people in terms of power, prestige, and resources. This universal phenomenon of social inequality is so important for the understanding of individual behavior and the structure of society that Chapters 9 through 12 are devoted to it. At the individual level, one's placement in the hierarchy directly affects self-perception, motivation, political attitudes, and the degree of advantage or disadvantage in school, in the economy, in the courts, and even for life itself. At the societal level, the extent of inequality affects the types and magnitude of social problems, societal stability, and economic growth.

Social Institutions

One distinguishing characteristic of societies is the existence of a set of institutions. The popular usages of this term are imprecise and omit some important sociological considerations. An institution is not anyone or anything that is established and traditional (for example, a janitor who has worked at the same school for forty-five years). An institution is not limited to specific organizations such as a school or a prison or a hospital. An institution is much broader in scope and importance than a person, a custom, or a social organization. **Institutions** are social arrangements that channel behavior in prescribed ways in the important areas of social life. They are interrelated sets of normative elements—norms, values, and role expectations—that the persons making up the society have devised and passed on to succeeding generations in order to provide "permanent" solutions to society's perpetually unfinished business.

Institutions are cultural imperatives. They serve as regulatory agencies, channeling behavior in culturally prescribed ways.

> Institutions provide procedures through which human conduct is patterned, compelled to go, in grooves deemed desirable by society. And this trick is performed by making the grooves appear to the individual as the only possible ones.[22]

For example, a society instills in its members predetermined channels for marriage. Instead of allowing the sexual partners a whole host of options, it is expected in American society that they will marry and set up a conjugal household. Although the actual options are many, the partners choose what society demands. In fact, they do not consider the other options as valid (for example, polygyny, polyandry, group marriage). The result is a patterned arrangement that regulates sexual behavior and attempts to ensure a stable environment for the care of dependent children.

Institutions arise from the uncoordinated actions of multitudes of individuals over time. These actions, procedures, and rules evolve into a set of expectations that appear to have a design, because the consequences of these expectations provide solutions that help maintain social stability. The design is accidental, however; it is a product of cultural evolution.

All societies face problems in common. Although the variety of solutions is almost infinite, there is a functional similarity in their consequence, which is stability and maintenance of the system. Table 2–1 gives a number of common societal problems and the resulting institutions. This partial list of institutions shows the type of societal problems for which solutions are continually sought. All societies, for instance, have some form of the family, education, polity, economy, and religion. The variations on each of

TABLE 2–1   Common Societal Problems and Their Institutions

Societal Problems	Institution
Sexual regulation; maintenance of stable units that ensure continued births and care of dependent children	Family
Socialization of the newcomers to the society	Education
Maintenance of order; the distribution of power	Polity
Production and distribution of goods and services; ownership of property	Economy
Understanding the transcendental; the search for meaning of life and death and the place of humankind in the world	Religion
Understanding the physical and social realms of nature	Science
Providing for physical and emotional health care	Medicine

these themes that are found in societies are almost beyond imagination. These variations, while most interesting, are beyond the scope of this book. By looking at the interrelated norms, values, and role expectations that provide "pat" solutions to fundamental societal problems, we shall begin to understand American society.

Institutions are, by definition, conservative. They are the answer of custom and tradition to questions of survival. While absolutely necessary for unity and stability, institutions in contemporary American society are often outmoded, inefficient, and unresponsive to the incredibly swift changes brought about by technological advances, population shifts, and increasing worldwide interdependence. Let us look briefly at problems within two institutions— the polity and the economy.

The polity is based on a set of norms that were for the most part appropriate for another age. Current laws, for example, penalize the cities, which have experienced an eroding tax base, and benefit the wealthier suburbs. The government bureaucracy is so large and unwieldy that it is unresponsive to all but the large and powerful interest groups. A final example is of ultimate importance. This is the inability to control the expansion and use of nuclear weapons throughout the world.

The American economic system, based on a philosophy of free enterprise, is also outmoded in many respects. Capitalism has always thrived in an environment when there were people to exploit (slaves, unskilled and semi-skilled labor, colonies), but these exploited groups worldwide are no longer passive. The free enterprise mentality, while appropriate in an expansionist setting with seemingly inexhaustible resources, is inappropriate in a world of shortages. Consumption for its own (and profit's) sake is no longer a legitimate goal, for it hastens the end of resources and eventual chaos. The profit orientation has also meant pollution and ecological catastrophes. The resistance to government planning increases the probability of booms and busts, surpluses and shortages, and high unemployment.

As we look at the institutions of American society we must not forget that institutions are made by people and can therefore be changed. We should be guided by the insight that while institutions appear to have the quality of being "sacred," they are not. They can be changed. But critical examination is imperative. Social scientists must look behind the facades. They must not accept the patterned ways as the only "correct" ways. This is in the American heritage—as found in the Declaration of Independence. As Skolnick and Currie have put it:

> Democratic conceptions of society have always held that institutions exist to serve man, and that, therefore, they must be accountable to men. Where they fail to meet the tests imposed on them, democratic theory holds that they ought to be changed. Authoritarian governments, religious regimes, and reformatories, among other social systems, hold the opposite: in case of misalignment between individuals or groups and the "system," the individuals and groups are to be changed or otherwise made unproblematic.[23]

SUMMARY

Sociologists are interested in two levels of social organization—relatively small groups (the micro level) and the societal (macro) level. The micro level is characterized by the same structural components and social processes as occur at the societal level except for social classes and institutions, which are strictly macro phenomena. Social organizations of all types are created and sustained by the social interaction of the members. Enduring social interaction is the basis for a social relationship. A social relationship requires the patterning and therefore the predictability of behavior. The shared knowledge that emerges from this continuous interaction guides the behavior, giving it a sacred quality. While social organizations are constantly changing, the rate of change is relatively slow because of the sanctity of the cultural components (norms, values, roles, and ideologies).

Although we shall refer occasionally to the micro level, the thrust of this book is on the societal level. The goal is to understand the structure of American society—its norms, values, roles, and institutions. This endeavor will provide the reader with a grasp of the sociological perspective and the tools to understand not only the machinery of society but also the bias of that machinery.

The focus of our inquiry throughout the remainder of this book, then, is on the positive and negative consequences of the way American society is structured. This is spelled out in Chapter 3. To anticipate the argument, the positive consequences of the traditional features of society are unity and stability—both necessary ingredients for social survival.

On the negative side, we shall focus on the structure of society as a source of social problems. Such social problems as poverty, racism, pollution, and unemployment are the result of the unequal distribution of wealth and power in society; the values of Americans; the tendency of Americans to blame individuals rather than the social environment ("blaming the victim"), which is translated into person-change solutions rather than system-change answers; and the inability of institutions to cope with the massive changes occurring in society and throughout the world.

CHAPTER REVIEW

1. Social organization refers to the observed regularities in the behavior of people that are due to social conditions rather than the physiology or psychology of individuals.

2. Social organization includes both social structure and culture. These emerge through enduring social interaction.

3. Social structure involves the linkages and network that transform individuals into a group. It includes the patterns of interaction that emerge, the division of labor, and the links and hierarchy of positions.

4. Culture, the shared beliefs of a group's members, guides conduct. The elements of culture include the norms (rules), roles (behavioral expectations for the occupants of the various positions), and values (the criteria for judging of people, things, and actions).

5. Norms are the rules specifying appropriate and inappropriate behaviors. The important norms are called mores and the less important ones are called folkways.

6. Each of us belongs to a number of social organizations and in each we occupy a position (status). These statuses are a major source of identity for individuals.

7. The behavior expected of a person occupying a status in a social organization is the role. The pressures to conform to role demands ensure that there is stability and predictability in social groups even though member turnover occurs.

8. There are three reasons, however, why role expectations do not make behavior totally predictable: (a) personality differences; (b) inconsistent messages as to what behavior is expected; and (c) multiple group memberships resulting in conflicting demands.

9. Social organizations employ positive sanctions (rewards) and negative sanctions (punishments) to enforce conformity to the norms, values, and roles of the group.

10. One way to classify social groups is on the basis of size and the quality of interaction. Primary groups are those whose members are involved in intimate, face-to-face interaction, with strong emotional attachments. The organization is informal and long lasting. The members identify strongly with each other and the group. In contrast, secondary groups are large, impersonal, and formally organized. The individual member is relatively unimportant.

11. Primary groups often emerge within secondary groups.

12. Social groups have enormous power over their members and affect their beliefs, behaviors, perceptions, and even health.

13. A society is the largest social organization to which persons owe their allegiance. The society provides the social

context for primary and secondary groups. Society places constraints on these groups and their members through its own norms, values, roles, and mechanisms for social control.

14. A society is a social system composed of interdependent parts that are linked together in a boundary-maintaining whole. There is order and predictability within. There is a division of labor providing for self-sufficiency.

15. A society, like other social organizations, has a culture involving norms, roles, values, symbols, and technical knowledge.

16. Unlike other social organizations, a society has a set of institutions. These are social arrangements that channel behavior in prescribed ways in the important areas of social life.

17. Institutions are conservative, providing the answers of custom and tradition to questions of social survival. While absolutely necessary for unity and stability, institutions can be outmoded, inefficient, and unresponsive to the swift changes of contemporary life.

FOR FURTHER STUDY

The Process of Social Organization

S. F. Nadel, *The Theory of Social Structure* (New York: Free Press, 1957).

Marvin E. Olsen, *The Process of Social Organization*, 2nd ed. (New York: Holt, Rinehart and Winston, 1976).

Max Weber, *The Theory of Social and Economic Organization*, A. M. Henderson and Talcott Parsons, trans. (New York: Free Press, 1947).

Micro Structure

Elliot Aronson, *The Social Animal*, 3rd ed. (San Francisco: W. H. Freeman, 1980).

Harold Garfinkel, *Studies in Ethnomethodology* (Englewood Cliffs, N.J.: Prentice-Hall, 1967).

Erving Goffman, *Presentation of Self in Everyday Life* (Garden City, N.Y.: Doubleday (Anchor Books), 1957).

A. Paul Hare, Robert F. Bales, and Edward Borgatta, eds., *Small Groups* (New York: Alfred A. Knopf, 1965).

Macro Structure

Gerhard Lenski, *Human Societies: A Macrolevel Introduction to Sociology* (New York: McGraw-Hill, 1970).

Robert Marsh, *Comparative Sociology* (New York: Harcourt Brace Jovanovich, 1967).

Robin Williams, Jr., *American Society: A Sociological Interpretation*, 3rd ed. (New York: Alfred A. Knopf, 1970).

NOTES AND REFERENCES

1. Muzafer Sherif and Carolyn W. Sherif, *Groups in Harmony and Tension* (New York: Farrar, Straus & Giroux (Octagon Books), 1966).
2. Two classic sociological studies of this phenomenon are: William F. Whyte, *Street Corner Society* (Chicago: University of Chicago Press, 1943); and Elliot Liebow, *Tally's Corner: A Study of Negro Street Corner Men* (Boston: Little, Brown, 1967). Other illustrations can be found in literature; see William Golding, *The Lord of the Flies* (London:

Faber & Faber, 1954); and George Orwell, *Animal Farm* (New York: Harcourt, Brace, 1946).

3. The view of social organization presented here is fundamentally indebted to Marvin E. Olsen, *The Process of Social Organization*, 2nd ed. (New York: Holt, Rinehart and Winston, 1976).

4. Peter M. Blau and W. Richard Scott, *Formal Organizations: A Comparative Approach* (San Francisco: Chandler, 1962), p. 2. Blau and Scott's distinction between social structure and culture is incorporated in the following analysis.

5. Olsen, *The Process of Social Organization*, p. 37.

6. See Emile Durkheim, *The Rules of Sociological Method,* 8th ed., Sarah A. Solovay and Hohn H. Mueller, trans. (Glencoe, Ill.: Free Press, 1938).

7. Charles K. Warriner, "Groups Are Real: A Reaffirmation," *American Sociological Review* 21 (October, 1956), pp. 549–554.

8. George Homans, "Bringing Men Back In," *American Sociological Review* 29 (December, 1964), pp. 809–818.

9. Blau and Scott, *Formal Organizations*, pp. 4–5.

10. Philip G. Zimbardo, "Pathology of Imprisonment," *Society* 9 (April, 1972), p. 6.

11. "Shun Thy Neighbor," *Newsweek* (December 8, 1975), p. 68.

12. The term "primary group" was coined by Charles H. Cooley, *Social Organization* (New York: Scribner's, 1909).

13. Edward A. Shils and Morris Janowitz, "Cohesion and Disintegration in the Wehrmacht in World War II," *Public Opinion Quarterly* 12 (Summer, 1948), pp. 280–315.

14. Charles C. Moskos, Jr., "The American Combat Soldier in Vietnam," *The Journal of Social Issues* 31 (Fall, 1975), pp. 25–37. 37.

15. Emile Durkheim, *Suicide*, reprinted ed. (Glencoe, Ill.: Free Press, 1951). For an update and a confirmation of Durkheim, see Jack P. Gibbs, "Suicide," in *Contemporary Social Problems*, 2nd ed., Robert K. Merton and Robert A. Nisbet, eds. (New York: Harcourt, Brace and World, 1966), pp. 281–321.

16. See Stephen Cole, *The Sociological Orientation: An Introduction to Sociology* (Chicago: Rand McNally, 1975), p. 9.

17. Solomon E. Asch, "Effects of Group Pressure upon the Modification and Distortion of Judgments," in *Readings in Social Psychology*, 3rd ed., Eleanor E. Maccoby, Theodore M. Newcomb, and Eugene L. Hartley, eds. (New York: Holt, Rinehart and Winston, 1958), pp. 174–183.

18. Muzafer Sherif, "Group Influences upon the Formation of Norms and Attitudes," in *Readings in Social Psychology*, pp. 219–232.

19. Leon Festinger, Henry W. Riecken, Jr., and Stanley Schacter, *When Prophecy Fails* (Minneapolis, Minn.: University of Minnesota Press, 1956).

20. Nathan L. Gerrard, "The Serpent Handling Religions of West Virginia," *Trans-action* 5 (May, 1968), p. 23.

21. Wilbert E. Moore, "Social Structure and Behavior," in *The Handbook of Social Psychology*, 2nd ed., Vol. IV, Gardner Lindzey and Elliot Aronson, eds. (Reading, Mass.: Addison-Wesley, 1969), p. 283.

22. Peter L. Berger, *Invitation to Sociology: A Humanistic Perspective* (Garden City, N.Y.: Doubleday, Anchor Books, 1963), p. 87.

23. Jerome H. Skolnick and Elliott Currie, "Approaches to Social Problems," in *Crisis in American Institutions*, Jerome H. Skolnick and Elliott Currie, eds. (Boston: Little, Brown, 1970), p. 15.

3

The Duality of Social Life:
Order and Conflict

Jerome Skolnick, an analyst of American society who is highly sensitive to the role of the powerful, has observed (in his report to the National Commission on the Causes and Prevention of Violence) that what is considered violence and what is not will actually be determined by those in power.

First, "violence" is the term used for any act that threatens the power structure. In this way the lynching of a black is less shocking (and therefore less violent) than the behavior of the black that provoked it. In other words, violence is perceived as a quality of those individuals and groups who challenge existing arrangements rather than those who uphold them. Thus, what the victimized group may see as "police brutality" is viewed by those in power as legitimate and not as violence.

Violence always refers to a disruption of some condition of order. But Skolnick has pointed out that order, like violence, is also politically defined. "Order" itself can be very destructive to some categories of persons. Carmichael and Hamilton illustrated this in their book *Black Power*. They noted that when white terrorists bombed a black church as they did in Birmingham, Alabama, and killed five children, the act was deplored by most elements of American society. But when hundreds of black babies die each year in Birmingham because of the effects of racism, no one in the power structure gets upset and calls this violence.[1] Although high infant mortality and rates of preventable disease, which are perpetuated through discrimination, take many times more lives than civil disorder, the term "violence" is not applied. Skolnick has suggested that we should indeed identify such outcomes as "institutional violence," implying that the system itself injures and destroys.

Violence is also defined politically through the selection process. Some acts of force (to injure persons or to destroy property) are not always forbidden or condemned in American society. Property damaged during football games, Halloween, or the Mardi Gras is often overlooked. Even 10,000 beer-drinking, noisy, and sometimes destructive college students on the beaches of Florida are allowed to go on such a binge because "boys will be boys." But if the same 10,000 college students were to destroy the same amount of property in a demonstration where the goal was to change the system, then the

acts would be defined as "violent" and the police called to restore order by force if necessary (which, of course, would not be defined as violence by the authorities). Thus, violence is condemned or condoned through political pressures and decisions. The basic criterion is whether the act is in approved channels or is supportive of existing social and political arrangements. If not supportive, then the acts are by definition to be condemned and punished.

The decision of whether or not to use violence to control protest is also a political one. Although the use of force by those in power ("official violence") is violent, it is not usually perceived as such. When the mayor of a large city tells his police to shoot looters, or when police officers injure persons for alleged violations of the law, we have instances of official violence.

Skolnick's analysis of the relationship between the power structure and violence is important and useful to the analyst of any society. It highlights the benefits accruing to those persons and groups highly situated because of existing social arrangements. It also aids in understanding the behavior of those not well situated who work to change the existing system.

Source: Summarized from Jerome Skolnick, *The Politics of Protest* (New York: Ballantine Books, 1969), pp. 3–8.

The analyst of society begins with a mental picture of its structure. For scientists, this image (or **model**) influences what they look for, what they see, and how they explain the phenomena that occur within the society.

SOCIAL SYSTEMS: ORDER AND CONFLICT

Among the characteristics of societies is one—the existence of segmentation— that is the basis for the two prevailing models of society. Every society is composed of parts. This differentiation may result from differences in age, race, sex, physical prowess, wisdom, family background, wealth, organizational membership, type of work, or any other characteristic considered to be salient by the members. The fundamental question concerning differentiation is this: What is the basic relationship among the parts of society? The two contradictory answers to this question provide the rationale for the two models of society—order and conflict.

One answer is that the parts of society are in harmony. They cooperate because of similar or complementary interests and because they need each other to accomplish those things beneficial to all (for example, production and distribution of goods and services, protection). Another answer is that the subunits of society are basically in competition with each other. This view is based on the assumption that the things people desire most (wealth, power, autonomy, resources, high status) are always in short supply; hence, competition and conflict are universal social phenomena.

The Order Model

The **order model*** attributes to societies the characteristics of cohesion, consensus, cooperation, reciprocity, stability, and persistence. Societies are viewed as social systems, composed of interdependent parts that are linked together into a boundary-maintaining whole. The parts of the system are basically in harmony with each other. The high degree of cooperation (and societal integration) is accomplished because there is a high degree of consensus on societal goals and on cultural values. Moreover, the different parts of the system are assumed to need each other because of complementary interests. Because the primary social process is cooperation and the system is highly integrated, all social change is gradual, adjustive, and reforming. Societies are therefore basically stable units.

For order theorists, the central issue is: What is the nature of the social bond? What holds the group together in a boundary-maintaining whole? This was the focus of one of the most important figures in sociology, Emile Durkheim, the French social theorist of the early 1900s. The various forms of integration were used by Durkheim to explain differences in suicide rates, social change, and the universality of religion.[3]

One way to focus on integration is to determine the manifest and latent consequences of social structures, norms, and social activities. Do these consequences contribute to the integration (cohesion) of the social system? Durkheim, for example, noted that the punishment of crime has the **manifest** (intended) **consequences** of punishing and deterring the criminal. The **latent consequence** of punishment, however, is the societal reaffirmation of what is to be considered moral. The society is thereby integrated through belief in the same rules.[4]

Taking Durkheim's lead, sociologists of the order persuasion have made many penetrating and insightful analyses of various aspects of society. By focusing on *all* the consequences of social structures and activities—intended and unintended, as well as negative (malintegrative)—we can see behind

*This model is most often referred to in sociology as the functional or structural-functional model. It is the basis for the analysis of American society by Robin M. Williams, Jr.[2]

the facades and thereby understand more fully such disparate social arrangements and activities as ceremonials (from rain dances to sporting events), social stratification, fashion, propaganda, and even political machines.*

The Conflict Model

The assumptions of the **conflict model** are opposite from those of the order model. The basic form of interaction is not cooperation but competition, which often leads to conflict. Because the individuals and groups of society compete for advantage, the degree of social integration is minimal and tenuous. Social change results from the conflict among competing groups and therefore tends to be drastic and revolutionary. The ubiquitousness of conflict results from the dissimilar goals and interests of social groups. It is, moreover, a result of social organization itself.

The most famous conflict theorist was Karl Marx, who, after examining history, theorized that there exists in every society (except, Marx believed, in the last historical stage of communism) a dynamic tension between two groups—those who own the means of production and those who work for the owners. The powerful will use and abuse the powerless, thereby "sowing the seeds" of their own destruction. The destruction of the elite is accomplished when the dominated unite and overthrow the dominants.

Ralf Dahrendorf, a contemporary conflict theorist, has also viewed conflict as a ubiquitous phenomenon, not because of economic factors as Marx believed, but because of other aspects of social organization. Organization means, among other things, that power will be distributed unequally. The population will therefore be divided into the "haves" and the "have-nots" with respect to power. Because organization also means constraint, there will be a situation in all societies where the constraints are determined by the powerful, thereby further ensuring that the "have-nots" will be in conflict with the "haves"—thus, the important insight that conflict is endemic to social organization.†

One other emphasis of conflict theorists is that the unity present in society is superficial because it results not from consensus but from coercion. The powerful, it is asserted, use force and fraud to keep society running smoothly, with benefits mostly accruing to those in power.

The basic duality of social life can be seen by summarizing the opposite ways in which order and conflict theorists view the nature of society. If asked, "What is the fundamental relationship among the parts of society?" the answers of order and conflict theorists would disagree. This disagreement leads to and is based upon a number of related assumptions about society. These are summarized in Table 3–1.

---

*See Robert K. Merton's *Social Theory and Social Structure* for an excellent discussion of sociological research from the order (functionalist) perspective.[5]

†This description is a very superficial account of a complex process that has been fully described by Ralf Dahrendorf.[6]

TABLE 3–1   Duality of Social Life: Assumptions of the Order and Conflict Models of Society

	Order Model	Conflict Model
Question:	What is the fundamental relationship among the parts of society?	
Answer:	Harmony and cooperation.	Competition, conflict, domination, and subordination.
Why:	The parts have complementary interests. Basic consensus on societal norms and values.	The things people want are always in short supply. Basic dissensus on societal norms and values.
Degree of integration:	Highly integrated.	Loosely integrated. Whatever integration is achieved is the result of force and fraud.
Type of social change:	Gradual, adjustive, and reforming.	Abrupt and revolutionary.
Degree of stability:	Stable.	Unstable.

One interesting but puzzling aspect of Table 3–1 is that these two models are held by different scientific observers *of the same phenomenon.* How can such different assumptions be derived by experts on society? The answer is that both models are correct. Each focuses on reality—but only part of that reality. Scientists have tended to accept one or the other of these models, thereby focusing on only part of social reality, for at least two reasons: (1) one model or the other was in vogue at the time of the scientist's intellectual development;* or (2) one model or the other made the most sense for the analysis of the particular problems of interest—for example, the interest of Emile Durkheim, who devoted his intellectual energies to determining what holds society together, or the fundamental concern of Karl Marx, who explored the causes of revolutionary social change. The analysis of social problems is one important area where sociologists have been influenced by the order and conflict models. Let us turn to these contrary ways to view social problems before examining a synthesis of the two models.

*Order theorists have dominated American sociology since the 1930s. This has led to the charge by "radical" sociologists that the contemporary sociology establishment has served as the official legitimator of the system—not the catalyst for changing the system.[7] This radical challenge to order theory gained momentum in the 1960s and has generated a great deal of subsequent conflict theorizing.

SOCIAL PROBLEMS FROM THE ORDER AND
CONFLICT PERSPECTIVES

There is a general agreement among sociologists that a **social problem** reflects a violation of normative expectations.[8] It is a situation that is incompatible with the values of a significant number of people, who agree that the situation should be altered. Under this rubric fall such different phenomena as unemployment, poverty, crime, discrimination, drug addiction, political extremism, and mental illness.

The order and conflict perspectives constrain their adherents to view the causes, consequences, and remedies of social problems in opposing ways. The order perspective focuses on deviants themselves. This approach (which has been the conventional way of studying social problems) asks: Who are the deviants? What are their social and psychological backgrounds? With whom do they associate? Deviants somehow do not conform to the standards of the dominant group; they are assumed to be out of phase with conventional behavior. This is believed to occur most often as a result of inadequate socialization. In other words, deviants have not internalized the norms and values of society because they either are brought up in an environment of conflicting value systems (as are children of immigrants or the poor in a middle-class school) or are under the influence of a deviant subculture such as a gang. Because the order theorist uses the prevailing standards to define and label deviants, the existing practices and structures of society are accepted implicitly. The remedy is to rehabilitate the deviants so that they conform to the societal norms.

The conflict theorist takes quite a different approach to social problems. The adherents of this perspective criticize order theorists for **"blaming the victim."**[9] To focus on the individual deviant is to locate the symptom, not the disease. Individual deviants are a manifestation of a failure of society to meet the needs of individuals. The sources of crime, poverty, drug addiction, and racism are found in the laws, the customs, the quality of life, the distribution of wealth and power, and in the accepted practices of schools, governmental units, and corporations. In this view, then, the schools are the problem, not the dropouts; the quality of life, not mental illness; the maldistribution of wealth, not poverty; the roadblocks to success for minority-group members, not apathy on their part. The established system, in this view, is not "sacred." Because it is the primary source of social problems, it, not the individual deviant, must be restructured.

Although most of this book attempts to strike a balance between the order and conflict perspectives, the conflict model is clearly favored when social problems are brought into focus. This is done explicitly for three reasons: (1) the focus on the deviant has dominated sociology and there is a need for balance; (2) the subject matter of sociology is not individuals, who are the special province of psychology, but society. If sociologists do not make a critical analysis of the social structure, who will? Also (3) I am convinced that the source of social problems is found within the institutional framework of society. Thus, a recurrent theme of this book is that social problems are societal in origin and not the exclusive function of individual pathologies.

SYNTHESIS OF THE ORDER AND CONFLICT MODELS

The assumptions of both models are contradictory for each comparison shown in Table 3–1, and their contradictions highlight the duality of social life. Social interaction can be harmonious or acrimonious. Societies are integrated or divided, stable or unstable. Social change can be fast or slow, revolutionary or evolutionary.

Taken alone, each of these perspectives fosters a faulty perception and interpretation of society, but taken together, they complement each other and present a complete and realistic model. A synthesis that combines the best of each model would appear, therefore, to be the best perspective for understanding the structure and process of society.[10]

The initial assumption of a synthesis approach is that *the processes of stability and change are properties of all societies*. There is an essential paradox to human societies: they are always ordered; they are always changing. These two elemental properties of social life must be recognized by the observer of society. Within any society there are forces providing impetus for change *and* there are forces insisting on rooted permanence. Allen Wheelis has labeled these two contrary tendencies as the instrumental process and the institutional process, respectively.[11]

The instrumental process is based upon the desire for technological change—to find new and more efficient techniques to achieve goals. The institutional process, on the other hand, designates all those activities that are dominated by the quest for certainty. We are bound in our activities, often by customs, traditions, myths, and religious beliefs. So there are rites, taboos, and mores that persons obey without thinking. So, too, are there modern institutions such as monotheism, monogamy, private property, and the sovereign state, all of which are coercive in that they limit freedom of choice, but they are assumed proper by almost all individuals in American society.

These two processes constitute the dialectic of society. As contrary tendencies, they generate tension because the instrumental forces are constantly prodding the institutions to change when it is not their nature to do so.

The second assumption is that *societies are organized but the very process of organization generates conflict*. Organization implies, among other things, differential allocation of power. Inequalities in power are manifested in at least two conflict-generating ways: differentials in decision making, and inequalities in the system of social stratification (social classes and minority groups). Scarce resources can never be distributed equally to all persons and groups in society. The powerful are always differentially rewarded and make the key decisions as to the allocation of scarce resources.

A third basic assumption for a synthesis model is that *society is a social system*. The term **"social system"** has several important implications: (1) that there is not chaos but some semblance of order—that action within the unit is, in a general way, predictable; (2) that boundaries exist which may be in terms of geographical space or membership; and (3) that there are parts which are interdependent—thus conveying the reality of differentiation and unity. A society is a system made up of many subsystems (for example, groups, organizations, communities). Although these are all related in some way, some are strongly linked to others, while others have only a remote linkage. The interdependence of the parts implies further that events and decisions in one sector may have a profound influence on the entire system. A strike in the transportation industry, for example, eventually impinges upon all individuals and groups. But some events have little or no effect upon all of American society. Most important for the synthesis approach is the recognition that the parts of the system may have complementary interests with other parts but may also have exclusive, incompatible interests and goals. There is generally some degree of cooperation and harmony found in society because of consensus over common goals and because of similar interests (for example, defense against external threats). Some degree of competition and dissensus is also present because of incompatible interests, scarcity of resources, and unequal rewards. Societies, then, are imperfect social systems.

A fourth assumption is that *societies are held together by complementary interests, by consensus on cultural values, but also by coercion.* Societies do cohere. There are forces that bind diverse groups together into a single entity. The emphasis of both order and conflict models provides twin bases for such integration—consensus and coercion.

Finally, *social change is a ubiquitous phenomenon in all societies. It may be gradual or abrupt, reforming or revolutionary.* All social systems change. Order theorists have tended to view change as a gradual phenomenon occurring either because of innovation or because of differentiation (for example, dividing units into subunits to separate activities and make the total operation more efficient within the society). This view of change is partially correct. Change can also be abrupt; it can come about because of internal violence, or it may result from forces outside the society (that is, reaction to events outside the system, or accepting the innovations of others).

To summarize, a synthesis of the order and conflict models views society as having ". . .two faces of equal reality—one of stability, harmony, and consensus and one of change, conflict, and constraint."[12]

The remainder of this chapter illustrates the duality of social life by examining American society from the perspectives of the conflict and order theorists. We will consider the sources of disunity in the United States and the major instances of violence that have occurred throughout American history. Despite the existence of division and violence, the United States is unified at least minimally. We will, therefore, also consider the factors that work to unify.

Division and Violence in American Society

Societies are integrated but disunity and disharmony also exist to some degree in all societies. It is especially important to examine the segmenting influences in American society, for they aid in explaining contemporary conflict and social change.

Social scientists studying the divisive forces in American society have found that in small groups, the more heterogeneous the group, the more likely cliques will form. A group composed of members of one religion, for example, cannot form cliques on the basis of religion, but one with three religions represented has the potential of subdividing into three parts.[13] This principle applies to larger organizations as well, including societies. The United States, then, has the potential of many, many subgroups since it is so diverse. The United States is, in effect, a mosaic of different groups— different on a number of dimensions, such as occupation, racial background, education, and economic circumstances. Let us briefly examine these and other dimensions and the manner in which they bring about segmentation in American society.

Size.   The United States is large in size, in both number of people and expanse of land. Both of these facts have a segmenting influence in American society. With respect to population size, there is an accepted sociological proposition that states: "As the population of a social organization increases, the number of its parts and the degree of their specialization also increases."[14] If, as in the United States, there is not only a large population (over 235 million) but also a high level of technology, then the division of labor becomes very refined. This division is so refined that there are over 30,000 different occupations recognized and catalogued by the Bureau of the Census.

If people have specialized occupations, they will probably interact most often with persons like themselves. Because of similar interests, they will tend to cooperate with each other and perhaps compete with other groups for advantage. An important social theorist of the early 1900s, Robert Michels, wrote about this tendency for exclusion and conflict as a universal tendency in all social organizations.

> By a universally applicable social law, every organ of the collectivity, brought into existence through the need for the division of labor, creates for itself, as soon as it becomes consolidated, interests peculiar to itself. The existence of these special interests involves a necessary conflict with the interests of the collectivity.[15]

A second segmenting factor related to size has to do with land rather than population. The United States, excluding Alaska and Hawaii, has an area of 3,615,123 square miles. Found within this large territory is a wide range in topography and climate. Some areas are sparsely settled, others not. Some regions are attracting new residents at a much faster rate than others.

Traditionally there have been pronounced regional differences (and sometimes rivalries) because each region had its own economic specialization (that is, its own industry and agriculture) and each was relatively isolated from the influences of the others. The revolutions in manufacturing, transportation, and communication have helped to break down this regionalism.

Although regionalism has been declining, it remains a force that sometimes divides Americans. As evidence of this, many votes in Congress show that regional considerations often outweigh national ones. Many nonsouthern

Americans have stereotyped ideas of southerners. Southerners often hold stereotypes of the "Yankee" that may cause the rejection of ideas and innovations from such a source. Consequently, communication within American society is often blocked and interaction stifled because persons from one region feel not only physically separate from but also superior to persons from other regions.

Social Class. Economic differences provide important sources of division in American society. There is the natural resentment of persons without the necessities of life toward those with a bountiful supply of not only the necessities but luxuries as well. There is also hostility toward a system that provides excessive benefits (or excessive hurdles) to persons not on the basis of demonstrated skills but on family background.

Status (prestige) differentials also divide Americans. Organizations, residential areas, and social clubs sometimes exclude certain persons and groups because of their social "inferiority."

Race. Throughout human history race has been used as a criterion for differentiation. If any factor makes a difference in American society, it is race. Blacks, American Indians, Mexican Americans, and other minority racial groups have often been systematically excluded from residential areas, occupations, and organizations, and even sometimes denied equal rights under the law. Although the overt system of racial discrimination has changed, racist acts continue in American society, with the result that these disadvantaged groups continue to be second-class citizens.

Racial strife has occurred throughout American history. Slave revolts, Indian battles, race riots, and lynchings have occurred with regularity. Racial conflict continues today not only in the ghettos of large cities but in most neighborhoods where the minority group is large enough to be perceived by the majority as a threat, in universities and secondary schools, in factories and other places of work, and in the armed forces. The rhetoric of violence has been escalated recently by minority-group leaders. The appeal of militant groups is even greater, particularly among the young. Minority-group members are no longer willing to wait for slow racial reform. They are bent upon seeing justice done now. It is equally clear that many majority-group members will do virtually anything to keep the status quo (that is, to retain an advantageous position for themselves). Many minority persons seeking to shake the status quo may participate in various acts of violence. This violence brings repression by the powerful which further angers and frustrates the minority—thus a treadmill of violence and division.

The racial composition of the United States is changing and this will likely lead to increased tension and conflict. The two largest racial minorities are increasing in number faster than the rest of the population. By 1990, blacks will number nearly 30 million (12.2 percent of the population) and Hispanics, the fastest growing minority, will likely number 17 million (7 percent of the population—up from 4 percent in 1970).[16] Also in recent years refugees in great numbers have fled to the United States. In 1980 there were a total of 375,000 Indochinese; 900,000 Cubans; and 100,000

Haitian refugees in the United States. Not classified as refugees are the millions of undocumented immigrants mostly from Mexico and South America, estimated to number between 3.5 and 12 million in 1980.[17] These refugees have brought problems that have led to growing hostility. Jobs are in short supply. Taxes are already high and these groups require large amounts of aid. The poor fear that these new refugees will take jobs, increase demands on cheap housing, and decrease welfare currently allocated to them. Schools and other public agencies cannot meet the demands of these new groups.

Ethnic Groups.   The United States is inhabited by a multitude of **ethnic groups** that migrated to this country in different waves and continue to do so. These groups have distinctive lifestyles and customs. One reason for this is that they have retained a cultural heritage brought to this country from another society. Another, and very important for their continued distinctiveness, is the structure of American society. The persistence of subordination, discriminatory housing and work patterns, and other forms of structured inequality encourages solidarity among the disadvantaged.[18] The uniqueness and strong ethnic identification of immigrant groups is a source of internal strength for them but causes resentment, negative stereotypes, competition, hatred, and conflict as other ethnic groups or members of the dominant majority question their loyalty, resent their success, fear being displaced by them in the job market, and worry about maintaining the integrity of their schools and neighborhoods (Panel 3–1).

PANEL 3–1

Los Angeles and the New Immigrants

More immigrants (legal and undocumented) are coming to Los Angeles than to any other American city. This is because of the warm climate and the easy access from Asia and Mexico. In 1960 the principal minority groups—blacks, Hispanics, and Asiatics—accounted for 28 percent of the city's population. The estimates in 1980 were: 20 percent black, 30 percent Hispanic, 10 percent Asiatic, and 40 percent Anglo out of a population of 2.9 million. Most of the change occurred from 1975 to 1980 with heavy migrations of Mexicans, Vietnamese, and Koreans.

The immigrants have strained city services and schools. There are 83 languages spoken in Los Angeles County and every government agency lacks employees who can communicate with the refugees. The schools, however, are especially affected. Hollywood High School,

for example, has students who speak 60 different languages and dialects. In Grant Elementary School, 95 percent of the new pupil enrolling in 1980 could speak no English.

The potential for social unrest in this situation is heightened in a number of ways, a noted in the following account from the *Wall Street Journal*:

"We're very concerned about the hostility here and the potential for a riot," says Carl Martin, executive director of the Los Angeles County Commission on Human Relations; he and everyone else here remember the carnage of the Watts riots in 1965. "We haven't had any overt, major incidents in recent years, and we're hoping the lid can be kept on," he adds.

But the pot is bubbling. There were 783 murders in the city last year, 50% more than in 1975. Many were due to gang warfare involving minorities battling for turf. For many immigrants, joining a gang gives them an identity and a measure of protection; in the sprawling barrio of East Los Angeles, three generations in the same house may belong to the same gang.

Blacks and Hispanics here have been fighting between and among themselves for many years, and so have rival Hong Kong and Taiwanese gangs, including the Wah Chings and Jo Fongs. Vietnamese of Chinese extraction now are joining them, and Korean gangs such as the American Burgers, Korean Killers, and Black Ji are slugging it out with black and Hispanic gangs from adjoining neighborhoods.

Ironically, immigrants also have trouble adjusting to the other immigrants and minorities they find here. Many Asians have ingrained prejudices against, and fear of, blacks. They don't necessarily get along with other Asians, either; though Anglos lump them together as one minority, the Asians include dozens of nationalities and regional groups with a history of animosity in their home countries. "We've been fighting each other for centuries," one Japanese-American says.

Unskilled immigrants from traditional rural societies have the hardest adjustment of all. Jo Marcel, head of the county's Indochina social-service project, says wife-beating, divorce, and alcoholism are all rising as the Indochinese struggle with a foreign urban culture, ideas such as women's liberation, and even indoor plumbing. . . .

Most newcomers must settle for rock-bottom jobs. Some become the pawns of employers who play off one minority against another to keep wages low. Recently more than a dozen Vietnamese hired by an assembly plant in the San Fernando Valley complained of harassment from Hispanic co-workers; the community agency that got them the positions discovered that the Vietnamese had replaced Hispanics fired because they had wanted to start a union.

The influx of foreigners also is creating restlessness in Watts and other predominantly black areas of south-central Los Angeles, where youth unemployment hovers at around 50 percent. "We are opening our arms to immigrants, but we aren't opening our arms to our own black citizens who've been here much longer," says John Mack, president of the Los Angeles Urban League. Adds an AFL-CIO official here: "Charity should begin at home."

Blacks, however, have political influence the others lack. Mayor Tom Bradley is black, and so are three of the 15 city councilmen—while Hispanics, by far the biggest minority and possibly a majority within 10 or 20 years, haven't any elected representatives in city government. That may change. One political analyst says: "As the Anglos fade, you may see the blacks running the political establishment and Chicanos fighting them for power."

Meanwhile, more people keep coming. Some 200 miles south, they penetrate the border, move north by night and melt into "East Los," uncounted and uncountable. They come from Russia, Samoa, Manila. Some 1,500 Indochinese are arriving every month, mostly after stays in other American cities; they like the climate in Los Angeles and are drawn by the presence of so many countrymen. Smiling in the sunlight, one recent arrival says cheerfully: "After a year or two, we all move here."

Religion. A wide variety of religious beliefs is found in the United States (see Figure 3–1). Although 59 percent of Americans are Protestants, the variations among them include snake handlers in Appalachia, the Amish who refuse modern conveniences, sects that refuse medical help, literalists who are dogmatic in their narrow views of the Scriptures, and other groups that accept religious pluralism. Among the 28 percent of Americans who are Roman Catholics, great differences exist in beliefs and lifestyles. The same is true when comparing Orthodox, Conservative, and Reformed Jews. And, outside the Judeo-Christian tradition are Buddhists, Muslims, and many other religious organizations and faiths.

Religion, like race and ethnicity, evokes an emotional response in individuals. It is difficult to be neutral about religion. It is almost impossible to accept the idea that religious beliefs other than one's own are equally legitimate. Religion also has a polarizing effect because it is often the basis for selecting (or rejecting) mates, friends, neighbors, schools, and employees.

FIGURE 3–1   Religious Preference of Major Faiths and Denominations, 1981

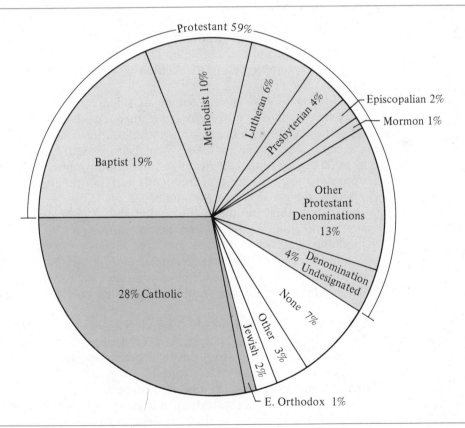

Source: The Gallup Report, "Religion in America," Report Nos. 201–202 (June-July 1982), p. 22.

Therefore, religious differences in the United States not only differentiate persons but also may provide the basis for conflict.[19]

Religious intolerance is not unknown in American history. Although the nation was founded on the principle of religious freedom, at various times and places Jews, Catholics, Quakers, Mennonites, and atheists have been targets of religious bigotry.

There have been political parties (Know-Nothing Party), organizations (Ku Klux Klan and the American Nazi Party), and demagogues (Gerald L.K. Smith and George Lincoln Rockwell) that have been anti-Catholic and anti-Semitic. Their moderate success in attracting followers demonstrates that some Americans are susceptible to such appeals. The effect has been to lessen the probability of interfaith cooperation and enhance the likelihood of conflict.

These segmenting factors create some groups in society that are advantaged and others that are disadvantaged. The former work to perpetuate their advantages while the latter sometimes organize to protest and change the system they consider unfair.[20] But how can these persons change the system if they are self-defined as powerless? A first step is legitimate, polite protest, which usually takes the form of voting, petitions, or writing public officials. A second option is to use impolite, yet legitimate forms of protest (for example, peaceful demonstrations, picket lines, boycotts, and marches). The third alternative, used when others fail, is to employ illegitimate forms of protest (for example, civil disobedience, riots, bombings, and guerilla warfare).[21]

Illegitimate protest is selected by dissident groups because of the intransigence of those in power toward change. The dissident groups consider their actions legitimate because they are for a just cause ("the ends justify the means"), but these protests are perceived as illegitimate by those in power. Those in authority resort to force, often intensifying the zeal and purpose of the protester, and frequently rallying previously uncommitted persons to the cause of the dissidents.

Implicit in this section is the notion that highly differentiated social systems, like that in the United States, must cope with the realities of disharmony, conflict of interest, and even violence. There is no alternative to conflict because of the diverse conditions of the American social structure. This is not to say that conflict is altogether bad. There can be positive consequences of conflict for both parties to the conflict and for society as well.[22]

All societies have the potential for cleavage and conflict because of the differential allocation of power. Concomitant with having power is the holding of other advantages (prestige, privilege, and economic benefits). Persons with advantage almost invariably wish to keep it, and those without typically want to change the reward system.

Coupled with the stratification system in the United States are other aspects of social structure that increase the probability of conflict. The United States, perhaps more than any other society, is populated by a multitide of ethnic groups, racial groups, and religious groups. The diversity is further increased by the existence of regional differences and a generation gap. Although assimilation has occurred to some degree, the different groups and categories have not blended into a homogeneous mass, but continue to remain separate—often with a pride that makes assimilation unlikely and conflict possible.

Violence in the United States and the Myth of Peaceful Progress

There are two beliefs held typically by Americans that combine to make the **"myth of peaceful progress."**[23] First, there is a widely held notion that the United States is made up of diverse groups that have learned to compromise differences in a peaceful manner. Second, there is the belief that any group in the United States can gain its share of power, prosperity, and respectability merely by playing the game according to the rules. Hence, there is no need for political violence in America, since the system works for the advantage of all.

It is precisely because these beliefs are widely shared that most Americans do not understand dissent by minority groups. These are believed to be aberrations, and are explained away by saying that they are communist-inspired, or that some groups (for example, blacks) are exceptions to the rule because they are basically immoral and irrational. Perhaps the most prevalent explanation locates the source of all violence in the individual psyches of the persons involved.

These explanations are incomplete because they locate the blame outside the system itself. American history shows that, with but few exceptions, powerless and downtrodden groups seeking power have not achieved it without a struggle. American institutions, Rubenstein has noted, are better designed to facilitate the upward mobility of talented individuals than of oppressed groups. "Most groups which have engaged in mass violence have done so only after a long period of fruitless, relatively nonviolent struggle in which established procedures have been tried and found wanting."[24] The problem is that the United States, like all other societies, has not and does not allow for the nonviolent transfer of power.

Throughout American history groups that were oppressed resorted to various legitimate and illegitimate means to secure rights and privileges which they believed to be rightfully theirs. Those in power typically reacted either by doing nothing or by repression—the choice depending upon the degree to which the minority groups' actions were perceived as a real threat. The following is a partial list of groups which at various times in American history have resorted to violence to achieve social, economic, or political objectives.[25]

Revolutionary Colonists.   The most notable case of violence by a minority in early American history was the Revolutionary War. The United States was literally born through violence. The American colonists first petitioned the King of England to redress grievances, and when this failed they turned to acts of civil disobedience and finally to eight years of war. "The Declaration of Independence," clearly a revolutionary document, provided the rationale for mass violence:

We hold these truths to be self-evident, that all men are created equal, that they are endowed by their Creator with certain unalienable Rights, that among these are Life, Liberty, and the pursuit of Happiness. That to secure these rights, Governments are instituted among Men, deriving their just powers from the consent of the governed. That whenever any Form of Government becomes destructive of these ends, it is the Right of the People to alter or to abolish it, and to institute new Government, laying its foundation on such principals and organizing its powers in such form as to them shall seem most likely to effect their Safety and Happiness. Prudence, indeed, will dictate that Governments long established should not be changed for light and transient causes; and accordingly all experiences hath shewn that mankind are more disposed to suffer, while evils are sufferable, than to right themselves by abolishing the forms to which they are accustomed. But when a long train of abuses and usurpations, pursuing invariably the same Object evinces a design to reduce them under absolute Despotism, it is their right, it is their duty, to throw off such Government, and to provide new Guards for their future security . . .

This document, a cornerstone of American heritage, legitimates the use of violence by oppressed peoples. It could have been written by a modern-day militant. While still revered, its content is no longer taken literally by the bulk of the American citizenry.

American Indians.   Long before the Revolutionary War, and continuing to the present day, Indians attempted to change the order established by whites. When white settlers took their land, ruined their hunting, and imprisoned them on reservations, the Indians fought these occurrences and were systematically suppressed by the United States government.[26] In recent years Indians have occasionally boycotted, used violence (for example, trashing of the Bureau of Indian Affairs headquarters in 1972), tried to take land by violence (for example, Alcatraz in 1969 and Wounded Knee, South Dakota, in 1973), or used legal offensives to regain former Indian lands. The last tactic has become especially popular. More than half of the 266 federally recognized tribes have claims in various federal courts. These are not trivial claims, as evidenced by the case brought by the Passamaquoddy and Penobscot tribes to regain 8 million sparsely settled acres in Maine.[27]

Exploited Farmers.   Farmers have used violence on occasion to fight economic exploitation. Between the Revolutionary War and 1800, for example, three such revolts took place—Shays's Rebellion, the Whiskey Rebellion, and Fries's Rebellion. The protesting farmer has used various forms of violence (destruction of property, looting, and killing) throughout American history. Some modern farmers have resorted to acts of violence to publicize their demands and to terrorize other farmers in order to present a united front against their opponents.

Slaveholders.   Feeling the threat of the abolitionist movement, white southerners beginning in about 1820 used violent means to preserve slavery. In the early stages this amounted to civil disobedience, and later it burst out into fighting in places like "bleeding Kansas." Eventually the South seceded and the Civil War was waged—a classic example of a minority group using violence to force a change and being suppressed by the power of the majority.

WASP Supremacists.   Following the Civil War and continuing to the present day, some whites have engaged in guerilla warfare, terrorism, and lynching in order to maintain the subjugation of blacks. From 1882 to 1903, for example, 1,985 blacks were killed by southern lynch mobs.[28]

Riots, lynchings, and mob actions are not solely southern phenomena. Many Americans from other sections of the country have used these techniques against various "alien" groups (usually Catholics and immigrants from non-Teutonic Europe) in order to maintain their superiority. American history is rife with examples of this phenomenon: "Native Americans" tore apart the Irish section of Philadelphia in 1844; a Catholic church and homes of Irish Catholics were destroyed in Boston in 1854; Chinese and Japanese immigrants were victims of both riots and discrimination, particularly on the West Coast; Japanese, even those who were American citizens, were put in "concentration camps" during World War II because their patriotism was suspect; and Jews have been the objects of physical attack, boycotts, intimidation, and discrimination throughout American history. Perhaps the best contemporary example of mob violence against intruders can be seen in some communities where an all-white neighborhood is faced with one or more black families moving in. Threats, burning crosses, ostracism, and occasional physical violence have occurred with alarming regularity where black "invasion" of previously all-white areas has taken place. This is not a southern phenomenon but an American one.*

Ethnic Minorities.   Immigrant groups (that is, those groups most recently immigrant) as well as racial groups, because they have been the target of discrimination, threats, and physical violence, have themselves participated in violence. Sometimes gangs have attacked the groups responsible for their deprived condition. Most often, however, hostility by immigrants has been aimed at groups with less power, either toward blacks or toward more newly arrived immigrants.

Violence by blacks has occurred throughout American history. Always the victims, they have sometimes responded to violence in kind. During the years of slavery more than 250 insurrections took place. Mass black violence has occurred in many major cities (for example, Chicago and Washington, D.C., in 1919, Detroit in 1943, and again in 1967, Los Angeles in 1965, and Newark in 1967).

The rage that blacks must feel against whites has surfaced sporadically in small and diffuse ways as well. Most commonly it has been manifested in individual crimes (murder, theft, and rape) or gang assaults on whites or in destruction of property owned by whites.

Labor Disputants.   Another relatively powerless group resorting to violence to achieve their aims was American labor. The workingmen of the 1870s attempted to organize for collective action against unfair policies of the industrialists. Unions, such as the Knights of Labor, American Federation of Labor, and the Industrial Workers of the World, formed. Their primary tactic was the strike, which in itself is nonviolent. But strikers often used force to keep persons from crossing the picket lines. Nor were the owners blameless. Their refusal to change existing wages, hours, and working con-

---

* Ironically, this type of violence usually occurs in blue-collar areas (black "invasion" is not a threat in the more expensive neighborhoods) where individuals are more prone toward "law-and-order" political candidates. Apparently when individuals feel personally threatened, "law and order" becomes vigilantism.

ditions was the source of grievance. They sometimes turned to violence themselves to suppress the unions (for example, threats and hiring persons to physically break up picket lines).

The intransigent refusal of the owners to change the truly awful conditions of nineteenth-century workers resulted in considerable violence in many industries, particularly in the coal mining, steel, timber, and railroad industries. Labor violence, as in other cases mentioned previously, was ultimately effective. Working conditions, wages, and security of the workers improved. Legislation was passed providing for arbitration of differences, recognition of unions, and so on. Clearly, the use of force was necessary to gain advances for the laboring man.

Given the evidence just cited, it is remarkable that people still hold to the "Myth of Peaceful Progress." Violence was necessary to give birth to the United States. Violence was used both to keep the blacks in servitude and to free them. Violence was used to defeat rebellious Indians and to keep them on reservations. Additionally, violence has been a necessary means for many groups in American society to achieve equality or something approaching parity in power and in the rights that all Americans are supposed to enjoy.

The powerful have not been munificent in giving a break to the powerless. To the contrary, much effort has been expended by the powerful to keep the powerless in that condition. Many times in American history, violence has been the only catalyst for change. Minority groups in the United States (for example, blacks, women, farmers) have repeatedly gone outside of existing law. To these groups, the use of force was justified because of the need to right insufferable wrongs—the very reason the colonists gave for breaking from England. We should note, however, that violence does not always work. The Indian revolts were not beneficial in any way to the Indians. Moreover, some groups, such as the Jews, have advanced with comparatively little violence.[29] Historically, however, "violence is as American as cherry pie." The Presidential Commissions on Civil Disorders and Violence have laid bare the inaccuracies of the "peaceful progress" idea held by so many Americans. The uniform remedy suggested by these commissions for minimizing violence is to solve the cause of social unrest and perceived injustice. It cannot be a surprise that minority groups occasionally use violence because they are reacting against a system that systematically disadvantages them with little hope for change through peaceful means.

The Integrative Forces in American Society

Most order theorists recognize that conflict, disharmony, and division occur within societies, particularly in complex, heterogeneous societies. They stress, however, the opposite societal characteristics of cooperation, harmony, and unity. They see American society as "We the people of the United States . . ." rather than a conglomerate of sometimes hostile groups.

In particular, order theorists focus on what holds society together. What are the forces that somehow keep anarchy from becoming a reality—or as the philosopher Hobbes asked long ago, "Why is there not a war of all against all?" The answer to this fundamental question is found in the combined effects of a number of factors.

Functional Integration. Probably the most important unifying factor is the phenomenon of **functional integration.** In a highly differentiated society such as the United States with its very specialized division of labor, interaction among different segments occurs with some regularity. Interdependence often results because no group is entirely self-sufficient. The farmer needs the miller, the processor, and retail agents, as well as the fertilizer manufacturer and the agricultural experimenters. Manufacturers need raw materials, on the one hand, and customers, on the other. Management needs workers and the workers need management.

These groups, because they need each other, because each gains from the interaction, work to perpetuate a social framework that maximizes benefits to both parties and minimizes conflict or the breaking of the relationship. Written and unwritten rules emerge to govern these relationships, usually leading to cooperation rather than either isolation or conflict, and to linkages between different (and potentially conflicting) groups.

Consensus on Societal Values. A second basis for the unification of diverse groups in American society is that almost all Americans hold certain fundamental values in common. Order theorists assume that commonly held values are like social glue binding otherwise diverse people in a cohesive societal unit. Unlike functional integration, unity is achieved here through similarity rather than through difference.

Most Americans believe that democracy is the best possible government. Americans accept the wishes of the majority on election day. Defeated candidates, for example, do not go off into the hills with their followers to blow up bridges and otherwise harass the government. Most Americans are patriotic. They revere American heritage and believe strongly in individualism, free enterprise, and the Judeo-Christian ethic.

There are many symbols that epitomize the consensus of Americans with respect to basic values. One such unifying symbol is the American flag. Although a mere piece of cloth, the flag clearly symbolizes something approaching the sacred. Reverence for the flag is evidenced by the shock shown when it is defiled and by the punishment given to defilers. The choice of the flag as an object to spit on, or burn, is a calculated one by dissident groups. They choose to defile it precisely because of what it represents and because most Americans revere it so stongly.

Similarly, such documents as the Declaration of Independence and the Constitution are held in high esteem and serve to unify Americans.

The American heritage is also revered through holidays such as Thanksgiving and Independence Day. Consensus is also achieved through the collective "worship" of such American heroes as George Washington, Abraham Lincoln, and Dwight Eisenhower.

The Social Order. A third factor that unifies all Americans, at least minimally, is that they are all subject to similar influences and "rules of the game." Americans are answerable to the same body of law (at the national level) and they are under the same government. Additionally, Americans use the same language, the same system of monetary exchange, the same standards for measurement, and so on. The order in society is evidenced by the fact that Americans take for granted such assorted practices as obeying traffic lights, the use of credit, and the acceptance of checks in lieu of money.

Group Membership. A source of unity (as well as cleavage) is group memberships. Some groups are exclusive, since they limit membership to a particular race, ethnic group, income category, religion, or other characteristic. The existence of exclusive organizations creates tension if persons are excluded who want to be included, because exclusiveness generally implies feelings of superiority. Country clubs, fraternities, some churches, and some neighborhoods are based on the twin foundations of exclusiveness and superiority. In American society, however, there are groups whose membership consists of persons from varying backgrounds (that is, the membership includes rich and poor or black and white). Consequently, heterogeneous organizations such as political parties, religious denominations or churches, and veterans' organizations allow members the chance not only to interact with persons unlike themselves but also to join together in a common cause.

Many, if not most, Americans who belong to several organizations belong to organizations with different compositions by race, religion, or other salient characteristics. To the extent that these cross-cutting memberships and allegiances exist, they tend to "cancel out" potential cleavages along social class, race, or other lines. Individuals belonging to several different organizations will probably feel some "cross-pressures" (that is, pulls in opposite directions), thereby preventing polarization.

Additionally, most Americans belong to at least one organization such as a school, church, or civic group with norms that support those of the total society. These organizations support the government and what it stands for and they expect their members to do the same.

International Competition and Conflict. External threats to the society's existence unify. The advice Machiavelli gave his "prince" is a regrettable truth: "if the Prince is in trouble he should promote a war." This was the advice that Secretary of State Seward gave to President Lincoln prior to the Civil War. Although expedient advice from the standpoint of preserving unity, it was, Lincoln noted, only a short-term solution.

A real threat to security unifies those groups, no matter how diverse, who feel threatened. Thus, a reasonable explanation for lack of unity in America's involvement in an Indochina war was that the Viet Cong were not perceived by most Americans as a real threat to their security. The

Soviet buildup in armaments in the late 1970s and early 1980s, on the other hand, was perceived as a real threat, unifying many Americans in a willingness to sacrifice in order to catch up with and surpass the Russians.

The Mass Media.   The world is in the midst of a communications revolution. Only in very recent times has television, for example, expanded to encompass virtually every home in the United States. This phenomenon—universal exposure to television—has been blamed, among other things, for rising juvenile delinquency, lowering cultural tastes, contributing to general moral deterioration, and suppressing creativity.[30] These damning criticisms are countered by order theorists, who see television and the other forms of mass media as performing several integrative functions. Government officials, for example, can use the media to shape public opinion (for example, to unite against an "enemy" or to sacrifice by paying higher taxes). The media also reinforce the values and norms of society. Newspaper editorials extol certain persons and events while decrying others. Soap operas are stories involving moral dilemmas, with virtue winning out. Newspaper and magazine stories under the caption, "It Could Only Have Happened in America," abound. The media do not, except for a few exceptions, "rock the boat." American heroes are praised and her enemies vilified. The American way is the right way; the ways of others are considered incorrect, or downright immoral.

Planned Integration.   Charismatic figures or other persons of influence may work to unite segmented parts of the system (conversely, they can promote division). Thus, a union leader or the archbishop of a Catholic diocese can, through personal exhortation or by example, convince group members to cooperate rather than compete, or to open membership requirements rather than maintain exclusiveness.

Public officials on the local, state, and national levels can use their power to integrate the parts of the society in three major ways: (1) by passing laws to eliminate barriers among groups; (2) by working to solve the problems that segment the society; (3) by providing mediators to help negotiate settlements between such feuding groups as management and labor.[31] High officials such as the President utilize various means of integration. First, there is the technique of **co-optation** (that is, appointing a member of a dissident group to a policy-making body to appease the dissenting group). Second, he can use his executive powers to enforce and interpret the laws in such a way as to unite groups within the society. Finally, the President may use the media to persuade the people. The President can request television time on all networks during prime time, thereby reaching most of the adult population in order to use whatever powers of persuasion he has to unite diverse groups.

False Consciousness.   Most Americans do not feel oppressed. Even many persons who do not have many material blessings tend to believe in the

American creed that anyone can be upwardly mobile—if not themselves, then at least their children.

Thus, contrary to Karl Marx's prediction over a century ago that capitalism would be overthrown by an oppressed majority, most Americans today consider themselves as "haves" rather than as "have-nots." There has been little polarization along purely economic lines because blue-collar workers are often relatively well-off financially (many make more money than persons with more prestigious jobs).

SUMMARY

There are two contradictory models of society—the order and conflict models. The order model views society as basically cooperative, consensual, and stable. The system works. Any problems are the faults of people, not society. At the other extreme, the adherents of the conflict model assume that society is fundamentally competitive, conflictual, coercive, and radically changing. Social problems are the faults of society, not individuals, in this view.

The order and conflict models of society are both significant, and they will be utilized in the remainder of this book. While each, by itself, is important, a realistic analysis must include both. The order model must be included because there is integration, order, and stability; because the parts are more or less interdependent; and because most social change is gradual and adjustive. The conflict model is equally important because society is not always a harmonious unit. To the contrary, much of social life is based on competition. Societal integration is fragile; it is often based on subtle or blatant coercion.

A crucial difference between the two models is the implicit assumption of each as to the nature of the social structure (rules, customs, institutions, social stratification, and the distribution of power). The order perspective assumes that the social structure is basically right and proper because it serves the fundamental function of maintaining society. There is, therefore, an implicit acceptance of the status quo, assuming that the system works. As we examine the major institutions of society in this book, one of the tasks will be to determine how each of these institutions aids in societal integration.

Although order theorists also look for the **dysfunctions** of institutions, rules, organizations, and customs (dysfunctions refer to those consequences that are malintegrative), the critical examination of society is the primary thrust of conflict theorists. While this book will describe the way American society is structured and how this arrangement works for societal integration, a major consideration will center around the question, "who benefits under these arrangements and who does not?" Thus, the legitimacy of the system will always be doubted.

CHAPTER REVIEW

1. Sociologists have a mental image (model) of how society is structured, how it changes, and what holds it together. There are two prevailing models—order and conflict—that provide contradictory images of society.

2. Order model theorists view society as ordered, stable, and harmonious, with a high degree of cooperation and consensus. Change is gradual, adjustive, and reforming. Social problems are seen as the result of problem individuals.

3. Conflict model theorists view society as competitive, fragmented, and unstable. Social integration is minimal and tenuous. Social change, which can be revolutionary, results from clashes among conflicting groups. Social problems are viewed as resulting from society's failure to meet the needs of individuals. Indeed, the structure of society is seen as the problem.

4. The order and conflict models present extreme views of society. Taken alone, each fosters a faulty perception and interpretation of society. A realistic model of society combines the strengths of both models. The assumptions of such a synthesis are: (a) the processes of stability and change are properties of all societies; (b) societies are organized but the very process of organization generates conflict; (c) society is a social system, with the parts linked through common goals and similar interests, and competitive because of scarce resources and inequities; (d) societies are held together by consensus on values and by coercion; and (e) social change may be gradual or abrupt, reforming or revolutionary.

5. The divisive forces bringing about segmentation in American society are size, social class, race, ethnic groups, and religion. Thus, society has the potential for cleavage and conflict.

6. Americans tend to believe in the "myth of peaceful progress"—that disadvantaged groups throughout history have gained prosperity and equality without violence. The evidence, however, is that oppressed groups have had to use force or the threat of force to achieve gains.

7. There are a number of integrative forces in American society. These are functional integration, consensus on values, the social order, group memberships, threats from other societies, the mass media, planned integration, and false consciousness.

FOR FURTHER STUDY

Sociological Theories: General

Thomas J. Bernard, *The Consensus-Conflict Debate* (New York: Columbia University Press, 1983).

Tom Bottomore and Robert Nisbet (eds.), *A History of Sociological Analysis* (New York: Basic Books, 1978).

E. Ellis Cashmore and Bob Mullen, *Approaching Social Theory* (London: Heinemann, 1983).

Graham C. Kinloch, *Sociological Theory: Its Development and Major Paradigms* (New York: McGraw-Hill, 1977).

George Ritzer, *Sociological Theory* (New York: Knopf, 1983).

George Ritzer, *Contemporary Sociological Theory* (New York: Knopf, 1983).

The Order Model

Kingsley Davis, *Human Society* (New York: Macmillan, 1937).

Robert K. Merton, *Social Theory and Social Structure*, Revised Edition (New York: Free Press, 1968).

Talcott Parsons, *Sociological Theory and Modern Society* (New York: Free Press, 1967).

Jonathan Turner and Alexandra Maryanski, *Functionalism* (Menlo Park, Calif.: Benjamin-Cummings, 1979).

Robin Williams, Jr., *American Society: A Sociological Interpretation*, 3rd ed. (New York: Knopf, 1970).

The Conflict Model

Charles H. Anderson and Jeffry R. Gibson, *Toward a New Sociology*, 3rd ed. (Homewood, Ill.: Dorsey Press, 1978).

William J. Chambliss, ed., *Sociological Readings in the Conflict Perspective* (Reading, Mass.: Addison-Wesley, 1973).

Ralf Dahrendorf, *Class and Class Conflict in Industrial Society* (Stanford: Stanford University Press, 1958).

Karl Marx and Friedrich Engels, *The Communist Manifesto*, Eden Paul and Cedar Paul, trans. (New York: Russell and Russell, 1963).

C. Wright Mills, *The Power Elite* (New York: Oxford University Press, 1956).

Michael Parenti, *Power and the Powerless* (New York: St. Martin's Press, 1978).

NOTES AND REFERENCES

1. Stokely Carmichael and Charles V. Hamilton, *Black Power: The Politics of Liberation in America* (New York: Random House (Vintage Books), 1967), p. 4.
2. Robin M. Williams, Jr., *American Society: A Sociological Interpretation*, 3rd ed. (New York: Alfred A. Knopf, 1970).
3. Emile Durkheim, *Suicide*, John A. Spaulding and George Simpson, trans. (New York: Free Press, 1951), originally published in 1897; Emile Durkheim, *The Division of Labor in Society*, George Simpson, trans. (New York: Free Press, 1933), first published in 1893; and Emile Durkheim, *The Elementary Forms of Religious Life*, Joseph Ward Swain, trans. (New York: Macmillan (Collier Books), 1961), first published in 1912.
4. Emile Durkheim, *The Rules of the Sociological Method*, 8th ed. (Glencoe, Ill.: Free Press, 1938), pp. 64–75.
5. Robert K. Merton, *Social Theory and Social Structure*, 2nd ed. (Glencoe, Ill.: Free Press, 1957), pp. 19–84.
6. Ralf Dahrendorf, *Class and Class Conflict in Industrial Society* (Stanford, Calif.: Stanford University Press, 1959).
7. *Sociological Inquiry* 40 (Winter, 1970).
8. This section depends largely on the insights from three sources: John Horton, "Order and Conflict Theories of Social Problems as Competing Ideologies," *American Journal of Sociology* 71 (May, 1966), pp. 701–713; Jerome H. Skolnick and Elliott Currie, "Approaches to Social Problems," in *Crisis in American Institutions*, Jerome H. Skolnick and Elliott Currie, eds. (Boston: Little, Brown, 1970), pp. 1–16; and Earl Rubington and Martin S. Weinberg, eds., *The Study of Social Problems: Five Perspectives* (New York: Oxford University Press, 1971).
9. William Ryan, *Blaming the Victim* (New York: Pantheon Books, 1971).
10. A number of contemporary analysts have attempted such a synthesis: Pierre van den Berghe, "Dialectics and Functionalism: Toward a Theoretical Synthesis," *American Sociological Review* 28 (October, 1963), pp. 697–705; Gerhard E. Lenski, *Power and Privilege: A Theory of Social Stratification* (New York: McGraw-Hill, 1966); and Chalmers Johnson, *Revolutionary Change* (Boston: Little, Brown, 1966).
11. Allen Wheelis, *The Quest for Identity* (New York: W. W. Norton, 1958).
12. Ralf Dahrendorf, "Out of Utopia: Toward a Reorientation of Sociological Analysis," *American Journal of Sociology* 64 (September, 1968), p. 127.

13. James A. Davies, "Structural Balance, Mechanical Solidarity, and Interpersonal Relations," *Sociological Theories in Progress I*, Joseph Berger, Morris Zelditch, Jr., and Bo Anderson, eds. (Boston: Houghton Mifflin, 1966), pp. 74–101.

14. Paul E. Mott, *The Organization of Society* (Englewood Cliffs, N.J.: Prentice-Hall, 1965), p. 50.

15. Robert Michels, *Political Parties*, Eden Paul and Cedar Paul, trans. (New York: Free Press, 1966), p. 389.

16. "U.S. Population Headed for Change in the '80s," *Intercom* 8 (January, 1980), p. 12. See also, Kurt Anderson, "The New Ellis Island," *Time* (June 13, 1983), pp. 18–25; and James Fallows, "Immigration," *The Atlantic Monthly* 252 (November 1983), pp. 45–106.

17. "Refugees: Stung by a Backlash," *U.S. News & World Report* (October 13, 1980), pp. 60–63.

18. See Ronald L. Taylor, "Black Ethnicity and the Persistence of Ethnogenesis," *American Journal of Sociology* 84 (May, 1979), pp. 1401–1423; and William L. Yancey, Eugene P. Ericksen, and Richard N. Juliani, "Emergent Ethnicity: A Review and Reformulation," *American Sociological Review* 41 (June, 1976), pp. 391–402.

19. Earl Raab (ed.), *Religious Conflict in America* (Garden City, N.Y.: Doubleday (Anchor Books), 1964); and Robert Lee and Martin E. Marty, (eds.), *Religion and Social Conflict* (New York: Oxford University Press, 1964).

20. See Lynne B. Iglitzin, *Violent Conflict in American Society* (San Francisco: Chandler, 1972).

21. David O. Arnold, "The American Way of Death: The Roots of Violence in American Society," *The Age of Protest*, Walt Anderson, ed. (Pacific Palisades, Calif.: Goodyear, 1969), pp. 262–268.

22. Lewis Coser, *The Functions of Social Conflict* (New York: Free Press, 1956); and Joseph S. Himes, "The Functions of Racial Conflict," *Social Forces* 45 (September, 1966), pp. 1–10.

23. The following discussion is drawn largely from three staff reports to the National Commission on the Causes and Prevention of Violence: Jerome H. Skolnick, *The Politics of Protest* (New York: Ballantine Books, 1969); Hugh Davis Graham and Ted Robert Gurr, *The History of Violence in America* (New York: Bantam Books, 1969); and James F. Kirkham, Sheldon G. Levy, and William J. Crotty, *Assassination and Political Violence* (New York: Bantam Books, 1970). Also helpful were: Richard E. Rubenstein, *Rebels in Eden: Mass Political Violence in the United States* (Boston: Little, Brown, 1970), and a series of analyses by a number of eminent social scientists appearing in *The New York Times Magazine* (April 28, 1968) under the title, "Is America by Nature a Violent Society?"

24. Rubenstein, *Rebels in Eden*, p. 8.

25. Graham and Gurr, *The History of Violence in America*; Skolnick, *The Politics of Protest*, pp. 10–15; Kirkham, Levy, and Crotty, *Assassination and Political Violence*, pp. 212–237; John Higham, *Strangers in the Land* (New Brunswick, N.J.: Rutgers University Press, 1955); David W. Chalmers, *Hooded Americanism* (Chicago: Quadrangle Books, 1968); Graham Adams, Jr., *Age of Industrial Violence* (New York: Columbia University Press, 1966); and Arthur I. Waskow, *From Race Riot to Sit-In* (Garden City, N.Y.: Doubleday, 1966).

26. Dee Brown, *Bury My Heart at Wounded Knee* (New York: Holt, Rinehart and Winston, 1971).

27. See "Should We Give the U.S. Back to the Indians?" *Time* (April 11, 1977), p. 51; and "If Indian Tribes Win Legal War to Regain Half of Maine—," *U.S. News & World Report*, April 4, 1977, pp. 53–54.

28. James E. Cutler, *Lynch-Law: An Investigation into the History of Lynching in the United States* (New York: Longmans, Green, 1905), p. 177.

29. Rubenstein, *Rebels in Eden*, p. 18.

30. Melvin L. DeFleur, *Theories of Mass Communication*, 2nd ed. (New York: David McKay, 1970), p. 5.

31. Paul E. Mott, *The Organization of Society* (Englewood Cliffs, N.J.: Prentice-Hall, 1965), pp. 283–284.

4

The Duality
of Social Life:
Stability and Change

Technological breakthroughs are a major source of social change. In modern society these occur with ever greater rapidity and often with dramatic impact on individuals. Consider, for example, the possible implications of the following technology-related incidents for individuals and society:

—Cancer kills some 400,000 Americans every year, and the Department of Health, Education and Welfare estimated that at least one-fourth of this total can be attributed to conditions of the workplace. Other estimates are that up to 90 percent of all cancers are environmentally related.[1]

—In March 1979 the risk of nuclear plant failure became clear when the people of Pennsylvania faced the real possibility of a fuel core meltdown at Three Mile Island.

—In 1980 the Supreme Court ruled that the new gene splicing technology could be patented. This ruling opened the door for patenting new life forms with genetic information never before in existence.[2]

—In 1981 it was reported that: "About once every four days, on the average, the Pentagon discovers that the United States is being attacked by Soviet missiles. In the last eighteen months there have been 151 nuclear alerts, each requiring a 'missile display conference' by radio or telephone among U.S. technicians in various parts of the world. Fortunately, all 151 alerts turned out to be equipment failures or false alarms that were identified in time—sometimes barely in time."[3]

There are some major economic and social problems that appear inevitable for the decade of the 1980s. Some of these are: (1) high unemployment will continue; (2) the standard of living will decline; (3) the cost of energy will remain high; (4) competing business and political interest groups will make central planning difficult, if not impossible, to achieve; (5) huge government expenditures for the military will reduce the monies spent for social projects; (6) the gap between the "haves" and the "have nots" will widen; (7) the large cities will be increasingly unable to meet their needs; (8) resources will grow short; and (9) businesses will continue to resist pollution control.

Given the strong probability of these and other problems escalating in proportion and severity, will the system adapt and stabilize or change, even dramatically?[4] There are adaptive mechanisms and trends that may neutralize or at least minimize the potential for social unrest and tumultuous change. These are: (1) the state's ability to adapt by increasing benefits such as unemployment compensation in times of crisis;[5] (2) the tendency of unrest by minorities and other groups to be localized and segmented; (3) the increasing frequency with which both spouses are in the labor force to offset declining personal incomes; (4) patriotism's ability to unify people in times of international tensions; and (5) patriotism's ability to foster a spirit of sacrifice in times of scarcity.

There is an alternative scenario. The problems could reach unprecedented proportions. The government could become more and more ineffective in solving problems. The masses or a significant number of people could focus on a major national problem whose source was clearly identified. Leaders could emerge. The people could become committed to activism with the goal of major structural changes.

The question, then, is just how resilient is our social system? Will the 1980s be a time of turmoil and major change or will this decade be characterized by adaptation and relative stability? The answer is not easy because there are structural forces that work to achieve change and there are others that operate to promote stability. The dialectic between these opposing forces is the subject of this chapter.

CHANGE IN SOCIAL SYSTEMS

Social systems, if they are to survive, require two opposite tendencies—stability and change. They require stability so that interaction and behaviors will be relatively predictable. These must be predictable for goods and services to be produced and distributed, for work to be coordinated, and for chaos in everything from traffic to politics to be averted.

But while societies and their members need stability and predictability, social change is both inevitable *and* necessary. To say that change is inevitable is another way of saying that it is normal. Inevitable changes in the environment or within a social system require changes in the social system. Changes occur in response to external forces that impinge on the system such as war, flood, famine, and economic conditions. Changes occur also because of conditions within the social system such as shortages or surpluses, technological innovations, population growth or decline, conflict between factions, and economic booms or declines. Because societies are never completely stable and tranquil, adjustments (minor or major) are necessary to meet members' needs. These changes may be gradual or abrupt, reforming or revolutionary, deliberate or accidental.

Thus, the duality of social systems introduced in the last chapter includes not only order and conflict but also the related conditions of stability and change. This chapter is organized to describe how society is buffeted by these two seemingly contrary tendencies. We will begin by examining the structural sources for stability, and follow by examining the sources of change.

FORCES FOR STABILITY

Societies strain toward persistence. We are bound in our activities, for example, by the constraints of customs, traditions, myths, and ideologies that we have been taught to accept without thinking. Some of these are so important that we will sacrifice—even our lives, if necessary—to perpetuate them. Religious beliefs and nationalism evoke this kind of response in most of us. Clearly, perceived threats to religious dogma and to the foundations of our political heritage will be resisted by most. We will consider four especially important impediments to social change—institutions, bureaucracy, ideology, and organizations bent on preserving the status quo—in addition to the values and ideologies held by the members of society:

Institutions All **institutions** are by definition reactionary. They provide answers from tradition and thus preserve stability. Each institution, whether it be the family, education, religion, the economy, or the polity, channels behavior in prescribed ways. Any deviation from these demands is punished, either formally or informally. For example, we do not have the option in American society to marry more than one spouse at a time. Similarly, school districts do not hire those who are known atheists, Communists, or homosexuals.

Let's look briefly at the institution of the polity and some other elements of society and see how they operate to resist change in American society.

The government is structured to inhibit change. For example, the choices of decisionmakers are often limited by various **systemic imperatives.** In other words, there is a bias that pressures the government to do certain things and not to do other things. Inevitably, this bias favors the status quo, allowing those with power to continue as they are, because no change is always easier than change. The current political and economic systems have worked and generally are not subject to question, let alone change. In this way the laws, customs, and institutions of society resist change. Thus the propertied and the wealthy benefit while the propertyless and the poor continue to be disadvantaged. As Parenti has argued, the law has such a bias:

> The law does not exist as an abstraction. It gathers shape and substance from a context of power, within a real-life social structure. Like other institutions, the legal system is class-bound. The question is not whether the law should or should not be neutral, for as a product of its society, it *cannot* be neutral in purpose or effect.[6]

In addition to the inertia of institutions, there are other systemic imperatives. One such imperative is for the government to strive to provide an adequate defense system against our enemies, which stifles any external threat to the status quo. Domestically, government policy is also shaped by the systemic imperative for stability. The government promotes domestic tranquility by squelching dissidents. This last point is significant. The job of the government is to keep order. By definition, this function works against change. The "enemies" of society therefore are harassed by the FBI, the CIA, and other government agencies.

The very way that the government is organized promotes stability. For example, the requirement that three fourths of the state legislatures, each by a two-thirds vote, must ratify proposed amendments, makes it extremely difficult to amend the Constitution. Thus, though a majority of the Congress, the people, and the state legislators favor the Equal Rights Amendment, it has failed to be ratified. Similarly the law resists change because the Courts use the principle of precedent to determine current cases. The way Congress is organized is another example. Committee chairs are selected on the basis of seniority not expertise. Longevity in public office is rarely achieved by taking radical stances. Thus the very powerful positions of committee chairs are occupied by people oriented toward the status quo.

As a final example, the two party system is organized to preserve the status quo. A multi-party system, as is common in Western Europe, means that each party has a narrow appeal because of its principles. Our system of two parties, in contrast, requires that both parties have wide appeal. A radical position is not acceptable in this system. Although there is no mention of political parties in the Constitution, our two party system has evolved in such a way as to make third parties inconsequential. Attempts to add parties are thwarted by the election laws, which make it difficult for candidates other than Republicans and Democrats to get on the ballots in each state.[7] At the presidential level, it is difficult for third party candidates to qualify for public campaign funds. They also have difficulty being allowed to participate in televised debates and receiving equal time on television, as John Anderson found out in 1980. Finally, the way Congress is organized, one must be a Republican or a Democrat to be effective.

Bureau-cracy

The process of **bureaucratization** refers to the changes within organizations toward greater rationality—that is, improved operating efficiency and more effective attainment of common goals. (See Panel 4–1.) As the size and complexity of an organization grow, there is a greater need for coordination if efficiency is to be maintained or improved. Organizational efficiency would be maximized (ideally) under the following conditions:

□ When the work is divided into small tasks performed by specialists;
□ When there is a hierarchy of authority (chain of command) with each position in the chain having clearly defined duties and responsibilities;
□ When behaviors are governed by standardized, written, and explicit rules;
□ When all decisions are made on the basis of technical knowledge, not personal considerations;
□ When the members are judged solely on the basis of proficiency, and discipline is impartially enforced.[8]

In short, a bureaucracy is an organization designed to perform like a machine.

The push toward increased bureaucratization pervades nearly all aspects of American life including the government (at all levels), the church (the Catholic Church, the Methodist Church), education (all school systems), sports (NCAA, A.A.U., athletic departments at "big time" schools, professional teams), corporations (General Motors, IBM), and even crime ("mafia").

The majority of social scientists have viewed with alarm what they conceive to be the trend toward greater and greater bureaucratization. Individuals will, it is typically predicted, increasingly become small cogs in very big machines. Narrowly defined tasks, a rigid chain of command, and total impersonality in dealing with others will be our organizational lot in the future. Human beings will be rigid conformists—the prototype of the organization man or woman.

Several aspects of bureaucracies as they operate in reality work to promote the status quo.* First, the blind obedience to rules and the unquestioned following of orders means that new and unusual situations cannot be handled efficiently because the rules do not apply. Rigid adherence to the rules creates automatons. Secondly, bureaucracies tend to be stagnant in selecting

---

*These forces promoting the status quo may actually foster change when bureaucracies are unable to adapt. Thus, individuals may subvert the bureaucracy or form new organizations to meet new conditions. Bureaucracies, then, provide the interesting paradox that in their quest for rationality, they may actually accomplish irrationality.[9]

The Bureaucracy as a Rational Tool: The Organization of Power

Bureaucracy is a remarkable product of gradual, halting, and often unwitting social engineering. Most elements were in place before the spurt of industrialization in the nineteenth century; it was this spurt and the associated control over employees that destroyed most other forms of large-scale organized activity. Without this form of social technology, the industrialized countries of the West could not have reached the heights of extravagance, wealth, and pollution that they currently enjoy. . . .

First . . . I would like to state my own biases. After twenty years of studying complex organizations, I have come to two conclusions that run counter to much of the organizational literature. The first is that the sins generally attributed to bureaucracy are either not sins at all or are consequences of the failure to bureaucratize sufficiently. In this respect, I will defend bureaucracy as the dominant principle of organization in our large, complex organizations. My second conclusion is that the extensive preoccupation with reforming, "humanizing," and decentralizing bureaucracies, while salutary, has served to obscure from organizational theorists the true nature of bureaucracy and has diverted us from assessing its impact upon society. The impact upon society in general is incalculably more important than the impact upon the members of a particular organization, that most critics concern themselves with . . .

By its very nature, and particularly because of its superiority as a social tool over other forms of organization, bureaucracy generates an enormous degree of unregulated and often unperceived social power; and this power is placed in the hands of a very few leaders. As bureaucracies satisfy, delight, and satiate us with their output of goods and services, they also shape our mentality, control our life chances, and define our humanity. They do so not so much in our role as members of one or more of these organizations, but as members of a society that is truly an organizational society. Those who control these organizations control the quality of our life, and they are largely self-appointed leaders.

Let me be quite clear about my position. . . . In my view, bureaucracy is a form of organization superior to all others we know or can hope to afford in the near and middle future; the chances of doing away with it or changing it are probably nonexistent in the West in this century. Thus, it is crucial to understand it and appreciate it. But it is also crucial to understand not only how it mobilizes social resources for desirable ends, but also how it inevitably concentrates those forces in the hands of a few who are prone to use them for ends we do not approve of, for ends we are generally not aware of, and more frightening still, for ends we are led to accept because we are not in a position to conceive alternative ones.

Source: *Complex Organizations: A Critical Essay*, Second Edition, by Charles Perrow. (Glenview, Ill.: Scott, Foresman, 1979, pp. 5–7. Copyright© 1979, 1972 Scott, Foresman and Company. Reprinted by permission of Random House, Inc.

people for leadership roles. Leaders in bureaucracies typically follow two principles when choosing new leaders. The first is to select from the pool of potential leaders those who in addition to being competent have not "rocked the boat;" have proven their loyalty to the organization; and are likely to continue the policies of the current leadership. The second has been labeled "The Peter Principle."[10] When a vacancy occurs, the leadership tends to choose an individual who has been successful at the lower level. That person will continue to advance in the hierarchy until he or she has reached his or her level of incompetence. A good teacher and researcher in college may not be a good department administrator, yet that is often the basis for selection. The Peter Principle taken to the extreme means that a bureaucracy will ultimately be staffed with people who have reached the level just above where they are competent. The result, noted by organizational researchers Blau and Meyer, is that people who realize they are "over their heads" will tend to relieve their feelings of insecurity by overemphasizing rules and regulations.[11] (See Panel 4–2.)

In sum, the bureaucratic form of organization inhibits social change because it encourages sameness. Office holders and those who replace them tend to be very much alike in expertise, outlook, and attitudes. As Leslie, Larson, and Gorman have put it: "Bureaucrats tend strongly to resemble past, present, and future bureaucrats."[12]

Ideology

Ideology can be a prime mover or an impediment to change. The following are a few examples from history of how ideological beliefs stifled change:[13]

- In China, Confucian thought acted as a barrier to change by idealizing the past.
- During the Middle Ages, economic progress was retarded by the Christian belief that usury (the loaning of money for interest) was sinful. The Church also channeled surplus wealth into building religious monuments rather than investing in trade and commercial development.
- The Church at various times has enforced rigid conformity through the Inquisition, heresy trials, and witchcraft trials.
- New scientific ideas challenging religious orthodoxy have routinely been fought by religious groups. Galileo's trial for heresy and the Scopes trial in Tennessee for teaching evolution are two blatant examples of this strong tendency.
- In Russia biological breakthroughs were retarded because the government insisted on a biological theory congruent with Marxian ideology—that socially acquired traits are genetically transmitted to the next generation. Thus, the insights of Mendelian genetics were ignored.

Groups Organized to Resist Change

A **social movement** is a collective attempt to promote or resist change. Such movements arise when people are sufficiently discontented that they will work for a better system. A social movement develops organization with leaders, a division of labor, an ideology, and a set of roles and norms for the members.[14] One type of social movement is explicitly organized to resist change. These **resistance movements** are organized to reinforce the old system by preventing change. Later in this chapter we will examine reform and revolutionary social movements. For now, let's look at those movements that work to resist change or are reactionary in that they want to reverse change that has already occurred.

The Bureaucracy as an Irrational Tool: "Laws" Governing the Behavior in Bureaucracies

Boren's Laws of the Bureaucracy. (1) When in doubt, mumble. (2) When in trouble, delegate. (3) When in charge, ponder.

Robertson's Second Order Rule of Bureaucracy. The more directives you issue to solve a problem, the worse it gets.

Dyer's Law. A continuing flow of paper is sufficient to continue the flow of paper.

Evelyn's Rules for Bureaucratic Survival. (1) A bureaucrat's castle is his desk . . . and parking place. Proceed cautiously when changing either. (2) On the theory that one should never take anything for granted, follow up on everything, but especially those items varying from the norm. The greater the divergence from normal routine and/or the greater the number of offices potentially involved, the better the chance a never-to-be-discovered person will file the problem away in a drawer specifically designed for items requiring a decision. (3) Never say without qualification that your activity has sufficient space, money, staff, etc. (4) Always distrust offices not under your jurisdiction which say that they are there to serve you.

Fowler's Law. In a bureaucracy, accomplishment is inversely proportional to the volume of paper used.

Hacker's Law of Personnel. It is never clear just how many hands—or minds—are needed to carry out a particular process. Nevertheless, anyone having supervisory responsibility for the completion of the task will invariably protest that his staff is too small for the assignment.

Imhoff's Law. The organization of any bureaucracy is very much like a septic tank— the really big chunks always rise to the top.

Parkinson's Laws. (1) Work expands so as to fill the time available for its completion. (2) Expenditure rises to meet income. (3) Expansion means complexity and complexity, decay; or to put it even more plainly—the more complex, the sooner dead.

Peter Principle and Corollaries. In every hierarchy, whether it be government or business, each employee tends to rise to his level of incompetence; every post tends to be filled by an employee incompetent to execute its duties. *Corollaries:* (1) Incompetence knows no barriers of time or place. (2) Work is accomplished by those employees who have not yet reached their level of incompetence. (3) If at first you don't succeed, try something else.

Rayburn's Rule. If you want to get along, go along.

Riesman's Law. An inexorable upward movement leads administrators to higher salaries and narrower spans of control.

Rigg's Hypothesis. Incompetence tends to increase with the level of work performed. And, naturally, the individual's staff needs will increase as his level of incompetence increases.

Smith's Principles of Bureaucratic Tinkertoys. (1) Never use one word when a dozen will suffice. (2) If it can be understood, it's not finished yet. (3) Never do anything for the first time.

Vail's First Axiom. In any human enterprise, work seeks the lowest hierarchical level.

Work Rules. (1) The boss is always right. (2) When the boss is wrong, refer to Rule 1.

Source: Paul Dickson, *The Official Rules: The Definitive, Annotated Collection of Laws, Principles, and Instructions for Dealing with the Real World* (New York: Delta, 1978). Reprinted with permission.

Since periods of rapid change foster resistance movements, there are numerous contemporary examples of this phenomenon. There are current efforts to stop the trend toward the use of nuclear power for energy. People have organized to resist the damming of rivers because they want to protect the environment. The move to make the Equal Rights Amendment part of the Constitution has met with considerable organized resistance. Anti-abortion groups have formed to reverse recent legislation and judicial acts legalizing abortion. These resistance movements are, by definition, political in nature. This is illustrated by the contemporary movement fostered by evangelicals to use their political clout to reverse trends they consider opposite to Christian principles.

FORCES FOR CHANGE

There are a variety of important forces that converge in contemporary American society which heighten the questioning of traditional behavior patterns, which alter roles and rules, and which shift modes of thought and action. These reforming and revolutionary forces—technological change, urbanization, population growth, the economy, the government, and social movements—are the subjects of this section.

Technology Technological change in the United States has been so rapid that it could be characterized as revolutionary. As Sykes has said, paraphrasing Michael Harrington,

> Our lives are becoming drastically transformed not by any self-conscious plan or the machinations of a few, but by the unanticipated consequences of economic and technological development in which we are all implicated. It is the man of business and industry, especially with his goal of productivity and his skillful allocation of resources, who has been the great revolutionary of our era. He has remade our existence far more than any ideologist, smashing institutions, shifting the landscape, stuffing some regions with people and depopulating others—all without a policy or overall purpose.[15]

Technological breakthroughs (for example, the assembly line, computers, birth-control pills) are indeed revolutionary since they create and destroy occupations. They may make some products obsolete and increase the demand for others. They alter behavior, and may even cause a shift in values. Thus, technology solves some problems but creates some new ones. As Charles Silberman has said:

> Economic growth reduces poverty, but it also produces congestion, noise, and pollution of the environment. Technological change widens the individual's range of choice and makes economic growth possible; it also dislocates workers from their jobs and their neighborhoods. Affluence plus new technology

frees men from slavery to the struggle for existence, from the brutalizing labor that had been man's condition since Adam; it thereby forces them to confront the questions of life's meaning and purpose even while it destroys the faith that once provided answers.[16]

The industrial techniques of the early 1900s, for instance, had a number of profound effects. They created a need for a large working class of semiskilled workers whose tasks were largely repetitive. They fostered the growth of cities (and conversely the decline of rural areas). They created products at a relatively low cost, thereby causing the decline of many skilled craftspersons. The high influx of goods through mass production increased the probability of economic booms and depressions, since production and distribution were not always synchronized.

As technology advances many of the jobs created in an earlier era are displaced. There is no longer the need for huge masses of semiskilled workers. The present demand is for educated white-collar workers with narrow specialties. In 1956, there were for the first time more white-collar workers than blue-collar workers. The problem now is that having a narrow specialty ensures obsolescence, since new techniques and knowledge undoubtedly will alter present arrangements very quickly.

Technological changes are the cause of many social problems as well as the source of varied blessings. The paradoxical nature of this trend is important to consider, because both aspects are real and have profound effects upon individuals, groups, and the society as a whole. Much of the current unrest is in reaction to the "bad" qualities engendered by these trends.

Contemporary technology has replaced tedious tasks and backbreaking tasks with labor-saving devices and more leisure time. Life without electricity, television, central heating, air conditioning, and other "necessities" would be difficult for most Americans to accept. For many Americans, however, people are viewed as victims of technology. In the words of Philip Slater:

> We talk of technology as the servant of man, but it is a servant that now dominates the household, too powerful to fire, upon whom everyone is helplessly dependent. We tiptoe about and speculate upon his mood. What will be the effects of such-and-such an invention? How will it change our daily lives? We never ask, for example, if the trivial conveniences offered by the automobile could really offset the calamitous disruption and depersonalization of our lives that it brought about. We simply say "You can't stop progress" and shuffle back inside.[17]

Recent technological advances in communications and transportation have had profound liberating consequences for Americans. Transoceanic flights, space travel, instantaneous worldwide communications, color television from the moon or Rangoon have had the effect of emancipating human beings from the provinciality of their local communities. We have seen alternatives. Dogma has less of a hold on our thinking. We have participated vicariously in historical events. The old customs, the status quo are brought into question as never before.

Television has had an especially important impact on American life. The exact nature of this impact is difficult to assess, however, since modern teenagers are the first generation to have been exposed to television from birth. The average American child by age 18 has watched 22,000 hours of television. The same average viewer has watched thousands of hours of inane situation comedy, fantasy, and soap opera (and an average of 4286 acts of violence). He or she also has watched great drama, debates, music, and has been educated to the wonders of nature. Additionally, the television medium has been used to persuade him or her to "need" certain products, to form certain opinions, and to vote for particular candidates. But more important, television has forced persons to broaden their horizons. One's experience is no longer limited to the local community. Through television we participate vicariously in wars, riots, demonstrations, assassinations, coronations, United Nations debates, festivals, famines, summit meetings, the Olympic Games, national disasters, and international crises. Whereas persons once were exposed to a consistent set of expectations and constraints, television (as well as the modern means of transportation) presents us with a variety of life styles and ideologies.[18]

We have seen that the technological revolution has an immense impact upon individuals and institutions because it is responsible for internal migration, changes in the occupational structure, and the freeing of individuals from the provinciality of localism. As a final demonstration of the magnitude of technological change, let us look at the gross national product. The United States and the other "have" nations of the world (21 nations according to the Organization for Economic Cooperation and Development) are doubling their total output of goods and services (gross national product) about every fifteen years.

> This means, generally speaking, that the child reaching teen age in any of these societies is literally surrounded by twice as much of everything newly made as his parents were at the time he was an infant. It means that by the time today's teen-ager reaches age thirty, perhaps earlier, a second doubling will have occurred. Within a seventy-year lifetime, perhaps five such doublings will take place—meaning, since the increases are compounded, that by the time the individual reaches old age the society around him will be producing thirty-two times as much as when he was born.[19]

Urbaniza-
tion

Technology is only one factor affecting social change. Change also results from political, economic, and social factors. Here we will consider how the concentration of people in limited geographical areas affects change.

The cities of the United States have undergone three major shifts that have important social consequences: accelerated growth, the growth of suburbs, and the racial transformation of the central cities. We will describe these and their implications in this section.

Population Implosion. As the United States grew from a tiny nation of several million in 1790 to one of 235 million in 1983 there was a related trend of an ever greater concentration of the people in urban places. Using the Census Bureau's definition of an urban place as an incorporated area exceeding 2,500 in population, the United States has moved steadily from a rural to an urban nation—the 1790 population was 5 percent urban, while the population in 1900 was 40 percent urban, and 74 percent urban in 1980. Looked at another way, in 1800 there were only six cities in excess of 8000 people, while in 1980 there were six exceeding 1 million in population and 50 cities exceeding 280,000.

This fantastic growth is the result of several factors: population increase (births over deaths), immigration, and the internal migration from rural to urban. Changes in technology were largely responsible for many rural persons leaving farms. The mechanization of agriculture, for example, significantly reduced the rural job market, resulting in a farm population decline from 32 million persons in 1940 to 10 million in 1970 and 6 million in 1980. The cities were also attractive to migrants because they offered a variety of jobs, entertainment, and the like. This trend had some negative consequences. Certainly many small rural towns declined and decayed as their population base eroded. Rural bankruptcy increased. Towns once served by doctors, dentists, lawyers, and other professionals were now denied these services at the local level. Also, many rural persons who moved to the city found that environment difficult and alien. Many of their skills were not transferable to urban jobs. This urban trend, then, was the source of dislocations for many newcomers and for their rural sources of origin. Also, of course, the cities undergoing this rapid growth had difficulty providing adequate housing, sewage disposal, and other services for the hordes of newcomers.

The Suburban Explosion.   Whereas the long-term strong trend has been from rural to urban, there has also been a recent trend outward from the central cities to separate communities contiguous with the large city. The growth of the suburbs is a twentieth-century phenomenon accompanying the building of the highway system, and the increased use of the automobile, commuter trains, and buses. The 1970 Census revealed that for the first time the suburban population of metropolitan areas exceeded that of the central city. This trend has continued, with the population of suburbs increasing 2.8 percent from 1970 to 1979 while the central cities *decreased* 1.9 percent.[20] From 1970 to 1980 only two of the six cities over one million (Houston and Los Angeles) increased in population and only 19 of the next largest 40 cities grew. (All but one of these were located in the rapidly growing sunbelt states.)

The population composition of the suburbs points to several problems. The suburbanites, when compared to the residents of the central city, are usually white and relatively affluent. In 1980, for example, only 6.1 percent of the suburban population was black, and these persons were primarily living in the older, fringe communities. Thus, there is the problem that suburbs constitute a white ring around an ever-blacker inner city. This homogenization also results in the services (including education) being superior in the suburbs because the tax revenues are relatively higher. Thus arise the inequality of educational opportunity and the cry by some for busing and other integration plans.

Another trend that tends to strangle the inner city is that places of work are increasingly being located in the suburbs. This loss of jobs in the central city reflects the trend of businesses and plants to relocate in the suburbs, where land may be cheaper, taxes lower, and traffic congestion and parking less of a problem.

The negative consequences of this trend for the central city are obvious. Foremost is that job opportunities are increasingly limited. High unemployment results in financial hardship for the city because of the decreased tax revenues but also because of increased welfare needs. Decreased tax revenues are also a consequence of the movement of taxpaying individuals and businesses away from the city.

Racial Transformation of the Central Cities. The 1960s and 1970s were decades of great growth for the suburbs and concomitant loss in population for the central cities. This fact, at first glance, would seem to reveal that the central cities were only losing people—that there was relatively little in-migration. Such an interpretation is incorrect, however. What occurred was a "white flight"—that is, whites leaving the cities for the suburbs and blacks, usually from the rural South, moving in. From 1970 to 1980, for instance, the total population in New York City declined by 10.4 percent while the black population in the city grew by 7 percent; the total population in Chicago lost 10.7 percent while its black population increased by 8.6 percent; and Detroit's total population dropped 20.4 percent while black population in Detroit increased by 14.9 percent during the decade.[21]

This change in the racial mix of the city has several implications. First, it reflects the rapid urbanization of the black population. Throughout most of American history, blacks have been rural and mainly in the South. But from World War II until 1970, 4.5 million more blacks left the South than moved into it—and these migrants mainly left rural life for life in the cities of the northern and border states.

The second consequence of this trend is that more and more cities will have black majorities. This fact has important implications for black power— the election of black leaders to political office at the city level and sending black representatives to the state and national legislatures. For the school system, it means de facto segregation, despite Supreme Court rulings to the contrary.

The central city is not only becoming increasingly populated by blacks, it is also the residence, disproportionately, of other minorities, the foreign born, and the aged. In other words, as the affluent leave the city for the suburbs, the people who remain tend to be the economic and social underdogs of the society. The central city, then, without an adequate tax base, is peopled by the very people who need the most social services (for example, welfare, unemployment compensation, housing subsidies, and special education programs).

The central city, lacking in resources and disproportionately peopled by society's outcasts, is surrounded typically by the affluent and white suburbs. This is a source of resentment and hostility for the citizens of the inner city and the governmental officials.

To summarize this section, let us examine where these trends of metropolitan growth are leading, as presented by The Commission on Population Growth and the American Future.[22] The commission concluded that the proportion of future Americans living in metropolitan areas will continue to increase. The proportion of Americans living in metropolitan areas (71 percent) will increase to 85 percent by 2000. City growth by the natural increase of births alone will add 40 million to the metropolitan areas by 2000 if families increase at the low rate of two children per family. Assuming natural increase and migration, the metropolitan areas will increase by some 81 to 129 million by 2000.

The size of the metropolitan areas will also increase. In 1970, about 40 percent of Americans lived in metropolitan areas of 1 million or more people. By 2000 this percentage will increase to 60. Moreover, the number of large metropolitan areas (1 million or more people) will increase from the 29 in 1970 to a total of 44 to 50 in 2000.

The growth of large metropolises will give rise to another phenomenon—the **urban region.** The metropolitan areas will continue to expand geographically as a consequence of suburban growth, resulting in a continuous zone of metropolitan areas. In 1920, there were 10 urban regions with over one third of the total population. By 1970, about three fourths of the population lived in urban regions and by 2000 about five sixths of the American people will be living in 25 urban regions.

Migration
and
Immigra-
tion

In addition to the movement of people to the cities and suburbs, another major migration trend has been toward the sunbelt states. From 1970 to 1980, for example, the Northeast *lost* 0.2 percent in population, the Northcentral gained 3.5 percent, while the South increased by 15.4 percent and the West by 19.5 percent.[23] The sunbelt, especially California, Arizona, Florida, and Texas are growing rapidly not only because of the favorable geographical climate but more importantly because businesses are moving there due to a favorable business climate (including lower taxes, lower wages, and less entrenched unions). This increases employment opportunities in these areas and encourages many to go where the jobs are more plentiful. The mountain states are also growing rapidly because of the vast energy resources located there, the growth of new industries, and the aesthetic appeal of the region.

These represent profound shifts in the population, leaving some areas of the country stagnant, with declining tax bases, and high unemployment, while other regions are experiencing vigorous development and relative prosperity. Politically, this internal migration has important implications as well. Reapportionment based on the 1980 Census will reflect the population shifts by adding representatives for states in the sunbelt and mountain

Reprinted by permission of United Feature Syndicate.

regions while states such as New York, New Jersey, and Illinois will lose some of their representation in Congress. This means a shift in regional power. Also, this trend increases the political clout of conservatives as the traditional individualism of the South and mountain states replaces the traditional liberalism of the Northeast.

Immigration has been a major source of population growth in the United States. The Census Bureau estimates that 20 percent of the annual population increase during the decade of the 1980s will result from legal immigration. This assumes an annual influx of about 400,000 immigrants. In addition it is estimated that somewhere between 1 and 2 million immigrants enter the United States illegally each year, mostly from Mexico.

Immigrants, legal and undocumented, added in these numbers add to the rich ethnic diversity in the United States. Many people resent them, however, because they are perceived as threats to jobs (although in fact they often do the work that others refuse to do), and put a major strain on local schools and social services. Because most of the recent immigrants live in cities, they add to the financial woes of these already overburdened municipalities.

Population Growth

The United States has experienced a rapid population growth in this century. The 1900 population of 76 million grew to 235 million by 1983, an increase of 159 million persons (and 310 percent) in just 83 years. This surge in population was the result of two factors. The first was that medical advances significantly decreased the mortality (death) rate. This resulted in extending life expectancy dramatically from 47 years in 1900 to 74.1 years in 1981. The second reason for this growth was immigration. During this span approximately 30 million more people moved to the United States than out of it. Remarkably, however, this great growth in population occurred despite a downward trend in fertility (the birth rate). In 1900, for example, women averaged 3.5 children in their lifetimes, but by 1981 this average had fallen to 1.9 children. In this section we will examine fertility rates in recent American history, determining the reasons for the rises and falls and the consequences of differing rates for the society. We will then project the population growth into the future to determine the eventual stable population size and the consequences of having a stable population of that magnitude.

Despite the tripling in U.S. population from 1900 to 1980, the United States does not have the population problem of the developing countries. Whereas the population of some countries is increasing at an annual rate of more than 3 percent, the United States is growing at a 0.6 percent rate. While some African nations have 51 births per 1,000 people, the U.S. rate is below 16 births per 1,000 people. In fact, as we will document shortly, the United States has achieved a birth rate below the replacement level. In other words, a zero population growth rate has been achieved. So the population problem that faces the world would appear to have bypassed America. We would argue that this is a false premise in two regards. First, population pressures anywhere affect the United States because of the resulting shortages in resources, ecological imbalances, and increased international tensions. Second, and a point that is stressed at the end of this section, population changes affect social life in a number of important ways. As the Commission on Population Growth and the American Future summarized:

> There is scarcely a facet of American life that is not involved with the rise and fall of our birth and death rates: the economy, environment, education, health, family life and sexual practices, urban and rural life, governmental effectiveness and political freedoms, religious norms, and secular life styles. If this country is in a crisis of spirit—environmental deterioration, racial antagonisms, the plight of the cities, the international situation—the population is part of that crisis.[24]

Fertility in Recent American History.   Table 4–1 documents the dramatic fall in birth rates in recent American history. In 1800 there were 58 live births per 1000 population (higher than the current rate in Africa, 46 per 1000, that makes it the fastest-growing continent) and this has steadily declined to a low of about 16 per 1000 in 1981. What is most significant about this current rate is that it is *below* the replacement rate and therefore will, if maintained, produce a stationary population—zero population growth. The ZPG rate is 2.11 children per woman and, as Table 4–1 shows, the rate dipped below this in 1972 and continues to decline. However, actual zero population growth did not occur at this point and will not for a number of years. A rate of 2.11 children per woman must be maintained for 70

TABLE 4–1   Declining Birth Rate in America: 1800–1981

Year	Births per 1000 Population	Average Number of Births per Adult Woman (15–44)
1800	58	7.0
1850	48	5.4
1900	32	3.5
1950	24	3.2
1957	25	3.8
1970	18	2.4
1972	16	2.0
1973	15	1.9
1974	14.8	1.8
1975	14.7	1.75
1978	14.8	1.8
1980	15.8	1.9
1981	15.9	1.9

years before a stationary population is accomplished (a consistent rate of 1.9 children per woman would take 50 years, and a rate of 1.0 would bring population growth to an immediate halt).[25] The reason for the growth in population after the ZPG rate has been reached is that it takes the age structure several generations to change so that it reflects the birth rates and death rates at each age that would produce a replacement level of children. In other words, the current age structure is so comprised that there is a relatively large proportion of persons of reproductive age. In 1956, for example, there were about 10 million women in the high-fertility age group (age 20–29) but in 1980 there were about 20 million in this age category. So while women on the average may have fewer babies, this low rate will still mean an increasingly large number of children until the number of women in this category is substantially fewer. Table 4–2 shows how the U.S. population will continue to grow until 2037, even if the zero fertility rate of 2.11 remains constant.

Consequences of the Birth Dearth.   Predicting the population at some future time based on current fertility trends is a faulty enterprise. However, let us assume that the birth rate will continue at the current 1.9 children per woman until the year 2000 instead of a rate of 2.8 (the rate in the early 1960s). What will be the consequences at the family and societal levels?

At the family level smaller size will have very positive consequences. First, it is expected that by the year 2000 the average family income will be relatively higher in today's dollars.[26] Families will have more wealth to spend on health and educational benefits for their children. But more than just spending more money on their children for doctors or college expenses,

TABLE 4–2   Total Population Projections for the United States, 1970 to 2100, Assuming a
Constant Fertility Rate of 2.11 Births per Woman

Year	Without Immigration	With Immigration of 400,000 per Year[b]
1970	204,800,000	204,800,000
1980	220,272,000	224,696,000
1990	237,060,000	246,593,000
2000	248,965,000	264,154,000
2010	260,347,000	281,636,000
2020	268,894,000	296,513,000
2030	273,003,000	307,032,000
2037[a]	273,793,000	—
2040	273,740,000	314,189,000
⋮	⋮	⋮
2100	273,046,000	352,092,000

[a]Year that zero growth is first reached.
[b]The annual immigration rate in 1975 was 400,000.

Source: Adapted from Bureau of the Census, *Illustrative Population Projections for the United States: The Demographic Effects of Alternate Paths to Zero Growth, Current Population Reports,* Series P-25, No. 480 (Washington, D.C.: Government Printing Office), p. 9.

small family size is related to physical and intellectual endorsements. Hartley has summarized the research findings in the following areas:

1. *Health* is better on the average for persons in small families than those in large families. Height, weight, vital capacity, and strength all decline as the number of children goes up. There is a tenfold increase in mental deficiency as one moves from first child to sixth. Even with father's occupation constant, short stature is related to large family size.
2. *Intelligence* tests have indicated that children from small families consistently score higher on the average than children from large families. We have tended to disregard these early studies because of the possible spuriousness of the relationship, since both are related to social class. However, when family income, social class, or the occupation of the father is held constant, there is still a substantial decline in IQ with increasing numbers of children in the family. The greatest differences are found in verbal intelligence, with declines noted even from the first to later children.[27]

Other benefits that would tend to accrue to small families are increased marital satisfaction (absence of unwanted children, fewer economic troubles), less complicated divorces for families with few or no children, and persons living longer, healthier lives.

At the societal level there will be negative consequences because the society will be composed of 250 million persons instead of 228 million as in 1980. There will be obvious problems with resource shortages, increased pollution, employment, and the like. But let's look at this 250 million persons as a blessing compared to the 300 million that would have populated the United States in 2000 if the birth rate had been 2.8 per woman instead of 1.8. What will be the benefits of having 50 million *fewer* persons in 2000? Here are a few possibilities.

It has been estimated that the average American living to age 70 consumes in a lifetime: 50 tons of food, 28 tons of iron and steel, 1200 barrels of petroleum products, 4500 cubic feet of paper and wood; and discards 60 tons of garbage and 10,000 nonreturnable bottles. If one would multiply each of these figures by 50 million, one would get an indication of what American society would save in resources and in the control of waste and pollution by having 50 million fewer persons.

Resources will also be saved because most families will be small. Families, therefore, will need less land, smaller dwellings, fewer clothes, smaller appliances, smaller cars, and less electricity, heat, and fuel.

Another saving for the society would be the smaller amount that the government (and therefore taxpayers) would have to pay for infrastructure services (roads, sewage disposal, water, schools, police and fire protection). Daniel Bell, a sociologist, has estimated that these services cost approximately $18,000 for each new person added to the population[28]—or a saving of $900 billion if the population were 50 million fewer.

It is interesting to speculate as to the impact of having 50 million fewer persons on social problems in the society. With 250 million people instead of 300 million, several predictions seem appropriate. Because wealth will be spread over fewer people, a smaller proportion of the population will likely be poor. The number of crimes will be less. Because there will be less overcrowding, intergroup tensions and violence will likely be less. Moreover, a smaller population would free governmental monies, if the officials were so inclined, to help alleviate material suffering and increase the probability of equality of opportunity.

The Boom Generation.   Birth rates in this century, while showing a definite downward trend, had one period that reversed the trend, resulting in a baby boom. This aberration has had and will continue to have a profound effect on American society.[29]

The depression period was a time of low fertility as families postponed having children or restricted their family size because of economic difficulties and uncertainties. These uncertainties were compounded further by World War II. Again fertility was kept low by the conscious acts of families or now because many husbands and wives were physically separated. So following 15 years of depression and war persons who had delayed child bearing began to make up for lost time. The result was a period of rising fertility from 1947 through 1960. Between 1947 and 1957, for example, 43 million babies were born—10 million more than in the previous decade—and one fifth of the present population. This created a 10-million-person bulge in the age structure. Like a pig that has been swallowed by a python, this bulge has been slowly moving through the age structure, creating problems and dislocations at every stage (see Figure 4–1). It will continue to create problems of adjustment for the duration of the 70-year life span of the baby boom—until 2020 or so.

FIGURE 4–1   Progress of Depression Cohort, Baby Boom Cohort, and Baby Bust Cohort Through U.S. Population Age-Sex Pyramid: 1960–2050

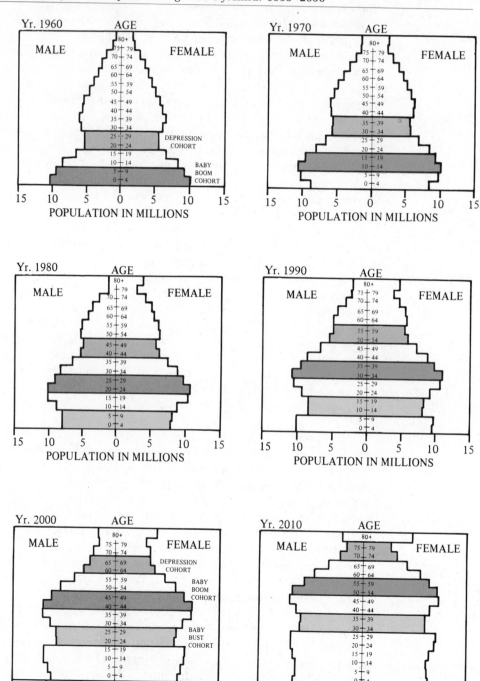

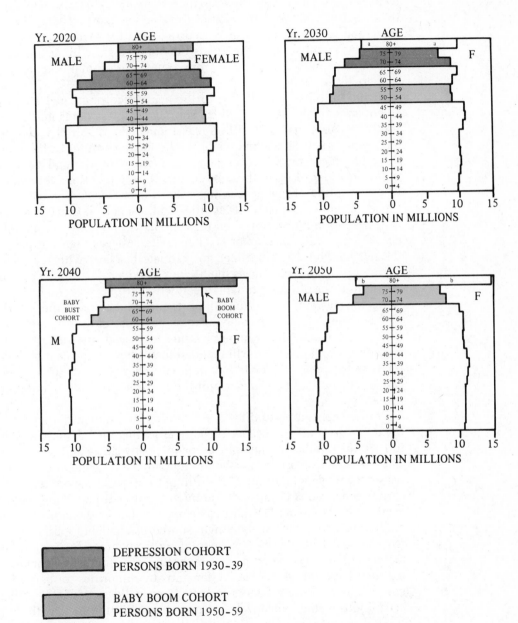

DEPRESSION COHORT
PERSONS BORN 1930-39

BABY BOOM COHORT
PERSONS BORN 1950-59

BABY BUST COHORT
PERSONS BORN 1970-79

Source: Leon F. Bouvier, "America's Baby Boom Generation: The Fateful Bulge," *Population Bulletin* Vol. 35, No. 1 (Population Reference Bureau, Inc., Washington, D.C., 1980), Figure 4.

The immediate effect of the baby boom was to reduce the number of women in the labor force. By 1950 there were 858,000 fewer women working than in 1945 and the proportion of working women was below that of 1940. Increased family size also increased the need for room, hence the trend to move to the suburbs. In the 1950s the suburbs grew by nearly 20 million, and homeownership increased from 44 percent of total housing in 1940 to 62 percent in 1960.[30]

In the mid-fifties this bulge in the age structure created a crisis for elementary schools—a tremendous shortage in classrooms and teachers. By 1960 the nation had 1.4 million classrooms, about half of which had been built since 1950 to accommodate the boom generation. In the early 1960s these shortages hit the secondary schools and by the end of that decade the colleges faced up to these problems. During this time, for example, one new institution of higher learning opened *every week*. The baby boom had caused a rapid expansion of facilities and teachers at every level but when the population bulge moved on the schools faced another problem—empty classrooms and a surplus of teachers. The colleges that had geared up to the teacher shortage continued to graduate teachers with the jobs rapidly drying up. Then the colleges themselves faced a difficult adjustment period as the number of their students declined sharply.

As the new wave of humanity entered adolescence, the society faced new problems. Traffic accidents increased because of the tremendous number of young drivers. The volume of crime increased dramatically. The Commission on Population Growth reported that "about 28 percent of the reported increase between 1960 and 1970 in the number of arrests for serious crimes can be attributed to an increase in the percentage of the population under 25."[31]

Employment opportunities are a continuing problem for society and for the boom generation, because they are crowding the job market. From 1965 to 1980 the number of unemployed people between 24 and 35 *quadrupled*.[32] The increased pressure for jobs by the baby boom generation will depress wages for those who occupy jobs. Promotions will be more limited than in earlier generations because of the intense competition. The problem is exacerbated further by: (1) the increasing number of women who will seek employment; (2) the largest single source of available jobs in the sixties, teaching, will offer very few openings; (3) openings for professional and technical jobs are created more slowly than the number of persons trained for such jobs; and (4) increased demands by minorities for better jobs. One consequence of these factors is that many college graduates will have to accept jobs *below* their level of competence and training. As these college-trained persons acquire jobs below their level (a condition known as **underemployment**) they will in turn "bump" many non-college-trained individuals also to a level below their training and competence. This will create a condition of **status inconsistency** for those individuals affected— that is, having an occupational status that does not measure up to one's educational attainment. This condition causes resentment for the individual who is underrewarded for his efforts (investment in education) and the potential increases for social unrest.[33] This status imbalance is not a trivial one. The estimate is that during the 1980s nearly one-fourth of college graduates will be overeducated for the jobs they get.[34]

The members of the boom generation will, as they move through the age structure, also affect the economy in a number of ways. For example, their large numbers will ensure a growing market for housing, furniture, and other items. There will be a continual problem of economic dislocations. Companies supplying goods for the boom generation will face expansion followed by a rapid decline as the "boomers" age and move on to another stage, just as the schools built rapidly and then found themselves overbuilt. These dislocations added to the problems of unemployment could be a continual source of economic booms and recessions.

A concern to demographers is what will happen to population growth as the members of the population bulge marry and have children. Although these couples will doubtless have small families, the overall effect will be a surge in population growth. We may experience a second baby boom (even with a low birth rate) as an "echo effect" of the postwar baby explosion.

In the decade from 2010 to 2020 the boom generation will reach retirement. The number of persons over 65 in 2030 will be 52 million (compared to 23 million in 1977). "That age group then would equal more than half of what the entire U.S. population was in 1900."[35] The problem, of course, is that these people on pensions and Social Security will have to be supported by the younger working population. Mayer has informed us of the magnitude of this burden in the following quote:

> In what may turn out to be the most dramatically unfair action against the outsize cohorts of the twenty-year bulge, their parents in 1971 rewrote the social-security laws to assure themselves a highly comfortable retirement at four to five times the monthly income that social security yields today—an income based not on the social-security taxes they were paying themselves but on the taxes that will be paid by the larger work force now coming on. But when the current demographic bulge reaches retirement age, its successors will be too few to support so many old people in so fine a style: the unfunded liabilities of the social-security system will then total well over 2 *trillion* of today's dollars. Assuming only minor growth in longevity from all the medical research now in progress, a social-security tax rate approaching 30 percent of the national payroll will then be necessary in order to meet the payouts prescribed by law, and nobody believes that social-security taxes of those dimensions will actually be assessed.[36]

Finally, 70 years after it had begun, the population bulge created by the baby boom will have passed through the age structure. By then, presuming a steady birth rate at or below the replacement rate, the U.S. population will have stabilized at about 270 million with a balanced age structure.

The Government

Although the government can resist change, it can also be a powerful force for change.[37] For example, in the United States the government has fought wars and made peace, been imperialistic, opened the West, subsidized the transcontinental railroad, seized land from the Indians, built dams and canals, harnessed the atom, and initiated space travel. Through laws the government has stimulated farming (the Homestead Act of 1862 gave farmers tracts of land), encouraged education (the Morrill Act of 1862 instituted land grant colleges in each state), desegregated schools (Brown v. Board of Education), and attempted to eliminate sexism in the schools (Title IX).

The government has been active in all major changes in American history. It has not been a disinterested bystander but rather an impetus for change in a particular direction. Most important, the government has tended to promote changes that benefitted those already affluent segments of society. Those actions providing equity for the lower strata of society generally have occurred when there was a threat of social unrest.[38]

Social Movements Oriented to Changing Society

There are three types of social movements that are political in nature. There are those that are organized to prevent changes, the "resistance" movements discussed earlier. There are **reform movements,** which seek to alter a specific part of society. These movements commonly focus on a single issue such as women's rights, gay liberation, or ecology. Typically there is an aggrieved group such as blacks, Indians, homosexuals, farmers, or workers that focuses its strategy on changing the laws and customs to improve their situation. As noted in the previous chapter, at various times in American history oppressed groups have organized successful drives to change the system to provide more equity. The Civil Rights Movement of the 1950s and 1960s provides an example. Blacks had long been exploited in American society. A series of events in this period such as the jailing of Rosa Parks, a black woman, for not giving her seat on a bus to a white man as was the custom, raised the consciousness of blacks and whites. A leader emerged, Martin Luther King, Jr., who inspired blacks to stand up against oppression. He and others organized marches, sit-ins, boycotts, and court cases, which eventually succeeded in destroying the racist laws and customs of the South. King's reform movement was bent on tearing down existing norms and values and substituting new ones. Many individuals and groups resisted these efforts.

The third type of social movement—**revolutionary movements**—seeks radical changes. These movements go beyond reform by seeking to replace the existing social structure with a new one. For example, a shift from a capitalist to a socialist economy would dramatically change all areas of social life. Castro's 1959 socialist revolution in Cuba illustrates this type of movement as do the French Revolution in 1789 and the Russian Revolution in 1918.

Several categories of persons are particularly susceptible to the appeal of social movements. Obvious candidates for recruits are the disadvantaged. The American economic system, because it encourages private property, profit, and accumulation, divides people into rich and poor, powerful and powerless.[39] The result, as suggested by the theory of Karl Marx, is a class which bears all the burdens of society without sharing its advantages.[40] At the other end of the scale there is a class that lives in affluence at the expense of the oppressed. The antagonism between these two groups will ultimately result in the attempt by the oppressed to change the system. Clearly, individuals who define themselves as oppressed are ripe for appeals to change a system they consider unjust.

There are other categories of persons who, because of their status in the social system, are also candidates for involvement in social movements.[41] These types share a condition called **status anguish**—a fundamental concern with the contradictions in the individual's status set. One type of status anguish results from **marginality**.[42] Some examples of categories experiencing marginality are second-generation immigrants, recent migrants from rural areas to urban centers, and interracial couples. These people are in two different worlds but not fully part of either. The result, commonly, is psychic stress which may manifest itself in attempts by the marginal group to seek change that would allow them to be accepted.

Another form of status anguish that occurs is the condition of **status inconsistency**. A black physician, for example, has high occupational status in American society but ranks low on the racial dimension of status. Such an individual is accepted and treated according to his or her high status by some while others ignore the occupational dimension and consider only his or her race. Faced with this kind of contradiction, individuals may react by withdrawal from painful situations, accommodation, or aggression.

The third form of status anguish—**status withdrawal**—occurs as a result of losing status. Those individuals whose occupations have lost out to new technology are included in this category. Another example would be small entrepreneurs who cannot compete with huge corporations. These downwardly mobile persons are typically going to blame outside conditions for their problems and seek reforming or revolutionary means to restore their lost status.

SUMMARY

This chapter has focused on an apparent contradiction—the co-existence of stability and change. Social systems are, on the one hand, ordered, stable, and predictable while on the other they are always changing. There are, as we have seen, elements of the social structure that impede change while others impel change. This tension leads to the inevitability of change, most often in gradual adjustments and reforms but occasionally in swift and revolutionary ways.

The changes in American history have generally been in the general direction of increased freedom. Although the freedom we now have is far from absolute, it is important to note that modern American women and men, while still greatly affected by traditional sex roles, are freer than ever before. This shift toward freedom is a mixed blessing, however, as Silberman has noted in the following passage:

In the past men inherited their occupations, their status, their religion, and their life style; their wives were selected for them, and their struggle to survive gave them little time to question anything. Today, by contrast, they are presented with a bewildering range of options; they are forced to choose their occupations, jobs, places to live, marital partners, number of children, religion, political allegiance and affiliation, friendships, allocation of income, and life style. This widening of the range of choice and enhancement of individuality have had the effect of reducing the authority of tradition, which in turn requires still more choices to be exercised.

The burden is heavy. The choices are frightening, for they require the individual, perhaps for the first time in history, to choose, and in a sense to create, his own identity.[43]

CHAPTER REVIEW

1. Within societies there are structural forces that work to achieve change while there are others that operate to promote stability. Both change and stability are inevitable and necessary for the survival of societies. These contradictory forces present another inherent duality in social systems.

2. The forces for stability are the constraints of customs, traditions, myths, and ideologies.

3. Institutions are barriers to social change because they provide answers from tradition. The institution of the government inhibits change because of systemic imperatives (the necessity of order, the stifling of dissent, enforcing the law, and promoting the political and economic systems). Also the organization of the government preserves the status quo.

4. Bureaucracies are complex organizations designed to increase efficiency by dividing work into small tasks performed by specialists; by having a chain of command in which each position has clearly defined responsibilities; by making decisions based on technical knowledge; and by judging performance by proficiency.

5. Bureaucracies promote the status quo in several ways. Unquestioned following of rules and orders means that new and unusual situations cannot be handled because the rules do not apply. Promotions within the hierarchy are made on the basis of conformity, loyalty, and productivity.

6. Ideological beliefs can stifle change. Religious beliefs, for example, have rejected new ideas and technologies throughout history.

7. A social movement is a collective attempt to promote or resist change. A resistance movement is explicitly organized to resist change.

8. Technology is a major force for change, altering roles, rules, ideas, and behaviors. A few examples are the automobile, television, contraceptives, and computers, which have affected the family, created and destroyed occupations, and changed perceptions.

9. Urbanization, the concentration of people in limited geographical areas, is another force for social change. The growth of cities and suburbs, and the racial transformation of the central cities in this century have greatly affected changes in American society.

10. Migration is having a profound effect on contemporary life. Migration patterns away from central cities to suburbs and from the industrial Northeast to the

sunbelt are bringing economic problems to the abandoned areas and increased economic and political power to the growing regions.

11. Immigration, legal and illegal, is adding as it always has to the ethnic diversity of the United States. It is also bringing problems, such as increased hostilities among competing groups and increased costs for social services.

12. Population growth is another source of societal change. The baby boom generation provides an excellent example. This bulge of an extra 10 million people has had dramatic effects on society as they move through the age structure.

13. The government, although it can resist change, can also be a prime mover by financing new technologies, opening or closing trade with other nations, stimulating the economy, and the like.

14. There are two types of social movements organized to promote change. A reform movement seeks to alter a specific part of society such as discrimination against a certain category. The goal of a revolutionary movement is more ambitious, seeking the transformation of the entire society.

15. Social movements to enhance or inhibit change appeal to certain categories of persons. These are the disadvantaged and oppressed and those who share a condition called "status anguish." These persons are marginal in status (such as children of immigrants, recent migrants from rural to urban areas, and interracial couples), have inconsistent status, or have lost status.

FOR FURTHER STUDY

Social Change: General

Barry Jones, *Sleepers Awake! Technology and the Future of Work* (Melbourne: Oxford University Press, 1982).

William Kornhauser, *The Politics of Mass Society* (New York: Free Press, 1959).

Robert Lauer, *Perspectives on Social Change*, 2nd ed. (Boston: Allyn and Bacon, 1977).

Alvin Toffler, *The Third Wave* (New York: Morrow, 1980).

Steven Vago, *Social Change* (New York: Holt, Rinehart and Winston, 1980).

Forces for Social Change

Daniel Bell, *The Cultural Contradictions of Capitalism* (New York: Basic Books, 1976).

Barry Bluestone and Bennett Harrison, *The Deindustrialization of America* (New York: Basic Books, 1982).

Herbert Blumer, "Collective Behavior," in Alfred M. Lee (ed.), *Principles of Sociology*, 2nd ed. (New York: Barnes and Noble, 1955), pp. 165–198.

Lawrence G. Brewster, *The Public Agenda: Issues in American Politics* (New York: St. Martin's, 1984).

Hugh Davis Graham and Ted Robert Gurr (eds.), *Violence in America: Historical and Comparative Perspectives*, rev. ed. (Beverly Hills, Calif.: Sage, 1979).

Michael Harrington, *Decade of Decision* (New York: Simon and Schuster, 1980).

Landon Y. Jones, *Great Expectations: America and the Baby Boom Generation* (New York: Ballantine, 1980).

Michael Parenti, *Power and the Powerless* (New York: St. Martin's, 1978).

Ralph H. Turner and Lewis M. Killian, *Collective Behavior*, 2nd ed. (Englewood Cliffs, N.J.: Prentice-Hall, 1972).

Max Weber, *The Theory of Social and Economic Organization*, A. M. Henderson and Talcott Parsons (trans.), (New York: Free Press, 1947).

NOTES AND REFERENCES

1. "The Politics of Cancer," *The Progressive* 43 (May, 1979), pp. 1–10.
2. "Out of the Bottle," *The Progressive* 44 (August, 1980), p. 8.
3. Sidney Lens, "The Doomsday Prerogative," *The Progressive* 45 (January, 1981), p. 10.
4. This debate is considered in a series of articles appearing in *Social Policy* 11 (May/June, 1980): S. M. Miller, "Turmoil and/or Acquiescence for the 1980s?" (pp. 22–25); Heather Booth and Steve Max, "Citizen vs. Corporation," (pp. 26–28); Robert Lekachman, "Acquiescence for Now," (p. 35); Peter Marcuse, "The Establishment in Crisis," (pp. 36–38); and Alan Wolfe, "Left: Out of Step," (pp. 39–40).
5. See Frances Fox Piven and Richard A. Cloward, *Regulating the Poor* (New York: Random House, 1971).
6. Michael Parenti, *Power and the Powerless* (New York: St. Martin's Press, 1978), p. 188.
7. Jim McClellan, "Two-Party Monopoly," *The Progressive* 45 (January, 1981), pp. 28–31.
8. See the classic statement on bureaucracy by Max Weber, *The Theory of Social and Economic Organization*, A. M. Henderson and Talcott Parsons (trans.), (New York: The Free Press, 1947), pp. 329–341. Originally published in 1922.
9. See Robert K. Merton, *Social Theory and Social Structure* (Glencoe, Ill.: The Free Press, 1968).
10. Laurence F. Peter and Raymond Hull, *The Peter Principle* (New York: Morrow, 1969).
11. Peter M. Blau and Marshall W. Meyer, *Bureaucracy in Modern Society*, 2nd ed. (New York: Random House, 1971), p. 104.
12. Gerald R. Leslie, Richard F. Larson, and Benjamin L. Gorman, *Introductory Sociology*, 3rd ed. (New York: Oxford University Press, 1980), p. 283.
13. The examples in this section are taken from Robert H. Lauer, *Perspectives on Social Change* (Boston: Allyn and Bacon, 1973), pp. 120–122.
14. For the classic treatment on social movements and other forms of collective behavior see Herbert Blumer, "Collective Behavior," in Alfred McClung Lee (ed.), *New Outline of the Principles of Sociology* (New York:

Barnes and Noble, 1951). See also Neil Smelser, *Theory of Collective Behavior* (New York: The Free Press, 1962).
15. Gresham M. Sykes, *Social Problems in America* (Glenview, Ill.: Scott, Foresman, 1971), p. 30; see also Michael Harrington, *The Accidental Century* (Baltimore, Md.: Penguin, 1965).
16. Charles E. Silberman, *Crisis in the Classroom* (New York: Random House, 1970), p. 22.
17. Philip Slater, *The Pursuit of Loneliness: American Culture at the Breaking Point* (Boston: Beacon Press, 1970), pp. 44–45.
18. See, James Mann, "What Is TV Doing to America," *U.S. News & World Report* (August 2, 1982), pp. 27–30.
19. Alvin Toffler, *Future Shock* (New York: Bantam, 1970), p. 24.
20. The data in this section on urban population are taken from two sources: Andrew Hacker (ed.), *U/S: A Statistical Portrait of the American People* (New York: Viking, 1983); and *Statistical Abstract of the United States, 1982–1983* (Washington, D.C.: U.S. Government Printing Office, 1983).
21. Associated Press release (August 20, 1981).
22. The data presented in this section are taken from *Population and the American Future: The Report of the Commission on Population Growth and the American Future* (New York: New American Library, 1972), pp. 37–43.
23. David L. Kaplan and Cheryl Russell, "What the 1980 Census Will Show," *American Demographics* (October, 1979), pp. 11–17.
24. *Population and the American Future*, p. 2.
25. *Population and the American Future*, p. 15; "Looking to the ZPG Generation," *Time* (February 28, 1977), pp. 71–72.
26. *Population and the American Future*, p. 46. See also "Next 25 Years—How Your Life Will Change," *U.S. News & World Report* (March 22, 1976), pp. 39–42.
27. Shirley Foster Hartley, "Our Growing Problem: Population," *Social Problems* 21 (Fall 1973), p. 195.
28. Daniel Bell, quoted in the *Kansas City Star* (September 30, 1973).
29. The following is taken primarily from three sources: Leon F. Bouvier, "America's Baby Boom Generation," *Population Bulletin* 35

(Washington, D.C.: Population Reference Bureau, April, 1980); Richard A. Easterlin, "What Will 1984 Be Like? Socioeconomic Implications of Recent Twists in Age Structure," *Demography* 15 (November, 1978), pp. 397–419; and Landon Y. Jones, *Great Expectations: America and the Baby Boom Generation* (New York: Ballantine, 1980).

30. James W. Kuhn, "The Immense Generation," *Intellectual Digest* 4 (February, 1974), p. 68.

31. *Population and the American Future*, p. 17. See also "Yesterday's 'Baby Boom' Is Overcrowding Today's Prisons," *U.S. News & World Report* (March 1, 1976), pp. 65–67.

32. *Newsweek* (March 30, 1981), p. 36.

33. See James O'Toole, "The Reserve Army of the Under-Employed," *Change* 7 (May 1975), pp. 28–30.

34. *Newsweek* (March 30, 1981), p. 35.

35. See David Stolberg, "American Population Aging; Over-75 Group Grows Fastest," *Rocky Mountain News* (February 5, 1975), p. 92; "The Graying of America," *Newsweek* (February 28, 1977), pp. 48–65; and "Age Distribution Shifts in U.S.," *The Futurist* 10 (April, 1976), p. 109.

36. Martin Mayer, "Growing Up Crowded," *Commentary* 60 (September, 1975), p. 45.

37. Lauer, *Perspectives on Social Change*, pp. 153–159.

38. Ibid., pp. 156–157; and Piven and Cloward, *Regulating the Poor*.

39. See Alan Wolfe, *The Limits of Legitimacy: Political Contradictions of Contemporary Capitalism* (New York: The Free Press, 1977).

40. See Karl Marx, *Capital: A Critique of Political Economy*, Vol. 1 (New York: International Publishers, 1967). Originally published in 1866.

41. Lauer, *Perspectives on Social Change*, pp. 159–165.

42. The classic statement on marginality is by Everett C. Hughes, "Dilemmas and Contradictions of Status," *American Journal of Sociology* 50 (July 1944–May 1945), pp. 353–359.

43. Silberman, *Crisis in the Classroom*, pp. 22–23.

Part 2

The Individual in Society; Society in the Individual

5

Culture

Let's begin with a bold assertion—American values taken to the extreme, kill. Although such a statement is too strong, there is some truth to it. The American values of individualism, according to which we are judged by our personal accomplishments, our success in competitive situations, and our accumulation of material goods as evidence of our success, drives many persons toward premature death from heart disease. The medical profession, following the pioneering work of Drs. Meyer Friedman and Ray H. Rosenman, has accepted the thesis that persons exhibiting "Type A" behavior (resulting from the intense drive to be No. 1) are likely candidates for early heart trouble.

The Type A Behavior Pattern: You possess this pattern:

1. If you always move, walk, and eat rapidly.
2. If you feel an impatience with the rate at which most events take place. The signs of such impatience are: (a)

hurrying the speech of others; (b) attempting to finish the sentences of persons speaking to you before they can; (c) becoming unduly irritated when a car ahead of you in your lane runs at a pace you consider too slow; (d) becoming irritated at having to perform necessary but repetitious duties (writing out the monthly checks); and (e) hurrying your own reading or always attempting to obtain condensations or summaries of truly interesting and worthwhile literature.

3. If you think of or do two or more things at once. Examples of this would be to eat breakfast, read the paper, and watch the Today Show simultaneously or to shave with an electric razor while driving to work.

4. If you find it always difficult to refrain from talking about or bringing the theme of any conversation around to those subjects that especially interest and intrigue you.

5. If you almost always feel vaguely guilty when you relax and do absolutely nothing.

6. If you fail to notice or be interested in your environment or things of beauty.

7. If you do not have any time to spare to become the things worth being because you are so preoccupied with getting the things worth having.

8. If you attempt to schedule more and more activities into less and less time.

A concomitant of this is a chronic sense of time urgency.

9. If you resort to certain characteristic gestures or nervous tics. For example, if you frequently clench your fist or bang your hand on a table in conversations you are exhibiting Type A gestures. Similarly, if you habitually clench your jaw or grind your teeth, this suggests the presence of a continuous struggle.

10. If you measure your own or others' successes in terms of numbers (number of books read, articles written, sales made).

11. If you play every game to win, even when playing with children.

The Type B Behavior Pattern: You possess this pattern:

1. If you are completely free of all the habits and exhibit none of the traits that harass the Type A person.

2. If you never suffer from a sense of urgency with its accompanying impatience.

3. If you feel no need to display or discuss either your achievements or accomplishments unless such exposure is demanded by the situation.

4. If, when you play, you do so to find fun and relaxation, not to exhibit your superiority at any cost.

5. If you can relax without guilt, just as you can work without agitation.

Source: from *Type A Behavior and Your Heart* by Meyer Friedman and Ray H. Rosenman. Copyright © 1974 by Meyer Friedman. Pp. 182–186.

An important focus of sociology is on the social influences on human behavior. As people interact over time two fundamental sources of constraints on individuals emerge—social structure and culture. As noted in Chapter 2, **social structure** refers to the linkages and network among the members of a social organization. **Culture,** the subject of this chapter, is the knowledge that these members share. Because this shared knowledge includes ideas about what is right, how one is to behave in various situations, religious beliefs, and communication, culture constrains not only behavior but how people think about and interpret their world.

This chapter is divided into two parts. The first describes the nature of culture and its importance for understanding human behavior. The second part focuses on one aspect of culture—values. This discussion is especially vital for understanding the organization and problems of society, in this case, American society.

CULTURE: THE KNOWLEDGE THAT PEOPLE SHARE

Social scientists studying a society foreign to them must spend months, perhaps years, learning the culture of that group. They must learn the meanings for the symbols (written and spoken language, gestures, and rituals) the individuals in that society employ. They must know the feelings people share as to what is appropriate or inappropriate behavior. Additionally, they need to know the rules of the society: which activities are considered important, the skills members have in making and using tools, as well as the knowledge members need to exist in that society. In short, the analyst must discover all the knowledge that people share—that is, he or she must know the culture. Let us examine each of the characteristics of this important social concept.

Character-
istics of
Culture

An Emergent Process.   As individuals interact on any kind of sustained basis, they exchange ideas about all sorts of things. In time they develop common ideas, common ways of doing things, and common interpretations for certain actions. In so doing, the participants have created a culture. The emergent quality of culture is an ongoing process; it is built up slowly rather than being present at the beginnings of social organization. The culture of any group is constantly undergoing change because the members are in continuous interaction. Culture, then, is never completely static.

A Learned Behavior.   Culture is not instinctive or innate in the human species; it is not part of the biological equipment of human beings. The biological equipment of humans, however, makes culture possible. That is, we are symbol-making creatures capable of attaching meaning to particular objects and actions and communicating these meanings to others. When a person joins a new social organization, she or he must learn the culture of that group. This is true for the infant born into a society as well as for a college girl joining a sorority or a young man inducted into the armed forces, or for immigrants to a new society. This process of learning the culture is called **socialization.**

A Channel for Human Behavior.   Culture, since it emerges from social interaction, is an inevitable development of human society. More important, it is essential in the maintenance of any social system because it provides two crucial functions—predictability of action and stability. To accomplish these functions, however, culture must restrict human freedom (although as we shall see, cultural constraints are not normally perceived as such); through cultural patterns the individual is expected to conform to the expectations of the group.

How does culture work to constrain individuals? Or put another way, how does culture become internalized in people so that their actions are controlled? Somehow culture operates not only outside individuals but also inside them. Sigmund Freud recognized this process when he conceptualized the "superego" as that part of the personality structure that inhibits people from committing acts considered wrong by their parents, a group, or the society.

The process of **internalization** (and therefore control) is accomplished mainly in three ways. First, culture becomes part of the human makeup through the belief system into which a child is born. This belief system, provided by parents and those persons immediately in contact with youngsters, shapes their ideas about the surrounding world as well as giving them certain ideas about themselves. The typical American child, for example, is taught to accept Christian beliefs without reservation. These beliefs are literally "force fed," since alternative belief systems are considered unacceptable by the "feeders." It is interesting to note that after Christian beliefs are internalized by the child, they are often used by the "feeders" as levers to keep the child in line.

Second, culture is internalized through psychological identification with the groups to which individuals belong (membership groups), or to which they want to belong (**reference groups**). Individuals want to belong; they want to be accepted by others. Therefore, they tend to conform to the behavior of their immediate group as well as to the wishes of society at large.

Finally, culture is internalized by providing the individual with an identity. People's age, sex, race, religion, and social class have an effect upon the way others perceive them and the way they perceive themselves. To be a male, for example, requires in American society that one be aggressive, ambitious, and competitive. Berger has said, "in a sociological perspective, identity is socially bestowed, socially sustained, and socially transformed."[1]

Culture, then, is not freedom but rather constraint. Of the entire range of possible behaviors (which probably are considered appropriate by some society somewhere), the person of a particular society can only choose from a narrow range of alternatives. The paradox, as Peter Berger has pointed out, is that while society is like a prison to the persons trapped in its cultural demands and expectations, it is not perceived as limiting to individual freedom. Berger has stated it well in the following passage:

> For most of us the yoke of society seems easy to bear. Why? . . . because most of the time we ourselves desire just what society expects of us. We *want* to obey the rules. We *want* the parts that society has assigned to us.[2]

Individuals do not see the prisonlike qualities of culture because they have internalized the culture of their society. From birth children are shaped by the culture of the society into which they are born. They retain some individuality because of the configuration of forces unique to their experience (gene structure, peers, parents' social class, religion, and race), but the behavioral alternatives deemed appropriate for them are narrow.

Culture even shapes thought and perception. What we see and how we interpret what we see is determined by culture. CBS News staged an experiment several years ago that illustrates this point. A black man with something in his hand ran down a crowded city street. White bystanders were asked what they saw. The typical response was that they had perceived the black as carrying a gun, knife, or stolen property, and running from the authorities. In fact, the man was running to catch a bus with a rolled-up newspaper in his hand. Would the respondents have interpreted the actions differently if the person were white? Many white Americans believe that blacks tend toward criminal activity. This stereotype can, therefore, affect negatively the interpretation of a socially acceptable act.

For a dramatic illustrative case of the kind of mental closure that may be determined by culture, consider the following riddle about a father and son driving down a highway:

> There is a terrible accident in which the father is killed, and the son, critically injured, is rushed to a hospital. There the surgeon approaches the patient and suddenly cries, "My God, that's my son!"

How is it possible that the critically injured boy is the son of the man in the accident as well as the son of the surgeon? Answers might involve the surgeon being a priest, or a stepfather, or even artificial insemination. The correct answer to this riddle is that the surgeon is the boy's mother. Americans, male and female alike, have been socialized to think of women as occupying roles less important than physician/surgeon. If Russians were given this riddle, they would almost uniformly give the correct answer since approximately three-fourths of Russian physicians are women. So culture may be confining—not liberating. It constrains not only actions but also thinking.

A Maintainer of Boundaries. Culture not only limits the range of acceptable behavior and attitudes but it instills in its adherents a sense of "naturalness" about the alternatives peculiar to a given society (or other social organization). Thus there is a universal tendency to deprecate the ways of persons from other societies as wrong, old-fashioned, inefficient, or immoral, and to think of the ways of one's own group as superior (as the only right way). The concept for this phenomenon is **ethnocentrism.** The word combines the Greek word *ethnikos*, which means nation or people, and the English word for center. So one's own race, religion, or society is the center of all and therefore superior to all.

Ethnocentrism is demonstrated in statements such as "My fraternity is the best," "Reincarnation is a weird belief," "We are God's chosen people," or "Polygamy is immoral." To name the playoff between the American and National Leagues the "World Series" implies that baseball outside the United States (and Canada) is inferior. Religious missionaries provide a classic example of one among several typical groups convinced that their own faith is the only correct one.

A resolution passed at a town meeting in Milford, Connecticut, in 1640 is a blatant example of ethnocentrism. It stated:

> Voted, the earth is the Lord's and the fulness thereof
> Voted, the earth belongs to the saints
> Voted, we are the saints.

Further examples of ethnocentrism taken from American history are: "manifest destiny," "white man's burden," exclusionary immigration laws such as the Oriental Exclusion Act, and "Jim Crow" laws. A current illustration of ethnocentrism can be seen in the activities of the United States as it engages in exporting the "American way of life," because it is believed that democracy and capitalism are necessities for the good life and therefore best for all peoples.

Ethnocentrism, because it implies feelings of superiority, leads to division and conflict between subgroups within a society and between societies, each of which feels "superior."

Ethnocentric ideas are real because they are believed and they influence perception and behavior. Analysts of American society (whether they are Americans or not) must recognize their own ethnocentric attitudes and the way these affect their own objectivity.

To summarize, culture emerges from social interaction. The paradox is that although culture is human-made, it exerts a tremendous complex of forces that *constrain* the actions and thoughts of human beings. The analyst of any society must be cognizant of these two qualities of culture, for they combine to give a society its unique character; culture explains social change as well as stability; culture explains existing social arrangements (including many social problems); culture explains a good deal of individual behavior because it is internalized by the individual members of society and therefore has an impact (substantial but not total) on their actions and personalities.

Types of Shared Knowledge

The concept of culture refers to knowledge that is shared by the members of a social organization. In analyzing any social organization and, in this case, any society, it is helpful to conceive of culture as combining six types of shared knowledge—symbols, technology, roles, ideologies, norms, and values.

Symbols. By definition, language refers to symbols that evoke similar meanings in different people. Communication is possible only if persons attribute the same meaning to stimuli such as sounds, gestures, or objects. Language, then, may be written, spoken, or unspoken. A shrug of the shoulders, a pat on the back, the gesturing with a finger (which one may be significant), a wink, or a nod are examples of unspoken language and vary in meaning from society to society.

Technology.   Technology refers to the information, techniques, and tools used by people to satisfy their varied needs and desires. For analytic purposes two types of technology can be distinguished—material and social. **Material technology** refers to knowledge of how to make and use things. It is important to note that the things produced are not part of the culture but represent rather the knowledge that people share and that makes it possible to build and use the object. The knowledge is culture, not the object.

Social technology is the knowledge about how to establish, maintain, and operate the technical aspects of social organization. Examples of this are procedures for operating a university, a municipality, or a corporation through such operations as Robert's Rules of Order, bookkeeping, or the kind of specialized knowledge citizens must acquire to function in society (knowing the laws, how to complete income tax forms, how to vote in elections, how to use credit cards and banks).[3]

Ideologies.   These are shared beliefs about the physical, social, and metaphysical worlds. They may, for example, be statements about the existence of supernatural beings, the best form of government, or racial pride.

Ideologies help individuals interpret events. They also provide the rationale for particular forms of action. They can justify the status quo or demand revolution. A number of competing ideologies exist within American society— for example, fundamentalism and atheism, capitalism and socialism, and white supremacy and black supremacy. Clearly, ideology unites as well as divides and is therefore a powerful human-made (cultural) force within societies.

Societal Norms.   There are societal prescriptions for how one is to act in given situations—for example, at a football game, concert, restaurant, church, park, or classroom. We also learn how to act with members of the opposite sex, with our elders, with social inferiors, and with equals. Thus, behavior is patterned. We know how to behave and we can anticipate how others will behave. This allows interaction to occur smoothly.

There is a subdiscipline in sociology called **ethnomethodology,** which is the scientific study of the commonplace activities of daily life. The goal is to discover and understand the underpinnings of relationships (the shared meanings that implicitly guide social behavior). The assumption is that much of social life is "scripted"; that is, the players act according to society's rules (the script). The conduct in the family, in the department store between customer and salesperson, between doctor and patient, between boss and secretary, between coach and player are, in a very real sense, determined by societal scripts.

But what happens when persons do not play according to the common understandings (the script)? Harold Garfinkel, an ethnomethodologist, has used this technique to discover the implicit bases of social interaction.[4] Examples of possible rule breaking include: (1) when answering the phone, you remain silent; (2) when selecting a seat in the audience, you ignore the empty seats and choose rather to sit next to a stranger (violating that person's privacy and space); (3) you act as a stranger in your family; (4) in talking with a friend, you insist that that person clarify the sense of his or her commonplace remarks; and (5) you bargain with clerks over the price of every item of food you wish to purchase. Now these behaviors violate the rules of interaction in American society. When they are violated, the other persons in the situation do not know how to respond. Typically, they become confused, anxious, and angry. This buttresses the notion that most of the time social life is very ordered and orderly. We behave in prescribed ways and we anticipate that others will do the same. The norms are strong and we tend to follow them automatically.

In addition to societal norms being necessary for the conduct of behavior in society, they vary in importance, as we saw in our discussion of norms at the micro level. There are those norms that are less important—the **folkways**—that are not severely punished if violated. Examples of folkways in American society are: it is expected that men should rise when a woman enters the room (unless she is the maid); women should not wear curlers to the opera; and one does not wear a business suit but go barefoot.

Violation of the **mores** of society is considered important enough by society that it must be punished severely. This type of norm involves morality. Some examples of mores are: one must have only one spouse at a time; "thou shalt not kill" (unless defending one's country or one's own property); and one must be loyal to the United States.

There is a problem, however, for many Americans in deciding the degree of importance for some norms. Figure 5–1 shows the criteria for deciding whether a norm should be classified as a folkway or a mos (the singular of the Latin term mores).

Figure 5–1 shows that on the basis of the two defining criteria there are four possibilities, not just two. It is difficult to imagine cases that would be located in cell (b). The only possibilities are activities that have only recently been designated as very harmful but against which laws have not

FIGURE 5–1   Classification of Norms

		Severity of Punishment	
		High	Low
Degree of Importance	High	Mores (a)	(b)
	Low	(c)	Folkways (d)

yet been passed for strict punishment (either because of the natural lag in the courts and legislatures or because powerful groups have been influential in blocking the necessary legislation). The best current example of cases that would fall in cell (b) would be the pollution of lakes, streams, and air by large commercial enterprises. These acts are recognized as having serious consequences for present and future generations, but either go unpunished or receive only minor fines.

Cell (c), on the other hand, is interesting because there are acts not important to the survival of society or the maintenance of its institutions that receive severe punishments (at least relative to the crime). Some examples would be a male student being suspended from school until he gets his hair cut; persons caught smoking marijuana being sentenced to a jail term; young men burning their draft cards being jailed or drafted; and a woman being fired from her job for not wearing a bra.

Both criteria used to delineate types of norms—degree of importance and severity of the punishments—are determined by those in power. Consequently, activities that are perceived by the powerful as being disruptive of the power structure or institutional arrangements that benefit some and not others are viewed as illegitimate and punished severely. For example, if 10,000 young persons protest against the political system with marches, speeches, and acts of civil disobedience, they are typically perceived as a threat and jailed, beaten, gassed, and harassed by the police and the National Guard. Compare the treatment of these young people with another group of 10,000 on the beaches of Florida during their annual spring break. These people often drink to excess, are sexually promiscuous, and are destructive of property. Generally, the police consider these behaviors as non-threatening to the system and therefore treat them relatively lightly.

Norms are also situational. Behavior expected in one societal setting may be inappropriate for another. Several examples should make this point clear. One may ask for change from a clerk, but one would not put money in a church collection plate and remove change. Clearly, behavior considered acceptable by fans at a football game (yelling, booing authority figures, even destroying property) would be inexcusable behavior at a poetry reading. Behavior allowable in a bar probably would be frowned upon in a bank. Or doctors may ask patients to disrobe in the examining room but not in the subway.

Finally, because norms are properties of groups, they vary from society to society and from group to group within societies. Thus, behavior appropriate in one group of society may be absolutely inappropriate in another. Some examples of this are:

> □ *Item:* The "couvade" is a practice surprisingly common throughout the world, but in sharp contrast to the expectations in the United States. This refers to the time when a woman is in childbirth. Instead of the wife suffering, the husband moans and groans and is waited on as though he were in greater pain. After his wife has had the baby she will get up and bring her husband food and comfort. The husband is so incapacitated

The Kiss as a Cultural Creation

Nothing seems more natural than a kiss. Consider the French kiss, also known as the soul kiss, deep kiss, or tongue kiss (to the French, it was the Italian kiss, but only during the Renaissance). Western societies regard this passionate exploration of mouths and tongues as an instinctive way to express love and to arouse desire. To a European who associates deep kisses with erotic response, the idea of one without the other feels like summer without sun.

Yet soul kissing is completely absent in many cultures of the world, where sexual arousal may be evoked by affectionate bites or stinging slaps. Anthropology and history amply demonstrate that, depending on time and place, the kiss may or may not be regarded as a sexual act, a sign of friendship, a gesture of respect, a health threat, a ceremonial celebration, or disgusting behavior that deserves condemnation. . . .

One of the first modern studies to dispel the belief that sexual behavior is universally the same (and therefore instinctive) was *Patterns of Sexual Behavior*, written in 1951 by Clellan Ford and Frank Beach. Ford and Beach compared many of the sexual customs of 190 tribal societies that were recorded in the Human Relations Area Files at Yale University.

Unfortunately, few of the field studies mentioned kissing customs at all. Of the 21 that did, some sort of kissing accompanied intercourse in 13 tribes—the Chiricahua, Cree, Crow, Gros Ventre, Hopi, Huichol, Kwakiutl, and Tarahumara of North America; the Alorese, Keraki, Trobrianders, and Trukese of Oceania; and in Eurasia, among the Lapps. Ford and Beach noted some variations: The Kwakiutl, Trobrianders, Alorese, and Trukese kiss by sucking the lips and tongue of their partners; the Lapps like to kiss the mouth and nose at the same time. (I would add Margaret Mead's observation of the Arapesh. They "possess the true kiss," she wrote; they touch lips, but instead of pressing, they mutually draw the breath in.)

But sexual kissing is unknown in many societies, including the Balinese, Chamorro, Manus, and Tinguian of Oceania; the Chewa and Thonga of Africa; the Siriono of South America; and the Lepcha of Eurasia. In such cultures the mouth-to-mouth kiss is consid-

by the experience that in some societies he stays in bed for as many as 40 days.

☐ *Item:* Among the Murgin of Australia, a woman giving birth to twins kills one of the babies because it makes her feel like a dog to have a litter instead of one baby. A tribe along the Niger Delta puts both the mother and the twins to death. With the Bankundo of the Congo valley, on the other hand, the mother of twins is the object of honor and veneration.

☐ *Item:* In some Latin American countries high-status males are expected to have a mistress. This practice is even encouraged by their wives because it implies high status (given the cost of maintaining two households). In the United States, such a practice is grounds for divorce. American wives would never find such a circumstance something to brag about.

☐ *Item:* In Pakistan one never reaches for food with his or her left hand. To do so would make the observers physically sick. The reason is that the left hand is used to clean oneself after a bowel movement. Hence, the right hand is symbolically the only hand worthy of accepting food.

ered dangerous, unhealthy, or disgusting, the way most Westerners would regard a custom of sticking one's tongue into a lover's nose. Ford and Beach report that when the Thonga first saw Europeans kissing they laughed, remarking, "Look at them—they eat each others saliva and dirt."

Deep kissing apparently has nothing to do with the degree of sexual inhibition or repression in a culture. Donald S. Marshall, an anthropologist who studied a small Polynesian island he called Mangaia, found that all Mangaian women are taught to be orgasmic and sexually active; yet kissing, sexual and otherwise, was unknown until Westerners (and their popular films) arrived on the island. In contrast, John C. Messenger found that on a sexually repressed Irish island where sex is considered dirty, sinful, and, for women, a duty to be endured, tongue kissing was unknown as late as 1966. . . .

Small tribes and obscure Irish islanders are not the only groups to eschew tongue kissing. The advanced civilizations of China and Japan, which regarded sexual proficiency as high art, apparently cared little about it. In their voluminous production of erotica—graphic displays of every possible sexual position, angle of intercourse, variation of partner and setting—mouth-to-mouth kissing is conspicuous by its absence. Japanese poets have rhapsodized for centuries about the allure of the nape of the neck, but they have been silent on the mouth; indeed, kissing is acceptable only between mother and child. (The Japanese have no word for kissing—though they recently borrowed from English to create "kissu.") Intercourse is "natural"; a kiss, pornographic. When Rodin's famous sculpture, *The Kiss*, came to Tokyo in the 1920s as part of a show of European art, it was concealed from public view behind a bamboo curtain.

Among cultures of the West, the number of nonsexual uses of the kiss is staggering. The simple kiss has served any or all of several purposes: greeting and farewell, affection, religious or ceremonial symbolism, deference to a person of higher status. (People also kiss icons, dice, and other objects, of course, in prayer, for luck, or as part of a ritual.) Kisses make the hurt go away, bless sacred vestments, seal a bargain. In story and legend a kiss has started wars and ended them, and awakened Sleeping Beauty and put Brunnhilde to sleep.

Values. Another aspect of a society's structure are the **values,** which are the bases for the norms. These are the criteria used in evaluating objects, acts, feelings, or events as to their relative desirability, merit, or correctness. Values are extremely important, for they determine the direction of individual and group behavior, encouraging some activities and impeding others. For example, efforts to get Americans to conserve energy and other resources run counter to the long-held American values of growth, progress, and individual freedom. Consequently, the prevailing values have thwarted the efforts of various presidents and others to plan carefully about future needs and restrict usage and the rate of growth now.

Role. Societies, like other social organizations, have social positions (**statuses**) and behavioral expectations for those who occupy these positions (**roles**). There are family statuses (son or daughter, sibling, parent, husband, wife); age statuses (child, adolescent, adult, aged); sex statuses (male, female); racial statuses (black, Chicano, Indian, white); and socioeconomic statuses (poor, middle class, wealthy). For each of these statuses there are societal constraints on behavior. To become 65 years old in American society is an especially traumatic experience for many. The expectations of society dramatically shift when one reaches this age. A sixty-five-year-old person is no longer considered an employable adult. The aged are forced into a situation of dependence rather than independence. To be a male or female in American society is to be constrained in a relatively rigid set of expectations. Similarly, blacks and other minorities, because of their minority status, have been expected to "know their place." The power of the social role is best illustrated, perhaps, by the person who occupies two relevant statuses—for example, the black physician or the woman airline pilot. Although each of these persons is a qualified professional, they will doubtless encounter many situations where persons will expect them to behave according to the dictates of the traditional role expectations of their **ascribed status** (race or sex, statuses over which the individual has no control) rather than their **achieved status** (that is, their occupation).

The Social Construction of Reality

A society's culture determines how the members of that society will interpret their environment.[5] Language, in particular, influences the ways in which the members of a society perceive reality. Two linguists, Edward Sapir and Benjamin Whorf, have shown this by the way the Hopi Indians and Anglos differ in the way each speak about time.[6] The Hopi language has no verb tenses and no nouns for times, days, or years. Consequently the Hopi think of time as continuous—without breaks. The English language, in sharp contrast, divides time into seconds, minutes, hours, days, weeks, months, years, decades, centuries, and the like. The use of verb tenses in English clearly informs everyone whether an event occurred in the past, present, or future (see Panel 5–2 for other examples of how time is conceived of in various societies). Clearly precision regarding time is important to English speaking peoples while unimportant to the Hopi.

There is an African tribe that has no word for the color gray. This implies that they do not see gray even though we "know" that there is such a color and readily see it in the sky and in hair. The Navajo do not distinguish between *blue* and *green* yet they have two words for different kinds of *black*.

The Aimore tribe in eastern Brazil has no word for *two*. The Yancos, an Amazon tribe, cannot count beyond *poettarrarorincoaroac*, their word for *three*. The Temiar people of West Malaysia also stop at three.[7] Can you imagine how this lack of numbers beyond two or three affects the way these people perceive reality?

Our language helps us to make order out of what we experience. Our particular language allows us to perceive differences among things or to recognize a set of things to be alike even when they are not identical. Language permits us to order these by what we think they have in common. As Bronowski has put it:

Habit makes us think the likeness obvious; it seems to us obvious that all apples are somehow alike, or all trees, or all matter. Yet there are languages in

Cultural Time

To find social time it is necessary to look beyond the individual perceptions and attitudes, to the temporal construct of the society or culture. Temporal constructs are not to be found in human experience, but rather in the cultural symbols and institutions through which human experience is construed. Our own Indo-European language imposes the concept of time on us at a very early age, so it is difficult to identify with the concept of timelessness. Societies do exist without a consciousness of time. But most societies possess a concept of time. Conceptualizations of time are as varied as the cultures, but most can be categorized by one of three images. Time in the broad sense is viewed as a line (linear), a wheel (cyclical), or as a pendulum (alternating phenomenon). But within these central images, numerous other distinctions must be made. One is tense. Is there a past or present or future, or all three? If more than one, to which is the society oriented and in what way? Another is continuity. Is time continuous or discontinuous? Does the continuity or hiatus have regularity? Another is progressiveness. Is evolutionary transformation expected with the passage of time? Still another is use. Is time used for measuring duration or is it for punctuality? The metaphysical distinctions are numerous. Is there a mode for measuring time? Is it reversible or irreversible? Subjective or objective, or both? Unidirectional? Rectilinear?

These distinctions come into focus when one studies various cultures. The Pawnee Indians, for example, have no past in a temporal sense; they instead have a timeless storehouse of tradition, not a historical record. To them, life has a rhythm but not a progression. To the Hopi, time is a dynamic process without past, present, or future. Instead, time is divided vertically between subjective and objective time. Although Indo-European languages are laden with tensed verbs and temporal adjectives indicating past, present, and future, the Hopi have no such verbs, adjectives, or any other similar linguistic device. The Trobriander is forever in the present. For the Trobriander and the Tiv, time is not continuous throughout the day. Advanced methods of calculating sun positions exist for morning and evening, but time does not exist for the remainder of the day. For the Balinese, time is conceived in a punctual rather than a durational sense. The Balinese calendar is marked off, not by even duration intervals, but rather by self-sufficient periods which indicate coincidence with a period of life. Their descriptive calendar indicates the *kind* of time, rather than what time it is. The Maya had probably the most complicated system of time yet discovered. Their time divisions were regarded as burdens carried by relays of divine carriers—some benevolent, some malevolent. They would succeed each other, and it was very important to determine who was currently carrying in order to know whether it was a good time or a bad time.

Source: Excerpted from F. Gregory Hayden, "A Critical Analysis of Time Stream Discounting for Social Program Evaluation," *The Social Science Journal* 17 (January 1980), pp. 26–27.

the Pacific Islands in which every tree on the island has a name, but which have no word for tree. To these islanders, trees are not at all alike; on the contrary, what is important to them is that the trees are different.[8]

The social interpretation of reality is not limited to language. For example, some people believe that there is such a thing as "holy water." Now there is no chemical difference between water and holy water but some people believe that the differences in properties and potential are enormous. To understand holy water we must examine priests and parishioners, not water.[9] Similarly, consider the difference between spit and saliva.[10] There is no chemical difference between them, the only difference being that in one case the substance is inside the mouth and in the other it is outside. We swallow saliva continuously and think nothing about it yet one would not gather his or her spit in a container and then drink it. Clearly saliva is defined positively and spit negatively, yet the only difference is a social definition.

There is a debate in philosophy and sociology on this issue of reality. One position—**ontology**—accepts the reality of things because their nature cannot be denied (a chair, a tree, the wind, a society). The opposite side—**epistemology**—argues that all reality is socially constructed. In this view all meaning is created out of a world that generates no meanings of its own.[11] The world is absurd and humans make sense out of it to fit their situation. This extreme position is expressed by two sociologists in the following quotation:

> Fundamental to our view is the assumption that the universe has no intrinsic meaning—it is, at bottom, absurd—and that the task of the sociologist is to discover the various imputed or fabricated meanings constructed by [people] in society. Or, to put it another way, the sociologist's job is to find out *by what illusions people live*. Without these artifacts, these delicately poised fantasies, most of us would not survive. Society, as we know it, could not exist. Meaninglessness produces terror. And terror must be dissipated by participating in, and believing in, collective fictions. They constitute society's "noble lie," the lie that there is some sort of inherent significance in the universe. It is the job of sociology to understand [how people] impute meaning to the various aspects of life.[12]

Cultural Relativity

A number of customs from around the world have been described in this chapter. These typically seem to us weird, cruel, or stupid. Anthropologists, though, have helped us to understand that in the cultural context of a given society, the practice may make considerable sense. For example, anthropologist Marvin Harris has explained why sacred cattle are allowed to roam the countryside in India while the people may be starving.[13] Outsiders see cow worship as the primary cause of India's hunger and poverty, because cattle do not contribute meat while eating crops that would otherwise go to humans. Harris, however, argues that cattle must not be killed for food because they are the most efficient producer of fuel and food. To kill them would cause the economy to collapse. Cattle contribute to the Indian economy in a number of significant ways. They are the source of oxen, which are the principal traction animals for farming. Their milk helps to meet the nutritional needs of many poor families. India's cattle annually excrete 700 million tons of recoverable manure, half of which is used for fertilizer and the rest for fuel. Cow dung is also used as a houshold flooring material. If cows were slaughtered during times of famine, the economy would not recover in good times. To Western experts it looks as if the Indian would rather starve to death than to eat his cow. But as Harris has argued, "They don't realize that the farmer would rather eat his cow than starve, but that he will starve if he does eat it."[14] The practice of cow worship also allows for a crude redistribution of wealth. The cattle owned by the poor are allowed to roam freely. In this way the poor are able to let their cows graze the crops of the rich and come home at night to be milked. As Harris has concluded:

> The sacredness of the cow is not just an ignorant belief that stands in the way of progress. Like all concepts of the sacred and the profane, this one affects the physical world; it defines the relationships that are important for the maintenance of Indian society.
>
> Indians have the sacred cow; we have the "sacred" car and the "sacred" dog. It would not occur to us to propose the elimination of automobiles and dogs from our society without carefully considering the consequences, and we should not propose the elimination of zebu cattle without first understanding their place in the social order of India.
>
> Human society is neither random nor capricious. The regularities of thought and behavior called culture are the principal mechanisms by which we human beings adapt to the world around us. Practices and beliefs can be rational or irrational, but a society that fails to adapt to its environment is doomed to extinction. Only those societies that draw the necessities of life from their surroundings, inherit the earth. The West has much to learn from the great antiquity of Indian civilization, and the sacred cow is an important part of that lesson.[15]

This extended example is used to convey the idea that the customs of a society should be evaluated in the light of the culture and their functions for that society. These customs should *not* be evaluated by our standards, but by theirs. This is called **cultural relativity.** The problem with cultural relativity, of course, is ethnocentrism—the tendency for the members of each society to assume the rightness of their own customs and practices and the inferiority, immorality, or irrationality of those found in other societies.

AMERICAN VALUES

While all of the components of culture are essential for an understanding of the constraints on human behavior, perhaps the quickest way to reach this understanding is to focus on its values. These are the criteria used by the members of society to evaluate objects, ideas, acts, feelings, or events as to their relative desirability, merit, or correctness.

Humans are valuing beings. They continually evaluate themselves and others. What objects are worth owning? What makes people successful? What activities are rewarding? What is beauty? Of course, different societies have distinctive criteria (values) for evaluating. People are considered successful in the United States, for example, if they accumulate many material things as a result of hard work. In other societies people are considered to be successful if they attain total mastery of their emotions or if they totally reject materialism.

One objective common to any social science course is the hope that students will become aware of the various aspects of social life in an analytical way. For Americans studying their own society this means that while immersed in the subject matter, they also become participant observers. This implies an objective detachment (as much as possible) so that one may understand better the forces which in large measure affect human behavior, individually and in groups.

The primary task for the participant observer interested in societal values is to determine what the values are. There are a number of clues that are helpful for such a task.* The first clue is to determine what most preoccupies people in their conversations and actions. So one might ask: Toward what do people most often direct their action? Is it, for example, contemplation and meditation or physical fitness or the acquiring of material objects? In other words, what gives individuals high status in the eyes of their fellows?

A second technique that might help delineate the values is to determine the choices that people make consistently. The participant observer should ascertain what choices tend to be made in similar situations. For example, how do individuals dispose of surplus wealth? Do they spend it for self-aggrandizement or for altruistic reasons? Is there a tendency to spend it for the pleasure of the present, save it for security in the future, or spend it on others?

A third procedure is used typically by social scientists—that is, to find out through interviews or written questionnaires what people say is good, bad, moral, immoral, desirable, or undesirable. There is often a difference between what people say and what people do. This is always a problem in the study of values because there will sometimes be a discrepancy between values and actual behavior. Even if there is a difference between what people write on a questionnaire or say in an interview and their actual behavior, they will probably say or write those responses they feel are appropriate, and this by itself is a valid indicator of what the values of the society are.

One may also observe the reward-punishment system of the society. What behavior is rewarded with a medal, or a bonus, or public praise? Alternatively, what behavior brings condemnation, ridicule, public censure, or imprisonment? The greater the reward or the punishment, the greater the likelihood that important societal values are involved. Consider, for example, the extraordinary punishment given to Americans who willfully destroy the private property of others (for example, a cattle rustler, a thief, a looter, or a pyromaniac).

---

*A good but partial list of methods to determine empirically the values of American society has been developed in a text by Robin M. Williams.[16]

Closely related to the reward-punishment system are the actions that cause individuals to feel guilt or shame (losing a job, living on welfare, declaring bankruptcy) or those actions which bring about ego enhancement (a better-paying job, getting an educational degree, owning a business). Individuals feel guilt or shame precisely because they have internalized the norms and values of society. When values and behavior are not congruent, feelings of guilt will be a typical response.

Another technique is to examine the principles that are held as part of "the American way of life." These principles are enunciated in historical documents such as the Constitution, the Declaration of Independence, and the Bible. We are continually reminded of these principles in speeches by elected officials, by editorials in the mass media, and from pulpits. The United States has gone to war to defend such principles as democracy, equality, freedom, and the free enterprise system. One question the analyst of values should ask, therefore, is, "For what principles will the people fight?"

The remainder of this chapter is devoted to the description of the American system of values. Understanding American values is essential to the analysis of American society, for they provide the basis for America's uniqueness as well as the source of many of its social problems.

American Values as Sources of Societal Integration and Social Problems

American society, while similar in some respects to other advanced industrial societies, is also fundamentally different. Given the combination of geographical, historical, and religious factors found in the United States, it is not surprising that its cultural values are unique.

Geographically, the United States has remained relatively isolated from other societies for most of its history. Americans have also been blessed with an abundance of rich and varied resources (land, minerals, and water). Until only recently, Americans were unconcerned with conservation and the careful use of resources (as many societies must be to survive) because there was no need. The country provided a vast storehouse of resources so rich they were often used wastefully.

Historically, the United States was founded by a revolution that grew out of opposition to tyranny and aristocracy. Hence, Americans have verbally supported such principles as freedom, democracy, equality, and impersonal justice.

Another historical factor that has led to American culture having its particular nature is that it has been peopled largely by immigrants. This fact has led, on the one hand, to a blending of many cultural traits, such as language, dress, and customs, and alternatively, to the existence of ethnic enclaves that resist assimilation.

A final set of forces that has affected American culture stems from its religious heritage. First is the Judeo-Christian ethic that has prevailed throughout American history. The strong emphases on humanitarianism, the inherent worth of all individuals, a morality based on the Ten Com-

Reprinted courtesy of the *Rocky Mountain News.*

mandments, and even the Biblical injunction to "have dominion over all living things" have had a profound effect upon how Americans evaluate each other.

Another aspect of America's religious heritage, the Protestant (Puritan) work ethic, has been an important determinant of the values that are believed to typify most Americans.[17] The majority of early European settlers in America tended to believe in a particular set of religious beliefs that can be traced back to two individuals, Martin Luther and John Calvin. Luther's contribution was essentially twofold: each person was considered to be his or her own priest (stressing the person's individuality and worth), and each person was to accept his or her work as a "calling." To be "called" by God to do a job, no matter how humble, was to give the job and the individual dignity. It also encouraged everyone to work very hard to be successful in that job.

The contribution of John Calvin was based upon his belief in "Predestination." God, because He is all-knowing, knows who will be "saved." Unfortunately, individuals do not know whether they are "saved" or not, and this is very anxiety-producing. Calvinists came to believe that God would look with more favor upon those preordained to be "saved" than those who were not. Consequently, success in one's business became a sign that one was "saved," and this was therefore anxiety-reducing. Calvinists worked very hard to be successful. As they prospered, the capital they accumulated could only be spent on necessities, for to spend on luxuries was another sign that one was not "saved." The surplus capital was therefore invested in the enterprise (purchasing more property or better machinery, hiring a larger work force, or whatever).

Luther and Calvin produced an ethic that flourished in America. This ethic stressed the traits of self-sacrifice, diligence, and hard work. It stressed achievement, and most importantly, it stressed a self-orientation rather than a collectivity orientation. Indirectly, this ethic emphasized private property, capitalism, rationality, and growth.

Thus geography, religious heritage, and history have combined to provide a distinctive set of values for Americans. However, before we describe these dominant American values, several caveats should be mentioned. First, the tremendous diversity of the United States precludes any universal holding of values. There are persons and groups that reject the dominant values. Moreover, there are differences in emphasis for the dominant values by region, social class, age, and religion. Second, the system of American values is not always consistent with behavior. Third, the values themselves are not always consistent. How does one reconcile the coexistence of individualism with conformity? or competition and cooperation? Robin Williams, an eminent analyst of American society, has concluded that:

> We do not find a neatly unified "ethos" or an irresistible "strain toward consistency." Rather, the total society is characterized by diversity and change in values. Complex division of labor, regional variations, ethnic heterogeneity, and the proliferation of specialized institutions and organizations all tend to insulate differing values from one another.[18]

To minimize the problem with inconsistencies, we will present only the most dominant of American values in this section.[19] Let's examine these in turn.

Success (Individual Achievement). The highly valued individual in American society is the self-made person—i.e., one who has achieved money and status through his or her own efforts in a highly competitive system. Our culture heroes are persons like Abe Lincoln and John D. Rockefeller, each of whom rose from humble origins to the top of his profession.

Success can be achieved, obviously, by outdoing all others, but it is often difficult to know exactly the extent of one's success. Hence, economic success (one's income, personal wealth, and type of possessions) is the most commonly used measurement. Economic success, moreover, is often used to measure personal worth. As Robin Williams has put it, "The comparatively striking feature of American culture is its tendency to identify standards of personal excellence with competitive occupational achievement."[20]

Competition.   Competition is highly valued in American society. Most Americans believe it to be the one quality that has made America great because it motivates individuals and groups to be discontented with the status quo and with being second best. Motivated by the hope of being victorious in competition, or put another way, by fear of failure, Americans must not lose a war or the Olympics or be the second nation to land men on the moon.

Competition pervades almost all aspects of American society. The work world, sports, courtship, organizations like the Cub Scouts, and schools all thrive on competition. The pervasiveness of competition in schools is seen in how athletic teams, cheerleading squads, debate teams, choruses, bands, and casts are composed. In each case, competition among classmates is used as the criterion for selection. Of course, the grading system is also often based on the comparison of individuals with each other.

The Cub Scouts, because of its reliance on competition, is an all-American organization. In the first place, individual status in the den or pack is determined by the level one has achieved through the attainment of merit badges. Although all boys can theoretically attain all merit badges, there is competition as the boys are pitted against each other to see who can obtain the most. Another example of how the Cub Scouts use competition is their annual event—the Pinewood Derby. Each boy in a Cub pack is given a small block of wood and four wheels that he is then to shape into a racing car. The race is held at a pack meeting with one boy eventually being the winner. The event is rarely questioned even though nearly all of the boys go home disappointed losers. Why is such a practice accepted—indeed publicized? The answer, simply, is that it is symbolic of the ways things are done in virtually all aspects of American life.

An important consequence of this emphasis on the "survival of the fittest" is that some persons take advantage of their fellows to compete "successfully." Perhaps the best recent example is the abuses by high administration officials during the 1972 election campaign (the Watergate break-in, bugging, "laundering of money," taking of illegal contributions from individuals and corporations, use of the Internal Revenue Service to punish enemies, and the "dirty tricks" against political opponents) were done in the cause of a "higher good"—i.e., insuring the reelection of Richard Nixon. Sociologist Amitai Etzioni has captured the essence of this relationship between "success" and illegal means in the following statement:

Truth to be told, the Watergate gang is but an extreme manifestation of a much deeper and more encompassing American malaise, the emphasis on success and frequent disregard for the nature of the means it takes to achieve it. Not only high level administration officials, but many Americans as well, seem to have accepted the late football coach Vince Lombardi's motto, "Winning is not the most important thing, it's the only thing." Thus, the executives of ITT who sought to overthrow the government of Chile to protect their goodies, the Mafia chieftains who push heroin, the recording company executives who bribe their records onto the top-40 list, and the citizens who shrug off corruption in the local town hall as "that's the way the cookie crumbles," all share the same unwholesome attitude. True, the Watergate boys have broken all known American precedents in their violation of fair play, but they are unique chiefly in the magnitude of their crime—not in the basic orientation that underlies it. John Mitchell captured the perverted spirit of Watergate best when he stated that "in view of what the opposition had to offer" (i.e., McGovern), he felt justified in doing anything necessary to secure Nixon's reelection.[21]

In the business world we find theft, fraud, interlocking directorates, and price-fixing are techniques used by some individuals to "get ahead" dishonestly. A related problem, abuse of nature for profit, while not a form of cheating, nevertheless takes advantage of others, while one pursues economic success. The current ecology crisis is caused by individuals, corporations, and communities, which find pollution solutions too expensive. Thus, in looking out for themselves, they ignore the short- and long-range effects on social and biological life. In other words, competition, while a constant spur for individuals and groups to succeed, is also the source of some illegal activities and hence social problems in American society.

Similar scandals are also found in the sports world. The most visible type of illegal activity in sports is illegal recruiting of athletes by colleges and universities. In the quest to succeed (i.e., win), some coaches have felt it necessary to violate NCAA regulations by altering transcripts to insure an athlete's eligibility, allowing substitutes to take admissions tests for athletes of marginal educational ability, paying athletes for nonexistent jobs, illegally using government work-study monies for athletes, and offering money, cars, and clothing to entice athletes to their schools.[22]

The Valued Means to Achieve.   There are three related highly valued ways to succeed in American society. The first is through hard work. Americans, from the early Puritans to the present day, have elevated persons who were industrious and denigrated those who were not. Most Americans, therefore, assume that poor people deserve to be poor because they are allegedly unwilling to work as hard as persons in the middle and upper classes. This type of explanation places the blame on the victim rather than on the social system that systematically thwarts efforts by the poor. Their hopelessness, brought on by their lack of education, or by their being black, or by their lack of experience, is interpreted as their fault and not as a function of the economic system.

The two remaining valued means to success are continual striving and deferred gratification. Continual striving has meaning for both the successful and the not-so-successful. For the former, one should never be content with what he or she has; there is always more land to own, more money to make, or more books to write. For the poor, continual striving means a never-give-up attitude, a belief that economic success is always possible through hard work, if not for yourself, at least for your children.

Deferred gratification refers to the willingness to deny immediate pleasure for later rewards. The hallmark of the successful person in American society is just such a willingness—to stay in school, to moonlight, or to go to night school. One observer has asserted that the difference between the poor and the nonpoor in this society is whether they are future or present-time oriented.[23] Superficially, this assessment appears accurate, but we would argue that this lack of a future-time orientation among the poor is not a subcultural trait but basically a consequence of their hopeless situation.

Progress.   Societies differ in their emphasis on the past, the present, and the future. American society, while giving some attention to each time dimension, stresses the future. Americans neither make the past sacred nor are they content with the present. They place a central value on progress—on a brighter tomorrow, a better job, a bigger home, a move to the suburbs, college education for their children, and on self-improvement.

Americans are not satisfied with the status quo; they want growth (bigger buildings, faster planes, bigger airports, more business moving into the community, bigger profits, and new world's records). They want to change and conquer nature (dam rivers, clear forests, rechannel rivers, seed clouds, and spray insecticides).

Although the implicit belief in progress is that change is good, some things are not to be changed, for they have a sacred quality (the political system, the economic system, American values, and the nation-state). Thus, Americans while valuing technological change, do not favor changing the system (revolution).

The commonly held value of progress has also had a negative effect on contemporary American life. Progress is typically defined to mean either growth or new technology. Every city wants to grow. Chambers of Commerce want more industry and more people (and incidentally more consumers). No industry can afford to keep sales at last year's figures. Everyone agrees that the gross national product (GNP) must increase each year. If all these things are to grow as Americans wish, then concomitant with such growth must be increased population, more products turned out (using natural resources), more electricity, more highways, and more waste. Continued growth will inevitably throw the tight ecological system out of balance since there are but limited supplies of air, water, and places to dump waste materials. Not only are these limited but they diminish as the population increases.

Progress also means a faith in technology. It is commonly believed by Americans that scientific knowledge will solve problems. Scientific breakthroughs and new technology have solved some problems and do aid in saving labor. But often new technology creates problems that were unanticipated.* Although the automobile is of fantastic help to humankind, it has polluted the air, and it kills about 60,000 Americans each year in accidents. It is difficult to imagine life without electricity, but the creation

---

*Sociologists have a term for this phenomenon—**latent functions**—which means, in effect, unintended consequences. The intended consequences of an activity or social arrangement are called **manifest functions.**

of electricity pollutes the air and causes the thermal pollution of rivers. Insecticides and chemical fertilizers have performed miracles in agriculture but have polluted food and streams (and even "killed" some lakes). Obviously, the slogan of the Du Pont Corporation—"better living through chemistry"— is not entirely correct.

Material Progress.   An American belief holds that "work pays off." The payoff is not only success in one's profession but also in economic terms— income and the acquisition and consumption of goods and services that go beyond adequate nutrition, medical care, shelter, and transportation. The superfluous things that we accumulate or strive to accumulate, such as country club memberships, jewelry, lavish homes, boats, second homes, pool tables, electric toothbrushes, and season tickets to the games of our favorite teams are symbols of success in the competitive struggle. But these have more than symbolic value because they are elements of what Americans consider the "good life" and, therefore, a right.

This emphasis on *having* things has long been a facet of American life. This country, the energy crisis notwithstanding, has always been a land of opportunity and abundance. Although many persons are blocked from full participation in this abundance, the goal for most is to accumulate those things that bring status and that provide for a better way of life by saving labor or enhancing pleasure in our leisure.

Individual Freedom.   Americans value individualism. They believe that people should generally be free from government interference in their lives and businesses and free to make their own choices. Implied in this value is the responsibility of each individual for his or her own development. The focus on individualism places responsibility on the individual for his or her acts—not on society or its institutions. The individual is blamed for being poor, not the maldistribution of wealth and other socially perpetuated disadvantages that blight many families generation after generation. Blacks are blamed for aggressive behavior, not the limits placed on social mobility for blacks by the social system. Individual students are blamed for dropping out of high school before graduation, not the educational system that fails to meet their needs. This attitude helps to explain the reluctance by persons in authority to provide adequate welfare, health care, and compensatory programs to help the disadvantaged. This common tendency of individuals to focus on the deviant rather than the system that produces deviants has also been true of American social scientists analyzing social problems.

Individual freedom is, of course, related to capitalism and private property. The economy is supposed to be competitive. Individuals, through their own efforts, business acumen, and luck can (if successful) own property and pyramid profits.

The belief that private property and capitalism are not to be restricted has led to several social problems: (1) unfair competition (monopolies, interlocking directorates, price fixing); (2) a philosophy by many entrepreneurs of *caveat emptor* ("Let the buyer beware"), whereby the aim is profit with total disregard for the welfare of the consumer; and (3) the current ecology crisis, which is due in great measure to the standard policy of many Americans and most corporations to do whatever is profitable—thus a total neglect for conservation of natural resources.

All these practices have forced the federal and state governments to enact and enforce regulatory controls. Clearly, Americans have always tended to abuse nature and their fellows in the name of profit. Freedom if so abused must be curtailed, and the government (albeit somewhat reluctantly, given the pressures from various interest groups) has done this.

The related values of capitalism, private property, and self-aggrandizement (individualism) have also led to an ecology crisis. Industries fouling the air and water with refuse, farmers spraying pesticides that kill weeds and harm animal and human life, are but two examples of how individual persons and corporations look out for themselves with an almost total disregard for the short- and long-range effects of their actions on life. As long as Americans hold a narrow self-orientation rather than a collectivity orientation this crisis will not only continue but steadily worsen. The use people make of the land (and the water on it or running through it, and the air above it) has traditionally been theirs to decide because of the American belief in private property. This belief in private property has meant, in effect, that individuals have had the right to pave a pasture for a parking lot, tear up a lemon grove for a housing development, put down artificial turf for a football field, dump waste products into the air and water, and so on. Consequently, individual decisions have had the collective effect of taking millions of acres of arable land out of production permanently, polluting the air and water, covering land where vegetation once grew with asphalt, concrete buildings, and astroturf even though green plants are the only source of oxygen.

Values and Behavior

The discrepancy between values and behavior has probably always existed in American society. Inconsistencies have always existed, for example, between the Christian ethic of love, brotherhood, and humanitarianism, on the one hand, and the realities of religious bigotry, the maximization of self-interest, and property rights over human rights on the other. The gap may be widening because of the tremendous rate of social change taking place (the rush toward urbanization, the increased bureaucratization in all spheres of social life). Values do not change as rapidly as do other elements of the culture. Although values often differ from behavior, they remain the criteria for evaluating objects, persons, and events. It is important, however, to mention behaviors that often contradict the values because they demonstrate the hypocrisy prevalent in American society that so often upsets young people (and others) who, in turn, develop countercultures (a topic that we shall cover shortly).

Perhaps most illustrative of the inconsistency between values and behavior is the belief in the American Creed held by most Americans—generally assumed to encompass equality of all persons, freedom of speech and religion,

The Giant Plates of Culture

Throughout the nineteen-sixties, while the news media focused on the ferment in American life—civil rights marches, the assassinations of John and Robert Kennedy and Martin Luther King, protests against the war in Vietnam, and other spectacular events—my work in studying cross sections of the public showed the vast majority of Americans going about their daily routines unruffled, their outlook on life hardly touched by these momentous happenings. In the past few years, however, as the media tell us that we have reverted to a nineteen-fifties-style normalcy—quiet campuses with well-dressed young people more concerned with finding jobs than bringing the Establishment to its knees, and much talk of a retreat from the liberal social attitudes of the post-World War II era toward more conservative values—our recent studies show evidence of startling cultural changes. These range from marginal changes (fewer V-8 engines, white wine instead of hard liquor before dinner) to changes that penetrate to the core of American life—into the private spaces of our inner lives, the semipublic space of our lives within the family, at work, in school, in church, in the neighborhood and into the public space of our lives as citizens.

Indeed, so far ranging are these changes that each time I encounter them a recurring image comes to mind, the image of the earth moving deep beneath the surface and so transforming the landscape that it loses its comfortable familiarity. According to the geological theory of plate tectonics, giant "plates" undergird the earth's surface and keep it stable and rigid. Sometimes these immense geologic formations, grinding against one another beneath the surface of the earth, shift their positions. Their movements may be slight, but the plates are so massive that along their fault lines even slight shifts cause volcanoes and earthquakes on the surface.

Increasingly in recent years, our studies of the public show the "giant plates" of American culture shifting relentlessly beneath us. The shifts create huge dislocations in our lives. Those living closest to society's fault lines are the first to be thrown into new predicaments. But even those living at a remote distance feel the tremors.

The shifts in culture manifest themselves in many different ways:

Every year through the nineteen-seventies, a million or so Americans had themselves sterilized. In just one decade, ten million Americans made sure that they would not have children. This is only one cause of a declining birth rate in a society that seems to have set itself against biological imperatives that prevailed in the past. At an anticipated 1.7 children for each woman of childbearing age, we have fallen below the 2.2 zero population replacement rate needed to keep the population from shrinking, and dramatically below the 3.7 rate of the nineteen-fifties. Our studies show that, unlike most American women in the recent past, tens of millions of women no longer regard having babies as self-fulfilling. Large-scale and deliberate childlessness is a new experience for our society.

Among the most startling changes are those in household composition. In the nineteen-fifties a typical American family consisting of a working father, a stay-at-home mother and one or more children constituted 70 percent of all households. This was the norm, the familiar American nuclear family.

It shocks most Americans to learn to what extent this norm has collapsed in a single generation. Far from being the dominant mode, the "typical American family" does not now constitute even a large minority of households. Rather, it accounts for only 15 percent of them. There are fewer "typical American families" today than households consisting of a single person—the fastest growing category of households counted by the U.S. cen-

(continued)

sus. Single households grew from 10.9 percent of all households in 1950 to 23 percent in the late seventies. We have moved from a society dominated by one type of arrangement, the husband-provider nuclear family, to a more variegated society with many types of households, no one of which predominates.

A General Motors plant in Tennessee gives its union, the UAW, first chance at fifty custodial jobs—janitoring, cleaning up, doing routine maintenance work. They expect ten or twenty applications from older workers who have not quite reached retirement age but have worn themselves out and are seeking a resting place. To the astonishment of both union and management, they receive not ten or twenty inquiries, but an overwhelming two thousand applications from men who hold higher-paying, higher-status jobs. Furthermore, most of the applicants are young, vigorous and far from retirement. The union doesn't know how to allocate the fifty jobs. Seniority rights were originally conceived with upward mobility in mind, giving the person with the longest service the right to higher-paying, not to lower-paying, jobs. Who ever heard of bargaining for downward mobility rights?

Vast shifts are taking place in the composition of the workplace. A generation ago, the typical worker was a man working full-time to provide complete support for his wife and children. Today, fewer than one out of five people who work for pay conform to this standard. By the late seventies a majority of women (51 percent) were working outside the home. By 1980, more than two out of five mothers of children age six or younger worked for pay. In families earning more than $25,000 a year, the majority now depend on two incomes: the husband's and the wife's. Ironically, while women have been clamoring to get in, men have been slowly edging out of the work force. Between 1947 and 1977, the number of men in the prime working years (from ages 16 to 65) who dropped out of the work force nearly doubled, from 13 percent to 22 percent.

Most jobs are still organized as if these changes had not taken place: they continue to be full-time, five-day-a-week, regular-hour jobs, with pay and fringe benefits based on the assumption that the jobholder is the sole earner in the family. We can expect vast changes in the future in how paid work and child care are organized.

In 1978, for the first time in our history, more women than men were admitted to U.S. institutions of higher learning. This trend reflects women's determination to achieve parity with men in education, training and job opportunities. But it also reflects a decline in the proportion of male high-school graduates going on to college—a reversal of the post–World War II pattern. For many American men, going to college is no longer the royal road to success as they define success.

In 1970, my firm's surveys of cultural trends identified almost two out of five Americans as having a "sour grapes" outlook on life. These people believed in the American dream of "bettering oneself" by acquiring education, money, possessions, recognition and status, but in their own lives the dream had failed. My associate, Florence Skelly, named these people "retreaters" because so many felt bitter, negative and withdrawn about their lives. Among the retreaters were many older Americans: their median age was fifty-three compared to twenty-eight for the population as a whole. Astonishingly, a decade later in 1980 the number of retreaters had been slashed in half—reduced from 38 percent to 18 percent, reflecting several changes in American life. One is that we are growing less fiercely competitive with each other: the average American no longer defines success as surpassing the Joneses. Far fewer Americans now than in 1970 judge their own fulfillment in life by the standards of competitive success. Therefore a failure to surpass others economically no longer stigmatizes a person in his own eyes.

A University of Michigan study discloses

another change. It shows older Americans becoming less miserable, anxious and depressed than in the past. On the other hand, it reveals that younger Americans are growing ever more fretful, anxious, off balance and goalless. Yankelovich, Skelly and White studies also show that as the retreater attitude of older Americans declines, a new restlessness is spreading among younger Americans. Each year for the past several years the number of young Americans who lack clearly defined goals and feel utterly aimless about their lives has increased.

Until a few years ago, I assumed that these various shifts signified no more than the normal accommodations our culture makes to new conditions. Change is the one constant we expect in our history, and yet, despite all the changes, certain themes in American culture persist generation after generation. In the nineteen-seventies, the National Science Foundation supported a team of social researchers who replicated, after a fifty-year hiatus, the classic Middletown study that sociologists Robert and Helen Lynd carried out in Muncie, Indiana, in 1923. The Lynds had compared their nineteen-twenties' findings to life in Muncie in the 1880s and 1890s. Almost a full century of American life passed under review.

The Middletown III researchers found abundant evidence of cultural change in the Muncie of the seventies: more divorce, pot smoking, overt pornography, greater tolerance. But what struck them most forcefully was not change, but continuity. In the midst of social upheaval, they were astonished to find that Muncie high-school students gave the same answers to certain questions in 1977 that their grandparents had given to the Lynds in the 1920s: the same numbers reported disputes with parents over getting home late at night, and a majority said they still regard the Bible as a "sufficient guide to all the problems of modern life."

The Muncie researchers are not wrong to stress the continuity of American life. In any culture there will usually be more continuity than change; ordinarily, cultural patterns persist for long periods of time. In my three decades as a student of changes in American mores, I too have grown accustomed to more continuity than change. Almost every survey measuring trends in American values and behavior exhibits extraordinary stability.

In American life, continuity and far-reaching change do coexist with each other. So variegated is American culture that an observer who wishes to highlight its continuity can easily do so; and conversely, an observer who wishes to document the changing nature of American life can also have his way. The subtle question of judgment is always: Have the important things remained the same, or have *they* changed? If important things have changed, as our findings seem to show, they will overflow the confines of culture and flood into our economic and political lives as well. And, if they are important enough, they will break the continuity of American experience in decisive ways, even when on the surface life follows its familiar path in Muncie and other typical American towns and cities.

The shifts in ways of life we will be examining in this study *are* important ones; they do mark a decisive break with the past, and they do affect our economic and political destiny as well as our cultural life styles.

Source: Daniel Yankelovich, *New Rules: Searching for Self-Fulfillment in a World Turned Upside Down* (New York: Bantam Books, 1982), pp. xi–xvi.

and the guarantees of life, liberty, and prosperity—as against the injustices perpetuated by the system and individuals in the system on members of minority groups.

Americans glorify individualism and self-reliance. These related traits, however, are not found in bureaucracies, where the watchword is, "don't rock the boat." Whyte in his classic *The Organization Man* has noted that bureaucracies are not tolerant of individualists (except at the highest levels). They desire persons who adjust to the wishes of the group. They generally prefer that committees reach decisions, not individuals.[24]

The value placed on "hard work" is still found in many Americans. But for many it has been replaced by a philosophy of "getting by." Unions sometimes enforce a policy of restricted output so as not to embarrass slower (or lazier) workers. Some observers have noted that the current generation, unlike its predecessor, is overrepresented by either: (1) "corner cutters" and "angle players"—persons interested in "easy money"; or (2) persons who value a subsistence existence.

Successful persons in America have always been self-made. They have been the ones who achieved wealth, fame, and power through their own achievements. The value placed on achievement rather than ascription (inherited advantages) began in American history as an antiaristocracy bias. This has changed over time, and now the wealthy are considered successful whether they made the money or not. Americans now tend to give great weight to the opinions expressed by the wealthy, as evidenced by the electorate's tendency to elect them to public office.

Americans have always placed high value on the equality of all persons (in the courts or in getting a job). This value is impossible to reconcile with the racist and superiority theories held by some individuals and groups. It is also impossible to reconcile with many of the formal and informal practices on jobs, in the schools, and in the courts.

Related to the stated belief in equality are the other fundamental beliefs enunciated by the Founding Fathers: the freedoms guaranteed in the Bill of Rights and the Declaration of Independence. Ironically, although the United States was founded by a revolution, the same behavior (called for by the Declaration of Independence) by dissident groups is now squelched (in much the same way as by King George III).

Americans value "law and order." This reverence for the law has been overlooked throughout American history whenever "law-abiding" groups, such as vigilante groups, took the law in their own hands (by threatening that anyone who disobeys vigilante law will be lynched). Currently, the very groups to make the loudest demands for "law and order" are ones who disobey certain laws—for example, southern politicians blocking federal court orders to integrate schools, American Legion posts that notoriously ignore local, state, and federal laws about gambling and liquor, and school administrators allowing prayer in public schools despite the ruling of the Supreme Court.

A final example of disparity between American values and behavior involves the pride Americans have in solving difficult problems. Americans are inclined to be realists. They are pragmatic, down-to-earth problem solvers ready to apply scientific knowledge and expertise to handle such technical problems as getting human beings to and from the moon safely. This realism tends to be replaced by mere gestures, however, when it comes to social problems. Americans have a compulsive tendency to avoid confrontation with chronic social problems. They tend to think that social problems will be solved if one has "nice" thoughts, such as "ban the bomb," "the population problem is everybody's baby," or "black is beautiful." Somehow the verbal level is mistaken for action. If we hear our favorite television personality end the program with a statement against pollution, the problem will somehow be solved.

This is evidenced at another level by proclaiming a "war on poverty," or setting up a commission to study violence, pornography, or civil disorders. Philip Slater has said that the typical American approach to social problems is to decrease their visibility—out of sight, out of mind.

> When these discarded problems rise to the surface again—a riot, a protest, an expose in the mass media—we react as if a sewer had backed up. We are shocked, disgusted, and angered. We immediately call for the emergency plumber (the special commission, the crash program) to ensure that the problem is once again removed from consciousness.[25]

The examples just presented make clear that while Americans express some values, they often behave differently. The values do, however, still provide the standards by which individuals are evaluated. These inconsistencies are sometimes important in explaining individual behavior (guilt, shame, aggression), and the emergence of insulating personal and social mechanisms such as compartmentalization and racial segregation.

Not only is there an inconsistency between values and behavior, but there is also a lack of unity among some of the values themselves. Some examples of this phenomenon, which has been called "ethical schizophrenia," are individualism vs. humanitarianism, materialism vs. idealism, and pragmatism vs. utopianism.[26]

Cultural Diversity

Americans are far from unanimous on a number of public issues. Table 5–1 shows this diversity. Despite inconsistencies and ambiguities, Americans do tend to believe in certain things—for example, that democracy is the best form of government; that capitalism is the best economic system; that success can be defined in terms of hard work, initiative, and the amassing of wealth and property; that Christianity should be the country's dominant religion; and that there should be equality of opportunity and equal justice before the law. It is important to note that while these values are held generally by the American populace, there is never total agreement on any of them. The primary reason for this is the tremendous diversity found within the United States.

It is composed of too many people who differ on important social dimensions: age, sex, race, region, social class, ethnicity, religion, rural/urban, and so on. These variables suggest that groups and categories will differ in values and behavior because certain salient social characteristics imply differential experiences and expectations. These will be noted often in the remainder of this book.

Let us examine a few differences held by various groups and categories to illustrate the lack of consistency among Americans. Values are the criteria used to determine, among other things, morality. A Gallup survey asked a

TABLE 5–1   Diversity of Public Opinion (percentages)

Issue	Favor	Oppose
Equal Rights Amendment	61%	39%
Ban on handguns	45	55
Freeze on nuclear weapons	45	55
Legalization of marijuana	30	70
Death penalty for murder	72	28
Increase military spending	42	58
Decrease spending on social programs	34	66
Prayer in public schools	73	27
Ban on federal financing of abortions	44	56
Busing children to achieve racial balance	28	72

Source: *Gallup Report*, Report No. 206 (November 1982), from a survey taken September 17–20, 1982.

national sample in 1983 their opinions on abortion. Table 5–2 breaks down the data by sex, race, age, income, and education. Clearly on this issue Americans differ. The differences are systematic rather than random. The older the person and the lower his or her income or education, the more likely to be anti-abortion.

There are rural-urban differences in American society that are well known. An interesting example is the probability that rural people are more humanitarian, yet more intolerant of deviance among their neighbors than are urban dwellers. But there are variations among rural communities as there are among urban places on these and other differences.

Region of the country accounts for some variation in values held. But the generalizations made about southerners, easterners, and midwesterners, while having some validity, gloss over many real differences. Within any one region there are differences among rural and urban people, among different religious groups, among different ethnic groups, and so on. Perhaps the best study of cultural variation within the United States (and even within one geographical region) was done by Kluckhohn and Strodtbeck.[27] These researchers studied five small communities in the same general area in the American southwest—a Mormon settlement, a Texan settlement, a village of Spanish-Americans, a Zuñi reservation, and a Navajo reservation. They found that these groups were quite different with respect to individual versus collective orientation, time dimension, the relationship of human beings to nature, and so on. Because each of these communities differed in their answers to various human dilemmas, their values also differed significantly.

Kluckhohn and Strodtbeck, of course, did not choose American communities at random. They were very selective, hoping to demonstrate the existence of real cultural differences within the United States. What they

TABLE 5–2   The Legality of Abortion (percentages)

Question: "Do you think abortions should be legal under any circumstances, legal under only certain circumstances, or illegal in all circumstances?"

	Legal, Any Circumstances	Legal, Certain Circumstances	Illegal, All Circumstances	No Opinion
National	23%	58%	16%	3%
Sex				
Men	24	57	16	3
Women	22	58	17	3
Race				
White	23	60	15	2
Nonwhite	23	46	26	5
Education				
College	32	56	10	2
High School	22	59	16	3
Grade School	10	55	29	6
Age				
Under 30	24	58	17	1
30–49 years	26	58	14	2
50 and older	19	58	18	5
Income				
$25,000 and over	29	59	10	2
$10,000–14,999	17	59	21	3
Under $5,000	16	47	30	7

Source: *The Gallup Report*, Report No. 215 (August 1983), p. 18. The survey was conducted June 24–27, 1983.

found were four subcultures (all but the Texas community) within one geographical region within the border of the United States.

The concept, **subculture,** has been defined typically as a relatively cohesive cultural system that varies in form and substance from the dominant culture. Under the rubric "subculture," then, there are ethnic groups, delinquent gangs, and religious sects. Milton Yinger has proposed that the concept "subculture" be defined more precisely. He has suggested that it be used for one type of group and "contraculture" for another type that has been previously called a subculture.[28] For Yinger the concept "subculture" should be limited to relatively cohesive cultural systems that differ from the dominant culture in such things as language, values, religion, and style of life. Typically, a group that is a subculture differs from the larger group because it has immigrated from another society and because of physical or social isolation has not been fully assimilated. The cultural differences, then, are usually based on ethnicity. Tradition keeps the culture of this group somewhat unique from the dominant culture. There are a number of examples of such

PANEL 5–4   Methods Panel

Participant Observation

A common method of data collection is the direct observation of social phenomena in natural settings. One way to accomplish this is for the researcher to become part of what he or she is studying. There are several roles that observers may take in this regard. One is to hide the fact that one is a researcher and participate as a member of the group being studied. Another is to let the subjects know that you are a scientist but remain separate and detached from the group. A third option is to identify oneself as a researcher and become friends with those being studied. Each of these alternatives has its problems, such as the ethics of deceiving subjects and the fundamental problem of subjects altering their behavior if they know they are being investigated.

Elliot Liebow—a white, Jewish, and middle-class researcher—investigated the **subculture** of poor black males in one section of the Washington, D.C. ghetto.* From the beginning Liebow identified himself as a

researcher. He became deeply involved with his subjects. He partied with them, visited in their homes, gave them legal advice, and just generally "hung around" with them in their leisure hours. As the research progressed he became more and more a part of the street-corner life he was investigating. As a white, though, he never escaped completely being an outsider.

At first Liebow's field notes concentrated on individuals: what they said, what they did, and the contexts in which they said or did them. Through this beginning he ultimately saw the patterns of behavior and how the subjects perceived and understood themselves. He was able to understand the social structure of streetcorner life. More important, his research enabled him to see the complexity of the social network of society's "losers" and how they continuously slip back and forth between the values and beliefs of the larger society and those of their own social system.

* *Tally's Corner* (Boston: Little, Brown, 1967).

subcultures in the United States—the Amish, the Hutterites, some Orthodox Jewish sects, many Indian tribes, Appalachian snake handlers, and Poles, Croatians, Hungarians, Italians, Greeks, and Irish groups at one time or another in American history. The existence of numerous subcultures within the United States explains much of the lack of consistency with respect to American values.

A **contraculture** as defined by Yinger, is a culturally homogeneous group that has developed values and norms that differ from the larger society because the group opposes the larger society. This type of group is in conflict with the dominant culture. The particular values and norms can only be understood by reference to the dominant group.

The values held by delinquent gangs are commonly believed to be a reaction against the values held by the larger society (and hence would represent a contraculture). Albert K. Cohen has noted, for example, that lower-class juvenile gangs not only reject the dominant value system but they exalt the exact opposite values.[29] These boys, Cohen argues, are ill-equipped because of their lower-class origins and other related drawbacks to be successful in the game as it is defined by the dominant society. They, therefore, repudiate the commonly held values for a new set that have meaning for them and under which they can perform satisfactorily. These values differ from the values of the larger culture because the delinquents actually want the larger values but cannot attain them. If Cohen's thesis is correct, then delinquent gangs indeed form a contraculture (although Cohen specifically names them subcultures).

SUMMARY

Culture, the knowledge that the members of a collectivity share, is the product of sustained interaction. At the societal level people create language and other symbols, norms, values, technical knowledge, and belief systems and pass them from generation to generation through socialization. (The process of socialization is the topic of the following chapter.) This human creation is a powerful determinant of people's subsequent behavior. It shapes their thoughts and perceptions. It guides their choices by providing the criteria for evaluation. It includes societal rules. In many ways culture provides the script for social life. Violating this script invites social ostracism, the label of mental illness, or even prison (see Chapters 7 and 8).

The second part of this chapter focused on American values. Values are the culturally prescribed criteria by which individuals evaluate persons, behavior, objects, and ideas as to their relative morality, desirability, merit, or correctness. Although there is not complete agreement on American values because of the diversity present in American society, there are some dominant value orientations that make Americans unique. These are success through individual achievement, competition, hard work, continual striving, and deferred gratification. Other American values are progress, materialism, and individual freedom.

These values are sources of both societal integration and social problems. Order theorists assume that sharing values solves the most fundamental problem of societal integration. The values are symbolic representations of the existing society and therefore promote unity and consensus among Americans. They must, therefore, be preserved.

Conflict theorists, on the other hand, view the mass acceptance of values as a form of cultural tyranny that promotes political conservatism, inhibits creativity, and gets people to accept their lot because they believe in the system rather than joining with others to try and change it. Thus, conflict theorists believe that slavish devotion to society's values inhibits necessary social change. Moreover, American values are assumed by conflict theorists to be the actual source of social problems such as crime, conspicuous consumption, planned obsolescence, the energy crises, pollution, and the artificial creation of winners and losers.

Regardless of which side one may take on the consequences of American values, most would agree that the traditional values of individual freedom, capitalism, competition, and progress have made America relatively affluent.

The future, however, will very likely be very different from the past, requiring a fundamental change in these values. The future of slow growth or no growth, lower levels of affluence, and resource shortages will require that Americans adapt by adopting values that support cooperation rather than competition, that support group goals over individual goals, and a mode of "making do" rather than the purchasing of unnecessary products and the relentless search for technological solutions.

CHAPTER REVIEW

1. Culture, the knowledge the members of society or other social organizations share, constrains behavior and how people think about and interpret their world.

2. Culture emerges as a result of continued social interaction.

3. Culture is learned behavior. The process of learning the culture is called socialization.

4. Through the socialization process, individuals internalize the culture. Thus the control that culture has over individuals is seen as natural.

5. Culture channels behavior by providing the rules for behavior and the criteria for judging.

6. Culture is boundary maintaining. One's own culture seems right and natural. Other cultures are considered inferior, wrong, or immoral. This tendency to consider the ways of one's own group superior is called ethnocentrism.

7. Six types of shared knowledge constitute the culture—symbols, technology, ideologies, norms, values, and roles.

8. Norms are divided into two types by degree of importance and severity of punishment for their violation. Folkways are less important while the mores are considered more vital and thereby more severely punished if violated.

9. Roles are the behavioral expectations of those who occupy the statuses in a social organization.

10. Through language and other symbols culture determines how the members of a society will interpret their environment. The important point is that through this "construction of reality" the members of a society make sense out of a world that has no inherent meaning.

11. The variety of customs found throughout the world is staggering. The members of one society typically view the customs found elsewhere as weird, cruel, and immoral. If we understand the cultural context of a given society, however, their practices generally make sense. This is called cultural relativity.

12. Knowing the values (the criteria for evaluation) of a society is an excellent way of understanding that society.

13. American values are the result of three major factors: (a) geographical isolation and being blessed with abundant resources; (b) founding of the nation in opposition to tyranny and aristocracy and supporting freedom, democracy, equality, and impersonal justice; and (c) a religious heritage based on the Judeo-Christian ethic and the Protestant work ethic.

14. The dominant American values are: success through individual achievement, competition, hard work, progress

through growth and new technology, material progress, and individual freedom.

15. These American values are the sources of societal integration as well as social problems.

16. Despite the power of culture and American values over individual conduct, the diversity present in American society means that for many there are inconsistencies between values and actual behavior. There are clear variations in how Americans feel on public issues based on their different social situations.

17. A major source of cultural variation in the United States is the existence of subcultures. Because of different religions and ethnicity some groups retain a culture different from the dominant one. Other groups form a culture because they oppose the larger society. The latter are called contracultures.

FOR FURTHER STUDY

Culture: General

Ruth Benedict, *Patterns of Culture* (Baltimore, Md.: Penguin, 1946).

Peter L. Berger and Thomas Luckman, *The Social Construction of Reality* (Garden City, N.Y.: Doubleday (Anchor Books), 1967).

Marvin Harris, *Cows, Pigs, Wars, and Witches: The Riddles of Culture* (New York: Random House (Vintage Books), 1974).

American Values

Florence Kluckhohn and Fred L. Strodtbeck, *Variations in Value Orientations* (New York: Harper & Row, 1961).

Philip Slater, *Wealth Addiction* (New York: E. P. Dutton, 1980).

Robin Williams, *American Society: A Sociological Interpretation*, 3rd ed. (New York: Alfred A. Knopf, 1970).

Daniel Yankelovich, *New Rules: Searching for Self-Fulfillment in a World Turned Upside Down* (New York: Bantam, 1982).

Subcultures

Elliot Liebow, *Tally's Corner* (Boston: Little, Brown, 1967).

Rosabeth M. Kanter, *Commitment and Community: Communes and Utopias in Sociological Perspective* (Cambridge, Mass.: Harvard University Press, 1972).

William M. Kephart, *Extraordinary Groups: The Sociology of Unconventional Life-Styles* (New York: St. Martin's Press, 1976).

NOTES AND REFERENCES

1. Peter L. Berger, *Invitation to Sociology* (Garden City, N.Y.: Doubleday (Anchor Books), 1963), p. 98. See also R. P. Cuzzort, *Humanity and Modern Sociological Thought* (New York: Holt, Rinehart and Winston, 1969), pp. 203–204.

2. Berger, *Invitation to Sociology*, p. 93.

3. Marvin E. Olsen, *The Process of Social Organization* (New York: Holt, Rinehart and Winston, 1968), p. 60; and Gerhard Lenski, *Human Societies: A Macrolevel Introduction to Sociology* (New York: McGraw-Hill, 1970), pp. 37–38.

4. See Harold Garfinkel, *Studies in Ethnomethodology* (Englewood Cliffs, N.J.: Prentice-Hall, 1967).

5. See Peter L. Berger and Thomas Luckman, *The Social Construction of Reality* (Garden City, N. Y.: Doubleday (Anchor Books), 1967).

6. John B. Carroll (ed.), *Language, Thought,*

and Reality: Selected Writings of Benjamin Lee Whorf (Cambridge, Mass.: MIT Press, 1956).

7. Norris and Ross McWhirter, Guinness Book of World Records, 11th ed. (New York: Sterling, 1972), p. 167.

8. J. Bronowski, The Common Sense of Science (Cambridge, Mass.: Harvard University Press, 1978), p. 21.

9. Thomas Szasz, Ceremonial Chemistry (Garden City, N.Y.: Doubleday (Anchor Books), 1974), p. 17.

10. This insight comes from my colleague Ronny Turner, Colorado State University.

11. Charles Edgley and Ronny E. Turner, "Masks and Social Relations," Humboldt Journal of Social Relations 3 (Fall/Winter 1975), p. 6.

12. Harvey Farberman and Eric Goode, Social Reality (Englewood Cliffs, N.J.: Prentice-Hall, 1973), p. 2.

13. Marvin Harris, Cows, Pigs, Wars, and Witches: The Riddles of Culture (New York: Random House (Vintage Books), 1975), pp. 11–32.

14. Ibid., p. 21.

15. Marvin Harris, "India's Sacred Cow," Human Nature 1 (February, 1978), p. 36.

16. Robin M. Williams, American Society: A Sociological Interpretation, 3rd ed. (New York: Alfred A. Knopf, 1970), pp. 444–446.

17. See especially the insights of Max Weber, The Protestant Ethic and the Spirit of Capitalism, Talcott Parsons (trans.) (New York: Scribner's, 1958). This work was first published in 1904.

18. Williams, American Society, p. 451.

19. Much of the following material is taken from D. Stanley Eitzen and George H. Sage, Sociology of American Sport, 2nd ed. (Dubuque, Iowa: Wm. C. Brown, 1982), chapter 3.

20. Williams, American Society, pp. 454–455.

21. Amitai Etzioni, "After Watergate—What?: A Social Science Perspective," Human Behavior 2 (November 1973), p. 7.

22. See George H. Hanford, "Controversies in College Sports," The Annals 445 (September 1979), pp. 66–79; and John Underwood, "The Writing is on the Wall," Sports Illustrated (May 19, 1980), pp. 36–72.

23. Edward C. Banfield, The Unheavenly City Revisited (Boston: Little, Brown, 1974).

24. William H. Whyte, Jr., The Organization Man (Garden City, N.Y.: Doubleday (Anchor Books), 1956), p. 150.

25. Philip Slater, The Pursuit of Loneliness: American Culture at the Breaking Point (Boston: Beacon, 1970), p. 15.

26. Jane C. Record and Wilson Record, "Ideological Forces and the Negro Protest," The Annals 357 (January, 1965), pp. 89–96.

27. Florence Kluckhohn and Fred L. Strodtbeck, Variations in Value Orientation (New York: Harper & Row, 1961).

28. J. Milton Yinger, "Contraculture and Subculture," American Sociological Review 25 (October, 1962), pp. 625–635. The following discussion relies principally upon this article.

29. Albert K. Cohen, Delinquent Boys: The Culture of the Gang (Glencoe, Ill.: Free Press, 1955).

6

Socialization

Oscar Stohr and Jack Yufe are identical twins separated as babies by their parents' divorce. Oscar was raised by his maternal grandmother in the Sudetenland of Czechoslovakia. He was a strict Catholic. As a loyal Nazi, he hated Jews. His brother, Jack, was raised by his Jewish father in Trinidad. During World War II he was loyal to the British and hated the Germans.

The twins were united briefly in 1954, but Jack was warned by the translator to not tell his brother that he was Jewish.

In 1979, at age 47, the brothers were reunited by scientists who wished to establish the degree to which environment shapes human behavior. Because they had the same genes, any differences between the brothers must result from how they were raised.

The scientists found not only that they were physically alike but that the twins were strikingly similar in temperament, tastes, tempo, and the way that they did things. Both had been excellent athletes. Both had had trouble in school with mathematics. But the twins also differed in many important respects. Jack is a workaholic, while Oscar enjoys his leisure time. Jack is a political liberal while Oscar is a traditionalist. This difference is seen in Jack's tolerance of feminism and Oscar's resistance to that movement. Jack is proud of being Jewish while Oscar never mentions his Jewish heritage.

In this chapter we will examine this process of socialization that is so powerful in shaping human thought and behavior as to make identical twins different.

Every day a horde of savages appears on the scene in American society. How do these savages become members of society? How do they lose their "savageness"? How do they become "human"? The answer to these questions is that they learn to be human by acquiring the meanings, ideas, and actions appropriate for that society. This process of learning the culture is called **socialization.***

Children are born with the limits and potential established by their unique genetic compositions. Their physical features, size and shape, rate of physical development, and even temperament will unfold within pre-determined boundaries. The limits of their intellectual capabilities are also influenced by biological heritage. But, while children are biologically human, they do not have the instincts or the innate drives that will make them human. They acquire their "humanness" through social interaction. Their concepts of themselves, personality, conception of love, freedom, justice, right and wrong, and interpretation of reality are all products of social interaction. In other words, human beings are essentially the social creations of society.

Evidence for this assertion is found by examining the traits and behaviors of children raised without much human contact. There have been occasional accounts of **feral** children throughout history. These are children believed to have been raised by animals. When found, they look human but act like the animals with whom they have had contact. A recent case involved a Tarzan-like child reported to have been raised by monkeys in the jungles of central Africa. The boy was discovered in 1974 at about the age of six with a troop of gray monkeys. Two years later after painstaking efforts to "rehabilitate" him, he remained more monkey than human. "He is unable to talk and communicates by 'monkey' grunts and chattering. He will eat only fruit and vegetables, and when excited or scared jumps up and down uttering threatening monkey cries."[1] If a child's personality were largely determined by biological heritage, this child would have been much more human than simian. But, there is a consistent finding in all cases of feral children—they are not normal. They cannot talk and have great difficulty

---

*That this chapter focuses on how children learn the culture should *not* be interpreted to mean that the socialization process stops at the end of adolescence. To the contrary, socialization is a lifelong process and occurs in all social groups, not just the society.

in learning human speech patterns. They do not walk or eat like human beings. They express anger differently. In essence, the behavior that arises in the absence of human contact is not what we associate with human beings.

The most famous case of a child who was raised with only minimal human contact was a girl named Anna.[2] Anna was an illegitimate child. Her grandfather refused to acknowledge her existence, and to escape his ire, the mother put her in an attic room and, except for minimal feeding, ignored her. Anna was discovered by a social worker at about age six and she was placed in a special school. When found, Anna could not sit up or walk. She could not talk and was believed to be deaf. She was immobile and completely indifferent to those around her. Staff members worked with Anna (during one year a single staff member had to receive medical attention more than a dozen times for bites she received from Anna[3]), and eventually Anna learned to take care of herself, walk, talk, and play with other children.

> By the time Anna died of hemorrhagic jaundice approximately four and a half years [after she was found], she had made considerable progress as compared with her condition when found. She could follow directions, string beads, identify a few colors, build with blocks, and differentiate between attractive and unattractive pictures. She had a good sense of rhythm and loved a doll. She talked mainly in phrases but would repeat words and try to carry on a conversation. She was clean about clothing. She habitually washed her hands and brushed her teeth. She would try to help other children. She walked well and could run fairly well, though clumsily. Although easily excited, she had a pleasant disposition. Her involvement showed that socialization, even when started at the late age of six, could still do a great deal toward making her a person. Even though her development was no more than that of a normal child of two or three years, she had made noteworthy progress.[4]

The conclusion from those who had observed Anna and other cases of isolated children is that being deprived of social interaction during one's formative years deprives individuals of their humanness.

The second essential to socialization is language. Language is the vehicle through which socialization occurs. In Anna's case, what little human contact she had during her first six years was physical and not communicative interaction. As Kingsley Davis has noted, Anna's case illustrates "that communicative contact is the core of socialization."[5] This principle is also illustrated by Helen Keller. This remarkable person became deaf and blind as a result of illness during infancy. She was locked into her own world until her teacher, Anne Sullivan, was able to communicate to her that the symbol she traced on Helen's hand represented water. That was the beginning of language for Helen Keller and the beginning of her understanding of who she was and the meaning of the world and society in which she was immersed.[6]

Learning language has profound effects on how individuals think and perceive. Through their languages societies differ in the way they conceive of time, space, distance, velocity, action, and specificity. To illustrate this last dimension—specificity—let's consider the Navajo language. With respect to rain, the Navajo make much finer distinctions than the English who generally leave it to: "It has started to rain;" "It is raining;" and "It has stopped raining." When the Navajo reports his or her experiences

> he uses one verb form if he himself is aware of the actual inception of the rain storm, another if he has reason to believe that the rain has been falling for some time in his locality before the occurrence struck his attention. One form must be employed if rain is general round about within the range of vision; another if, though it is raining about, the storm is plainly on the move. Similarly, the Navaho must invariably distinguish between the ceasing of rainfall (generally) and the stopping of rain in a particular vicinity because the rain clouds have been driven off by the wind. The [Navaho] people take the consistent noticing and reporting of such differences . . . as much for granted as the rising of the sun.[7]

In short, the languages of different societies are not parallel methods for expressing the same reality. Our perception of reality depends on our language. In this way experience itself is a function of language. As the distinguished linguist B. L. Whorf has put it: ". . . no individual is free to describe nature with absolute impartiality but is constrained to certain modes of interpretation even while he thinks himself most free."[8]

In learning language we discover the meaning of symbols not only for words but also for objects, such as the cross, the flag, and traffic lights. Through language we can think about the past and the future. Language symbolizes the values and norms of the society, thus enabling the user to label and evaluate objects, acts, individuals, and groups. The words we use in such instances can be positive, such as beautiful, wise, moral, friend, and appropriate, or negative, such as ugly, dumb, immoral, enemy, or inappropriate. Moreover, the description of the same act can portray a positive or a pejorative image. This can be seen in the sports world, as reported by syndicated columnist Jim Murray:

> "On our side, a guy is 'colorful.' On their side, a 'hotdog'."
>
> "Our team is 'resourceful.' Theirs is 'lucky'."
>
> "Our guys are 'trusted associates.' Theirs are 'henchmen'."
>
> "Our team gives rewards. Theirs, bribes."
>
> "Our team plays 'spirited' football. Theirs plays dirty."
>
> "Our team is 'opportunistic.' Theirs gets all the breaks."
>
> "Our guy is 'confident.' Theirs is an egotist."[9]

Thus, language is a powerful labeling tool, clearly delineating who is "in" and who is "out." Finally, children learn who they are by using words to describe themselves. The words they use are those that others, in turn, have used in talking about them and their actions.

THE PERSONALITY AS A SOCIAL PRODUCT

In Chapter 2, we noted the dialectic character of society. Society is at once a product of social interaction, yet that product continuously acts back on its producers. As Berger has put it, "Society is a product of man. . . . Yet it may also be stated that man is a product of society."[10] In this section, the emphasis will be on this second process—human beings as a product of society. In particular, we shall examine the emergence of the human personality as a social product.

We develop a sense of self (our personality) in interaction with others. Newly born infants have no sense of self-awareness. They are unable to distinguish between themselves and their surroundings. They cry spontaneously when uncomfortable. They eventually become aware that crying can be controlled and that its use can bring a response from others. In time, and especially with the employment of language, the child begins to distinguish between "I" and "you" and "mine" and "yours"—signs of self-awareness. But this is just the beginning of the personality-formation process. Let us look now at several classical theories of how children develop personalities and how they learn what is expected of them in the community and society.

Charles H. Cooley: The Looking-Glass Self

Cooley (1864–1929) believed that children's conceptions of themselves arise through interaction with others.[11] He used the metaphor of a looking glass to convey the idea that all persons understand themselves through the way in which others act toward them. They judge themselves on how they think others judge them. Cooley believed that each of us imagines how we look to others and what their judgment of us is. Bierstedt has summarized this process: "I am not what I think I am and I am not what you think I am. I am what I think you think I am."[12]

The critical process in Cooley's theory of personality development, then, is the feedback the individual receives from others. Others behave in particular ways with regard to an individual. The individual interprets these behaviors positively or negatively. When the behaviors of others are perceived as consistent the individual accepts this definition of self, which in turn has consequences for his or her behavior. In sum, there is a self-fulfilling prophecy—the individual is as defined by others. Suppose, for example, that whenever you entered a room and approached a small knot of people conversing with each other, they promptly melted away with lame excuses. Clearly, this experience, repeated many times, would affect your feelings about yourself. Or, if wherever you appeared, a conversational group quickly formed around you, would not such attention tend to give you self-confidence and ego strength?

Cooley's insight that our self-concepts are a product of how others react to us is important in understanding behavior. Why are some categories of persons more likely to be school dropouts or criminals or malcontents or depressed while others fit in? As we will see in Chapter 8, deviance is the result of the successful application of a social label, a process akin to the "looking-glass self." So, too, does this concept help us to understand the tendency of minority-group members to have low self-esteem. If black children, for example, receive a consistent message from whites that they are inferior, that they are incapable of success in intellectually demanding tasks, and that they are not trustworthy, the probability is that they will have these traits. Many black children and adults fulfill this prophecy, thereby reinforcing the stereotypes of the majority and the low self-esteem of the blacks.

George Herbert Mead: Taking the Role of the Other

Mead (1863–1931) theorized about the relationship of self and society.[13] In essence, he believed that children find out who they are as they learn about society and society's expectations. This occurs in several important stages. Infants learn to distinguish between themselves and others from the actions of their parents. By the age of two or so, children have become self-conscious. By this Mead meant that the children are able to react to themselves as others will react to them. For example, they will tell themselves "No-No," as they have been told many times by their parents, and not touch the hot stove. The importance of this stage is that the children have internalized the feelings of others. What others expect has become a part of them. They have become conscious of themselves by incorporating the way others are conscious of them.

The next stage is the play stage. Children from age four to seven spend many hours a day in a world of play. Much of this time is spent in pretending to be mothers, teachers, doctors, police officers, ministers, grocers, and other roles. Mead called this form of play "taking the role of the other." As children play at a variety of social roles, they act out the behavior associated with these social positions and thus develop a rudimentary understanding of adult roles and why people in those positions act the way they do. They also see how persons in these roles interact with children. Thus, children learn to look at themselves as others see them. As McGee has put it, "he learns who he is by 'being' who he is not."[14] The play stage, then, accomplishes two things. It provides further clues for children as to who they are and it prepares them for later life.

The game stage occurs at about age eight and is the final stage of personality development in Mead's scheme. In the play stage the children's activities were fluid and spontaneous. The game stage, in contrast, involves activities that are structured. There are rules that define, limit, and constrain the participants. Mead used the game of baseball to illustrate what occurs in the game stage. In baseball children must understand and abide by the rules. They must also understand the entire game—that is, when playing second base what they and the other players must do if there is a player on first, one out, and the batter bunts down the first base line. In other words, the various individuals in a game must know the role of all the players and adjust their behavior to that of the others. The assessment of the entire situation is what Mead called the discovery of the "generalized

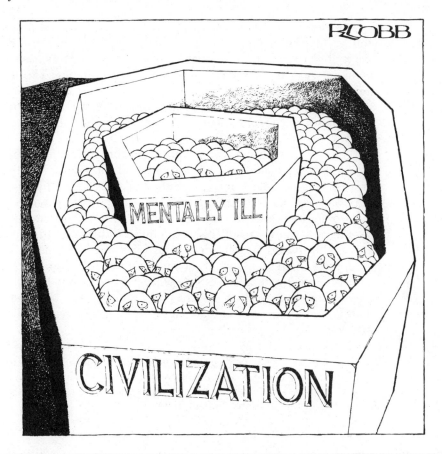

other.'' In the play stage, children learned what was expected of them by ''significant others'' (parents, relatives, teachers). The game stage provides children with constraints from many others, including people they do not know. In this way children incorporate and understand the pressures of society. By passing through these stages children have finally developed a social life from the expectations of parents, friends, and society.

Sigmund Freud: The Psycho-analytic View

Freud (1856–1939) emphasized the biological dimension along with social factors in personality development.[15] For Freud, the infant's first years are totally egocentric, with all energies directed toward pleasure. This is an expression of a primitive biological force—the **id**—that dominates the infant. The id, although a force throughout life, is gradually stifled by society. Parents, as the agents of society, hamper children's pleasure seeking by imposing schedules for eating, punishing them for messy behavior and masturbation, forcing them to control their bowels, and the like.

The process of socialization is, in Freud's view, the process of society controlling the id. Through this process children develop egos. The **ego** is the rational part of the personality that controls the id's basic urges, finding realistic ways of satisfying these biological cravings. The individual also develops a superego (conscience) which regulates both the id and ego. The **superego** is the consequence of the child's internalizing the parents' morals. A strong superego represses the id and channels behavior in socially acceptable ways.

Freud presents a view of socialization that differs significantly from the theories of Mead and Cooley. Whereas Mead and Cooley saw the socialization process as a complete and nonconflictual one, Freud believed the process to be incomplete and accomplished by force. Freud saw the person pulled by two contradictory forces—the natural impulses of biology and the constraints of society—resulting in the imperfection and discontent of human beings. Mead and Cooley, in contrast, did not view the child as one who is repressed, led kicking and screaming into adulthood. For Mead the child passed through natural stages as a willing apprentice to become a conforming member of society. Thus, Mead's conception of the socialization process is deterministic—the individual is a creature of society. Freud's view is quite different.

> To Freud man is a *social* animal without being entirely a *socialized* animal. His very social nature is the source of conflicts and antagonisms that create resistance to socialization by the norms of any of the societies which have existed in the course of human history.[16]

Society's Socialization Agents

Two themes stand out in this section. First, the personality of the child is, to a large degree, socially created and sustained. Second, through the process of socialization, the child internalizes the norms and values of society. In a sense, the child learns a script for acting, feeling, and thinking that is in tune with the wishes of society. Before we leave this topic, let us look briefly at the special transmitters of the cultural patterns—the family, the schools, and the media.

The Family.   Aside from the obvious function of providing the child with the physical needs of food, clothing, and shelter, the family is the primary agent of socialization. The family will indoctrinate the child in the ways of society. The parents equip the child with the information, etiquette, norms, and values necessary for the functioning member of society. Parents in blatant and subtle ways emit messages of what is important, appropriate, moral, beautiful, correct, and what is not. There is no option for young children. They must accept the messages of their parents of what is and what ought to be. As Everett Wilson has put it:

> But when he [the child] enters the human group, he is quite at the mercy of parents and siblings. They determine both what and when he shall eat and wear, when he shall sleep and wake, what he shall think and feel, how he

shall express his thoughts and feelings (what language he shall speak and how he shall do it), what his political and religious commitments shall be, what sort of vocation he shall aspire to. Not that parents are ogres. They give what they have to give: their own limited knowledge, their prejudices and passions. There is no alternative to this giving of themselves; nor for the receiver is there any option. Neither can withhold the messages conveyed to the other.[17]

Thus, children learn from their parents. They learn from them the meaning of physical objects such as the Bible, poison, and the police officer's badge. They also learn the relative worth of social groups such as Jews or blacks. Panel 6–1 provides an example of how one southern white girl was raised to hate blacks.

PANEL 6–1

The Teaching of Prejudice

A southern child's basic lessons were woven of such dissonant strands as these; sometimes the threads tangled into a terrifying mess; sometimes archaic, startling designs would appear in the weaving; sometimes, a design was left broken while another was completed with minute care. Bewildered teachers, bewildered pupils in homes and on the street, driven by an invisible Authority, learned their lessons:

The mother who taught me what I know of tenderness and love and compassion taught me also the bleak rituals of keeping Negroes in their "place." The father who rebuked me for an air of superiority toward schoolmates from the mill and rounded out his rebuke by gravely reminding me that "all men are brothers," trained me in the steel-rigid decorums I must demand of every colored male. They who so gravely taught me to split my body from my mind and both from my "soul," taught me also to split my conscience from my acts and Christianity from southern tradition.

Neither the Negro nor sex was often discussed at length in our home. We were given no formal instruction in these difficult matters but we learned our lessons well. We learned the intricate system of taboos, of renunciations and compensations, of manners, voice modulations, words, feelings, along with our prayers, our toilet habits, and our games. I do not remember how or when, but by the time I had learned that God is love, that Jesus is His Son and came to give us more abundant life, that all men are brothers with a common Father, I also knew that I was better than a Negro, that all black folks have their place and must be kept in it, that sex has its place and must be kept in it, that a terrifying disaster would befall the South if ever I treated a Negro as my social equal and as terrifying a disaster would befall my family if ever I were to have a baby outside of marriage. I had learned that God so loved the world that He gave His only begotten Son so that we might have segregated churches in which it was my duty to worship each Sunday and on Wednesday at evening prayers. I had learned that white southerners are a hospitable, courteous, tactful people who treat those of their own group with consideration and who carefully segregate from all the richness of life "for their own good and welfare" thirteen million people whose skin is colored a little differently from my own.

I knew by the time I was twelve that a member of my family would always shake hands with old Negro friends, would speak graciously to members of the Negro race unless they forgot their place, in which event icy peremptory tones would draw lines beyond which only the desperate would dare take one step. I knew that to use the word "nigger" was unpardonable and no well-bred southerner was quite so crude as to do so; nor would a well-bred southerner call a Negro "mister" or invite him into the living room or eat with him or sit by him in public places.

I knew that my old nurse who had cared for me through long months of illness, who had given me refuge when a little sister took my place as the baby of the family, who soothed, fed me, delighted me with her stories and games, let me fall asleep on her deep warm breast, was not worthy of the passionate love I felt for her but must be given instead a half-smiled-at affection similar to that which one feels for one's dog. I knew but I never believed it, that the deep respect I felt for her, the tenderness, the love, was a childish thing which every normal child outgrows, that such love begins with one's toys and is discarded with them, and that somehow— though it seemed impossible to my agonized heart—I too, must outgrow these feelings. I learned to use a soft voice to oil my words of superiority. I learned to cheapen with tears and sentimental talk of "my old mammy" one of the profound relationships of my life. I learned the bitterest thing a child can learn: that the human relations I valued most were held cheap by the world I lived in.

From the day I was born, I began to learn my lessons. I was put in a rigid frame too intricate, too twisting to describe here so briefly, but I learned to conform to its slide-rule measurements. I learned it is possible to be a Christian and a white southerner simultaneously; to be a gentlewoman and an arrogant callous creature in the same moment; to pray at night and ride a Jim Crow car the next morning and to feel comfortable in doing both. I learned to believe in freedom, to glow when the word *democracy* was used, and to practice slavery from morning to night. I learned it the way all of my southern people learn it; by closing door after door until one's mind and heart and conscience are blocked off from each other and from reality.

I closed the doors. Or perhaps they were closed for me. One day they began to open again. Why I had the desire or the strength to open them, or what strange accident or circumstance opened them for me would require in the answering an account too long, too particular, too stark to make here. And perhaps I should not have the wisdom that such an analysis would demand of me, nor the will to make it. I know only that the doors opened, a little; that somewhere along that iron corridor we travel from babyhood to maturity, doors swinging inward began to swing outward, showing glimpses of the world beyond, of that bright thing we call "reality."

Source: Reprinted from *Killers of the Dream* by Lillian Smith (New York: Norton, 1949), pp. 17–19. By permission of W. W. Norton & Company, Inc. Copyright © 1949, © 1961 by Lillian Smith.

The Schools.   In contrast to families who may differ somewhat in their attitudes, interests, and emphases, the schools provide a more uniform indoctrination of youth in the culturally prescribed ways. Formal education in any society serves to enculturate young persons. The schools have the avowed goal of preparing persons for their adult roles. Youngsters in school must learn appropriate skills and incorporate character traits and attitudes (such as patriotism) that pay off. In the United States some of the character traits are competitiveness, ambition, and conformity.

As we will see in Chapter 15, the formal system of education is most conservative—transmitting the attitudes, values, and training necessary for the maintenance of society. Thus, schools are preoccupied with order and control. This emphasis on order teaches the norms and prepares the youth for the organizational life they are expected to experience as adults. Unlike the family, where the child is part of a loving relationship, the school is impersonal. The rules are to be obeyed. Activities are regimented rather than spontaneous. Thus, the child learns how to function in the larger society by learning the formal prescriptions of society and by learning that to get along one must go along. (See Panel 6–2.)

The Media. The mass media—consisting of newspapers, magazines, movies, radio, and television—play a vital role in promoting the existing values and practices of society. For example, they *select* most of the information that helps us to define socio-political reality. As Parenti has suggested:

> Almost all the political life we experience is through the media. How we view issues—indeed, what we even define as an issue or event—what we see and hear and what we do *not* see and hear are greatly determined by those who control the mass media. By enlarging our vision through technology, we have actually surrendered control over much of our own sensory experience.[18]

The media promote traditional American values. In his study of *CBS Evening News, NBC Nightly News, Newsweek,* and *Time,* sociologist Herbert Gans found that these news sources portrayed eight clusters of enduring values: ethnocentrism, altruistic democracy, responsible capitalism, small-town pastoralism, individualism, moderatism, social order, and national leadership.[19] The promotion of these values is especially effective because it appears to the consumers as independent and objective.

Television, through its entertainment shows, also functions to promote the status quo. Stereotypes of the aged, women, and minorities are promoted on these programs.[20] Crime shows, for example, provide a series of morality plays in which:

> Wrongs are righted, victims avenged, and victimizers awarded for just deserts. The timing is the same, the rhythm, the choreography, the cast, the denouement—everyone has learned just what to expect. On the top of the heap are television's Good Guys, for years mainly mature white males. On the bottom of the heap lie the Victims—piled up bodies of children, old people, poor people, nonwhites, young people, lone women—all done in by Bad Guys recruited principally from the lower social strata many of the so-called victims come from. . . . Our modern morality plays . . . point the finger at the social strata from which evil emanates and signal the conditions that make it quite proper to shoot, kill, maim, hurt, rip, smash, slash, crush, tear, burn, bury, excise. What starts out as shocking becomes routine then is converted into ritual.[21]

The impact of television is of special importance because children are so exposed to it. Children age two through five, for example, watch television an average of 27 hours a week.[22] The messages they receive are consistent: they are bombarded with materialism and consumerism, what it takes to

What Is the Purpose of Education?

What is the purpose of education? The typical answer to this question is that the task of formal education is to preserve the culture by passing it on to the newcomers of society. This is traditionally done by teaching the accumulated wisdom of the past. This has often meant, in effect, that the schools have taught dogma, insisting that certain ideas and practices are considered correct, perhaps even sacred (nationalism, capitalism, Christianity, monogamy), while other ideas and practices are believed to be wrong and even immoral.

In the late 1960s a social science curriculum for grade-school children was developed by the National Science Foundation that had a different purpose. This curriculum, known by the acronym MACOS (Man: A Course of Study), was designed to acquaint children with what makes us human (by contrasting us with other animals) and with the alternative ways human beings have adapted to their environment. About one half of the course is devoted to an in-depth study of the Netsilik Eskimos. This society is composed of people living in the harshest of physical environments. They have adapted by being unusually inventive and cooperative. Most important, they have customs very different from those found in the United States. Some of these are senilicide, infanticide (especially of first-born daughters), trial marriage, wife swapping, and occasional cannibalism.

By 1976, some 1700 schools throughout the United States had adopted the MACOS curriculum. There has been a considerable amount of controversy in many of these schools generated by the concerns of many parents and conservative political and religious organizations. The fundamental issues raised by these critics are that: (1) children are exposed to alternatives rather than indoctrinated with our ways; (2) this may lead children to question America's cherished values; (3) children will be tolerant of practices that we consider deviant; (4) children would implicitly receive the message that there are no moral absolutes, leading to the adoption of situational ethics; and (5) the long-range consequences will be a breakdown of nationalism and the consensus that unites Americans.

If you were a parent of a child in a MACOS program, how would you feel? Would you want some modifications in a program that presents alternative cultures and lifestyles to small children? How far would you agree with the critics of MACOS?

One group of concerned parents in Fort Collins, Colorado, was so upset by the MACOS program in the local schools and its presumed effects on the values of children that they drafted a document, which each individual parent would address to his or her child's principal. This letter said, in part:

This letter is to inform you that certain rights and privileges with regard to the instruction of our child are permanently specifically reserved by us, the parents. The familial relationship involving personal relationships, attitudes, responsibilities, religious and social training are the sole prerogative of the parents. We demand that you not enroll, prepare or instruct our child in any course or class, workshop, study group, etc., known as, or including 'sensitivity training,' 'MACOS,' Human Development programs, social awareness, self-awareness, situation ethics, value judgment, values clarification, Ethnic Studies, 'Humanities,' the philosophies of the Humanist religion, the Occult or any other additional specific courses attempting to modify moral values without our prior informed written consent, which shall also be required for any sex education program, course or study whatever.

Other parents hailed MACOS as a necessary program to prepare children for a shrinking world undergoing ever-faster-paced change.

The School Board in Fort Collins resolved the issue by providing a traditional program in any school where a parent objected to MACOS. Thus, parents were given a very important choice because exposure to one or the other curriculum will make a difference in their children. Children will be more tolerant of deviance, more receptive to alternatives, and less bound by tradition than those children denied access to MACOS. How would you feel about this issue if your children were in a MACOS school?

be a success, and the value of law and order. In short, the media have tremendous power to influence us all, but particularly our youth. This influence can be in the direction of acceptance or criticism of the system. Overwhelmingly, the media are supportive of that system.

SIMILARITIES AND DIFFERENCES AMONG MEMBERS OF SOCIETY

Modal Personality Type

In Chapter 2, we described the condition that Durkheim called "anomie." This refers to a situation where an individual is unsure of his or her social world—the norms are ambiguous or conflicting. In other words, an anomic situation lacks consistency, predictability, and order. Since this condition is upsetting, individuals and groups seek order. Every society provides a common **nomos** (meaningful order) for its members.[23] "Every society has its specific way of defining and perceiving reality—its world, the universe, its overarching organization of symbols."[24] Through the socialization process, the newcomer to society is provided a reality that makes sense. By learning the language and the ready-made definitions of society, the individual is given a consistent way to perceive the world. The order that is created for each of us is taken for granted by us; it is the only world that we can conceive of; it is the only system in which we feel comfortable.

> This order, by which the individual comes to perceive and define his world, is thus not chosen by him, except perhaps for very small modifications. Rather it is discovered by him as an external datum, a ready-made world that simply is *there* for him to go ahead and live in, though he modifies it continually in the process of living in it.[25]

Each society has its unique way of perceiving, interpreting, and evaluating reality. This common culture, and nomos, is internalized by the members of society through the process of socialization—thus, people are a product of their culture. It follows, then, that the members of a society will be similar in many fundamental respects. Although there are individual exceptions and subcultural variations, we can say that Americans differ fundamentally from Mexicans, Germans, the French, and others. Let us illustrate how people in a society will develop similarly by briefly characterizing two categories of Indians of North America.[26]

1. *The Pueblo Indians of the southwest.* The Zuñi and Hopi Indians are submissive and gentle peoples. Children are treated with warmth and affection. They live in highly cooperative social structures where individualism is discouraged. One who thirsts for power is ridiculed.

Life in these societies is highly structured. The rules are extremely important and order is highly valued. They never brew intoxicants and reject the use of drugs. In these orderly and cooperative settings, people are trusted. Life is pleasant and relatively free from hatred. The kind of person that develops in these societies tends to be confident, trusting, generous, polite, cooperative, and emotionally controlled.

2. *The Indians of the northern plains.* The Plains Indians are aggressive peoples. They are fierce warriors exhibiting almost suicidal bravado in battle. They stress individuality with fierce competition for prestige. They boast of their exploits. They stress individual ecstasy in their religious experiences, brought about by fasting, self-torture, and the use of drugs (peyote and alcohol).

The Plains Indians, in contrast to the Pueblo Indians, are more individualistic, competitive, and aggressive. They are more expressive as individuals and less orderly in group life.

These examples show that each society tends to produce a certain type of individual—a **modal personality type.** The individual growing up in American society, with its set of values, will tend to be individualistic, competitive, materialistic, and oriented toward work, progress, and the future. While this characterization of Americans is generally correct, there are some problems with the assumption that socialization into a culture is so all-powerful. First, the power of socialization can vary by the type of society. Small, homogeneous societies like those of American Indian tribes provide the individual member of society with a consistent message, while in a heterogeneous society like the United States, individuals are confronted with a number of themes, variations, and counterthemes. More fundamental, though, is the second problem—is the socialization process completely deterministic? The views of Cooley and Mead noted earlier would seem to suggest this. Dennis Wrong has criticized this position. He has argued that, from a Freudian position, the individual and society are never completely in harmony. While individuals are socialized and generally comply with the demands of society, the process is never complete.[27] The distance from complete socialization is maximized in modern, heterogeneous societies.

Why We
Aren't All
the Same

Every society has its deviants. Clearly, people are not robots. Given the power of society, through the socialization process, what are the forces that allow for differences in people in the United States? We begin with a discussion of the major agencies of socialization.

Family.   We have said that the family is the ultimate societal agency for socialization. Families teach their children the language, etiquette, skills, and the like that will enable the child to find his or her niche in society. But families differ in a variety of important ways (for example, in religion, political views, optimism, and affluence). Socioeconomic status is an especially important variable. In Chapter 14 we shall provide the details as to how the different social classes tend to rear children and the consequences. Two examples will suffice for the present discussion. Working-class parents tend to be authoritarian, demanding control of their youngsters, and providing punishment for failure to comply. Authority figures are to be obeyed without question. In contrast, upper-middle-class parents have tended to allow their children to explore, experiment, and question. The family is democratic. Rules are not necessarily absolute. Clearly, children growing up in authoritarian and permissive families will differ in their acceptance of authority, political proclivities, and view of the world.

The family may have little influence on the child if the parents disagree on politics, religion, values, and the like. Or, if the parents' values are consistent, they may be neutralized by contrary values held by their friends. This is facilitated by the decreasing amount of time that parents spend with the children compared to the time spent in previous generations.[28] As parents spend less and less time raising and influencing their children, their youngsters are influenced more and more by not only peers but also baby sitters, schools, and television.

Some families may have little or negative influence on their children because they are hopelessly disorganized. One or both parents may be alcoholics, unstable, or uncommunicative.

In sum, although children raised in American society are affected by a common culture, family experiences and emphases can vary enough to result in behavioral and attitudinal differences. That children and families can be fundamentally different is seen in the occasional value conflicts between parents and school authorities on sex education, the use of certain literature, rules, and the proper way to enforce rules. But the schools themselves also vary, resulting in different products by type of school.

Schools.   American schools, as are schools in all societies, are conservative. But, there are differences that have a substantial impact on students. There are schools, for example, where the curriculum, schedule, and philosophy are very rigid. Children sit in straight rows, may talk only with permission, wear the prescribed clothing, and accept without question the authority of the teacher. There are other schools, however, where the curriculum, schedules, teachers, and rules are flexible. The products of these two types of schools are likely to differ in much the same way as do the children of autocratic or permissive homes.

Religion.   In general, organized religion in the United States reinforces American values and the policies of the government (see Chapter 16). But there are significant differences among and within the various religious

Socialization of Children for the Future

American youth have been socialized to be individualistic and highly competitive. Through institutions such as the family, school, and sport, Americans have been socialized to be restless, ambitious, self-reliant strivers who are intolerant of losers, and who place the individual above the group. These traits may have had positive consequences when the United States was isolated, underpopulated, and blessed with abundant resources. But Americans are now part of an interdependent worldwide economic system. The planet's resources are rapidly being depleted and its environment is being fouled with pollutants and waste.

Are the typical American traits that we pass on to our children proper for a world that will be overcrowded and characterized by shortages? A strong case can be made that if we continue to raise individualistic, competitive, grasping children, then we will produce a society whose inhabitants will be increasingly irrational—that is, unable to cope with the demands of a future that will likely include rationing and other forms of sacrifice for the good of the society and the world.

Do you think that your children will be better prepared for the future if they learn less competitiveness and more cooperation? If so, how much should you do to help them learn more cooperation in a competitive society? There are societies that appear to inculcate a predominantly cooperative ethic.* How far should these form partial models for rewarding cooperation while discouraging aggressiveness? For example, what if we established a general principle that parents, teachers, and other authorities should reward cooperative behavior by children and either ignore or punish competitive, individualistic behavior. Parents might then also reward their children whether they achieved or not. Games can be used that encourage teamwork. Honors could be equally distributed for participation in sports and other activities that presently glorify the achievements of stars. Schools could abolish tournaments and playoffs. Grades, if used at all, could be based on meeting universal standards, and never on outdoing one's classmates. Absolutely forbidden should be contests such as those sponsored by various corporations and civic groups that reward a small elite at the expense of the masses (for example, the Punt, Pass, and Kick competition).

Do you think that you should encourage a modification of our competitive society by raising your children along these lines? If so, or if not, what modifications would you suggest for the upbringing of your children to cope with life in the future?

* See Ruth Benedict, *Patterns of Culture* (Baltimore, Md.: Penguin Books, 1946); Urie Bronfenbrenner, *Two Worlds of Childhood: U.S. and U.S.S.R.* (New York: Pocket Books, 1973); and Linden L. Nelson and Spencer Kagan, "Competition: The Star-Spangled Scramble," *Psychology Today* 6 (September, 1972), pp. 53–56, 90–91.

bodies. There are religious disagreements on morality, birth control, abortion, capital punishment, evolution, and other volatile issues. Moreover, religious ideas can conflict with those of one's peers, and with what is taught in school. The more salient one's religion, then, the more likely one will differ from those who do not share one's religious views.

Social Location.   Each of us is located in society, not only geographically, but also socially. Depending on our wealth, occupation, education, ethnic or racial heritage, and family background, we see ourselves and others see us as being superior to some persons and inferior to others (see Chapters 9 through 12). Our varying positions in this hierarchy will have an effect on our attitudes and perceptions. In particular, those who are highly placed will tend to be supportive of the status quo, while those who are less advantaged will likely be more antagonistic to the way things are and desirous of changes beneficial to them.

Contradictory Influences.   We have seen that youngsters may experience pulls in opposite directions from their family, church, and school. Other sources of contradictory attractions are peer groups and the media. Parents may insist, for instance, that their children not fight. Yet, their peers might demand such behavior. Moreover, children are bombarded by violence (much of which is considered appropriate) in the movies and on television. How are these children to behave, faced with such opposing and powerful stimuli? Some will follow their parents' dictates, while others will succumb to other pressures.

Conflicts in Role Definition.   Some societies are clear and consistent in their expectations for members' behavior. There is no such consensus in American society. An examination of a few fundamental social roles illustrates the disagreement on the expectations of the occupants. Adolescents are often unsure of what is expected of them. The law sometimes defines them as children and at other times as adults. Parents and other adults often lack consistency in what they expect of teenagers. The aged are another category that experiences ill-defined expectations. At times they are treated as adults and at other times they are not taken seriously. Some must retire from work at age 65 while others may continue.

Sex roles provide another example of varying expectations depending on the individual, audience, and community. Traditional masculine and feminine roles are in flux. What precisely is expected of a man and woman as they enter a building? Does the man open the door for the woman? This was appropriate behavior in the past and it may be now, but one is never sure, for some women find such behavior offensive. What are the expectations of a newly married husband and wife? How will they divide the household chores? Who is to be the breadwinner? And later, if there is a divorce, who will take the children? Twenty years ago, or even five years ago, the answers to these questions were certain, but no longer.

SUMMARY

The theme of this chapter is that people are the products of society. Society shapes our identity, our thoughts, our emotions, our perceptions, and our behavior. Through the various agencies of the society—the family, school, church, voluntary associations, and the media—children internalize the norms and values of society. In short, they learn the societal script for living successfully in society.

The socialization process tends to create a relatively uniform product (modal personality type). But, while there is some uniformity in language, understanding, perception, world view, values, and personality, there are differences. A heterogeneous society like the United States will have a good deal of variance among its members because families, churches, and schools may differ in their emphases and because there is often no solid agreement about societal expectations.

Both order and conflict theorists acknowledge the power of the socialization process. They differ, however, in their interpretation of this universal process. The order theorists view this as necessary to promote unity and law-abiding citizens. Conflict theorists, on the other hand, view the process as one in which persons are led to accept the customs, laws, and values of society uncritically and therefore become willing participants in a society that may be in need of change. The ultimate irony is that most of the powerless in American society do not rebel because they actually believe in the system that systematically disadvantages them.

Although the emphasis of this chapter has been on how the individual is shaped by powerful social forces, we must not forget that people are not utterly predictable. Moreover, human beings are actively involved in shaping the social landscape. In sum, the person is, as Kenneth Westhues has said, "a two-sided being, at once created and creating, predictable and surprising."[29]

CHAPTER REVIEW

1. Socialization is the process of learning the culture. Children must learn the culture of the society in which they are born. Socialization, however, is a lifelong process and occurs in all social groups, not just society.

2. Infants become human only through learning the culture.

3. The socialization of youth requires social interaction.

4. Another essential to socialization is language, which has profound effects on how individuals think and perceive.

5. The personality emerges as a social product. We develop a sense of self only through interaction with others.

6. One theory of how personality develops is Cooley's "looking-glass self." Through interaction children define themselves according to how they interpret how others think of them.

7. Mead's theory of self development involves several stages. Through interaction with their parents, infants are able to distinguish between themselves and others. By age two they are able to react to themselves as others react to them. In the play stage (from age four to seven) children pretend to be in a variety of adult roles (taking the role of the other). In the game stage (about age eight) children play at games with rigid rules. They begin to understand the structure of the

entire game with the expectations for everyone involved. This understanding of the entire situation is called the "generalized other."

8. According to Freud's theory, socialization is the process by which society controls the id (the biological needs for pleasure). Through this process children develop egos (the control of the id by finding appropriate ways to satisfy biological urges). A superego also emerges which is the internalization of the morals of the parents, further channeling behavior in socially acceptable ways.

9. Through interaction children internalize the norms and values of society. There are three special transmitters of the cultural patterns—the family, the schools, and the media.

10. Because the socialization agents of society present a relatively consistent picture, the members of a society tend to be alike in fundamental ways (modal personality type). The smaller and more homogeneous the society, the more alike the members of that society will be.

11. Despite the tendency for the members to be alike, people, especially in large, heterogeneous societies, are not all the same. The sources of deviation are the differences found in families (e.g., in social class, religion, ethnic background); schools with differing philosophies (rigid or flexible, public or sectarian); religions, social locations, contradictory influences, and conflicts in role definitions.

FOR FURTHER STUDY

The Socialization Process

Charles Horton Cooley, *Human Nature and the Social Order* (New York: Schocken, 1964).
Erik Erikson, *Childhood and Society* (New York: W. W. Norton, 1950).
Frances Fitzgerald, *America Revised* (Boston: Atlantic-Little, Brown, 1979).
Sigmund Freud, *Civilization and Its Discontents*, Joan Riviere, trans., (London: Hogarth, 1946).
Herbert J. Gans, *Deciding What's News* (New York: Pantheon, 1979).
Erving Goffman, *The Presentation of Self in Everyday Life* (Garden City, N.Y.: Doubleday, 1959).
Rose K. Goldsen, *The Show and Tell Machine: How Television Works and Works You Over* (New York: Delta, 1977).
George Herbert Mead, *Mind, Self and Society* (Chicago: University of Chicago Press, 1934).
Jean Piaget and Barbara Inhelder, *The Psychology of the Child* (New York: Basic Books, 1969).

Gail Sheehy, *Passages: Predictable Crises in Adult Life* (New York: Dutton, 1976).

Modal Personality

Victor Barnouw, *Culture and Personality*, 3rd ed. (Homewood, Ill.: Dorsey, 1979).
Ruth Benedict, *Patterns of Culture* (Baltimore, Md.: Penguin Books, 1946).
Urie Bronfenbrenner, *Two Worlds of Childhood: U.S. and U.S.S.R.* (New York: Simon and Schuster (Pocket Books), 1973).
Stanley Elkins, *Slavery: A Problem of American Institutional and Intellectual Life* (New York: Universal Library, 1963).
Margaret Mead, *Sex and Temperament in Three Primitive Societies* (New York: William Morrow, 1935).
David Reisman, *The Lonely Crowd* (New York: Doubleday, 1953).

NOTES AND REFERENCES

1. "Jungle Boy Remains More Like Monkey," Associated Press release, May 15, 1976. See also J. A. L. Singh and Robert M. Zingg, *Wolf-Children and Feral Man* (New York: Harper, 1942).

2. Kingsley Davis, *Human Society* (New York: Macmillan, 1948), pp. 204–205; Kingsley Davis, "Extreme Social Isolation of a Child," *American Journal of Sociology* 45 (January, 1940), pp. 554–564.

3. Bruno Bettelheim, "Feral Children and Autistic Children," *American Journal of Sociology* 54 (March, 1959), p. 458.

4. Davis, *Human Society*, p. 205.

5. Ibid.

6. Helen Keller, *The Story of My Life* (Garden City, N.Y.: Doubleday, 1954).

7. Clyde Kluckhohn and D. Leighton, *The Navaho* (Cambridge, Mass.: Harvard University Press, 1946), p. 194.

8. B. L. Whorf, "Science and Linguistics," in E. E. Maccoby, T. M. Newcomb, and E. L. Hartley (eds.), *Readings in Social Psychology* (New York: Holt, 1956), p. 1. See also Alfred R. Lindesmith, Anselm L. Strauss, and Norman K. Denzin, *Social Psychology*, 4th ed. (Hinsdale, Ill.: Dryden, 1975), pp. 161–166.

9. Jim Murray, "Vocabulary Takes on a Ruddy-Faced Look," *Rocky Mountain News* (December 9, 1976), p. 150.

10. Peter Berger, "Religion and World Construction," *Life as Theatre*, Dennis Brissett and Charles Edgley, eds. (Chicago: Aldine, 1975), p. 234.

11. Charles Horton Cooley, *Human Nature and the Social Order* (New York: Schocken, 1964).

12. Robert Bierstedt, *The Social Order*, 4th ed. (New York: McGraw-Hill, 1974), p. 197.

13. George Herbert Mead, *Mind, Self and Society* (Chicago: University of Chicago Press, 1934). For a summary, see Reece McGee, *Points of Departure: Basic Concepts in Sociology*, 2nd ed. (New York: Dryden Press, 1975), pp. 63–77.

14. McGee, *Points of Departure*, pp. 74–75.

15. Sigmund Freud, *Civilization and Its Discontents*, Joan Riviere, trans. (London: Hogarth Press, 1946).

16. Dennis Wrong, "The Oversocialized Conception of Man in Modern Sociology," *Sociological Theory*, 3rd ed., Lewis A. Coser and Bernard Rosenberg, eds. (New York: Macmillan, 1969), p. 130.

17. Everitt K. Wilson, *Sociology: Rules, Roles and Relationships* (Homewood, Ill.: Dorsey Press, 1966), p. 92.

18. Michael Parenti, *Democracy for the Few*, 3rd ed. (New York: St. Martin's, 1980), p. 168. See also Robert Cirino, *Don't Blame the People* (New York: Vintage, 1972), pp. 30–31.

19. Herbert J. Gans, *Deciding What's News* (New York: Pantheon, 1979), pp. 39–69, 196–203.

20. *Window Dressing On the Set: An Update*, A Report of the U.S. Commission on Civil Rights (Washington, D.C., 1979).

21. Rose K. Goldsen, *The Show and Tell Machine: How Television Works and Works You Over* (New York: Delta, 1977), pp. 223–224, 234.

22. Kate Moody, "The Research on TV: A Disturbing Picture," *The New York Times* (April 20, 1980), EDUC 17.

23. This discussion is dependent on the insights of Peter Berger on the "social construction of reality," especially Peter L. Berger and Thomas Luckman, *The Social Construction of Reality: A Treatise in the Sociology of Knowledge* (Garden City, N.Y.: Doubleday (Anchor Books), 1967); and Peter Berger and Hansfred Kellner, "Marriage and the Construction of Reality," in Brissett and Edgley, *Life as Theatre*, pp. 219–233.

24. Berger and Kellner, "Marriage and the Construction of Reality," p. 219.

25. Ibid., p. 220.

26. These accounts are taken from Victor Barnouw, *Culture and Personality*, 3rd ed. (Homewood, Ill.: Dorsey, 1979), pp. 59–75.

27. Wrong, "The Oversocialized Conception of Man," p. 130.

28. The evidence is summarized in Sarane S. Boocock, "Is U.S. Becoming Less Child Oriented?" *National Observer* (February 22, 1975), p. 12.

29. Kenneth Westhues, *First Sociology* (New York: McGraw-Hill, 1982), p. viii.

7

Social Control in Society

At 9:34 P.M. on July 13, 1977 the electricity went out in New York City and in some areas did not work again for twenty-five hours. Under the cover of darkness many areas of the city were pillaged. More than two thousand stores were broken into with property losses estimated at $1 billion. The plunderers were of all ages. They stole appliances, jewelry, shoes, groceries, clothes, furniture, liquor, and automobiles (fifty new Pontiacs from one dealer). The atmosphere was a mixture of revenge, greed, and festival. Observers characterized the looting binge as a carnival atmosphere in which the actors had no concept of morality. It was as if they were immune from the law and from guilt. All of society's constraints were removed resulting in anarchy. When the lights went out, the social controls on behavior left as well for many citizens.

All social groups have mechanisms to ensure conformity—mechanisms of **social control.** The socialization process is one of these ways by which individuals internalize the norms and values of the group. Persons are taught what is proper, moral, and appropriate. This process is generally so powerful that individuals conform, not out of fear of punishment, but because they *want* to. In other words, group demands *out there* become demands *inside* us. But socialization is never perfect—we are not all robots. As we will see in Chapter 8, people deviate. To cope with this, social groups exert external control—that is, rewards and punishments. These controls are the subject of this chapter.

The focus of this chapter is on social control at the societal level. The dominant modes of socialization vary by type of society. Small, homogeneous societies, for example, are dominated by tradition, while large, modern societies are very much less affected by the force of tradition. Traditional societies tend to have an overriding consensus on societal values; therefore, the family, religion, and the community convey to each individual member a consistent message on which behaviors are appropriate and which ones are not. Although the formal punishment of norm violators does occur in traditional societies, informal controls are usually quite effective and more typical.

In a complex society such as the United States, social control is more difficult to attain because of the existence of different groups with values that are often competing. Therefore, social control tends to be more formal and appears more repressive (because it is more overt) than that which is found in traditional societies. It occurs in many forms and disguises. Social control is accomplished in the home and school and through various other institutions. It is attained through the overt and covert activities of political agencies, psychotherapists, and even genetic engineers. Efforts to manipulate the masses through various techniques of persuasion also keep deviance in check.

The remainder of this chapter is devoted to an extensive examination of the various agents of social control in American society. These are divided into two types by the means used to achieve social control: ideological and direct intervention. The former aims at control through manipulation of ideas and perceptions, while the latter controls the actual behavior of citizens.[1]

AGENTS OF IDEOLOGICAL SOCIAL CONTROL

Ideological social control is the attempt to manipulate the consciousness of citizens so that they accept the ruling ideology and refuse to be moved by competing ideologies. Other goals are to persuade the members of society to comply willingly with the law and to accept without question the existing distribution of societal power and rewards. These goals are accomplished in at least three ways. First, ideological social control is accomplished through the socialization of youth. Young people, for example, are taught the values of individualism, competition, patriotism, and respect for authority at home, in school, in scouting organizations, in sports, and through the media. The socialization process could be referred to as cultural control, since the individual is given authoritative definitions of what should and should not be done, which make it appear as if there were no choice.[2] Second, ideological conformity occurs by frontal attacks on competing ideologies by politicians, ministers, teachers, and other persons in authority. Finally, there are propaganda efforts by political authorities to persuade the public what actions are moral, who the enemies are, and why certain courses of governmental action are required. Let us examine these in detail by describing the agents of social control that are especially important in accomplishing the goal of ideological conformity.

The Family The primary responsibility of parents is to teach their children the attitudes, values, and behaviors considered appropriate by the parents (and society). Parents universally want their children to succeed. Success is not only measured in terms of monetary achievement but also in whether the child fits in society. This requires that the child learn to behave and think in the ways that are deemed "proper." Although, as noted in Chapter 6, there is a wide latitude in the actual mode of socialization in the family,[3] most children do behave in acceptable ways.

The School The formal system of education is an important societal agent for conformity. The school insists that the behavioral standards of the community be maintained in speech, dress, and demeanor. More than this, the schools indoctrinate their pupils in the "correct" attitudes about work, respect for authority, and patriotism. The textbooks used in schools have typically not provided an accurate account of history, for example, but rather an account that is biased in the direction the authorities wish to perpetuate. The treatment given minorities in these texts is one indicator of the bias. Another is the contrast between descriptions of the behavior of the United States and the behavior of its enemies in wars.[4]

   The schools promote respect for American institutions and the "American Way of Life." State legislatures, for instance, have passed laws similar to the one in Arizona requiring every student to take a one-semester course in "the essentials and benefits of the free enterprise system."[5] Florida requires a course for high school graduation called *Americanism versus Communism.* The legislation requiring this course noted that the best method for meeting the challenge of communism is "to have the youth of the state and nation thoroughly and completely informed as to the evils, dangers and fallacies of Communism. . . ."[6] Clearly, the goal of such a course is not education but indoctrination.

   One critic of the schools is concerned with the problem of conformity, which taken to the extreme results in blind obedience to such malevolent authority figures as Adolph Hitler, Charles Manson, and the Rev. Jim Jones.

Rather than turning out conformists the schools should be turning out individuals with the courage to disobey false prophets.

> The power of socialization can conceivably be harnessed so as to develop individuals who are rational and skeptical, capable of independent thought, and who can disobey or disagree at the critical moment. Our society, however, continues systematically to instill exactly the opposite. The educational system pays considerable lip service to the development of self-reliance, and places huge emphasis on lofty concepts of individual differences. Little notice is taken of the legions of overly obedient children in the schools; yet, for every overly disobedient child, there are probably twenty who are obeying too much. There is little motivation to encourage the unsqueaky wheels to develop as noisy, creative, independent thinkers who may become bold enough to disagree.[7]

Religion   Established religion in America tends to reinforce the status quo. Few clergy and their parishioners work actively to change the political and economic system. Instead they preach sermons extolling the virtues of "the American Way of Life," and "giving unto Caesar the things which are Caesar's." Directly or indirectly there has been a strong tendency for religious groups throughout American history to accept existing government policies, whether they are slavery, war, or the conquest of the Indians.

PANEL 7–1   Cross-Cultural Panel

The Amish

The Amish are a religious sect found mainly in Pennsylvania, Indiana, and Kansas. They are farmers who resist modern technology. They forbid the use of motorcycles, automobiles, and electricity. They wear simple clothes of the nineteenth century. They believe that they are only temporary visitors on earth, and hence remain aloof from it. This explains why they insist on being different. Most important, the Amish insist on conformity within their community.

The Amish descend from Jacob Amman, a Mennonite preacher in Switzerland. The Mennonites and other Anabaptists of that day differed from mainstream Protestants because they believed in the separation of church and state, adult baptism, refusal to bear arms and take oaths. Amman and his followers split away from the Mennonites in 1700 over an issue of church discipline—the *Meidung*.

Amman felt that the Mennonites were too lax in their discipline of deviants and that the *Meidung* must be enforced in severe cases. The *Meidung* is one of the most potent of all social control mechanisms. The following is a description by William Kephart of this device used by the Amish to ensure conformity within the community.

> The ultimate sanction is imposition of the *Meidung*, or ban, but because of its severity, this form of punishment is used only as a last resort. The Amish community relies heavily on the individual's conscience to tell him what is right and wrong. And since the typical Amishman has a finely developed conscience, actions like gossip or reprimand are usually sufficient to bring about conformity. The *Meidung* would be im-

posed only if a member were to leave the church, or marry an outsider, or break a major rule (such as buying an auto) without being repentant.

Although the *Meidung* is imposed by the bishop, he will not act without the near-unanimous vote of the congregation. The ban, however, is total. No one in the district is permitted to talk or associate with the errant party, including members of his own family. Even normal marital relations are forbidden. Should any member of the community ignore the *Meidung*, that person would also be placed under the ban. As a matter of fact, the *Meidung* is honored by *all Amish districts*, including those which are not in full fellowship with the district in question. There is no doubt that the ban is a mighty weapon. Jacob Amman intended it to be.

On the other hand, the ban is not irrevocable. If the member admits the error of his ways—and asks forgiveness of the congregation in person—the *Meidung* will be lifted and the transgressor readmitted to the fold. No matter how serious the offense, the Amish never look upon someone under the ban as an enemy, but only as one who has erred. And while they are firm in their enforcement of the *Meidung*, the congregation will pray for the errant member to rectify his mistake.

Although imposition of the ban is infrequent, it is far from rare. Males are involved much more often than females, the young more frequently than the old. The *Meidung* would probably be imposed on young males more often were it not for the fact that baptism does not take place before age sixteen, and sometimes not until eighteen. Prior to this time, young males are expected to be— and often are—a little on the wild side, and allowances are made for this fact. The prebaptismal period thus serves as a kind of safety valve.

Baptism changes things, however, for this is the rite whereby the young person officially joins the church and makes the pledge of obedience. Once the pledge is made, the limits of tolerance are substantially reduced. More than one Amish youth has been subjected to the *Meidung* for behavior which, prior to his baptism, had been tolerated.

Religious groups also preserve the status quo by teaching that people should accept an imperfect society (poverty, racism, and war) because they are born sinners. In this way, religion, as Marx suggested, *is* an opiate of the masses because it convinces them to accept an unjust system rather than work to change it. The downtrodden are advised to accept their lot because they will be rewarded in the next life. Thus, they have no need to change the system from below. As Szymanski has argued:

> The doctrine of the omnipotence of God and total submission to His will pervades the general world views of religious people, and hence is sublimated as submission to political rulers and the upper class. Religion provides a consolation for the suffering of people on earth and a deflection of one's hopes into the future. Combined with its advocacy of the earthly status quo, religion thus typically serves as a powerful legitimatizing force for upper-class rule. Further, most religions, especially the religions of the working class and the poor—Baptism, Methodism, the Messianic sects, and Catholicism—in their

sermons typically condemn radical political movements and preach instead
either political abstention or submission to government authority.[8]

Sport

School and professional sports work to reinforce conforming attitudes and
behaviors in the populace in several ways.[9] First, there is the strong relationship between sport and nationalism. Success in international sports
competition tends to trigger pride among that nation's citizens. The Olympics
and other international games tend to promote an "us vs. them" feeling
among athletes, coaches, politicians, the press, and fans. It can be argued,
then, that the Olympic Games is a political contest, a symbolic world war
in which nations win or lose. Because this interpretation is commonly held,
citizens of the nations involved unite behind their flag and their athletes.[10]

The integral interrelationship of sport and nationalism is easily seen in
the blatantly militaristic pageantry that surrounds sports contests. The playing
of the national anthem, the presentation of the colors, the jet-aircraft fly-
overs, the band forming a flag or a liberty bell, are all political acts supportive
of the existing political system.

For whatever reason, sport competition and nationalism are closely intertwined. When American athletes compete against those of another country,
national unity is the result (for both sides, unless one's athletes do poorly).
Citizens take pride in their representatives' accomplishments, viewing them
as collective achievements. This identification with athletes and their cause
of winning for the nation's glory tends to unite a nation's citizens regardless
of social class, race, and regional differences. Thus, sport can be used by
political leaders whose nations have problems with divisiveness.

We have seen that sport success can unite a nation through pride. After
Brazil won the world cup in soccer (*futebol*) for the third time in succession,
one observer noted:

> The current *futebol* success has promoted a pride in being Brazilian and a
> unifying symbol without precedent. Even the lower classes of the cities,
> thanks to television, felt a sense of participation in something representing na-
> tional life. They know that Brazil is now internationally significant, not neces-
> sarily for reasons of interest to the scholar or public figure, but of importance
> to the common man. It is estimated that over 700 million soccer fans through-
> out the world watched Brazil defeat England and Italy. The Englishman in his
> pub, the French worker, the German with a Volkswagen all know that Brazil
> is not just another large "tropical country," but the homeland of the world's
> best *futebol* and a legend named Pelé.[11]

This pride in a nation's success, because it transcends the social classes,
serves as an opiate of the masses. Sanders has asserted that *futebol* in Brazil
enables the poor to forget partially the harshness of their life. It serves also
as a safety valve for releasing tensions that might otherwise be directed
toward disrupting the existing social order.[12]

The same situation appears to be true of the United States. Virtually all
homes have television sets, making it possible for almost everyone to par-

ticipate vicariously in and identify with local and national sports teams. Because of this, their minds and energies are deflected away from the hunger and misery that are disproportionately the lot of the lower classes in American society.

Sport also acts as an opiate by perpetuating the belief that persons from the lowest classes can be upwardly mobile by success in sports. Clearly this is a myth since for every major leaguer who has come up from poverty, tens of thousands have not. The point, however, is that most Americans *believe* that sport is a mobility escalator and that it is merely a reflection of the opportunity structure of the society in general. Again, poor youth who might otherwise invest their energies to changing the system, work instead on a jump shot. The potential for revolution is thus impeded by sport.

Another way that sport serves to control persons ideologically is by reinforcing American values among the participants.[13] Sport is a vehicle by which the American values of success in competition, hard work, perseverance, discipline, and order are transmitted. This is the explicit reason given for the existence of little league programs for youngsters and the tremendous emphasis on sports in American schools. While vice president, Spiro Agnew voiced the prevailing view well in a speech delivered to the Touchdown Club of Birmingham, Alabama. The following are some excerpts from that speech:

> Not the least of these values is the American competitive ethic which motivates young Americans . . . to strive toward excellence in everything they undertake. For such young Americans—whether on the athletic field, in the classroom, or on the job—the importance of our competitive ethic lies in the fact that it is only by trial of their abilities—by testing and challenging—can they discover their strengths and, yes, their weaknesses. Out of this process of self-discovery, painful though it may be at times, those young Americans who compete to excel learn to cope with whatever challenges lie ahead in life.
> And having given their best, they also emerge from the competitive test with greater ability to determine for themselves where their individual talents lie. Life is a great competition. In my judgment it will remain so despite the efforts of the social architects to make it a bland experience, controlled by their providing what they think is best for us. Success is sweet but it entails always the risk of failure. It is very, very important to learn how to lose a contest without being destroyed by the experience. For a man who has not known failure—cannot fully appreciate success. . . .
> And so, to me, that is the message of competitive sports: not simply trying to win, and to achieve, but learning how to cope with a failure—and to come back. In this regard, let me say something about my personal philosophy concerning the meaning of success and failure in sports for young Americans.
> First, I believe that sports—all sports—is one of the few bits of glue that holds society together, one of the few activities in which young people can proceed along avenues where objectives are clear and the desire to win is not only permissible but encouraged.
> Opponents of the free-enterprise system tell our young people that to try for material success and personal status is bad; that the only thing worthwhile

is to find something to wring your hands about; that the ultimate accomplishment is to make everybody feel better.

I, for one, would not want to live in a society that did not include winning in its philosophy; that would have us live our lives as identical lemmings, never trying to best anybody at anything, all headed in the same direction, departing not from the appointed route, striving not for individual excellence. In short, I would rather be a failure in a competitive society which is our inheritance than to live in a waveless sea of nonachievers.[14]

One explicit goal of sports is to build character. The assumption is that participation in sports from the Little Leagues through the Big Leagues (professional ranks) provides the athletes with those values that are American: achievement in competitive situations through hard work, materialism, progress, and respect for authority. As David Matza has put it: "The substance of athletics contains within itself—in its rules, procedures, training, and sentiments—a paradigm of adult expectations regarding youth."[15] Schools want individuals to follow rules, be disciplined, to work hard, to fit in, and sports accomplish these goals.

Not only do schools insist that athletes behave a certain way during practice and games, but they also strictly monitor the behavior of the athletes in other situations as well. The athletes must conform to the school's norms in dress, speech, demeanor, and grades if they want to continue to participate. In this way, school administrators use athletes as models of decorum. If others in the school and community admire athletes, then athletes serve to preserve the community and school norms.

The Media

The movies, television, newspapers, and magazines also serve basically to reinforce the system. There is clearly a conservative bias among the various corporations involved because their financial success depends on whether the public will buy their product and whether advertisers will use their vehicles. As Wolfe has put it:

> Because the media are part of the capitalist system, and because a change in the system would significantly alter the power of a small group of men, it is not surprising that the media engage much of their time in preserving the existing state of affairs. They do this by being conscious propagandists for the system, by reinforcing indirect consciousness manipulation, and by *not* serving as an information vehicle.[16]

That the media reinforce the values and norms of society is seen in newspaper editorials that extol certain persons and events while decrying others and in stories under the caption, "It Could Only Have Happened in America." Soap operas also accomplish this since they are stories involving moral dilemmas with virtue winning out. Television, in particular, has had a significant impact on the values of Americans. The average American child will watch 4000 hours of television before he or she enters elementary school. What are the consistent messages that television emits? One study has concluded that:

> Television influences the way children think about jobs, job values, success and social surroundings. It stresses the prestige of upper-middle-class occupations: the professions and big business. It makes essentially middle-class value judgments about jobs and success in life.[17]

In short, the media shape how we evaluate ourselves and others. Just as important, they affect directly the way viewers or readers perceive and interpret events. The media, therefore, have tremendous power to influence us to accept or question the system. Although the media do investigative reporting and occasionally question the system (for example, Watergate, the CIA scandal), the overall impact of the media is supportive of the system.

The Government

Governmental leaders devote a great deal of energy toward ideological social control. One governmental effort is to convince the public that capitalism is good and communism is bad. This is done in political speeches and books. Blatant examples were noted earlier in this chapter of how state legislatures have tried to control the ideological content (patriotism, pro-capitalism, anticommunism) in schools. Another example of ideological control is seen in government agencies such as the Defense Department and the departments of Agriculture, Commerce, and Education. Each maintains active public relations programs which spend millions of dollars to persuade the public of their views.

The public can also be manipulated by being convinced that their security is threatened by an enemy. This could be done to unify a nation troubled by internal strife. The advice Machiavelli gave his "prince" is a regrettable truth: "if the Prince is in trouble, he should promote a war." This was the advice that Secretary of State Seward gave to President Lincoln prior to the Civil War. Although expedient advice from the standpoint of preserving unity, it was, Lincoln noted, only a short-term solution. Similar efforts to unite by suggesting an external threat, although short of declaring war, have been tried by various American political leaders or candidates for office.

Perhaps the most obvious way that government officials attempt to shape public opinion is through speeches, especially on television. The President can request free prime-time television to speak to the public. These efforts are typically intended to unite the American people against an enemy (inflation, deflation, the energy crisis, communism).

Conclusion

We have described how the various agents of ideological social control operate. Perhaps the best evidence that they are successful is that few of the downtrodden in American society question the legitimacy of the political and economic system. Karl Marx theorized that the "have-nots" in a capitalist

The Politics of the "Non-Partisan" Advertising Council

The nation's second-largest advertiser is not Sears, Roebuck & Company, as the trade statistics indicate, nor is it General Foods, General Motors, or McDonald's. The number-two huckster does not peddle autos, cigarettes, washing machines, or hamburgers. Rather, it hawks ideas and causes to Americans, and it does so without ever purchasing an inch of space in newspapers or magazines or a second of broadcast time.

The Advertising Council, a New York–based nonprofit corporation, ranks second among advertisers (behind Procter & Gamble) thanks to about $650 million worth of space and time the media donate each year for its "public service" campaigns. Though the Council itself is relatively unknown, its work is ubiquitous: Smokey the Bear, Crime Dog McGruff, television spots for the Red Cross and the United Way, and the slogans "Take stock in America," "Give to the college of your choice," and "A mind is a terrible thing to waste" are some of the Council's creations.

Founded in 1942 by a group of leading advertising executives, the Council promotes voluntary, individual actions "to help solve national problems." Each year it conducts about two dozen "non-partisan public service campaigns in the interest of Americans generally," some in cooperation with government agencies, others in conjunction with private organizations. In each case, an ad agency volunteers to produce a campaign for the Council and its client; the client pays agency out-of-pocket expenses, estimated at $150,000 to $200,000. Major corporations contribute just under $1 million annually to sustain Council operations.

The Council's campaigns include pitches on behalf of the Peace Corps, the National Endowment for the Arts, the Alliance to Save Energy, and the National Alliance of Business. It promotes the prevention of child abuse, support for colleges and universities, education about high blood pressure, "equality for all," and other ways to make "our system work better."

Through its television and radio spots, billboards, subway and bus signs, and advertisements in the press, the Council dominates the public service advertising (PSA) market—and reaches millions with its diverse but remarkably consistent set of messages which, taken together, make up a distinct view of what American society is and ought to be. Without exception, Council ads and Council-based organizations convey one theme: Personal charity can untangle any mess, solve any problem; collective or governmental action is never necessary in a land of good neighbors.

"They are promoting a vision of America that is not susceptible to solutions by government, that solves its problems through volunteerism, and is very middle-class in its orientation," says Andrew Schwartzman, executive director of the Media Access Project, a public-interest law firm in Washington, D.C.

G. William Domhoff, professor of sociology and psychology at the University of California–Santa Cruz, says of the Advertising Council, "They feel that we're one big happy family, that there are no serious differences among people of different social classes. They present the image that solving every problem is a matter of good will, that no group or class has to make any particular sacrifice."

Indeed, the preeminent partisan of national consensus and diminished government, Ronald Reagan, has called the Council "indispensable." "You know," he told the organization last November, "those words, 'the Ad Council,' evoke for me the whole idea of what our American spirit and volunteerism are all about."

The American spirit—the bootstrap ideology—was more accurately described as "the myth of individual influence, the illusion of individual political competence" by the authors of a 1977 study, *Politics in Public Service*

Advertising on Television. "PSAs encourage pseudo-participation," the Duke University political scientists wrote, "by exhorting Americans to act in a limited and predetermined manner."

"We're directing our message to individual people around the country, telling what they can do," says Council spokesman Benjamin Greenberg. "It's like in commercial advertising they're telling you that you can buy aspirin to get rid of a headache."

Of course, people do not embrace a particular view of the world—or purchase aspirin—simply because a television spot urges them to do so, "but a message gets repeated over and over and it becomes part of the lexicon of images we're exposed to," notes Michael Singsen, media director of the San Francisco-based Public Media Center, which prepares PSAs for social-action organizations. "Who hasn't heard of Smokey the Bear or 'Don't be a litterbug'? It's more of an insidious nature than an overt one."

According to both Singsen and Domhoff, the Advertising Council does not induce direct changes in attitude or behavior; it simply reinforces existing conceptions of acceptable civic activity. As University of California—Berkeley sociologist Todd Gitlin puts it, the Council "contributes to the general cultural stock of symbols." But more important, all three emphasize, is the Council's role in keeping alternative—more systemic—visions from gaining access to the media.

"Simply by occupying this [PSA] space, the Council has enabled television stations to argue that they've discharged their public service responsibility," Gitlin points out.

"Because of its dominance," Singsen says, "a lot of other ideas do not get out. And because of the way they've been able to set the tone for public-service announcements, by making them noncontroversial and nonpolitical, they've been able to get a lot of stations to buy into the notion that PSAs *should* be noncontroversial and nonpolitical."

By refusing to back controversial causes,

the Council has persuaded most media enterprises that its products are safe because they are nonpartisan, nondenominational, and noncommercial—and in a literal sense that is correct. But the Council's campaigns are, in fact, intensely if subtly political, for they assert that private interests can invariably meet the demands of the public interest. The faith in charitable stop-gap measures as a substitute for structural reform sustains the status quo and the entrenched position of American business.

What's more, some of the Council's work renders direct assistance to specific segments of corporate America. For example, the familiar antipollution ads featuring an Indian shedding tears over roadside trash have been employed for more than two decades to persuade Americans that pollution is primarily a problem of careless littering. The damage done by litter is, of course, inconsequential compared to the damage done by industrial pollution, but the images and the Ad Council's slogan—"People start pollution, people can stop it"—suggest that individuals, not government or industry, are responsible for the foul condition of the environment, and are therefore personally responsible for finding a solution.

* * *

People who watch conventional television, read magazines, ride mass transit, or listen to the radio—in essence, most of us—will continue to be exposed to large doses of the Council's individualist vision of America. Indeed, according to a recent issue of the Council's *Bulletin*, the Ad Council is undertaking the largest number of new campaigns in its history.

And Smokey will still be with us, and McGruff, and all the other cute or compelling critters in the Council's stable, assuring us that all is well in America or, if it isn't, that we can fix it by sending a dollar here, ordering a pamphlet there, doing something, anything, except rocking the boat.

Source: Excerpts from Keenen Peck, "Ad Nauseam," *The Progressive* 47 (May 1983), pp. 43–47. Reprinted by permission from *The Progressive*, 409 East Main Street, Madison, Wisconsin 53703. Copyright © 1983, *The Progressive*, Inc.

society (the poor, the minority group members, the workers) would eventually feel their common oppression and unite to overthrow the owners of capital. That this has not happened in America is due, in large part, to the success of the various agents of ideological social control.[18]

AGENTS OF DIRECT SOCIAL CONTROL

Direct social control refers to attempts to punish or neutralize organizations or individuals who deviate from society's norms. The deviant targets here are essentially four: the poor, the mentally ill, criminals, and political dissidents. This section will be devoted to three agents of social control whose efforts are directed at these targets—social welfare, sciences/medicine, and the government.

Welfare

Piven and Cloward, in their classic study of public welfare, have argued that public assistance programs serve a social control function in times of mass unemployment by defusing social unrest.[19] When large numbers of people are suddenly barred from their traditional occupations, the legitimacy of the system itself may be questioned. Crime, riots, looting, and social movements bent on changing the existing social and economic arrangements become more widespread. Under this threat, relief programs are initiated or expanded by the government. Piven and Cloward show how during the Great Depression, for example, the government remained aloof from the needs of the unemployed until there was a great surge of political disorder. The function of social welfare, then, is to defuse social unrest through direct intervention of the government. Added proof for Piven and Cloward's thesis is the contraction or even abolishment of public assistance programs when political stability is restored.*

Science and Medicine

The practitioners and theoreticians in science and medicine (physicians, psychotherapists, geneticists, electrical engineers, and public health officials) have devised a number of techniques for shaping and controlling the behavior of nonconformists.

---

*The second function of welfare mentioned by Piven and Cloward is more subtle (and fits more logically as an agent of ideological social control). Even in good times some people must live on welfare (the disabled, the husbandless who must care for dependent children). By having a category of persons on welfare who live in wretched conditions and who are continuously degraded, work is legitimized. Thus, the poor on welfare serve as an object lesson—keeping even those who work for low wages relatively satisfied with their lot. As Piven and Cloward have concluded:

> In sum, market values and market incentives are weakest at the bottom of the social order. To buttress weak market controls and ensure the availability of marginal labor, an outcast class—the dependent poor—is created by the relief system. This class, whose members are of no productive use, is not treated with indifference, but with contempt. Its degradation at the hands of relief officials serves to celebrate the virtue of all work and deters actual or potential workers from seeking aid.[20]

Drugs are often used to control the behavior of deviants. Powerful drugs have revolutionized the practice of psychiatry.[21] These drugs, called neuroleptics, are used to quell the disordered thoughts of schizophrenics, shorten psychotic episodes, and control violent behavior. They do not cure the problems, however, only mask them. Moreover, critics have charged, the use of drug therapy for mental problems too often replaces talking to people and making them feel wanted.

Drugs are often used in nursing homes to control disruptive behaviors in the elderly. A 1980 study, for example, found that in 173 nursing homes in Tennessee, 43 percent of the nearly 6,000 residents received antipsychotic drugs.[22]

Drugs are prescribed by school psychologists to tranquilize hyperactive students in American schools.[23] They are also commonly used in mental hospitals and prisons to calm aggressive inmates. Rebellious prison inmates have been given such drugs as Anectine, which induces sensations of extreme terror, suffocation, and imminent death. After such an episode the individual is told to reform or face another dose of the drug. In one Iowa prison the drug Apomorphine, which causes uncontrolled vomiting, has been used on inmates who used abusive language or smoked illegally. The drug Prolixin, which produces a catatonic state, has also been used on prison inmates who are judged by their captors to need additional control.

Another social control use of drugs is through methadone maintenance.[24] In these programs heroin addicts are provided by an official agency with an addictive drug that is cheap and easy to administer—methadone. The purpose of such programs is to reduce the crime rate among heroin addicts by eliminating their dependence on that drug, the costs of which are so prohibitive that criminal activity is almost mandatory. In some of the more responsible programs addicts are eventually weaned from the methadone over a period of months. While such programs do serve this social control function, most do not attempt to treat the source of the addiction.

Psychologists and psychotherapists are clearly agents of social control. Their goal is to aid persons who, in the patient's eyes and the eyes of others, do not follow the expectations of the society. In other words, they attempt to treat persons considered "abnormal" in order to make them "normal." By focusing on the individual and his adjustment, the mental health practitioners validate, enforce, and reinforce the established ways of society. The implicit assumption is that the individual is at fault and needs to change, not that society is the root cause of mental suffering.

A special category of psychiatrists—forensic psychiatrists—are explicitly involved as agents of social control. These persons are employed as consultants by the courts to advise whether a particular defendant: (1) is competent to stand trial or not; (2) should be involuntarily committed to a mental hospital or not; and (3) can, if already confined to a mental hospital, be released. Obviously, these duties give forensic psychiatrists unusual powers. They, because of their expertise, can determine the defendant's fate. Especially powerful is their ability to even take away the defendant's right to a trial by recommending that he or she is incompetent. Studies have shown that forensic psychiatrists are quite conservative in their judgments—that is,

The Control of Illicit Sex Among the Arabs

In the kinship culture of the Arab world . . . family bonds are so strong that all members suffer "blackening of the face" after the dishonorable act of any one. However, within this general context, there is for the Arab mind a sharp distinction between those shameful events that do involve women and those that do not. In the Arab world, the greatest dishonor that can befall a man results from the sexual misconduct of his daughter or sister, or *bint 'amm* (one's father's brother's daughter). The marital infidelity of a wife, on the other hand, brings to the Arab husband only emotional effects and not dishonor.

The roots of this particular view of male honor go deep into the structure and dynamics of the Arab kin group. The ties of blood, of patrilineal descent, can never be severed, and they never weaken throughout a person's life. This means that a woman, even though she marry into a different kin group, never ceases to be a member of her own paternal family. Her paternal family, in turn, continues to be responsible for her. This has beneficial effects for the married woman, especially during that difficult period in her life which precedes the time when her sons reach maturity and become her supporters and defenders. Prior to that time, the young wife, who is considered something of an outsider by her husband's family, can always count on the aid and sympathy of her own father and brothers. The very knowledge that these men are lined up solidly behind her, and are ready, if need be, even to fight for her, puts a restraint on her husband's family in their treatment of a young daughter-in-law.

Whatever credit or discredit a woman earns reflects back on her own paternal family. This continuing responsibility comes powerfully into play if a woman becomes guilty of a sexual indiscretion, or if her behavior arouses as much as a suspicion that she may be tempted to do something forbidden by the traditional code. The most powerful deterrent devised by Arab culture against illicit sex (which means any sexual relations between a man and a woman who are not married to each other) is the equation of family honor with the sexual conduct of its daughters, single or married. If a daughter becomes guilty of the slightest sexual indiscretion (which is defined in various terms in various places), her father and brothers become dishonored also. Family honor can be restored only by punishing the guilty woman; in conservative circles, this used to mean putting her to death.

That the sexual conduct of women is an area sharply differentiated from other areas of the honor-shame syndrome is reflected in the language. While honor in its non-sexual, general connotation is termed "*sharaf*," the specific kind of honor that is connected with women and depends on their proper conduct is called " *'ird*" Sharaf is something flexible: depending on a man's behavior, way of talking and acting, his *sharaf* can be acquired, augmented, diminished, lost, regained, and so on. In contrast, *'ird* is a rigid concept: every woman has her ascribed *'ird*; she is born with it and grows up with it; she cannot augment it because it is something absolute, but it is her duty to preserve it. A sexual offense on her part, however slight, causes her *'ird* to be lost, and once lost, it cannot be regained. It is almost as if the physical attribute of virginity were transposed in the *'ird* to the emotional-conceptual level. Both virginity and *'ird* are intrinsically parts of the female person; they cannot be augmented, they can only be lost, and their loss is irreparable. The two are similar in one more respect: even if a woman is attacked and raped, she loses her *'ird* just as she loses her virginity. Where the two differ, of course, is in the circumstance that the legal, approved, and expected loss of virginity during the wedding night has no counterpart in the *'ird*: a good woman preserves it, guards it jealously until her dying day.

What is even more remarkable is that the *sharaf* of the men depends almost entirely on the *'ird* of the women of their family. True, a man can diminish or lose his *sharaf* by showing lack of bravery or courage, or by lack of hospitality and generosity. However, such occurrences are rare because the men learn in the course of their early enculturation to maintain at all cost the appearances of bravery, hospitality, and generosity. Should a man nevertheless become guilty of an open transgression of any of these, he will, of course, lose his honor, but this is not accompanied by any institutionalized and traditionally imposed physical punishment. Over crimes which are outside the focus of the code of ethics, such as killing, stealing, breaking promises, accepting bribes, and other such misdeeds, Arab opinion is divided: some say such acts would affect a man's *sharaf*, others feel they would not. But as to the results of a woman's transgression of the *'ird* there is complete and emphatic unanimity: it would destroy the *sharaf* of her menfolk. This led one student of Arab ethics to the conclusion that the core of the *sharaf* "is clearly the protection of one's female relatives' *'ird*." To which we can add that this attitude is characteristic of the Arab world as a whole, and that, moreover, a transgression of the *'ird* by a woman and by her paramour is the only crime (apart from homicide) which requires capital punishment according to the Arabic ethical code. Since any indiscretion on her part hurts her paternal family and not her husband's, it is her paternal family—her father himself, or her brothers, or her father's brother's son—who will punish her, by putting her to death, which is considered the only way of repairing the damage done to the family honor.

Source: Excerpt from *The Arab Mind* by Raphael Patai, pp. 119–122. Copyright © 1973 by Raphael Patai. Reprinted by permission of Charles Scribner's Sons.

they are prone to err in the direction of confinement rather than freedom. The reasons for this tendency are two. First, the community pressures are usually for confinement of persons thought to act abnormally. Second, there is always the fear that a person released on their recommendation might be charged later with a serious crime. If this were to happen, the credibility of the psychiatrist would be challenged and he or she probably would not be asked to consult for the court again. One observer, Henry Steadman, has summed up the role of the forensic psychiatrist this way: "Forensic psychiatry is intimately connected with the political forces of social control. Its legitimation appears to be greatly tied up in its ability to apply social control in a manner favorable to existing power structures."[25]

Psychosurgery is yet another method with important implications for social control. As with drug therapy or psychotherapy, individuals who are considered abnormal are treated to correct the problem, but this time through brain surgery.[26] With modern techniques, surgeons can operate on localized portions of the brain that govern particular behaviors (for example, sex, aggression, appetite, or fear). The technology has advanced to the point where surgeons can now implant small electrodes that not only make it possible to record the brain's electrical activity but also, by stimulating a particular area of the brain, to control the behavior of the subject.

Clearly, such a telemetric system, with its ability to monitor and control behavior by remote control, approaches the ultimate technique of social control. All deviants or potential deviants could be outfitted with the electronic device and they would remain "normal." The procedure could replace jails. Instead of jail, or as a condition of parole, individuals could be equipped with a telemetric control system. This would presumably benefit the offender because it is an alternative to jail. Society would benefit in three ways: (1) telemetry is less costly than maintaining jails; (2) the offender would continue to support his or her dependents; and (3) the offender is conditioned to nondeviant behavior, thus reducing to zero the probability of recidivism.[27]

Although some of the preceding techniques have the potential for absolute social control in a "Brave New World," another scientific endeavor, **genetic engineering,** if successfully applied, would herald its ultimate achievement. The rationale of **eugenics,** the improvement of the human race through control of hereditary factors, has operated for some time in American society. Through sterilization, categories of persons labeled defective have not been allowed to reproduce. From 1907 to 1964, for instance, over 64,000 persons in 30 states were legally sterilized for abnormalities such as drunkenness, criminality, sexual perversion, and feeblemindedness.[28] By 1971, 21 states still had laws authorizing eugenic sterilization of "mental defectives."

The sterilization of the poor is accomplished also by more subtle techniques.[29] In 1975, for example, the Department of Health, Education and Welfare proposed that the government pay 90 percent of the costs of sterilization of the poor but only 50 percent for abortions. By such a tactic, of course, HEW encourages the long-term eugenics solution of sterilization over abortions.

Experts inform us that the potential for eugenics will progress dramatically in the next few decades. **Cloning,** the creating of large numbers of genetically identical individuals (with the traits deemed desirable by society) may be possible in the future.[30] An important question, if cloning were feasible, is which human traits will be included and which ones will be excluded? Should aggression be omitted from the behavioral traits of future people? If so, passive subjects could be totally controlled without fear of revolution. The social–political–economic system, whatever its composition, would go unchallenged and society would be tranquil. The logic of genetic engineering, while positive in the sense of ridding future generations of hereditary diseases, is frightening in its basic assumption that problems arise, not from the faults of society, but from the genes of individuals in society.

Should the poor be forbidden to reproduce? They should if one accepts the argument of psychologist Richard Herrnstein that the poor are poor (see Chapter 10) for genetic reasons.[31] Or should those males with an extra Y chromosome be sterilized since some research findings have noted that these persons tend to have a greater probability than those with a normal XY arrangement to be criminals or mentally ill? Or should blacks be sterilized because they score noticeably lower than whites on IQ tests and they are more likely to be adjudicated as criminals?

Similar questions can be raised about the other techniques in this section. The creativity of the scientific community has presented the powerful in society with unusually effective means to enforce conformity. The aggressive

The Sterilization Solution

Throughout recent American history various public officials have supported the involuntary sterilization of persons considered undesirable. Four examples make this point.

In 1924 Virginia passed a law permitting the involuntary sterilization of mental patients, the mentally retarded, habitual criminals, and others considered misfits by society. Three years later the U.S. Supreme Court upheld this law by a vote of 8 to 1. Justice Oliver Wendell Holmes declared in the majority opinion:

> In order to protect us from being swamped by incompetents it is better for all the world instead of waiting to execute degenerate offspring for crimes or let them starve for their imbecility, if society can prevent those who are manifestly unfit from continuing their kind. . . . The principle that sustains compulsory vaccination is broad enough to cover cutting Fallopian tubes. . . .

A representative in the Oklahoma House sponsored a bill in 1979 that would provide for the castration of rapists whose victims were under the age of 18, whose crime was especially cruel, or who seem to demonstrate a high probability of recidivism. Requiring 51 votes for passage, the bill received 49 votes for and 47 against.

In 1980 the chairperson of the Texas Welfare Board and mayor of Richmond, Texas for thirty-two years said that he supported sterilization of welfare recipients. "I've always felt that when you cannot support yourself or your family, you give up certain rights. One of these is bringing in more children, and if you don't want to give them up, then get a job and get off welfare."

In 1983 a Bexar County (Texas) jury agreed to give probation to a convicted rapist provided he undergo 10 years of treatment with the drug Depo-Provera, a medication that would have the effect of chemical castration.

in schools, prisons, mental hospitals, and in society can be anesthetized. But what is aggressive behavior? What is violence? In 1973, for example, the then-Governor of California, Ronald Reagan, endorsed a proposal, which came from his Director of Corrections, that would allow psychosurgery as a "cure" for violence. But who is violent? Should psychosurgery have been used on the protestors in the political demonstrations of the late 1960s? Was Martin Luther King, Jr., violent? Although he advocated nonviolent techniques, his goal was to change a system oppressive to blacks and this brought violence in its wake. Society would have been much more tranquil without a Martin Luther King, Jr., aggressively seeking changes the majority did not want. Thus, it could be argued, he would have been a likely candidate for psychosurgery to cure him of his "violent" inclinations.

The Justice Department has proposed a test of 2,000 boys ages 9 to 12 who have already had their first contact with the police. The goal of this test is to identify the chronic offender. Proponents of the proposal argue that chronic offenders have certain characteristics that the tests could identify—for example, left handedness, dry or sweaty palms, below normal reactions to noise and shocks, high levels of the male hormone testosterone, abnormalities in alpha waves emitted by their brains, and physical anomalies such as malformed ears, high steeped palate, furrowed tongue, curved fingers, and a wide gap between first and second toes.[32] Such a plan, if implemented, has frightening implications. Will these tests actually separate chronic offenders from one-time offenders? Is criminal behavior actually related to the formation of one's tongue, ears, and toes? And, if the tests do identify potential problem people accurately, should such persons be punished for their potential behaviors rather than their actual behaviors? Most significant, what are the negative effects of being labeled a chronic offender? Such a label would doubtless have a self-fulfilling prophecy effect as those who interact with labeled persons do so on the basis of that label.

The Government

The government, as the legitimate holder of power in society, is directly involved in the control of its citizens. A primary objective of the government is to provide for the welfare of its citizens. This includes protection of their lives and property. It requires, further, that order be maintained within the society. There is a clear mandate, then, for the government to apprehend and punish criminals. Not so clear, however, is the legitimacy of a government in a democracy to stifle dissent, which is done in the interests of preserving order. The American heritage, best summed up in the Declaration of Independence, provides a clear rationale for dissent:

> Governments are instituted among men, deriving their just powers from the consent of the governed. That whenever any form of government becomes destructive of these ends [the rights of life, liberty, and the pursuit of happiness], it is the right of the people to alter or to abolish it, and to institute a new government, laying its foundation on such principals and organizing its powers in such form as to them shall seem most likely to effect their safety and happiness.

The American government, then, is faced with a dilemma. American tradition and values affirm that dissent is appropriate. Two facts of political life work against this principle, however. First, for social order to prevail, a society needs to ensure that existing power relationships are maintained over time (otherwise anarchy will result). Second, the well-off in society benefit from the existing power arrangements so they use their influence (which is considerable, as noted in the previous chapter) to encourage the repression of challenges to the government. The evidence is strong that the American government has opted for repression of dissent. Let us examine this evidence.

To begin with, we must peruse the processes of law enactment and law enforcement. These two processes are both directly related to political authority. Some level of government determines what the law will be (that is, which behaviors are to be allowed and which ones are to be forbidden) and the agents of political authorities then apprehend and punish violators. Clearly, the law is employed to control behaviors that might otherwise endanger the general welfare (for example, the crimes of murder, rape, and theft). But laws also promote certain points of view at the expense of others (for example, the majority instead of the minority, or the status quo rather than change). With this in mind, let us turn to the two schools of thought on the function of the law—the prevailing liberal view and the Marxist interpretation.[33]

The dominant view in American society is based on liberal democratic theory and is congruent with the order model. The state exists to maintain order and stability. Law is a body of rules enacted by representatives of the people in the interests of the people. The state and law, therefore, are essentially neutral, dispensing rewards and punishments without bias. A basic assumption of this view is that the political system is pluralistic— that is, the existence of a number of interest groups of more-or-less equal power. The laws, then, reflect compromise and consensus among these various interest groups. In this way the interests of all are protected.

Contrary to the prevailing view of law based on consensus for the common good is the view of the radical criminologists, which is based on conflict theory. The assumptions of this model are: (1) the state exists to serve the ruling class (the owners of large corporations and financial institutions); (2) the law and the legal system reflect and serve the needs of the ruling class; and (3) the interests of the ruling class are served by the law when domestic order prevails and challenges to changing the economic and political system are successfully thwarted. In other words, the law does not serve society as a whole, but the interests of the ruling class prevail.

Closely related to the Marxian view of the role of law in capitalist societies is the interest-group theory of Richard Quinney.[34] The essence of this theory is that a crime is behavior that conflicts with the interests of those segments of society that have the power to shape criminal policy.

> Law is made by men, representing special interests, who have the power to translate their interests into public policy. Unlike the pluralist conception of politics, law does not represent a compromise of the diverse interests of society, but supports some interests at the expense of others.[35]

Quinney's view is in the conflict model tradition. Society is held together by some segments coercing other segments. Interest groups are unequal in power. The conflict among interest groups results in the powerful getting their way in determining public policy. Evidence for this position is seen in the successful efforts of certain interest groups to get favorable laws: the segregation laws imposed by whites on blacks, the repression of political dissidents whose goal is to transform society, and the passage of income tax laws that benefit the rich at the expense of wage earners.

Quinney's model makes a good deal of sense. The model is not universally applicable, however, because certain crimes—burglary, murder, and rape— would be regarded as crimes no matter which interest group was in power.[36] A very important part of his theory that does fit almost universally is his proposition that: "*The probability that criminal definitions will be applied varies according to the extent to which the behaviors of the powerless conflict with the interests of the power segments .*"[37]

I CAN'T TAKE IT ANYMORE... THE BURGLARIES.. THE BREAK-INS..
RUNNING FROM THE COPS... HIDING OUT IN FLEA-RIDDEN
MOTELS... CHARLIE, YOU'VE GOT TO QUIT THE FBI.

Reprinted by permission of United Feature Syndicate.

The law, of course, provides the basis for establishing what is criminal behavior. Enforcement of the law is accomplished by the police and the courts. The evidence is overwhelming that the law is unequally enforced in American society. Let us direct our attention here, rather, to the efforts of other agencies in the political system to control deviance, especially political deviance.[38]

Government agencies have a long history of surveillance of citizens.[39] The pace quickened in the 1930s and increased further with the Communist threat in the 1950s. Surveillance reached its peak during the height of antiwar and civil rights protests of the late 1960s and early 1970s. The FBI's concern with internal security, for example, dates back to 1936 when President Roosevelt directed J. Edgar Hoover to investigate domestic Communist and Fascist organizations in the United States.[40] In 1939, as World War II began in Europe, President Roosevelt issued a proclamation that the FBI would be in charge of investigating subversive activities, espionage, and sabotage, and directed that all law enforcement offices should give the FBI any relevant information on suspected activities. These directives began a pattern followed by the FBI under the administrations of Presidents Truman, Eisenhower, Kennedy, Johnson, Nixon, Ford, Carter, and Reagan.

The scope of these abuses by the FBI and other government agencies such as the CIA, the National Security Agency, and the Internal Revenue Service, is incredible. In the name of "national security" the following actions have been taken against American citizens:

- □ *Item:* The Internal Revenue Service monitored the activities of 99 political organizations and 11,359 individuals during the period of 1969 to 1973. During and since that period the IRS has used a variety of methods to invade the private lives of individuals, including the use of seizure-liens, assessments, penalties, wiretaps, and even hiring prostitutes to occupy suspects while agents photocopied the contents of briefcases.[41]
- □ *Item:* From 1967 to 1973 the NSA (National Security Agency) monitored the overseas telephone calls and cables of approximately 1,650 Americans and U.S. organizations, as well as almost 6,000 foreign nationals and groups.[42]
- □ *Item:* The CIA opened and photographed nearly 250,000 first class letters in the United States between 1953 and 1973.[43]
- □ *Item:* As Director of the CIA, William Colby acknowledged to Congress that his organization had opened the mail of private citizens and accumulated secret files on more than 10,000 Americans.[44]
- □ *Item:* The FBI over the years conducted about 1,500 break-ins of foreign embassies and missions, mob hangouts, and the headquarters of such organizations as the Ku Klux Klan and the American Communist Party.[45]
- □ *Item:* The FBI confessed to the Senate Intelligence Committee that it had committed 238 burglaries against 14 domestic organizations during a 26-year period ending in 1968.[46]
- □ *Item:* The FBI collected over 500,000 dossiers between 1959 and 1971 on Communists, black leaders, student radicals, and feminists.[47]
- □ *Item:* The husband of an officer in ACTION, a St. Louis civil rights organization, received a handwritten note that said: "Look man, I guess your old lady doesn't get enough at home or she wouldn't be shucking and jiving with our black men in ACTION, you dig? Like, all she wants to integrate is the bedroom and we black sisters ain't gonna take no second best from our men. So lay it on her man or get her the hell off Newstead (Street)." The couple soon separated and the local FBI officer wrote to headquarters: "This matrimonial stress and strain should cause her to function much less effectively in ACTION."[48]
- □ *Item:* In 1972 the FBI paid 7,402 "ghetto informants" to provide information about racial extremists.[49]
- □ *Item:* In 1970 actress Jean Seberg helped raise money for a militant organization, the Black Panthers. According to documents released by the FBI after the suicide of Ms. Seberg in 1979, the FBI tried to discredit the actress by planting the rumor that the father of her baby was a prominent Black Panther leader. This false story led to a miscarriage and psychotic behavior, and possibly to her suicide.[50]
- □ *Item:* In its annual report for 1982 on electronic surveillance by Federal and state officials, the Office of the U.S. Courts stated that the FBI and

the Drug Enforcement Administration installed 129 taps and bugs (up from 106 in 1981 but still below the all-time high of 281 in 1971 under President Nixon).[51]

These are but a few examples of government abuses against its citizens. To make the point clearer, we will describe in greater detail two nefarious (but representative) campaigns of the government: (1) the FBI's vendetta against Martin Luther King, Jr.; and (2) the FBI's campaign to nullify the effectiveness of the Socialist Workers party.

The FBI had a campaign to destroy civil rights groups. The most infamous of these was the attempt to negate the power of Martin Luther King, Jr. King had been openly critical of the Bureau's ineffectual enforcement of civil rights laws, which apparently led the Director, J. Edgar Hoover, to label King "the most notorious liar in the U.S." and to launch a vendetta against him.[52] From 1957, when King became prominent in the Montgomery Bus Boycott, the FBI monitored King's activities under its vague authority to investigate "subversives." The more powerful King became the greater the FBI's surveillance of him. King was indexed in the files as a Communist and someone to be imprisoned in the event of a "national emergency." This charge against King was based on the allegation that two of his associates in the Southern Christian Leadership Conference were Communists.

Because Hoover had convinced the Attorney General, Robert Kennedy, of the possible link between King and the Communists, Kennedy authorized wiretaps of King's phones, which continued for the next two years. Unknown to Kennedy was that the FBI planned to use the wiretaps to discredit King.

The FBI's efforts to neutralize or even destroy King were intensified with King's increasing popularity as exemplified by his *I had a Dream* speech before 250,000 in Washington, D.C. in August of 1963. King was thus characterized in an FBI memo:

> He stands head and shoulders over all other Negro leaders put together when it comes to influencing great masses of Negroes. *We must mark him now . . . as the most* dangerous Negro of the future of this Nation from the standpoint of Communism, the Negro and national security.[53]

The efforts now escalated to include physical and photographic surveillance and the placement of illegal bugs in his living quarters. The tapes of conversations in a Washington hotel were used by the FBI to imply that King engaged in extramarital sexual activities. They used these tapes, which may or may not have been altered, to dishonor King. At the very time King was receiving great honors such as the Nobel Peace Prize, *Time* magazines's "Man of the Year" award, and numerous honorary degrees, the FBI countered with briefings, distribution of the "tapes" to newspeople and columnists, and congressional testimony about King's "Communist" activities and "private" behavior. The FBI even briefed officials of the National Council of Churches and other church bodies about King's alleged deviance.

The smear campaign against King reached its zenith when the FBI mailed the "tapes" to the Southern Christian Leadership Conference offices in

Atlanta with a covering letter suggesting that he commit suicide or face humiliation when the tapes were made public on the eve of the Nobel award ceremonies in Sweden.

Summing up the sordid affair, Halperin and his associates have editorialized:

> The FBI had turned its arsenal of surveillance and disruption techniques on Martin Luther King and the civil rights movement. It was concerned not with Soviet agents nor with criminal activity, but with the political and personal activities of a man and a movement committed to nonviolence and democracy. King was not the first such target, not the last. In the end we are all victims, as our political life is distorted and constricted by the FBI, a law enforcement agency now policing politics.[54]

This comment is justifiably critical of the FBI. I believe that the FBI's tactics were illegal whether King was a communist or not. But that is a moot point because King was not a communist. In testimony before a Senate committee, the FBI's assistant deputy director James Adams was asked by Senator Frank Church if the FBI ever found that King was a communist. Replied Adams, "No, we did not."[55]

Another example of an FBI vendetta against a non-existent threat involved the Socialist Workers Party, a small, peaceful, and legal political party.[56] This party became the target of FBI abuses because it supported such causes as Castro's Cuba and worked for racial integration in the South. For these transgressions, the FBI kept the SWP under surveillance for 34 years. FBI documents have revealed that in one 6½-year period in the early 1960s the agency burglarized the offices of the party in 94 raids, often with the complicity of the New York City police department. Over this period FBI agents photographed 8,700 pages of party files and compiled dossiers totaling 8 million pages.

The FBI tried to destroy the party by sending anonymous letters to members' employers, working to keep the party's candidates off the ballot, and by otherwise sabotaging political campaigns. They also used informants to collect information about the political views of the organization.*

Several points need to be made about these FBI activities. Obviously, these were a thorough waste of time and money. As one observer put it: "If they had devoted tens of thousands of man-hours to pursuing true criminals—say, those involved in organized crime—they might have served the public interest as they were meant to."[57] Most important, the FBI's tactics were not only illegal but they were directed at an organization that was working legally *within* the system.

> Just as the FBI's illegal assumption of the authority to investigate subversive activities led to illegal methods, the failure of those methods to produce evidence that could be used to take legal action against radical and liberal political movements led to further lawlessness: active efforts to destroy them. In

---

*The SWP has sued the FBI (and won) for its violations of the SWP's civil rights.

Genetic Control of Future Generations

A long-time dream of science, genetic engineering, is at hand. Scientists have been able to combine segments of the DNA from the bacterium known as *Escherichia coli* (*E. coli*) with the DNA of plants, animals, and other bacteria. The *E. coli* combined with a DNA molecule from another source can reproduce billions of exact duplicates of the hybrid in a single day. This technology for genetic manipulation will eventually be applied to higher organisms, and this has fantastic potential for good and ill. Positively, it may lead to a cure for cancer, eliminate hereditary diseases, and create plants that take their nitrogen from the air rather than fertilizers. There are great dangers, however, many that are unforeseeable, such as new diseases for which humans have no immunity, or the creation of new human forms.

Despite these dangers, varied experimentation with genetic manipulation will continue on a number of fronts. In the near future, we will very likely be able to test unborn fetuses and abort them if they possess undesirable traits (mongoloidism and other genetic defects, which can be detected now, but also "aggressive" fetuses). Cloning (the genetic recreation of an individual from a single cell) has been accomplished in a submammalian species and soon may be possible for humans. Eventually, too, we may be able to "order" a child with just the right characteristics (sex, height, hair color, disposition, mental ability).

These possibilities lead to the question: will this genetic technology lead to a higher level of evolution, or will it threaten humankind with a new source of bondage? Other ethical and political questions we must answer are: Who has the power over the unborn fetus? Should society remove certain undesirable genetic traits from the population (hemophilia, Tay-Sachs disease, cystic fibrosis, diabetes, sickle cell anemia) by insisting on a prenatal test and automatic abortion if the tests determine that the fetus has the undesirable trait? Or should eugenics be voluntary, even if this runs the risk of the undesirable traits being passed on to unborn generations that might have been saved this grief?

What kind of political/social interference would you agree to or vote for? What kind of restraints would you advocate to limit government power in this area? Would you advocate any restraints to limit the power of individuals over their offspring? The answers to these questions have important implications for individuals and society. For example, if you favor governmental intervention to control physical defects, there is the important question of limits. How can you be sure the government will promote the genes you favor? Most important, a totalitarian political regime could use genetic manipulation as the ultimate means of social control, ensuring that all offspring will be docile, compliant, and willing workers—shades of Orwell's *1984*.

October, 1961, for example, the FBI put into operation its "S.W.P. Disruption Program." The grounds for this program, as a confidential Bureau memorandum described them, were that the Socialist Workers Party had been "openly espousing its line on a local and national basis through running candidates for public office. . . ." The memorandum is astonishingly revealing about the political sophistication of the FBI. If these Socialists were openly espousing their line by running candidates for public office, including the Presidency, these activities obviously weren't illegal. And if their support for the civil-rights movement was subversive, then so was that of many millions of Americans.[58]

One should remember that the government *must* exert some control over its citizens. There must be a minimum of control if the fabric of society is to remain intact. But in exerting control, there are serious problems that came to the forefront during the Nixon years. First, there is the problem of the violation of individual rights as guaranteed in the Constitution. Under what conditions can these be violated by the government—if ever? A closely related problem can be framed in the form of a question: Who monitors the monitors? The problem inherent in this question is not only the tactics of the monitors but also the criteria used to assess who should be controlled or who should not.

A most serious charge is that the government squelches protest, which Thomas Jefferson said is the hallmark of a democracy. The implication is that the government is beyond questioning—the dissidents are the problem. But as Donner has put it:

> To equate dissent with subversion, as intelligence officials do (the FBI, CIA, IRS, Justice Department, and the Department of Defense), is to deny that the demand for change is based on real social, economic, or political conditions.[59]

SUMMARY

In 1949 George Orwell wrote a novel about life as he envisioned it to be in 1984. The essence of his prediction was that every word, every thought, and every facial expression of citizens would be monitored by government using sophisticated electronic devices. The computer age has fulfilled in part Orwell's prophecy. The federal government has an average of 18 computer files on each American; each state has an average of 15 files per person, and local governments average 6 files. In the private sector (e.g., credit, insurance, banks, employers) we have another 40 files. The average citizen's name emerges in computers 35 times a day and gets passed between computers 5 times a day.[60] Not only is such computer knowledge an invasion of one's privacy, but it provides the government with the technology to monitor closely the activities of those who threaten it. And, as we have seen in this chapter, the government is strongly inclined to do so. But the political dissident is not the only person whose freedoms are being threatened. As Howard Zinn has put it:

> Our actual freedom is determined . . . by the power the policeman has over us on the street, or that of the local judge behind him; by the authority of our employers; by the power of teachers, principals, university presidents, and boards of trustees if we are students; by parents if we are children; by children if we are old; by the welfare bureaucracy if we are poor; by prison guards if we are in jail; by landlords if we are tenants; by the medical profession or hospital administration if we are physically or mentally ill.[61]

The technology for "1984" exists in drugs, psychosurgery, and telemetry. Currently, various arms of the government have used some of these techniques in their battle to fight crime, recidivism, political dissidence, and other forms of nonconformity. But at what point does the government go too far in its control of nonconformity? The critical question, as stated earlier, is who monitors the monitors? One can easily envision a future when the government, faced with anarchy or political revolution, might justify ultimate control of its citizens—in the name of national security. If this were to take place, then obviously, the freedoms rooted in 200 years of history will have been washed away.

The future may resemble Orwell's vision, however, not because of a tyrannical government, but rather because it is in the interests of society that people be controlled. The time may come when people, because human survival depends on it, will not have the freedom to have as many children as they want or the freedom to squander energy on eight-cylinder cars or air-conditioned homes, or to own a gun. B. F. Skinner, the famous behavioral psychologist, has argued that we must give up our outmoded notions of freedom and dignity and build a society in which the behavior of people will be controlled for their own good—for the sake of their survival, happiness, and satisfaction.[62] In other words, if not enough people exercise self-control, the government, for the common good, may be forced to impose controls from the outside. And with the technology available to the government, absolute control is a real threat.

CHAPTER REVIEW

1. All societies have mechanisms to ensure conformity—mechanisms of social control.

2. The socialization process through which the demands of the group become internalized is a fundamental mechanism of social control. This process is never complete, however, otherwise we would be robots.

3. Ideological social control is the attempt to manipulate the consciousness of citizens so they accept the status quo and ruling ideology.

4. The agents of ideological social control are the family, education, religion, sport, and the media.

5. Direct social control refers to attempts to punish or neutralize organi-

zations or individuals who deviate from society's norms, especially the poor, the mentally ill, criminals, and political dissidents.

6. According to Piven and Cloward, public assistance programs serve a direct social control function in times of mass unemployment by defusing social unrest.

7. Science and medicine provide the techniques for shaping and controlling the behavior of nonconformists. Drugs, psychosurgery, and genetic engineering are three such techniques.

8. The government is directly involved in the control of its citizens. It apprehends and punishes criminals. It is also involved in the suppression of dissent, which, while important for preserving order, runs

counter to the American democratic heritage. Order theorists argue that the state
exists to maintain order. The state and
the law in this view are neutral, dispensing rewards and punishments without

bias. Conflict theorists, however, believe
that the state and the law exist to serve
the ruling class. Squelching political dissent, therefore, benefits the powerful.

FOR FURTHER STUDY

Ideological Social Control

Martin Carnoy, *Education as Cultural Imperialism* (New York: Longman, 1974).

Jules Henry, *Culture Against Man* (New York:
Random House (Vintage Books), 1963).

Donald B. Kraybill, *Our Star-Spangled Faith*
(Scottsdale, Pa.: Herald Press, 1976).

Elliot S. Valenstein (ed.), *The Psychosurgery
Debate: Scientific, Legal, and Ethical Perspectives* (San Francisco: W. H. Freeman,
1980).

Alan Wolfe, *The Seamy Side of Democracy:
Repression in America*, 2nd ed. (New York:
Longman, 1978).

Direct Social Control

Philip Agee, *Inside the Company: CIA Diary*
(New York: Bantam, 1975).

Michael Dorman, *Witch Hunt: The Underside
of American Democracy* (New York: Dell,
1976).

Jack D. Douglas and John M. Johnson (eds.),
Official Deviance: Readings in Malfeasance,

Misfeasance, and Other Forms of Corruption
(Philadelphia: J. B. Lippincott, 1977).

Vance Packard, *The People Shapers* (Boston:
Little, Brown, 1977).

Frances Fox Piven and Richard A. Cloward,
*Regulating the Poor: The Functions of Public
Welfare* (New York: Random House, 1971).

Richard Quinney, *Critique of Legal Order: Crime
Control in Capitalist Society* (Boston: Little,
Brown, 1973).

David R. Simon and D. Stanley Eitzen, *Elite
Deviance* (Boston: Allyn and Bacon, 1982).

B. F. Skinner, *Beyond Freedom and Dignity* (New
York: Alfred A. Knopf, 1972).

Thomas Szasz, *The Manufacture of Madness*
(New York: Harper & Row, 1970).

Roy Wilkins and Ramsey Clark, in *Search and
Destroy: A Report of the Commission of In-
quiry into the Chicago Police Raid on the
Black Panther Headquarters* (New York:
Harper & Row, 1973).

David Wise, *The American Police State: The
Government against the People* (New York:
Random House, 1976).

NOTES AND REFERENCES

1. This distinction and much of the material
that follows is taken from Alan Wolfe, *The
Seamy Side of Democracy: Repression in
America* (New York: David McKay, 1973).

2. Richard Stivers, "Introduction to the Social
and Cultural Control of Deviant Behavior,"
in *The Collective Definition of Violence*, F.
James Davis and Richard Stivers, (eds.) (New
York: Free Press, 1975), p. 372.

3. There are a number of sources that document

the differences in mode of socialization by
social class. Especially important is the article
that summarizes twenty-five years of studies
of parent-child relationships by Urie Bronfenbrenner, "Socialization and Social Class
though Time and Space," in *Readings in
Social Psychology*, E. E. Maccoby, T. M.
Newcomb, and E. L. Hartley, (eds.) (New
York: Holt, Rinehart and Winston, 1958),
pp. 400–425. See also Melvin L. Kohn, "So-

cial Class and Parental Values," *American Journal of Sociology* 64 (January, 1959), pp. 337–351.

4. See Francis FitzGerald, *America Revised: History Schoolbooks in the Twentieth Century* (Boston: Atlantic-Little, Brown, 1979).

5. James J. Kilpatrick, "Education, Not Indoctrination," *Washington Star* (Jan. 20, 1974).

6. Quoted in Wolfe, *The Seamy Side of Democracy*, p. 162.

7. Sarah J. McCarthy, "Why Johnny Can't Disobey," *The Humanist* (September/October 1979), p. 34.

8. Albert Szymanski, *The Capitalist State and the Politics of Class* (Cambridge, Mass.: Winthrop, 1978), p. 253.

9. Most of the material in this section is taken from D. Stanley Eitzen and George H. Sage, *The Sociology of American Sport*, 2nd ed. (Dubuque, Iowa: Wm. C. Brown, 1982), Chap. 7.

10. See Donald W. Ball, "Olympic Games Competition: Structural Correlation of National Success," *International Journal of Comparative Sociology* 13 (September/December, 1972), pp. 186–199; and Phillip Goodhart and Christopher Chataway, *War without Weapons* (London: W. H. Allen, 1968).

11. Thomas G. Sanders, "The Social Functions of Futebol," *American Universities Field Staff Reports*, East Coast South America Series 14 (July, 1970), p. 7.

12. Sanders, "The Social Functions," pp. 8–9. See also Janet Lever, "Soccer: Opium of the Brazilian People," *Trans-action* 7 (December, 1969), pp. 36–43.

13. See Eitzen and Sage, *The Sociology of American Sport*, Chap. 4; and Harry Edwards, *Sociology of Sport* (Homewood, Ill.: Dorsey Press, 1973), Chap. 5.

14. Excerpts from the press release of the address by the Vice President of the United States, Spiro Agnew, Birmingham, Alabama (January 18, 1972), pp. 5–6. For a critique of the Agnew position see Nicholas von Hoffman, "The Sport of Politicians," *The Washington Post* (January 24, 1972), p. B1.

15. David Matza, "Position and Behavior Patterns of Youth," *Handbook of Modern Sociology*, Robert E. L. Faris, (ed.) (Chicago: Rand McNally, 1964), p. 207.

16. Wolfe, *The Seamy Side of Democracy*, p. 145.

17. Hilde Himmelweit, A. N. Oppenheim, and Pamela Vance, *Television and the Child* (London: Oxford University Press, 1958).

18. Michael Parenti, *Power and the Powerless* (New York: St. Martin's Press, 1978).

19. The following section is taken from Frances Fox Piven and Richard A. Cloward, *Regulating the Poor: The Functions of Public Welfare* (New York: Random House, 1971).

20. Frances Fox Piven and Richard A. Cloward, "The Relief of Welfare," *Trans-action* 8 (May, 1971), p. 52.

21. See "Drugs and Psychiatry: A New Era," *Newsweek* (November 12, 1979), pp. 98–104.

22. Cited in Dava Sobel, "Psychiatric Drugs Widely Misused, Critics Charge," *The New York Times* (June 3, 1980), pp. C1–C2.

23. Charles Witter, "Drugging and Schooling," *Trans-action* 8 (July/August, 1971), pp. 31–34. See also "About Drugs for 'Unruly' Schoolchildren," *U.S. News & World Report* (April 5, 1976).

24. Florence Heyman, "Methadone Maintenance as Law and Order," *Society* 9 (June, 1972), pp. 15–25.

25. Henry J. Steadman, "The Psychiatrist as a Conservative Agent of Social Control," *Social Problems* 20 (Fall, 1972), p. 270.

26. For an elaboration on the psychosurgery debate, see Elliot S. Valenstein (ed.), *The Psychosurgery Debate: Scientific, Legal, and Ethical Perspectives* (San Francisco: W. H. Freeman, 1980); Lani Silver, et. al., "Surgery to the Rescue," *The Progressive* (December, 1977), p. 23; and Vernon H. Mark, "A Psychosurgeon's Case for Psychosurgery," *Psychology Today* 8 (July, 1974), pp. 28–33, 84–86.

27. Barton L. Ingraham and Gerald W. Smith, "The Use of Electronics in the Observation and Control of Human Behavior and Its Possible Use in Rehabilitation and Parole," *Issues in Criminology* 7 (Fall, 1972), pp. 35–53.

28. Associated Press release (March 23, 1980).

29. See Sheila M. Rothman, "Sterilizing the Poor," *Society* 14 (January/February 1977), pp. 36–40.

30. See Martin Ebon, *The Cloning of Man: A Brave New Hope—or Horror?* (New York: New American Library, 1978).

31. Richard Herrnstein, "I.Q." *The Atlantic* 228 (September, 1971), pp. 43–64.

32. Reported in Jack Anderson, "Plans to Test Adolescents Smack of 1984," *Rocky Mountain News* (October 13, 1983), p. 106.

33. The following is taken from Richard Quinney, *Criminal Justice in America: A Critical Understanding* (Boston: Little, Brown, 1974), pp. 18–25. See also Richard Quinney, *Critique of Legal Order: Crime Control in Capitalist Society* (Boston: Little, Brown, 1973).

34. Richard Quinney, *The Social Reality of Crime* (Boston: Little, Brown, 1970), especially pp. 29–42.

35. Quinney, *The Social Reality of Crime*, p. 35.

36. Marshall B. Clinard, *Sociology of Deviant Behavior*, 4th ed. (New York: Holt, Rinehart and Winston, 1974), p. 258.

37. Quinney, *The Social Reality of Crime*, p. 18.

38. Of special importance to this section is Frank Donner's "The Theory and Practice of American Political Intelligence," *The New York Review of Books* 16 (April 22, 1971), pp. 27–39; and David Wise, *The American Police State: The Government against the People* (New York: Random House, 1976).

39. The remainder of this chapter is taken from David R. Simon and D. Stanley Eitzen, *Elite Deviance* (Boston: Allyn and Bacon, 1982), Chapter 7. For a history of the government's monitoring of its citizens, see Alan Wolfe, "Political Repression and the Liberal Democratic State," *Monthly Review* 23 (December, 1971), pp. 18–38; Donald B. Davis, "Internal Security in Historical Perspective: From the Revolution to World War II," *Surveillance and Espionage in a Free Society*, Richard H. Blum, ed. (New York: Praeger, 1972), pp. 3–19; "It's Official, Government Snooping Has Been Going On for 50 Years," *U.S. News & World Report* (May 24, 1976), p. 65; and Select Committee to Study Governmental Operations with Respect to Intelligence Activities, U.S. Senate, *Intelligence Activities and the Rights of Americans: Book II*, Report 94–755 (April 26, 1976), pp. 1–

20, found in *Corporate and Governmental Deviance*, M. David Ermann and Richard J. Lundman, eds. (New York: Oxford University Press, 1978), pp. 151–173.

40. This brief history of the FBI is taken from Richard Harris, "Crime in the FBI," *The New Yorker* (August 8, 1977), pp. 30–42.

41. See Blake Fleetwood, "The Tax Police: Trampling Citizens' Rights," *Saturday Review* (May, 1980), pp. 33–36.

42. "Project Minaret," *Newsweek* (November 10, 1975), pp. 31–32.

43. U.S. Senate, *Intelligence Activities*, in Ermann and Lundman, p. 156. See also, "Who's Chipping Away at Your Privacy," *U.S. News & World Report* (March 31, 1975), p. 18.

44. Ibid.

45. "The FBI's 'Black-Bag Boys,' " *Newsweek* (July 28, 1975), pp. 18, 21.

46. Associated Press release (March 29, 1979).

47. United Press International release (November 19, 1975).

48. "Tales of the FBI," *Newsweek* (December 1, 1975), p. 36.

49. "Curbing the Spooks," *The Progressive* 42 (November, 1978), pp. 10–11.

50. "The FBI vs. Jean Seberg," *Time* (September 24, 1979), p. 25.

51. Cited in Herman Schwartz, "Reagan's Bullish on Bugging," *The Nation* (June 4, 1983), p. 697.

52. The following account is taken from several sources: Morton H. Halperin, et al., *The Lawless State: The Crimes of the U.S. Intelligence Agencies* (New York: Penguin, 1976), pp. 61–89; "The Truth about Hoover," *Time* (December 22, 1975), pp. 14–21; "Tales of the FBI," and "The Crusade to Topple King," *Time* (December 1, 1975), pp. 11–12.

53. Final Report of the Select Committee to Study Governmental Relations with Respect to Intelligence Activities, U.S. Senate, *Supplementary Detailed Staff Reports on Intelligence Activities and the Rights of Americans: Book III*, "Dr. Martin Luther King, Jr., Case Study" (Washington, D.C.: U.S. Government Printing Office, 1976), pp. 107–198, cited in Halperin, et al., *The Lawless State*, p. 78.

54. Halperin, et al., *The Lawless State*, p. 89.

55. Quoted in "The Crusade to Topple King," p. 11.

56. The evidence presented on the FBI's campaign against the SWP is taken from Harris, "Crime in the FBI," Associated Press release (March 29, 1976); and "Monitoring Repression," *The Progressive* 41 (January, 1977), p. 7.

57. Harris, "Crime in the FBI," p. 40.

58. Ibid.

59. Donner, "The Theory and Practice of American Political Intelligence," p. 35.

60. John Hillkirk, "Computer Age Brings New Fears," *USA Today* (October 4, 1983), pp. B1–2; see also, *U.S. News & World Report* (July 12, 1982), p. 35.

61. Quoted in Tom Wicker, "The Long Arm of the Military," *The New York Times* (December 31, 1973).

62. B. F. Skinner, *Beyond Freedom and Dignity* (New York: Alfred A. Knopf, 1972).

8

Deviance

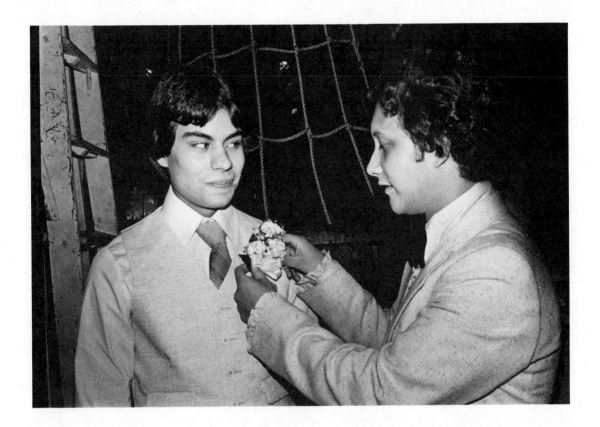

Who are the deviants in American society? There is considerable evidence that most of us at one time or another break the laws. For example:

□ In 1980 it was estimated that about 80 million Americans shoplifted about $8 billion worth of goods (more than the combined 1979 net incomes of Exxon and IBM). During the 1979 Christmas buying season alone approximately $2 billion in goods were stolen by shoppers and dishonest employees.[1]

□ In 1979 between $250 and $400 billion earned in business transactions (10 percent of the entire United States economy) went unreported to the Internal Revenue Service (a loss in revenues to the federal government of as much as $100 billion). Most of these monies come from the selling of goods or services for cash, tips received, and second incomes. An estimated 15 to 20 million Americans do not report all or part of their income from otherwise legal practices.[2]

□ In a 1982 nationwide survey, the Internal Revenue Service found that 3 out of 10 persons were less than honest in completing their taxes. This number translates into an estimated loss to the government of $180 billion.[3]

□ In the United States there are approximately 200,000 growers of marijuana—the most valuable cash crop worth in excess of $13.9 billion in 1983.[4]

□ Company executives were asked by the *Harvard Business Review* if they would abide by a code of business ethics and 4 out of 7 said that they would violate such a code whenever they thought they could avoid detection.[5]

These illustrations indicate that many of us are guilty of cheating and stealing—behaviors clearly considered wrong. But are those of us who commit these illegal or immoral acts deviant? The complexities of the designation of "deviant" are the topics of this chapter.

The previous three chapters have analyzed the ways in which human beings, as members of society, are constrained to conform. We have seen how society is not only outside of us coercing us to conform but also inside of us making us *want* to behave in the culturally prescribed ways. But despite these powerful forces, people deviate from the norms. These acts and actors are the subjects of this chapter.

WHAT IS DEVIANCE?

Deviance is that behavior which does not conform to social expectations. It violates the rules of a group (custom, law, role, or moral code). *Deviance, then, is socially created.*[6] Social organizations create right and wrong by originating norms, the infraction of which constitutes deviance. This means that nothing inherent in a particular act makes it deviant. Whether an act is deviant or not depends on how others react to it. As Kai Erikson has put it: "Deviance is not a property *inherent* in any particular kind of behavior; it is a property *conferred upon* that behavior by the people who come into direct or indirect contact with it."[7] This means that *deviance is a relative, not an absolute notion.* Evidence for this is found in two sources: inconsistencies among societies as to what is deviance and inconsistencies in the labeling of behavior as deviant within a single society.

There is abundant anthropological evidence that what is right or wrong varies from society to society. The following are a few examples:

□ *Item:* The Ila of Africa encourage sexual promiscuity among their adolescents. After age ten girls are given houses of their own during harvest time, where they can play at being husband and wife with boys of their choice. In contrast the Tepoztlan Indians of Mexico do not allow girls to speak to or encourage a boy after the time of the girl's first menstruation.

□ *Item:* Egyptian royalty were required to marry their siblings, whereas this was prohibited as incestuous and sinful for European royalty.
□ *Item:* Young men of certain Indian tribes are expected, after fasting, to have a vision. This vision will be interpreted by the tribal elders to decide that young man's future occupation and status in the tribe. If an American youth were to tell his elders that he had had such a vision, he would likely be considered mentally ill.

Differential treatment for the same behavior by different categories of persons within a single society provides further proof that deviance is *not* a property of the act but depends upon the reaction of the particular audience. Several examples illustrate that it is not the act but the situation that determines whether the behavior is interpreted by others as deviant or not:

□ *Item:* Unmarried fathers escape the severe censure that unmarried mothers typically receive.
□ *Item:* Sexual intercourse between consenting adults is not deviant except if one partner pays another for his or her services and then the deviant is the recipient of the money, not the donor.
□ *Item:* Murder is a deviant act but the killing of an enemy during wartime is rewarded with praise and medals.
□ *Item:* A father would be considered a deviant if he removed his bathing suit at a public beach but his two-year-old son could do this with impunity. The father can smoke a cigar and drink a martini every night, but if his young son did, the boy (and his parents, if they permitted this) would be considered deviant.[8]
□ *Item:* Women smokers were once considered deviants but are no longer considered so.

In a heterogeneous society there will often be widespread disagreement on what the rules are and therefore what constitutes deviance. There are differences over, for example, sexual activities between consenting adults (regardless of sex, marital status), smoking marijuana, public nudism, pornography, drinking alcohol, remaining seated during the national anthem, and refusal to fight a war. Concerning this last instance, who was the deviant in the Vietnam war, for example, the person who killed Viet Cong or the person who refused to kill them? There is a difference of opinion among Americans on this with the majority likely to define the draft evaders and protesters as the deviants even though they were officially pardoned by President Carter.

This leads to a further insight about deviance: *the majority determines who is a deviant.* If most people believe that the Viet Cong are the enemy, then napalming them and their villages is appropriate and refusal to do so is deviant. If most people believe there is a God you can talk to, then such a belief is not deviance (in fact, the refusal to believe in God may then be deviant). But if the majority are atheists, then those few who believe in God would be deviant and subject to ridicule, job discrimination, and mental treatment.

Another example of this "safety in numbers" principle is the effort by some parents to deprogram their children if they have adopted a different religion—for example, pentecostal Christian, Children of God, or Hare Krishna. These parents had their children kidnapped. The children were confined for days with little food or sleep and badgered by hired experts into recanting their beliefs. As Mewshaw has described it:

> Euphemistically called "deprogramming," the process amounts to little more than a methodical and sometimes violent attempt to exorcise not Satan, but unpopular, misunderstood, or inarticulate notions about God.[9]

Erikson has summarized how deviance is a relative rather than an absolute notion in the following:

> Definitions of deviance vary widely as we range over the various classes found in a single society or across the various cultures into which mankind is divided, and it soon becomes apparent that there are no objective properties which all deviant acts can be said to share in common—even within the confines of a given group. *Behavior which qualifies one man for prison may qualify another for sainthood, since the quality of the act itself depends so much on the circumstances under which it was performed and the temper of the audience which witnessed it.*[10] (italics added)

An insight of the order theorists is important to note. Deviance is an integral part of all healthy societies.[11] Deviant behavior, according to Durkheim, actually has positive consequences for society because it gives the nondeviants a sense of solidarity. By punishing the deviant, the group expresses its collective indignation and reaffirms its commitments to the rules.

> Crime brings together upright consciences and concentrates them. We have only to notice what happens, particularly in a small town, when some moral scandal has just been committed. They stop each other on the street, they visit each other, they seek to come together to talk of the event and to wax indignant in common. From all the similar expressions which are exchanged, for all the temper that gets itself expressed, there emerges a unique temper . . . which is everybody's without being anybody's in particular. That is the public temper.[12]

Durkheim believed that the true function of punishment was not the prevention of future crimes. He asserted, rather, that the basic function of punishment is to reassert the importance of the rule being violated. It is not that a murderer is caught and put in the electric chair to keep potential murderers in line. That argument assumes people to be more rational than they really are. Instead, the extreme punishment of a murderer reminds each of us that murder is wrong. In other words, the punishment of crimes serves to strengthen our belief as individuals and as members of a collectivity in the legitimacy of society's norms. This enhances the solidarity of society as we unite in opposition to the deviant.

Crime, seen from this view, has positive functions for society. In addition to reaffirming the legitimacy of the society, defining certain acts as crimes creates the boundaries for what is acceptable behavior in the society.

Deviance, from the order perspective, is not only a consequence of social order (a violation of society's rules) but also is necessary for social order. As Rubington and Weinberg have said: "Each [social order and deviance] presupposes the other. And from studying one, sociologists frequently learn more about the other."[13]

The conflict theorists have pointed out that all views of rule violations have *political* implications.[14] When persons mistreat rule breakers they are saying, in effect, that the norms are legitimate. Thus, the bias is conservative, serving to preserve the status quo, which includes the current distribution of power. The opposite view, that the norms of society are wrong and should be rejected, is also political. When people and groups flaunt the laws and customs (for example, the draft, segregation, and marijuana smoking) they are not only rejecting the status quo but also questioning the legitimacy of those in power. As Edwin Schur has argued:

> Deviance issues are inherently political. They revolve around some people's assessments of other people's behavior. And power is a crucial factor in determining which and whose assessments gain an ascendancy. Deviance policies, likewise, affect the distribution of power and always have some broad political significance.[15]

TRADITIONAL THEORIES FOR THE CAUSES OF DEVIANCE[16]

The Individual as the Source of Deviance

Biological, psychological, and even some sociological theories have assumed that the fundamental reason for deviance is a fatal flaw in certain people.[17] The criminal, the dropout, the addict, the schizophrenic, have something wrong with them. These theories are deterministic, arguing that the individual ultimately has no choice but to be different.

Biological Theories. Biological explanations for deviance have focused on physiognomy (the determination of character by facial features), phrenology (the determination of mental abilities and character traits from the configuration of the skull), somatology (the determination of character by physique), genetic anomalies (for example, XYY chromosome in males), and brain malfunctions.

Some of these theories have been discredited (for example, Lombroso's theory that some distinct body types are more likely to be criminal because they are throwbacks to an earlier stage of human development—closer to the ape stage than nondeviants). Other biological theories have shown a statistical link between certain physical characteristics and deviant behavior. Chances are, though, that when such a relationship is found, it is likely a

Reprinted by permission of United Feature Syndicate.

result of social factors. The learning disability known as dyslexia, for example, is related to school failure, emotional disturbance, and juvenile delinquency. A survey of all youngsters admitted to reform schools in Colorado found that 90 percent had clinically provable learning disabilities. Another study in Cleveland found that 74 percent were afflicted in that way.[18] This disability is a brain malfunction where visual signs are scrambled. Average skills in reading, spelling, and arithmetic are impossible to attain if the malady remains undiagnosed. Teachers and parents often are unaware that the child is dyslexic and assume, rather, that she or he is retarded, lazy, or belligerent. The child (who actually may be very bright—Thomas Edison and Woodrow Wilson were dyslexic) finds school frustrating. Such a child is therefore much more likely than those not affected to be a troublemaker, to be alienated, to be either pushed out of school or a dropout, and to never reach full intellectual potential.

Psychological Theories. These theories also consider the source of deviance to reside within the individual, but they differ from the biological theories in that they assume conditions of the mind or personality to be the fault. Deviant individuals, depending on the particular psychological theory, are psychopaths (asocial, aggressive, impulsive) as a result of a lack of affection during childhood, Oedipal conflict, psychosexual trauma, or other early life experience.[19] Using Freudian assumptions, the deviant is one who has not developed an adequate ego to control deviant impulses (the id). Or, alternatively, deviance can result from a dominating superego. Persons with this condition are so repulsed by their own feelings (such as sexual fantasies, or ambivalence toward parents and siblings) that they may commit deviant acts in order to receive the punishment they deserve. Freudians, therefore, place great stress on the relationship between children and their parents. The parents, in this view, can be too harsh or too lenient, or too inconsistent in their treatment of the child. Each situation leads to inadequately socialized children and immature, infantile behavior by adolescents and adults.

Since the fundamental assumption of the biological and psychological theories of deviance is that the fault lies within the individual, the solutions are aimed at changing the individual. Screening of the population for those individuals with the presumed flaws is considered the best preventive. Doctors could routinely determine which boys had the XXY or XYY chromosome pattern. Psychological testing in the schools could find out which persons were unusually aggressive, guilt ridden, or fantasy oriented. Although the screening for potential problem people may make some sense (to detect dyslexics, for example), there are some fundamental problems with this type of solution. First, the screening devices likely will not be perfect, thereby mislabeling some persons. Second, screening is based on the assumption that there is a direct linkage between certain characteristics and deviance. If identified as a predeviant by these methods, the subsequent treatment of that individual and his own new definition of self would likely lead to a self-fulfilling prophecy and a false validation of the screening procedures, increasing their usage and acceptability.

A related problem with these screening procedures is the tendency to overpredict. In one attempt to identify predelinquents, a panel of experts examined a sample of youths already in the early stages of troublemaking and made predictions regarding future delinquency. Approximately 60 percent of the cases were judged to be predelinquents. A follow-up twenty years later revealed, however, that less than one third actually became involved with the law.[20]

For those identified as potential deviants or those who are actually deviants, the "kinds-of-people" theorists advocate solutions aimed at changing the individuals. The person is treated by drug therapy, electrical stimulation of the brain, electronic monitoring, surgery, operant conditioning, counseling, psychotherapy, probation with guidance of a psychiatric social worker, or incarceration. The assumption is clearly that deviants are troubled and sick persons who must be changed to conform to the norms of society.

The Socialization Approach. There are a number of sociological theories that are also "kinds-of-people" explanations for deviance. Instead of individual characteristics distinguishing the deviant from the nondeviant, these focus on differing objective social and economic conditions. These are based on the empirical observations that crime and mental illness rates, to name two forms of deviance, vary by social class, ethnicity, race, place of residence, and sex.

> From these gross differences, the sociologist infers that something beyond the intimacy of family surroundings is operative in the emergence of delinquent patterns; something in the cultural and social atmosphere apparent in certain sectors of society.[21]

Let us look at some of these theories, which emphasize that certain social conditions are conducive to the internalization of values that encourage deviance.

Urbanism.   One theory that purports to explain the high crime rates in cities rests its argument on the characteristics of the city and city living.[22] The assumption is that people living in cities are crowded together, and that urban relations tend to be impersonal and anonymous. A fundamental difference between rural and city living is that the former is characterized by face-to-face relations as a form of social control while the latter is basically free of these constraints. Interaction is often with strangers. Thus, "city life does not provide the restraints on social behavior formerly built into the rural social structure."[23] Free of the constraints of rural life, individuals in the city may engage in activities that they would have foregone in rural settings.

A variant of this theory is that some places in the city are especially conducive to criminal activity because of their characteristics. The highest crime rates, for example, occur precisely in those geographical areas of the city where poverty, substandard housing, overcrowding, disease, and population instability are also the highest. As Hartjen has summarized it, "crime and human wretchedness seem to go hand in hand."[24]

Cultural transmission.   Sutherland's theory of differential association sought to explain why some persons are criminals while others are not, even though both may share certain social characteristics such as social class position.[25] Sutherland believed that through interaction, one learns to be a criminal. If our close associates are deviants, there is a strong probability that we will learn the techniques and the deviant values that make criminal acts possible. In sum,

> the significant feature of Sutherland's theory is his claim that procriminal sentiments are acquired, as are all others, by association with other individuals in a process of social interaction. Criminal orientations do not, thus, stem from faulty metabolism, inadequate superego development, or even poverty.[26]

Societal goals and differential opportunities.   Robert Merton has presented an explanation for why the lower classes (who coincidentally live in the cities) disproportionately commit criminal acts.[27] In Merton's view, societal values determine both what are the appropriate goals (success through the acquisition of wealth) as well as the approved means for achieving these goals. The problem, however, is that some people are denied access to the legitimate means of achieving these goals. The poor, especially those from certain racial and ethnic groups, in addition to the roadblocks presented by negative stereotypes, often receive a second-class education or they have to drop out of school prematurely because of financial exigencies, all of which effectively exclude them from high-paying and prestigious occupations. Because legitimate means to success are inaccessible to them, they often resort to certain forms of deviant behavior to attain success. Viewed from this perspective, deviance is a result of social structure and not the consequence of individual pathology. McGee makes this point in his analysis of Merton's scheme.

> [In each of the deviant adaptations] the individuals are behaving as they have been taught by their societies. They are not sinful or weak individuals who choose to deviate. They are, in fact, doing what they have learned they are supposed to do in order to earn the rewards which their society purports to offer its members. But either because their positions in the social structure do not permit them access to the means through which to seek the rewards they have learned to want, or because the means do not in fact guarantee goal attainment, they become frustrated and experience loss of self-esteem. In a final attempt to do and be what they have been taught they must, they engage in what is called deviant behavior. Such behavior is simply an attempt to gain the same self-esteem which others are presumed to have and which the society has made it intolerable to be without.[28]

Although Merton's analysis provides many important insights, the emphasis is on the adjustments people make to the circumstances of society. Deviance is a property of people because they cannot adapt to the discrepancy between the goals and the means of society. The problem is that Merton accepts the American success ethic. In the words of Doyle and Schindler:

> What is missing is the perspective that the winner, firster, money mentality could be a pathology rather than a value in America, a pathology that so powerfully corrupts our economy, polity, and way of life that it precludes any possibility of a cohesive, healthy, community. Certainly it is valid and worthwhile to explore the situation of the deprived in a success oriented society, but it is also valid to question the viability of a social system with such a "value" at its core. The sociology of deviance has turned too quickly and too exclusively to hypotheses about "bad" people. The analysis of "bad" societies has been neglected.[29]

Subcultural differences by social class.   We shall explore the **culture of poverty** hypothesis in Chapter 10. Since it has special relevance for explaining differential crime rates, we will briefly characterize it here with that emphasis. The argument is that people because of their social class position differ in resources, power, and prestige and hence have different experiences, lifestyles, and ways of life. The lower-class culture has its own values, many of which run counter to the values of the middle and upper classes. There is a unique morality (a "right" action is one that works and can be gotten away with) and a unique set of criteria that make one successful in the lower-class community (being tough, willingness to take risks).[30] Panel 8–1 provides what Banfield considers the elements of propensity to crime by the lower class. Banfield may be correct in his assertions about the "lower-class culture," but there is strong evidence that it is incorrect (see Chapter 10).[31] Assuming that Banfield's characterization of the lower-class propensity to crime is correct, the critical question is whether these differences are durable or not. Will a change in monetary status or peer groups make a difference because the individual has a dual value system— one that is a reaction to his deprived situation and one that is middle class? This is a key research question because the answer determines where to attack the problem—at the individual or societal level.

PANEL 8–1

The Lower-Class Propensity to Criminal Activity

The elements of propensity [toward criminal activity] seem to be mainly these:

Type of morality. This refers to the way in which an individual conceptualizes right and wrong and, therefore, to the weight he gives to legal and moral rules in making choices. One whose morality is "preconventional" understands a "right" action to be one that will serve his purpose and that can be gotten away with; a "wrong" action is one that will bring ill success or punishment. An individual whose morality is preconventional cannot be influenced by authority (as opposed to power). One whose morality is "conventional" defines "right" action as doing one's "duty" or doing what those in authority require; for him, laws and moral rules have a constraining effect even in the absence of an enforcement apparatus. One whose morality is "postconventional" defines "right" action as that which is in accord with some universal (or very general) principle that he considers worthy of choice. Such an individual is constrained by law as such only if the principle that he has chosen requires him to be; if it requires him to obey the law only when he thinks that the law in question is just, he is, of course, not under the constraint of law at all.

Ego strength. This refers to the individual's ability to control himself—especially to his ability to adhere to and act on his intentions (and therefore to manage his impulses) and to his ability to make efforts at self-reform. One who is radically deficient in ego strength

cannot conceive or implement a plan of action; he has a succession of fleeting resolves, the last of which eventuates in action under the pressure of circumstances.

Time horizon. This refers to the time perspective an individual takes in estimating costs and benefits of alternative courses of action. The more present-oriented an individual, the less likely he is to take account of consequences that lie in the future. Since the benefits of crime tend to be immediate and its costs (such as imprisonment or loss of reputation) in the future, the present-oriented individual is *ipso facto* more disposed toward crime than others.

Taste for risk. Commission of most crimes involves a certain amount of risk. An individual who places a very low (perhaps even a negative) value on the avoidance of risk is thereby biased in the direction of crime.

Willingness to inflict injury. Most crimes involve at least the possibility of injury to others and therefore a certain willingness on the part of the actor to inflict injury. It may be useful to distinguish among (a) individuals with a distaste for inflicting any injury ("crimes without victims" would still be open to them, of course); (b) those with a distaste for injuring specifiable individuals (they might steal from a large enterprise, but they would not cheat the corner grocer); (c) those with a distaste for doing bodily (but not necessarily other) injury to people; and (d) those with no distaste for inflicting injuries, along with those who positively enjoy inflicting them.

These several elements of propensity tend to exist in typical combinations. In general, an individual whose morality is preconventional also has little ego strength, a short time horizon, a fondness for risk, and little distaste for doing bodily harm to specifiable individuals. The opposites of these traits also tend to be found together.

It also happens that individuals whose propensity toward crime is relatively high— especially those with high propensity for violent crime—tend to be those whose situation provides the strongest incentive to crimes of common sorts. The low-income individual obviously has much more incentive to steal than does the high-income one. Similarly, a boy has much more incentive to "prove he is not chicken" than does a girl. In general, then, high propensity and high inducement go together.

Source: Excerpted from Edward C. Banfield, *The Unheavenly City Revisited* (Boston: Little, Brown, 1974), pp. 182–183. Copyright © 1968, 1970, 1974 by Edward C. Banfield. By permission of Little, Brown and Co.

The "Blaming-the-Victim" Critique of the Individual-Oriented Explanations for Deviance

Although the socialization theories focus on forces external to individuals that push them toward deviant behavior, they, like the biological and psychological theories, are "kinds-of-people" theories that find the fault within the individual. The deviant has an acquired trait—the internalization of values and beliefs favorable to deviance—that is social in origin. The problem is that this results in **"blaming the victims,"** as William Ryan has forcefully argued:

> The new ideology attributes defect and inadequacy to the malignant nature of poverty, injustice, slum life, and racial difficulties. The stigma that marks the victim and accounts for his victimization is acquired stigma, a stigma of social, rather than genetic origin. But the stigma, the defect, the fatal difference—though derived in the past from environmental forces—is still located *within* the victim, inside his skin. With such an elegant formulation, the humanitarian can have it both ways. He can, all at the same time, concentrate his charitable interest on the defects of the victim, condemn the vague social and environmental stresses that produced the defect (some time ago), and ignore the continuing effect of victimizing social forces (right now). It is a brilliant ideology for justifying a perverse form of social action designed to change, not society, as one might expect, but rather society's victim.[32]

Let us contrast, then, two ways to look at deviance—blaming the victim or blaming society. The fundamental difference between these two approaches to deviance is whether the problems emanate from the pathologies of individuals or because of the situation in which deviants are immersed. The answer is doubtless somewhere between these two extremes, but since the individual blamers have held sway, let us look carefully at the critique of this approach.[33]

Let us begin by considering some victims. One group of victims is composed of children in slum schools who are failures. Why do they fail? Victim blamers point to the children's **cultural deprivation.*** They do not do well in school because their families speak a different dialect, because their parents are uneducated, because they have not been exposed to all the educational experiences of middle-class children (for example, visits to the zoo, extensive travel, attendance at cultural events, exposure to books). In other words, the defect is in the children and their families. System blamers, however, look elsewhere for the sources of failure. They ask: What is there about the schools that makes slum children more likely to fail? The answer for them is found in the irrelevant curriculum, the class-biased IQ tests, the tracking system, the overcrowded classrooms, the differential allocation of resources within the school district, and insensitive teachers whose low expectations for poor children comprise a prophecy that is continually fulfilled.

Another victim is the criminal. Why is the **recidivism** rate (reinvolvement in crime) of criminals so high? The individual blamer would point to the faults of the individual criminals: their greed, feelings of aggression, weak impulse control, and lack of a conscience (superego). The system blamers' attention is directed to very different sources for this problem. They would look, rather, at the penal system, the employment situation for ex-criminals, and the schools. For example, studies have shown that 20 to 30 percent of inmates are functionally illiterate.[34] This means they cannot meet minimum reading and writing demands in American society such as filling out job applications. Yet these persons are expected to leave prison, find a job, and stay out of trouble. Because they are illiterate and ex-criminals, they face unemployment or at best the most menial jobs (where there are low wages, no job security, and no fringe benefits). The system blamer would argue that these persons are not to blame for their illiteracy but rather that the schools at first and later the penal institutions have failed to provide these people with the minimum requirements for citizenship. Moreover, the lack of employment and the unwillingness of potential employers to train functional illiterates forces many to return to crime in order to survive.

While still President, Richard Nixon made the following statement:

> Americans in the last decade were often told that the criminal was not re-sponsible for his crimes against society, but that society was responsible. I to-tally disagree with this permissive philosophy. Society is guilty of crime only when we fail to bring the criminal to justice. When we fail to make the crimi-nal pay for his crime, we encourage him to think that crime will pay. Such an attitude will never be reflected in the laws supported by this Administration, nor in the manner in which we enforce those laws.[35]

---

* The term "cultural deprivation" is a loaded ethnocentric term. It implies that the culture of the group in question is not only deficient but that it is inferior. This label is applied by members of the majority to the culture of the minority group. It is not only a malicious "putting down" of the minority, but the concept itself is patently false because no culture can be inferior to another; it can only be different. The concept does remind us, however, that people can and do make invidious distinctions about cultures and subcultures. Furthermore, they act on these definitions as if they were true.

Aside from the obvious irony of this statement by the now-disgraced former president, it does present a classic statement that blames the victim. In support of Nixon's position, an editorial writer for *The National Observer* said that the system is not to blame for crime because of the opportunity for upward mobility that exists. The poor do not have to stay poor. There is not, in his opinion, a cycle of poverty that dooms the individual.[36] The system blamer, on the other hand, would argue that for every individual who breaks out of a cycle of poverty, many are trapped by their inferior education, their lack of salable skills, their greater likelihood to be ill because of poor nutrition and inadequate medical care, and their lack of self-esteem because of the negative labels the system gives them. As Tom Wicker, in response to the Nixon speech, argued:

> Conditions of poverty and unemployment, social and economic disadvantage tend to breed criminal behavior. . . . Poverty and inequity lead more and more young people into the only career that seems to offer them any hope—crime. And an ineffective and counterproductive prison system tends to keep them in that career.[37]

Blacks (and other racial minorities) constitute another set of victims in American society. What accounts for the greater probability for blacks than whites to be failures in school, to be unemployed, to be criminals, and to be heroin addicts? The individualistic approach places the blame on the blacks themselves. They are "culturally deprived," they have high rates of illegitimacy, a high proportion of transient males, and a relatively high proportion of black families have a matriarchal structure. But this approach neglects the pervasive effects of racism in American society, which limits the opportunities for blacks, provides them with a second-class education, and renders them powerless to change the system through approved channels.

Why is there a strong tendency to place the blame for deviance on individuals rather than on the social system? The answer lies in the way that persons tend to define deviance. Most people define deviance as behavior that deviates from the norms and standards of society. Because people do not ordinarily question the norms or the way things are done in society, they tend to question the exceptions. The system is not only taken for granted, but it has, for most people, an aura of sacredness because of the traditions and customs behind it. Logically, then, those who deviate are the source of trouble. The obvious question, then, is why do these people deviate from the norms? Because most persons abide by society's norms, the deviation of the exceptions must be the result of some kind of unusual circumstance—accident, illness, personal defect, character flaw, or maladjustment.[38] The key to this approach, then, is that the flaw is within the deviant and not a function of societal arrangements.

The position taken in this debate has serious consequences. Let us briefly examine the effects of interpreting social problems solely within a person-blame framework.[39] First, this interpretation of social problems frees the government, the economy, the system of stratification, the system of justice, and the educational system from any blame. The established order is protected against criticism, thereby increasing the difficulty encountered in trying to change the dominant economic, social, and political institutions. A good example is found in the strategy of social scientists studying the origins of poverty. Since the person blamer studies the poor rather than the nonpoor, the system of inequality (buttressed by the tax laws, welfare rules, and employment practices) goes unchallenged. A related consequence of the person-blame approach, then, is that the relatively advantaged segments of society retain their advantages.

Not only is the established order protected from criticism by the person-blame approach, but the authorities can control dissidents under the guise of being helpful. Caplan and Nelson have provided an excellent illustration of this in the following quote:

> Normally, one would not expect the Government to cooperate with "problem groups" who oppose the system. But if a person-blame rather than system-blame action program can be negotiated, cooperation becomes possible. In this way, the problem-defining process remains in the control of the would-be benefactors, who provide "help" so long as their diagnosis goes unchallenged.
>
> In 1970, for example, while a group of American Indians still occupied Alcatraz Island in San Francisco Bay, a group of blacks took over Ellis Island in New York Harbor. Both groups attempted to take back lands no longer used by the Federal Government. The Government solved the Ellis Island problem by getting the blacks to help establish a drug-rehabilitation center on it. They solved the Alcatraz problem by forcibly removing the Indians. Had the Indians been willing to settle for an alcoholism-treatment center on Alcatraz, thereby acknowledging that what they need are remedies for their personal problems, we suspect the Government would have "cooperated" again.[40]

Another social control function of the person-blame approach is that troublesome individuals and groups are controlled in a publicly acceptable manner. Deviants, whether they be criminals, homosexuals, or social protestors are controlled by incarceration in prison or mental hospital, drugs, or other forms of therapy. In this manner, not only is blame directed at individuals and away from the system, but the problems (individuals) are in a sense eliminated.

A related consequence is the manner in which the problem is to be treated. A person-blame approach demands a person-change treatment program. If the cause of delinquency, for example, is defined as the result of personal pathology, then the solution lies clearly in counseling, behavior modification, psychotherapy, drugs, or some other technique aimed at changing the individual deviant. Such an interpretation of social problems provides and legitimates the right to initiate person-change rather than system-change treatment programs. Under such a scheme, norms that are racist or sexist, for example, will go unchallenged.

The person-blame ideology not only invites person-change treatment programs but also programs for person control. If local governments spent less than 2 percent for social services while 75 percent were for public safety, chiefly to police departments, as was the case in the 1970s, then the system blamer would argue that such an emphasis treats the symptom rather than the disease.[41]

A final consequence of person-blame interpretations is that they reinforce social myths about the degree of control we have over our fate. It provides justification for a form of Social Darwinism—that is, a person's placement in the stratification system is a function of ability and effort. By this logic, the poor are poor because they *are* the dregs of society. In short, they deserve their fate, as do the successful in society. Thus, there is little sympathy for governmental programs to increase welfare to the poor.

We should recognize, however, that the contrasting position—the system-blame orientation—also has its dangers. First, it is only part of the truth. Social problems and deviance are highly complex phenomena that have both individual and systemic origins. Individuals, obviously, can be malicious and aggressive for purely psychological reasons. Perhaps only a psychologist can explain why a parent is a child abuser, or why a sniper shoots at cars passing on the freeway. Clearly, society needs to be protected from some individuals. Moreover, some persons require particular forms of therapy, remedial help, or special programs on an individual basis if they are to function normally. But much that is labeled deviant is the end product of social conditions.

A second danger in a dogmatic system-blame orientation is that it presents a rigidly deterministic explanation for social problems. Taken too far, this position views individuals as robots controlled totally by their social environment. A balanced view of people is needed, since human beings have autonomy most of the time to choose between alternative courses of action. This raises the related question as to the degree to which people are responsible for their behavior. An excessive system-blame approach absolves individuals from the responsibility of their actions. To take such a stance would be to argue that society should never restrict deviants. This extreme view invites anarchy.[42]

Despite the problems with the system-blame approach just noted, it will be emphasized in this chapter. The rationale for this is, first, that the contrasting view (individual-blame) is the prevailing view in American society. Since average citizens, police personnel, legislators, judges, and social scientists tend to interpret social problems from an individualistic perspective, a balance is needed. Moreover, as was noted earlier, to hold a strict person-blame perspective has many negative consequences, and citizens must realize the effects of their ideology.

A second basis for the use of the society-blaming perspective is that the subject matter of sociology is not the individual, who is the special province of psychology, but society. If sociologists do not emphasize the social determinants of behavior and if they do not make a critical analysis of the social structure, then who will? As noted in Chapter 1, an important ingredient of the sociological perspective is the development of a critical stance toward societal arrangements. The job of the sociologist is to look behind the facade to determine the positive and negative consequences of societal arrangements.

The persistent question is: Who benefits under these arrangements and who does not? This is why there should be such a close fit between the sociological approach and the societal-blaming perspective. Unfortunately, this has not always been the case.

SOCIETY AS THE SOURCE OF DEVIANCE

We have seen that the traditional explanations for deviance, whether they be biological, psychological, or sociological, have found the source of deviance in individual deviants, their families, or their immediate social settings. The basic assumption of these theories is that because deviants do not fit in society, something is wrong with them.[43] In this section we shall provide an antidote to the medical analogy implicit in those theories by focusing instead on two theories that place the blame for deviance on the role of society—labeling theory and conflict theory.

Labeling Theory

All the explanations for deviance described so far assume that deviants differ from nondeviants in behavior, attitude, and motivation. This is buttressed by the commonly held belief that deviance is the actions of a few weird people who are either criminals, insane, or both. In reality, however, most persons break the rules of society at one time or another. The evidence from this comes from a number of studies. For example, two researchers asked 700 middle-class citizens if they had ever committed (after age 15) any one or more of 49 crimes that were punishable in New York State by at least one year in prison. The results were that 99 percent of the respondents admitted committing at least one such offense. The average number of offenses by men was 18 and by women, 11. Moreover, about two thirds of the men admitted at least one serious crime—a felony—as did about one third of the women.[44] There is also a considerable amount of evidence that indicates little or no difference in magnitude between lower-class delinquent behavior and middle-class delinquent behavior.[45] Hirschi has summarized these studies by saying:

> While the prisons bulge with the socioeconomic dregs of society, careful quantitative research shows again and again that the relation between socioeconomic status and the commission of delinquent acts is small, or nonexistent.[46]

These studies do not mesh with our perceptions and the apparent facts. Crime statistics do show that the lower classes are more likely to be criminals. Even data on mental illness demonstrate that the lower classes are more prone than the middle classes to have serious mental problems.[47] The difference is that most persons break the rules at one time or another, even serious rules for which they could be placed in jail (for example, theft, statutory rape, vandalism, violation of drug or alcohol laws, fraud, violations of the Internal Revenue Service), but only some get the *label* of deviant.[48]

As one adult analyzed his ornery but normal youth:

> I recall my high school and college days, participating in vandalism, entering locked buildings at night, drinking while under age—even while I made top grades and won athletic letters. I was normal and did these things with guys who now are preachers, professors, and businessmen. A few school friends of poorer families somehow tended to get caught and we didn't. They were failing in class, and we all believed they were too dumb not to know when to have fun and when to run. Some of them did time in jail and reformatories. *They* were "delinquents" and *we* weren't.[49]

This chapter began with the statement that society creates deviance by creating rules, the violation of which constitutes deviance. But rule breaking itself does "not a deviant make." The successful application of the label "deviant" is crucial.[50]

Who gets labeled as a deviant (criminal, psychotic, queer, or junkie) is not just a matter of luck or random selection but the result of a systematic societal bias against the powerless. Chambliss has summarized the empirical evidence for criminals:

> The lower class person is (1) more likely to be scrutinized and therefore be observed in any violation of the law, (2) more likely to be arrested if discovered under suspicious circumstances, (3) more likely to spend the time between arrest and trial in jail, (4) more likely to come to trial, (5) more likely to be found guilty, (6) if found guilty, more likely to receive harsh punishment than his middle- or upper-class counterpart.[51]

We can see how the well-to-do tend to avoid the criminal label by examining the disposition of those persons actually found guilty of a felony (major crime) by their socioeconomic characteristics. The judicial procedures in Florida provide a revealing glimpse of this bias. For persons accused of a felony but placed on probation, Florida law allows a judge the option of withholding adjudication of guilt. The importance of avoiding this label is that such persons lose none of their civil rights and may truthfully assert that they have never been convicted of a felony. To be a "convicted felon," on the other hand, means that one loses the rights to vote, hold public office, serve on juries, and possess certain firearms. The stigma of "felon" also makes employment more difficult as well as acceptance in other situations. A study of the legal and social characteristics of 2419 consecutive felony probation cases found that defendants who were older, black, poorly educated, had a prior record, and were defended by a court-appointed attorney were the most likely to be so labeled.[52] Clearly, the judges reflected the bias present in society by formally imposing criminal labels on those persons *expected* to be the most criminal (the poor, the uneducated, racial minorities), who coincidentally are the least powerful segments in society.

Not only are the more well-to-do less likely to receive a punishment of imprisonment, but those who are imprisoned receive advantages over the lower-class and minority inmates. The most blatant example of this is found by examining what type of person actually receives the death penalty. A former Attorney General has summarized the findings in the following quote:

> The poor and the black have been the chief victims of the death penalty. Clarence Darrow observed that "from the beginning, a procession of the poor, the weak, the unfit, have gone through our jails and prisons to their deaths. They have been the victims." It is the poor, the sick, the ignorant, the powerless and the hated who are executed.
>
> Racial discrimination is manifest from the bare statistics of capital punishment. Since we began keeping records in 1930, there have been 2,066 Negroes and only 1,751 white persons put to death. Hundreds of thousands of rapes have occurred in America since 1930, yet only 455 men have been executed for rape—and 405 of them were Negroes. There can be no rationalization or justification of such clear discrimination. It is outrageous public murder, illuminating our darkest racism.[53]

The social class of the prisoner on death row is also related to whether an individual receives the ultimate punishment or not. In a study of death row in Pennsylvania from 1914 to 1958, those offenders with court-appointed counsel were much more likely to be executed than offenders with private counsel. Likewise, there is a greater probability of the death penalty being imposed on persons of low-prestige occupations than for those of higher prestige.[54]

Who gets paroled is another indicator of a bias in the system. Parole is a conditional release from prison that allows prisoners to return to their communities under the supervision of a parole officer before the completion of their maximum sentence. Typically, parole is granted by a parole board set up for the correctional institution or for the state. Often the parole board members are political appointees without training.[55] The parole board reviews a prisoner's social history, past offenses, and behavior in prison and makes its judgment. The decision is rarely subject to review and can be made arbitrarily or discriminatorily.

The bias that disadvantages minorities and the poor throughout the system of justice continues as parole board members, corrections officers, and others make judgments that often reflect stereotypes. What type of prisoner represents the safest risk, a black or a white? An uneducated or an educated person? A white-collar worker or a chronically unemployed unskilled worker? One study shows vividly how the parole system tends to continue the bias against blacks and those of low socioeconomic status. Petersen and Friday compared prisoners in Ohio who were granted "shock probation" (release after a short period of incarceration) with those who were eligible for early release but were not.[56] They found that while 44 percent of whites received "shock probation," only 20 percent of blacks did. Educational attainment was also a significant variable affecting early release from prison. Only 25 percent of those inmates with less than nine years of education were released early, while 53 percent of those with some college were. Especially interesting to note is the effect of race and education combined (see Table 8–1). These

TABLE 8–1	Early Release from Prison According to the Race of the Offender, with Education Held Constant (percentages)			
	Shock probation		Incarceration	
Education	White	Black	White	Black
Less than 9 years	31.9	11.9	68.1	88.1
Some high school	51.4	25.4	48.6	74.6
High school graduate	64.4	30.8	35.6	69.2
Some college	56.3	33.3	43.8	66.7

Source: Adapted from David M. Petersen and Paul C. Friday, "Early Release from Incarceration: Race as a Factor in the Use of 'Shock Probation,'" *The Journal of Criminal Law and Criminology* 66 (March, 1975), p. 82. Reprinted by special permission of the Journal of Criminal Law and Criminology. Copyright © 1975 by Northwestern University School of Law.

data show that blacks have about one half of the choice of early release that whites have *at each educational level.* The researchers also examined the effects of race, holding constant a number of other variables (for example, type of offense, number of previous adult arrests, and father's education) and found invariably that whites are much more likely than blacks to receive the preferential treatment of "shock probation" by the authorities. The conclusion that the procedure favors whites over blacks, then, is inescapable.

Currently in the United States there are about 5000 city and county jails, 400 state and federal prisons, plus a variety of other forms of detention centers. On an average day about 1.3 million persons are confined in these places. We have shown that the underdogs in society (the poor and the minorities) are disproportionately represented in the prison population. An important consequence of this is that it reinforces the negative stereotypes already present in the majority of the population. The large number of blacks and the poor in prison "prove" that they have criminal tendencies. This belief is reinforced further by the high recidivism rate of 70 percent of ex-prisoners.

At least four factors relative to the prison experiences operate to fulfill the prophecy that the poor and the black are prone toward criminal behavior. The first is that the entire criminal justice system is viewed by the underdogs as unjust. There is a growing belief among prisoners that because the system is biased against them, all prisoners are, in fact, political. This "consciousness raising" increases the bitterness and anger among them.[57]

A second reason for the high rate of crime among those processed through the system of criminal justice is the accepted fact that prison is a brutal, degrading, and altogether dehumanizing experience. Mistreatment by guards, sexual assaults by fellow prisoners, overcrowding, unsanitary conditions, are commonplace in American prisons.[58] Prisoners cannot escape the humiliation, anger, and frustration. These feelings, coupled with the knowledge that the entire system of justice is unjustly directed at certain categories of persons, creates within many ex-cons the desire for revenge.

A third factor is that prisons provide learning experiences for prisoners in the art of crime. Through the interaction of the inmates, individuals learn the techniques of crime from the masters and develop the contacts that can be used later.

Finally, the ex-con faces the problems of finding a job and being accepted again in society. Long-termers face problems of adjusting to life without regimentation. More important, since good-paying jobs, particularly in times of economic recession, are difficult for anyone to find, the ex-con who is automatically assumed to be untrustworthy is faced with either unemployment or those jobs nobody else will take. Even the law works to his disadvantage by prohibiting certain jobs to ex-cons.

In 46 states and the District of Columbia, for example, they cannot become barbers. In New York, he or she is prohibited from being an auctioneer, junk dealer, pharmacist, undertaker, embalmer or poolroom operator, among other things. In Kentucky, ex-cons are not even allowed to perform the foul job of cleaning septic tanks.[59]

The result of nonacceptance by society is often to return to crime. Previous offenders, on the average, are arrested for crime within six weeks after leaving prison. This, of course, justifies the beliefs by policemen, judges, parole boards, and other authorities that certain categories of persons should receive punishment while others should not.

The Consequences of Labeling. We have just seen that the labeling process is a crucial factor in the formation of a deviant career. In other words, the stigma of the label leads to subsequent deviance. This is what Lemert meant by the concept of secondary deviance.[60] **Primary deviance** is the rule breaking that occurs prior to labeling. **Secondary deviance** is that behavior resulting from the labeling process. Being labeled a criminal means being rejected by society, by employers,[61] by friends, and even relatives. There is a high probability that such a person will turn to behavior that fulfills the prophecies of others. Put another way, persons labeled as deviants tend to become locked into a deviant behavior pattern. Looking at deviance this way turns the tables on conventional thought.

Instead of assuming that it is the deviant's difference which needs explanation, [the labeling perspective] asks why the majority responds to this difference as it does. This shift of the question reverses the normal conception of causation; the labeling school suggests that the other person's peculiarity has not caused us to regard him as different so much as our labeling hypothesis has caused his peculiarity.[62]

Ex-mental patients, like ex-convicts, usually have difficulty in finding employment and establishing close relationships because of the stigma of the label. This, of course, leads to frustration, anger, low self-esteem, and other symptoms of "mental illness." Moreover, the consistent messages from others (remember Cooley's looking-glass self) that one is sick will likely lead the individual to behavior in accord with these expectations. Even while a patient is in the mental hospital, the actions of the staff may actually foster in the person a self concept of "deviant" and behavior consistent with that definition. Patients who show insight about their "illness" confirm the medical and societal diagnosis and are positively rewarded by psychiatrists and other personnel.[63] The opposite also occurs, as illustrated so vividly by the character R. P. McMurphy in *One Flew Over the Cuckoo's Nest.*[64] Although the mythical McMurphy fought this tendency to confirm the expectations of powerful others, the pressures to conform were great. Cole has summarized this process of how the deviant role is sustained in the following:

> After someone is labeled as deviant, he often finds it rewarding to accept the label and act deviant. Consider, for example, a patient in a mental hospital who has been diagnosed as a schizophrenic. If the patient refuses to accept the diagnosis, claims that he is not mentally ill, and demands to be immediately released, the staff will consider him to be hostile and uncooperative. He may be denied privileges and treated as hopelessly insane. After all, the person who cannot even recognize that he is ill must be in a mental state in which he has no perception of reality! On the other hand, if the patient accepts the validity of the diagnosis, admits his illness, and tries to cooperate with the staff in effecting a cure, he will be rewarded. He will be defined as a good cooperative patient who is sincerely trying to get better. Any weird or unusual behavior he engages in will be ignored; after all, he is mentally ill, and such types of behavior should be expected from a person in his mental state. He may even be rewarded for engaging in behavior which is considered to be characteristic of schizophrenia. Such behavior serves to reassure the staff that the patient is indeed mentally ill and that the social organization of the mental hospital makes sense.[65]

The labeling perspective is especially helpful in understanding the bias of the criminal justice system. It shows, in summary, that when society's underdogs are disproportionately singled out for the criminal label, the subsequent problems of stigmatization and segregation they face result in a tendency toward further deviance, thereby justifying the society's original negative response to them. This tendency for secondary deviance is especially strong when the imposition of the label is accompanied by a sense of injustice. Lemert argued that a stronger commitment to a deviant identity is greatest when the label (stigma) is believed by the individual to be inconsistently applied by society.[66] The evidence of such inconsistency is overwhelming.

From this perspective, then, the situations which show that society's underdogs engage in more deviance than persons from the middle and upper classes are invalid, since they reflect the differential response of society to the deviance by them at every phase in the process of criminal justice.

Hartjen has provided an excellent statement that summarizes this process.

> Criminal sanctions are supposedly directed toward a person's behavior—what he does, not what kind of person he is. Yet, the research on the administration of criminal justice . . . reveals that just the opposite occurs. A person is likely to acquire a social identity as a criminal precisely because of what he is—because of the kind of personal or social characteristics he has the misfortune to possess. Being black, poor, migrant, uneducated, and the like increases a person's chances of being defined as a criminal. . . . What I am suggesting here is that the very structure and operation of the judicial system, which was created to deal with the problem called crime, are not only grounded in an unstated image of the criminal but also—merely because the system exists— serve to produce and perpetuate the "thing" it was created to handle. That is to say, the criminal court (and especially the juvenile court) does not exist in its present form because the people it deals with are what they are. Rather, the criminals and delinquents become the way they are characterized by others as being because the court (and the world view it embodies) exists in the form that it does. *The criminal, thus, is a "product" of the structural and procedural characteristics of the judicial system.*[67]

"Solutions" for Deviance from the Labeling Perspective. The labeling theorist's approach to deviance leads to unconventional solutions.[68] The assumption is that deviants are not basically different—except that they have been processed (and labeled) by official sources (judges and courts; psychiatrists and mental hospitals). The primary target for policy, then, should be neither the individual nor the local community setting, but the process by which some persons are singled out for the negative label. From this approach, organizations produce deviants. Speaking specifically about juvenile delinquency, Schur has argued that the solution should be what he has called **"radical nonintervention."**

> We can now begin to see some of the meanings of the term "radical nonintervention." For one thing, it breaks radically with conventional thinking about delinquency and its causes. Basically, radical nonintervention implies policies that accommodate society to the widest possible diversity of behaviors and attitudes, rather than focusing as many individuals as possible to "adjust" to supposedly common societal standards. This does not mean that anything goes, that all behavior is socially acceptable. But traditional delinquency policy has proscribed youthful behavior well beyond what is required to maintain a smooth-running society or to protect others from youthful depredations.
>
> Thus, the basic injunction for public policy becomes: *leave kids alone wherever possible.* This effort partly involves mechanisms to divert children away from the courts but it goes further to include opposing various kinds of intervention by diverse social control and socializing agencies. . . . Subsidiary policies would favor collective action programs instead of those that single out specific individuals; and voluntary programs instead of compulsive ones. Finally, this approach is radical in asserting that major and intentional sociocultural change will help reduce our delinquency problems. Piecemeal socioeconomic reform will not greatly affect delinquency; there must be

through-going changes in the structure and the values of our society. If the choice is between changing youth and changing society (including some of its laws), the radical noninterventionist opts for changing the society.[69]

One way to accomplish this "leave the deviants alone whenever possible" philosophy would be to treat fewer acts as criminal or deviant. For adults this could be accomplished by decriminalizing victimless crimes, such as gambling, drug possession, prostitution, and homosexuality. Youth should not be treated as criminals for behavior that is legal if one is old enough. Truancy, running away from home, curfew violations, and purchasing alcohol are acts for which persons below the legal age can receive the label "delinquent," yet they are not crimes for adults. Is there any wonder, then, why so many youthful rule breakers outgrow their "delinquency," becoming law-abiding citizens as adults?

Acts dangerous to society do occur, and these must be handled through legal mechanisms. But when a legal approach is required, justice must be applied evenly. Currently, the criminal label is disproportionately applied to individuals from the "other side of the tracks." This increases the probability of further deviance by these persons because of "secondary deviance" and justifies further stern punishment for this category. This unfair cycle must be broken.

The strengths of labeling theory are: (1) that it concentrates on the role of societal reactions in the creation of deviance, (2) the realization that the label is applied disproportionately to the powerless, and (3) that it explains how deviant careers are established and perpetuated. There are problems with the theory, however.[70] First, it avoids the question of causation (primary deviance). Labeling, by definition, occurs after the fact. It disregards undetected deviance. As McCaghy has put it,

> By minimizing the importance of explaining initial (primary) deviance, whatever meaning the behavior originally had for the deviant is ignored as a contributor to subsequent behavior. Although societal reaction may become a crucial factor in behavior, it is questionable that whatever purpose of reward the behavior first held is invariably replaced. For example, if a person first steals for thrills, do thrills fail to be a factor once societal reaction has taken its toll?[71]

Another problem with labeling involves the assumption that deviants are really normal—because we are all rule breakers. Thus, it overlooks the possibility that some persons are unable to cope with the pressures of their situation. Some people are dangerous. Individuals who are disadvantaged tend to be more angry, frustrated, and alienated than their more fortunate fellows. The result may be differences in quantity and quality of primary deviance.

This perspective also relieves the individual deviant from blame. The underdog is seen as victimized by the powerful labelers. Further, individuals enmeshed in the labeling process are so constrained by the forces of society that they are incapable of choice. Once again, McCaghy has put it well: "Although it is true that deviants may be pawns of the powerful, this does not mean that deviants are powerless to resist, to alter their behavior, or to acquire power themselves."[72]

Perhaps the most serious deficiency of labeling theory, though, is that it focuses on certain types of deviance but ignores others. The attention is directed at society's underdogs, which is good. But those forms of deviance emanating from the social structure or from the powerful are not considered a very serious omission. As Liazos has put it, the themes of labeling theory focus attention on those who have been successfully labeled as deviants ("nuts, sluts, and perverts"), the deviant subculture, and the self-fulfilling prophecy that perpetuates their deviant patterns.[73] While this is appropriate and necessary, it concentrates on the powerless. The impression is that deviance is an exclusive property of the poor in the slum, the minorities, and street gangs.

But what of the deviance of the powerful members of society and even society itself? Liazos has chronicled these for us.[74]

1. The unethical, illegal, and destructive actions found in the corporate world, such as robbery through price fixing, low wages, pollution, inferior and dangerous products, deception, and outright lies in advertising.
2. The covert institutional violence committed against the poor by the institutions of society: schools, hospitals, corporations, and the government.
3. The political manipulators who pass laws that protect the interests of the powerful and disadvantage the powerless.
4. The power of the powerful is used to deflect criticism, labeling, and punishment even when deserved.

In short, labeling overlooks the deviant qualities of the society and its powerful members. Although social structure should be central to sociologists, the labeling theorists have minimized its impact on deviance. Liazos has summarized the problem this way:

> We should banish the concept of "deviance" and speak of oppression, conflict, persecution, and suffering. By focusing on the dramatic forms, as we do now, we perpetuate most people's beliefs and impressions that such "deviance" is the basic cause of many of our troubles, that these people (criminals, drug addicts, political dissenters, and others) are the real "troublemakers"; and, necessarily, we neglect conditions of inequality, powerlessness, institutional violence, and so on, which lie at the bases of our tortured society.[75]

Another way deviance is explained—conflict theory—extends labeling theory by focusing on social structure, thereby overcoming the fundamental criticisms of Liazos and others.

Conflict
Theory

Why is certain behavior defined as deviant? The answer, according to conflict theorists, is that powerful economic interest groups are able to get laws passed and enforced that protect their interests.[76] We must begin, then, with the law.

Of all the requirements for a just system, the most fundamental is the foundation of nondiscriminatory laws. Many criminal laws are the result of a consensus among the public as to what kinds of behaviors are a menace and should be punished (for example, murder, rape, theft). The laws devised to make these acts illegal and the extent of punishment for violators are nondiscriminatory (although, as we have seen, the administration of these laws is discriminatory) since they do not single out a particular social category as the target.

There are laws, however, that discriminate because they result from special interests using their power to translate their interests into public policy.[77] These laws may be discriminatory because some segments of society (for example, the poor, minorities, youth, renters, debtors) rarely have access to the lawmaking process and therefore often find the laws unfairly aimed at them. Vagrancy, for example, is really a crime that only the poor can commit.[78] Perhaps a better example of this interest group approach to the law is to examine certain crimes of the Jim Crow days in the South. The majority created laws to keep the races separate and unequal. Burns has summarized the situation this way:

> In classical theories of democracy, the laws are supposed to reflect "the will of the people"—or at least of the majority. From the point of view of black people in this country, American law has been all too successful in this regard; for, in a country permeated by white racism, the legal system has been and continues to be racist in character.[79]

Let's examine a few specific examples of the historical bias of the law against blacks.[80]

□ *Item:* The law played a critical role in defining and sanctioning slavery. For instance, the law made slavery hereditary and a lifetime condition.
□ *Item:* The slave codes denied blacks the rights to bring law suits or testify against a white person.
□ *Item:* Jim Crow laws codified the customs and usages of segregation.
□ *Item:* After reconstruction, the grandfather clause, the literacy test, and the poll tax were all legal devices designed to block blacks from the polls.
□ *Item:* In the nineteenth century, the law reserved exclusively for white men the right to sit on juries.

Not only is the formation of the law political, but so, too, is the administration of the law.[81] This is because at every stage in the processing of criminals, choices are made by authorities based on personal bias, pressures from the powerful, and the constraints of the status quo. Some examples of the political character of law administration are: (1) the attempt by the powerful to coerce others to their view of morality, hence laws against homosexuality, pornography, drug usage, and gambling; (2) the powerful may exert pressure on the authorities to crack down on certain kinds of violators, especially those individuals and groups who are disruptive (protesters); (3) there may be political pressure exerted to keep certain crimes from public view (embezzlement, stock fraud, the Watergate coverup); (4) there may be pressure to protect the party in power, the elected officials, the police, CIA, and FBI; and (5) any effort to protect and preserve the status quo is a political act. Hartjen has summarized why the administration of justice is inherently political in the following quote:

> Unless one is willing to assume that law-enforcement agents can apply some magic formula to gauge the opinions of the public they serve, unless one is willing to assume that citizens unanimously agree on what laws are to be enforced and how enforcement is to be carried out, unless one is willing to assume that blacks, the poor, urbanites, and the young are actually more criminalistic than everyone else, it must be concluded, at least, that discriminatory law enforcement is a result of differences in power and that actual decisions as to which and whose behavior is criminal are expressions of this power. One need only ask himself why some laws, such as those protecting the consumer from fraud, go largely unenforced while the drug addict, for example, is pursued with a paranoiac passion.[82]

PANEL 8–2   Social Dilemmas and Critical Choices

The Politics of Pot

Until about 1965 public consensus supported strict enforcement of the marijuana laws. Marijuana was believed to be a dangerous drug associated with other forms of deviance, such as sexual promiscuity and crime. Even college students were virtually unanimous in their condemnation of marijuana smokers as deviants of the worst sort. But the social upheavals of the 1960s included experimentation with drugs and the questioning of society's mores. Rapid changes in attitudes and behavior, especially among the young and college educated, took place. Most significantly, the use of marijuana skyrocketed. In 1965 some 18,815 persons were arrested for violations of state and local marijuana laws, but this number rose to 420,700 in 1973. A survey of high school seniors in 1976 revealed that 53 percent had tried marijuana

(up 5 percent from the previous year) and 30 percent were regular users. By 1980 some 44 million Americans had tried marijuana and 22 million used the drug on a regular basis.

While behavior patterns have changed since the mid-1960s, the laws have essentially remained punitive to marijuana users. This gap between the law and behavior has had some interesting consequences: (1) many white, affluent, and middle-class parents saw their children treated as criminals; (2) many persons spent time in jail and were stigmatized as drug users, making reintegration into society hard and thereby creating a deviant drug culture (that is, repressive societal controls created secondary deviance); (3) there was a growing disrespect for the law, because the law was perceived by many of the users and their families as governmental interference in a private matter; and (4) insolence for the law was also encouraged by those who saw the crackdown on marijuana as discrimination, not based on pharmacological grounds but on political laws—laws that made marijuana use a crime but not the use of other drugs, such as alcohol and tobacco. Informed persons also realized that some drugs were illegal and others were not because of the particular distribution of power. Powerful interests promoted the use of tobacco and alcohol (corporations and the Department of Agriculture), whereas marijuana had only the support of isolated individuals (and underworld suppliers who benefited by its illegality).

Essentially, there are four options to solve this "problem." The first option would be to make the penalties harsh for the use and sale of marijuana. In this way, society could continue to impose its will to protect the health, safety, and morals of its citizens. A second possibility would be to decriminalize the smoking of pot. The penalty for usage would be reduced from a crime to a civil infraction akin to a traffic violation. This solution would recognize that persons likely will continue to use marijuana for recreational purposes

but that society mildly disapproves. Another alternative would be to legalize the sale and use of marijuana. Similar to the present sale and use of tobacco and alcohol, the state and local governments would permit over-the-counter purchases with some regulations, such as restricting the age of the buyer. Finally, there is the suggestion by libertarians that it is none of the government's business what drug people put into their bodies. Therefore, there should be no governmental interference in this private act.

Obviously, the decision to use drugs is your personal choice to make. But there are also the larger questions of society's role in the control of their usage. The political apparatus is slowly moving in the direction of greater liberalization of the drug laws. So, too, the people, especially middle-class young people, are becoming more tolerant of marijuana use. What can you do to clarify the discrepancy between law and society? Where are the boundaries to society's control of its citizens? Once these boundaries are established, should society be consistent for all types of drugs?

The fundamental assumption of the conflict approach to deviance is that the state is a political organization that is controlled by the ruling class for its advantage. This assumption has been summarized by Sykes:

At the heart of this orientation lies the perspective of a stratified society in which the operation of the criminal law is a means of controlling the poor (and members of minority groups) by those in power who use the legal apparatus to (1) impose their particular morality and standards of good behavior on the entire society; (2) protect their property and physical safety from the depredations of the have-nots, even though the cost may be high in terms of the legal rights of those it perceives as a threat; and (3) extend the definition of illegal or criminal behavior to encompass those who might threaten the status quo. . . . The coercive aspects of this arrangement are hidden—at least in part—by labeling those who challenge the system as "deviants" or "criminals" when such labels carry connotations of social pathology, psychiatric illness and so on. If these interpretative schemes are insufficient to arouse widespread distaste for the rule-breaker as "bad" or "tainted," official statistics can serve to create a sense of a more direct and personal danger in the form of a crime wave that will convince many people (including many of the people in the lower classes) that draconian measures are justified.[83]

The Collective Effort to Change Society: The Gay Rights Movement

The forces of society converge to restrict the behavior of individuals to those activities considered socially acceptable. But occasionally some who find these demands too confining organize to change society. One contemporary example is the Gay Rights Movement.

Experts agree that about 10 percent of adult Americans (about 17 million persons) are homosexuals. Although homosexuals have been accepted by some societies (e.g., ancient Greece and Rome), they have never been accepted in the United States. The erotic sexual attraction and behaviors between members of the same sex has always been severely sanctioned in our society. Formal laws forbidding such behaviors have been enacted. Employers, typically, have not knowingly hired homosexuals. Persons assumed to have such aberrent proclivities have been the objects of ridicule throughout society—in the media, on playgrounds, in factories, and in boardrooms. Because of discrimination against them, fear of social ostracism, and other forms of rejection even by friends and family, most homosexuals have felt it necessary to conceal their sexual preference.

These compelling fears have kept homosexuals for most periods of American history from organizing to change a repressive situation. A few homosexual organizations were formed (the first in 1925 and others in the 1950s) for mutual support, but a relatively few homosexuals were willing at these times to declare publicly their deviance from the norm of society.

The 1960s provided a better climate for change as youths, blacks, women, pacifists, and other groups questioned the norms and ideologies of the dominant society. This time clearly was one of heightened awareness among the oppressed of their oppression and of the possibility that through collective efforts they could change what seemed before as unchangeable.

The precipitating event for homosexual unity occurred at 3 A.M. on June 28, 1969 when police raided the Stonewall Inn of New York's Greenwich Village. But instead of dispersing, the 200 homosexual patrons, who had never collectively resisted the police before, threw objects at the police and set fire to the bar. The riot lasted 45 minutes, but it gave impetus to a number of collective efforts by gays to publicize police harassment of the gay community, job discrimination, and other indignities that homosexuals face. Gay liberation groups emerged in numerous cities and on university campuses. By 1980 over 4,000 homosexual organizations existed in the United States. Many neighborhoods in major cities became openly homosexual—most notably the Castro district in San Francisco, New Town in Chicago, and Greenwich Village in New York City. Gay organizations now include: churches, associations of professionals, health clinics, and networks of gay-owned businesses to supply the gay community's needs. The proliferation of these organizations for homosexuals has provided a supportive climate allowing many of them to "come out of the closet."

The increased numbers of "public" homosexuals have provided the political base for changing the various forms of oppression that homosexuals experience. A Gay Media Task Force promotes accurate and positive images of gays in television, films, and advertising; a Gay Rights National Lobby promotes favorable legislation; and a National Gay Task Force serves to further gay interests by attacking the minority group status of homosexuals in a variety of political and ideological arenas.

The positive results of these political activities, although limited, have been encouraging to the gay community. Since 1983, Wisconsin and most of the larger cities in the United States have enacted gay-rights laws. More than one-half of the states have repealed their sodomy statutes (in Colonial times sodomy was a crime punishable by death). The Civil Service Reform Act of 1978 prohibits federal agencies from discriminating against gays in employment practices. And, although still rare, a few avowed homosexuals have been elected to public office.

The successes of gay-rights political activists have not yet achieved their ultimate goal—the full acceptance of homosexuality as an alternative lifestyle. Homosexuals are still not allowed to marry. Discrimination in housing and jobs still occurs. Polls show that only about one-third of Americans consider it an acceptable lifestyle. And gay-rights movements have met fierce resistance by fundamentalist religious groups such as the Moral Majority who believe homosexuality to be morally offensive and dangerous. But clearly during the past 15 years, the collective efforts of homosexuals have had an enormous and positive impact for homosexuals.

Thus, the focus of the conflict perspective is on the political and economic setting in society. The power of certain interests determines what gets defined as deviance (and who, then, is a deviant), and how this "problem" is to be solved. Since the powerful benefit from the status quo, efforts to reform society are vigorously thwarted by them. The solution, from the conflict theorists, however, requires not only reform of society but its radical transformation. It is the structure of society that is the problem. The radical therapists, for example, assume that society is the root cause of all mental suffering.[84] Mental illness in this view is really a process that an individual is going through in a relationship to his environment. The depressed person, the chronic alcoholic, and the schizophrenic are each trying to survive in a mad world. Rather than focusing on the individual and his adjustment (although this may be necessary in the short term), which validates and reinforces the established system, the radical therapist argues that the only real and lasting form of therapy is a radical transformation of society.

The strengths of the conflict perspective on deviance are[85]: (1) its emphasis on the relationship between political order and nonconformity; (2) the understanding that the most powerful groups use the political order to protect their interests; (3) that it emphasizes how the system of justice is unjust, and that the distribution of rewards in society is skewed; and (4) the realization that the institutional framework of society is the source of so many social problems (for example, racism, sexism, pollution, unequal distribution of health care, poverty, and economic cycles). There are some problems with this perspective, however. First, there is the tendency to assume a conspiracy by the well-to-do. Because the empirical evidence is overwhelming that the poor, the uneducated, and the members of minority groups are singled out for the deviant label, some persons make the too facile imputation of motive.

Second, the answer of the conflict theorists is too utopian. The following quotation by Quinney is representative of this naivete:

The alternative to the contradictions of capitalism is a truly democratic society, a socialist society in which human beings no longer suffer the alienation inherent in capitalism. When there is no longer the need for one class to dominate another, when there is no longer the need for a legal system to secure the interests of a capitalist ruling class, then there will no longer be the need for crime.[86]

But, would crime and other forms of deviance disappear under such a socialist system? This, like Marx's final stage of history, is a statement of faith rather than one based on proof.

SUMMARY

The preceding descriptions of the theories on the causes of deviance indicate clearly their social nature. To recapitulate, they are social because they involve: (1) the violation of societal norms, values, and expectations; (2) the perceptions of the citizenry which are shaped, of course, by the way they have been socialized; (3) the labeling process, whereby society designates certain persons as deviants; (4) the role of the powerful in all these processes; and (5) the structure of society itself as a source of human suffering.

Despite the social nature of deviance, however, there is a very strong tendency for individuals (laypeople, police personnel, judges, lawmakers, and social scientists alike) to perceive social problems and prescribe remedies from a psychological perspective. The individual is blamed for being poor, not the maldistribution of wealth and other socially perpetuated disadvantages which blight many families generation after generation. The black is blamed for his or her aggressive behavior, not the limits placed on social mobility for blacks by the social system. Dropouts are blamed for leaving school prematurely, not the educational system that fails to meet their needs. This type of explanation helps to explain the reluctance by persons in authority to provide adequate welfare, health care, and compensatory programs to help the disadvantaged. This common tendency of individuals to focus on the deviant rather than the system that produces deviants has also been true of American social scientists analyzing social problems. Although one might logically expect psychologists to have such a bias, sociologists, because their unit of analysis is society, should logically focus on institutions rather than the deviant. Since this has not been the case, let us examine more closely the theoretical perspectives within sociology to determine why sociology has tended to view social problems as a result of individual pathologies rather than the structure of society.

The two contrasting theoretical perspectives in sociology—the order model (functionalism) and the conflict model—constrain their adherents to view the causes, consequences, and remedies of social problems in opposing ways (see Table 8–2).

The order perspective focuses on deviants themselves. This approach (which has been the conventional way of studying social problems) asks: Who are the deviants? What are their social and psychological backgrounds? With whom do they associate? Deviants somehow do not conform to the standards of the dominant group; they are assumed to be out of phase with conventional behavior. This is believed to occur most often as a result of

TABLE 8–2   Assumptions of the Order and Conflict Models about Deviance[87]

Order model	Conflict model
Who is deviant?	
Those who break the rules of society.	Those who break the rules but also those who make the rules. Deviance is created by the powerful, who make the rules. Enactment and enforcement of these rules are used by the powerful to control potentially dissident groups and to maintain their own interests at the expense of those being ruled.
The legitimacy of deviance:	
Deviance is illegitimate, by definition.	Deviance of rule breakers can be legitimate because the rules are arbitrarily made and reflect a class bias. Deviance is also necessary to change an unjust society.
The causes of deviance:	
People are deviant because they have not been socialized to accept and obey the customs of society.	Deviance is caused by society, which makes the rules, the violation of which constitutes deviance. The inequities of society generate the behavior that the powerful label as deviant.
The solutions for deviance:	
Control by punishment and rehabilitation of deviant individuals (therapy, behavior modification, incarceration).	Restructure society (eliminate inequities, provide adequately for the needs of all members, a fair system of justice, laws that reflect the interest of all groups).

inadequate socialization. In other words, deviants have not internalized the norms and values of society because they are either brought up in an environment of conflicting value systems (as are children of immigrants or the poor in a middle-class school) or are under the influence of a deviant subculture such as a gang. Since the order theorist uses the prevailing standards to define and label deviants, the existing practices and structures of society are accepted implicitly. The remedy is to rehabilitate the deviants so that they conform to the societal norms.

The conflict theorist takes a quite different approach to social problems. The adherents of this perspective criticize order theorists for "blaming the victim." To focus on the individual deviant is to locate the symptom, not the disease. Individual deviants are a manifestation of a failure of society to meet the needs of individuals. The sources of crime, poverty, drug addiction, and racism are found in the laws, the customs, the quality of life, the distribution of wealth and power, and in the accepted practices of schools, governmental units, and corporations. The established system, in this view, is not "sacred." Since it is the primary source of social problems, it, not the individual deviant, must be restructured.

Since this is a text on society, we have emphasized and will continue to emphasize the conflict approach. The insights of this approach will be clarified further in the remainder of this book as we examine the structure and consequences of social inequality in the next five chapters, followed by four chapters describing the positive and negative effects of institutions.

CHAPTER REVIEW

1. Deviance is behavior that violates the laws and expectations of a group. This means that deviance is not a property inherent in a behavior but a property conferred upon that behavior by others. In short, deviance is socially created.

2. What is deviant varies from society to society and within a society the same behavior may be interpreted differently as it is done by different categories of persons.

3. The norms of the majority determine what behaviors will be considered deviant.

4. Order theorists point out that deviant behavior has positive consequences for society because it gives the nondeviants a sense of solidarity and it reaffirms the importance of society's rules.

5. Conflict theorists argue that all views of rule violations have political implications. Punishment of deviants reflects a conservative bias by legitimating the norms and the current distribution of power. Support of the deviant behavior is also political because it rejects the legitimacy of those in power and their rules.

6. There are several traditional theories for the causes of deviance that assume the source as a fatal flaw in certain people. These are theories that focus on physical or psychological reasons for deviant behavior.

7. "Kinds-of-people" explanations for deviance also apply to some theories by sociologists. One theory argues that crime results from the conditions of city life. Another places the blame on the influences of peers. A third focuses on the propensity of the poor to be deviants because of the gap between the goal of success and the lack of the means for these people to attain it. Finally, some have argued that lower-class culture is responsible.

8. These "kinds-of-people" theories have been criticized for blaming the victim. Because they blame the victim, the society (government, system of justice, education) is freed from blame. Because the established order is protected from criticism, necessary social change is thwarted.

9. An alternative to person-blame theories is labeling theory. This approach argues that while most people break the rules on occasion, the crucial factor in establishing a deviant career is the successful application of the label "deviant."

10. Who gets labeled as a deviant is not a matter of luck but the result of a systematic societal bias against the powerless.

11. Primary deviance is the rule breaking that occurs prior to labeling. Secondary deviance is that behavior resulting from the labeling process.

12. Labeling theorists argue that because deviants are not much different from nondeviants, the problem lies in organizations that label. Thus, these organizations should: (a) leave the deviants alone whenever possible; and (b) apply justice fairly when the legal approach is required.

13. Labeling theory has been criticized because it: (a) disregards undetected deviance; (b) assumes that deviants are really normal because we are all rule-breakers; (c) relieves the individual from blame; and (d) focuses on certain types of deviance but ignores deviance by the powerful.

14. Conflict theory focuses on social structure as the source of deviance. There is an historical bias in the law that favors the powerful. The administration of justice is also biased. In short, the state is a political organization controlled by the ruling class for its own advantage. The power of powerful interests in society determines what and who is deviant.

15. From the conflict perspective the only real and lasting solution to deviance is the radical transformation of society.

FOR FURTHER STUDY

Howard S. Becker, *The Outsiders: Studies in the Sociology of Deviance*, 2nd ed. (New York: Free Press, 1973).

Kai Erikson, *Wayward Puritans: A Study in the Sociology of Deviance* (New York: John Wiley, 1966).

Erving Goffman, *Stigma: Notes on the Management of Spoiled Identity* (Englewood Cliffs, N.J.: Prentice-Hall, 1963).

Clayton Hartjen, *Crime and Criminalization*, 2nd ed. (New York: Praeger, 1978).

Edwin M. Lemert, *Human Deviance, Social Problems, and Social Control*, 2nd ed. (Englewood Cliffs, N.J.: Prentice-Hall, 1972).

Charles H. McCaghy, *Deviant Behavior: Crime, Conflict, and Interest Groups* (New York: Macmillan, 1976).

Gwynn Nettler, *Explaining Crime*, 3rd ed. (New York: McGraw-Hill, 1984).

Richard Quinney, *The Social Reality of Crime* (Boston: Little, Brown, 1970).

Jeffrey H. Reiman, *The Rich Get Richer and the Poor Get Prison: Ideology, Class, and Criminal Justice* (New York: John Wiley & Sons, 1979).

Earl Rubington and Martin S. Weinberg, *The Study of Social Problems: Five Perspectives*, rev. ed. (New York: Oxford University Press, 1977).

William Ryan, *Blaming the Victim*, rev. ed. (New York: Vintage Books, 1976).

Edwin M. Schur, *The Politics of Deviance* (Englewood Cliffs, N.J.: Prentice-Hall, 1980).

Edwin M. Schur, *Interpreting Deviance: A Sociological Introduction* (New York: Harper & Row, 1979).

David R. Simon and D. Stanley Eitzen, *Elite Deviance* (Boston: Allyn and Bacon, 1982).

Steven Vago, *Law and Society* (Englewood Cliffs, N.J.: Prentice-Hall, 1981).

NOTES AND REFERENCES

1. "Shoplifting Soars—and Merchants Strike Back," *U.S. News & World Report* (December 3, 1979), pp. 71–72; Associated Press release (August 25, 1980); and Pat Cloud, "Shoplifting Deterrents Cut Deeply into Profit Margins," Colorado State University *Collegian* (October 9, 1980), p. 4.

2. "The Underground Economy," *U.S. News & World Report* (October 22, 1979), pp. 49–56; and Terri Schultz, "How Millions Cheat (and Beat) the IRS," *Dallas Times Herald* (March 30, 1980), pp. 1M, 6M.

3. Cited in Robert L. Jackson, "Tax-Cheating Loss," *The Denver Post* (March 18, 1982), pp. 1A, 7A.

4. Ward Sinclair, "Harvest Highs," *Denver Post* (April 5, 1984), pp. 1A, 25A.

5. Reported in "Ripoffs—New American Way of Life," *U.S. News & World Report* (May 31, 1976), p. 30.

6. Howard S. Becker, *The Outsiders: Studies in the Sociology of Deviance* (New York: Free Press, 1963), pp. 8–9.

7. Kai T. Erikson, *Wayward Puritans: A Study in the Sociology of Deviance* (New York: John Wiley, 1966), p. 6.

8. Deena Weinstein and Michael Weinstein, *Living Sociology: A Critical Introduction* (New York: David McKay, 1974), p. 271.

9. Michael Mewshaw, "Irrational Behavior or Evangelical Zeal?" *The Chronicle of Higher Education*, (October 18, 1976), p. 32.

10. Erikson, *Wayward Puritans*, pp. 5–6.

11. See Emile Durkheim, *The Rules of Sociological Method*, S. A. Solovay and J. H. Mueller, trans. (Glencoe, Ill.: Free Press, 1958); and Emile Durkheim, *The Division of Labor in Society*, George Simpson, trans. (Glencoe, Ill.: Free Press, 1960); and Robert A. Dentler and Kai T. Erikson, "The Functions of Deviance in Groups," *Social Problems* 7 (Fall, 1959), pp. 98–107.

12. Durkheim, *The Division of Labor in Society*, p. 102.

13. Earl Rubington and Martin S. Weinberg, *Deviance: The Interactionist Perspective*, 2nd ed. (New York: Macmillan, 1973), p. 1.

14. See Becker, *Outsiders*, p. 4; Weinstein and Weinstein, *Living Sociology*, p. 273; and

Robert Ross and Graham L. Staines, "The Politics of Analyzing Social Problems," *Social Problems* 20 (Summer, 1972), pp. 18–40.

15. Edwin M. Schur, *The Politics of Deviance* (Englewood Cliffs, N.J.: Prentice-Hall, 1980), p. xi.

16. The section that follows is dependent on the organization and insights of Edwin M. Schur, *Radical Non-intervention: Rethinking the Delinquency Problem* (Englewood Cliffs, N.J.: Prentice-Hall (Spectrum Books), 1973).

17. For a summary of the biological and psychological theories on deviance, see Charles H. McCaghy, *Deviant Behavior: Crime, Conflict, and Interest Groups* (New York: Macmillan, 1976), pp. 5–40; Sue Titus Reid, *Crime and Criminology* (Hinsdale, Ill.: Dryden Press, 1976), pp. 130–171; and Albert K. Cohen, *Deviance and Control* (Englewood Cliffs, N.J.: Prentice-Hall, 1966), pp. 48–62. For a formal review of the sociological theories of deviance, see summaries provided by: Nanette J. Davis, *Sociological Construction of Deviance* (Dubuque, Iowa: Wm. C. Brown, 1975); McCaghy, *Deviant Behavior*; Earl Rubington and Martin S. Weinberg, *The Study of Social Problems: Five Perspectives* (New York: Oxford University Press, 1971); and Charles E. Frazier, *Theoretical Approaches to Deviance: An Evaluation* (Columbus, Ohio: Charles E. Merrill, 1976).

18. Chester D. Poremba, "Learning Disabilities, Youth and Delinquency: Programs for Intervention," in *Progress in Learning Disabilities*, Vol. III, Helmer R. Myklebust, ed. (New York: Grune & Stratton, 1975), pp. 123–149; Herb Stoenner, "Youth Crime, Learning Disability Found 90% Linked," *Denver Post*, April 9, 1974, p. D1; and Charles A. Murray, *The Link between Learning Disabilities and Juvenile Delinquency* (Washington, D.C.: U.S. Department of Justice, 1976).

19. Cohen, *Deviance and Control*, pp. 41–45.

20. Edwin Powers and Helen Witmer, *An Experiment in the Prevention of Delinquency* (New York: Columbia University Press, 1951).

21. David Matza, *Delinquency and Drift* (New York: John Wiley, 1964), p. 17.

22. Two representative sources for this approach are: Louis Wirth, "Urbanism as a Way of Life," *American Journal of Sociology* 44 (July, 1938), pp. 1–24; and Clifford R. Shaw and Henry D. McKay, *Juvenile Delinquency and Urban Areas* (Chicago: University of Chicago Press, 1942).

23. Milton L. Barron, "The Crimogenic Society: Social Values and Deviance," *Current Perspectives on Criminal Behavior*, Abraham S. Blumberg, ed. (New York: Alfred A. Knopf, 1974), p. 81.

24. Clayton A. Hartjen, *Crime and Criminalization* (New York: Praeger, 1974), p. 175. Excerpts from this work are reprinted by permission of Praeger Publishers, a division of Holt, Rinehart and Winston, © 1974 by Praeger Publishers.

25. Edwin H. Sutherland and Donald R. Cressey, *Principles of Criminology*, 7th ed. (Philadelphia: J. B. Lippincott, 1966), pp. 81–82.

26. Clayton A. Hartjen, *Crime and Criminalization*, p. 51.

27. Robert K. Merton, *Social Theory and Social Structure*, rev. ed. (Glencoe, Ill.: Free Press, 1957), pp. 131–160.

28. Reece McGee, *Points of Departure: Basic Concepts in Sociology* (Hinsdale, Ill.: Dryden Press, 1975), pp. 211–212.

29. Jack Doyle and Paul T. Schindler, "The Incoherent Society," paper presented at the meetings of the American Sociological Association, Montreal, August 25–29, 1974, p. 2.

30. See, especially, Walter B. Miller, "Lower Class Culture as a Generating Milieu of Gang Delinquency," *Journal of Social Issues* 14 (No. 3, 1958), pp. 5–19; and Edward C. Banfield, *The Unheavenly City Revisited* (Boston: Little, Brown, 1974), especially pp. 179–210.

31. For other criticisms of this approach, see Gwynn Nettler, *Explaining Crime* (New York: McGraw-Hill, 1974), pp. 150–153.

32. William Ryan, *Blaming the Victim* (New York: Random House (Vintage Books), 1972), p. 7.

33. Many of the insights that follow come from William Ryan, *Blaming the Victim* (New York: Pantheon Books, 1971); and two articles by Nathan Caplan and Stephen D. Nelson: "On Being Useful: The Nature and Consequences of Psychological Research on Social Problems," *American Psychologist* 28 (March, 1973), pp. 199–211; and "Who's to Blame?" *Psychology Today* 8 (November, 1974), pp. 99–104.

34. "Illiteracy: Invitation to Failure," editorial in *Kansas City Times*, January 26, 1974.

35. Quoted in *The New York Times*, March 11, 1973.

36. Edwin A. Roberts, Jr., ". . . It Is Dangerous for the Nation to Project a Tolerant Attitude Toward the Criminal," *The National Observer*, March 24, 1973.

37. Tom Wicker, "Nixon's Rhetoric on Crime Ignores the Real Problem," *Kansas City Times*, March 14, 1973.

38. Ryan, *Blaming the Victim*, pp. 10–18.

39. The following enumeration of the consequences of the person-blame model are taken primarily from Caplan and Nelson, "On Being Useful," and Caplan and Nelson, "Who's to Blame?"

40. Caplan and Nelson, "Who's to Blame?" p. 104.

41. Lee Stillwell, "Revenue Sharing Fails to Aid Poor, Study Says," *Rocky Mountain News*, December 11, 1974, p. 36.

42. Caplan and Nelson, "On Being Useful," p. 209.

43. For a critique of the traditional sociological assumptions of such pathology by deviants, see C. Wright Mills, "The Professional Ideology of Social Pathologists," *American Journal of Sociology* 49 (September, 1942), pp. 165–180.

44. James S. Wallerstein and Clement J. Wyle, "Our Law-Abiding Law Breakers," *Probation* 22 (April, 1947), pp. 107–112.

45. See F. Ivan Nye, James F. Short, Jr., and Virgil J. Olson, "Socioeconomic Status and Delinquent Behavior," *American Journal of Sociology* 63 (January, 1958), pp. 381–389; Ronald I. Akers, "Socioeconomic Status and Delinquent Behavior: A Retest," *Journal of Research and Delinquency* 10 (January, 1964), pp. 38–46; Harwin L. Voss, "Socioeconomic Status and Reported Delinquent Behavior," *Social Problems* 13 (Winter,

1966), pp. 314–324; and Maynard L. Erickson and LaMar T. Empey, "Class Position, Peers, and Delinquency," *Sociology and Social Research* 49 (April, 1965), pp. 268–282.

46. Travis Hirschi, *Causes of Delinquency* (Berkeley, Calif.: University of California Press, 1969), p. 66.

47. See August B. Hollingshead and Frederick C. Redlich, *Social Class and Mental Illness* (New York: John Wiley, 1958); and Jerome K. Myers and Lee L. Bean, *A Decade Later: A Follow-Up of Social Class and Mental Illness* (New York: John Wiley, 1968).

48. Becker, *Outsiders*, p. 14.

49. David Janzen, "Love 'em and Leave 'em Alone," *The Mennonite*, June 11, 1974, p. 390. See also William J. Chambliss, "The Saints and the Roughnecks," *Society* 11 (November/December, 1973), pp. 24–31.

50. For a complete discussion of the labeling approach to deviance, see Edwin M. Schur, *Labeling Deviant Behavior: Its Sociological Implications* (New York: Harper & Row, 1971).

51. William J. Chambliss, *Crime and the Legal Process* (New York: McGraw-Hill, 1969), p. 86.

52. Theodore G. Chiricos, Philip D. Jackson, and Gordon P. Waldo, "Inequality in the Imposition of the Criminal Label," *Social Problems* 19 (Spring, 1972), pp. 553–572. These data focus on the poor and the blacks. Similar results are found when examining the differential treatment of other minority groups in the criminal justice system. One study, for example, of native Americans and the system of justice substantiates the finding comparing whites and blacks; see Edwin L. Hall and Albert A. Simkus, "Inequality in the Types of Sentences Received by Native Americans and Whites," *Criminology* 13 (August, 1975), pp. 199–222.

53. Ramsey Clark, *Crime in America: Observations on Its Nature, Causes, Prevention and Control* (New York: Simon and Schuster, 1970), p. 335. See also Marvin E. Wolfgang and Marc Riedel, "Race, Judicial Discretion and the Death Penalty," *The Annals* 477 (May, 1973), pp. 119–133; and William J. Bowers, *Executions in America* (Lexington, Mass.: Lexington Books, 1974).

54. Marvin E. Wolfgang, Arlene Kelly, and Hans C. Nolde, "Comparisons of the Executed and the Commuted Among Admissions to Death Row," *Journal of Criminal Law, Criminology and Police Science* 53 (September, 1962), p. 311.

55. *The Challenge of Crime in a Free Society*, A Report by the President's Commission on Law Enforcement and Administration of Justice (New York: Avon Books, 1968), pp. 80–429.

56. David M. Petersen and Paul C. Friday, "Early Release from Incarceration: Race as a Factor in the Use of 'Shock Probation,'" *The Journal of Criminal Law and Criminology* 66 (March, 1975), pp. 79–87.

57. See Martin R. Haskell and Lewis Yablonsky, *Crime and Delinquency*, 2nd ed. (Chicago: Rand McNally, 1974), pp. 629–630. See also Charles E. Reasons, "The Politicizing of Crime, the Criminal, and the Criminologist," *The Journal of Criminal Law and Criminology* 64 (December, 1973), pp. 471–477.

58. See Campbell et al., *Law and Order Reconsidered*, pp. 628–637; Ronald L. Goldfarb, "American Prisons: Self-Defeating Concrete," *Psychology Today* 7 (January, 1974), pp. 20–24, 85–90; Haskell and Yablonsky, *Crime and Delinquency*, pp. 622–624; and Gresham Sykes, *The Society of Captives* (Princeton, N.J.: Princeton University Press, 1958), pp. 65–78.

59. "The Ex-Con's Unhappy Lot," *Newsweek*, February 25, 1974, pp. 84–85.

60. Edwin M. Lemert, *Social Pathology: A Systematic Approach to the Theory of Sociopathic Behavior* (New York: McGraw-Hill, 1951), pp. 75–78.

61. For an empirical verification of this assertion, see Richard D. Schwartz and Jerome H. Skolnick, "Two Studies of Legal Stigma," *Social Problems* 10 (Fall, 1962), pp. 133–138.

62. Nettler, *Explaining Crime*, p. 203.

63. See Thomas J. Scheff, *Mentally Ill* (Chicago: Aldine, 1966); and M. Balint, *The Doctor, His Patient, and the Illness* (New York: International Universities Press, 1957).

64. Ken Kesey, *One Flew Over the Cuckoo's Nest* (New York: Signet Books, 1962).

65. Stephen Cole, *The Sociological Orientation:*

An Introduction to Sociology (Chicago: Rand McNally, 1975), pp. 141–142. See also Eli Glogow, "The 'Bad Patient' Gets Better Quicker," Social Policy 4 (November/December, 1973), pp. 72–76.

66. Edwin M. Lemert, Human Deviance, Social Problems and Social Control (Englewood Cliffs, N.J.: Prentice-Hall, 1967), pp. 42–43.

67. Hartjen, Crime and Criminalization, pp. 120–121.

68. Schur, Radical Non-intervention, pp. 117–173.

69. Ibid., pp. 154–155. Reprinted by permission of Prentice-Hall, Inc., Englewood Cliffs, N.J.; © 1973.

70. For critiques of labeling theory, see Carol A. B. Warren and John M. Johnson, "A Critique of Labeling Theory from the Phenomenological Perspective," in Theoretical Perspectives on Deviance, Jack D. Douglas and Robert Scott, eds. (New York: Basic Books, 1973); Jack P. Gibbs, "Conceptions of Deviant Behavior: the Old and the New," Pacific Sociological Review 9 (Spring, 1966), pp. 9–14; Davis, Sociological Constructions of Deviance, pp. 164–191; and, most important, Alexander Liazos, "The Poverty of the Sociology of Deviance: Nuts, Sluts, and Preverts," Social Problems 20 (Summer, 1972), pp. 103–120.

71. McCaghy, Deviant Behavior, p. 87.

72. Ibid., p. 88.

73. Liazos, "The Poverty of the Sociology of Deviance."

74. Ibid.

75. Ibid., p. 119.

76. Richard Quinney, The Social Reality of Crime (Boston: Little, Brown, 1970); Richard Quinney, Critique of Legal Order: Crime Control in a Capitalist Society (Boston: Little, Brown, 1974).

77. The following is taken largely from Richard Quinney, The Social Reality of Crime, pp. 29–97.

78. For a historical analysis of the role of powerful interest groups in the formation of laws concerning activities on Sunday, theft, antitrust, adulterated food, sex, drunkenness, drugs, and vagrancy, see Quinney, The Social Reality of Crime, pp. 65–97; and Hartjen, Crime and Criminalization, pp. 21–33.

79. Haywood Burns, "Black People and the Tyranny of American Law," The Annals 407 (May, 1973), p. 157.

80. The following examples are taken from Burns, "Black People and the Tyranny of American Law," pp. 156–166.

81. For discussions of the political nature of the system of justice, see George F. Cole, Politics and the Administration of Justice (Beverly Hills, Calif.: Sage Publications, 1973).

82. Hartjen, Crime and Criminalization, p. 11.

83. Gresham M. Sykes, "Criminology: The Rise of Critical Criminology," The Journal of Criminal Law and Criminology 65 (June, 1974), p. 210.

84. See Walt Anderson, "Breaking Out of the Establishment Vise," Human Behavior 2 (December, 1973), pp. 10–18; and Jerome Agel, The Radical Therapist (New York: Ballantine Books, 1971).

85. See Sykes, "Criminology," and Reid, Crime and Criminology, pp. 203–205.

86. Richard Quinney, Criminal Justice in America (Boston: Little, Brown, 1974), p. 25.

87. See Nanette J. Davis, Sociological Constructions of Deviance: Perspectives and Issues in the Field (Dubuque, Iowa: Wm. C. Brown, 1975), pp. 192–244; Gresham M. Sykes, "Criminology: The Rise of Critical Criminology," The Journal of Criminal Law and Criminology 65 (June, 1974), pp. 206–213; John Horton, "Order and Conflict Theories of Social Problems as Competing Ideologies," American Journal of Sociology 71 (May, 1966), pp. 701–713; Jerome H. Skolnick and Elliott Currie, "Approaches to Social Problems," in Crisis in American Institutions, Jerome H. Skolnick and Elliott Currie, eds. (Boston: Little, Brown, 1970), pp. 1–16; William J. Chambliss, Functional and Conflict Theories of Crime, Module 17 (New York: MSS Modular Publications, 1974), pp. 1–23; and William J. Chambliss, "Functional and Conflict Theories of Crime: The Heritage of Emile Durkheim and Karl Marx," in Whose Law, What Order? A Conflict Approach to Criminology, William J. Chambliss and Milton Mankoff, eds. (New York: John Wiley & Sons, 1976), pp. 1–28.

Part 3

Social Inequality

9

The American System

of

Social Stratification

A sample of the income and wealth extremes found in the United States includes:

- In 1983 the ZIP code area with the highest median household income ($81,926) was 90077—an area in southern Los Angeles that includes swanky Bel Air. The ZIP code area with the lowest median household income ($5,833) was 30313—in the southwest section of Atlanta.[1]
- In 1982 average annual income for production workers was $17,200 while chief executive officers in the Forbes 500 companies enjoyed a median income of $400,000.[2]
- The 1982 average income for physicians was about $110,000 compared to registered nurses who averaged $19,318.[3]
- In 1980, 4,112 family units had incomes of over $1 million while 3,736,000 family units had incomes of under $5,000.[4]

□ In 1980 the wealthiest 20 percent of the population had an aggregate income of $601,472,768,000 (41.6 percent of the total U.S. income) while the poorest 20 percent had an aggregate income of $73,738,248,000 (5.1 percent of the total U.S. income).[5]

□ In 1983 *Forbes* magazine reported that 400 individuals had wealth in excess of $125 million, 15 members of this group had fortunes above $1 billion.[6] In stark contrast were the 31.8 million individuals living below the poverty line in that year.

Inequality is a fact of social life. All known societies have some system of ranking individuals and groups along a superiority–inferiority scale. The thrust of this chapter is that the particular placement of individuals in the ranking system makes a significant difference—a difference in lifestyle, behavior, attitude, and self-images.

MAJOR CONCEPTS, ASSUMPTIONS, AND THEORIES

People differ in age, physical attributes, and in what they do for a living. The process of categorizing persons by age, height, occupation, or whatever is called **social differentiation.** When people are ranked in a vertical arrangement (hierarchy) that differentiates them as superior or inferior, we have **social stratification.** The key difference between differentiation and stratification is that the process of ranking or evaluation occurs only in the latter. What is ranked and how it is ranked are dependent upon the values of the society.

Social stratification refers, in essence, to structured social inequality. The term "structured" refers to stratification being socially patterned.[7] This implies that inequalities are not caused by biological differences (for example, sex or race). Biological traits do not become relevant in patterns of social superiority or inferiority until they are socially recognized and given importance by being incorporated into the beliefs, attitudes, and values of the people in the society. Americans, for example, tend to believe that sexual and racial characteristics make a difference—therefore they do.

The social patterning of stratification is also found in the distribution of rewards in any community or society, since that distribution is governed by social norms. In American society few individuals seriously question the income differential between medical doctors and primary school teachers because the norms and values of society dictate that such inequalities are just.

Patterned behavior is also achieved through the socialization process. Each generation is taught the norms and values of the society and of its social class. The children of slaves and the children of the ruling family in a society are each taught the behavior "proper" for persons of their station in life.

Finally, the system of stratification is always connected with other aspects of the society. The existing stratification arrangements are affected by and have effects upon such matters as politics, marriage and the family, economics, education, and religion.

Harold Kerbo has summarized what is meant by social stratification:

> *Social stratification* means that inequality has been hardened or *institutionalized*, and there is a *system of social relationships* that determines who gets what, and why. When we say *institutionalized* we mean that a system of layered hierarchy has been established. People have come to expect that individuals and groups with certain positions will be able to demand more influence and respect and accumulate a greater share of goods and services. Such inequality may or may not be accepted equally by a majority in the society, but it is recognized as the way things are.[8]

An individual's position (**social status**) in the social stratification system is determined by the degree to which he or she possesses those qualities highly valued by the society. The important criteria by which people are evaluated and ranked in the United States are (1) family background, which includes the status of the preceding generations of one's family, their ethnic and racial background, and religious affiliation; (2) the amount and type of an individual's wealth; (3) personal qualities, such as sex, age, beauty, and intelligence; (4) personal achievements, such as amount of education, type of job, and job performance; and (5) the amount of power and authority of the individual.

These criteria for evaluation can be viewed as either ascribed or achieved characteristics. **Ascribed characteristics** befall individuals regardless of their efforts. Individuals cannot control their age, sex, their race, or their family background—therefore, these characteristics are ascribed. **Achieved characteristics,** on the other hand, are those attained by individuals because of their own efforts, such as amount of education and type of job.* Ascribed characteristics determine an individual's **ascribed status,** while achieved characteristics determine his or her **achieved status.** An individual's **social rank** is determined by both types of status.

When a number of persons occupy the same relative economic rank in the stratification system, they form a **social class.** Persons of similar status form a **status group.** The members of a status group view one another as social equals. Interaction tends to occur most frequently among status equals. Although social classes and status groups often overlap, they may not— leading to the phenomenon of status inconsistency.

The rigidity of the stratification system varies from society to society. The key indicator of rigidity is the extent to which ascribed characteristics "lock" the individual into a social class or status group. The more that

---

*This distinction between ascribed and achieved characteristics is a somewhat artificial one made for analytical purposes, since ascribed characteristics can and do have an effect upon educational attainment, type of job, and the other achieved characteristics.

achieved characteristics determine class or status position, the more open the system—the more movement is possible from one rank to another (**social mobility**).

As we examine inequality in American society, let us keep in mind the alternative ways order and conflict theorists view this phenomenon. The position of the order theorists is basically supportive of inequality, since the unequal distribution of rewards is assumed to be not only inevitable but necessary. Conflict theorists, on the other hand, tend to denounce the distributive system as basically unjust, unnecessary, and the source of many social problems.

Adherents of the order model begin with the fact that social inequality is a ubiquitous and apparently unavoidable phenomenon. They reason that inequality must, therefore, serve a useful function for society. The argument, as presented in the classic statement by Davis and Moore, is as follows:[9] The smooth functioning of society requires that various tasks be accomplished through a division of labor. There is a universal problem, then, of allocation— of getting the most important tasks done by the most talented people. Some jobs are more important for societal survival than others (typically persons involved in decision making, medicine, religion, teaching, and the military). The societal problem is how to get the most talented people motivated to go through the required long periods of training and to do these important tasks well. The universally found answer, according to Davis and Moore, is differential rewards. Society must provide suitable rewards (money, prestige, and power) to induce individuals to fill these positions. The rewards must, it is argued, be distributed unevenly to various positions because the positions are not equally pleasant or equally important. Thus, a differential reward system guarantees that the important societal functions are fulfilled, thereby ensuring the maintenance of society. In this way, differential ranks actually serve to unify society (functional integration through a division of labor and through the socialization of persons to accept their positions in the system). Although there probably is some truth to this argument, the analyst of American society must also ask: Is inequality primarily integrative or divisive? Is it necessary? Must the poor always be with us?[10]

Conflict theorists view stratification in a wholly different manner. Rather than accepting stratification as a source of societal integration, the conflict perspective assumes it to be a major source of discord and coercion. It is a source of discord because the "have-nots" will not be satisfied but rather resentful of their lowly position and lack of rewards. Coercion results from stratification as the powerful (who are coincidentally the wealthy) prey on the weak. The powerful make and enforce the laws, determine the distribution of rewards, and through control of the media and education make their value system paramount.

A major contention of the conflict theorists is that most oppressed peoples accept their deprivation because of **false consciousness**.[11] This concept refers to the acceptance of an untrue belief that works to one's disadvantage. The argument is that people adhere to beliefs damaging to their interests because of the power of the socialization process in society. The working classes and the poor in the United States, for example, tend to accept their lack of monetary rewards, power, and prestige because they believe that the system is truly meritocratic—and they lack the skills and brains to do the better-rewarded tasks in society. In short, they believe that they deserve their fate.[12] Consequently, they accept a differential reward system and the need for their supervision and decision making left to "experts."

While it is true that social stratification is an important source of societal friction, the conflict theorists have not answered the important question as to its necessity (neither have the order theorists for that matter, although they address themselves directly to that question). Both models have important insights that we must consider. The order theorists see stratification serving the useful function of societal maintenance by providing a mechanism (differential rewards) to ensure that all the slots in the division of labor are filled. Conflict theorists are equally valid in their contention that stratification is unjust, divisive, and a source of social instability or change.

SOCIAL CLASSES IN THE UNITED STATES

There are several questions to be raised in this section: Is the United States a classless society? If not, how many classes are there and what are their characteristics? Are there real gaps between each of these classes? Are the classes national in scope or are they community-specific?

Economic and Status Differences in the United States

There is a great deal of evidence that Americans differ greatly on a number of socioeconomic dimensions. Americans are also very status-conscious. Let us examine some of the documentation of the existence of economic and status differences in the United States.

In the first place, wealth is unquestionably maldistributed in the United States. There exists in the United States unbelievable wealth in the hands of a few and wretched poverty for some others. This is not to say that the bulk of Americans lack enough wealth to live comfortably, for most are reasonably comfortable. The median family income in 1981 was $22,388. The differences in family income by race were substantial for that year: white families, $23,517, black families, $13,266, and Hispanic families, $16,401. It is also important to note that in that year 6 percent of all families had incomes of less than $5,000.[13] Those at the low end of the wealth continuum experience malnutrition and inadequate health care while at the other end of the spectrum, a few other Americans have a superabundance of material blessings.*

Americans also vary considerably in educational attainment. The amount of formal education an individual receives is a major determinant of his or her occupation and income. Despite the standard belief by Americans in

---

*Chapters 10 and 13 will provide much greater detail about the unequal distribution of income in American society.

Status Seeking Among the Kwakiutl

Competition for prestige so obsesses the Kwakiutl Indians of British Columbia that they act in what appears to outsiders in irrational ways. The Kwakiutl engage in activities where they destroy or give away their possessions to gain status. This practice of "conspicuous waste" (as opposed to "conspicuous consumption," the American practice of trying to outdo others in the accumulation and display of material possessions) occurs in a ceremony known as the potlatch.

Competition among the various village chiefs is heightened because each is insecure about his status and the status he will transmit to his heirs. The competition for status among the contenders occurs at the potlatch. Here a host chief and his followers give a rival chief and his followers great quantities of valuable gifts, thereby gaining in prestige. The recipients, though, belittle these gifts and vow to hold a return potlatch where they would give even more valuable gifts.

The gifts transferred are fish, fish oil, berries, animal skins, blankets, canoes, and others.

The gifts are piled neatly before the guests while the host chief boasts of his incredible generosity and the relative poverty of his rivals. Accountants for each side carefully record the wealth being given away. Occasionally the ultimate is conspicuous waste—the destruction of valuable property—is accomplished in front of those the chief most wants to outdo. Blankets and even a house might be burned as a display of fabulous wealth. This will cause shame for the guests who then feel compelled to have an even bigger potlatch to shame their competitors.

The goal of the potlatch ceremony is to solidify a man's hereditary claims to chiefdom and the right to transmit them to his heirs. If he miscalculates, however, and is unable to give away or destroy more than his competitor, the prestige of the chief and his heirs will be in doubt and subject to serious challenge from within and outside the village. This fear of miscalculation causes the chief and his followers to work extra hard to produce the goods to be given away.

free mass education and the almost uniform requirement that persons complete at least eight years of formal schooling, very real differences in educational attainment exist. In 1981 the data for male adults age 25 and over revealed that 22 percent of white males had a college degree while only 10 percent of Hispanic and 8 percent of black males had a college degree. At the low end of educational attainment, 54 percent of Hispanic adult males had not completed high school, compared to 47 percent of black males and only 28 percent of white males.[14]

There is an obvious correspondence between being inadequately educated and receiving little or no income. There is not only a generational correlation between these two variables but an intergenerational one as well. The children of the poor and uneducated tend not to do well in school and eventually drop out (regardless of ability), while the children of the educated well-to-do tend to continue in school (regardless of ability). Thus, the cycle of inequality is maintained.

Another demonstration that persons diverge in status is that occupations vary systematically in prestige. The degree of prestige and difference accorded to occupations is variable. A justice of the Supreme Court obviously enjoys more prestige than a bartender. But society makes much more subtle prestige distinctions. There is a rather uniform tendency to rate physicians slightly higher than college professors, who in turn are somewhat higher in rank than dentists. Further down the prestige scale, mail carriers outrank carpenters, who in turn have higher prestige than automobile mechanics.*

---

*C. C. North and Paul K. Hatt, the two sociologists who gathered these prestige rankings in 1947, found some degree of variation but a substantial agreement among a cross section of American adults ($N = 3000$).[15] This study was replicated in 1963 to ascertain if Americans had changed their ranking of occupations. The correlation between the two studies of 0.99 suggests that the rating of occupations by Americans has remained remarkably stable.[16] Incidentally, sociologists have found a high correlation in the ratings for occupations for a number of industrialized nations.[17]

The culture provides a ready-made and well-understood ranking system. It provides a relatively uniform system based on several related factors. These are: (1) the importance of the task performed (that is, how vital the consequences of the task are for the society), (2) the degree of authority and responsibility inherent in the job, (3) the native intelligence required, (4) the knowledge and skills required, (5) the dignity of the job, and (6) the financial rewards of the occupation.

But society also presents us with warped images of occupations, which leads to the acceptance of stereotypes. The media, for example, through advertisements, television, and movie portrayals, evoke positive images for middle- and upper-class occupations and negative ones for lower-prestige occupations. Professional and business leaders are white, male, cultured, and physically attractive. They are decisive, intelligent, and authoritative. At the other end of the occupational spectrum very different characteristics are portrayed:

> It is the incumbents of the lowest-prestige occupations who are portrayed in the least enhancing light. Blue-collar workers of all kinds are either the butt of comedy or the embodiment of ignorance or deviance. They are often ethnic, always lower class, sometimes immoral, generally unattractive, frequently bigoted, and not-too-bright. They are not superhuman; they are subhuman, often with personalities bent by a warp that evokes laughter or disgust.[18]

Occupation, then, is a very important variable that sorts people into hierarchically arranged categories. It is highly correlated with income and education level (see Table 9–1). There is a strong probability that highly educated persons will also have a high-prestige job and have a good deal of wealth. Of these three variables, occupational level is the best single indicator of status position in the United States. However, as the data in Table 9–1 indicate, the gender of the worker makes a tremendous difference. A woman working full time as a professional, for example, makes less than a male employed full time in the operative category.

Additional evidence for Americans being status-conscious is the importance attached to family background. An individual's social status is not immutably fixed by birth in American society, but family background remains an important determinant of status. Race and ethnicity are inherited from one's parents, and they have had and continue to have a profound effect upon socioeconomic status. Offspring almost invariably adopt the religion of their parents, and this, too, may have consequences for placement in the status hierarchy. Most important, the extent of family wealth determines in very large measure the lifestyle, amount and type of education, with whom one associates as equals, whom one marries, and the occupational niche one occupies. Family status is especially important at either extreme of the status hierarchy. In the middle range there is much greater fluidity, with family background being less important either as an obstacle (as with the lowest social category) or as a passport to prestige and wealth (as with the very highest category).

TABLE 9–1	Income Differentials by Gender, Occupation, and Education, 1980 (median incomes for full-time, year-round workers)

Occupation Category	Men	Women	Women's Income as Percentage of Men's Income
Professional	$23,026	$15,285	66.4%
Managerial	23,558	12,936	54.9
Sales	19,910	9,748	49.
Clerical	18,247	10,997	60.
Craft	18,671	11,701	62.
Operatives	15,702	9,440	60.
Laborers	12,757	9,747	76.
Service workers	13,064	7,853	60.1
Educational attainment			
5 + years college	27,690	18,100	65.4
4 years college	24,311	15,143	62.3
1–3 years college	20,909	12,954	61.9
4 years high school	19,469	11,537	59.3
1–3 years high school	16,101	9,676	60.1
Less than high school	13,117	8,216	62.6

Source: U.S. Bureau of the Census, "Money Income and Poverty Status of Families and Persons in the United States: 1980," *Current Population* Reports, Series P–60 (August 1981).

There is no doubt that most Americans are status seekers. They spend a great amount of effort seeking to rise in status. Many Americans "moonlight" (that is, work at two jobs), or both husband and wife work to get ahead financially. Others sacrifice to further their education so that they might be better able to secure a more prestigious (and better-paying) job.

There is also the propensity of Americans to purchase material goods that they feel will impress others. Presumably this is done in order that persons might be accepted as social equals by others higher in the stratificational "pecking order." The purchase of jewelry, furs, large homes, art objects, luxury cars, the latest in clothing styles, and other ostentatious displays are examples of this phenomenon of **conspicuous consumption.**

A final piece of evidence leading to the conclusion that social inequality is a real phenomenon in American society is the existence of patterns of deference. Persons of wealth are treated differently than poor persons in schools, churches, and community organizations. With few exceptions, their opinions are given greater weight, they are more likely to be elected or appointed to official posts, and they are automatically treated with greater respect.

American
Social
Classes:
Statistical
Categories
or Social
Groups?

The preceding section established that Americans are conscious of their position in the status hierarchy and that the range in status is quite large with respect to income, education, and occupation. This means, in effect, that there is social inequality in the United States and that it can be perceived as a continuum of status. This raises a question upon which social scientists are not in agreement: Are there breaks in this continuum that allow us to distinguish social classes and/or status groups? Put another way, are American social classes real, or are they artificial constructs?

The techniques employed by many sociologists ensure that the social strata they delineate are not real. Persons are assigned a social class position on the basis of their education, occupation, income level, place of residence, or other status characteristics. With such a technique, placement is arbitrary, to say the least. The procedure is invalid if the goal is to delineate the exact boundaries of classes and their memberships. It is a valid technique, however, if the goal is to compare the behaviors and/or attitudes of persons at different status levels. The sociologists who use this technique tend either to accept the continuum approach to stratification, or to use it as a quick method to delineate approximately the members of real classes.

The "classes-are-real" adherents claim that there are distinct social strata whose members are conscious of their unity. They share common goals, interests, and values. Furthermore, they contend that there are boundaries separating each of the strata. The problem is that class consciousness, class unity, and the understanding of class boundaries are variables. They may be quite pronounced in some communities and not so in others. The valid point made by proponents of the "realist" perspective, however, is that persons in communities tend to think in terms of classes. They see themselves in a class and they can place others in the stratification system.

There is conflicting evidence for the "classes-are-real" thesis. A. B. Hollingshead found evidence in his study of Morris, Illinois, for the existence of five discrete classes. He found that respondents in that community believed in the existence of social classes, identified persons as members of specific classes, thought of themselves as members of classes, and associated behavior with class level. At one point in the research Hollingshead asked twelve knowledgeable persons to rank twenty representative families into classes. No instructions were given regarding the number of strata into which the families should be divided. Ten of the twelve raters divided the families into five strata. This ranking Hollingshead interpreted as conclusive evidence for the existence of five discrete social class groups in that community.[19]

In contrast, Gerhard Lenski's study of Danielson, Connecticut, suggests the very opposite of Hollingshead's. Lenski selected 24 residents who were old enough (between 20 and 70) and who had lived in the community long enough (at least 7 years) to be considered "well-informed" members of that community of 6000. Each rater was given a pack of cards with the names and addresses of 173 families. They were asked to select from the pack only the names they knew and rank these families according to their relative "standing." They were not given any instructions regarding the number of classes or levels into which the families were to be divided. The raters, it was found, lacked a consensus on the number of strata and the placement of families within strata. For example, one rater identified three strata in the community, four raters discerned four strata, seven raters noted five strata, eight raters perceived six strata, and four raters believed the community to have seven strata. Lenski noted that the raters, in the course of the rating interview, constantly changed the number of strata they were using to classify the sample families. He concluded that, for this community at least, there was no system of discrete social classes. But Lenski delved further into the data. Perhaps some of the raters perceived the actual number of classes while others just were not keen observers of the community. If this were so, perhaps all the raters who agreed on the number of strata would agree as to the families belonging in each. There was virtually no agreement, however, among the raters who perceived the same number of strata. For example, the most common number of strata perceived was six, but some raters defined the top stratum in very narrow terms, including only two or three families in it. Others, by contrast, defined the top stratum so as to include twelve families in it. Lenski's findings, therefore, present the consistent conclusion that although status differences occur in the community, there are no real social classes.[20]

The studies by Hollingshead and Lenski suggest that the extent of class boundaries varies from community to community. The analyst of any particular community or the total society should look for two basic indicators of the existence of separate classes: the existence of **class consciousness** and **class segregation.**

The Extent of Class Consciousness. Karl Marx believed that capitalist societies were composed of two broad classes—those persons who owned the instruments of production (bourgeoisie) and those who worked for the owners (proletariat). In other words, there would be a dichotomy based on the relationship to the means of production. Marx predicted (based upon his analysis of history and of how capitalism was working in mid-nineteenth-century England) that persons in these two classes would develop class consciousness—a necessary precondition for class conflict. The essential characteristics of class consciousness for Marx were, first, that persons in a similar economic position should realize they have common interests. In Marx's analysis, the proletariat will be profoundly dissatisfied with the distribution of economic rewards while the bourgeoisie will work to keep the status quo. The bourgeoisie will cooperate among themselves because they are outnumbered and fear the potential power of the lower class. These feelings of common interests lead naturally to the second characteristic of class consciousness—each class becomes hostile to the other. Marx designated these two classes as the oppressors and the oppressed. If these words describe the situation accurately, then hostility between them would be a natural outcome. Finally, class consciousness entails a collective commitment to a political ideology for the attainment of economic interests.

Implied in these three characteristics of class consciousness is the uniformity of belief by persons in a similar economic situation. Marx believed this would occur because of the unequal distribution of economic rewards. Because of similar economic interests, the bourgeoisie would unite to exert control over the proletariat, while the proletariat would band together for power. Finally, the relative ease of communication among the individuals in the same class position should lead to relatively uniform beliefs within each class.

Marx predicted that the natural development of class consciousness would lead ultimately to class conflict in capitalist societies. Does his prediction appear to hold for the United States? To answer this, we need to ask: Do Americans identify themselves with a class? Are blue-collar workers (or businesspersons) unified? Are they allied in a common cause? Do they vote for the same candidates and perceive issues in the same way? Are they organized? Is it clear who are members and who are not?

The empirical evidence for the existence of class consciousness suggests that this phenomenon is relatively low in the United States but not absent.

Table 9–2 provides the data on political preferences from 1952 to 1980 in presidential elections. These data reveal that the voting patterns are relatively stable—the higher the education, the more likely to vote for the Republican candidate (although the data are not supplied here, the results are similar for occupation, with the holders of the higher-prestige jobs the greatest supporters of the Republican Party). Despite the apparent uniformity, the data also reveal that within each educational category, a minimum of one third of the persons differ in their political views from the others.

Other studies also document that people in various occupational, educational, and income levels differ significantly in their opinions on a number of social and political issues.[21]

Are Americans aware of class boundaries? Do they know what class they are in? Do they owe great allegiance to that class? These related questions lie at the core of class consciousness. Most of the evidence from studies of the United States suggests negative answers to these questions.

The study cited most often as a basis for the existence of class consciousness in the United States was conducted by Richard Centers.[22] Centers gathered data from a representative cross section of American adult white males in 1945. Among other things, he asked if they belonged to the middle class, lower class, working class, or upper class. Here are the results:

Upper class	3%
Middle class	43%
Working class	51%
Lower class	1%
Don't know	2%

Centers felt that since only 2 percent of Americans did not know what class they belonged to, he had overwhelming evidence of a strong class consciousness in the United States.

Centers's study, however, raises more questions than it answers. Let us look at several of the criticisms, because they weaken what on the surface appears to be a very strong argument for class consciousness.[23] First, self-

TABLE 9–2   Voting Preferences by Education in Presidential Elections (percentages)

Election	Educational Attainment		
	College	High school	Grade school
1952			
Stevenson (D)	34	45	52
Eisenhower (R)	66	55	48
1956			
Stevenson (D)	31	42	50
Eisenhower (R)	69	58	50
1960			
Kennedy (D)	39	52	55
Nixon (R)	61	48	45
1964			
Johnson (D)	52	62	66
Goldwater (R)	48	38	34
1968			
Humphrey (D)	37	42	52
Nixon (R)	54	43	33
Wallace (I)	9	15	15
1972			
McGovern (D)	37	34	49
Nixon (R)	63	66	51
1976			
Carter (D)	42	54	58
Ford (R)	55	46	41
McCarthy (I)	2	a	1
1980			
Carter (D)	35	43	54
Reagan (R)	53	51	42
Anderson (I)	10	5	3

[a]Less than 1 percent.
Source: *The Gallup Opinion Index*, Report No. 183 (December, 1980), pp. 6–7.

identification as to class in a questionnaire may not be reliable. Some individuals may claim a class position that represents only wish fulfillment or fantasy. For instance, 18 percent of the unskilled workers in Centers's study said they were middle class. Conversely, some individuals may be inclined to downgrade their actual class position because they are influenced by equalitarian ideology. In Centers's study 10 percent of the professionals identified themselves as working class instead of middle or upper.

A second criticism is the use of a forced-choice type of question. The situation was structured for the respondents, as they had four response categories. What if Centers had used five or six categories? Or better yet, what if the respondents were not given any prearranged choices? Neal Gross tested this in a study of 935 heads of households in Minneapolis. The

respondents were asked to identify their social class with no hint as to
what was meant by social class or how many the interviewer thought there
might be. Over one third of the responses were in the "don't know" category
(Centers only found 2 percent in this category).[24] Obviously, the open-ended
method provides an opportunity for the respondent to express his lack of
class identification as well as identification. We must conclude, therefore,
that Centers did not measure class consciousness.

Oscar Glantz conducted a study better designed than Centers's to determine
the extent of class consciousness. He gathered data from 400 white, adult
males in Philadelphia. But rather than a cross section of citizens, he selected
occupational groups that would most likely be class-conscious in the Marxian
sense—big and small businessmen, on the one hand, and union and nonunion,
on the other. To get at class consciousness, he asked: "To which of these
groups do you feel you owe allegiance—business or labor?" He further
asked them to respond to six questions, three of which were statements
adopted by the National Association of Manufacturers and three from the
Congress of Industrial Organizations. On the basis of group identification
and the answers to the six questions, Glantz ascertained the degree of class
consciousness. The methods, it would appear, were "stacked" in favor of
finding class consciousness (as was the case for Centers), but the results
revealed the opposite. He found that 40 percent of all big businessmen and
25 percent of small businessmen were class-conscious. Only 28 percent of
all union members and 13 percent of nonunion workers were so designated.
These findings, striking because the percentages are so much less than
expected in the most class-conscious-prone groups, indicate that class consciousness certainly must be at a relatively low level in the United States.[25]
Although this is the obvious conclusion, we should not ignore its existence
for some individuals and groups. The very uppermost stratum in American
society, the group that has had a great deal of money over several generations,
whose children go to exclusive schools, and where intermarriage is the
highest, constitute a social class with a high degree of class identification
by the members. Toward the other end of the continuum there are persons
who feel oppressed and who lack economic security. It has been demonstrated
that these persons are especially likely to be conscious of their class and
feel antipathy toward other classes.[26]

Marx's prediction of the class consciousness and the polarization of the
classes has occurred but only minimally in the United States. Class conflict
occurs only rarely, and more in the context of specific issues rather than
a proletarian revolution. There are labor disputes and strikes, but they do
not threaten the fabric of American society. The poor can, if organized,
exert greater pressure for better living conditions. The Poor People's March
on Washington, D.C., late in the 1960s is just such an example. Welfare
mothers in various cities have also organized to bring about change.

Perhaps the two best examples of group consciousness in American society
are not based on economics (as Marx envisioned) but rather on race and
gender. Some black leaders emphasize racial pride, separateness, and even
violence and considerable in-group solidarity (race consciousness) is found

among some black groups. A similar situation exists among the Hispanic population, but loyalties are commonly divided along place of origin (e.g., Mexico, Cuba, and Puerto Rico). Many women's groups also generate an "us" versus "them" feeling. But while feminist groups show considerable solidarity, their views are not shared by many women. In fact, some women are openly antagonistic toward efforts to liberate women from the constraints and discrimination they experience.

Although racial and gender groups approach the group consciousness that Marx envisioned, this consciousness has not really developed among social classes in the United States.* There are a number of possible explanations for the relatively low level of class consciousness in the United States. First, Americans, rich and poor alike, tend to share the belief that upward mobility is possible. Even workers who know they will never move to a better job often hold the hope that their children will be upwardly mobile. Because of this widespread belief in the opportunities for upward mobility, efforts to improve status are typically individual efforts rather than concerted collective effort.

A second reason for the low level of class consciousness is that mass consumption patterns of Americans have impeded the development of distinctive life styles found in more status-conscious societies. Skilled laborers (electricians, plumbers, masons) are paid more than many white-collar workers (clerks, bank tellers, nurses, teachers). Many dual-earner families, even when both spouses work at relatively low status jobs, are sometimes able to achieve middle-class levels of consumption.

A third reason is that complexity and segmentation within the middle and working classes limit occupational identification and loyalty to a narrow field and discourage class awareness across fields that otherwise share a common economic situation.[27]

Fourth, the two major political parties are not sharply defined along class lines. Within either the Democratic or Republican party, members are found that represent both rich and poor, whites and people of color, and owners of capitalist enterprises as well as common laborers. Minor political parties that have a sharp ideological focus that correlates with class ideologies are without power and therefore have few followers.

Fifth, the unions, both historically militant and politically forceful throughout most of this century, have for the most part lost members, power, and zeal. Significant reasons for this recent turnabout include: high unemployment rates, reduced profits during economic downturns, threats of employers to move their operations overseas or to the nonunion climate of the sunbelt states, and a Congress and administration generally unsympathetic to the unions during the 1970s and early 1980s.

The development of class consciousness is also inhibited by the existence of organizations whose memberships cut across class lines. Religious de-

---

* Marx's theory, however, has provided a fairly accurate model for considering the development process in the emerging nations of Latin America, Africa, and Asia.

nominations, local churches, and organizations such as the American Legion have as members persons from a number of social strata.

Finally, the blue-collar category, the most likely stratum to develop class consciousness according to Marx, is composed not only of whites but all manner of racial and ethnic group members as well. The animosities among these groups within the ranks of the blue collars is often so great that the possibility of unity, coordinated effort, and group pride necessary for class consciousness is precluded.

PANEL 9–2   Social Change Panel

The Structural Conditions for Class Consciousness Among the Proletariat: The Potential for Social Change

The recent past has been characterized by a relatively low level of class consciousness among the working and impoverished classes in the United States. These classes have displayed division instead of unity, apathy rather than zeal, and atomized individuals rather than a collective political force organized to change their oppressive situation.

A critical barrier to the development of class consciousness in American society has been the strong tendency for Americans to explain success and failure in individualistic (psychological and genetic) terms.[28] Some contemporary conditions, if they persist, will work toward replacing this explanation with an ideology that places the blame on the social structure rather than on the individual. And, if people in a common economic situation perceive the system as the problem, they will, according to Marx, develop a heightened class consciousness, a common bond, and a political organization aimed at change. Let's consider some current trends that have the potential for building class consciousness.

The economy is undergoing a major transformation from its traditional manufacturing base to a high technology and service industries base (see Chapter 13). The increased use of new technologies (e.g., robots and computers) has accelerated the loss of jobs. The owners of economic enterprises are ever more inclined to shift their operations to more favorable economic climates (to foreign countries or to the sunbelt in the U.S.) where wages are lower, materials cheaper, and unions

impotent. These profound economic facts and related trends are having some significant consequences.

Foremost, for the first time in American history, downward mobility is more likely to occur than upward mobility. A generation ago blue-collar families outnumbered white-collar families leaving plenty of room for people to move up in status. Also, the past was characterized by rising prosperity. Each generation had more material wealth than the preceding one. The economy, however, is no longer capable of maintaining this trend. Since the late 1970s, more and more people are being excluded from the prosperous life. The numbers of poor are increasing (from 11 percent in 1973 to 15 percent in 1982). Official unemployment now hovers around 10 percent. Home ownership, long the symbol of middle class membership, is now beyond the budgets of most young families (75 percent of Americans cannot afford the averaged price home).[29]

Diminished chances for upward mobility and prosperity are not just problems for the workers in declining industries, the already poor, and the minorities. In the middle classes persons with college educations are also negatively affected by contemporary economic conditions. In the past a college education assured opportunities for advancement but that assurance is now relatively rare. Underemployment (i.e., a job below one's training) is rapidly becoming the rule. Will these underemployed blame themselves for this situation? Hardly. They have invested in an education, but society has not provided the proper rewards for such an investment.

Job opportunities today seem to offer a few top jobs and many low paying ones. The Bureau of Labor Statistics has projected, for example, that by 1990 the United States will require 120,000 more computer programmers, 125,000 more electrical engineers, 600,000 janitors, 500,000 more sales clerks, and some 3 million more secretaries and office clerks. Workers in the fastest growing job areas now earn an average of $5,000 a year less than workers in declining industries (such as production line assembly plants and steel mills).[30]

In effect these current trends are evidence of widening inequality and blocked opportunities in America. The current distribution of jobs is increasing the number of persons toward the bottom of the economic ladder and diminishing those in the middle. Karl Marx's prediction that under capitalism the conditions of the labor force can only worsen appears to be occurring. The critical question now becomes, will this time of ever-diminishing rewards for so many Americans increase their sense of a common condition with others in similar circumstances? Moreover, will they share an ideology that holds the structure of society, in particular the organization of the economy, as the source of the problem? In short, will they develop a class consciousness that results in a unified collective attempt to change the structure of society?

Class Segregation.   A second empirical technique that may be employed to ascertain whether there are distinct boundaries among the social classes is to determine the extent to which there is class segregation. There are two types of segregation to look for: social and spatial. Social segregation refers to barriers that restrict social interaction to the members of a certain category. This is often accomplished by economic factors. High rent, high cost of property, entrance fees, and dues have the function of restricting residents in some parts of town and membership in some clubs. "Undesirables" may also be kept out of certain areas or clubs by the vote of the members. This practice of "blackballing," as well as the economic factors, explains the separation of the wealthiest from the rest of the population.

There is also a voluntary segregation by status that occurs at all levels in the hierarchy. The status character of many organizations is well known and is accomplished often without restrictive entrance requirements. People just feel more comfortable interacting with others like themselves (in wealth, amount of education, type of occupation). Society matrons just have no desire to belong to the women's auxiliary of plumbers local 371, and the wives of plumbers would probably not be comfortable sipping tea with the ladies of the Junior League. Lower-class persons probably would feel uneasy in prestigious Episcopal, Presbyterian, or Unitarian churches, while the well-to-do probably would feel just as uncomfortable in a Pentecostal church.

To determine the extent of voluntary status separation, the analyst can: (1) compare the status characteristics of marriage partners, (2) determine the status characteristics of persons who spend their leisure time together, (3) ascertain the status characteristics of the members of voluntary associations (from the African Violet Society to the Veterans of Foreign Wars), and (4) compare the status characteristics of close friends.

Segregation also occurs in space. Residential segregation may be forced (as is often the case with minority racial groups) or voluntary. Some residential areas go to great lengths to remain exclusive. Devices such as "gentleman's agreements," restrictive covenants, and point systems have been used for such a purpose.

In summary, the evidence shows that class consciousness has not developed in the United States as Karl Marx predicted (that is, to the point of political unity). The degree of class consciousness varies with locality and status group. The best evidence for the existence of class consciousness seems to be the social and spatial boundaries separating the highest classes from the rest of the populace.

The Hierarchy of "Classes"

Although class consciousness is relatively low in the United States, Americans do have a conception of a stratification structure, and evaluate persons as social superiors, equals, or inferiors.

Since actual class boundaries are virtually nonexistent (or fuzzy beyond recognition), we will put some artificial closure around a number of strata and call them social classes. The reason for this exercise is to enumerate the characteristics that tend to cluster in the persons located at particular points along the status hierarchy. These characteristics aid in the understanding of behavioral and attitudinal differences found when comparing persons in different strata. They also aid in understanding and analyzing power differentials on the community and national levels. We should keep in mind, however, that the dividing line between strata is arbitrary and that we should conceive of the stratification system as a continuum with artificial lines designating social classes for analytical purposes only.

The assumption of this analysis is that at different points on this "class" continuum persons will have more or less distinctive characteristics. The units designated as social classes are aggregates of individuals and families who are in similar economic positions and therefore have similar opportunities. Moreover, there is a strong likelihood that they probably consider other persons in the aggregate as social equals.

The Upper Class (the Old Rich). Of the various social classes in the United States, the upper class of the old rich is the only class with real boundaries. There is strong in-group solidarity and it is clear to the members who is and who is not included. G. William Domhoff, after an extensive analysis, concluded that this category makes up 0.5 percent of the American population. His criteria for inclusion in the upper class are found in Panel 9–3.

Domhoff's criteria for inclusion suggest that the very uppermost stratum in American society is not only wealthy but exclusive. They belong to exclusive clubs and attended equally exclusive boarding schools. These clubs and schools are exclusive because they have very elaborate screening mechanisms to ensure that only certain people are allowed in—usually the persons whose parents were also wealthy. Great wealth by itself is not enough, for persons who acquired it only during their lifetime will never be fully accepted by the persons in the highest stratum.

One characteristic of the upper class is physical and social separation from the other strata. As mentioned above, members of the elite go to very private schools and they belong to private clubs where interaction is restricted

The Criteria for Upper-Class Membership

G. William Domhoff provides a number of criteria that distinguish the uppermost social stratum from all others:

1. A person will be considered a member of the upper class if he, his parents, his wife's parents, or any of his siblings are listed in any of the following registers and blue books: *The Social Register* (which has editions in twelve major cities), *Social Secretary* (Detroit), *Social Register* (Houston), *Blue Book* (Los Angeles), *Social Register* (New Orleans), and the *Blue Book* (Seattle).

2. A person will be considered a member of the upper class if he, his father, brother, or father-in-law attended any of the following schools: thirty-seven very private schools, including Choate (Wallingford, Connecticut), Deerfield (Deerfield, Massachusetts), Groton (Groton, Massachusetts), and St. Mark's (Southborough, Massachusetts).

3. A person will be considered a member of the upper class if he, his father, brother, or father-in-law belongs to any one of the following social clubs: forty exclusive clubs, including the Century and Knickerbocker Clubs (New York), Pacific Union (San Francisco), Idlewild (Dallas), Somerset (Boston), and the Racquet Club (St. Louis).

4. A person will be considered a member of the upper class if his sister, wife, mother, or mother-in-law attended one of the following schools: sixty-seven private schools, including Abbot Academy (Andover, Massachusetts), Baldwin (Bryn Mawr, Pennsylvania), Chatham Hall (Chatham, Virginia), Lenox (New York), and Westover (Middlebury, Connecticut).

5. A person will be considered a member of the upper class if his sister, wife, mother, or mother-in-law belongs to one of the following clubs: ten, including Acorn (Philadelphia), Chilton (Boston), Colony (New York), Fortnightly (Chicago), and Sulgrave (Washington, D.C.).

6. A person will be considered a member of the upper class if his or her father was a millionaire entrepreneur or a $100,000-a-year corporation executive or corporation lawyer, *and* (a) if he or she attended one of the 130 private schools listed in the back of Kavaler's *The Private World of High Society*, or (b) if he or she belongs to any of the exclusive clubs mentioned in Baltzell's *Philadelphia Gentleman: The Making of a National Upper Class* or in Kavaler. The list of private schools and exclusive clubs can be larger here than for the second, third, fourth, and fifth criteria because it is known that the person is a member of the second generation of a wealthy family.

Source: Summarized from G. William Domhoff, *The Higher Circles: The Governing Class in America* (New York: Random House, 1970), pp. 21–27. Copyright © by G. William Domhoff. Reprinted by permission of Random House, Inc.

to people like themselves. Living in restricted residential areas is another dimension of the exclusiveness prevalent in the upper strata. The lifestyle of the very wealthy also distinguishes it from the other strata. Expensive clothes, jewelry, furs, and cars, as well as distinctive speech and manners, serve to separate this group further from others.

The possession of great wealth and the benefits concomitant to having great wealth serve to make the elite very powerful, both in the local communities where each of the members resides, and nationally. Persons of wealth accumulate not only power, but also honor and deference. It is natural that such persons exude self-confidence, for their opinions are sought, their lifestyle is emulated, and they, by their presence, can legitimize an otherwise questionable activity.

Upper-class persons tend to be family oriented. There is a sense of extended family solidarity. This is a consequence of the emphasis on family heritage among the elite. Family solidarity is also maintained often by the joint holding of property. The main source of wealth for the elite is interest and dividends from investment of inherited wealth. Their typical jobs are those of high-ranking executives in established corporations or banks.

Persons in this category tend toward attitudes of political and economic conservatism. Because they benefit so much from existing political and economic arrangements, they work to maintain the status quo. The holding of similar interests (for example, maintaining the status quo) promotes class consciousness—a condition not found to any extent elsewhere in the stratification hierarchy.

Since the American system of social stratification is a continuum of social "classes," there are no rigid boundaries that mark this continuum into clearly defined classes except at the highest level. As Domhoff has asserted, "the social structure is made up of strata that shade off one into the other until we arrive at the highest level, where the continuum hardens into a social class with more or less definite boundaries and class consciousnness."[31]

Domhoff argued that through in-group interaction and differential lifestyles, class consciousness is intensified among the elite. Evidence of in-group interaction is found in the large proportion of intermarriage that occurs among the very rich. The marriage between two elite young people provides further linkage between the two families. The linked families are often widely separated in space, but the marriage occurred because the children attended the same or neighboring private boarding schools or colleges.

The prestigious private schools that provide the milieu for mate selection have stringent requirements that usually admit only the uppermost stratum. The evidence is also that these schools provide havens for the interaction of rich children from all over the country. As an example of this, "Hotchkiss graduates are listed in the Social Register for the following cities: New York, 552; Chicago, 125; Philadelphia, 94; Cleveland, 64; Pittsburgh, 64; Boston, 59; San Francisco, 40; Washington, 35; and St. Louis, 34."[32]

The nationwide interaction of the rich is also found in club memberships. The exclusive clubs of the upper class have nationwide memberships.

Summer resorts are further evidence for the cohesiveness of the national upper class. Around the island of Mt. Desert in Maine, for example, are found the summer homes of Social Register listees from the following cities: Philadelphia, 92; New York, 80; Boston, 40; Washington, 12; Chicago, 7; Baltimore, 7; Cincinnati-Dayton, 6; and St. Louis, 5.[33] The same is true of such winter resorts as Palm Beach in Florida and Palm Springs in California.

In summary, the "old rich" are a distinct social class. They are separated from others in the stratification system by where they live, where they attend school, by lifestyle, and by the deference they receive from others. There is, therefore, a clear-cut boundary between the old rich and others.

The persons within the old rich category form a real social class because the members consider themselves as such—they know who belongs and who does not. Additionally, there are linkages between the members—through marriage, business, school, neighborhood, club, and mutual acquaintance. The members interact and hence form a social group.

The old rich social class, unlike any of the other strata, is national in scope. There is a considerable amount of intermarriage and social interaction linking wealthy families living in different cities. While it is clear that not everyone in the old rich category knows each other, it is highly probable (as Domhoff has asserted after a great deal of research on the subject) that everyone has friends and relatives who know someone from the uppermost stratum in every major American city. The upper-class person, therefore, has an entree into the highest social circles all over the country.[34]

The "New Rich." We shall inaccurately refer to the "new rich" and the remaining status categories as "classes." They are not classes in the sense that the old rich are. Class consciousness is weak, within-stratum interaction is not as restrictive as in the elite, and the boundaries, which are fuzzy in the minds of many citizens, and therefore set arbitrarily according to objective criteria by social researchers. This arbitrariness of the boundaries, however, does not negate the existence of status differentials.

The new rich differ from the uppermost stratum in prestige, not wealth. Great wealth alone does not ensure acceptance by the elite as a social equal. A family tradition of wealth (of more than two generations) is a necessary condition for inclusion in the elite. The *nouveaux riches* of Houston, for example, could buy a membership in River Oaks Country Club with an initiation fee of many thousands of dollars, but membership in the Houston Country Club is closed except to members of old-guard families.[35] To have acquired wealth in one's lifetime means that one will not have had the time required to learn the ways of the wealthy (for example, language, manners, grace). This is accomplished only if one has been totally immersed from birth in the ways of the wealthy (private schools, extensive travel, interaction limited to others of equivalent status and background).

The *nouveaux riches* often try to buy their way into elite circles by giving lavish parties, building very expensive homes, and by means of other forms of conspicuous consumption. Such overly ostentatious behavior is perceived typically by the elite as "too gauche" and therefore further evidence for exclusion from the most elite circles. One tenet of the old rich faith is that one should not have to prove oneself with ostentatious displays. This behavior, although it is often motivated by a desire to be accepted by the old rich, actually causes the opposite reaction.

The new rich stratum is thus composed of the self-made wealthy. These families have amassed fortunes typically through business ventures, or because of special talent in sports, music, or motion pictures. Additionally, some professionals (doctors, lawyers) may become wealthy because of their practice and/or investments. Finally, a few persons because of their own talent may become very wealthy by working their way in corporations to top executive positions, where high salaries and stock options are common.

The new rich tend to be political conservatives. They are inclined toward the radical right groups that oppose the welfare state, the graduated income tax, and unions. They vigorously oppose communism and socialism because under these economic systems hard work and initiative are penalized while the ne'er-do-wells benefit. As the political sociologist S. M. Lipset has noted:

> New wealth most often tends to have extremist ideologies, to believe in extreme conservative doctrines in economic matters. The man who makes money himself feels more insecure about keeping it than do people who possess inherited wealth. He feels more aggrieved about social reform measures which involve redistribution of the wealth, as compared with individuals, still wealthy, who have grown up in an old traditionalist background, which inculcates the values of tolerance traditionally associated with upper-class aristocratic conservatism. It is not without reason that the new millionaires, such as those in Texas, have given extensive financial support to radical right movements, politicians, and to such propaganda organizations as Facts Forum.[36]

The Upper-Middle Class.   The key distinguishing feature of this category is high-prestige jobs (but not the most remunerative in the society) that require a good deal of formal education and have a high degree of autonomy, responsibility, and security. This stratum is largely composed of professional people, executives, and business people. They do not make nearly as much money as the new rich but, as a category, they are usually better educated. Education is of particular importance to persons in this class because the members have found it important to their own careers. The children of this class are expected by the parents to receive a college education.

Much like the two upper classes, the upper-middle class is a bastion of conservatism in American society. They believe in the work-success ethic and capitalism. They are self-made persons, having accomplished prestige and a comfortable economic situation through hard work and sacrifice. They tend, therefore, to oppose many socialistic programs, especially welfare. Many of the more highly educated, however, tend toward liberalism on civil rights, civil liberties, and international issues (but some notable exceptions may be doctors, dentists, and engineers).

The Middle Class.   This category is composed of white-collar workers who may work primarily in minor jobs in bureaucracies. Also included are clerks, technicians, the owners of small businesses, and salespeople.

These workers are paid an adequate wage, but substantially lower than upper-middle-class persons. Their jobs require less skill, less responsibility, and do not involve as much decision making as the class above them in the stratification hierarchy.

These persons usually have some education beyond high school. Some college or training in specialized schools is typical. Most, however, have not graduated from college. This presents a severe limitation to career mobility unless they possess exceptional skills.

The heterogeneity of this stratum is clearly evident. There is a vast difference, for example, between white-collar workers in huge bureaucracies and the owners of small businesses. They differ in amount and type of education, income, degree of autonomy on the job, and job security. These differences affect attitudes, perceptions, motivation, and behaviors. Even child-rearing patterns are noticeably different between these two social categories. An interesting study by Miller and Swanson showed the diversity found within this stratum by comparing entrepreneurial parents (self-employed) with bureaucratic parents (employed in large-scale organizations). The researchers assumed that the different settings and demands of each category would be revealed in the way children were reared. They found that entrepreneurial families stressed self-control, self-reliance, and individual initiative because these traits were needed in the competitive business world. Bureaucratic parents, on the other hand, reared their children to adjust and accommodate to the wishes of others because these traits were especially appropriate for success in large organizations.[37]

The wide diversity found within the middle class demonstrates that this category is not a real social class. The persons designated as members by social scientists lack class consciousness and the boundaries are not well defined.

The Lower-Middle Class.   This category is composed of skilled craftsmen such as mechanics, electricians, plumbers, cabinetmakers, and masons, many of whom are self-employed. It also includes supervisors in large industrial plants, who have authority over other workers.

This category receives relatively high wages, often higher than white-collar workers, allowing them to own homes and other possessions typical of middle-class Americans.

They differ from white-collar workers in that they are manual workers with less formal education. Although they rank relatively low in the hierarchy, they are "aristocrats" of the blue-collar workers.

Many persons in this stratum are likely to be status inconsistents (as are the "new rich"). This means that an individual's status attributes are unbalanced—that is, their income is higher than their educational background would appear to warrant. This condition often leads to strain and hostility in individuals, since they may not be accepted as equals by persons they feel are their equals (neighbors, colleagues, customers), who have similar incomes but more education and different lifestyles.

The Upper-Lower Class.   Semiskilled operatives who work in the mass production industries are the main component of this class. They are manual workers whose jobs allow little if any autonomy, are simple and repetitive, and require no creativity. Along with the boredom of these jobs is their relative insecurity because of strikes or because of unemployment brought about by economic recession.

These persons have not gone beyond high school and many have not even achieved that. Because of their lack of education and limited skills, they are severely blocked if they have aspirations to be upwardly mobile. There is really quite a large gap between semiskilled workers and white-collar workers. The gulf, for many, is too large to breach.

The Lower-Lower Class. This class is composed of unskilled laborers whose formal education is often less than eight grades. The chronically unemployed are in this class. The bulk of those on welfare are in this class. Minority-group members—blacks, Puerto Ricans, Mexican Americans, Indians—are disproportionately found in this category.

These persons are those that are looked down upon by all others in the community. They live "on the other side of the tracks." They are considered by others to be undesirable as playmates, friends, organization members, or marriage partners. Lower-lowers are viewed as lazy, shiftless, dependent, and immoral—traits exactly opposite "good middle-class virtues."

SOCIAL MOBILITY

Societies vary in the degree to which individuals may move up in status. Probably the most rigid stratification system ever devised was the **caste system** of India. In brief, this system (1) determined status by heredity, (2) allowed marriage to occur only within one's status group (endogamy), (3) determined occupation by heredity, and (4) restricted interaction among the status groups. Even the Indian caste system, however, was not totally rigid, for some mobility has been allowed under certain circumstances.*

In contrast to the closed stratification system of India, the United States is a relatively open system. Social mobility is not only permitted, but it is part of the American value that upward mobility is good and should be the goal of all Americans.

The United States, however, is not a totally open system. All American children have the social rank of the parents while they are youths. As we shall see in the four chapters of Part 3, the status of parents has a tremendous influence on a child's attitudes and behaviors (particularly performance in school) and these determine in large measure whether the child can be mobile (upward or downward).

Concepts **Social mobility** refers to an individual's movement within the class structure of society. **Vertical mobility** is movement upward or downward in social class. **Horizontal mobility** is the change from one position to another of about equal prestige. The shift in occupations from being an electrician to a plumber is an example of horizontal mobility.

Social mobility occurs in two ways. **Intergenerational mobility** refers to vertical movement comparing a daughter with her mother or a son with his father. **Intragenerational mobility** is the vertical movement of the individual through his or her adult life.

Societal Factors Affecting Social Mobility. There are societal factors that increase the likelihood of people's vertical mobility regardless of their

---

*Some observers have charged that the stratification system of the United States is castelike with reference to race. Race, in many ways, presents a barrier that determines status, range of marriage partners, and discriminatory treatment of all kinds.[38]

individual efforts. The availability of cheap and fertile land with abundant resources gave many thousands of Americans in the nineteenth century opportunities for advancement no longer present. Similarly, the arrival of new immigrants to the United States from 1880 to 1920 provided a status boost for those already here. Economic booms and depressions obviously affect individuals' economic success. Technological changes too can provide increased chances for success as well as diminish the possibilities for those trained in occupations now obsolete. Finally, the size of one's age cohort can limit or expand opportunities for success (see Panel 9–4).

PANEL 9–4   Methods Panel

Baby Boomers and Social Mobility: A Cohort Analysis

An important tool of social scientists is the longitudinal study—research designed to permit observations over a long period. One type of longitudinal study is the *trend study,* in which changes in a population are noted over time. Figure 1 shows the results of a trend study noting the differences in birth rate (the ratio of births in a given year to the average population) for the United States since World War I.

This figure shows that following World War II (roughly from 1947 to 1960) there was a very high birth rate, preceded and followed by periods of relatively low birth rates.

Another type of longitudinal study—a *cohort study*—follows an age group (such as the people born in the depression, or those born in the 1950s) across time. As we saw

in Chapter 4, the baby boom generation consists of an extra 10 million persons. Because of these extra numbers, those born in this cohort are having a more difficult time economically than those born during the "birth dearth" depression years. The baby boom generation is and will continue to find it tough sledding economically because of the pressure of numbers and the resulting keen competition for jobs and resources. Jobs are scarcer. The possibilities for advancement are rarer. Salaries are lower. Even "stagflation," a combination of high unemployment and accelerating inflation, is partly the consequence of this cohort. The result is that this accident of birth—being born in an overly populated cohort—will negatively affect the members of that cohort throughout their lives.

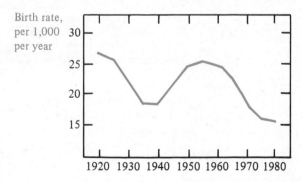

Source: Richard A. Easterlin, *Birth and Fortune: The Impact of Numbers on Personal Welfare* (New York: Basic Books, 1980), p. 8.

The Extent of Vertical Mobility in the United States. The most comprehensive study of intergenerational mobility has been conducted by Peter Blau and Otis Dudley Duncan.[39] Figure 9–1 summarizes their findings on the probability of mobility in American society for males. Some of their conclusions are that: (1) few sons of white-collar workers become blue-collar workers; (2) most mobility moves are short in distance; (3) occupational inheritance is highest for sons of professionals (physicians, lawyers, professors); and (4) the opportunities for the sons of nonprofessionals to become professionals are very small. Another study, this one by the Carnegie Council on Children, found that only one male in five exceeds his father's social status through individual effort and achievement.[40] The advantages of the children of the rich over those of the poor are enormous, as seen in the following example from this study:

FIGURE 9–1   Percentage Distribution of U.S. Males' Intergenerational Mobility: Distance and Direction by Educational Level

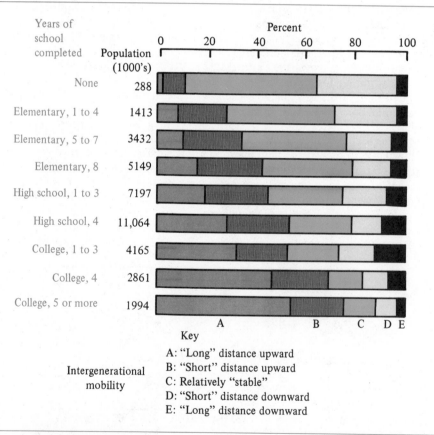

Key

Intergenerational mobility

A: "Long" distance upward
B: "Short" distance upward
C: Relatively "stable"
D: "Short" distance downward
E: "Long" distance downward

Source: Reprinted with permission of Macmillan Publishing Co., Inc. from *The American Occupational Structure* by Peter M. Blau and Otis Dudley Duncan, p. 159. Copyright © 1967 by Peter M. Blau and Otis Dudley Duncan.

Jimmy is a second grader. He pays attention in school, and enjoys it. School records show he is reading slightly above grade level and has a slightly better than average I.Q. Bobby is a second grader in a school across town. He also . . . enjoys school and his test scores are quite similar to Jimmy's. Bobby is a safe bet to enter college (more than four times as likely as Jimmy) and a good bet to complete it—at least twelve times as likely as Jimmy.

Bobby will probably have at least four years more schooling than Jimmy. He is twenty-seven times as likely as Jimmy to land a job which by his late forties will pay him an income in the top tenth of all incomes. Jimmy has one chance in eight of earning a median income.

These odds are the arithmetic of inequality in America. . . . Bobby is the son of a successful lawyer whose annual salary of $35,000 puts him well within the top 10 percent of the United States income distribution in 1976. Jimmy's father, who did not complete high school, works from time to time as a messenger and a custodial assistant. His earnings, some $4,800, put him in the bottom 10 percent.[41]

This example clearly demonstrates that the commonly accepted belief of Americans that ours is a meritocratic society is largely a myth. Equality of opportunity does not exist because (1) employers may discriminate on the basis of race, sex, or ethnicity of their employees or prospective employees; (2) educational and job training opportunities are unequal; and (3) the family has great power to enhance or retard a child's aspirations, motivation, and cognitive skills.[42]

Education and Social Mobility

The schools play a major part in both perpetuating the meritocratic myth and legitimizing it by giving and denying educational credentials on the basis of "open and objective" mechanisms that sift and sort on merit.[43] The use of I.Q. tests and tracking, two common devices to segregate students by cognitive abilities, are highly suspect because they label children, resulting in a positive self-fulfilling prophecy for some children and a negative one for others. Moreover, the results of the tests and the placement of children in "tracks" because of the tests, are biased toward middle and upper class experiences.

Educational attainment, especially receiving the college degree, is the most important predictor of success in America. Bowles and Gintis have shown, for example, that those in the lowest tenth of the population in years of schooling have a 3.5 percent chance of being in the top fifth of the population in monetary income. At the other end, though, those in the highest tenth of the population in education have a 45.9 percent chance of being in the top 20 percent in income.[44] Moreover, among people with identical I.Q. test scores, those in the top tenth in schooling are eight times more likely to be in the top fifth in income than those in the lowest tenth in education.[45] Clearly, mental skills alone are not enough. They must be coupled with formal schooling to maximize the likelihood of economic success.

Just as important, Bowles and Gintis have also shown that family socioeconomic background determines how much education one receives: those in the lowest tenth in socioeconomic family background *with the same average I.Q. scores* as those in highest tenth in socioeconomic family background will receive an average of 4.9 *fewer years of education.*[46] In short, educational level determines socioeconomic position—and one's family's socioeconomic background determines one's educational opportunities. Thus, the ascribed status of family background has a profound impact on the probability of educational achievement and upward mobility.

Christopher Jencks and his associates have added to the work of Bowles and Gintis, providing the most current and methodologically sophisticated analysis of the determinants of upward mobility in their book *Who Gets Ahead?*[47] Their findings, summarized, show the following as the most important factors leading to success.

1. Family background is the most important factor. Children coming from families in the top 20 percent in income will, as adults, have incomes of 150 to 186 percent of the national average whereas those from the bottom 20 percent will earn 56 to 67 percent of the national average.

2. Educational attainment—especially graduating from college—is very important to later success. It is not so much what one learns in school but obtaining the credentials that counts. The probability of high educational attainment is closely tied to family background.

3. Scores from intelligence tests are by themselves poor predictors of economic success. Intelligence test scores are related to family background and educational attainment. The key remains the college degree. If high I.Q. people do not go to college they will tend *not* to succeed economically.

4. Personality traits of high school students, more than grades and I.Q., have an impact on economic success. No single trait emerges as the decisive determinant of economic success but rather the combined effects of many different traits are found to be important. These are self-concept, industriousness (as rated by teachers), and the social skills or motivations that lead students to see themselves as leaders and to hold positions of leadership in high school.

The picture drawn by Jencks and other experts on social mobility in America is of a relatively rigid society in which being born to the right family has a profound impact, especially on the probability of graduating from college. There are opportunities for advancement in society but they are clustered among the already advantaged. If the stratification system were open with equality of opportunity it would make sense that people, even the disadvantaged, would support it. The irony is that although the chances of the poor being successful are small indeed, the poor tend to support the inequality generated by capitalism—truly a case of false consciousness. This irony will become clearer as we see the consequences of inequality for individuals.

THE CONSEQUENCES OF SOCIOECONOMIC STATUS

We have conceived of social strata as aggregates of individuals and families with more or less similar economic positions, similar educational attainment, and holding occupations similar in prestige. These aggregates are ranked, and this creates a stratification hierarchy. Even though these "classes" do not possess real boundaries and class consciousness (except, as we have noted, at the very top), there are very real differences between an aggregate of people at one level of the status hierarchy and persons at another level. This section will illlustrate these differences from research that has focused on the life chances of the various strata.

Perhaps Marx was right that the key to the class structure is economics. The extent of one's wealth is the determining factor in a number of crucial areas, including the chance to live and the chance to obtain those things (for example, possessions, education) that are highly valued in society. The term **life chances** refers to the chances throughout one's life cycle to live and to experience the good things in life. This is dependent almost exclusively on the economic circumstances of the family to which one is born. Gerth and Mills have contended that life chances refer to

> everything from the chance to stay alive during the first year after birth to the chance to view fine art, the chance to remain healthy and grow tall, and if sick to get well again quickly, the chance to avoid becoming a juvenile delinquent—and very crucially, the chance to complete an intermediary or higher educational grade. . . .[48]

Life
Expectancy

Economic position has a great effect upon how long one will live or in a crisis who will be the last to die. For instance, the official casualty lists of the trans-Atlantic luxury liner, the *Titanic*, which rammed an iceberg in 1912, listed 3 percent of the first-class female passengers as lost; 16 percent of the second-class female passengers drowned, and among the third-class females 45 percent were drowned.[49] Apparently, even in a disaster, socioeconomic position makes a very real difference—the higher the economic status of the individual, the greater the probability of survival.

The greater advantage toward longer life by the well-to-do is not limited to disasters such as that of the *Titanic*. A consistent research finding is that health and death are influenced greatly by social status.*

Probably the most complete and valid (methodologically) study in this area was conducted by Kitagawa and Hauser, who matched 340,000 death certificates (for deaths occurring during the months May–August, 1960) to the 1960 Census records.[51] Using educational attainment level as an indicator of socioeconomic status, the researchers found the expected strong inverse correlation between mortality and educational attainment. Among white

---

*There is an excellent summary article (by Aaron Antonovsky) surveying over thirty studies done prior to 1950 in the United States and elsewhere which lead to the conclusion that socioeconomic status influences one's chance of staying alive.[50]

women between the ages of 25 and 64 years, for example, the mortality rate for those with less than eight years of school was 61 percent higher than among college educated women. Among white males in this age bracket, the mortality rate for those with less than eight years of school was 48 percent higher than for the college-educated men.

Principal
Cause of
Death

The data from Kitagawa and Hauser show very clearly the relationship between socioeconomic status (as measured by educational attainment) and the principal cause of death. The most striking finding was for white males between 25 and 64; those with less than eight years of education had a mortality rate from tuberculosis of more than 800 percent higher than the college-educated. This relationship, although not as strong as found for tuberculosis, was also noted for death from influenza, pneumonia, accidents (motor vehicle and all others), and cancer of the stomach, lung, bronchus, and trachea.

Among the women of this sample, the same general pattern of the less educated having higher mortality rates from specific diseases was found with one exception. Cancer of the breast was found to be the cause of death more frequently in the more educated category.

Among men over 65 there were two interesting differences. The lower-educated persons were more likely to die of cardiovascular disease and cancer than the higher educated. But one form of cancer—cancer of the prostate—was much more likely to be the cause of death among the more highly educated men.

Physical
Health

The physical health of poor persons is more likely to be impaired than the health of the more well-to-do because of differences in diet, sanitation facilities, and adequate clothing and shelter. Poor people also cannot afford the best medical care. The following quotation from the United States Public Health Service summarizes the special health problems of the poor, in this case poor children:

> Poor children are more likely to be in poor health or to have functional disabilities than children in families with adequate incomes. They are more likely to develop communicable diseases. They are no more likely to develop other conditions, such as myopia or asthma, but because they are less likely to receive adequate medical care, they are more likely to have some degree of functional disability as a result.
>
> Physical illness, disability, and death are not independent of one another, nor are they independent of emotional illness and disability or the environment in which the child's life is spent. Emotional or behavioral problems can both cause and result from physical problems. The environment, both physical and social, affects physical and emotional health. Crowded and dilapidated housing, poor schools and teachers, poverty, and discrimination all increase the risk of physical and emotional illness and impairment. Adequate housing, good schools and teachers, enough money for food and clothing, and social acceptance all decrease the risk.
>
> Strong relationships exist between family income and certain health indica-

tors. The proportion of children in "fair" or "poor" health drops significantly as family income rises. About 9 percent of the children and youth in families with incomes of less than $5,000 per year, compared with 2 percent in families with incomes of $15,000 or more, are reported as being in "fair" or "poor" health. Children and youth in low income families are more likely to have days when their activity is restricted, when they are confined to bed, or when they are out of school. For example, school-age children in low income families lost an average 6.6 days from school per year during 1975–76 because of acute illnesses, while school-age children in high income families lost an average 4.7 days.[52]

Table 9–3 provides government data on the relationships between health and income. For example, children from families with incomes of less than $5,000 visit dentists less than once a year while those from families with incomes over $15,000 average 2.2 visits to the dentist annually. This does not mean that the teeth of the well-to-do are worse than those of the poor but rather that they can afford to do more to ensure that they will continue to have good teeth. The data also show that money translates into fewer days away from work, a lower incidence of respiratory conditions, feeling healthy, and adequate medical insurance.

Mental Health

The most consistent relationship reported in social psychiatric studies is the inverse relationship between socioeconomic status and psychological disorder. Probably the most often cited study is that conducted by Hollingshead and Redlich in New Haven, Connecticut.

Hollingshead and Redlich used objective variables to determine social class—level of occupation and education and quality of neighborhood. Despite the artificiality of the class boundaries, the findings are dramatic in that they show that the prevalence of all types of psychoses increases

TABLE 9–3   Selected Indicators of Health by Level of Income, 1980

Family Income	Average Number of Days of Disability per Person	Incidence of Diabetes (rate per 1000 population)		Median per Capita Daily Intake of Protein	Median per Capita Daily Intake of Vitamin C
Under $5,000	37.5	40.7	below poverty line[a]	59.77g	50.96mg
$5,000–$9,999	25.8	36.8			
$10,000–$14,999	19.4	24.1	above poverty line	67.56g	71.57mg
$15,000 and over	13.8	19.0			

[a]The official line denoting poverty in 1980 was an annual income of $8,414 for a nonfarm family of four.
Source: *Bureau of the Census, Statistical Abstract of the United States, 1982–83* (Washington, D.C.: U.S. Government Printing Office, 1982), Tables 185, 192, 205.

as the index of occupation, education, and neighborhood decreases. This classic study by Hollingshead and Redlich is representative of the findings of countless other studies.[53]

Family
Instability

Research relating socioeconomic status to family discord and marital disruption has found an inverse relationship—the lower the status, the greater the proportion of divorce or desertion. An explanation for this relationship is that lower-class families experience greater economic and job insecurity. Given the tremendous emphasis in the United States on success and achievement, lower-class persons (particularly men) will tend to define themselves and be perceived by others in the society as a failure. Such a belief will, doubtless, hinder rather than help a marriage relationship.

The Draft

The draft system works to the disadvantage of the uneducated. In 1969 only 10 percent of the men drafted were college men—yet over 40 percent of college-age men go to college. The Supreme Court has further helped the educated by ruling that a person can be a conscientious objector either on a basis of religion or philosophy. Young intellectuals can use their knowledge of history, philosophy, and even sociology to argue that they should not serve. The uneducated will not have the necessary knowledge or sharpened intellect to make such a case.

For those educated young men who end up in the armed services, there is a greater likelihood of their serving in noncombat supply and administrative jobs than for the non-college-educated. Persons who can type, do bookkeeping, or know computer programming will generally be selected to do jobs where their skills can be used. Conversely, the nonskilled will generally end up in the most hazardous jobs. The chances for getting killed while in the service are greater, therefore, for the less educated than for the college educated.[54]

Justice

Chapter 8 provided strong evidence that the administration of justice is unequal in the United States. Low-status persons are more likely to be arrested, to be found guilty, and to serve longer sentences for a given violation than persons of middle and upper status. Let us review a small but representative portion of the evidence.

A study of California court decisions involving first-degree murder found blue-collar workers to stand a better chance of being sentenced to death than white-collar workers. This study, conducted by five Stanford University Law School students, examined 200 separate factors that might be related to getting the death penalty. Occupation was found to be the most important determinant.[55]

White-collar crime (for example, price fixing, using fraudulent advertising claims, embezzlement, and issuing fraudulent stock) often involves much more money than burglary or robbery, but the offenders of white-collar

TABLE 9–4	Sentences for Different Categories of Crime, Federal Offenders in U.S. District Courts, 1982

Crime Categories	Average Sentence (in months)
Crimes of the poor	
Marijuana violations	56.5
Robbery	128.2
Burglary	39.0
Auto theft	33.4
Larceny/theft	41.8
Assault	76.7
Crimes of the affluent	
Embezzlement	32.3
Fraud	32.5
Income tax evasion	24.6

Source: Administration Office of the U.S. Courts, *Federal Offenders in U.S. District Courts, 1982* (Washington, D.C.: U.S. Government Printing Office, 1983), Table 6, Table H–2a.

crimes seldom receive proportionate jail sentences or fines as Table 9–4 shows.

For example, a partner in a New York stock brokerage firm pleaded guilty to trading illegally $20 million in Swiss banks. He hired a prestigious lawyer, who got the judge to issue a fine of $30,000 and a suspended sentence. That same judge, when confronted a few days later with the case of an unemployed black shipping clerk who pleaded guilty to stealing a television set worth $100 from an interstate shipment, sentenced him to one year in jail.[56]

Why does justice let its blindfold slip? The rich can afford the services of the very best lawyers for their defense, detectives to gather supporting evidence, and expert witnesses such as psychiatrists. The rich can afford to appeal the decision to a series of appellate courts. The poor, on the other hand, must take court-appointed lawyers, who are usually among the least experienced lawyers in the community. All the evidence points to the regrettable truth that a defendant's wealth makes a significant difference in the administration of justice.

There is a class bias held by most citizens, including arresting officers and judges, that affects the administration of justice. There is a set of assumptions about persons according to their socioeconomic status. In a study of a small South Dakota community, police officials were found to deal severely with lower-class delinquents on the theory that they came from bad stock and therefore required strict punishment. Upper-class teenagers who violated the same laws were deemed by officials to be "accidental" cases to which their families were not accountable, and the cases were consequently dismissed after a warning.[57]

A Philadelphia attorney who specializes in representing juveniles has said:

> A middle-class white juvenile delinquent—even if caught red-handed—almost never goes to jail, but for a poor kid, it's another story. I have represented many white middle-class girls caught shoplifting, and almost none of them went to prison. This isn't due to my talents, but to the system. I'd say to the court: "Your honor, this girl wants to go to college, and her family is sending her to a psychiatrist." Then I'd put Momma on the stand, have her mention the psychiatrist's name—and that's all it would take.[58]

Education

In general, life chances are dependent upon wealth—they are purchased. The level of educational attainment (except for the children of the elite, where the best in life is a birthright) is the crucial determinant of one's chances of income.

Inequality of educational opportunity exists in all educational levels in many subtle and not so subtle ways. It occurs in the quality of education when schools are compared by district. The districts with a better tax base have superior facilities, better-motivated teachers (because the districts can pay more), and better techniques than the poorer districts. Within each school, regardless of the type of district, children are given standardized tests that have a middle-class bias. Armed with these data, children are placed in "tracks" according to "ability." These tracks thus become discriminatory, because the lowest track is composed disproportionately of the lower socioeconomic category. These tracks are especially harmful in that they structure the expectations of the teacher.

The classic study that demonstrates empirically the reinforcement of the stratification system by the educational system was done by A. B. Hollingshead.[59] He found that the lower the socioeconomic status of the high school student's family:

1. The higher the dropout rate.
2. The lower the vocational aspirations.
3. The lower the proportion planning on college.
4. The lower the course grades and the higher the percentage of failures.
5. The lower the IQ scores.
6. The greater the number of recorded discipline problems.

The net effect of these facts is that children tend to repeat the educational experience of their parents. Consequently, even bright youngsters from the lower classes have difficulty in school and probably will not attend college. These data are interpreted by social scientists as demonstrating that American schools systematically disadvantage the lower-class children in favor of upper- and middle-class children.

Political Ideologies and Inequality

Is inequality what has made the United States a powerful and affluent nation? If so, will it continue to do so? Are we responsible for those who are unsuccessful in society? Governmental decision makers may reduce or increase the extent of inequality in society by subsidies and tax reform. What would you encourage them to do?

There are essentially four political ideologies held by various groups and individuals in American society. You will certainly find political figures representing each position, whom you can work for or against. Let's briefly review the spectrum of political ideologies with respect to their positions on inequality in society.

Conservatism. This political philosophy favors inequality. Similar to the order model, this ideology believes that competition for unequal rewards is necessary to motivate people and ensure that the best people will do the most important tasks. The key is the need for unequal wages to persuade people to work harder and unequal profits to promote managerial efficiency. The government should, therefore, leave individuals alone and let the competitive market work unencumbered.

Liberalism. This political ideology prevails in contemporary American society. Governmental aid is advocated to provide minimum welfare payments, food stamps, and the like to reduce the misery of the poorest segments of society. Governmental intervention to limit inequality is minimal, however, so as not to displace the basic functioning of the competitive free market.

New populism. The goal of this philosophy is to change the American political and economic system from one that further enriches the rich and powerful to one that responds to the less-than-rich and the not-so-powerful. Leaders of this reform movement advocate the closing of tax loopholes, the increase of inheritance and estate taxes, the lowering of taxes that disproportionately hurt the poor (for example, the sales tax), free medical care for all, the expansion of Social Security, and the public ownership of all utilities.

Democratic socialism. Unlike the three previous political-economic ideologies, socialism rejects capitalism. Socialists would take over the ownership of private corporations, commit an enormous investment in welfare for all citizens (health, housing, food, minimum annual wage), and make the tax structure truly progressive (treat all income alike for tax purposes and increase the rate as income increases). The goal of these programs is to halt gross inequalities by guaranteeing adequate goods and services to all citizens.

These ideologies represent four possible responses to the societal problem of inequality. The dilemma is that at one extreme, conservatism condones people living in poverty, while at the opposite end, persons must give up some freedoms and sacrifice for the good of all. What is your position? Which direction should our government take?

SUMMARY

Social stratification, the ranking of persons into superior and inferior statuses, is a universal phenomenon. Order theorists view this characteristic of society as having positive consequences. It provides for the smooth functioning of society by providing for a division of labor and ensuring that the most talented persons will be motivated to do the most sensitive and crucial tasks. Conflict theorists, however, see stratification not as a source of societal integration and survival, but as the major source of social problems and social discord. It leads to coercion by the powerful, who wish to retain their advantages, and to conflict between the "haves" and the "have-nots."

Both sides in this debate recognize the consistent relationship between socioeconomic status and achievement of the desirable things in life. The general pattern is that lower-status persons are disadvantaged—in school, in marriage, in the courts, in health, and so on. The research findings are consistent, regardless of whether socioeconomic status is measured by income, educational attainment, or occupational prestige, or a combination of these status characteristics.

CHAPTER REVIEW

1. The process of categorizing people on some dimension(s) is called social differentiation.

2. When people are ranked in a hierarchy that differentiates them as superior or inferior this is called social stratification.

3. An individual's position (social status) in the stratification system is determined by the degree to which he or she possesses those qualities highly valued by the society.

4. Those persons occupying the same relative economic rank form a social class.

5. Persons who consider themselves social equals constitute a status group.

6. Movement from one class or status position to another is called social mobility.

7. Order model theorists accept social inequality as universal and natural. They believe that inequality serves a basic function by motivating the most talented people to perform the most important tasks.

8. Conflict theorists tend to denounce social inequality as basically unjust, unnecessary, and the source of many social problems. The irony is that the oppressed often accept their deprivation. Conflict theorists view this as the result of false consciousness—the acceptance through the socialization process of an untrue belief that works to one's disadvantage.

9. Americans vary greatly on a number of socioeconomic dimensions. Wealth and income are maldistributed. Educational attainment varies. Occupations differ greatly in prestige and pay.

10. The extent of class boundaries varies from community to community. The two indicators of the existence of separate classes are class consciousness and class segregation.

11. Class consciousness is relatively low in the U.S. There are clusters of characteristics along the status hierarchy that individuals recognize and that make it possible to designate "social classes" more or less artificially.

12. Societies vary in the degree to

which individuals may move up in status. The most rigid are called caste systems which are essentially closed to hereditary groups. Class systems are more open, permitting vertical mobility.

13. Although the U.S. is a relatively open class system, the extent of inter-generational mobility (a son or daughter surpassing his or her parents) is limited.

14. The prime determinants of upward mobility appear to be: (a) family background; (b) educational attainment; (c) graduation from college; and (d) personality traits.

15. The consequences of one's socioeconomic status are best expressed in the concept of "life chances," which refers to the chances to live and the chances to obtain those things highly valued in society. The data show that the higher one's economic position: the longer one's life; the healthier (physically and mentally) one will be; the more stable one's family; the less likely one will be drafted; the less likely one will be processed by the criminal justice system; and the higher one's educational attainment.

FOR FURTHER STUDY

Paul Blumberg, *Inequality in an Age of Decline* (New York: Oxford University Press, 1980).

Samuel Bowles and Herbert Gintis, *Schooling in Capitalist America* (New York: Basic Books, 1976).

Ralf Dahrendorf, *Class and Class Conflict in Industrial Society* (Palo Alto, Calif.: Stanford University Press, 1959).

John Dalpin, *The Persistence of Social Inequality in America* (Cambridge, Mass.: Schenkman, 1981).

Dennis Gilbert and Joseph A. Kahl, *The American Class Structure: A New Synthesis* (Homewood, Ill.: Dorsey, 1982).

Vincent Jeffries and H. Edward Ransford, *Social Stratification: A Multiple Hierarchy Approach* (Boston: Allyn and Bacon, 1980).

Christopher Jencks, and others, *Who Gets Ahead? The Determinants of Economic Success in America* (New York: Basic Books, 1979).

Harold R. Kerbo, *Social Stratification and Inequality: Class Conflict in the United States* (New York: McGraw-Hill, 1983).

Louis Kriesberg, *Social Inequality* (Englewood Cliffs, N.J.: Prentice-Hall, 1979).

Gerhard Lenski, *Power and Privilege: A Theory of Social Stratification* (New York: McGraw-Hill, 1966).

Celeste Mac Leod, *Horatio Alger, Farewell: The End of the American Dream* (New York: Seaview, 1980).

Frances Fox Piven and Richard A. Cloward, *The New Class War: Reagan's Attack on the Welfare State and Its Consequences* (New York: Pantheon, 1982).

Jeffrey H. Reiman, *The Rich Get Richer and the Poor Get Prison* (New York: Wiley, 1979).

William Ryan, *Equality* (New York: Vintage Books, 1981).

Beth Ensminger Vanfossen, *The Structure of Social Inequality* (Boston: Little, Brown, 1979).

NOTES AND REFERENCES

1. Philip Lerman, "Latest Status Symbol: Swanky ZIP Code," *USA Today* (September 23, 1983), pp. 1A, 4A.

2. "The Man in the Middle," *Forbes* (February 28, 1983), p. 8.

3. David Osborne, "Rich Doctors, Poor Nurses," *Harper's* 265 (September 1982), pp. 8–17.

4. Andrew Hacker (ed.), *U/S: A Statistical Portrait of the American People* (New York: Viking, 1983), pp. 142–143.

5. *Ibid.*, p. 144.

6. Harold Seneker (ed.), "The Forbes Four Hundred," *Forbes* (Fall 1983), pp. 71–192.

7. The following discussion is indebted in part to the insights provided by Melvin M. Tumin, *Social Stratification: The Forms and Functions of Inequality* (Englewood Cliffs, N.J.: Prentice-Hall, 1967), pp. 12–18; and Celia Heller, *Structured Social Inequality* (New York: Macmillan, 1969).

8. Harold R. Kerbo, *Social Stratification and Inequality: Class Conflict in the United States* (New York: McGraw-Hill, 1983), p. 11.

9. Kingsley Davis and Wilbert E. Moore, "Some Principles of Stratification," *American Sociological Review* 10 (April, 1945), pp. 242–249. For an elaboration of the order model's view of stratification, see Leonard Beeghley, *Social Stratification in America: A Critical Analysis of Theory and Research* (Santa Monica, Calif.: Goodyear, 1978), Chap. 3.

10. There are some powerful criticisms of the Davis-Moore argument. See especially Melvin M. Tumin, "Some Principles of Stratification," *American Sociological Review* 18 (August, 1953), pp. 387–393; and George A. Huaco, "The Functionalist Theory of Stratification: Two Decades of Controversy," *Inquiry* 9 (Autumn, 1966), pp. 215–240.

11. L. Richard Della Fave, "Mass Support for Inequality," paper presented at the meeting of the Society for the Study of Social Problems, New York (August, 1975), pp. 5–7; Michael Parenti, *Power and the Powerless* (New York: St. Martin's Press, 1978), pp. 15–18; Albert J. Szymanski and Ted George Goertzel, *Sociology: Class, Consciousness, and Contradictions* (New York: D. Van Nostrand, 1979), pp. 137–138. For the original statement on "false consciousness" see Karl Marx and Friedrich Engels, "Manifesto of the Communist Party" in L. Feuer (ed.), *Marx and Engels: Basic Writings on Politics and Philosophy* (New York: Doubleday, 1959), pp. 15–17. This was originally written in 1848.

12. See especially Richard Sennett and Jonathan Cobb, *The Hidden Injuries of Class* (New York: Random House (Vintage Books), 1973).

13. Cary Davis, Carl Haub, and Jo Anne Willette, "U.S. Hispanics: Changing the Face of America," *Population Bulletin* 38 (June 1983), p. 37; and *U.S. News & World Report* (August 2, 1982), p. 8.

14. Davis, Haub, and Willette, "U.S. Hispanics," p. 32.

15. C. C. North and Paul K. Hatt, "Jobs and Occupations: A Popular Evaluation," *Public Opinion News* 9 (September, 1947), pp. 3–13.

16. Robert W. Hodge, Paul M. Siegel, and Peter H. Rossi, "Occupational Prestige in the United States, 1925–63," *American Journal of Sociology* 70 (November, 1964), pp. 286–302.

17. Robert W. Hodge, Donald J. Treiman, and Peter H. Rossi, "A Comparative Study of Occupational Prestige," in *Class, Status, and Power*, 2nd ed., Reinhard Bendix and S. M. Lipset, eds. (New York: Free Press, 1966), pp. 309–321.

18. Linda Burzotta Nilson and Murray Edelman, "The Symbolic Evocation of Occupational Prestige," *Society* 16 (March/April 1979), p. 60.

19. A. B. Hollingshead, *Elmtown's Youth: The Impact of Social Classes on Adolescents* (New York: John Wiley, 1949).

20. Gerhard Lenski, "American Social Classes: Statistical Strata on Social Groups," *American Journal of Sociology* 58 (September, 1952), pp. 139–144.

21. See, for example, William H. Form and Joan Huber (Rytina), "Ideological Beliefs on the Distribution of Power in the United States," *American Sociological Review* 34 (February, 1969); and any current poll by the Gallup or Roper organizations where the data are presented by income, education, and/or occupation levels.

22. Richard Centers, *The Psychology of Social Classes: A Study of Class Consciousness* (Princeton, N.J.: Princeton University Press, 1949).

23. For a summary of the criticisms of Centers's study, see especially Milton M. Gordon, *Social Class in American Sociology* (New York: McGraw-Hill, paperback edition, 1963), pp. 193–202.

24. Neal Gross, "Social Class Identification in the Urban Community," *American Sociological Review* 18 (August, 1953), pp. 398–404.

25. Oscar Glantz, "Class Consciousness and Po-

litical Solidarity," *American Sociological Review* 23 (August, 1958), pp. 375–382.

26. John C. Leggett, "Economic Insecurity and Working-Class Consciousness," *American Sociological Review* 29 (April, 1964), pp. 226–234. For other studies on class consciousness in the United States, see R. Vanneman and F. C. Pampel, "The American Perception of Class and Status," *American Sociological Review* 42 (June, 1977), pp. 422–437; and E. M. Schreiber and G. T. Nygreen, "Subjective Social Class in America: 1945–68," *Social Forces* 48 (March, 1970), pp. 348–356.

27. Beth Ensminger Vanfossen, *The Structure of Social Inequality* (Boston: Little, Brown, 1979), p. 242.

28. Daniel W. Rossides, *The American Class System* (Boston: Houghton Mifflin, 1976), p. 265.

29. Celeste Mac Leod, *Horatio Alger, Farewell: The End of the American Dream* (New York: Seaview, 1980).

30. Bob Kuttner, "The Declining Middle," *The Atlantic Monthly* 252 (July 1983), pp. 60–72.

31. G. William Domhoff, *The Higher Circles: The Governing Class in America* (New York: Random House, 1970), p. 74.

32. *Ibid.*, p. 78.

33. *Ibid.*, p. 80.

34. *Ibid.*, p. 87; see E. Digby Baltzall, *Philadelphia Gentlemen: The Making of a National Upper Class* (New York: Free Press, 1958); and C. Wright Mills, *The Power Elite* (Fair Lawn, N.J.: Oxford University Press, 1959).

35. Lucy Kavaler, *The Private World of High Society* (New York: Pyramid Books, 1961), p. 184.

36. Seymour Martin Lipset, "The Sources of the 'Radical Right,'" in *The Radical Right*, Daniel Bell, ed. (Garden City, N.Y.: Doubleday (Anchor Books), 1963), p. 341.

37. Daniel R. Miller and Guy E. Swanson, *The Changing American Parent* (New York: John Wiley, 1958).

38. For an excellent discussion of the extent to which American society parallels Indian society, see Gerald D. Berreman, "Caste in India and the United States," *American Journal of Sociology* 66 (September, 1960), pp. 120–127.

39. Peter M. Blau and Otis Dudley Duncan, *The American Occupational Structure* (New York: Wiley, 1967).

40. Richard H. De Lone, *Small Futures: Children, Inequality, and the Limits of Liberal Reform* (Carnegie Council on Children), cited in Patricia McCormack, "Economic Gap Between Classes," *Rocky Mountain News* (August 22, 1979), p. 66.

41. De Lone, *Small Futures*, cited in Murray Kempton, "Arithmetic of Inequality," *The Progressive* 43 (November, 1979), pp. 8–9.

42. Christopher Jencks, et al., *Who Gets Ahead? The Determinants of Economic Success in America* (New York: Basic Books, 1979); and Herbert Gintis, "Who Gets Ahead?" *Saturday Review* (June 2, 1979), pp. 29–33.

43. Samuel Bowles and Herbert Gintis, *Schooling in Capitalist America* (New York: Basic Books, 1976), Chapter 4.

44. *Ibid.*, pp. 110–112.

45. *Ibid.*, p. 113.

46. *Ibid.*, p. 31.

47. Jencks, *Who Gets Ahead?*

48. Hans Gerth and C. Wright Mills, *Character and Social Structure: The Psychology of Social Institutions* (New York: Harcourt, Brace, and World, 1953), p. 313.

49. Walter Lord, *A Night to Remember* (New York: Henry Holt, 1955), p. 107.

50. Aaron Antonovsky, "Social Class, Life Expectancy and Overall Mortality," *Millbank Memorial Fund Quarterly* 45 (April, 1967), pp. 31–73.

51. Evelyn M. Kitagawa and Philip M. Hauser, "Education Differentials in Mortality by Cause of Death: United States, 1960," *Demography* 5 (1968), pp. 318–353.

52. Public Health Service, *Health: United States 1978* (Department of Health, Education, and Welfare, Publication No. (PHS) 78–1232, December 1978), p. 55.

53. Robert Faris and H. Warren Dunham, *Mental Disorders in Urban Areas* (Chicago: University of Chicago Press, 1939); and Leo Srole, Thomas S. Langner, Stanley T. Michael, Marvin K. Oplea, and Thomas A. C. Rennie, *Mental Health in the Metropolis* (New York: McGraw-Hill, 1962).

54. Maurice Zeitlin, Kenneth G. Lutterman, and James W. Russell, "Death in Vietnam: Class, Poverty, and the Risks of War," in *American Society, Inc.*, 2nd ed., Maurice Zeitlin, ed. (Chicago: Rand McNally, 1977), pp. 143–155; and Laurence M. Baskir and William A. Strauss, *The Draft, The War, and the Vietnam Generation* (New York: Knopf, 1978). See also, Michael Useem, "Equity and the Draft," *Working Papers* 10 (January/February 1983), pp. 62–64; and Jeremy Feigelson, "Our Next War: Who Will Fight It? *Civil Rights Quarterly Perspective* 14 (Spring 1982), pp. 16–21.

55. "California Juries," *Parade*, November 2, 1969.

56. Glynn Mapes, "Unequal Justice: A Growing Disparity in Criminal Sentences Troubles Legal Experts," *The Wall Street Journal* (September 9, 1970), p. 21.

57. John Useem, Pierre Langent, and Ruth Useem, "Stratification in a Prairie Town," *American Sociological Review* 7 (June, 1942), p. 341.

58. Mapes, "Unequal Justice," p. 21.

59. A. B. Hollingshead, *Elmtown's Youth: The Impact of Social Classes on Adolescents* (New York: John Wiley, 1949).

10

Poverty
in the United States

. . . but I do not mean to ignore the bodily ills of these children [of migrant workers]: the hunger and the chronic malnutrition that they learn to accept as unavoidable; the diseases that one by one crop up as the first ten years of life go by; diseases that go undiagnosed and untreated; diseases of the skin and the muscles and the bones and the vital organs; vitamin deficiency diseases and mineral deficiency diseases; and untreated congenital diseases and infectious diseases and parasitic diseases, and in the words of one migrant mother, "all the sicknesses that ever was." She goes on: "I believe our children get them, the sicknesses, and there isn't anything for us to do but pray, because I've never seen a doctor in my life, except once, when he delivered my oldest girl; the rest, they was just born, yes sir, and I was lucky to have my sister near me, and that's the way, you know." . . .

That is what the migrant child eventually learns about "life," and once learned finds hard to forget. He learns that each day brings toil for his parents, backbreaking toil: bending and stooping and reaching and carrying. He learns that each day means a trip: to the fields and back from the fields, to a new county or on to another state, another region of the country. He learns that each day means not aimlessness and not purposeless motion, but compelled, directed (some would even say *forced*) travel. He learns, quite literally, that the wages of work are more work, rather than what some of us call "the accumulation of capital." He learns that wherever he goes he is both wanted and unwanted, and that, in any case, soon there will be another place and another and another. I must to some extent repeat and repeat the essence of such migrancy (the wandering, the dis-

approval and ostracism, the extreme and unyielding poverty) because children learn that way, learn by repetition, learn by going through something ten times and a hundred times and a thousand times, until finally it is there, up in their minds in the form of what I and my kind call an "image," a "self-image," a *notion*, that is, of life's hurts and life's drawbacks, of life's calamities—which in this case are inescapable and relentless and unremitting.

Source: Excerpts from Robert Coles, *Uprooted Children: The Early Life of Migrant Farm Workers* (Pittsburgh: University of Pittsburgh Press, 1970), pp. 123–126. Reprinted by permission of the University of Pittsburgh Press. © 1970 by University of Pittsburgh Press.

The United States is envied by most peoples of the world. It is blessed with great natural resources, the most advanced technology known, and a very high standard of living. Despite these facts, a significant portion of American citizens live in a condition of poverty. Millions of Americans are ill-fed, ill-clothed, and ill-housed. These same millions are discriminated against in the schools, in the courts, in the job market, and in the marketplace, and discrimination has the effect of trapping many of the poor in that condition. The "American Dream" is just that for millions of Americans— a dream that will not be realized.

The purpose of this chapter is both descriptive and practical. On the one hand, we shall examine the facts of poverty—who the poor are, how many are there, where they are located, is the proportion of poor people increasing or decreasing, and what it means to be poor. On the practical level, we shall explore what needs to be done if extreme poverty is to be eliminated.

There are two underlying themes in this chapter. The first: The victims of poverty are not to be blamed for their condition; rather, the inequities present in American society are responsible. This is because the essence of poverty is inequality—in money and in opportunity. The second theme is most important when we take up the possible solutions to this social problem: The United States has the resources to eliminate poverty if it will give that problem a high enough priority.

THE EXTENT OF POVERTY IN THE UNITED STATES

What separates the poor from the nonpoor? In a continuum there is no absolute standard for wealth. The line separating the poor from the nonpoor is necessarily arbitrary. The Social Security Administration (SSA) sets the official poverty line based on what it considers the minimal amount required for a subsistence level of life. To determine the poverty line, the SSA computes the cost of a basic nutritionally adequate diet and multiplies that figure by three. This figure is based on a government research finding that poor people spend one-third of their income on food. If we use this standard, in 1982 15 percent of the population (34.4 million, an increase of 2.6 million from 1981) were defined as living in poverty.

In this chapter we shall consider the poor as those below this arbitrary line. However, the government procedure is not only arbitrary; it actually minimizes the extent of poverty in America. Some economists have argued that a more realistic figure would be 50 percent of the median income. In 1982, for example, the official poverty line was $9,862 for a nonfarm family of four. If the 50 percent of median income standard were used, the line would have been $11,716, adding many millions to the poverty category.[1] Such a procedure might shock the government into more action to alleviate suffering in this country. In effect, though, "the poor" is anyone denied adequate health, diet, clothing, and shelter because of lack of resources.

Exact figures on the number of poor are difficult to determine. For one thing, the amount of money needed for subsistence varies drastically by locality. Compare, for example, the money needed for rent in New York City with that needed in rural Arkansas. Another difficulty is that those most likely to be missed by the U.S. Census are the poor. People most likely to be missed in the census live in ghettos (where several families may be crowded into one apartment) or in rural areas, where some homes are inaccessible and where some workers follow the harvest from place to place and therefore have no permanent home. Transients of any kind may well be missed by the census. The conclusion is inescapable that the proportion of the poor in the United States is underestimated, because the poor tend to be invisible, even to the government.[2] This underestimate of the poor has important consequences, since U.S. Census data are the basis for political representation in Congress. These data are also used as the basis for instituting new governmental programs or abandoning old ones. Needless to say, an accurate count of the total population is necessary if the census is so used.

Despite these difficulties and the understanding of actual poverty by the government's poverty line, we do know some facts about the poor.

□ *Racial minorities are disproportionately poor.* Income in the United States is maldistributed by race—the median family income in 1982 was $24,603 for whites and $13,598 for blacks. Similarly, measures of the extent of poverty by race in 1982 were 12.0 percent white, 29.9 percent Hispanic, and 35.6 percent black.[3]

□ *The aged are disproportionately poor.* Almost 15 percent of the persons age 65 and over are poor. Although the overall rate has remained fairly stable over the past ten years or so, the aged poor are increasingly women and minority group members.

□ *Female-headed households are disproportionately poor.* Families headed by a woman with no husband present constitute the fastest-growing category of persons living below the government's poverty line. One-half of the poor families are headed by females and the numbers are growing rapidly. This trend, termed the **"feminization of poverty,"**[4] is the result of rising frequency of marital disruption and of poor job and earnings opportunities for women (see Chapter 12).[5]

□ *Children are disproportionately poor.* In 1982, 13.5 million children under age eighteen were poor, up from 10.2 million in 1979. This means that of all children one in five lives in poverty. And, more startling, one in two black children and one in three Hispanic children grow up in poverty.

□ *The gap between the poor and the nonpoor is widening.* There are a number of reasons for this, the two most prominent being inflation and the reduction of government programs for the needy (to be discussed later). The government's poverty line is determined by trebling the cost of food needed. Not included in the formula is the cost of energy and other necessities also affected by inflation. A government report has noted:

In 1979 the high rate of inflation in the basic necessities was led by a 37.4 percent increase in energy costs (heating fuel, electricity and gasoline). Shelter costs rose 17.4 percent, food prices rose 10.2 percent and medical costs rose 10.1 percent. For the decade of the 1970s, energy prices rose nearly 200 percent, shelter costs rose 121 percent, food prices rose 114 percent and medical costs rose 117 percent. This inflation rate hits the poor the hardest because households in the lowest 20 percent of income distribution spend 90 percent of their average after-tax income on these necessities, and the very poorest families have to go into debt to provide themselves with the basic necessities of life.[6]

THE COSTS OF POVERTY

Some 15 percent of Americans were officially poor (1982). These people and those just above the poverty line generally receive inferior educations, live in substandard housing, are malnourished, and have health problems. Some examples follow.

□ One of every four Americans lives in substandard housing.[7]

□ Twenty percent of American adults are functionally illiterate.

□ Premature births among the poor are three times higher than among middle-income people, and some 5 percent are born mentally retarded because of prenatal malnourishment. Over one million babies and young children suffer from brain damage caused by poverty-induced malnutrition.[8]

□ The National Health Service in 1981 estimated that 22–25 million Americans have no health insurance.[9]

□ Economic hardships increase the likelihood of a number of pathologies such as alcoholism, suicide, and child abuse.[10]

The psychological consequences of being poor are many. The poor are rejected and despised by others in the society, looked down upon as lazy, shiftless, dirty, and immoral. Being poor is therefore degrading. The poor are not wanted by the more well-to-do as neighbors, friends, mates, or colleagues. Thus, many of the poor define themselves as failures. They are the rejects of society and they feel it.

Being poor also engenders hopelessness, and thus, apathy. The poor have virtually no power. They cannot afford lawyers or lobbyists. They cannot afford to go on strike against low wages or high rent. Consequently, they tend to feel that their fates are in the hands of powerful others.

There is also a great deal of anger among the poor. They pay higher interest rates (because they are poor credit risks—another vicious circle); they are the last to be hired and the first to be fired; they must live in poor housing and often filthy conditions.[11] One of the most important sources of anger is that they see affluence all about them but, no matter how hard they try, are unable to share in it.

Given the propensity for alienation, hostility, and lack of ego strength among the poor, there are three ways in which the individual poor cope with the conditions in which they find themselves.

One coping device is accommodation, that is, trying to make it as best as possible by hard work and obeying the law. A second psychological mechanism is avoidance. This is escaping the harshness of reality through mental illness, alcohol, drugs, television, or religion. A variant of this mechanism is withdrawal in total apathy (not working, and seeming to not care). A third possibility is aggression. Some individuals respond by openly attacking the system, through participation in revolutionary or reform organizations, threats, complaints, destruction of property, or theft. In general, then, any repressed group (like any minority group, as we will note in Chapter 11) has three basic responses: to put up with the aversive situation, to withdraw from it, or to fight it.

What are the consequences for society if a significant proportion of the populace is poor? In economic terms, the cost is very high. In the first place, the poor constitute a relatively unproductive mass of people. In a sense these persons are wasted: their work output is marginal; they pay few or no taxes (usually only sales tax, since they have little property and low incomes). The cost to other taxpayers is quite large, in the form of welfare programs, urban renewal, and crime prevention. If poverty were eliminated through more better-paying jobs and more adequate monetary assistance to the permanently disabled or elderly, the entire society would prosper from the increased purchasing power and the larger tax base.

But economic considerations, though important, are not as crucial as humanitarian ones. A nation that can afford it must, if it calls itself civilized, eliminate the physical and psychological misery associated with poverty.

THE CAUSES OF POVERTY

Who or what is to blame for poverty? There are two very different answers to this question.[12] One is that the poor are in that condition because of some deficiency: either they are biologically inferior or their culture fails them by promoting character traits that impede their progress in society. The other response places the blame on the structure of society: some persons are poor because society has failed to provide equality in educational opportunity, because institutions discriminate against minorities, because private industry has failed to provide enough jobs, because automation has made some jobs obsolete, and so forth. In this view, society has worked in such a way as to trap certain persons and their offspring in a condition of poverty.

Deficiency Theory 1: Biological Inferiority

In 1882 the British philosopher and sociologist Herbert Spencer came to the United States to promote a theory later known as social Darwinism. He argued that the poor were poor because they were unfit. Poverty was nature's way of "excreting . . . unhealthy, imbecile, slow, vacillating, faithless members" of society in order to make room for the "fit," who were duly entitled to the rewards of wealth. Spencer preached that the poor should not be

helped through state or private charity, because such acts would interfere with nature's way of getting rid of the weak.[13] Social Darwinism has generally lacked support in the scientific community for fifty years, although it has continued to provide a rationale for the thinking of many individuals. Recently, however, the concept has resurfaced in the work of two respected scientists. Both suggest that the poor are in that condition because they do not measure up to the more well-to-do in intellectual endowment.

Arthur Jensen, professor of educational psychology at the University of California, has argued that there is a strong possibility that blacks are less well endowed mentally than whites. From his review of the research on IQ, he found that approximately 80 percent of IQ is inherited, while the remaining 20 percent is attributable to environment. Since blacks differ significantly from whites in achievement on IQ tests and in school, Jensen claimed that it is reasonable to hypothesize that the sources of these differences are genetic as well as environmental.[14]

Richard Herrnstein, a Harvard psychologist, agrees with Jensen that intelligence is largely inherited, and goes one step further positing the formation of hereditary castes based on intelligence.[15] For Herrnstein, social stratification by inborn differences occurs because: (1) mental ability is inherited, and (2) success (prestige of job and earnings) depends on mental ability. Thus, a meritocracy (social classification by ability) develops through the sorting process. This reasoning assumes that persons close in mental ability are more likely to marry and reproduce, thereby ensuring castes by level of intelligence. According to this thesis, "in times to come, as technology advances, the tendency to be unemployed may run in the genes of a family about as certainly as bad teeth do now."[16] This is another way of saying that the bright people are in the upper classes and the dregs are at the bottom. Inequality is justified just as it was years ago by the social Darwinists.

To buttress their claim for the overwhelming primacy of heredity over environment in intelligence, both Jensen and Herrnstein used data from the classic studies of identical twins by the famous British psychologist Sir Cyril Burt. These studies from the 1940s and 1950s have come under a cloud of suspicion. Burt, who died in 1971, has been accused of fraud, of having faked much of his research, of reporting tests that were never done, and of signing fictitious names as coauthors.[17]

Notwithstanding the flaws in the logic and in the evidence used by Jensen and Herrnstein, it is important to consider the implications of this thesis for dealing with the problem of poverty.

Jensen and Herrnstein have argued that dispassionate study is required to determine whether intelligence is inherited to the degree that they state. Objectivity is the *sine qua non* of scientific inquiry, and one cannot argue with its merits. We should recognize, however, the important social consequences implied by the Jensen-Herrnstein argument. First, it is a classic example of blaming the victim. The individual poor person is blamed instead of schools, culturally biased IQ tests, or social barriers of race, religion, or nationality. By blaming the victim, this thesis claims a relationship between lack of success and lack of intelligence. This is a spurious relationship because it ignores the advantages and disadvantages of ascribed status. According to William Ryan, "Arthur Jensen and Richard Herrnstein confirm regretfully that black folks and poor folks are born stupid, that little rich kids grow up rich adults, not because they inherited Daddy's stock portfolio, but rather because they inherited his brains."[18]

A second implication is the belief that poverty is inevitable. The "survival of the fittest" capitalist ideology is reinforced, justifying both discrimination against the poor and privilege for the privileged. Inequality is rationalized so that little will be done to aid its victims. The acceptance of this thesis, then, has obvious consequences for what policy decisions will be made or not made in dealing with poverty.

This thesis divides Americans further by appealing to bigots. It provides scientific justification for their beliefs in the racial superiority of some groups and the inferiority of others. By implication, it legitimates segregation and unequal treatment of "inferiors." The goal of integration and the fragile principle of egalitarianism are seriously threatened to the degree that members of the scientific community give this thesis credence or prominence.[19]

Another serious implication of the Jensen-Herrnstein argument is the explicit validation of the IQ test as a legitimate measure of intelligence. The IQ test attempts to measure "innate potential," but to do this is impossible, because the testing process must inevitably reflect some of the skills that develop during the individual's lifetime. For the most part, intelligence tests measure educability—that is, the prediction of conventional school achievement. Achievement in school is, of course, also associated with a cluster of other social and motivational factors, as Joanna Ryan observes.

> The test as a whole is usually validated, if at all, against the external criterion of school performance. It therefore comes as no surprise to find that IQ scores do in fact correlate highly with educational success. IQ scores are also found to correlate positively with socio-economic status, those in the upper social classes tending to have the highest IQs. Since social class, and all that this implies, is both an important determinant and also an important consequence of educational performance, this association is to be expected.[20]

The Jensen-Herrnstein thesis, however, overlooks the important contribution of social class to achievement on IQ tests. This oversight is crucial, since most social scientists feel that these tests are biased in favor of those who have had a middle- and upper-class environment and experience. IQ tests discriminate against the poor in many ways. They discriminate obviously in the language that is used, in the instructions that are given, and in the experiences they assume the subjects have had. The discrimination can also be more subtle. For minority-group examinees, the race of the person administering the test influences the results. Another, less well-known fact about IQ tests is that in many cases they provide a self-fulfilling prophecy, as this observer notes:

> IQ scores obtained at one age often determine how an individual is subsequently treated, and, in particular, what kind of education he receives as a

consequence of IQ testing will in turn contribute to his future IQ, and it is notorious that those of low and high IQ do not get equally good education.[21]

The Jensen-Herrnstein thesis also provides justification for unequal schooling. Why should school boards allot comparable sums of money for similar programs in middle-class schools and lower-class schools if the natural endowments of children in each type of school are so radically different? Why should teachers expect the same performance from poor children as from children from the more well-to-do? The result of such beliefs is, of course, a self-fulfilling prophecy. Low expectations beget low achievement.

Finally, the Jensen-Herrnstein thesis encourages policymakers either to ignore poverty or to attack its effects rather than its causes in the structure of society itself.

Deficiency Theory 2: Cultural Inferiority

One prominent explanation of poverty, called the "culture of poverty" hypothesis, contends that the poor are qualitatively different in values and life styles from the rest of society *and that these cultural differences explain continued poverty.* In other words, the poor, in adapting to their deprived condition, are found to be more permissive in raising their children, less verbal, more fatalistic, less apt to defer gratification, and less likely to be interested in formal education than the more well-to-do. Most important is the contention that this deviant cultural pattern is transmitted from generation to generation. Thus, there is a strong implication that poverty is perpetuated by defects in the lifeways of the poor. If poverty itself were to be eliminated, the former poor would probably continue to prefer instant gratification, be immoral by middle-class standards, and so on. Panel 10–1 provides an illustration by Edward Banfield, an eminent political scientist, who views the poor in this manner. Banfield presents a classic example of blaming the victim. To him, the poor have a subculture with values that differ radically from the other social classes. He does not see the present-time orientation of the poor as a function of the hopelessness of their situation. Yet it seems highly unlikely that the poor see little reason to complain about the slums: What about the filth, the rats, the overcrowded living conditions, the high infant mortality? What about the lack of jobs and opportunity for upward mobility? This feeling of being trapped seems the primary cause of a hedonistic present-time orientation. If the structure were changed so that the poor could see that hard work and deferred gratification really paid off, they could adopt a future-time orientation. Needless to say, there have been many severe criticisms of Banfield's position.[22]

Critics of the "culture of poverty" hypothesis argue that the poor are an integral part of American society; they do not abandon the dominant values of the society, but rather, retain them while simultaneously holding an alternative set of values. This alternative set is a result of adaptation to the conditions of poverty. Elliot Liebow, in his classic study of lower-class black men, has taken this view. For him, streetcorner men strive to live by American values but are continually frustrated by externally imposed failure.

Blaming the Poor

A continuing controversy is what to do about the urban poor. Edward Banfield, a distinguished professor of urban government at Harvard and chairperson of President Nixon's task force on model cities, has written a highly controversial book that presents the conservative assessment of the urban condition.

In Banfield's view, the urban poor have a culture of poverty that dooms them and their descendants to the lowest social class. The essence of the poor subcultures is a present-time orientation.

> The lower-class individual lives from moment to moment. If he has any awareness of a future, it is of something fixed, fated, beyond his control: things happen to him, he does not make them happen. Impulse governs his behavior, either because he cannot discipline himself to sacrifice a present for a future satisfaction or because he has no sense of the future. He is therefore radically improvident: whatever he cannot consume immediately he considers valueless. His bodily needs (especially for sex) and his taste for "action" take precedence over everything else—and certainly over any work routine. He works only as he must to stay alive, and drifts from one unskilled job to another, taking no interest in his work.

The poor are doomed by their hedonism. But according to Banfield, the culture of poverty is such that it makes the slums actually desirable to the slum dwellers.

> Although he has more "leisure" than almost anyone, the indifference ("apathy" if one prefers) of the lower-class person is such that he seldom makes even the simplest repairs to the place that he lives in. He is not troubled by dirt and dilapidation and he does not mind the inadequacy of public facilities such as schools, parks, hospitals, and libraries;

indeed, where such things exist he may destroy them by carelessness or even by vandalism. Conditions that make the slum repellent to others are serviceable to him in several ways. First, the slum is a place of excitement—"where the action is." Nothing happens there by plan and anything may happen by accident—a game, a fight, a tense confrontation with the police; feeling that something exciting is about to happen is highly congenial to people who live for the present and for whom the present is often empty. Second, it is a place of opportunity. Just as some districts of the city are specialized as a market for, say, jewelry or antiques, so the slum is specialized as one for vice and for illicit commodities generally. Dope peddlers, prostitutes, and receivers of stolen goods are all readily available there, within easy reach of each other and of their customers and victims. For "hustlers," the slum is the natural headquarters. Third, it is a place of concealment. A criminal is less visible to the police in the slum than elsewhere, and the lower-class individual, who in some parts of the city would attract attention, is one among many there. In the slum one can beat one's children, lie drunk in the gutter, or go to jail without attracting any special notice; these are things that most of the neighbors themselves have done and that they consider quite normal.

As Banfield sees it, the poor are the cause of urban problems:

> So long as the city contains a sizeable lower class, nothing basic can be done about its most serious problems. Good jobs may be offered to all, but some will remain chronically unemployed. Slums may be demolished, but if the housing that replaces them is occupied by the

lower class it will shortly be turned into new slums. Welfare payments may be doubled or tripled and a negative income tax substituted, but some persons will continue to live in squalor and misery. New schools may be built, new curricula devised, and the teacher-pupil ratio cut in half, but if the children who attend these schools come from lower-class homes, they will be turned into blackboard jungles, and those who graduate or drop out from them will, in most cases, be functionally illiterate. The streets may be filled with armies of policemen, but violent crime and civil disorder will decrease very little. If, however, the lower classes were to disappear—if say, its members were overnight to acquire the attitudes, motivations, and habits of the working class—the most serious and intractable problems of the city would all disappear with it. . . . The lower-class forms of all problems are at bottom a single problem: the existence of an outlook and style of life which is radically present-oriented and which therefore attaches no value to work, sacrifice, self-improvement, or service to family, friends, or community.

Source: Edward C. Banfield, *The Unheavenly City Revisited* (Boston: Little, Brown, 1974), pp. 61, 72, 234–235. Copyright © 1968, 1970, 1974 by Edward C. Banfield. By permission of Little, Brown and Company.

From this perspective, the streetcorner man does not appear as a carrier of an independent cultural tradition. His behavior appears not so much as a way of realizing the distinctive goals and values of his own subculture, or of conforming to its models, but rather as his way of trying to achieve many of the goals and values of the larger society, of failing to do this and of concealing his failure from others and from himself as best he can.[23]

Most Americans, however, believe that the poor are poor because they have a deviant system of values that encourages behaviors leading to poverty.[24]

Structural Theories

In contrast to blaming the biological or cultural deficiencies of the poor, there is the view that the way in which society is organized creates poverty and makes certain kinds of people especially vulnerable to being poor.

Institutional Discrimination. Michael Harrington, whose book *The Other America* was instrumental in sparking the federal government's War on Poverty, has said, "The real explanation of why the poor are where they are is that they made the mistake of being born to the wrong parents, in the wrong section of the country, in the wrong industry, or in the wrong racial or ethnic group."[25] This is another way of saying that the society is to blame for poverty, not the poor. Customary ways of doing things, prevailing attitudes and expectations, and accepted structural arrangements work to the disadvantage of the poor. Let us look at several examples of the way in which the poor are trapped.

Most good jobs require a college degree, but the poor cannot afford to send their children to college. Scholarships go to the best-performing students. Children of the poor most often do not perform well in school, largely because of low expectations for them among teachers and administrators. This is reflected in the system of "tracking" by ability as measured on class-biased examinations. Further evidence is found in the disproportionately low amounts of money given to schools in impoverished neighborhoods. All of these acts result in a self-fulfilling prophecy—the poor are not expected to do well in school and they do not. Since they are failures as measured by "objective" indicators (such as the disproportionately high number of dropouts and discipline problems and the very small proportion who desire to go to college), the school feels justified in its discrimination toward the children of the poor.

The poor are also trapped because they get sick more often and stay sick longer than the more well-to-do. The reasons, of course, are that they cannot afford preventive medicine, proper diets, and proper medical attention when ill. The high incidence of sickness among the poor means either that they will be fired from their jobs or that they will not receive money for the days missed from work (unlike the more well-to-do, who usually have jobs with such fringe benefits as sick leave and paid-up medical insurance). Not receiving a paycheck for extended periods means that the poor will have even less money for proper health care—thereby ensuring an even higher incidence of sickness. Thus, there is a vicious cycle of poverty. The poor will tend to remain poor, and their children tend to perpetuate the cycle.

The traditional organization of schools and jobs in American society has limited the opportunities of racial minorities and women. The next two chapters describe at length how these groups are systematically disadvantaged by the prevailing laws, customs, and expectations of society. Suffice it to say in this context that:

☐ Racial minorities are deprived of equal opportunities for education, jobs, and income.
☐ Women typically work at less prestigious jobs than men and when working at equal status jobs receive less pay and fewer chances for advancement.

The Political Economy of Society.   The basic tenet of capitalism—that who gets what is determined by private profit rather than collective need—explains the persistence of poverty.[26] The primacy of maximizing profit works to promote poverty in several ways. First, employers are constrained to pay their workers the least possible in wages and benefits. Only a portion of the wealth created by the laborers is distributed to them; the rest goes to the owners for investment and profit. This means that it is important for employers to keep wages low. That they are successful in this is demonstrated by data from 1981 that showed 9.5 million employed persons had earned income under the poverty level.[27] Second, since the price of labor is determined by the suppply, it is in the interest of employers to have a surplus of laborers.[28] It is especially important to have a supply of undereducated and desperate people who will work for very low wages. A large supply of these marginal people (such as minorities, women, undocumented workers) aid the ownership class by depressing the wages for all workers in good times and provide the obvious category of people to be laid off from work in economic downturns.

A third impact of the primacy of profits in capitalism is that employers make investment decisions without regard for their employees (potential or actual). If costs can be reduced, employers will purchase new technologies to replace workers (such as robots to replace assembly line workers and word processors to replace secretaries). Similarly, owners may shut down a plant and shift their operations to a foreign country where wages are significantly lower.

In sum, the fundamental assumption of capitalism is individual gain without regard for what the resulting behaviors may mean for others. The capitalist system, then, should not be accepted as a neutral framework within which goods are produced and distributed, but rather as an economic system that perpetuates inequality.

A number of political factors complement the workings of the economy to perpetuate poverty. Political decisions made recently to fight inflation with high interest rates, for example, have hurt several industries, particularly automobiles and home construction, causing high unemployment.

The powerful in society also use their political clout to keep society unequal.

> Poverty exists in America because the society is unequal, and there are overwhelming political pressures to keep it that way. Any attempt to redistribute wealth and income will inevitably be opposed by powerful interests. Some people can be relatively rich only if others are relatively poor, and since power is concentrated in the hands of the rich, public policies will continue to reflect their interests.[29]

Clearly, the affluent in a capitalist society will resist efforts to redistribute their wealth to the disadvantaged. Their political efforts are, rather, to increase their benefits at the expense of the poor and the powerless. (See Panel 10–2.) The policies of the Reagan administration provide an excellent example of how political decisions have adversely affected the poor.

Beginning with his inaugural in 1981, President Reagan along with a conservative Congress instituted a new economic program designed to curtail government spending for social programs, reduce the national debt, and stimulate the economy. These policies, known collectively as Reaganomics, increased the numbers of people living in poverty and widened the gap between the poor and the nonpoor.

The first part of President Reagan's economic platform was a tight monetary policy designed to raise interest rates and thereby curb inflation. This goal was achieved (helped in large measure by a worldwide oil glut that reduced energy costs significantly) but at a heavy cost. The highly restrictive money policy resulted in hard times for industries selling products usually purchased on credit. The resulting recession especially affected the home building, automobile, and steel manufacturing industries, which in turn had a negative impact in other industries as well, causing bankruptcies, plant relocations,

Who Benefits from Poverty?

Herbert Gans, a sociologist, has some interesting insights about the benefits of poverty. He begins with the assumption that if some social arrangement persists, it must be accomplishing something important (at least in the view of the powerful in society). What, then, does the existence of a relatively large number of persons in a condition of poverty accomplish that is beneficial to the powerful?

1. Poverty functions to provide a low-wage labor pool that is willing (or unable to be unwilling) to do society's necessary "dirty work." The middle and upper classes are subsidized by the existence of economic activities that depend on the poor (low wages to many workers in restaurants, hospitals, and in truck farming).

2. The poor also subsidize a variety of economic activities for the affluent by supporting, for example, innovations in medicine (as patients in research hospitals or as guinea pigs in medical experiments) and providing servants, gardeners, and house cleaners who make life easier for the more well-to-do.

3. The existence of poverty creates jobs for a number of occupations and professions that serve the poor or protect the rest of society from them (penologists, social workers, police, pawn shop owners, numbers racketeers, and owners of liquor stores). The presence of poor people also provides incomes for doctors, lawyers, teachers, and others who are too old, poorly trained, or incompetent to attract more affluent clients.

4. Poor people subsidize merchants by purchasing products that others do not want (seconds, dilapidated cars, deteriorated housing, day-old bread, fruit, and vegetables) and that otherwise would have little or no value.

5. The poor serve as a group to be punished in order to uphold the legitimacy of conventional values (hard work, thrift, honesty, and monogamy). *The poor provide living proof that moral deviance does not pay,* and thus, an indirect rationale for blaming the victim.

6. Poverty guarantees the status of those who are not poor. The poor, by occupying a position at the bottom of the status hierarchy, provide a reliable and relatively permanent measuring rod for status comparison, particularly by those just above them (that is, the working class, whose politics, for example, are often influenced by the need to maintain social distance between themselves and the poor).

7. The poor aid in the upward mobility of others. A number of persons have entered the middle class through the profits earned from providing goods and services in the slums (pawn shops, secondhand clothing and furniture stores, gambling, prostitution, and drugs).

8. The poor, being powerless, can be made to absorb the costs of change in society. In the nineteenth century they did the back-breaking work that built the railroads and the cities. Today they are the ones pushed out of their homes by urban renewal, the building of expressways, parks, and stadia. Many economists assume that a degree of unemployment is necessary to fight inflation. The poor, who are "first to be fired and the last to be hired," are the ones who make the sacrifice for the economy.

Gans notes:

This analysis is not intended to suggest that because it is often functional, poverty *should* exist, or that it *must* exist. For one thing, poverty has many more dysfunctions than functions; for another, it is possible to suggest functional alternatives. For example, society's dirty work could be done without poverty, either by automation or by paying "dirty workers" decent wages. Nor is it necessary for the poor to subsidize the many activities they support through their low-wage jobs. This would, however, drive up the costs of these activities, which would result in higher prices to their customers and clients. . . .

In sum, then, many of the functions served by the poor could be replaced if poverty were eliminated, but almost always at higher costs to others, particularly more affluent others. Consequently a functional analysis [equivalent to the order model] must conclude that poverty persists not only because many of the functional alternatives to poverty would be quite dysfunctional for the affluent members of society. . . . Poverty can be eliminated only when they become dysfunctional for the affluent or powerful, or when the powerless can obtain enough power to change society (p. 24).

Source: Herbert J. Gans, "The Uses of Power: The Poor Pay All," *Social Policy* 2 (July-August 1971): 20–24. Copyright © 1971 by Social Policy Corporation.

and massive layoffs. This economic downturn did have the desired effect of reducing inflation, but it also was the source of high unemployment where about one out of ten workers wanting jobs was not working. Many persons became poor for the first time, and with changes in industries such as new forms of automation, even prosperous times will leave many of them permanently dislocated.

The second part of President Reagan's economic plan was a change in the tax policies to increase incentives for investment. Taxes were reduced and new tax subsidies (loopholes) created to accelerate economic growth and allow the benefits to "trickle down" to the less fortunate. It is too early to determine whether these measures will have the desired effect of stimulating economic growth, but we do know that they have *increased* the gap between the affluent and the poor. Three facts make this point:

▫ The tax cuts and tax subsidies provided those families in the top 20 percent (in family income) with $36 billion in cash income, while those in the bottom 20 percent lost $1.2 billion.[30]

▫ When the tax cuts under the new tax laws are considered along with social security taxes, those making an income under $10,000 paid taxes of $125 more than before the cuts, while those making in excess of $200,000 paid $19,427 less tax.[31]

▫ The same imbalance is found in the new taxing policies for corporations. The corporations were given tax breaks amounting to $40 billion annually. Eighty percent of these savings go to the 1,700 (out of 2 million) largest corporations.[32]

The third part of the president's plan was the drastic reduction in expenditures for social programs. The magnitude of these budget cuts was substantial. Especially affected by the cuts were the poor and those hovering just above the poverty line. Budgets were reduced for programs such as food stamps, legal services for the poor, Medicaid, school lunches, subsidized housing, public jobs, and Meals on Wheels for the housebound. Also affected were special nutritional programs and special programs for the handicapped. The following lists some specifics:

- □ One million recipients of food stamps were declared ineligible. Seventy-five percent of the $2 billion cut came from reductions in benefits for families below the poverty line.
- □ About 725,000 poor women and children lost the comprehensive medical services provided by Medicaid.
- □ Over 200 community health centers (28 percent of the nation's total) were forced to close or curtail their operations significantly.
- □ About 365,000 families receiving cash benefits from Aid to Families with Dependent Children were cut off.

The final part of the president's economic program was to reduce the scope of the federal government by granting money to the states to be used at their discretion. This "home rule" strategy, based on the assumption that local governments know what is best for their constituents, has several important negative consequences. First, it allows local patterns of discrimination against women, blacks, Hispanics, native Americans, the elderly, and other relatively powerless minorities to flourish unhindered by federal restrictions. Second, it permits legislatures dominated by certain interests to withhold monies from other interests. Third, and a point elaborated later in this chapter, the states vary markedly in their ability or willingness to provide welfare to the needy.

THE ELIMINATION OF POVERTY

In 1981 the National Advisory Council on Economic Opportunity—soon before its own demise as a result of budget cuts—issued a grim warning: the economic policies of the Reagan administration, Congress, and budget cuts aimed at the poor, if continued, would plunge the nation into social chaos.[33] About 35 million are officially poor, and another 30 million hover just above the poverty level. Continued budget cuts will devastate about one-fourth of the nation's population, particularly the elderly, women, minorities, and the young. The results are predictable: more crime, physical and psychological illness, broken families, racial division, and potential for violence. Thus, it is imperative on humanitarian grounds as well as for the well-being of society that the United States solve its poverty problem. But can poverty be eliminated? The answer is yes, if by poverty we mean the condition of life that is intolerable because the necessities of adequate health facilities, diet, clothing, and shelter are denied certain persons. The methods to accomplish this goal, however, are elusive. The remainder of this chapter enumerates some of the assumptions that appear basic to such a goal and some of the general programs that adoption of these assumptions demand.

Assumption 1: Poverty can be eliminated in the United States. Michael Harrington has argued forcefully that poverty must be eliminated because America has the resources: "In a nation with a technology that could provide every citizen with a decent life, it is an outrage and a scandal that there should be such social misery."[34] The paradox of poverty in the midst of plenty need not exist if the people wish to make such a commitment. The elimination of economic misery would require a reordering of the nation's priorities. And the commitment need not be that great: less than 2 percent of our gross national product, or less than one-fifth what we spend annually on defense, would raise all impoverished persons and families above the poverty line.[35]

Assumption 2: Poverty is caused by a lack of resources, not a deviant value system. Basic to a program designed to eliminate poverty is the identification of what keeps some people in a condition of poverty. Is it lack of money and power, or the maintenance of deviant values and life styles? This question is fundamental because the answer determines the method for eliminating poverty. The "culture of poverty" proponents would address non-middle-class traits. The target would be the poor themselves, and making them more socially acceptable. Developing the social competence of the poor—not changing the system—would bring an end to poverty. This approach treats the symptom, not the disease. The disease can only be cured by attacking its sources within the society—the structural arrangements that maintain inequality. Thus, the attack must be directed at the structural changes that will enable lower-class persons to earn a living to support their families adequately.

Assumption 3: Poverty is not simply a matter of deficient income; it results from other inequities in the society as well. Poverty involves a reinforcing pattern of restricted opportunities, deficient community services, powerful predators who profit from the poor, prejudiced attitudes, and unequal distribution of resources. These can be eliminated through structural changes, including first, the enforcement of the laws regarding equal opportunity for jobs, advancement, and schooling, and second, the redistribution of power on the local and national levels. The present system works in such a way as to keep the poor powerless. What is needed, rather, is the organization of the poor into viable groups with power to determine or at least shape policy in local communities. The poor need to have some power over school policies. They need to have a voice in the decisions about the distribution of resources within the community (such as money for parks and recreation, fire protection, street maintenance, refuse collection). The American system of representative democracy is one of "winner take all" and is therefore to blame for the powerlessness of all minorities. A system of proportional representation would guarantee a degree of power.

A third structural change involves an increasing reliance upon central planning and action at the national level to alleviate the causes of poverty. This shift from a relative laissez-faire policy toward a relative socialism will be outlined in greater detail toward the end of the chapter.

Assumption 4: Poverty cannot be eliminated by the efforts of the poor themselves. The poor have neither the power nor the resources to bring about the structural changes necessary to eliminate poverty. A few of the individual poor may escape poverty by their own efforts, but the others remain poor unless the people and groups with the power and the resources do change the system. This is not to say that the poor cannot have some effect. They can, but usually only indirectly through influential persons or groups who become concerned about their plight.

Assumption 5: Poverty cannot be eliminated by the efforts of the private sector of the economy. Assuming that private enterprises will not engage in unprofitable activities, we can assume also that private-enterprise efforts will never by themselves eliminate poverty. This is another way of saying that private profit will tend to subvert the human needs that are of public concern; businesses will not provide jobs that they consider unnecessary or not immediately profitable, nor will they voluntarily stop activities that are profitable (for example, renting deteriorated housing because the un-improved land may increase in value, or lobbying to keep certain occupational categories outside minimum-wage restrictions).

Conventional wisdom, however, suggests that private business is the answer, because it will generate new and better-paying jobs. This simply is not the case, because the "new poor," as Harrington has referred to them, differ dramatically from the "old poor."[36] The "old poor"—that is, the poor of other generations—had hopes of breaking out of poverty; if they did not break out themselves, at least they believed their children would. This hope was based on the needs of a rapidly expanding economy. There were jobs for immigrants, farmers, and grade-school dropouts because of the needs of mass production. The poor of the present generation, the "new poor," however, are much more trapped in poverty. There is now a much greater probability that poverty will persist from generation to generation, and hence a much greater pessimism among poor persons. The "new poor" could be called the "automation poor." They are workers (and their families) displaced by technological advancement. They left coal mining or the small farms, not because of the attraction of the cities, but because they were forced out. The jobs that required only the muscle of unskilled immigrants are now done by machines.

The year 1956 marked the first time in history that there were more white-collar than blue-collar workers in the United States. The proportion of workers needed in blue-collar positions continues to decline. The less skillful white-collar jobs are also being replaced by computers and automated techniques. At the same time, however, the labor force is growing. The private sector, with its emphasis on profit (and therefore efficiency), will not generate the new jobs needed to meet this need, let alone reduce the unemployment rate.

Assumption 6: Poverty will not be eliminated by the efforts of state and local governments themselves. A basic tenet of political conservatism is decentralization of government. Relatively small and locally based governmental units are believed to be best suited for meeting the needs of the people. This theory, though logical, has not always worked in practice. In fact, it has increased the problems of some localities.

A good deal of money is gathered and dispensed at the city, county, and state levels for the purpose of alleviating the misery associated with poverty. Some federal programs function only through local units of government. The basic problem is that these local units differ dramatically in their willingness to attack poverty. For example, there are vast differences among states in levels of welfare assistance. Table 10–1 provides 1981 data on the average monthly payments to needy children by state. The least generous states were Mississippi ($29.64 per child), Alabama ($37.91), Tennessee ($41.04), and South Carolina ($42.56). The most generous states were Alaska ($186.18), California ($141.73), Minnesota ($138.61), and Vermont ($134.61). These wide disparities by states lead to an important consequence of home rule—the migration of the needy to the more generous states.

> The size of cash allotments differs widely according to the politics, prevailing wage levels, and intensity of racial feeling in assorted jurisdictions. The least generous states, almost entirely in the South, have exported in the last generation a large percentage of their welfare population to the North and Midwest where standards of support have been comparatively generous. . . . As long as states can define their own standards of need and even determine the percentage of those that they decide to fund, politically reactionary legislatures and governors will be in a position to push their neediest citizens into the direction of communities less barbarously inclined.[37]

Assumption 7: Poverty is a national problem and must be attacked with massive, nationwide programs financed largely and organized by the federal government. Poverty can be eliminated through the massive infusion of money and compensatory programs, coupled with centralized planning. This is a form of socialism and therefore is suspect by many. Governmental control and government subsidies are not new phenomena in the United States, yet it is a curious fact that subsidies for the poor are generally decried while the others go unnoticed or even praised. The federal government has subsidized, for example, defense industries (loans), the oil industry (oil depletion allowance), all corporations (tax writeoffs), students (government scholarships and interest-free loans), professors (research grants), homeowners (the interest on mortgages is tax deductible, usually saving homeowners hundreds of dollars a year), newspapers and magazines (through lower-cost postage), churches (no property tax or income tax), and farmers (farm subsidies).

What can the federal government do to achieve the goal of getting all persons permanently above the poverty line? Three quite different programs are needed, because there are three kinds of poverty: (1) those who are unemployed (or employed at jobs that pay below the minimum wage) because they lack the skills needed in an advanced technological society; (2) those who cannot work because they are too old, physically or mentally handi-

TABLE 10–1   Welfare Payments to Needy Children by State, 1981

State	Families	Dependent Children	Average Family Payment	Average per Child Payment
Ala.	59,806	119,070	$105.60	$37.91
Alaska	6,652	10,855	$447.35	$186.18
Ariz.	22,809	45,437	$160.90	$58.33
Ark.	28,887	59,148	$135.90	$47.96
Calif.	523,771	1,015,834	$416.20	$141.73
Colo.	29,068	54,994	$256.70	$92.34
Conn.	49,093	95,946	$354.05	$124.68
Del.	11,525	21,751	$227.31	$82.27
D.C.	28,226	54,661	$258.99	$91.68
Fla.	102,005	194,646	$167.82	$62.41
Ga.	89,861	168,423	$149.57	$57.22
Hawaii	19,924	40,374	$388.98	$127.26
Idaho	7,086	12,933	$251.60	$92.56
Ill.	232,880	492,380	$286.61	$93.37
Ind.	59,399	117,028	$202.75	$71.45
Iowa	38,482	68,574	$307.45	$113.72
Kan.	27,485	50,772	$264.54	$100.21
Ky.	65,086	117,264	$180.17	$69.25
La.	69,475	153,596	$156.39	$51.57
Maine	20,703	37,869	$236.57	$87.93
Md.	79,819	145,996	$233.88	$85.66
Mass.	120,932	213,805	$355.26	$128.84
Mich.	243,950	487,475	$377.50	$122.15
Minn.	53,564	95,824	$382.52	$138.61
Miss.	59,809	127,867	$86.51	$29.64
Mo.	72,447	141,073	$218.63	$75.46
Mont.	7,095	13,547	$221.56	$78.57
Neb.	14,076	26,662	$282.62	$102.50
Nev.	5,273	9,761	$195.21	$72.13
N.H.	8,412	15,058	$266.37	$97.76
N.J.	151,674	315,400	$293.34	$96.58
N.M.	19,456	38,027	$197.93	$69.90
N.Y.	367,254	752,623	$352.03	$116.96
N.C.	78,695	137,611	$165.22	$66.40
N.D.	4,813	8,887	$274.09	$101.84
Ohio	207,276	393,720	$247.81	$85.67
Okla.	29,915	63,015	$247.84	$85.19
Ore.	33,362	56,960	$272.55	$102.98
Pa.	219,736	435,797	$290.52	$99.44
R.I.	19,030	36,785	$345.48	$120.38
S.C.	57,787	109,711	$114.45	$42.56
S.D.	6,691	12,659	$212.84	$78.51
Tenn.	63,577	116,989	$107.75	$41.04
Texas	106,530	231,685	$104.66	$34.82
Utah	13,254	25,644	$308.00	$100.58

TABLE 10–1   (Continued)

State	Families	Dependent Children	Average Family Payment	Average per Child Payment
Vt.	8,304	15,388	$396.93	$134.61
Va.	63,836	117,417	$227.16	$84.51
Wash.	54,974	94,666	$348.06	$130.18
W.Va.	28,336	60,140	$177.60	$63.57
Wis.	88,751	160,933	$371.97	$134.40
Wyo.	2,625	4,697	$266.70	$104.22
Total	3,835,489	7,527,016	$282.05	$97.64

Source: Office of Research and Statistics, Social Security Administration, reported in Warren Isensee, "When USA's Children Need Help, Some States Dig Deeper Than Others," USA Today (April 11, 1983), p. 4A. Reprinted with permission. USA Today.

capped, or are mothers with dependent children; and (3) the children of the poor.

The able-bodied poor need three things: (1) adequate training; (2) guaranteed employment; and (3) a guaranteed minimum income that provides the necessities of food, clothing, shelter, and medical care. It is important to create new jobs and even new occupational categories. Michael Harrington has suggested that these new jobs may involve working as "indigenous" neighborhood social workers, teacher's aides, community organizers, or research assistants. These new opportunities would be in the service sector of the economy rather than in the goods-producing sector where automation occurs.[38] Other jobs could be in such public-works areas as highway construction, mass transit, recycling waste materials, and park maintenance. An important component of such jobs is social usefulness. Jobs with high social productivity would also have some beneficial by-products (latent consequences) in the form of less estrangement of workers from their jobs and in overall improvements for the society itself.

All segments of society benefit under full employment. If the poor are paid adequately and therefore have more money to purchase products, the private sector of the economy will be stimulated by increased demand for goods and services. At the same time, full employment and decent pay will give power to the poor. The greater their resources are, the greater their likelihood to organize for political and social power, to vote their interests, and to become respected by others.

The disabled and incapacitated who cannot or should not be employed require government subsidies to get above the poverty line. These subsidies may be in the form of money, food, housing, recreational facilities, or special care centers for the physically and mentally handicapped. An important need is adequate low-cost housing, since most of the poor currently live in deteriorated housing units. Whatever the cost, there must be a nationwide commitment to provide a decent standard of living for these persons. According to an editorial in *Saturday Review*, "One hallmark of a civilized society is its willingness to care for its poor, ill, elderly, dependent young, and permanently handicapped."[39]

About one half of the poor are children. Present-day poverty tends to be passed on to succeeding generations, since the poor often drop out of school early because of financial difficulties at home or because they do not perform well in school. Changing this will require a crash program with massive investment of quality education both in the ghetto and in rural pockets of poverty. Harrington has pointed to the need for compensatory programs:

> The poor, so to speak, cannot be given the same voucher as everyone else. Having been systematically deprived for so long, they require the use of federal power to make the schooling market more favorable to them than to the children of affluent homes.[40]

In another article, Harrington argued:

> We should have a GI bill in the war against poverty and pay people to go to school, pay for their tuition, their books, and give them an additional living allowance if they have a family. The GI bill was one of the most successful social experiments this society ever had. Why does it require a shooting war for us to be so smart? Why can't we in the war on poverty say that the most productive thing a young person between ages 16 and 21 can do is go to school, and that this is an investment in the Great Society?[41]

The positive consequences of this plan would be, first, that a significant segment of potential workers would be kept out of the labor force for a time, thereby reducing the number of jobs needed. Second, individuals would learn the skills needed in an automated society. Third, the educated workers could command greater wages and therefore pay more in taxes. The lifetime earnings for veterans who took advantage of the GI bill were significantly greater than for those who chose to bypass the plan—so much so that they will pay back to the government in taxes approximately six times the amount the government invested in their education. A similar approach could work for the poor.

The problem with this emphasis on education (and with alleviating poverty in general) is the difficulty of creating enough socially useful jobs with a decent American standard of pay. Leon Keyserling, former chairman of the Council of Economic Advisors, had said that "education and training as a conduit to a job is itself a travesty unless the jobs are created first: training for jobs can be meaningful only if the jobs are going to be available, and the training itself does not create jobs."[42] The creation of jobs, then, is the key to eliminating poverty. Since most of these jobs will no doubt be in the public sector of the economy, the government must divert its best minds to tackling this immense problem.

Poverty: The Problem and a Proposal

This recession, the longest since World War II, is not like previous ones. Millions of laid-off workers will never be rehired because their industries, such as autos and steel, are shrinking. Although they produce the greatest abundance in history, our farmers are devastated by low prices, soaring costs and increasing concentration of farm ownership; farm bankruptcy rates are the highest since the Great Depression. Housing prices are out of reach for most Americans, and the Social Security system that many older people depend on seems to be in trouble.

In fact, most Americans are losing ground. Over the last decade, the purchasing power of the average worker's earnings has shrunk 16 percent. The U.S. economy, which offered an ever increasing standard of living to many Americans for several generations, is disappointing a lot of their children.

While President Reagan's programs have made things worse, earlier economic plans also failed to eliminate hunger and poverty. That's because neither economic expansion nor the government programs tried so far have ever created enough jobs for all who want to work, or economic security for those who can't provide for themselves (such as children or people unable to work). The social programs introduced in the 1960s and 1970s, such as food stamps and school lunch programs, did reduce hunger—an important advance. But they couldn't get to the root of American poverty because they refused to alter the structures that keep so many Americans poor and disenfranchised.

The failure of past programs to change these structures, and the economic crisis we face today, bring us to a crossroads, an opportunity to try a new approach. By establishing our economic rights, we could use our vast material wealth and human energies to end hunger and poverty and create a new, more democratic economy that would serve all Americans better.

1. *The right to a decent job with decent pay.* Without this right, there will be no security even for those who are working now. In the last two years alone, over one million people lost their jobs due to plant closings. Millions of Americans work fulltime for the minimum wage and still can't get by. (Could you support a family on $3.35 an hour, about $540 a month?)

Until a decent job is a right, guaranteed with government help if necessary, joblessness will continue to dash the dreams of millions. With more than 12 million of us officially out of work, the unemployment rate today is triple what was considered acceptable in the 1960s.

2. *The right to income with dignity for those out of work or unable to work.* Without this right, there's no guarantee that people in need will get unemployment insurance or welfare payments, or that this aid will cover their basic needs. While many jobless Europeans receive 80 percent of their regular pay when they're laid off, the average American gets only half. And regardless of our needs, the size and duration of benefits can be cut at any time—as they have under the Reagan administration. Despite the highest unemployment in four decades, only 41 percent of jobless Americans are getting unemployment benefits, compared to 60 percent during the 1975 recession.

Many Americans are unable to work—even if there were jobs—because they are too old, too sick, or taking care of children. Yet Social Security payments are inadequate for many elderly people and only about half those eligible get food stamps. And in no state do welfare payments and food stamps combined even bring families up to the poverty line. Until we establish the right to income with dignity, millions of Americans will continue to suffer needless deprivation and indignity, no matter how high the Dow Jones goes.

(continued)

3. *The right to participate in democratic decisions about how the nation's resources are used.* While we accept as a given our right to vote on many *political* issues, we've come to accept as normal and natural that a few thousand men in corporate boardrooms make most of the key *economic* decisions. We invest our work, our savings, our pension funds to create our country's wealth, but we let others have the final word about our pay, about our health, safety and working conditions, about whether the factory where we work should be shut down and moved to Taiwan or the Philippines.

Should American factories produce more cars, or should we use the same resources to build a new train system? Should we spend billions on an MX missile system that not even the Joint Chiefs of Staff agree on, or should we use the money to rebuild our cities? Without more democratic participation in decision-making on such key economic issues, corporate executives and the legislators who go along with them will continue to make the big decisions for us.

In the United States, 500 corporations control over 80 percent of all industrial assets and this concentration of control is increasing every year; the richest one-half of one percent of Americans control half of all privately owned corporate stock. American consumers are overcharged $20 billion a year because of monopoly in the food industry. The Fortune 500 corporations use their wealth both to influence the political process and to shape our very understanding of democracy—so that we don't even think in terms of economic rights.

Today we're paying for the bad decisions an elite group of corporate planners has made, thanks to what President Reagan calls "the magic of the marketplace." Naturally enough, corporate planners make their decisions in their interests—short-term profits and corporate growth—not ours. Instead of investing in useful, job-creating production, *they* decided to spend over $136 billion on mergers in the last two years, creating no jobs and drying up credit that smaller businesses needed just to stay afloat. In the last year alone, they decided to bring us 2,400 new food products—including 58 new salad dressings and 125 "light" foods—when some Americans could afford only dog food. They decided to continue to build big, gas-guzzling cars while more and more Americans were switching to small cars imported from Japan or Europe. They decided to develop expensive, dangerous nuclear power, when we needed greater emphasis on conservation and solar power.

Over the past 30 years, business interests have used their political power to reduce their share of taxes by 62 percent, while individuals are paying 28 percent more. Early in the Reagan administration, a Congressional committee voted cuts in corporate income taxes worth $500 billion over the next decade. Small wonder: 30 of the committee's 35 members had received corporate contributions totaling $1,739,119 for their 1980 campaigns.

The corporate message, communicated through advertising, free classroom materials, corporate-financed "think tanks" and politicians, is simple: the economy works best when people keep their hands off and the "laws" of the marketplace are liberated. Only a "free market"—that is, one they control—is consistent with political liberty.

But political liberty flourishes, and people live more secure lives, in some other nations whose citizens have already started claiming their economic rights. In France, England and Denmark, for example, health care is a right. In Sweden, voters recently elected a party proposing that workers buy into ownership of major corporations so they can begin to set corporate priorities that make sense for workers too. While these advances are very limited, they are steps in the right direction.

Now we too must take steps toward an Economic Bill of Rights, because an economy constructed around these rights could provide more democratic control over the economy and economic security for every American. While no one has a blueprint, people around the world are exploring innovative ways to build stronger, more just economies that meet the needs of all their citizens. We Americans can also devise new ways to claim our economic rights.

Source: Excerpt from "Don't Just Blame Reagan," a pamphlet distributed by the Institute for Food and Development Policy (San Francisco, 1983). Used with permission of the Institute for Food and Development Policy.

General programs such as these are indeed necessary if the United States is to get everyone above the absolute minimum level of economic security. This goal is easily attainable because the productive capacity of the United States is great enough to make it possible without too great a strain. *These programs, however, will not solve the basic problem of inequality:* there is no insurance that they will eliminate urban riots, demonstrations, or crime; they will not eliminate the anger and bitterness that persons feel as they experience deprivation. They can, however, eliminate the human suffering associated with extreme deprivation.

SUMMARY

Approximately one out of seven Americans is legally poor. Why are some people poor in a land of affluence? Order theorists see the fault in the individual poor. American society is an open society and people with the proper motivation and perseverance will eventually succeed. Clearly, if some do not succeed in such a system, they must lack the traits essential for success. The fatal flaws within the poor that keep them and their children poor are believed to be a deviant value system ("culture of poverty") and the inheritance of inferior genes.

Conflict theorists see the origins of poverty in the structure of society: (1) in the problems of the economy (inadequate wages for some types of work, unemployment, and automation); (2) in the schools where the poor receive an inferior education; (3) in the discrimination aimed at minority groups; and (4) in the political machinery of society that operates to keep the advantages of society among the already advantaged (for example, tax benefits and the exclusion of certain industries from minimum-wage laws). This last point is especially relevant, because American society has the resources to redistribute wealth and eliminate extreme poverty without undue hardship to the more favored segments of society. But the political apparatus continues to protect the nonpoor, passing legislation the effect of which has been to even increase the gap between the "haves" and the "have-nots."

CHAPTER REVIEW

1. According to the government's arbitrary dividing line, which minimizes the actual extent of poverty, 15 percent of the U.S. population (1982) is officially poor. Disproportionately represented in this category are blacks and Hispanics, the elderly, and female heads of families.

2. One explanation for poverty is that the poor themselves are to blame. The "culture of poverty" hypothesis, for example, contends that the poor are qualitatively different in values and life styles from the successful and that these differences explain their poverty and the poverty of their children.

3. Another position that blames the poor for their condition is the "innate inferiority" hypothesis. This theory, a variant of social Darwinism promoted by Arthur Jensen and Richard Herrnstein, holds that certain categories of people are disadvantaged because they are less well endowed mentally.

4. Critics of the "culture of poverty" and the "innate inferiority" hypotheses charge that, in blaming the victim, both theories ignore how social conditions trap individuals and groups in poverty.

5. Aside from negative life chances, the consequences of being poor are: rejection, isolation, hopelessness, degradation, and anger. Three coping devices are: accommodation, avoidance, and aggression.

6. The elimination of poverty requires: (a) a commitment to accomplish that goal; (b) a program based on the assumption that poverty results from a lack of resources rather than a deviant value system; (c) a program based on the assumption that poverty results from inequities in the society; (d) recognition that poverty cannot be eliminated by the efforts of the poor themselves, by the private sector, or by the efforts of state and local governments alone; and (e) recognition that poverty is a national problem and must be attacked by massive, nationwide programs largely financed and organized by the federal government.

7. Three quite different programs are needed because there are three kinds of poverty. The unemployed or underpaid need adequate training, guaranteed employment, and a guaranteed minimal income that is adequate to provide the necessities. The disabled and incapacitated require government subsidies to meet their needs. Finally, the children of the poor need education and opportunities to break the cycle.

FOR FURTHER STUDY

Edward C. Banfield, *The Unheavenly City Revisited* (Boston: Little, Brown, 1974). Herbert J. Gans, *More Equality*. (New York: Pantheon, 1973).

Stephen Jay Gould, *The Mismeasure of Man* (New York: W. W. Norton, 1981).

Michael Harrington, *The Other America: Poverty in the United States* (Baltimore: Penguin, 1963).

———. *The New American Poverty*. (New York: Holt, Rinehart and Winston, 1984).

R. J. Herrnstein, *I.Q. in the Meritocracy* (Boston: Little, Brown, 1973).

Arthur R. Jensen, *Bias in Mental Testing* (New York: Free Press, 1980).

Robert Lekachman, *Greed is Not Enough: Reaganomics* (New York: Pantheon, 1982).

Oscar Lewis, *Five Families: Mexican Case Studies*

in the *Culture of Poverty*. (New York: New American Library, 1971).

Elliot Liebow, *Tally's Corner*. (Boston: Little, Brown, 1967).

James T. Patterson, *America's Struggle Against Poverty, 1900–1980*. (Cambridge, Mass.: Harvard Univ. Press, 1983).

Frances Fox Piven and Richard A. Cloward, *The New Class War: Reagan's Attack on the Welfare State and Its Consequences*. (New York: Pantheon, 1982).

Harrell R. Rodgers, Jr., *Poverty amid Plenty: A Political and Economic Analysis*. (Reading, Mass.: Addison-Wesley, 1979).

William Ryan, *Equality*. (New York: Vintage Books, 1982).

Karin Stallard, Barbara Ehrenreich, and Holly Sklar, *Poverty in the American Dream*. Institute for New Communications, pamphlet no. 1. (Boston: South End Press, 1983).

NOTES AND REFERENCES

1. For problems with the various measures of poverty, see John B. Williamson and Kathryn M. Hyer, "The Measurement and Meaning of Poverty," *Social Problems* 22 (June 1975): 652–663. See also Michael Harrington, *Decade of Decision* (New York: Simon and Schuster, 1980), pp. 225–231; and Elizabeth Evanson, "The Dynamics of Poverty," *Focus* 5 (Institute for Research on Poverty, University of Wisconsin–Madison, September 1981): 9–11, 19–20.

2. For a survey of problems with missing census data, see "The Census—What's Wrong with It, What Can Be Done," *Trans-action* 5 (May 1968): 49–56. For a complete analysis see Jacob S. Siegal, "Completeness of Coverage of the Nonwhite Population in the 1960 Census and Current Estimates, and Some Implications," *Social Statistics and the City*, ed. David M. Heer (Cambridge, Mass.: Harvard University Press, 1968), pp. 13–54. See also Beth Brophy, "The Billion-Dollar Count," *Forbes*, November 12, 1979, p. 185; and Bryce Nelson, "5% of Blacks, 4.4% of Latins Not Counted," *Los Angeles Times*, November 6, 1981, pt. 1, p. 16.

3. *U.S. News & World Report* (August 15, 1983), p. 8.

4. Diane Pierce, "The Feminization of Poverty—Women, Work, and Welfare," (Department of Sociology, University of Illinois–Chicago Circle, 1978); Barbara Ehrenreich and Karin Stallard, "The Nouveau Poor," *Ms.* 11 (August 1982), pp. 217–224; Karin Stallard, Barbara Ehrenreich, and Holly Sklar, *Poverty in the American Dream: Women and Children First* (Boston: South End Press, 1983); Alice McKee, "The Shifting of Poverty to Women," *Graduate Woman* 76 (July–August 1982), pp. 34–36; and U.S. Commission on Civil Rights, *Disadvantaged Women and Their Children*, Clearing House Publication 78 (Washington, D.C.: U.S. Government Printing Office, 1983).

5. National Advisory Council on Economic Opportunity, *Critical Choices for the 80's*, Twelfth Report (Washington, D.C., 1980), p. 17.

6. Ibid., p. 157.

7. See MIT–Harvard Joint Center for Urban Studies, "The Nation's Housing Needs: 1975–1985" (Cambridge, Mass., 1977).

8. Michael Parenti, *Democracy for the Few*, 4th ed. (New York: St. Martin's, 1983), p. 29.

9. Harry Nelson, "22–25 Million Not Covered, Study Finds," *Los Angeles Times*, November 4, 1981, part 1, p. 3.

10. Abigail Trafford, "New Health Hazard: Being Out of Work," *U.S. News & World Report* (June 14, 1982), pp. 81–82. See especially, Harvey Brenner, *Mental Illness and the Economy* (Cambridge, Mass.: Harvard University Press, 1973).

11. See Daniel Zwerdling, "Poverty and Pollution," *The Progressive* 37 (January 1973): 25–27.

12. The theories presented here are also used in Chapter 4. They are elaborated fully in Mario Barrera, *Race and Class in the South-*

west: A Theory of Racial Inequality (Notre Dame, Ind.: University of Notre Dame Press, 1979), pp. 2, 174–219.

13. From an editorial in The Progressive (August 1980): 27–28. See also Richard Hofstadter, Social Darwinism in American Thought, rev. ed. (Boston: Beacon Press, 1955).

14. Arthur R. Jensen, "How Much Can We Boost IQ and Scholastic Achievement?" Harvard Educational Review 39 (Winter 1969): 1–123. Subsequent issues of the Harvard Educational Review include a large number of replies to Jensen's article. See especially the articles appearing in the spring and summer 1969 issues; and Arthur R. Jensen, Bias in Mental Testing (New York: Free Press, 1980).

15. Richard J. Herrnstein, "I.Q.," Atlantic Monthly, September 1971, pp. 43–64; and I.Q. in the Meritocracy (Boston: Little, Brown, 1973). For critiques, see Noam Chomsky, "The Fallacy of Richard Herrnstein's IQ," Social Policy 3 (May–June 1972): 19–25; Karl W. Deutsch and Thomas Edsall, "The Meritocracy Scare," Society 9 (September–October, 1972): 71–79; and Arthur S. Goldberger, "Mysteries of the Meritocracy" Institute for Research on Poverty, University of Wisconsin–Madison, October 1974).

16. Herrnstein, "I.Q.," p. 63. For a discussion of what might occur in a meritocracy, see Michael Young, The Rise of the Meritocracy, 1870–2033: An Essay on Education and Equality (Baltimore: Penguin, 1961).

17. See "An Epitaph for Sir Cyril?" Newsweek, December 20, 1976, p. 76; "Basic Study on IQ Pattern Challenged," Christian Science Monitor, November 30, 1976, p. 15; Oliver Gillie, "Did Sir Cyril Burt Fake His Research on Heritability of Intelligence?" Phi Delta Kappan, 58 (February 1977): 469–471; and the rejoinder by Arthur Jensen pp. 471, 492. See also "The Father of Jensenism," Psychology Today 13 (December 1979).

18. William Ryan, "Postscript: A Call to Action," Social Policy 3 (May–June 1972): 54. For an empirical study that verifies the importance of environment on IQ, see Sandra Scarr-Salapatek and Richard A. Weinberg, "When Black Children Grow Up in White Homes. . . ." Psychology Today 9 (December 1975), pp. 80–82.

19. See Rick McGahey, "In Search of the Undeserving Poor," Working Papers 8 (November/December 1981), pp. 62–64.

20. Joanna Ryan, "IQ—The Illusion of Objectivity," in Race and Intelligence, ed. Ken Richardson and David Spears (Baltimore: Penguin, 1972), p. 54. For new attempts to solve the intelligence testing dilemmas, see Berkeley Rice, "Brave New World of Intelligence Testing," Psycholgy Today 13 (September 1979): 27–41; and in the same issue, Robert J. Sternberg, "Stalking the IQ Quark," pp. 42–54. For a critique of intelligence by a natural scientist, see Stephen Jay Gould, The Mismeasure of Man (New York: W. W. Norton, 1981).

21. Ryan, "IQ—The Illusion of Objectivity," p. 44.

22. For an especially acerbic review of the first edition of Banfield's book, see William Ryan, "Is Banfield Serious?" Social Policy 1 (November–December 1970): 74–76. For a series of papers on the culture of poverty, see Eleanor Burke Leacock, ed., The Culture of Poverty: A Critique (New York: Simon and Schuster, 1971). For a summary of the culture of poverty theory, see Beth E. Vanfossen, The Structure of Social Inequality (Boston: Little, Brown, 1979), pp. 355–365.

23. Elliot Liebow, Tally's Corner: A Study of Negro Streetcorner Men (Boston: Little, Brown, 1967), p. 222. See also Hyman Rodman, "The Lower Class Value Stretch," Social Forces 42 (December 1963): 205–215; and Ulf Hannerz, "Roots of Black Manhood: Sex, Socialization, and Culture in the Ghettos of American Cities," Trans-action 6 (October 1969): 20.

24. Attitude surveys find consistently that Americans believe that the poor would not be poor if they just worked harder. See, for example, Joe R. Feagin, "Poverty: We Still Believe That God Helps Those Who Help Themselves," Psychology Today 6 (November 1972): 101–110, 129; and New York Times–CBS News Poll (1978).

25. Michael Harrington, The Other America: Poverty in the United States (Baltimore: Penguin, 1963), p. 21.

26. Michael Parenti, Power and the Powerless (New York: St. Martin's, 1978), pp. 54–55.

27. Sar A. Levitan and Robert Taggart, cited in *USA Today* (February 22, 1983).

28. Joan Smith, *Social Issues and the Social Order: The Contradictions of Capitalism* (Cambridge, Mass.: Winthrop, 1981), pp. 299–331.

29. Ian Robertson, *Sociology*, 2nd ed. (New York: Worth, 1981), p. 271.

30. *Denver Post* (October 22, 1982), p. 11A.

31. Robert Lekachman, *Greed is Not Enough: Reaganomics* (New York: Pantheon, 1982), p. 66.

32. *Ibid.*, p. 71.

33. National Advisory Council on Economic Opportunity, Thirteenth Report (Washington, D.C.: 1981), cited in Henry Weinstein, "U.S. Cuts Will Devastate Poor, Panel Charges," *Los Angeles Times*, September 21, 1981, pt. 1, p. 3.

34. Harrington, *The Other America*, p. 24.

35. U.S. Bureau of the Census, "Characteristics of the Population Below the Poverty Line," *Current Population Reports*, Series P-60, no. 115 (Washington, D.C.: Government Printing Office, 1978), cited in Robertson, *Sociology*, p. 271.

36. The following is taken largely from two sources: Michael Harrington, "The Politics of Poverty," in *Poverty Views from the Left* ed. Jeremy Larner and Irving Howe (New York: William Morrow, 1965), pp. 13–38; and Michael Harrington, "Introduction," in *Poverty in America: A Book of Readings,* ed. Louis A. Ferman, Joyce L. Kornbluh, and Alan Haber (Ann Arbor: University of Michigan Press, 1965), pp. vii–xiv.

37. Lekachman, *Greed is Not Enough*, p. 92. See also, Walter Guzzardi, Jr., "Who Will Care for the Poor?" *Fortune* 105 (June 28, 1982), pp. 34–42.

38. Harrington, "The Politics of Poverty," p. 35.

39. "Welfare: Time for Reform," *Saturday Review* (May 23, 1970), p. 19.

40. Michael Harrington, "The Urgent Case for Social Investment," *Saturday Review* (November 23, 1968), p. 34.

41. Harrington, "Introduction," pp. xii–xiii.

42. Leon H. Keyserling, "Programs: Present and Future," in *Dialogue on Poverty*, Paul Jacobs et al. (eds.) (Indianapolis: Bobbs-Merrill, 1966), p. 93.

11

Racial and Ethnic Minorities

A heroic figure in American history died in Mississippi on March 14 [1977]. The relative lack of notice given to her passing reveals how little we honor our saints and prophets—reveals, in fact, how little we know and appreciate them when they are among us.

To the majority of Americans, the name of Fannie Lou Hamer was not a familiar one. For the first forty-five years of her life, she was completely unknown except to her black family and friends in the Mississippi delta, and to the few whites for whom they labored. During her last fifteen years, she inspired and influenced and challenged a much larger circle of people; still, too few ever knew who she was or what she had done to advance the cause of freedom and justice for us all.

She was born the last of twenty children in a family of sharecroppers, one generation removed from slavery and still confined under the oppressive grip of white supremacy. She was allowed six abbreviated years of education in a segregated school before she was compelled to work full-time on the land, even though she had been crippled by polio. She always remembered a lesson her mother taught her. "God made you black. Respect yourself." With that as her compass, and with the deep love and respect she felt for her parents, she arrived at middle age angry at injustice, determined to attack it, and yet miraculously free of bitterness and vengeance. "Hate is something destructive," she used to say. "If I hate you, then we're just two miserable people."

If anyone ever had justification to hate, Mrs. Hamer did. In 1962, she was thrown off the farm where she lived and worked because she had tried to register to vote, and her husband and their daughters were subsequently evicted too. They were harassed and threatened repeatedly. In 1963, in the town of Winona, she was arrested with five other persons and jailed for three days, during which she was viciously whipped and beaten.

She survived to tell that tale of horror at the Democratic Convention in Atlantic City the following year. Nonetheless, the Democrats could not bring themselves to unseat the white delegation from Mississippi which steadfastly resisted voter registration and political participation by blacks. The FBI and the Justice Department investigated the Winona assault, and the whites responsible were tried but acquitted.

Mrs. Hamer and others who formed with her the Mississippi Freedom Democratic Party tried again to stir the conscience of the nation's leaders, taking their challenge to the floor of the U.S. House of Representatives, but again they were rebuffed. "I don't want no *equal* rights anymore," Mrs. Hamer said. "I'm fightin' for *human* rights. I don't want to become equal to men like them that beat us." To

a nation still unwilling to listen, she spoke the plain and terrible truth: "This ain't just Mississippi's problem," she said. "It's America's problem."

Slowly and reluctantly in the decade since then, Mississippi and the rest of America have moved to acknowledge that fact, and to begin to correct the injustice of it. Mrs. Hamer lived to see some evidence of improvement in the lives of some black and poor Americans, and she was gratified by it. But she was not—and could not have been—satisfied by it. Too many lives remained untouched, and too much justice remained undelivered, for her to consider the job done. "I ain't givin' up," she said later in her life. "I'm stayin' right here in the South, in Mississippi. We got to treat each other right, 'cause we're in this thing together, and if the white people survive, we're gonna survive too."

She stayed, and with the serene self-assurance she persisted in her nonviolent struggle for simple justice. She continued the fight until the day she died, at the age of sixty, of cancer, heart problems, and diabetes.

When Mrs. Hamer first dared to challenge the tyranny of white supremacy in the early 1960s, two of the people who gave assistance to her and were in turn inspired and strengthened by her courage were Andrew Young of the Southern Christian Leadership Conference and John Lewis of the Student Nonviolent Coordinating Committee. They, too, were later jailed and beaten, and like her, they held firmly to their faith in the ultimate power of nonviolence.

No doubt she was pleased by the accomplishments of Young and Lewis, and by the hundreds of other Americans, young and old, black and white, who have been emboldened by her example to commit themselves to the pursuit of human rights. But she would surely say now, to them and all of us, what she said many times over, and what her life spoke with such eloquence: Don't stop now. Discrimination is still alive. Racism and poverty still exist. People are sick, hungry, uneducated, out of work. We are still waiting for justice.

Not enough honor ever came to the life of Fannie Lou Hamer, but if that bothered her, she gave no indication of it. Honor and praise were not what she was about. What she was about was being right, and bringing justice like a mighty wave over the land and people she loved—over all of us. Honor came not so much to her life as from it, to the rest of the world. It was a gift outright. If she were awarded the Nobel Peace Prize posthumously—and she should be, for no one could be more deserving of it— our debt to her would still be enormous, and unpaid.

Source: John Egerton, "Fannie Lou Hamer," *The Progressive* (May 1977), p. 7. Reprinted by permission from *The Progressive*, 408 West Gorham Street, Madison, Wisconsin 53703. Copyright © 1977, The Progressive, Inc.

The United States is a mosaic of different social groups and categories. These are not equal in power, resources, prestige, or presumed worth. They are differentially ranked on each of these dimensions. But why is one group alleged to be superior to another? The basic reason is differential power— power derived from superior numbers, technology, weapons, property, or economic resources. Those holding superior power in a society establish a system of inequality by successfully imposing their will upon less-powerful groups, and this system of inequality is then maintained and perpetuated by power.[1] Inequality is maintained because the dominant group provides the standards (values and norms) by which individuals and groups are judged, and the reward–punishment system; thus the dominant group's institutions systematically disadvantage some groups while favoring others.[2]

Minority groups are among those that are disadvantaged by the standards of the majority in power. They experience injustice in the courts. They are discriminated against in schools, on the job, and in communities. Nevertheless people commonly think of these social injustices as some kind of aberration rather than in terms of a prevailing bias in the political-economic structure of society.

Racism, like poverty, is extremely difficult to abolish. The fundamental reason for the existence of both inequities is that they serve important functions for the society. The existence of minorities, for example, ensures that there are categories of people to do society's dirty work at low wages. More subtly, racism has positive consequences for the maintenance of the status quo; it is one means by which the powerful remain in power and retain their other advantages. This is accomplished in two ways. First, minority groups provide a justification for the existing inequalities in society; after all, the minorities do not deserve better jobs or schools because they are lazy, immoral, untrustworthy, and the like. Such negative stereotypes about the minority groups help to keep them "in their place," which seems natural to the majority and perhaps even to the members of the minority.

Second, racism works to maintain the system by dividing the working class into majority and minority group members and thereby forestalls the unity necessary for class consciousness and rebellion against the oppression of the powerful. Instead of rallying together with others in the same (or worse) economic predicament, white-collar workers direct their hostility against their minority-group colleagues and neighbors. Their anger should be directed instead at the powerful in society who get tax breaks and other legal subsidies, and who rake off enormous profits at the expense of the workers. Thus, ironically, although minority groups are oppressed by the structure of society, they are held responsible for helping to perpetuate it. They are blamed for their plight, which is another instance of blaming the victim. "The oppression is seen as being caused by the victim rather than by the system which victimizes them."[3]

This chapter focuses on the three most victimized racial/ethnic groups in the United States—blacks, Chicanos, and Native Americans. The chapter discusses the characteristics of minority groups, the characteristics of racial and ethnic groups, and the reasons for the oppression of racial and ethnic minorities, and assesses the effects of this oppression on blacks and Hispanics in terms of income, jobs, education, and health.

THE CHARACTERISTICS OF MINORITY GROUPS

Because majority-minority relations operate basically as a power relationship, conflict (or at least the potential for conflict) is always present. Overt conflict is most likely when the subordinate group attempts to alter the distribution of power.[4] Size is not crucial in determining whether or not a group is the most powerful. A numerical minority may in fact have more political representation than the majority, as is the case in the Union of South Africa and in most colonial situations. Thus, the most important characteristic of a subordinate "minority" group is that it is dominated by a more powerful group.

A second characteristic of a minority group is that it is composed of people with similar characteristics that differ significantly from the dominant group. These characteristics are salient: they are visible, though not necessarily physical, and they make a difference.

The behavior and/or characteristics of minority-group members are stereotyped and systematically condemned by the dominant or majority group. Minority groups typically inspire stereotypes in the minds of the dominant group, presumably because these negative generalizations keep them "down." In the following passage S. I. Hayakawa has shown vividly how stereotyped ideas of minority groups are variable, irrational, and negative in their consequences.

Mr. Miller is a Jew. If Mr. Miller succeeds in business that proves that "Jews are smart"; if he fails in business, it is alleged that he still has "money salted away somewhere." If Mr. Miller has different customs than ours, that proves that "Jews don't assimilate." If he is indistinguishable from other Americans, he is "trying to pass himself off as one of us." If Mr. Miller fails to give to charity, that is because "Jews are tight"; if he gives generously, he is "trying to buy his way into society." If he lives in the Jewish section of town, that is because "Jews are so clannish"; if he moves to a locality where there are no other Jews, that is because "they try to horn in everywhere." In other words, because of our feelings towards Jews in general, Mr. Miller is automatically condemned, no matter who he is or what he does.[5]

One last characteristic that all minority groups have in common is that they are singled out for differential and unfair treatment. The discrimination may be subtle or blatant, but it is always detrimental. A sizable portion of this chapter will focus on the various manifestations of discrimination toward minority groups in the United States.

By these criteria—relative powerlessness, visible differentiation from the majority, negative stereotyping, and unfair discrimination—eight categories of people are commonly designated as minority groups. *Race*, which refers to genetic and therefore immutable differences among individuals, is a typical basis for differential treatment in most societies. For some Americans, racial differences determine behavioral differences as well as skin color, shape of lips, and color of eyes. Although science belies this statement, some segments of society perceive behavioral differences as racial in nature, thereby justifying differential treatment.

A second category, *ethnicity*, is also a traditional basis for inequality. An ethnic group has a culture distinctive from the dominant one. An Amish rural community and an Italian neighborhood in Boston are examples of ethnic groups. Of course, racial groups may also differ culturally from the dominant group—say, the Chinese in San Francisco's Chinatown or any tribe of Native Americans.

The third classification, *religion*, also places some categories in inferior positions. Throughout most of their history Jews have been persecuted because of their religion (or assumed religious ties) in one country after another. Much of the unrest in Northern Ireland stems from religious differences. The Protestants in that country are dominant, and the Catholics are the objects of discrimination.

Another category, the *impoverished*, constitutes a minority group in all societies. As we found in Chapter 10, the American poor are powerless and victims of varied forms of discrimination.

One basis for differentiation, *sex*, has only recently been recognized as a basis for minority status. Women in American society are relatively powerless, perceived in terms of stereotyped qualities (for example, incapable of leadership because of being highly emotional), and victimized by discrimination, as you will see in Chapter 12.

Certain *deviant* groups also have the characteristics of minority groups (see Chapter 8). Hippies, unmarried mothers (and their offspring), homosexuals, ex-criminals, and ex-mental patients are examples of deviant groups with minority status.

A seventh category, the *aged*, meet the criteria for a minority group in many societies. The elderly in the United States are clearly objects of discrimination, possess negative stereotypes, and are relatively powerless.

The *physically different* also have minority-group status.[6] The deformed, the handicapped, the obese, the ugly, and the short experience discrimination because they are different.

RACIAL AND ETHNIC GROUPS

Racial and ethnic minorities are very significant in American society. An ethnic group is a group socially defined on the basis of a common culture.[7] Ethnicity refers, then, to identifying with a particular ethnic group. The culture that binds the members together is distinct from the culture of the majority. Some of the ethnic groups found in the United States are Vietnamese, Jews, Czechs, Mennonites, Chicanos, and Poles. A racial group is socially defined on the basis of a presumed common genetic heritage resulting in distinguishing physical characteristics. Crucial to understanding race is that these physical differences thought to cluster forming a race are socially defined. Scientists, however, do not agree on how many races there are or even if races exist. What happens is that "when people become convinced that two or more races exist, then those races do, in fact, exist in the everyday lives of the people who are labeled accordingly."[8]

Confusing the issue further, many racial groups also have ethnic characteristics. A racial group that has a distinct culture or subculture, shares a common heritage, and has developed a common identity is also an ethnic group. This chapter focuses on two groups—blacks and Chicanos—that have the characteristics of both. Both minority groups are subordinated by and discriminated against by the dominant majority.

Differences among Ethnic Groups

Some ethnic groups have moved into the mainstream of society while others have remained in a subordinate status. The Germans, Italians, and Irish, for example, experienced discrimination when they migrated here in the late nineteenth century but have been accepted into the dominant majority. Native Americans, blacks, Chicanos, and others, however, have not become assimilated and continue to be objects of discrimination. Two factors combine to explain much of this apparent anomaly.

The most obvious reason is color. Those groups easily identified by physical characteristics find it difficult if not impossible to escape the devalued label. Second, the conditions under which the ethnic groups came into contact with the dominant majority appear to be crucial. A key to the way ethnic groups were ultimately treated is whether or not they migrated to the United States voluntarily.[9] Voluntary migrants came to the New World to enhance their inferior status or to market their skills in a land of opportunity. They came with hope and sometimes with resources to provide a foundation for their hoped-for upward mobility. Most also had the option of returning if they found the conditions here unsatisfactory.

The voluntary migrants came to the United States in several waves. In colonial times the English, Scotch-Irish, and Germans were the most notable ethnic groups. The Catholic Irish came in great numbers just before the Civil War as a result of the great potato famine in Ireland. They were rural, unskilled, Catholic, and anti-English in sentiment. They settled in urban areas and experienced a good deal of discrimination. During this same period Chinese and later the Japanese migrated to western states. They experienced great discrimination by whites apprehensive about jobs.

From about 1870 to 1920 a great wave of voluntary migrants came to America, mainly from the Catholic areas of Europe—Poland, Italy, and eastern Europe. These new immigrants were different from the dominant English Protestant culture. As a result they experienced more discrimination than many of the earlier immigrants. The antimigrant feeling was exposed in a 1924 federal law, the National Origins Act, which restricted immigrants from southern and eastern Europe and stopped it altogether for Asians.

The voluntary migrants came to America and experienced varying forms of labor exploitation and other forms of discrimination. In general, though, they fared better than those who came involuntarily. Those forced to enter a country are by definition powerless; they are victimized from the beginning. Also, unlike the voluntary migrants, they were unable to return home if dissatisfied with the move. To understand the special plight of the involuntary migrants, let's look at three such groups—blacks, Chicanos, and Native Americans.

Blacks

The slave trade brought blacks to America from Africa from 1619 until the Civil War, when they constituted one-eighth of the population.[10] The slaves were defined as property and denied the rights given to other members of society. Families could be broken up for economic or punitive reasons. The slave owners used their power in several ways to maintain their dominance over their slaves. They demanded absolute obedience; to question the authority of the master meant physical punishment, often severe. Second, blacks were taught to defer to their masters and to accept their own inferiority. Third, the masters used public displays of power to create in slaves a sense of awe. Fourth, slaves were taught to identify with their masters' economic success. Finally, slaves were made to feel dependent on their masters, primarily by restrictions on their education. Typically, it was illegal in the South to teach a slave to read or write.

Following Emancipation the newly-freed blacks, except for the brief period of Reconstruction, remained powerless. They did not have the skills and resources to break away from their dependence on whites.[11] Since whites owned the land, blacks were forced to enter into sharecropping agreements, where they would farm the land, take all the risks, and return a percentage of the crops harvested to the owner. Typically the sharecroppers would borrow on the next year's crop to purchase equipment, food, and clothing. This often meant a cycle of indebtedness that bound the sharecroppers as if they were slaves.

During this same period many states passed "Jim Crow" laws mandating racial segregation in almost all areas of life (separate schools, transportation, neighborhoods, drinking fountains, public eating establishments). These laws, which legalized white domination, remained in effect until about 1965.

The hallmark of representative democracy is that all citizens have the fundamental right to vote for those who will administer and make the laws. Those in power have often defied this principle of democracy by minimizing, neutralizing, or even negating the voting privileges of blacks.[12] Although the Fourteenth Amendment gave blacks the right to vote after the Civil War, the white majority in the southern states used a variety of tactics to keep them from voting. Most effective was the strategy of intimidation. Blacks who tried to assert their right to vote were often beaten, sometimes lynched, or their property destroyed. A more subtle approach, however, was quite effective in eliminating the black vote in the southern states: through legal means, laws were passed to achieve illegal discrimination. One tactic was the white primary, which excluded blacks from the party primary.[13] The Constitution prohibited the states from denying the vote on the basis of race. A political party, however, because it was a private association, *could* discriminate. The Democratic party throughout most of the South chose the option of limiting the primary to whites. Blacks could legally vote in the general election, but only for the candidates already selected by whites. And since the Democratic party in the South was supreme, whoever was selected in the primary would be the victor in the general election. This practice was nullified by the Supreme Court in 1944.

Other legal obstacles for blacks in the South were the literacy test and the poll tax, which were finally prohibited by the twenty-fourth amendment, passed in 1964. Both obstacles were designed as southern suffrage requirements to admit whites to the electorate and exclude blacks (without mentioning race). The literacy test and its related requirements were blatantly racist.[14] Its object was to allow all adult white males to vote while excluding all blacks. The problem with this test was that many whites would also be excluded because they were also illiterate. Legislators in various southern states contrived alternatives to the literacy requirements that would allow the illiterate whites to vote. One loophole was the "grandfather clause." This provision, based on Louisiana law, "exempted persons from the literacy test who were registered voters in any state on January 1, 1867, or prior thereto, the sons and grandsons of such persons, and male persons of foreign birth naturalized before January 1, 1898."[15] Obviously, the use of these dates prevented blacks from voting and thereby served to maintain white domination.

Beginning with World War I, a time of labor shortage and industrial expansion, blacks began to move from the rural South to the urban North. After the war, blacks in the North experienced large-scale discrimination as jobs became scarce. World War II brought another great wave of migrants to the industrial cities of the North, and again after the war blacks faced unemployment and discrimination from many fronts.

Several conditions following World War II made the black experience different the second time. Blacks were now concentrated in cities more than ever, increasing the likelihood of group actions to alter their oppression. Also more blacks were educated and could provide leadership. Very important, many blacks had served the country in the war and now were unwilling to accept continued inferiority. The result of these factors and others was the civil rights movement of the 1960s. Although there were significant positive changes for blacks resulting from this movement, including favorable legislation and court decisions, the lot of blacks in the 1980s (documented fully later in this chapter) remains one of inferiority and subordination.

Chicanos   Mexican Americans represent another ethnic group that experienced involuntary migration. Unlike the blacks, who were transported to a hostile environment, Chicanos involuntarily became part of the United States largely because of military conquest.[16]

Beginning around 1600 the southwestern part of the present United States was controlled by Spain. Mexico gained control over this area when it gained independence from Spain in 1821. Mexico permitted immigrants to settle in this territory (primarily in what is now Texas), and by 1830 there were some 20,000 Anglo* settlers.[17] By 1835 these settlers were hostile toward Mexico and Mexicans. As one historian has described it, "The Texans saw themselves in danger of becoming the alien subjects of a people to whom they deliberately believed themselves morally, intellectually, and politically superior."[18] This feeling of superiority, Mexico's abolition of slavery, and other factors led to the Texas revolt of 1835 and an independent Texas republic. When the United States granted statehood to Texas in 1845 despite the fact that Mexico still claimed it, war was inevitable. Many U.S. politicians and business interests supported the war because of the high probability of winning and of subsequent territorial expansion.[19] As a result of the war, which lasted from 1846 to 1848, Mexico lost half its national territory and the United States increased its area by a third (Arizona, California, Colorado, New Mexico, Texas, Nevada, Utah, and parts of Kansas, Oklahoma, and Wyoming).† Under the Treaty of Guadalupe Hidalgo (1848), Mexicans living on the U.S. side of the new border who decided to remain would have all the rights of U.S. citizens according to the Constitution.

Despite the guarantees to the Mexicans who remained, their status under the new regime was clearly secondary. Their civil and property rights were routinely violated.[20] Most important, the U.S. military, judicial system, and government were used to establish Anglos in positions of power in the economic structures that Mexicans had developed in mining, ranching, and agriculture.[21] The techniques used to accomplish this were taxation; a court

---

* *Anglos*, as used by Chicanos, refers to all Caucasian Americans, not just those who trace their origins to the British Isles.
† In 1853 the United States purchased from Mexico (the Gadsden Purchase) an additional 45,000 square miles in Arizona and New Mexico.

system unfamiliar with Mexican and Spanish landowning laws, traditions, and customs; and the appropriation of land for the National Forest Service with little if any compensation. In short, Mexican Americans were largely dispossessed of power and property. With the coming of the railroads and the damming of rivers for irrigation, the Southwest became an area of economic growth, but the advantages accrued mainly to Anglos. Mexican Americans no longer owned the land; now they were the source of cheap labor, an exploited group at the bottom of the social and economic ladder. As Barrera has summarized:

> Dispossession from the land . . . depleted the economic base of Chicanos and put them in an even less favorable position to exercise influence over the political process. In addition, it had other far-ranging consequences, including facilitating the emergence of a colonial labor system in the Southwest, based in large part on Chicano labor.[22]

What emerged in the nineteenth-century Southwest was a segmented labor force, which Barrera refers to as a colonial labor system: "A colonial labor system exists where the labor force is segmented along ethnic and/or racial lines, and one or more of the segments is systematically maintained in a subordinate position."[23]

The twentieth century has been a period of large-scale immigration from Mexico to the Southwest. The number of persons born in Mexico living in the United States was 103,393 in 1900, 221,915 in 1910, and 639,017 in 1930.[24]

The Great Depression was an especially difficult time for Chicanos. Not only were they vulnerable because of their marginal jobs; they were also the object of hostility from many Anglos, who believed they were flooding an overcrowded labor market, depressing wages, and functioning as a drain on the welfare system. As a result, from 1929 to 1934 more than 400,000 Mexicans, many of them U.S. citizens, were forced to repatriate in Mexico. Those who applied for welfare benefits were the most likely to be victims: "Those who applied for relief were referred to 'Mexican Bureaus,' whose sole purpose was to reduce the welfare rolls by deporting the applicants. Indigence, not citizenship, was the criterion used in identifying Mexicans for repatriation."[25]

In contrast, after World War II, when the economy was booming and jobs were plentiful, the U.S. government instituted the bracero program, which permitted Mexicans to migrate to the United States to work in agriculture. Farmers favored such a program because it assured them of a steady supply of cheap labor. This program was terminated in 1964, after nearly 5 million Mexicans had come to the United States, and a total annual immigration quota of 120,000 was imposed on all nations in the Western Hemisphere.

Since World War II there has been another source of migrants—"illegals" or "undocumented workers" who came to the United States in great numbers seeking work. A current estimate is that perhaps more than a million people a year cross the border to work in the United States without legal permission.

These illegal immigrants are especially vulnerable to low wages and other abuses by employers and landlords.

The Census Bureau estimates the current Chicano population at 8.7 million, with perhaps another 7 million "undocumented workers" (1980).* Both figures are likely to be too low, since the Census Bureau misses a significant portion of those who are poor, work in migrant jobs, live in overcrowded conditions; and, of course, those who are in the United States illegally do everything they can to avoid detection.

Currently, Chicanos experience discrimination not only in jobs and wages but also through segregated schools, the use of Anglo-oriented tests for placement in schools, residential segregation, and exclusionary policies by private organizations.

Native Americans

American Indians have lived continuously in North America for at least 30,000 years.[26] The tribes located in North America were and are extremely heterogeneous, with major differences in physical characteristics, language, and social organization. There were theocracies, democracies, and hereditary chiefdoms; matrilineal and patrilineal systems; hunters and farmers; nomads and villagers. Some tribes were basically cooperative; others were fiercely competitive.

> In 1492, when Columbus landed at Watling's Island in the Bahamas, the North American continent was an area of astonishing ethnic and cultural diversity. North of the Rio Grande was a population of 12 million people, something like 400 separate and distinct cultures, 500 languages, and a dazzling variety of political and religious institutions and physical and ethnic types.[27]

Native Americans, then, lived in a pluralistic world, with tribes of quite different cultures and social organizations coexisting. In contrast, the Europeans who settled in the New World were quite similar: they spoke some variant of Indo-European language; they had a common religious tradition— Christianity; political and social conventions were similar (patrilineal descent, male dominance, property rights, and political organization as a nation-state). They shared a belief in what they considered the international law of the right of discovery. This was the belief that the European nation first landing on and claiming the right to territory not formerly held by other Europeans had the exclusive authority to negotiate with the natives for the absolute ownership of the land. This ethnocentric notion was buttressed further by the Europeans' belief that they represented the highest level of civilization. They were convinced of their superiority to the natives of the New World, whom they considered to be not only infidels but inferior beings.

From the beginning, the Europeans took the land once owned by the natives. One way of doing this was through treaties. The English and the

---

*Chicanos represent about 60 percent of the total U.S. Hispanic population of 14.6 million (1980). Fourteen percent are Puerto Rican, 5.5 percent Cuban, 8 percent Central or South American, and 21 percent of other Spanish origin.

Reprinted by permission of United Feature Syndicate.

French offered inducements to tribes to cede some of their land in exchange for the promise of material goods, health benefits, and the guaranteed security of Indian lands. Often these treaties included a perpetuity clause—that the treaty would remain in effect and the Indians could live in peace, security, and independence in their lands "as long as the waters flow and the grasses grow." The Indians accepted the treaties but were quickly disillusioned; "virtually all were broken by the European signatores."[28]

Another tactic was outright genocide. In 1755 the following proclamation was issued in Boston against the Penobscot Indians:

At the desire of the House of Representatives . . . I do hereby require his majesty's subjects of the Province to embrace all opportunities of pursuing, captivating, killing and destroying all and every of the aforesaid Indians. . . . The General Court of this Province have voted that a bounty . . . be granted: For the capture of every male Penobscot Indian above the age of twelve and brought to Boston, fifty pounds. For every scalp of a male Indian above the age aforesaid, brought in as evidence of their being killed as aforesaid, forty pounds. . . . For every scalp of such female Indian or male Indian under the age of twelve years that shall be killed and brought in as evidence of their being killed as aforesaid, twenty pounds.[29]

As new waves of settlers moved westward, the lands the Indians had been promised were forcibly taken. Native Americans protecting their lands fought battles with settlers and with U.S. troops. Always the result was that Native Americans were forced to move farther west to remote areas.

Indians were also forced to move to other places against their will. Although the Supreme Court ruled that the Cherokees had legal title to their lands in the South, President Andrew Jackson forcibly evicted them and forced them to walk a thousand miles in midwinter from Carolina and Georgia to Oklahoma. Four thousand died in this forced march. The Indians had been promised that the land that they settled in the Indian territory would never be made part of a state; yet this area became part of Oklahoma in 1907.

In 1871 all Indians were made "wards" of the federal government and were placed on federal reservations on lands considered of little value. As wards, Native Americans had no control of their communities and no power to effect federal policies over them. They were under the jurisdiction of the Bureau of Indian Affairs, which decided "what they would eat, where they would live, and ultimately what style of living they would adopt."[30] Thus, they were stripped of their political rights and even their culture.

Native Americans were first granted U.S. citizenship and the right to vote in 1924. Some states, including New York and North Carolina, disputed their right to vote even into the 1970s.[31] Recent legislation and court decisions have restored some rights and powers to Native American tribes. This is significant in two major respects. First, various tribes are claiming in the courts that they have the legal rights to millions of acres of land. Second, Indian lands are teeming with riches that the Indians also claim.

> It is one of history's more stunning ironies. The 51.9 million acres in the U.S. reserved for the Indians were lands the white man could not see any conceivable reason to reserve for himself. They were too wet or too dry, too barren or too remote. Now, at a time when the U.S. seems to be running out of practically everything, the 272 federally recognized Indian reservations constitute one of the largest and least known mineral repositories on the continent— nearly 5 percent of the U.S.'s oil and gas, one-third of its strippable low-sulfur coal, one-half of its privately owned uranium.[32]

It will be instructive to see how the powerful decide on these claims. If history is a guide, Native Americans will not receive their share.

The treatment of Native Americans throughout their history of contact with Europeans and Caucasian Americans has been brutal. From a population of 12 million at the time of Columbus, their numbers were reduced to an estimated 210,000 in 1910.* This remarkable decrease was the result of three major factors: death in battle; death from such Old World diseases as smallpox, cholera, and measles, to which they lacked immunity; and the poverty and misery forced on them by the decisions of the powerful.

Today, Native Americans are the poorest, the least educated, least employed, unhealthiest, and worst-housed ethnic group in America.[33] A few statistics confirm their appalling condition.

---

*The 1980 Census counted as Indians all who identified themselves as such—1,361,869.

□ More than one-third live below the poverty line. In some areas of Arizona and Utah, the proportion below this line is as high as 65 percent.

□ Only about one-third of Indian males are high school graduates.

□ Sixty-two percent of all housing units on Indian reservations are substandard, compared with 12.9 percent in the general U.S. population.

□ Deaths from tuberculosis, dysentery, and accidents are four times higher for Indians than for non-Indians.

□ For 1976–1978, the Indian Health Service reported 16.1 infant deaths per 1,000 live births, compared with 14.1 per 1,000 for the total population.[34]

□ The life expectancy of the average Indian is ten years below that of the nation as a whole.[35]

□ Unemployment generally ranges between 45 and 55 percent.

□ The suicide rate is double the national average and the alcoholism rate is at least five times as high.

Blacks, Chicanos, and Native Americans, then, have been and are the three most disadvantaged minorities in the United States. Although each group differs in racial and ethnic characteristics, some important shared characteristics help to explain their continuing secondary status in American society. Unlike most other minorities, each of these groups is distinguished from the majority by *color*. Second, each group became part of the United States *involuntarily*. Third, blacks, Chicanos, and Native Americans were *colonized*. These three features of their minority experience are crucial to understanding the institution and maintenance of their oppression. The next section elaborates on the explanations given for this phenomenon.

EXPLANATIONS OF RACIAL AND ETHNIC INEQUALITY

Why have some racial and ethnic groups been consistently disadvantaged throughout American history? Some ethnic groups, such as the Irish and Jews, have experienced discrimination but managed to overcome their initial disadvantages.[36] Others, such as the blacks, Chicanos, and Indians, have not been able to cast off their secondary status. Three types of theories have been used to explain why some groups are consistently singled out for discrimination: deficiency theories, bias theories, and structural discrimination theories.[37]

Deficiency Theories

A number of analysts have argued that some groups are inferior because they *are* inferior. That is, when compared with the majority, they are deficient in some important way. There are three varieties of deficiency theory.

Biological Deficiency.   This classical explanation for the inferiority of certain groups maintains that their inferiority is the result of flawed genetic—and, therefore, hereditary—traits. This is the position of Arthur Jensen and Richard Herrnstein, as we saw in the last chapter, that blacks are mentally inferior to whites. Despite the work of these and others of their persuasion, there is no definitive evidence for the thesis that racial groups differ in intelligence. Biological deficiency theories are generally not accepted in the scientific community.

Deficiency in Social Structure. This type of explanation argues that some flaw in the social structure of minorities is responsible for their secondary status. An example of this type of explanation is the theory of Daniel Moynihan (former Harvard social scientist and the present senator from New York) that a weak family structure prevalent among blacks is the reason for their disadvantaged position in society.[38]

> The fundamental source of weakness in the black community is an unstable family structure caused by the experience of slavery, the absence of husbands and a high rate of illegitimacy. The modal family type, then, is a matriarchy. A matriarchal form of family is detrimental because it is at variance with the standard pattern in American society. It is especially harmful to boys who will be denied adequate sex role models. Thus, the institution of the black family is assumed to be defective. Black culture produces a weak and disorganized form of family life, which, because it is self-perpetuating, is the obstacle to full realization of equality.

There are a number of criticisms of the Moynihan report.[39] They are important, because by itself the report indicts blacks rather than society (the racism that perpetuates unequal opportunities and the massive overrepresentation of blacks among the poor) and masks the relationship between poverty and family stability regardless of race.

An initial criticism is directed at the common practice of overgeneralization. To speak of "the black family" is a fiction. There is a wide diversity of family forms in different geographic regions, at different income levels, and at different social status levels throughout American society. Blacks are not a homogeneous group.

A related criticism addresses Moynihan's contention that black family structure, compared with white family structure, is highly unstable. In general, Moynihan's assertion is correct, but it incorrectly implies that the crucial difference in family structure is race. The more important differences are the relative economic positions of the two categories. Poor families are disproportionately unstable when compared to the more well-to-do, regardless of race. Since nearly half of all black families are poor, compared to 10 to 15 percent of white families, the higher instability rates for blacks are explained not by race itself, but by the racism that systematically disadvantages blacks and advantages whites. Moynihan bases his claim on the breakup of the black family on data from the early 1960s. These data show that 23 percent of all nonwhite homes were headed by a woman, 24 percent of all black births were illegitimate, and 36 percent of black children live in broken homes. Although these figures reflect marital instability, they do not in themselves validate the claim that black families are unstable. To the contrary, the same figures show that 77 percent of all nonwhite homes are headed by a male, 76 percent of all black babies are born to a man and woman who are legally married, and 64 percent of black children are living with both parents. Thus, these same statistics show that *the overwhelming majority of black families are stable.*

The fact that the majority of black families are stable belies Moynihan's contention that deviant family forms are part of black culture. Matriarchy and desertion by the husband are believed to result from the continual humiliation of the black male under slavery and the Jim-Crow laws of the South. Without question these practices were humiliating, but these occurrences do not prove the existence of a black culture that transmits a peculiar family form (as well as mode of socialization, power relations, family roles) from generation to generation. It may just be a matter of economics. In black families that have attained middle-class status, for example, nine of ten children have both parents present in the home. That finding directly contradicts the Moynihan thesis, which argues that economic aid alone would not solve the tangle of pathology for blacks. Historical data also refute the Moynihan argument. Herbert Gutman, a historian who spent ten years examining letters, plantation records, marriage applications, and other data on black families during and after slavery, found that the two-parent household and enduring marriages have been typical among blacks for most of their American experience.[40]

A final objection to the Moynihan report is that it is a classic case of blaming the victim. According to this thesis, the pathology lies within black Americans, especially black males, not in social institutions. Thus, Moynihan's solution was that "a national effort towards the problems of Negro Americans must be directed towards the question of family structure. The object should be to strengthen the Negro family so as to enable it to raise and support its members as do other families."[41]

The problem, however, lies not in the black family but in the oppressive white racist society. The target should be not the black family, but discrimination in the schools and on the job. Furthermore, power and wealth need to be more equally distributed. Then the "problem" black family will cease being a problem, for whatever problem it presents is an artifact of economic and social inequality.

Cultural Deficiency. Cultural deficiency theories argue that the culture (attitudes, values, and language) of a minority keeps its members from competing successfully in society. The culture of poverty, considered in the last chapter, is the explanation given by Edward Banfield and others for the perpetuation of disadvantage for some groups. This view holds that members of these groups want instant gratification and are unwilling to sacrifice now for future payoffs. Their "culture" devalues education.[42] Some analysts have argued that the Chicano culture has held the members of this group back.[43] From this perspective, Chicanos are viewed as culturally disadvantaged because the Chicano heritage and customs value the present rather than the future, dependency rather than independence, and low rather than high motivation for achievement. These traits, coupled with the difficulty that many have with the English language, mean that Chicanos will be less likely to be successful in Anglo schools and Anglo work settings.

The latest promoter of the cultural deficiency theory is Thomas Sowell. Sowell, a black economist, has argued that ethnic groups in America such as the Italians and Jews have overcome obstacles to become part of the mainstream because their cultures were congruent with the values of American society. The progress of blacks and Chicanos, on the other hand, has been impeded by their culture.

> What determines how rapidly a group moves ahead is not discrimination but the fit between elements of its culture and the requirements of the economy. To get ahead, you have to have some ability to work, some ability at entrepreneurship or something else that the society values.
>
> In that regard, the cultural legacy of slavery has retarded the progress of blacks. Under slavery, there was no possibility of advancement. The only incentive was to avoid being punished. If you did enough to avoid punishment, that was about all you ought to do.
>
> Because slaves did the menial work, the white population in the South became disdainful of menial labor. But the immigrant groups who came over here did not have the intellectual baggage holding them back, and so, though often destitute when they got here, they typically ended up earning more than Southern whites because of their willingness to take any job.[44]

Sowell, Banfield, and others who argue for the culture deficiency thesis are criticized on a number of grounds. For one, they argue that the cultural attributes of the disadvantaged explain their secondary status, not discrimination. But these cultural traits are likely to be the result of discrimination. It is hard to be success oriented and willing to sacrifice now for a better future when there is little hope of success regardless of one's efforts. Moreover, as we saw in the last chapter, minority-group members have a dual value system—they hold the values of the minority and the majority simultaneously. Research has shown that given a chance, members of minority groups quickly adopt competition and success values.

In effect, culture deficiency theorists blame the victim and ignore the structural constraints that deny certain groups the same opportunities that others have. Roger Wilkins has said of Sowell's argument:

> A society that was bent and twisted out of shape in order to deny opportunity to minorities and to women can't be fixed by two and a half decades of vigorous protest, by laws and court decisions or even by the pieties and half-truths of neoconservative politicians and pundits. The system is still substantially skewed, and so are the minds of a good number of white Americans—particularly males. So, when I see Labor Department statistics that tell me that 15 percent of all minorities are out of work, that 45.7 percent of all black teenagers who want work can't get it and that women still earn less than 60 percent of what men make, I do not conclude that the sun spins around the earth and that these results flow from a society in which all opportunity is equal.

Sowell, who believes that it is, seems to have arrived at this conclusion by examining the experiences of Italians in Argentina and explicitly ignoring the history and the current social conditions of America. He has published nonsense.[45]

Bias Theories

The deficiency theories just discussed blame the minorities for their plight. Bias theories, on the other hand, blame the members of the majority—in particular, they blame the prejudiced attitudes of majority members. Gunnar Myrdal, for example, argued in his classic, *An American Dilemma*, that prejudiced attitudes are the source of discriminatory actions, which in turn keep minorities subordinate.[46] The inferior status of minorities reinforces negative stereotypes that in turn justify the prejudice of the majority; the process is a vicious cycle that perpetuates the secondary status from generation to generation.

PANEL 11–1   Methods Panel

Scientific Reasoning

Science uses methods that are logical, systematic, and verifiable. It is exactly opposite to forms of analysis using dogma, intuition, and revelation. The objective of science is to search for facts. This quest is guided by a number of postulates that scientists agree maximize the chances for finding facts. These are:

1. All behavior is naturally determined.
2. Human beings are part of the natural world.
3. Nature is orderly and regular.
4. Nature is uniform.
5. Nature is permanent.
6. All objective phenomena are eventually knowable.
7. Nothing is self-evident.
8. Truth is relative; absolute or final truth may never be achieved.
9. All perceptions are achieved through the senses.
10. People can trust their perceptions, memory, and reasoning as reliable agencies for acquiring facts.

Once verifiable facts are obtained, they must be assembled and arranged into useful structures. It requires the use of logic (valid reasoning) to achieve reliable conclusions about the facts. There are a number of rules and prescriptions for logical reasoning that have been established over the course of twenty-five centuries of Western thought.

As an example of the role that *faulty* logic plays in our interpretations, let's consider the following discussion:

Negroes have a proportionately higher crime rate than do Whites. This common contention (made even by chiefs of police, prison officials and legislators) illustrates several facets of faulty logic: (a) It implicitly infers that *all* Negroes have a higher potential for committing crimes; and this is not a fact—only some classes of urban Negroes in the United States exhibit a higher rate of some types of popularly-noticed crimes. (b) It also infers that Negroes—even if they should in fact commit proportionately more crimes—do so *because* they are Negroes. This implication is also false in fact, as any social psychologist well knows. Without elaborating this example, it is interesting to note that here is a case of a partially-true assertion which is valid for the wrong reason (i.e., wrong in the sense of popular attribution or causative reasoning). In the cases where Negroes have a proportionately higher crime rate than do Whites, they apparently do so because (1) crime rates are proportionately higher in urban than in rural areas; and the Negro-criminal allegation is largely an outgrowth of Negro immigration into urban areas; (2) popularly-noted crimes are generally of a lower criminal class variety (e.g., rape, robbery, burglary and assault); and Negroes predominate in the lower classes due to the racial discrimination exhibited against them in jobs, housing, etc.; and because (3) crime rates as indicated by the population of penal establishments (where Negroes are proportionately high) simply reflect disproportionate social (i.e., police, the courts, the press) sensitivity to lower-class crimes.

There is no substantial evidence, for example, that Negroes commit proportionately as many (let alone more) upper-class crimes (e.g., embezzlement, big-time gambling, forgery, espionage,) than do Whites; in fact, growing evidence strongly suggests that they commit proportionately fewer of such kinds of crimes. If, however, it is clearly established as a matter of fact that one's criminal-behavior potential is in no way a direct and necessary consequence of his racial inheritance, then it may be validly deduced that—if and when Negroes achieve complete social, economic, political and legal equality with Whites—they probably will commit the same proportion of all types of crimes as will Whites.

The foregoing argument suggests the fundamental role that sound reasoning plays in the scientific approach.

Source: Carlo L. Lastrucci, *The Scientific Approach: Basic Principles of the Scientific Method* (Cambridge, Mass.: Schenkman, 1967). An elaboration of the postulates of science is found on pp. 37–47, and the excerpt is from pp. 50–51.

David Wellman has made an extensive critique of bias theories and presented an alternative.[47] He has raised a number of objections to the traditional view that the attitudes of white Americans are the major cause of racism. The typical view is that whites, particularly lower-class whites, have hostile feelings toward and make faulty generalizations about minorities. Minorities are thus prejudged and misjudged by the majority, and the result is discrimination. Prejudiced attitudes, however, do not explain the behaviors of unprejudiced whites who defend the traditional arrangements that negatively affect minorities. Unbiased persons fight to preserve the status quo by favoring, for example, the seniority system in occupations, or they oppose affirmative action, quota systems, busing to achieve racial balance, and open enrollment in higher education. As Wellman has argued:

The terms in which middle-class professionals defend traditional institutional arrangements are, strictly speaking, not examples of racial prejudice. They are neither overtly racial nor, given these people's *interests*, misrepresentations of facts. However, while the sentiments may not be prejudiced, they justify arrangements that in effect, if not in intent, maintain the status quo and thereby keep blacks in subordinate positions.[48]

Thus, to focus strictly on prejudice is to take too narrow a view. It presents an inaccurate portrayal of racism because it concentrates only on the bigots and ignores the discriminating acts of those who are not prejudiced. Moreover, according to Wellman, prejudice is not the cause of discrimination. Rather, it is the racial organization of society that is the cause of people's racial beliefs. The determining feature of majority-minority relations is not prejudice, but rather the superior position of the majority and the institutions that maintain this superiority. "The subordination of people of color is functional to the operation of American society as we know it and the color of one's skin is a primary determinant of people's position in the social structure."[49] Thus, institutional and individual racism generate privilege for whites. Discrimination provides the privileged with disproportionate advantages in the social, economic, and political spheres. Racist acts, in this view, are not only based on hatred, stereotyped conceptions, or prejudgment but are rational responses to the struggle over scarce resources by individuals acting to preserve their advantage.

Structural Discrimination Theories

Critics of the deficiency and bias theories argue that these explanations focus, incorrectly, on individuals—the characteristics and attitudes of the prejudiced majority and the flaws of the minority. Both kinds of theories ignore the politicoeconomic system that dominates and oppresses minorities. Parenti has criticized those who ignore the system as victim-blamers. "Focusing on the poor and ignoring the system of power, privilege, and profit which makes them poor, is a little like blaming the corpse for the murder."[50] Structural theory corrects this fundamental fault by focusing on institutionalized patterns of discrimination that operate independently of people's attitudes.

Institutional racism refers to the established, customary, and respected ways in which society operates to keep the minority in a subordinate position. For Carmichael and Hamilton there are two types of racism—individual and institutional. Individual racism consists of overt acts by individuals that harm other individuals or their property. This type of action is usually publicly decried and is probably on the decline in the United States. Institutional racism is more injurious than individual racism to more minority-group members, but it is not recognized by the dominant-group members as racism. Carmichael and Hamilton illustrated the two types as follows:

> When a black family moves into a home in a white neighborhood and is stoned, burned or routed out, they are victims of an overt act of individual racism which many people will condemn—at least in words. But it is institutional racism that keeps black people locked in dilapidated slum tenements, subject to the daily prey of exploitative slumlords, merchants, loan sharks, and discriminatory real estate agents. . . . Respectable individuals can absolve themselves from individual blame: *they* would never plant a bomb in a church: *they* would never stone a black family. But they continue to support political officials and institutions that would and do perpetuate institutionally racist policies. Thus *acts* of overt, individual racism may not typify the society, but institutionalism racism does. . . .[51]

We have noted that some individuals and groups discriminate whether they are bigots or not. These individuals and groups operate within a social milieu that is also discriminatory. The social milieu includes laws, customs, religious beliefs, social stratification, the distribution of power, and the stable arrangements and practices through which things get done in society. These social arrangements and accepted ways of doing things may consciously or unconsciously disadvantage some social categories while benefiting others. The major sectors of society—the system of law and the administration of justice, the economic system, the formal educational structure, and health care—are all possible discriminators. Thus, the term *institutional discrimination* is a useful one. As Knowles and Prewitt have said, the institutions of society

> have great power to reward and penalize. They reward by providing career opportunities for some people and foreclosing them for others. They reward as well by the way social goods and services are distributed—by deciding who receives training and skills, medical care, formal education, political influence, moral support and self-respect, productive employment, fair treatment by the law, decent housing, self-confidence, and the promise of a secure future for self and children.[52]

Analysts of society, pursuing the phenomenon of discrimination, need to ask, how are things normally done in the society? Who gets preferential treatment under these normal arrangements? Who is automatically excluded because of these arrangements? The answers to these questions are not always easy because the arrangements are "natural" and the discrimination often unintentional or disguised. The task is especially difficult because the exact placement of responsibility is often impossible to pinpoint. Who is responsible for the low scores of ghetto children on standard IQ tests? Who is responsible for residential segregation? Who is responsible for the high unemployment rate of minority-group members?

There are four basic themes of institutional discrimination.[53] First is the importance of history in determining present conditions and affecting resistance to change. Historically, institutions defined and enforced norms and role relationships that were racially distinct. The American nation was founded and its institutions established when blacks were slaves, uneducated, and different culturally from the dominant whites. From the beginning blacks were considered inferior (the Constitution, for example, counts a slave as three-fifths of a person). Religious beliefs buttressed this notion of the inferiority of blacks and justified the differential allocation of privileges and sanctions in society. Laws, customs, and traditions usually continue to reinforce current thinking. Institutions have an inertial quality: once set in motion, they tend to continue on the same course. Thus institutional racism is extremely difficult to change without a complete overhaul of society's institutions.

The second theme of institutional discrimination is that discrimination can occur *without* conscious bigotry. All it takes for institutional discrimination to continue is for employers to insist that prospective employees take aptitude or IQ tests that are based on middle-class experiences, or for decisions on who must be fired in times of financial exigency to be based on seniority, or for employers to stress educational requirements for hiring. These conditions, seemingly fair and neutral, are biased against minorities.

Institutional discrimination is also more invisible than individual discrimination. Institutional discrimination is more subtle and less intentional than individual acts of discrimination. As a result it is extremely difficult to establish blame for this kind of discrimination.

Finally, institutional discrimination is reinforced because institutions are interrelated. The exclusion of minorities from the upper levels of education, for example, is likely to affect their opportunities in other institutions (type of job, level of remuneration). Similarly, being poor means that your children will probably receive an inferior education, be propertyless, suffer from bad health, and be treated unjustly by the criminal justice system. These inequities are cumulative. As Benokraitis and Feagin have argued:

> Once a minority is excluded from one institution, chances are greater that it will also be excluded from other institutional privilege. Thus, institutional racism theorists agree that once, historically, institutions have evolved differential opportunities for wealth, power, prestige, privilege, and authority based on racial criteria, unequal resources will produce unequal qualifications to compete for goods and services, unequal qualifications will limit access to goods and services and unequal access to goods and services will result in unequal resources.[54]

Let us examine some illustrations of how various aspects of the society work to derogate minority groups, deny them equality, and even do them violence. Institutional derogation occurs when minority groups and their members are made to seem inferior or possess negative stereotypes through legitimate means by the powerful in society. The portrayal of minority group members in the media (movies, television, newspapers, and magazines) is often derogatory.[55] Only recently has there been an effort to thwart the negative images of minorities in the media. The "Amos 'n' Andy" radio program that was popular in the 1940s and 1950s used almost all the black stereotypes—and America laughed. The early Shirley Temple movies had an adult black by the name of Stepin Fetchit, whose role was to be more childlike than Miss Temple. The traditional roles of blacks, Indians, and women in movies, novels, and television have typically focused on the negative stereotypes of these groups. These stereotypes are similarly reinforced in textbooks.[56]

A much more subtle form of derogation works within the English language itself. Panel 11–2 reprints a portion of a speech by a distinguished black actor, dramatic artist, and writer, who shows how invidious the English language can be.[57]

The system (customs, practices, expectations, laws, beliefs) also works to deny equality to minority-group members—most often without malicious intent. Because it is the system that disadvantages, discrimination would continue even if tomorrow all Americans were to awake with all animosity toward minority groups obliterated from their hearts and minds. All that is needed for minorities to suffer is that the law continue to favor the owners of property over renters and debtors. All that is needed for job opportunities to remain unequal is for employers to hire those with the most conventional training and experience and to use machines when they seem more immediately economical than manual labor. All that is needed to ensure that poor children get an inferior education is to continue "tracking," using class-biased tests, making education irrelevant in their work, rewarding children who conform to the teachers' middle-class concepts of the "good student," and paying disproportionately less for their education (buildings, supplies, teachers, counselors).[58] In other words, all that is needed to perpetuate discrimination in the United States is to pursue a policy of "business as usual."

Skolnick has described institutional discrimination as it applies to blacks, but the same could be said for the treatment of other minority groups as well:

> It is theoretically possible to have a racist society in which most of the individual members of that society do not express racist attitudes. A society in which most of the good jobs are held by one race, and the dirty jobs by the people of another color, is a society in which racism is institutionalized, no matter what the beliefs of its members are. For example, the universities of America are probably the least bigoted of American institutions. One would rarely, if ever, hear an openly bigoted expression at schools like Harvard, Yale, the University of Chicago, the University of California. At the same time, university faculties and students have usually been white, the custodians black. The universities have concerned themselves primarily with the needs and interests of the white upper middle and upper classes, and have viewed the lower classes, and especially blacks, as objects of study rather than of service. In this sense, they have, willy-nilly, been institutionally "white racist."[59]

Approximately 1 percent of American lawyers are black, Puerto Rican, Chicano, or members of other recognized minority groups. Six-tenths of 1 percent of American medical doctors are black. Racial minority groups are underrepresented in the professions because they receive a "disadvantaged" education for the reasons given above.

Educational deficiencies and lack of finances for most minority groups make colleges and graduate schools the almost exclusive havens of the majority group. Through discrimination, the system victimizes certain groups and perpetuates inequality. Because such a small percentage of minority group members go on to college and graduate school, school boards and legislatures can justify not spending more for their education. This brings about the conditions that the dominant group consider proof of the minority's inferiority. The great British playwright George Bernard Shaw is reported to have said, "The haughty American nation . . . makes the Negro clean its boots, and then proves the . . . inferiority of the Negro by the fact that he is a bootblack."

The English Language Is My Enemy

I stand before you, a little nervous, afflicted to some degree with stage fright. Not because I fear you, but because I fear the subject.

The title of my address is, "Racism in American Life—Broad Perspectives of the Problem," or, "The English Language Is My Enemy."

In my speech I will define culture as the sum total of ways of living built up by a group of human beings and transmitted by one generation to another. I will define education as the act or process of imparting and communicating a culture, developing the powers of reasoning and judgment and generally preparing oneself and others intellectually for a mature life.

I will define communication as the primary means by which the process of education is carried out.

I will say that language is the primary medium of communication in the educational process and, in this case, the English language. I will indict the English language as one of the prime carriers of racism from one person to another in our society and discuss how the teacher and the student, especially the Negro student, are affected by this fact.

The English language is my enemy.

Racism is a belief that human races have distinctive characteristics, usually involving the idea that one's own race is superior and has a right to rule others. Racism.

The English language is my enemy.

But that was not my original topic—I said that English was my goddamn enemy. Now why do I use "goddamn" to illustrate this aspect of the English language? Because I want to illustrate the sheer gut power of words. Words which control our action. Words like "nigger," "kike," "sheeny," "Dago," "black power"—words like this. Words we don't use in ordinary decent conversation, one to the other. I choose these words deliberately, not to flaunt my freedom before you. If you are a normal human being these words will have assaulted your senses, may even have done you physical harm, and if you so choose, you could have me arrested.

Those words are attacks upon your physical and emotional well being; your pulse rate is possibly higher, your breath quicker; there is perhaps a tremor along the nerves of your arms and your legs; sweat begins in the palms of your hands, perhaps. With these few words I have assaulted you. I have damaged you, and there is nothing you can possibly do to control your reactions—to defend yourself against the brute force of these words.

These words have a power over us; a power that we cannot resist. For a moment you and I have had our deepest physical reactions controlled, not by our own wills, but by words in the English language.

A superficial examination of Roget's *Thesaurus of the English Language* reveals the following facts: The word "whiteness" has 134 synonyms, 44 of which are favorable and pleasing to contemplate. For example: "purity," "cleanness," "immaculateness," "bright," "shiny," "ivory," "fair," "blonde," "stainless," "clean," "clear," "chaste," "unblemished," "unsullied," "innocent," "honorable," "upright," "just," "straightforward," "genuine," "trustworthy"—and only 10 synonyms of which I feel to have been negative and then only in the mildest sense, such as "gloss-over," "whitewash," "gray," "wan," "pale," "ashen," etc.

The word "blackness" has 120 synonyms, 60 of which are distinctly unfavorable, and none of them even mildly positive. Among the offending 60 were such words as "blot," "blotch," "smut," "smudge," "sullied," "begrime," "soot," "becloud," "obscure," "dingy," "murky," "low-toned," "threatening," "frowning," "foreboding," "forbidding," "sinister," "baneful," "dismal," "thundery," "wicked," "malignant," "deadly," "unclean," "dirty," "unwashed," "foul," etc. In addition, and this is what really hurts, 20 of those words—and I exclude the villainous 60 above—are related directly to race, such as "Negro," "Negress," "nigger," "darkey," "blackamoor," etc.

If you consider the fact that thinking itself is subvocal speech (in other words, one must use words in order to think at all), you will appreciate the enormous trap of racial pre-

judgment that works on any child who is born into the English language.

Any creature, good or bad, white or black, Jew or Gentile, who uses the English language for the purpose of communication is willing to force the Negro child into 60 ways to despise himself, and the white child, 60 ways to aid and abet him in the crime.

Source: Ossie Davis, "The English Language Is My Enemy," IRCD *Bulletin* 5 (Summer 1969): 13.

The labor market also operates so as to trap minority-group members. Job opportunities are segmented in American society into a dual labor market.[60] There are essentially two types of employers, with the labor market operating differently for each. Employers in the primary core enterprises are heavily capitalized and unionized; they offer jobs with relatively high wages, good working conditions, security, fringe benefits, and the chance for advancement. The other type, the marginal employers, pay the lowest wages and often have deplorable working conditions (such as in the garment industry, restaurants, and in farming). These jobs require few skills. Employers are interested in workers who will make minimal demands. Workers who agitate for better wages and working conditions are soon replaced because they have no job security and there is generally a large pool of persons available (teenagers, ex-convicts, recent immigrants from rural areas, recent immigrants, and the poor). Very few people at the bottom of the labor market ever have access to the jobs considered part of the "American Dream"— those with security, good pay, and chances for advancement. Low educational attainment and lack of skills keep minority-group members in jobs that are unstable, below average in wages, and dead end. The poor black or Chicano is most likely to end up in these jobs because the institutions of society are programmed for sifting and sorting individuals, usually according to predetermined categories such as age, race, sex, and socioeconomic background. Inner-city minority schools, for example, actually prepare youth for these dead-end jobs by encouraging those of "disadvantaged" backgrounds to drop out and by socializing them in particular ways. Joan Moore has argued that

the young school dropout is *well* prepared for jobs in the peripheral firms. He has been thoroughly socialized in the schools to expect very little: he learns to cope with, and finally abandon all hope of, pleasing the teacher, and he establishes patterns of "truancy, tardiness and evasion of school rules." Finally, the young dropout acquires habits and attitudes that can qualify him (or her) only for jobs in the secondary labor market. It is essential for peripheral employers that their workers not expect much, as they must be hired and fired as finances permit and as the market demands.[61]

Not only are minorities trained for lower-level jobs; they are also restricted from better jobs by lack of geographic access to them. Because of residential segregation and/or lack of money, they commonly live in ghetto concentrations in large cities. Jobs nearby have become increasingly scarce recently as factories and firms have moved to the sunbelt states or to the edge of cities. When jobs are a considerable distance away, the prospect of high commuting costs may deter people from even trying for a job there.

Minorities are also thwarted by the increasing demands for education, especially a college education. The baby-boom generation (those born in the years 1945–1960) is now flooding the job market along with increasing numbers of women. Competition for jobs is increasing, with the more educated applicants getting the best ones.

> As the trend continues, minorities will find "credentialism" even more frustrating. It is an endless game of "catch-up." At the other end, jobs that traditionally go to uneducated people probably would expand fast enough to match the supply of poorly educated workers *if* employers were concerned only with skill. Almost certainly, however, employers will continue to discriminate.[62]

All this is not to say that minority group members are always unsuccessful in American society. Many have become wealthy and famous, particularly in the sports or entertainment fields, but also in education, science, business, and politics. The solitary minority member, through unusual achievement, has been able to make it in the white world of middle-class America. The point is, however, that these individuals made it as individuals *despite* the roadblocks provided by the system. Ironically, the system ("the American way") takes credit for the success of these individuals. The even greater irony is that when individuals fail, they are blamed rather than the system.

One structural theory—colonial theory—addresses directly the question of why some minorities have overcome their disadvantaged status while others have not. This is an important issue because the answer informs us as to whether the United States is a melting pot or not. Many social scientists have assumed that America is a land of opportunity and that all groups— ethnic and racial—will eventually be assimilated into the mainstream. As soon as minorities give up their distinctive ethnic characteristics and learn the skills and acquire the education required by the larger society, they will achieve equality. From the conflict perspective used throughout this book, the assimilation model, which does fit the case of European immigrants, does not apply to racial groups such as blacks, Chicanos, and Native Americans. The fact that they were colonized determined their asymmetrical relation to the dominant society and their continuing experience in America. According to Robert Blauner, internal colonialism is manifested in four ways: (1) colonization is involuntary, with the colonized becoming part of a new society through force or coercion; (2) the colonizing power attempts to change or eliminate the culture of the colonized people; (3) the colonized people are legally controlled by the colonizers; and (4) the colonizers discriminate against the colonized.[63] These conditions make assimilation into the larger society a myth, because the colonial experience subjected the oppressed in a system of stratification far more structurally rooted than that experienced by European immigrants. The key ingredient in internal colonialism is that there is a dominant-subordinate relationship in all spheres— social, economic, and political—that began as a result of conquest.[64] The superordinate group exploits this relationship for its own economic advantage. The structure, in turn, traps the disadvantaged. Clearly, blacks, Chicanos and Native Americans were, from the beginning, colonized peoples in this country. This explains why these groups have been blocked in their efforts to achieve equality. The following section provides ample evidence that they are victims of discrimination.

DISCRIMINATION AGAINST BLACKS AND HISPANICS: CONTINUITY AND CHANGE

The treatment of blacks and Hispanics* has been disgraceful throughout American history. Members of both categories have been denied equality in money, jobs, services, housing, and even the right to vote. Since World War II, however, under pressure from civil rights advocates, the government has led the way in breaking down these discriminatory practices. Segregated public schools were determined to be unconstitutional in 1954; poll taxes were prohibited by the Twenty-fourth Amendment; the Equal Employment Opportunity Commission was established in 1964; the Voting Rights Act of 1965 struck down discriminatory voting practices; government contracts stipulated the proportion of minorities to be hired; and in 1976 the Supreme Court ordered that special seniority rights be granted to minorities previously denied jobs because of their race, and that white suburbs must accept public housing projects for blacks and other low-income families.

These and other acts brought about a marked improvement in the situation of these minorities. Although there have been real improvements, the important question remains whether racial minorities have closed the gap with whites. This section examines the extent of improved conditions for blacks and Hispanics and how they have fared relative to the gains made by whites.

Income

Table 11–1 shows clearly that the average income for white families is greater than the average income for black and Hispanic families. Two patterns are apparent: (1) Hispanics fare relatively better than blacks (for example, in 1981 Hispanic family income was 70 percent of white family income, compared to black family income, which was only 56 percent of

*Unless otherwise noted, this section uses statistics on Hispanics rather than Chicanos because most often the data supplied by the government provide information only on the total Spanish-speaking population. Hispanics, although they share the Spanish language and Catholicism, are quite diverse, so that few generalizations are possible.

TABLE 11–1	Median Income of White, Hispanic, and Black Families: 1972–1981 (in constant 1981 dollars)

| | Median Family Income | | |
Year	White	Hispanic	Black
1972	$25,107	$17,790	$14,922
1973	25,777	17,836	14,877
1974	24,728	17,594	14,765
1975	24,110	16,140	14,835
1976	24,823	16,390	14,766
1977	25,124	17,141	14,352
1978	25,606	17,518	15,166
1979	25,689	18,255	14,590
1980	24,176	16,242	13,989
1981	23,517	16,401	13,266

Source: Bureau of the Census, "Money Income and Poverty Status of Families and Persons in the United States: 1981," *Current Population Reports*, Series P–60, No. 134 (July 1983), Table 3.

white family income);* and (2) the gap between whites and both minorities is *not* narrowing.

In terms of poverty, as noted in Chapter 10, the pattern is consistent—blacks are disproportionately poor, followed by Hispanics and then whites. The data for 1982 showed that 35.6 percent of blacks, 29.9 percent of Hispanics, and only 12 percent of whites were below the poverty line. An important fact to remember is that the government actually understates the gap between whites and minorities, because the census misses part of the poor population. (In 1980, for example, the government estimated that it missed 0.5 percent of the population—but 4.4 percent of the Hispanics and 5 percent of blacks were uncounted.)[66] Poverty is especially prevalent in families headed by females. In these instances, race once again makes a key difference: 22.3 percent of whites in this category live below the poverty line, compared with 49.2 percent of blacks and 49.3 percent of Hispanics.[67] At the other end of the income spectrum, minorities are disproportionately underrepresented: in 1980, 36.7 percent of white families had incomes of $25,000 or more, compared with only 17.1 percent of black families and 20.7 percent of Hispanic families.

Perhaps the explanation for the gap between whites and nonwhites lies in differential education, geographic location (minorities of color tend to live in the South and Southwest, where incomes are lower for everyone),

---

*The figures vary from state to state. In Colorado, for example, a state where Hispanics outnumber blacks, the pattern is reversed. In 1981, the average income in Colorado was $26,059 for white families, $19,898 for black families, and $16,815 for Hispanic families. Similarly, the proportion of Hispanics in poverty in Colorado was significantly larger than for blacks.[65]

or some other variable. Johnson and Sell have examined this question carefully for whites and blacks to determine the effects of race. They concluded:

> The overall gap between white and nonwhite income has *increased* during the 1960–70 decade. Although nonwhite income expressed as a proportion of white income has increased, suggesting improvement in the situation in one sense ... [the data indicate] that while the differences due to white-nonwhite social position in terms of education, occupation, and region of the country have decreased, the labor shift has shifted upward to an educational level at which the gap between whites and nonwhites within educational levels, occupational categories, and regions of the country is large. The increase during the decade in the total difference between white and nonwhite income is due to the increase in ... "the cost of being Negro." In 1969 dollars, the fee for being black was $1380 in 1959 and $1647 in 1969.[68]

Comparing income by race in 1959 and 1973, Reynolds Farley found that the differences in income between white and black men (about $1,900) were attributable to blacks having less education, working at less prestigious jobs, working less, and living in the South more than whites. Subtracting for that differential, he found that the cost of being black was $2,700. Moreover, this cost did not change during the 1960s or the early 1970s.[69]

Education   Blacks and Hispanics have made significant gains in educational attainment, but an important gap remains. For example, the proportion of blacks age twenty-five and older who graduated from high school increased from 8 percent in 1940 to 51 percent in 1980, while the comparable gain for whites was from 26 percent to 71 percent.[70] Despite these gains, relatively few members of racial minorities are successful in the schools. Table 11–2 shows

TABLE 11–2   Recipients of Doctorates by Discipline and by Race/Ethnicity, 1980–1981

Discipline	Race/Ethnicity			
	American Indian	Black	Hispanic	White
Arts and Humanities	12	93	104	2954
Computer Science	—	2	—	162
Education	42	589	160	5561
Engineering	4	19	16	1092
Life Science	11	80	61	4021
Math	1	9	5	446
Physical Science	1	28	36	2199
Social Science	14	223	122	4960

Source: Adapted from, "A Profile of 1980–81 Recipients of Doctorates," *The Chronicle of Higher Education* (October 6, 1982), p. 8. Copyright © 1982 *The Chronicle of Higher Education*. Reprinted by permission.

just how few complete the highest educational achievement—the attainment of the doctorate.

Table 11–3 provides data for 1981 on educational attainment for whites, blacks, and Hispanics. Clearly, whites complete the most years of formal education and Hispanics the least. Two other measures of discrepancy in educational attainment are the dropout rate and the median years of school completed. For example, 36 percent of Hispanics ages eighteen and nineteen were not enrolled in school yet were not high school graduates, compared with 19 percent for blacks and 16 percent for whites in the same age group;[71] and one-half of adult Hispanics have 8.8 years of formal schooling, compared with 12.5 years for whites and 12.0 years for blacks. The tremendous diversity among Hispanics helps to explain the relatively low median years of school completed. Among Chicanos, for example, immigrants have completed 5.8 years of education, first-generation Chicanos have 9.1 years, and the second generation have a median of 11.1 years.[72]

The relatively low level of educational attainment for Hispanics is the result of several factors. Poverty drives many young Hispanics (and blacks) out of school and into the labor force to help their families. A large proportion of the migrant labor force in the United States is Hispanic, and following the harvests makes schooling different and difficult. Another factor robbing Hispanics of education is the poor schooling in low-income districts, where they are found disproportionately (see Chapter 15). Contrary to the intent of court decisions, more Hispanics were attending segregated schools in 1980 than in 1970.[73] Children of undocumented workers are denied education in many places unless they pay tuition. Houston charged a tuition of $172 per month, a prohibitive sum for most because of their marginal economic situation. In 1980 this practice kept approximately 100,000 Texas children out of school.[74] In 1982 the Supreme Court in a 5–4 decision ruled that this practice was unconstitutional.

Historically the schools have not met the needs of Hispanic children. Often schools have not provided the extra resources required for bilingual programs. These programs are critical because they allow youngsters to learn the intricacies of various subjects in their native language while becoming proficient in the new language. If thrust immediately into situations

TABLE 11–3   Years of School Completed by Race by Persons 25-Years Old and over, 1981

Race	4 or More Years of High School	1 or More Years of College	4 or More Years of College
White	71.6%	33.1%	17.8%
Black	52.9	21.2	8.2
Hispanic	44.5	18.2	7.7

Source: U.S. Bureau of the Census, "Population Profile of the United States: 1981," *Current Population Reports*, Series P–20, No. 374 (September 1982), Table 6–3.

where English is the only language, many Hispanic children will be unable to keep up and, regardless of their inherent abilities or motivation, will be placed in "slow" tracks. Also, research has shown that Hispanic children born in the United States who speak both English and Spanish do better in school than those who speak only English.[75]

The schools have also discriminated against Hispanic children by testing them with Anglo-biased tests, which then are used to classify children according to ability. A Carnegie Foundation report has concluded that the schools often contribute to the obstacles facing Hispanic students: "Schools discriminate against Hispanics by shunting them into educational tracks designed for low achievers, by classifying them as mentally retarded, by denigrating their heritage and by giving them the message that they are not expected to succeed."[76]

Despite being behind whites in educational attainment, blacks and Hispanics have made significant gains in recent years. These gains are now jeopardized, however, by some recent trends. The general movement against increased taxes hurts public schools, especially the costly programs for the disadvantaged (bilingual, Head Start, and the like). Inner-city schools, where minorities are concentrated and which are already understaffed and underfinanced, face even greater financial pressures because of the current trend to reduce federal programs to aid the disadvantaged. The effects of this can be predicted from the famous Coleman report, which noted that the longer blacks remain in school, the worse they score on standardized tests compared to whites.[77] The fault, then, is with the schools, and as their resources shrink, they will become even less effective.

Another trend that may reduce the number of minorities attending college is the increased cost of higher education. Since they are more likely to be poor than whites, minorities are less able to afford college. This decline should accelerate as the costs of education rise.

These pessimistic trends are compounded by the reality that minority members, regardless of their level of education, are underpaid compared with whites of similar education. Many of the disadvantaged, knowing that race is the significant variable keeping minorities down, have little motivation to do well in school because they regard education as having no payoff. Table 11–4 shows that at each educational level there is a significant difference in income between blacks and whites, clearly demonstrating the racial discrimination present in American society. Although the government has not furnished similar data for Hispanics, we can safely assume that the same relationship is true for this group as well.

Unemploy-
ment

Late in 1982 the United States was in a severe economic slump. Although many Americans were negatively affected by those economic hard times, minorities were especially hard hit. The unemployment data for the last quarter of 1982 showed, for example, that while the overall unemployment rate was 10.7 percent, 15.2 percent of Hispanic workers and 20.4 percent of black workers were out of work.[78] Although the economic conditions of

TABLE 11–4 Median Family Income, by Education of Head of Household, by Years of School Completed, and by Race, 1981

Race of Head of Household	Elementary School		High School		College	
	Less Than 8 Years	8 Years	1–3 Years	4 Years	1–3 Years	4 or More Years
White	$12,541	$14,935	$18,025	$23,864	$27,607	$33,126
Black	9,541	10,118	10,836	16,039	18,865	27,353
Difference	$ 3,000	$ 4,817	$ 7,189	$ 7,825	$ 8,742	$ 5,773

Source: U.S. Bureau of the Census, "Money Income of Households, Families, and Persons in the United States: 1981," *Current Population Reports*, Series P–60, No. 137 (March 1983), table 32.

1982 were unusual, these proportions are typical. The jobless rate of blacks is usually double the national rate, and the jobless rate of Hispanics is commonly 40 to 50 percent higher than the overall unemployment rate.[79] Figure 11–1 shows that this gap between whites and minorities has been consistent regardless of the economic conditions in society. But the gap is even greater than the official statistics reveal. The unemployment rate is

FIGURE 11–1 Black and White Unemployment Rates: 1960–1982

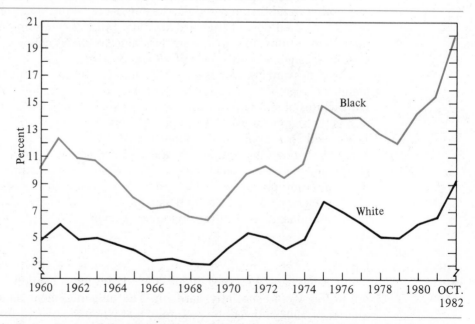

Source: Bureau of the Census, *Historical Statistics of the United States, Colonial Times to 1970*, Part 1, 1975. Series D 87–101: and Bureau of Labor Statistics.
Note: Black data for 1960–1971 are for "Blacks and other races."

based on the number of people who actually seek employment; people who have ceased looking for work are simply omitted. In 1982, approximately 1½ million Americans were not counted in the unemployment figures for just such a reason. Given the low pay for jobs that minorities receive if they can find work, more of them than whites would likely become discouraged enough to stop looking for a job.

The existence of pockets of disproportionately high minority unemployment suggests great potential for social unrest. Minorities from urban slums are those most affected by few job opportunities. The rate of unemployment for black teenagers, for example, exceeded 50 percent in 1982, compared with an unemployment rate around 20 percent for all teenagers. With such a large percentage of black youth unemployed (and we can assume a similarly high proportion for Hispanic teenagers), the potential for social unrest is especially high. Young people tend to be more militant than their elders. When these unemployed youth are concentrated in one area—as youths are in urban slums—the probability of unified militant action becomes even greater.

Type of Employ-ment

Not only are minorities twice as likely as whites to be unemployed; those who do work are overrepresented in jobs whose pay, power, and prestige are low. Table 11–5 shows that in 1980 far more blacks and Hispanics than whites were blue-collar and service workers, while whites held a majority of the white-collar jobs, which are physically safer, better paying, more stable, and offer more chance for advancement.

Although these data show that minorities are in the least rewarding jobs, there have been positive changes since 1960. Because of greater educational attainment and affirmative action programs (see Panel 11–3), nonwhites hold a greater number of management, white-collar, and upper-level blue-collar jobs than before. Despite these gains, however, a huge gap remains. Consider the job distribution in 1981 in the city government of Denver, which has a nonwhite population of 30 percent.[80]

TABLE 11–5   Occupation by Race, in Percentages, 1980

Occupational Category	White	Black	Hispanic
White-collar workers	53.9	36.6	35.0
Blue-collar workers	31.1	37.3	45.6
Service workers	12.1	24.4	16.2
Farm workers	2.9	1.7	3.3

Source: U.S. Bureau of the Census, "Population Profile of the United States: 1980." *Current Population Reports*, Series P–20, No. 363 (Washington, D.C.: Government Printing Office, 1981), p. 55.

Reverse Discrimination

One of the most explosive controversies facing society and especially young people today is the dilemma of whether minorities should receive preferential treatment in admission to schools, hiring, and promotion. The goal is honorable—giving racial minorities chances for success denied them for centuries—but the reality is that many majority-group members who are better qualified (as measured by scores on entrance examinations, grades, experience) will be denied in favor of minority-group members. To be denied admission to a medical school, for example, because of race (being white) is, according to opponents, a violation of the equal protection clause of the Fourteenth Amendment to the Constitution. At the same time, however, it would seem a reasonable societal goal that the professions reflect a sensible racial, ethnic, and sexual mix. Therein lies the dilemma. Let me review the arguments for both sides in this argument, so that you can consider the problems, as well as your own position and your own feelings on this issue.

Arguments for reverse discrimination

1. Since the Civil Rights movement of the 1960s, great advances have been made by blacks in jobs. However, although integration has occurred, it has been mostly in low-level jobs. If blacks are to be incorporated into the mainstream of American society, they must be given preferential treatment to break the bonds of past and present injustices. As President Johnson said in 1965:

   Freedom is not enough. You do not wipe out scars of centuries by saying "now you're free to go where you want and do as you desire." You do not take a person who for years has been hobbled by chains and liberate him, bringing him up to the starting line of a race and then say "you're free to compete"

and justly believe that you have been completely fair. All of our citizens must have the ability to walk through those gates; and this is the next and most profound stage of the battle for civil rights.

2. The so-called merit system for jobs or entrance to schools has been unfair to minorities because it has assumed the characteristics and traits of the dominant group. Moreover, the presence of prejudiced people has meant that minorities have not had to be merely as qualified as the majority, they had to be better (sports offers a visible example of this).

3. Similarly, to look only at formal test scores or other criteria ignores past cultural or social disadvantages that are the root cause of lower scores.

4. To employ or admit minorities in rough proportion to their presence in the population is not reverse discrimination but only equal representation.

5. Women and minorities need more, not fewer, anti-bias efforts, because there are still great differences between their incomes and those of the majority.

6. The law presently gives preferences to certain groups (veterans for civil service jobs, schools give preference to in-state residents, athletes, and children of alumni). If it is socially and legally acceptable to allow preferences for some social categories, then why not for another—the victims of discrimination.

Arguments against reverse discrimination

1. There is no constitutional right for any race to be preferred over another.

2. Of course, minorities have been discriminated against in the past and that was wrong, but "two wrongs don't make a right."

3. Equality is now being defined in terms of "results" rather than "opportunity."

4. Reverse discrimination is actually a quota system that disregards talent, ability, and skill.
5. It is unfair to ask the present generation of the majority group to pay for the sins of previous generations.
6. Racial preference is dynamite. Resentment of blacks receiving preferential treatment may nullify whatever positive gains have been achieved since the civil rights movement.

In sum, the present generation is asked to bear the burden to redress past wrongs. In the name of justice, the children of the previously favored groups are asked to accept a reduction below parity. Is this fair? Is it legal?

In 1978 the Supreme Court made its first major decision on this issue in *Regents of the University of California vs. Bakke*. Allan Bakke had applied to enter the medical school at the University of California at Davis. The school had a policy of reserving sixteen of the one hundred openings for disadvantaged minority students. Bakke was twice denied admission in 1973 and 1974, although his test scores surpassed those of some minority students who were admitted in those years. He charged the University with reverse discrimination, claiming that he was denied admission because of his race.

A lower court ruled in Bakke's favor, and this decision was affirmed by the Supreme Court. The Court's decision, however, was mixed. By a vote of 5 to 4 the Court ruled that Bakke must be admitted to the medical school because its quota system based entirely on race was illegal. However, also by a 5 to 4 vote, the Court declared that a university could continue to take race into account in admissions. In other words, it approved, on the one hand, affirmative action programs to help blacks and other minorities to overcome the effects of past discrimination. But, on the other hand, the Court rejected strict numerical quotas. This split decision may have partially clarified racial treatment in university admissions, but it left considerable doubt in other potentially explosive areas such as sex discrimination and employment practices.

In the city government:

☐ Twenty-two percent of city administrators were nonwhite.
☐ Seventeen percent of city professionals were nonwhite.
☐ One-half of the clerical employees were nonwhite.
☐ Over two-thirds of the service and maintenance workers were nonwhite.

In the city fire department:

☐ The fire chief, 27 of the 28 assistant chiefs, and all 64 captains were Anglo.
☐ Twenty-six percent of the firefighters were nonwhite.

In the city police department:

☐ The chief, 5 of the 6 division chiefs, 21 of 23 captains, and 44 of 46 lieutenants were Anglos.
☐ Twenty-four percent of the patrol officers were nonwhite.

These data show that even after a period of civil rights activism, minority recruitment, and affirmative action, racial minorities still hold disproportionately few responsible positions. The example of Denver reflects the situation in industry, banking, and other sectors of the economy.

The conclusion that racism continues to prevail is inescapable. Fom his analysis comparing the employment opportunities of whites and blacks (which can be generalized to Hispanics as well), Reynolds Farley has concluded:

> The occupational distribution of blacks has been upgraded more than that of whites throughout the period following the Depression. Particularly substantial gains were registered by blacks after 1960 and there is no evidence that the improvements among employed blacks have ceased during the present recession. Nevertheless these gains have not eliminated the very large gap between the occupations held by whites and those held by non-whites. *Despite three and one-half decades of improvements, the average prestige score for non-white workers in 1975 was inferior to that of white workers at the end of the Depression and the proportion of workers with white collar jobs was greater among whites in 1940 than among blacks in 1975.* (italics added)[81]

Health   The differences between whites and nonwhites are revealed most vividly in the facts concerning health and life itself. On virtually every measure of health, nonwhites are disadvantaged. They do not live as long (white males in 1982 could expect to live 6.6 years longer than black males), their children are less likely to survive infancy (the death rate for black babies is twice that of white babies during the first year), nonwhite mothers are much more likely to die during childbirth, and for almost every disease nonwhites have higher rates than whites. Table 11–6 provides some representative statistics showing the discrepancy between whites and nonwhites on health. Two of those statistics are especially revealing. First, whites go to the doctor more than nonwhites. This does not mean that whites are

TABLE 11–6   Selected Health Statistics by Race

Health Category	Whites	Nonwhites
Number of deaths per 1,000 population	6.0	8.3
Number of deaths for persons under age 25 per 10,000 population	6.4	12.5
Percentage of population age 5–9 immunized for polio (3 or more doses)	73.3	52.1
Percentage of infants weighing 2,500 grams or less at birth	5.8	11.1*
Visits to doctor per 1,000 population	3,489.1	2,768.4
Percentage of population with no health insurance	10.2	16.3

Source: U.S. Department of Health, Education and Welfare, *Health: United States, 1978* (Washington, D.C.: Government Printing Office, 1978), pp. 173, 199, 209, 257, 267, and 404.
*Blacks only.

sick more. Actually nonwhites are sick more because of inadequate diets, more dangerous jobs, and the greater likelihood of being exposed to pollutants. But nonwhites, because they are more likely to be poor, cannot afford to see physicians. Moreover, their access to doctors is less because fewer are available in the poor sections of cities and rural areas. The other statistic of special interest is that 16 percent of nonwhites are not covered by any health insurance. For these people adequate health care, even when sick or injured, is out of the question because it is so expensive.

SUMMARY

This chapter has chronicled the differences between blacks and whites in American society. In 1963 some 250,000 civil rights marchers gathered at the Lincoln Memorial in Washington to hear Martin Luther King, Jr. deliver his most eloquent and famous speech (see Panel 11–4). King told his friends that he "had a dream" that one day racism would end in America. Twenty-one years later data showed that while blacks had made some absolute progress, they had not made progress relative to the majority. There remains a gap between the races in educational attainment. Unemployment is twice as high for blacks, the same as it was in 1963. Jobs for blacks are less prestigious and less rewarding financially than they are for whites. Finally, blacks receive less medical attention and die younger than whites. Although there is less conscious bigotry now, institutional racism persists, and King's dream evades fulfillment.

The differences between blacks and whites have remained despite the breakdown of legalized discrimination (voting rights, public accommodations, housing, and schooling). But the laws have often been circumvented to continue de facto segregation and discrimination. Building codes have been used to restrict homeowners in a neighborhood to a certain income bracket. Schools have remained segregated in the South by the creation of private academies for whites and in the North by faculty assignment, school site selection, and "optional attendance zones." A final example of continued discrimination despite the law is the "last hired, first fired" layoff provision of many union contracts. Thus, there remains systematic institutional barriers to first-class citizenship for blacks. There have been changes: forty years ago the discrimination was blatant; now it is subtle. The effects, however, are essentially the same.

There is the danger today that the minimal gains blacks and other minorities have won in recent years may be eroded with the reduction of government programs and the cancellation of progressive legislation and court decisions. The election of President Reagan and a decidedly more conservative Congress in 1980 enhances the likelihood of *increased* inequality. Although many of their plans may curb inflation and reduce unemployment, the overall impact suggests the distinct possibility that the gap between the "haves" and the "have nots" will increase. This prediction is based on:

"I Have a Dream"
Martin Luther King, Jr.

I have a dream that my four little children will one day live in a nation where they will not be judged by the color of their skin but by the content of their character.

I have a dream today.

I have a dream that one day the state of Alabama, whose governor's lips are presently dripping with the words of interposition and nullification, will be transformed into a situation where little black boys and black girls will be able to join hands with little white boys and white girls and walk together as sisters and brothers.

I have a dream today.

I have a dream that one day every valley shall be exalted, every hill and mountain shall be made low, the rough places will be made plain, and the crooked places will be made straight, and the glory of the Lord shall be revealed, and all flesh shall see it together.

This is our hope. This is the faith with which I return to the South. With this faith we will be able to hew out of the mountain of despair a stone of hope. With this faith we will be able to transform the jangling discords of our nation into a beautiful symphony of brotherhood. With this faith we will be able to work together, to pray together, to struggle together, to go to jail together, to stand up for freedom together, knowing that we will be free one day.

This will be the day when all of God's children will be able to sing with new meaning, "My country 'tis of thee, sweet land of liberty, of thee I sing. Land where my fathers died, land of the pilgrim's pride, from every mountainside, let freedom ring."

And if America is to be a great nation this must become true. So let freedom ring from the prodigious hilltops of New Hampshire! Let freedom ring from the mighty mountains of New York! Let freedom ring from the heightening Alleghenies of Pennsylvania!

Let freedom ring from the snowcapped Rockies of Colorado!

Let freedom ring from the curvaceous peaks of California!

But not only that; let freedom ring from Stone Mountain of Georgia!

Let freedom ring from every hill and mole hill of Mississippi. From every mountainside, let freedom ring.

When we let freedom ring, when we let it ring from every village and every hamlet, from every state and every city, we will be able to speed up that day when all of God's children, black men and white men, Jews and Gentiles, Protestants and Catholics, will be able to join hands and sing in the words of that old Negro spiritual, "Free at last! Free at last! Thank God almighty, we are free at last!"

1. The professed desire of the newly powerful to reduce social expenditures (Social Security, Medicare, food stamps, school lunch subsidies, youth employment programs, subsidized housing, and other forms of welfare), while expanding the military budget significantly.
2. The new Republican majority in the Senate has meant a major change

in important committee chairs. The new chair of the Labor and Human Resources Committee, Orrin Hatch, has vowed to abolish affirmative action for women and minorities. The new chair of the Judiciary Committee, Strom Thurmond, has consistently opposed civil rights legislation since joining the Senate in 1954. Jesse Helms, the new chair of the Agriculture Committee, now has jurisdiction over food stamps and other nutritional programs for the needy, yet he has vowed to reduce such programs.

3. President Reagan's commitment to eliminating busing to achieve racial integration.

4. A number of measures to reduce civil rights, narrowly defeated in the past, which now seem more likely to pass: (a) the prohibition on using quotas or other numerical requirements in employment or admissions policies; (b) the prohibition on spending federal funds for bilingual education; (c) the repeal of Title IX, which insists on sexual equity in education programs receiving federal monies; and (d) the prohibition on spending federal funds for racial-integration busing.

5. The mood in government and among the majority of Americans to reduce or eliminate many social programs.

The implementation of these and other similar plans will directly impact minorities. Some will eliminate monetary, occupational, and educational gains of the recent decades. There may be increased hostility between the "haves" and the "have nots." The economic and social gulf between the two will widen. Violence, especially in urban ghettos, may escalate. In the short term, the "more guns and less butter" approach will bring increased misery to those already suffering. Vernon Jordan, executive director of the National Urban League, has called this governmental trend the "new minimalism." This philosophy, he has asserted, is a blueprint for continued inequality.

> Less government means less protection for people without resources; less spending means fewer desperately needed social programs and stark hunger for those in poverty; fewer government employees means fewer public services, and less interference means abandonment of civil-rights enforcement. The "new minimalism," then, is a blueprint for rolling back progressive social policies and laying waste the hopes of those who look for a more just, more equal America. . . . the new minimalism proposes to institutionalize intolerable living conditions for the black and the poor, and to perpetuate continued decay of America's cities and rural poverty pockets.[82]

Finally, this "new minimalism" further reduces the credibility of the order theorists' belief in the assimilation model. The claim that racial minorities will assimilate into the mainstream of society seems further and further removed from the realities of race relations as found in the United States.

CHAPTER REVIEW

1. The characteristics of a minority group are that: it is dominated by a more powerful group, the members have some characteristics that make them different from the dominant group, the characteristics of the group are stereotyped and systematically condemned, and the members are the objects of discrimination.

2. Eight categories of people are commonly designated as minority groups: racial groups, ethnic groups, religious groups, the poor, women, deviants, the aged, and the physically different.

3. An ethnic group is socially defined on the basis of a common culture that is distinct from the culture of the majority.

4. A racial group is socially defined on the basis of a presumed common genetic heritage.

5. Whenever a racial group has a distinct culture, shares a common heritage, and has developed a common identity, then that group is also an ethnic group.

6. Ethnic groups that have difficulty escaping the devalued status generally are easily identified by physical characteristics and became part of the United States involuntarily. Blacks, Chicanos, and Native Americans are three such groups.

7. Blacks came to the United States involuntarily as slaves. Following the Civil War, they were freed from slavery but remained oppressed by the economic, legal, and social practices of the majority.

8. Chicanos became part of the United States involuntarily as a result of military conquest and a change in political boundaries. With few exceptions they were dispossessed of power and property.

They became the major source of cheap labor in the Southwest. They continue to be the objects of discrimination today.

9. The lands of the Native Americans were taken by the Europeans and their descendants by force and fraud. The Indians were made wards of the federal government and placed on reservations. Today, they are the poorest, lowest in educational attainment, least employed, unhealthiest, and worst-housed ethnic group in America.

10. Deficiency theories maintain that some groups are unequal because they lack some important feature common among the majority. These deficiencies may be biological (such as low intelligence), structural (such as weak family ties), or cultural (such as the "culture of poverty").

11. Bias theories place the blame for inequality on the prejudiced attitudes of the members of the dominant group. These theories, however, do not explain the discriminatory acts of the unprejudiced, which are aimed at preserving privilege.

12. Structural theories argue that inequality is the result of the politico-economic system that dominates and oppresses minorities. There are four main features of institutional discrimination: (a) the forces of history shape present conditions; (b) discrimination can occur without conscious bigotry; (c) this type of discrimination is less visible than individual acts of discrimination; and (d) discrimination is reinforced by the interrelationships among the institutions of society.

13. The segmented labor market is a

structural source of inequality. There are two kinds of jobs: those that are secure, pay well, have fringe benefits, and offer a chance for advancement; and those that are unstable, poorly paid, and dead end. Large numbers of minorities are found at the bottom of the labor market because of institutional discrimination, particularly in the educational and economic sectors.

14. The assimilation model—that minorities will eventually become part of the mainstream once they give up their distinctive ethnicity and learn the skills required by society—is not applicable to colonized people of color. The colonization of people means their subordination in all spheres—social, economic, and political. The superordinate group exploits the colonized for its own advantage. This exploitation traps the minority in a subordinate status.

15. Although blacks and Hispanics have made some impressive gains in income, educational attainment, and type of employment, their position relative to whites has not improved.

FOR FURTHER STUDY

"American Indians, Blacks, Chicanos, and Puerto Ricans," *Daedalus* 110 (Spring, 1981), entire issue.

Mario Barrera, *Race and Class in the Southwest* (Notre Dame, Ind.: University of Notre Dame Press, 1979).

Robert Blauner, *Racial Oppression in America* (New York: Harper & Row, 1972).

Dee Brown, *Bury My Heart at Wounded Knee* (New York: Bantam, 1970).

Cary Davis, Carl Haub, and JoAnne Willete, "U.S. Hispanics: Changing the Face of America," *Population Bulletin* 38 (June, 1983), entire issue.

Vine Deloria, Jr. and Clifford M. Lytle, *American Indians, American Justice* (Austin: University of Texas Press, 1983).

Terry Eastland and William J. Bennett, *Counting by Race: Equality from the Founding Fathers to Bakke and Weber* (New York: Basic Books, 1979).

Reid Luhman and Stuart Gilman, *Race and Ethnic Relations: The Social and Political Experience of Minority Groups* (Belmont, Calif.: Wadsworth, 1980).

Joan W. Moore et al., *Homeboys: Gangs, Drugs, and Prison in the Barrios of Los Angeles* (Philadelphia: Temple University Press, 1978).

Thomas F. Pettigrew, ed., *The Sociology of Race Relations: Reflection and Reform* (New York: Free Press, 1980).

John Reid, "Black America in the 1980s," *Population Bulletin* 37 (December 1982), entire issue.

Thomas Sowell, *Ethnic America: A History* (New York: Basic Books, 1981).

David T. Wellman, *Portraits of White Racism* (Cambridge: Cambridge University Press, 1977).

William Wilson, *The Declining Significance of Race: Blacks and Changing Institutions* (Chicago: University of Chicago Press, 1978).

Norman R. Yetman and C. Hoy Steele, eds., *Majority and Minority: The Dynamics of Racial and Ethnic Relations*. 3rd ed. (Boston: Allyn and Bacon, 1982).

Maxine Baca Zinn, ed., "Chicanos." *Social Science Journal* 19 (April 1982), entire issue.

NOTES AND REFERENCES

1. Norman R. Yetman and C. Hoy Steele, "Introduction," in *Majority and Minority: The Dynamics of Racial and Ethnic Relations,* ed. Norman R. Yetman and C. Hoy Steele (Boston: Allyn and Bacon, 1971), p. 4.

2. Robert Bierstedt, "The Sociology of Majorities," *American Sociological Review* 13 (December 1948): 709.

3. Michael Parenti, *Power and the Powerless* (New York: St. Martin's, 1978), p. 97.

4. D. Stanley Eitzen, "A Conflict Model for the Analysis of Majority-Minority Relations," *Kansas Journal of Sociology* 3 (Spring 1967): 76–89.

5. S. I. Hayakawa, *Language in Thought and Action* (New York: Harcourt, Brace, 1949), pp. 190–191.

6. See John Gleidman and William Roth, "The Unexpected Minority," *New Republic,* February 2, 1980, pp. 26–30; Bruce P. Hillam, "You Gave Us Your Dimes . . .," *Newsweek,* November 1, 1976, p. 13; Terri Schultz, "The Handicapped, a Minority Demanding Its Rights," *New York Times,* February 13, 1977, p. E9; and "Now, a Drive to End Discrimination against 'Ugly' People," *U.S. News & World Report,* August 23, 1976, p. 50.

7. For further conceptual clarification on race and ethnicity see George Ritzer, Kenneth C. W. Kammeyer, and Norman R. Yetman, *Sociology: Experiencing a Changing Society,* 2d ed, (Boston: Allyn and Bacon, 1982), ch. 12; and Reid Luhman and Stuart Gilman, *Race and Ethnic Relations* (Belmont, Calif.: Wadsworth, 1980), pp. 5–6.

8. Luhman and Gilman, *Race and Ethnic Relations,* p. 6.

9. The following discussion is based on *ibid.,* pp. 8–27.

10. Ritzer, Kammeyer, and Yetman, *Sociology: Experiencing a Changing Society,* pp. 350–364. See also David Musick and Jonathan H. Turner, "Political Oppression of Black Americans: A Historical Study of the Maintenance of Inequality" (paper presented at the annual meeting of the Society for the Study of Social Problems, Toronto, August 21–24, 1981).

11. Luhman and Gilman, *Race and Ethnic Relations,* pp. 21–23; and Pete Daniel, *The Shadows of Slavery: Peonage in the South, 1901–1969* (New York: Oxford University Press, 1972).

12. This section is based on David R. Simon and D. Stanley Eitzen, *Elite Deviance* (Boston: Allyn and Bacon, 1982), pp. 190–191.

13. V. O. Key, Jr., *Southern Politics* (New York: Random House Vintage, 1949), pp. 619–643.

14. The following is taken from *ibid.,* pp. 555–577.

15. *Ibid.*

16. The details of Chicano history in this section are taken from Leobardo F. Estrada *et al.,* "Chicanos in the United States: A History of Exploitation and Resistance," *Daedalus* 110 (Spring 1981): 103–131. See also Joan Moore, *Mexican Americans* (Englewood Cliffs, N.J.: Prentice-Hall, 1976).

17. Mario Barrera, *Race and Class in the Southwest* (Notre Dame, Ind.: University of Notre Dame Press, 1979), pp. 1, 4.

18. Eugene C. Barker, *Mexico and Texas, 1821–1835* (New York: Russell and Russell, 1965), p. 52.

19. See Rudolfo Acuña, *Occupied America* (San Francisco: Canfield, 1972).

20. *Ibid.,* pp. 44–46; and Barrera, *Race and Class in the Southwest,* pp. 7–33.

21. Carey McWilliams, *North from Mexico* (Philadelphia: Lippincott, 1949).

22. Barrera, *Race and Class in the Southwest,* p. 33. See also Joan W. Moore, "Colonialism: The Case of Mexican Americans," *Social Problems* 17 (Spring 1970): 463–472.

23. Barrera, *Race and Class in the Southwest,* p. 39.

24. *Ibid.,* p. 66.

25. Estrada *et al.,* "Chicanos in the U.S.," p. 117.

26. This section is taken primarily from Michael A. Dorris, "The Grass Still Grows, the Rivers Still Flow: Contemporary Native Americans," *Daedalus* 110 (Spring 1981): 43–69.

27. James Cook, "The American Indian through Five Centuries," *Forbes,* November 9, 1981, p. 118.

28. Dorris, "The Grass Still Grows," p. 49.

29. Quoted in Nathaniel Paine, "Early American Broadsides, 1680–1800," *Proceedings, American Antiquarian Society* (1897); cited

in Ian Robertson, *Sociology*, 2d ed. (New York: Worth, 1981), p. 303.

30. Luhman and Gilman, *Race and Ethnic Relations*, p. 37.

31. *Ibid.*, p. 38.

32. James Cook, "New Hope on the Reservation," *Forbes*, November 9, 1981, p. 108.

33. Dorris, "The Grass Still Grows," pp. 63, 69.

34. Amalia Cabib, "Indians of the Americas: Refugees in Their Own Land," *Intercom* 9 (June 1981): 3.

35. This and the next two generalizations are taken from Robertson, *Sociology*, p. 304.

36. See Thomas Sowell, *Ethnic America: A History* (New York: Basic Books, 1981).

37. This section depends largely on the excellent discussion of these theories in Barrera, *Race and Class in the Southwest*, pp. 174–219.

38. *The Negro Family: The Case for National Action* (Washington, D.C.: U.S. Department of Labor, Office of Policy Planning and Research, 1965).

39. This material is taken from D. Stanley Eitzen, *In Conflict and Order* (Boston: Allyn and Bacon, 1978), pp. 378–380.

40. Herbert Gutman, *The Black Family in Slavery and Freedom: 1750–1925* (New York: Pantheon, 1976).

41. *The Negro Family*, p. 47.

42. Edward Banfield, *The Unheavenly City Revisited* (Boston: Little, Brown, 1977).

43. See Herschel Manuel, "The Mexican Population of Texas," *Southwestern Social Science Quarterly* 15 (June 1934): 29–51; and Florence Kluckholn and Fred Strodtbeck, *Variations in Value Orientation* (Evanston, Ill.: Row, Peterson, 1961). For strong statements of the opposite position see Maxine Baca Zinn, "Sociological Theory in Emergent Chicano Perspectives," *Pacific Sociological Review* 24 (April 1981), pp. 255–272; and idem, "Urban Kinship and Midwest Chicano Families: Evidence in Support of Revision," *De Colores Journal* 6 (Summer 1982), pp. 85–98.

44. Interview with Thomas Sowell, "Culture—Not Discrimination—Decides Who Gets Ahead," *U.S. News & World Report*, October 12, 1981, p. 74. See also Sowell, *Ethnic America*.

45. Roger Wilkins, "Sowell Brother?" *The Nation*, October 10, 1981, p. 333. For two other critiques of the Sowell position, see Andrew M. Greeley, "Ethnics' Progress: Is Data Fact?" *Psychology Today* 15 (September 1981): 90–94; and Martha Farnsworth Riche, "Immigration Waves," *Civil Rights Digest Perspectives* 13 (Spring 1981): 46–48.

46. Gunnar Myrdal, *An American Dilemma* (1944; reprint. New York: Pantheon, 1962).

47. This section is taken from David T. Wellman, *Portraits of White Racism* (Cambridge: Cambridge University Press, 1977), Chapter 1.

48. *Ibid.*, p. 8.

49. *Ibid.*, p. 35.

50. Parenti, *Power and the Powerless*, p. 24.

51. Stokely Carmichael and Charles V. Hamilton, *Black Power: The Politics of Liberation in America* (New York: Random House/Vintage, 1967), pp. 4–5.

52. Louis L. Knowles and Kenneth Prewitt, eds., *Institutional Racism in America* (Englewood Cliffs, N.J.: Prentice-Hall/Spectrum, 1965), p. 5.

53. Nijole Benokraitis and Joe R. Feagin, "Institutional Racism: A Review and Critical Assessment of the Literature" (Paper presented at the meeting of the American Sociological Association, Montreal, August 1974).

54. *Ibid.*, p. 6.

55. U.S. Commission on Civil Rights, *Window Dressing on the Set* (Washington, D.C.: Government Printing Office, 1979); and Christine Noschese, "The Ethnic Image in the Media," *Civil Rights Digest* 11 (Fall 1978): 28–34.

56. U.S. Commission on Civil Rights, *Character in Textbooks: A Review of the Literature* (Washington, D.C.: Government Printing Office, 1980).

57. See John E. Williams and John R. Stabler, "If White Means Good, Then Black . . .," *Psychology Today* 7 (July 1973): 51–54, see also "Reversing the Bigotry of Language," *Psychology Today* 7 (March 1974): 57.

58. David Steinberg, "Racism in America: Definition and Analysis," in *People against Racism* (Detroit, n.d.), p. 3.

59. Jerome S. Skolnick, *The Politics of Protest* (New York: Ballantine, 1969), p. 180.

60. This section is taken from Joan W. Moore et al., *Homeboys: Gangs, Drugs, and Prison in the Barrios of Los Angeles* (Philadelphia: Temple University Press, 1978), pp. 27–34;

idem, "Minorities in the American Class System," *Daedalus* 110 (Spring 1981), especially pp. 283–288; and Rick McGahey, "In Search of the Undeserving Poor," *Working Papers* 8 (November/December 1981), pp. 62–64.

61. Moore, *Homeboys*, p. 28.

62. Moore, "Minorities in the American Class System," p. 283.

63. Robert Blauner, *Racial Oppression in America* (New York: Harper & Row, 1972).

64. Barrera, *Race and Class in the Southwest*, pp. 188–204.

65. Census Bureau, reported in George Louis Archuleta, "The Decade of Hispaños?" *Rocky Mountain News* (November 28, 1982), p. 92.

66. Bryce Nelson, "5% of Blacks, 4.4% of Latins Not Counted," *Los Angeles Times*, November 6, 1981, pt. 1, p. 16.

67. Census Bureau, "Population Profile, 1980," p. 51.

68. Michael P. Johnson and Ralph R. Sell, "The Cost of Being Black: A 1970 Update," *American Journal of Sociology* 82 (July 1976): 189–190.

69. Reynolds Farley, "The Economic Status of Blacks: Have the Gains of the 1960s Disappeared in the 1970s?" (Ann Arbor, Mich.: Population Studies Center, 1975), pp. 31–32.

70. John Reid, "Black America in the 1980s," *Population Bulletin* 37 (December 1982), p. 25.

71. Cary Davis, Carl Haub, and JoAnne Willette, "U.S. Hispanics: Changing the Face of America," *Population Bulletin* 38 (June 1983), p. 29.

72. Estrada *et al.*, "Chicanos in the U.S.," p. 129.

73. Pachon and Moore, "Mexican Americans," p. 121.

74. Estrada *et al.*, "Chicanos in the U.S.," p. 129.

75. National Center for Education Statistics report, cited in "Bilingual Hispanics Do Better in School," *Phi Delta Kappan* 62 (December 1980): 235.

76. Carnegie Foundation report, cited in "Hispanics Make Their Move," *U.S. News & World Report*, August 24, 1981, p. 64. See, John U. Ogbu, "Minority Education and Caste," in Yetman and Steele (eds.), *Majority and Minority*, 3rd ed., pp. 426–439.

77. Department of Health, Education and Welfare, *Equality of Educational Opportunity* (Washington, D.C.: Government Printing Office, 1966), p. 20.

78. Davis *et al.*, "U.S. Hispanics," p. 35.

79. *Ibid.*

80. Dave Krieger, "Minorities Low on Supervisory Ladder," *Rocky Mountain News* (December 14, 1981), p. 79.

81. Farley, "The Economic Status of Blacks," pp. 17–18.

82. Vernon E. Jordan, Jr., "The New Minimalism," *Newsweek* (February 23, 1976), p. 9.

12

Sex Roles and Sex Stratification

Maxine Baca Zinn

In the past decade, the American public has been made dramatically aware of women's rights to equality. Despite the broadening of awareness, equality for women has not been achieved.

□ The Equal Rights Amendment has been defeated after a ten-year effort to make discrimination by sex unconstitutional.

□ Although the situation is improving slowly, most women are trapped in a "pink-collar ghetto" with about 80 percent of them working in 20 out of 420 occupations.

□ For every dollar earned by a working man, a working woman earns 62 cents. This earning gap has not narrowed much in recent decades.

□ Over half of all poor families are headed by women, and this proportion grows each year.

Senior author of this chapter is Maxine Baca Zinn, Department of Sociology, the University of Michigan-Flint.

The United States, like all other societies, has clear expectations for its members on the basis of sex. Women and men are assigned different expectations for personality traits, expressions of emotion, behaviors, and occupations. These classifications are so pervasive that they seem natural. It is increasingly clear that differentiation by sex is not "natural" at all, but actually a product of social organization. This differentiation ranks the sexes in such a way that women are unequal in power, resources, prestige, or presumed worth. At the same time, both women and men are denied the full range of human and social possibilities. The social inequalities created by sex differentiation have far-reaching consequences for the society at large.

This chapter examines sex stratification in American society at both structural and individual levels of social organization. The overriding theme is that sex inequality cuts across all aspects of life in American society.

THE ROLES AND RANKING OF WOMEN AND MEN

The concept **role** is borrowed directly from the theater and is a metaphor intended to convey the idea that conduct adheres to positions (statuses) in a social system. The social system that assigns roles to women and men is the gender system. It consists of two complimentary, yet mutually exclusive categories into which all human beings are placed on the basis of sex— sex is the biological fact of femaleness or maleness, while **gender** is the cultural and social definition of feminine and masculine. The gender system specifies behaviors, activities, and values of the sexes. Because behavioral expectations are associated with biological distinctions, they are referred to as sex roles. The gender system also operates as a system of stratification by ranking and rewarding sex roles unequally. Sex stratification is the differential ranking and rewarding of women's and men's roles. **Sexism** refers to the individual and institutional arrangements that discriminate against women.

Are Sex Roles Based on Physiological Differences?

A controversy among scientists concerns the basis for sex roles. One school argues that there is a biogenetic foundation for the observed differences in male and female behavior, while their counterparts are convinced that the differences are explained largely by differential learning.[1] We know that there are biological differences between the two sexes. The key question is whether these unlearned differences in the sexes contribute to the sex role differences found in societies. To answer this question, let's first review the evidence for both positions.

The Biological Bases for Sex Roles. Males and females are different from the moment of conception. Chromosomal and hormonal differences make males and females physically different. These differences, for example, give the female health superiority. At every age, from conception until old age, more males than females get sick and die. Approximately 120 males are conceived for every 100 females, yet there are only 105 live male births for each 100 female births, meaning that fetuses spontaneously aborted (miscarried) or stillborn are typically males. Various studies have shown that males are more susceptible than females to respiratory, bacterial, and viral infections, hepatitis, and childhood leukemia. The explanation for females being the healthier sex is that they have twice as many of a group of genes that program the production of immunological agents.[2] This means that females, compared to males, produce larger amounts of antibodies to combat a number of infectious agents.

Hormonal differences in the sexes are significant. The male hormones (androgens) and female hormones (estrogens) direct the process of sex differentiation from about six weeks after conception throughout life. They make males taller, heavier, and more muscular. At puberty they trigger the production of secondary sexual characteristics. In males, these include body and facial hair, a deeper voice, broader shoulders, and a muscular body. In females, puberty brings pubic hair, menstruation, the ability to lactate, prominent breasts, and relatively broad hips. Actually, males and females have both sets of hormones. It is the relative proportion of androgens and estrogens that gives one masculine or feminine physical traits.

These hormonal differences may explain in part why males tend to be more active, aggressive, and dominant than females.[3] Studies in animals provide some evidence for this assertion. Castrated rats and monkeys, deprived of the sex hormones created by the testes, have decreased levels of aggression. When testosterone is injected into these castrated males, their aggression levels increase.[4]

Critics of the biological determinist approach have argued that research on animals is irrelevant for humans because of the importance of socialization and culture.

Biological differences that do exist between women and men are only averages, and they are often influenced by other factors. For example, although men are on the average larger than women, body size is influenced by diet and physical activity, which in turn may be influenced by culture, class, and race. Greater variation exists within one sex than between the sexes.[5] The sociocultural variation of sex roles suggests that pressures of society are more important than innate physiological conditions.

The Social Bases for Sex Roles.   Sex roles are not uniform throughout the world. Every society has certain expectations for both women and men, as well as elaborate ways of producing people who are much like these expectations. The cross-cultural evidence shows a wide variation of behaviors for the sexes. Table 12–1 provides some interesting cross-cultural data from 224 societies on the division of labor by sex. This table shows that for the majority of activities, societies are not uniform in their sexual division of labor. Even activities requiring strength, presumably a male trait, are not strictly apportioned to males. In fact, activities such as burden bearing and

TABLE 12–1   Sex Allocation in Selected Technological Activities in 224 Societies

| | Number of Societies in Which the Activity Is Performed by: | | | | |
Activity	Males Exclusively	Males Usually	Both Sexes Equally	Females Usually	Females Exclusively	% Male
Smelting of ores	37	0	0	0	0	100.0
Hunting	139	5	0	0	0	99.3
Boat building	84	3	3	0	1	96.6
Mining and quarrying	31	1	2	0	1	93.7
Land clearing	95	34	6	3	1	90.5
Fishing	83	45	8	5	2	86.7
Herding	54	24	14	3	3	82.4
House building	105	30	14	9	20	77.4
Generation of fire	40	6	16	4	20	62.3
Preparation of skins	39	4	2	5	31	54.6
Crop planting	27	35	33	26	20	54.4
Manufacture of leather products	35	3	2	5	29	53.2
Crop tending	22	23	24	30	32	44.6
Milking	15	2	8	2	21	43.8
Carrying	18	12	46	34	36	39.3
Loom weaving	24	0	6	8	50	32.5
Fuel gathering	25	12	12	23	94	27.2
Manufacture of clothing	16	4	11	13	78	22.4
Pottery making	14	5	6	6	74	21.1
Dairy production	4	0	0	0	24	14.3
Cooking	0	2	2	63	117	8.3
Preparation of vegetables	3	1	4	21	145	5.7

Source: Adapted from George P. Murdock and Caterina Provost, "Factors in the Division of Labor by Sex: A Cross-Cultural Analysis," *Ethnology* 12 (April, 1973), p. 207.

water carrying are done by females more than by males. Even an activity like house building is not exclusively male.

While there is a wide variety in the social roles assigned to women and men, their roles "do not vary randomly."[6] In most societies of the world, the domestic and familial is the world of women and that of the public and political is the world of men. These differences are due at least indirectly to biology. Males are physically larger and stronger. Females give birth to children and are equipped to feed the newborn children. Since women in preindustrial societies tend to have a large number of children, they are bound by biology to domestic duties. Males, however, can leave their offspring for extended periods, and therefore are logically more likely to become engaged in activities such as hunting and fighting.

The
Differential
Ranking of
Women
and Men

In all societies, the activities of males are defined as more important than those of females. Pioneer anthropologist Margaret Mead noted that, no matter how trivial an activity may be, if it was performed by males it was more prestigious than if performed by females.[7] Male dominance refers to the beliefs, values, and cultural meanings that give higher value and prestige to masculinity than to femininity, that value males over females, men over women;[8] and to the male control of and privileged access to socially valued resources. **Patriarchy** is the term used for forms of social organization in which men are dominant over women. All societies exhibit some form of patriarchy in marriage and family forms, in division of labor, and in society at large. Men, it appears, "have gained in every society, the power of the legendary King Midas; they are able to transmute whatever they touch into the social gold of authority, while whatever women do is base metal by comparison."[9]

While sex stratification exists in all societies, it does not take the same form. What is universal is the imbalance in the evaluation of female and male activities.[10] The causes of this imbalance are not fully understood, but the most compelling explanations are economic, based on women's unequal access to such highly valued resources and rewards as property and economic rewards, power, and prestige.[11]

SEX STRATIFICATION FROM THE ORDER AND CONFLICT PERSPECTIVES

The Order
Perspective

From the order perspective biology, history, and the needs of society combine to separate men and women into distinctive roles. Biologically, men are stronger and women bear and nurse children. These facts have meant that men have tended to be the providers while women have "naturally" dealt with childrearing and family nurturance.

The necessity for women to nurse their infants and stay near home meant that for most of human history they have done the domestic chores while men were free to hunt and leave the village for extended periods. Thus, a whole set of customs and traditions supporting men as the providers and women as the nurturers set the expectations for future generations of men and women.

Although modern technology has freed women from the necessity of staying at home and has allowed them to work at jobs formerly requiring great strength, the order theorists believe that the traditional division of labor is beneficial for society as a whole. The clear-cut expectations for each sex fulfill many needs for individuals and provide order (see Panel 12–1). The traditional roles for men and women—for example, women as housekeepers and rearers of children and men as breadwinners—promote stable families and an efficient system of specialized roles with boys and girls trained throughout their youth to take their "natural" places in society.

Second-Class Citizens?

Little girls, it is said, are made of sugar and spice and everything nice. These days, however, "everything nice" includes the ability to operate and, in general, feel comfortable with the computer. We believe that little girls possess this ability, but the so-called computing culture places obstacles before them. These obstacles, while not insurmountable, present genuine problems. Unless they are removed, the girls of today may find themselves second-class citizens in the computer intensive world of tomorrow.

Consider the video arcade. Peer inside and, save for the electronic bells and whistles, you will see the poolroom of yesterday. Like the poolroom, it is largely a male preserve, a place where boys and young men gather. For many, it provides the first taste of the computer and, as such, serves as a doorway into a culture that is rapidly transforming the fabric of work. Closing that doorway to girls may inadvertently stack the deck against women in the electronic work place.

Within a few years, according to some industry estimates, computers will be the primary tools in 25 percent of all jobs. Increasingly, computer literacy is becoming an essential skill in the marketplace.

Children who are exposed to computers early on are most likely to develop "computer efficacy," learn procedural thinking and programming, and develop the sense of mastery that will encourage them to tackle more complex computer tasks.

The culture of computing is overwhelmingly male. With few exceptions, men design the video games, write the software, sell the machines, and teach the courses. Until recently, boys outnumbered girls in programming courses and in computer camps by as much as eight to one. (In recent years, however, according to officials at several computer camps, the enrollment ratio has dropped to about three to one.) If this bias leads to an equivalent gap in competence and confidence, the girls of today will undoubtedly become second-class citizens.

At first, computing is a strange and potentially humiliating activity, and girls need to be encouraged to take the initial plunge. The stylized nature of computing, and its arbitrary conventions, can be threatening. But those boys and girls who do acquire some proficiency usually advance rapidly. They learn discriminating attitudes toward games, machines, software, and programming styles.

Source: Sarah Kiesler, Lee Sproul, and Jacqueline S. Eccles, "Second Class Citizens," *Psychology Today* (March 1983), pp. 41–48. Used by permission of *Psychology Today*.

Talcott Parsons, a major order theorist, has argued that with industrialization, the family and the role of women as nurturers and caretakers have become more important than ever before. The husband in the competitive world outside the home needs a place of affection. As women take on the "expressive" roles of providing affection and emotional support within the family, men perform "instrumental" roles outside the family that provide economic support. Not only is this division of labor practical, it is necessary because it assures that the important societal tasks are accomplished.[12]

The
Conflict
Perspective

A very different view of sex roles has emerged from the conflict perspective. Conflict theorists are critical of the order model because it neglects what is most important about sex roles, namely that they are unequal in power, resources, and prestige. According to this conflict view, sex roles are not neutral ways of meeting societies' needs but are part of the larger system of sex stratification.

Many different conflict interpretations of sex stratification may be found. All emphasize male control and domination of both women and valued resources. For example, Randall Collins has traced sex stratification in simple societies as well as those that are more complex. In simple societies, men dominate by virtue of sheer strength. As societies become more developed, male domination takes the form of control of valued economic resources. Women use their femininity to acquire resources through marriage, but they become subordinated in the process.[13]

Most conflict theories explain sex stratification as the outcome of male control over property, the means of production, and the distribution of goods. This idea originated in the work of Friedrich Engels and Karl Marx who viewed marriage as a means of enforcing male power and control. As societies moved beyond subsistence stages and private property developed, men instituted the monogamous family in order to pass on wealth to their biological children:

> Because of the . . . importance attached to property and inheritance, the paternity of children becomes a paramount concern of the males. The patriarchal family form arises in response to the new conditions. The wife becomes the property of the husband who can use whatever means necessary to guarantee her sexual fidelity and, thereby, the paternity of his children.[14]

Contemporary conflict theorists stress control of the distribution of goods as the crucial fact in producing sex stratification. They point out that sex stratification is greater where women's work is directed inward to the family and men's work is directed outward to trade and the marketplace.[15] The division between domestic and public spheres of activity is particularly constraining to women and advantageous to men. The domestic and public spheres of activity are associated with different amounts of property, power, and prestige. Women's reproductive roles and their responsibilities for domestic labor limit their association with the resources that are highly valued.[16] Men are freed from these responsibilities. Their economic obligations in the public sphere assure them control of highly valued resources and give rise to male privilege.

In capitalist societies the domestic-public split is even more significant, because highly valued goods and services are exchanged in the public, not the domestic, sphere. Women's domestic labor, though important for survival, ranks low in prestige and power because it does not produce exchangeable commodities.[17] Because of the relationship between the class relations of production (capitalism) and the sexual hierarchical relations of its society (patriarchy),[18] the United States can be defined as a capitalist patriarchy.

Capitalism and patriarchy "are interrelated in complex ways and they must be analyzed together to understand the position of women."[19] Women and men are found doing different work both in the family and in the labor force. This division of labor between the sexes preserves power and prestige for men.

Sex stratification, like stratification systems based on class and race, generates privileges for some in society while denying equal access to others.

The Implications of Conflict and Order Perspectives

A point should be made about the implications of the conflict and order perspectives on sex stratification. Each position, with its emphasis on different factors, tends to call forth a different approach to the study of sex inequality. One consequence of the focus on sex roles by the order model has been to treat sex inequality as a problem of roles. Outmoded masculine and feminine roles are thought to be responsible for keeping women from achieving their full potential. This approach fails to recognize that sex stratification is a system of power and ranking that is found throughout the social structure.[20]

We must distinguish between (1) a sex roles approach, which focuses on learning behaviors that are defined as masculine or feminine, and (2) a structural approach, which focuses on features of social organization that produce sex inequality. The difference between the two lies in whether the individual or the society is the primary unit of analysis. The *sex roles approach* emphasizes characteristics that individuals acquire during the course of socialization, such as independent or dependent behaviors and ways of relating. The *structural approach* emphasizes factors that are external to individuals, such as the organization of social institutions, including the concentration of power, the legal system, and organizational barriers.[21] These approaches tend to differ in how they view the sexes, in how they explain the causes and effects of sexism, and in the solutions they suggest for elimination of inequality. Both individual and structural approaches are necessary to a complete understanding of sexism. This chapter places primary emphasis on social structure as the cause of inequality. Although sex roles are learned by individuals and produce differences in the personalities, behaviors, and motivations of women and men, essentially sex stratification is maintained by societal forms.

THE LEARNING OF TRADITIONAL SEX ROLES

The most complex, demanding, and all-involving role that a member of society must learn to play is that of male or female.

"Casting" takes place immediately at birth, after a quick biological inspection; and the role of "female" or "male" is assigned. It is an assignment that will last one's entire lifetime and affect virtually everything one ever does. A large part of the next 20 years or so will be spent gradually learning and perfecting one's assigned sex role; slowly memorizing what a "young lady" should do and should not do, how a "little man" should react in each of a million frightening situations—practicing, practicing, playing house, playing cowboys, practicing— and often crying in confusion and frustration at the baffling and seemingly endless task.[22]

From infancy through early childhood and beyond, children learn what is expected of boys and girls, and they learn to behave according to those expectations.

The characteristics associated with traditional sex roles are those valued by the dominant society. Keep in mind that the research on sex role socialization reflects primarily the experience of white middle-class persons— those who are most often the research subjects of these studies.[23] Sex roles and learning vary by race, ethnicity, and class. Still, society molds boys and girls along different lines.

The Child
at Home

Girls and boys are perceived and treated differently from the moment of birth. Parents describe newborn daughters as tiny, soft, and delicate, and sons as strong and alert,[24] and interact differently with newborn daughters and sons.

The way parents treat their children may be the most important factor of all in the creation of sex stereotypes. When one compares the life of the young girl to that of the young boy, a critical difference emerges: She is treated more protectively and she is subjected to more restrictions and controls; he receives greater achievement demands and higher expectations.[25] Girl infants are talked to more. Girls are the objects of more physical contact such as holding, rocking, caressing, and kissing.[26] We also know that fathers, especially working-class fathers, are more concerned than mothers about their young children engaging in behaviors considered inappropriate for their sex.[27] Mothers have a more covert role in the sex role socialization process, with the same result. They provide role models for their daughters. The mother's work status (at home, blue collar, professional) has a pronounced effect on the aspirations of daughters.[28]

In addition to the parents' active role in reinforcing conformity to society's sex role demands, a subtler message is emitted from picture books for preschool children that parents purchase for their children. One study of eighteen award-winning children's books from 1967 to 1971 found the following to be true:

1. Females were virtually invisible. The ratio of male pictures to female pictures was 11:1. The ratio of male to female animals was 95:1.
2. The activities of boys and girls varied greatly. Boys were active in outdoor activities, while girls were passive and most often found indoors. The activity of the girls typically was that of some service for boys.
3. Adult men and women (role models) were very different. Men led, women followed. Females were passive and males active. Not one

woman in these books had a job or profession; they were always mothers and wives.[29]

Two books by the same author best illustrate how children's books are biased toward traditional occupational roles apportioned by sex. The first, *What Boys Can Be*, lists fourteen occupations: fireman, baseball player, bus driver, policeman, cowboy, doctor, sailor, pilot, clown, zoo manager, farmer, actor, astronaut, and president.[30] The book, *What Girls Can Be*, also lists fourteen occupations: nurse, stewardess, ballerina, candyshop owner, model, actress, secretary, artist, nursery school teacher, singer, dress designer, bride, housewife, and mother.[31] In analyzing these two books, Weitzman et al., make several interesting observations. First, the ultimate goal presented for boys is to become president and for girls to be mothers. Second, while three of the male occupations are performed inside, eleven of the female jobs are. Third, the jobs for women are either glamorous or service-oriented. Males, in contrast, have a much greater range of choice. Finally, the male jobs tend to be more prestigious, better paid, and require more education than those for females.[32]

Before formal schooling, parents often send their child to day-care centers and nursery schools. The teachers there serve as surrogate parents, also reinforcing traditional sex roles. A study of fifteen preschools found that teachers act and react in quite different ways to boys and girls. The teachers, for example, responded over three times as often to males as to females who hit or broke things. Boys were typically punished by a loud public reprimand while girls were taken aside for a soft rebuke. In task-learning situations, boys were twice as likely as girls to receive individual instructions on how to do things. Summarizing their study, the researchers noted:

> As nursery-school children busily mold clay, their teachers are molding behavior. Unwittingly, teachers foster an environment where children learn that boys are aggressive and able to solve problems, while girls are submissive and passive. The clay impressions are transient, but the behavioral ones last into adulthood and present us with people of both sexes who have developed only parts of their psychological and intellectual capabilities.[33]

The last decade has undoubtedly seen changes in parents' sex-stereotyped attitudes. Unfortunately, attitude changes do not always translate into changes in behavior. Psychologist Beverly Fagot recently completed a study in which she compared parents' attitudes and their behavior towards their two-year-old children. While parents' attitudes were not sex-stereotyped, their behavior often contradicted the attitudes they had expressed. They still treated their daughters and sons differently in important areas of development.[34]

The Child at Play

According to the great social psychologist George Herbert Mead, through play and game activities children develop a sense of who they are and what the expectations of others and society are. If Mead's contention is correct, these activities should also contribute to the preservation of sex-role distinctions by stressing particular social skills and capacities for boys and others for girls. Janet Lever studied this possibility among fifth graders, most of whom were white and middle class. Her research found that boys, more than girls: (1) played outdoors; (2) played in larger groups; (3) played in age-heterogeneous groups; (4) were less likely to play in games dominated by the opposite gender; (5) played more competitive games; and (6) played in games that lasted longer.[35]

These differences in play by sex reinforce the traditional sex roles: Boys play at competitive games that require aggressiveness and toughness, while girls tend to play indoors with dolls and play-acting scenarios of the home. Lever's conclusions suggest that the skills and patterns of relating developed by girls are different from those developed by boys. These gender differences may be most characteristic of white middle-class children. An important study on black adolescent girls by Joyce Ladner has shown that black girls develop in a more independent fashion.[36]

Formal Education.   By the time youngsters graduate from high school, they have each spent approximately thirteen thousand hours in the classroom. Obviously, school has a profound influence on a child's world. The question to be answered in this section is: To what degree do the schools contribute to channeling people into narrow roles according to sex? To answer this question, we shall examine several areas: course offerings, textbooks, teacher-student interactions, sports, female role models, counseling, and teacher education.

Curriculum.   Home economics, business education, shop classes, and vocational agriculture have traditionally been rigidly sex-segregated. Reflecting society's expectations, schools taught girls child rearing, cooking, sewing, and secretarial skills. Boys, on the other hand, were taught mechanics, woodworking, and other vocationally oriented skills. (See Panel 12–1.) These courses were usually segregated by custom and sometimes by official school policy.

Separate programs for boys and girls persist even though Title IX of the Education Amendments Act, passed in 1972, requires any school that receives federal money to offer equal opportunities for males and females. In one Huron Valley, Michigan, school, for example, descriptions of a particular course were nearly identical, but one class was called "Slimnastics" and the other "Body Conditioning." The physical education department of the school told counselors that one was for girls and one was for boys, and that is how they were scheduled.[37]

Textbooks.   The content of textbooks transmits messages to readers about society, about children, and about what adults are supposed to do. For this reason, individuals and groups concerned about the potential for sexist bias in schools have looked carefully at how males and females are portrayed in textbooks assigned to students. Their findings provide a consistent message: textbooks commonly used in American schools are overtly and covertly sexist. This has become a recent concern of publishers, and a number have created guidelines for creating positive sexual and racial images in educational materials.[38]

Sex stereotypes abound in textbooks. A study of 134 books from twelve different publishers found that the ratio of boy-centered stories to girl-centered stories was 5:2; of male biographies to female biographies, 6:1; and of clever girls to clever boys, 33:131.[39] Another study found that the stereotypes occur in spelling, mathematics, science, and social studies texts as well as in readers. Stereotyping was found to be most extreme in the science textbooks. The researchers hypothesized that "the presentation of science as a prototypical masculine endeavor may help to explore how young girls are 'cooled' out of science and channeled into more traditional feminine fields."[40]

An extensive survey of the words used in elementary texts revealed that *he* occurred three times as often as *she,* and that *boy* occurred twice as often as *girl.* In an interesting switch, however, *wife* was found three times more than the word *husband.* This is not necessarily inconsistent, because the emphasis on wife suggests that society heavily stresses that role, whereas the husband's is not necessarily such an important role.[41]

Textbooks, then, have given official sanction to the subordinate roles that society imposes on women in real life.

Teacher-student interactions.   The purpose of schools at every level is to educate everyone based on the assumption of equal opportunity for all. This idealistic goal is not met in a number of areas which include a bias against females. Here we will examine how this works in only one area— teacher expectations for pupils by sex.

Typically, teachers expect boys to be aggressive, active, and independent achievers while girls should be submissive, quiet, and conforming.[42] These expectations result in a self-fulfilling prophecy that is beneficial to boys, for the "masculine" traits encouraged are exactly the ones that promote achievement, motivation, and success. Conversely, the "feminine" traits encouraged by teachers suppress creativity and inhibit achievement.

The differing attitudes teachers hold for boys and girls have other subtle effects that result in advantages for boys. One representative study of twenty-one fourth and sixth grade classes found that male and female teachers interacted *more* with boys than with girls in four major categories of teaching behavior: approval, instruction, listening to the child, and disapproval.[43] The boys got more attention than girls which likely encourages them to participate in classroom discussions, to be inquisitive, to be tougher in their thinking processes, and to be more confident in their ability to solve problems.

The reinforcement of sex roles in school sports.   Sport in American schools has historically been almost exclusively a male preserve. This is clearly evident as one compares by sex the number of participants, facilities, support of school administrators, and financial support.

Such disparities are based on the assumption that competitive sport is basically a masculine activity and that the proper role of girls is that of spectator and cheerleader. What is the impact on a society that encourages its boys and young men to participate in sports while expecting its girls and young women to be spectators and cheerleaders? The answer is that sport thereby serves to reinforce societal expectations for males and females. Males are to be dominant, aggressive—the doers—while females are expected to be passive supporters of men, attaining status through the efforts of their menfolk.

> The overemphasis on protecting girls from strain or injury, and underemphasis on developing skills and experiencing teamwork, fits neatly into the pattern of the second sex. Girls are the spectators and the cheerleaders. They organize the pep clubs, sell pompons, make cute, abbreviated costumes, strut a bit between halves and idolize the current football hero. This is perfect preparation for the adult role of women—to stand decoratively on the sidelines of history and cheer on the men, who make the decisions.[44]

A very important consequence of minimizing sport participation for women is that approximately one-half of the population is denied access to all that sport has to offer (enjoyment, teamwork, goal achievement, ego enhancement, social status, competitiveness, and character building). School administrators, school boards, and citizens of local communities have long assumed that sports participation has general educational value. If so, then clearly girls should also be allowed to receive the benefits.

In June, 1975, the federal government set forth guidelines to equalize opportunities for females in education. Every school that receives federal aid is affected: 2700 colleges and universities and 16,000 public school districts. With respect to sport, these guidelines insist that schools: integrate their physical education classes; provide athletic supplies, equipment, facilities, and travel allowances for women equal to those of men; sponsor separate women's teams for contact sports if requested; and allow women and men to participate together on teams in noncontact sports.

The results of this legislation guaranteeing women equal opportunity in school sports are mixed. On the positive side, sports for girls have become more popular in the last decade. Many girls who previously might not have participated and might have considered sports unfeminine are now joining teams. Some women's sports have become popular with spectators as well. Women's basketball is well on its way to becoming a spectator draw to rival women's tennis. Women are beginning to have an opportunity to achieve recognition by participating in physical competitive activities.[45] On the other hand, coed sports have not been successful in attracting girls largely because they still do not offer males and females equal opportunities.[46]

Female role models in education. A subtle form of sex-role reinforcement in education is found in the types of jobs held by men and women. The pattern is the familiar one found in hospitals, business offices, and throughout the occupational world: women occupy the bottom rungs while men are in the prestigious and decisionmaking positions. In 1979, only a handful of women were school superintendents in the United States, and more than half the school boards had no women members. Although 88 percent of American elementary school teachers are female, 88 percent of elementary school principals are male. Only 6 percent of high school principals are female and the imbalance has been increasing over the past seventy years.[47] As the level of education increases, the proportion of women teachers declines. In 1983, eleven years after the Office for Civil Rights issued guidelines spelling out the obligations of colleges and universities in the development of affirmative action programs, the proportion of women on college faculties was only 33 percent.[48] In the academic world, a definite prestige and pay pyramid extends from lowly instructorships to full professorships. Women tend to be lower in academic rank than men, make less money (even when statistically controlling for academic level), are less likely to have tenure, and are virtually excluded from administrative positions.

A study by the American Association of University Women showed no gains in the proportion of women faculty during the 1970s and only slight gains in administrative posts held by women.[49]

Today at the University of Michigan, the first university to incorporate an affirmative action plan for hiring and promotion of women, the distribution of women among faculty ranks remains distinctly pyramidal; the lower the rank, the higher the proportion of women (see Table 12–2). In 1983, only 6 percent of all full professors were women—while 45 percent of all instructors were women.[50]

TABLE 12–2   Average Faculty Salaries for Men and Women, 1981–1982

Academic Rank	Average Salary		Women as a Percent of Total Faculty	Percentage Distribution by Rank		Percentage Increase in Salary	
	Men	Women		Men	Women	Men	Women
Category I							
Professor	$36,750	$32,900	6.5%	44.4%	12.8%	9.5%	8.3%
Associate	27,010	25,270	17.5	29.3	25.8	9.0	8.4
Assistant	22,270	20,480	31.4	21.6	41.0	9.7	11.4
Instructor	17,400	16,190	54.0	3.0	14.3	7.5	8.6
Lecturer	20,540	17,600	46.0	1.7	6.1	—	—
All ranks	29,920	22,510	19.4	100.0	100.0	9.4	9.3
Category IIA							
Professor	31,500	30,430	12.3	37.1	15.0	8.1	8.8
Associate	25,150	24,040	21.0	32.4	24.9	8.8	8.7
Assistant	20,810	19,740	36.6	24.3	40.4	8.4	7.0
Instructor	17,030	16,110	53.5	5.3	17.6	10.1	7.5
Lecturer	17,830	15,500	44.5	0.9	2.1	—	—
All ranks	25,950	21,680	25.8	100.0	100.0	8.5	7.9

TABLE 12–2

Academic Rank	Average Salary		Women as a Percent of Total Faculty	Percentage Distribution by Rank		Percentage Increase in Salary	
	Men	Women		Men	Women	Men	Women
Category IIB							
Professor	27,510	25,660	13.2	30.1	11.0	9.3	8.5
Associate	22,130	20,710	22.6	31.1	21.8	9.2	8.7
Assistant	18,540	17,560	38.0	30.1	44.3	8.7	8.2
Instructor	15,450	14,520	52.7	8.2	21.9	8.7	7.7
Lecturer	18,210	19,220	44.3	0.5	1.0	—	—
All ranks	22,100	18,490	29.4	100.0	100.0	9.1	8.3
Category III							
Professor	27,670	26,700	22.1	22.3	10.7	9.0	9.6
Associate	24,070	23,330	31.5	31.7	24.6	8.6	8.9
Assistant	20,360	19,500	40.5	30.5	35.1	8.8	8.2
Instructor	17,300	16,270	52.6	15.3	28.7	8.9	7.7
Lecturer	16,820	14,990	73.5	0.2	0.9	—	—
All ranks	22,690	20,240	37.2	100.0	100.0	8.8	8.5
Category IV							
No rank	23,390	21,040	36.6	—	—	8.6	8.5
All Categories Except IV							
Professor	33,920	30,290	9.7	38.8	13.0	9.1	3.5
Associate	25,570	23,960	20.6	30.7	24.7	8.9	8.6
Assistant	21,070	19,620	35.1	24.1	40.6	9.1	9.1
Instructor	16,890	15,870	53.3	5.2	18.5	8.8	6.8
Lecturer	19,730	17,110	46.4	1.2	3.2	—	—
All ranks	27,200	21,300	24.3	100.0	100.0	9.0	8.6

Category I: Doctoral-granting institutions that have conferred an average of at least 15 earned doctorates in the last three years in at least three nonrelated disciplines.
Category IIA: Institutions awarding degrees above the baccalaureate not included in Category I.
Category IIB: Institutions awarding only the baccalaureate or equivalent degree.
Category III: Two-year institutions with academic ranks.
Category IV: Institutions, mostly two-year, without academic ranks.
Source: *On Campus* 2 (September 1982), p. 21.

More women than men now attend college. But on most campuses, women are left with few role models. Male students, too, should have outstanding women among their mentors, according to Dr. Muriel Ross, University of Michigan Professor of Anatomy,

> . . . so that the next generation will understand that femaleness and excellence are not a rare simultaneous occurrence. Male faculty members need to see their female colleagues as achievers, in order to better prepare women to compete successfully in the world of business and industry.[51]

Counseling.   A fundamental task of school guidance personnel is to aid students in their choice of a career. This involves testing students for their occupational preference and aptitude, advising them on course selection and what kind of post-high-school training they should get. The guidance that students receive on career choice tends to be biased in at least two ways. Foremost are the attitudes of the counselors themselves. As products of society, they typically hold traditional assumptions about what is a "normal" career for a boy and what is "normal" for a girl. Several research studies provide some proof that counselors do retain traditional sex role stereotypes. One study found that there is a counselor bias against women entering a "masculine" profession.[52] Another found that male school counselors tended to think of women in feminine roles characterized by feminine personality traits; they also associated college-bound girls with traditionally feminine occupations at the semiskilled level, while female counselors associated college-bound girls with occupations requiring a college education.[53]

In the past, aptitude tests have themselves been sex biased, listing occupations as either female or male.[54] Despite changes in testing, counselors may inadvertently channel students into traditional sex-typed choices.

Social-
ization as
Blaming
the Victim

It is clear from the discussion so far that there are many ways in which gender differences are learned. As philosopher Simone de Beauvoir has argued, women are created, not born.[55] Thus, socialization appears useful for "explaining" women. However, the socialization perspective on sexism can be misused in such a way that it blames women themselves for sex inequality. A critique of the socialization perspective by Elaine Enarson and Linda Peterson contends that, when used uncritically, socialization diverts attention from the oppression imposed by the dynamics of contemporary social structure:

> Misuse of the concept of socialization plays directly into the Blaming the Victim ideology; by focusing on the victim, responsibility for "the woman problem" rests not in the social system with its sex-structured distribution of inequality, but in socialized sex differences and sex roles.[56]

Not only is the cause of the problem displaced; so are the solutions. Enarson and Peterson concluded:

> Rather than directing efforts toward radical social change, the solution seems to be to change women themselves, perhaps through exhortation ("If we want to be liberated, we'll have to act more aggressive...") or, for example, changing children's literature and mothers' child rearing practice.[57]

This raises the critical question: If the socialization perspective is limited and perhaps biased, what is a better way of analyzing sex inequality? In answering this question, let us look at the ways in which male dominance affects our society.

THE REINFORCEMENT OF MALE DOMINANCE

Male dominance is both a socializing and structural force. It exists at all levels of society, from the interpersonal interactions of women and men, to the sex patterning that is found in all cultural forms and social institutions. This section describes the interpersonal and institutional reinforcement of male dominance.

Language

Language perpetuates male dominance by ignoring, trivializing, and sexualizing women. Use of the pronoun *he* when the sex of the person is unspecified and of the generic terms *mankind* to refer to humanity in general are obvious examples of how the English language ignores women. Common sayings like "that's women's work" (as opposed to "that's men's work!"), jokes about women drivers, phrases like "women and children first", or "wine, women, and song"[58] are trivializing. Women, more than men, are commonly referred to in terms that have sexual connotations. Terms referring to men ("studs," "jocks") that do have sexual meanings imply power and success, while terms applied to women ("broads," "dogs," "chicks") imply promiscuity or being dominated. In fact, the term promiscuous is usually applied only to women, although its literal meaning applies to either sex.[59] Terms such as dogs and chicks tell us a great deal about how women are regarded by society. Their cumulative effect is illustrated in the following passage:

> In her youth she is a "chick" and then she gets married and feels "cooped up" and goes to "hen parties" and "cackles" with her women friends. Then she has her "brood" and begins to "henpeck" her husband. Finally, she turns into an "old biddy."[60]

Inter-personal Behavior

Day-to-day interaction between women and men perpetuates male dominance. Gender differences in conversational patterns reflect differences in power. Women's speech is more polite than men's. Women end statements with tag questions ("don't you agree?" "you know?").[61] Men are more direct, interrupt more, and talk more, notwithstanding the stereotype that women are more talkative. Men also have greater control over what is discussed.[62] Another indication of women's lack of power lies in the work they do to keep conversations going. Fishman studied male-female conversations and found that women work harder in conversations, even though they have less control over the subject matter.[63] Males typically initiate interaction with women; they pursue, while females wait to be asked out.

Male dominance is also sustained by various forms of nonverbal communication. Men take up more space than women, touch women without permission more than women touch men. Women, on the other hand, engage in more eye contact, smile more, and generally exhibit behavior associated with low status. Sex differences in nonverbal behavior may be traced to differences in power, and these differences strengthen the system of dominance and privilege that exists.[64]

Mass
Communi-
cations
Media

The mass media (television, newspapers, magazines, movies, and popular music) reflect the culture of society, and nowhere more than in the sex role assumptions. Since the 1950s there has been relatively little change in the presentation of women. In contemporary American magazines, for example,[65] the picture of women that emerges from various stories and articles has been the happy housewife meeting the demanding but fulfilling needs of her husband and children.[66] The wife tends to be younger than her spouse and dependent upon him in almost a childlike way.

Even today, the lives of women in women's magazine fiction have been defined in terms of men, husbands, or lovers, or in terms of male absence.[67]

In spite of some recent improvements, television overwhelmingly portrays stereotyped sex roles. Women are sexual objects of mates in marriages rather than responsible individuals in their own right, while men are worldly and independent.[68] This situation applies to blacks as well as whites even though blacks appear on the screen far less frequently. Numerous studies have found differences in the portrayal of women and men.[69] In prime time, six times as many men as women are seen. These men work at many more occupations and they support families:

> In the family show, the male is almost invariably portrayed as the provider. For example, in "The Brady Bunch," the father supported six children, a wife who stayed home, and a domestic employee. "All in the Family" showed Edith Bunker as a totally dependent housewife. The Waltons, who were barely scraping along, never thought of having mother take a job; the father supported them all. Although women are shown working, as on "Maude," they are not shown as contributing in a meaningful way to family support. "Mary Tyler Moore" was the notable exception, but Mary was portrayed as a single woman. Only about 25 percent of the married women in prime-time shows work, and both married and single women usually work in traditional female occupations. In soap operas, women workers are shown, but they are subservient to men.[70]

Television commercials also present the sexes in stereotyped ways. A review of the research on television advertising has shown, for example, that: (1) almost all commercials with voice-overs are spoken or sung by men; (2) men are found in a wider variety of roles than women; (3) the roles depicted for females are typically family roles; (4) women tend to be doing activities in the home that benefit men; (5) women tend to be inside the home and men outside; (6) women are younger than men; and (7) in commercials during children's programming, women and girls are seen less often than men and boys.[71]

The sexism prevalent in advertising can be very subtle, as Erving Goffman has noted:

(1) Overwhelmingly a woman is taller than a man only when the man is her social inferior; (2) a woman's hands are seen just barely touching, holding or caressing—never grasping, manipulating, or shaping; (3) when a photograph of men and women illustrates an instruction of some sort the man is always instructing the woman—even if the men and women are actually children (that is, a male child will be instructing a female child); (4) when an advertisement requires someone to sit or lie on a bed or a floor that someone is almost always a child or a woman, hardly ever a man; (5) when the head or eye of a man is averted it is only in relation to a social, political, or intellectual superior, but when the eye or head of a woman is averted it is always in relation to *whatever* man is pictured with her; (6) women are repeatedly shown mentally drifting from the scene while in close physical touch with a male, their faces lost and dreamy, "as though his aliveness to the surroundings and his readiness to cope were enough for both of them"; (7) concomitantly, women, much more than men, are pictured at the kind of psychological loss or remove from a social situation that leaves one unoriented for action (e.g., something terrible has happened and a woman is shown with her hands over her mouth and her eyes helpless with horror).[72]

The advertising industry has been modifying very slowly this image as it has realized the potential buying power of larger numbers of working women, who have become targets of advertising campaigns designed to sell everything from three-piece suits to scotch. The underlying message is that women were discriminated against in the past but that mistake has been remedied.[73]

One cigarette advertiser directed an entire campaign to such a segment of the market with a slogan—"You've come a long way, baby"—intended to reach the "new woman." It should be understood that such advertising actually exploits women by masking their position in society (women, as we shall see, have not come such a long way), by trivializing them ("baby"), and by fostering excessive consumption. The advertising aimed at the "new woman" places additional stresses on women and at the same time upholds male privilege.

When a television commercial shows a woman breezing in from her job to sort the laundry, or pop a roast in the oven, it reinforces the notion that it's all right for a woman to pursue a career, as long as she can still handle the housework.[74]

Advertising aimed at such women increasingly relays the message that they should be superwomen, managing multiple roles of wife, mother, career woman, and so on and be glamorous as well. Such multifarious expectations are not imposed upon men. A recent cologne advertisement illustrates well the new expectations placed on employed women. Appealing to the "24-hour woman," the advertisement suggested that she "bring home the bacon, fry it up in a pan, and never let him forget he's a man." Under the guise of liberation, advertisers contribute to women's oppression by reinforcing the notion that domestic labor, child rearing, and pleasing men are women's responsibilities.

Religion   The customs, beliefs, and laws that discriminate against women are clearly reinforced and perpetuated by religious doctrines. Limiting discussion to the Judeo-Christian heritage, let's examine some of the teachings from the Old and New Testaments regarding the place of women. The Old Testament clearly established male supremacy in a number of ways.[75] To begin, God is believed to be a male. Women were obviously meant to be second to males because Eve was created from Adam's rib. According to the scriptures, only a male could divorce a spouse. A woman who was not a virgin at marriage could be stoned to death. Girls could be purchased for marriage. Even employers were enjoined to pay women only three-fifths the wages of men: "If a male from 20 to 60 years of age, the equivalent is 50 shekels of silver by the sanctuary weight; if it is a female, the equivalent is 30 shekels."[76]

> The Old Testament devotes inordinate space to the listing of long lines of male descent to the point where it would seem that for centuries women "begat" nothing but male offspring. Although there are heroines in the Old Testament—Judith, Esther and the like—it's clear that they functioned like the heroines of Greek drama and later of French: as counterweights in the imaginations of certain sensitive men to the degraded position of women in actual life. The true spirit of the tradition was unabashedly revealed in the prayer men recited every day in the synagogue: "Blessed art Thou, O Lord . . . for not making me a woman."[77]

The New Testament generally continued the tradition of male dominance. Jesus was a male. He was the son of a male God, not of Mary, who remained a virgin. All the disciples were male. The great leader of the early church, the Apostle Paul, was especially adamant in arguing for the primacy of the male over the female. According to Paul, "the husband is supreme over his wife," "woman was created for man's sake," and "women should not teach, nor usurp authority over the man, but to be silent."

Contemporary religious thought reflects this heritage. Some conservative denominations severely limit or even forbid women from any decision-making. Others allow women to vote but limit their participation in leadership roles.

There are, however, some indications of change. Recently the National Council of Churches called for elimination of sexist language and the use of "inclusive language" in the Revised Standard Version of the Bible.[78] Terms such as *man, mankind, brothers, sons, churchmen,* and *laymen* would be replaced by neutral terms that include reference to female gender.

Women are pursuing equal rights in all denominations and faiths, and the sexual revolution is causing upheaval and resistance at every level of organized religion.

From 1972 to 1980 in seminaries of Protestant denominations, the enrollment of women grew from 3,358 to 10,830—a rate of increase seven times greater than that of men.[79] Women are making advances in religious status despite the reluctance of established churches.

The Law That the law has been discriminatory against women is beyond dispute. One need only to recall that women were specifically denied the right to vote prior to passage of the Nineteenth Amendment. Less well known, but very important, was the 1824 Mississippi Supreme Court decision upholding the right of husbands to beat their wives (the U.S. Supreme Court finally prohibited this practice in 1891). Another interesting case that shows the bias of the legal system is *Minor v. Happerset* (1874). Here the Supreme Court ruled that the "equal protection" clause of the Fourteenth Amendment did not apply to women. Another ruling by the Supreme Court, at the time of the early feminist Susan B. Anthony, ruled that women were entitled to counsel, but that it must be male counsel.

But legal discrimination against women is not limited to the distant past. Only in the past decade have major obstacles to equality been removed by new laws or court decisions (see Panel 12–2). For example, sexist discrimination in the granting of credit has been ruled illegal: discrimination against pregnant women in the work force is now prohibited by law;[80] the structural bias against women has been removed by affirmative action; sexist discrimination in housing is prohibited; and the differential requirements by gender as traditionally practiced in the airline industry have been eliminated.[81]

Legal discrimination remains, however, in a number of areas. There are still problems with Social Security and other pension programs. State laws vary considerably concerning property ownership by spouses, welfare benefits, and the legal status of homemakers. A major area of concern continues in the area of reproductive choice. In 1973 the Supreme Court ruled that a state could not prohibit any abortion during the first three months of pregnancy. During the second three months the state's only legal actions regarding abortion may be related to regulations providing for safety in the abortion procedure. This controversial ruling was a major breakthrough for women, giving them the ultimate right to control their bodies. Several later decisions by the Court have reaffirmed this principle (a major one occurred in 1979 when the Court struck down a state law requiring unwed women under the age of 18 to have the consent of their parents for an abortion). In 1980, however, the Court ruled that although a woman has the right to an abortion she does not have a constitutional right to have the federal government pay for it. This decision, which reaffirmed the Hyde Amendment, passed by Congress in 1976, was a setback for abortion advocates because it made the option less likely for those women least able to afford children. The states have tended to pass similar laws restricting the use of state monies for abortion. These actions place a difficult burden on the poor who cannot afford the typical cost of $150 to $300. In effect the denial of money to pay for the abortion is the equivalent of denying the poor a legal abortion.

Sampling

In 1980 the Roper Organization selected a sample of 3,000 women age eighteen and over to determine the attitudes of women on various issues. The results from that survey (and one taken in 1970) for one question are found in the following table.

Efforts to Strengthen Women's Status

Question: There has been much talk recently about changing women's status in society today. On the whole, do you favor or oppose most of the efforts to strengthen and change women's status in society today?

	1980			1970		
	Favor	Oppose	Not Sure	Favor	Oppose	Not Sure
	%	%	%	%	%	%
Total Women	64	24	11	40	42	18
Single	75	15	10	53	33	14
Married	64	25	11	38	45	17
Divorced/separated	75	18	8	61	27	12
Widowed	48	35	17	36	41	23
White	62	26	12	37	46	17
Black	77	14	9	60	20	20
18 to 29	74	16	10	46	39	15
30 to 39	70	19	11	40	44	16
40 to 49	60	31	9	39	43	18
50 and over	55	31	14	35	45	20
Non-high school graduate	54	30	16	36	38	26
High school graduate	63	26	11	38	45	17
College	73	18	8	44	40	16
Northeast	68	21	11	41	40	19
Midwest	61	26	12	38	46	16
South	60	27	13	39	41	20
West	70	21	9	42	43	15
Cities	72	19	9	47	36	17
Suburbs	68	20	12	41	44	15
Towns	60	28	12	37	46	17
Rural	58	29	12	34	45	21

Source: Roper Organization, Inc.: *The 1980 Virginia Slims American Women's Opinion Poll*, p. 17. [machine-readable data file]. New York: Roper Organization producer, 1980; Storrs, CT: Roper Public Opinion Research Center, University of Connecticut distributor.

(continued)

The data in this table lead to several generalizations: (1) American women in 1980 when compared to American women in 1970, regardless of their social characteristics, were more favorable to the strengthening of women's status in society; (2) single and divorced women are more liberal on this question than married and widowed women; (3) blacks are more liberal than whites; (4) the younger the woman, the more liberal; (5) the higher the education, the more favorable to changing women's status; (6) women in the Northeast and West are more sympathetic to change than women in the Midwest and South; and (7) the larger the community in which a woman lives, the more liberal she will be on this issue.

How confident can we be about these generalizations? Do they represent the attitudes of American women? After all, Roper asked 3,000 women out of a potential pool of almost 100 million. How similar are these 3,000 to the 100 million they are supposed to represent? Our confidence depends on the sampling procedures used. Since it is too costly and even impossible to contact all women in America age 18 and over, a subset of that population—a sample—is drawn to represent the category investigated. A sample will probably never perfectly represent the actual population, but the error can be estimated statistically. This amount of error can be very small, if the sample is carefully drawn.

There are two fundamental types of sampling designs. In a *random sample* each member of the population to be studied has an equal chance of being selected. For example, every woman's Social Security number could be stored in a computer and a sample of 3,000 selected at random by the computer.

A *stratified sample* (the method used by Roper) is based on choosing persons whose characteristics are representative of the total population. If the investigator knows, for instance, the percentage of American women by age category, size of community, race, amount of education, and marital status, then she or he would select individuals for inclusion in the sample so that the total sample would have the characteristics of the population under investigation *in the correct proportion*. For example, if 12 percent of the nation's women are black, then 12 percent of the sample must be black. The key, though, is that the individuals selected because of their social characteristics be selected randomly.

Properly done, sampling can provide very accurate information about those groups too large to investigate in their entirety. Thus, it is appropriate to generalize from the findings of a survey when we have confidence about the representativeness of the sample.

For further information on sampling see: Earl R. Babbie, *The Practice of Social Research*, Second Edition (Belmont, Ca.: Wadsworth, 1979), Chapter 7; and Robert Sommer and Barbara B. Sommer, *A Practical Guide to Behavioral Research* (New York: Oxford University Press, 1980), Chapter 16.

The June 1982 defeat of the Equal Rights Amendment represents a major setback to women's newly won rights. The amendment reads "Equality of rights under the law shall not be denied or abridged by the United States or by any state on account of sex." What the amendment would have done is to render unconstitutional all state and federal laws and practices that treat men and women unequally. It would have prohibited all levels of government from discriminating against women in public employment and in job training programs. Ratification would have declared equality of the sexes a national policy and would have provided a sound constitutional basis for challenging sex discrimination.[82]

TABLE 12–3 Estimated Number of Women Holding Elective Office, 1976–1983

Level of Government	1976	1978	1980	1983
Congress	19	20	17	24
State wide offices	28	29	32	37
Legislatures	611	702	766	991
County offices	456	660	950	1,128
Mayors and other local posts	6,830	10,732	14,764	14,462
Total	7,944	12,143	16,529	16,642

Source: *U.S. News & World Report*, October 6, 1980, p. 68; *U.S. News & World Report*, August 14, 1983, p. 41.

Politics

Women's political participation has always been different from that of men. They received the right to vote only in 1920, when the Nineteenth Amendment was ratified. Today, although women vote in about the same proportions as men, they make up a very small percentage of officeholders. The recent appointment of the first woman to serve on the Supreme Court came at a time when women are seriously underrepresented at local, state, and national levels of government.

Women are increasingly seeking elective office and have made some gains in the last decade. Table 12–3 shows that the largest increases in women's elective political participation since 1975 have occurred at the county and local levels. The number of women in mayoralities and on municipal and township bodies has climbed dramatically. Legislatures, statewide offices, and Congress likewise show increases; yet, even at current rates of increase, women are many years away from equal participation.[83]

Evidence, however, shows a growing political influence of women in the voting booth. The marked differences between the political views of women and men voters, now called "the gender gap" by the media, could well determine elections at all political levels.[84]

STRUCTURED SEX INEQUALITY

In this discussion of structured sex inequality, we shall examine specific processes that limit women's access to highly valued resources and thereby "place" them in subordinate roles and activities. Women's oppression in both the work world and the family is part of the reinforcing systems of capitalism and patriarchy.

Occupational Distribution

In the past four decades, the proportion of women in the labor force has changed dramatically. In 1940, less than 20 percent of the female population age sixteen and older was in the labor force.[85] By 1980, the figure had risen to 52 percent.[86] The composition of the female labor force has changed as a result of new demand for workers in service and clerical jobs. Despite the change in composition and volume, some characteristics of women's participation remain amazingly resistant to change: their concentration in sex-typed jobs, their disproportionate share of low-ranking positions, and their low earnings relative to those of men with similar training and experience.[87]

Throughout the 1970s and in the mid 1980s, women were clustered in a relatively small number of occupations defined as female jobs—clerical workers, retail sales workers, sewers and stitchers, waitresses, private household workers, nurses, and noncollege teachers. Women make up more than 70 percent of retail sales persons and of noncollege teachers. The other occupations listed are over 80 percent female.[88] Job segregation is extreme and persistent with most occupations male dominated and very few integrated. (See Table 12–4.)

Women's surge into the work force has taken place in what Howe calls "pink-collar" occupations.[89] The most overwhelming increases have occurred in jobs where women have been working all along, simply because of the soaring demand for workers in the traditionally female occupations.

Recently, the media has given attention to women's gains in traditionally male jobs. *The New York Times,* for example, in 1983 referred to a turbulent labor market in which people moved into jobs held by the opposite sex.[90]

In fact the labor department says there are six major job categories in which women have become the majority in the last decade. Those categories are insurance adjusters, examiners, and investigators; bill collectors, real estate agents and brokers; photograph process workers, checkers, examiners and inspectors, and production-line assemblers.[91]

TABLE 12–4   Occupation, by Sex, 1980

Occupation	Women as Percent of Total in Occupation
Mainly male occupations	
Craft and kindred workers	6.0%
Nonfarm laborers	11.6
Managers and administrators, except farm	20.7
Mixed occupations	
Factory operatives, except transport	40.1
Professional and technical workers	44.3
Salespeople	45.3
Mainly female occupations	
Service (other than domestic)	58.9
Clerical workers	80.1
Private household workers	97.5

Source: U.S. Department of Commerce, *Population Profile of the United States: 1980,* Series P–20, No. 363, July 1981, p. 36.

This news must be balanced with figures pointing to the small reduction in the overall extent of sex segregation in the labor force between 1970 and 1980. For example, in blue-collar fields gains look dramatic at first glance with the number of women in blue-collar jobs rising by 80 percent in the 1970s. But this increase is so high because women were virtually excluded from these occupations until then. Today, only 3 percent of machinists, 2 percent of electricians, and 1 percent of auto mechanics are women. Overall, women now hold 2 percent of all skilled craft jobs compared to 1 percent in 1961.[92]

Women have made inroads in the high-paying and high-prestige professions (see Table 12–5). Still, the proportion of women in the professions remains low. In 1980 only 4 percent of engineers, 13 percent of lawyers, 13.4 percent of doctors, and 33 percent of university and college teachers were women.[93]

Actually, the reduction in the overall extent of sex segregation has been small despite unprecedented rates of change for women in formerly male-dominated occupations. One reason for this contradiction is that very few women, absolutely and proportionately, are employed in the occupations where positive change has occurred. The concentration of women in several large, predominately female occupations (bookkeepers and most clerical occupations) actually increased between 1970 and 1980.[94] Most women are still employed in low-paid, highly segregated jobs. Women of color, in particular, are concentrated in the lowest-paying, lowest-prestige jobs.

Although women have made some progress in entering fields dominated by men, major change is not expected in the degree of occupational sex segregation in the near future.[95] As the economy is being transformed from its traditional manufacturing base to a base in high-technology and service industries, more key punchers, salesclerks, food-service workers, secretaries, and cashiers will be needed.[96] Clerical and service occupations, characterized by low pay and limited opportunities for advancement, are projected to increase at faster rates than all other occupational groups.[97] The increased demand for clerical and service workers probably will be met by women.

Earning
Discrimi-
nation

The earning gap between women and men has been widely documented. Men traditionally earn more than women, and the differential has not changed substantially in recent years.

In 1980 the median income for a full time year-round working woman was $11,590 versus $19,172 for her male counterpart.[98] These figures mean that the average working woman earns 59 cents for every dollar earned by a man. This income differential has remained at about the same level throughout the past two decades. Working women continue to earn less than two-thirds the amount earned by working men (see Table 12–6).

The earning gap persists for several reasons:

□ Women are concentrated in lower-paying occupations.
□ Women enter the labor force at different and lower-paying levels than men.

TABLE 12–5   The Percentage of Women Graduates in Four Professional Fields, 1969–1981

Year	Medicine	Dentistry	Veterinary Medicine	Law
1969–1970	8.5	1.0	7.5	5.6
1975–1976	16.2	4.5	18.1	19.3
1980–1981	23.4	13.5	32.8	30.2

Source: Data from the National Center for Education Statistics, reported in *Chronicle of Higher Education*, January 16, 1978, p. 15 and October 4, 1981, p. 10.

TABLE 12–6   Occupations of Fully Employed Workers, 1980

	All Men	Both Sexes	White Women	Black Women	Hispanic Women	Ratio of Median Earnings of Women and Men
Total	100%	100%	100%	100%	100%	59.4%
Professional, technical, and kindred	17.6	18.2	19.5	17.6	10.9	65.6
Managers and administrators, except farm	18.2	15.3	11.0	4.3	7.1	55.3
Sales workers	6.1	5.5	4.7	2.6	4.0	48.9
Clerical and kindred workers*	6.2	17.9	40.2	34.8	36.2	59.1
Craftworkers, foremen, and kindred	21.5	14.6	2.2	1.4	3.2	61.5
Operatives, except transport	10.1	10.1	9.7	11.3	22.0	60.4
Transport equipment operatives	5.2	3.5	0.4	0.3	0.1	61.5
Laborers, except farm and mine	4.5	3.3	1.0	1.4	1.4	59.0
Private household workers	(^{1})	0.3	0.6	2.0	2.3	75.1
Service workers	6.9	8.7	10.1	24.4	13.0	(^{1})
Farmers and farm managers	2.5	1.7	0.3	(^{1})	(^{1})	61.2
Farm laborers and foremen	1.1	0.9	0.4	(^{1})	0.1	(^{1})

*This item may be read as follows: In 1980, 17.9 percent of all fully employed workers were in clerical and kindred jobs; however, 6.2 percent of all men, compared to 40.2 percent of white women, were in these occupations. The median earnings of all women in these jobs were 59.1 percent of the earnings of men in these jobs.

[1] Data not shown where base is less than 75,000.

Source: U.S. Department of Labor, Bureau of Labor Statistics, calculated from unpublished data, 1980.

Reprinted from: *A Growing Crisis, Disadvantaged Women and Their Children*. United States Commission on Civil Rights, *Clearinghouse Publication* 78 (May 1983).

□ Women as a group have less education and experience than men; therefore, they are paid less than men.
□ Women tend to work less overtime than men.[99]

These conditions explain only part of the earning gap between women and men. They do not explain why women workers earn substantially less than men workers with the same number of years of education.

Differential earning can be found even within occupational classifications. Table 12–2, for example, shows that female faculty members earn less than male faculty members at all levels. It is obvious that fully employed women, when compared with fully employed men, are consistently underpaid by thousands of dollars even when equal in educational attainment or type of occupation.

Double Discrimination: Women of Color

If women are disadvantaged due simply to their sex, minority women are doubly disadvantaged. Black and Hispanic women are overrepresented in low-paying, low-status jobs. They tend to have few fringe benefits, poor working conditions, high labor turnover, and little chance of advancement. Black and Hispanic women are clustered in service jobs such as cooks, dishwashers, food counter and fountain workers, cleaning service workers, waitresses, nurses' aides and child care workers.[100] Because of their race, black and Hispanic women are crowded into society's "dirty work" sectors. The gender system works with and through the system of racial stratification to place women of color at the bottom of the work hierarchy.

The Organization and Operation of Work

Researchers have long assumed that women's status in the labor force was a result of their low aspirations, their submissive personalities, and their greater commitment to family than to work. New sociological research on women has found that conditions inherent in work itself disadvantage women. The new research unmasks processes that assign women to sex-segregated jobs, exposes the working conditions of poor women in the most menial jobs, examines the mechanisms that truncate opportunity for women, and lays bare the reasons women earn less than men.[101]

Let us examine the structure of the labor market that places women unequally. The differential placement of women and men stems from forces in American capitalism. The capitalist labor market is divided into two separate segments with different characteristics, different roles, and different rewards. The primary segment is characterized by stability, high wages, promotion ladders, opportunities for advancement, good working conditions, and provisions for job security. The secondary market is characterized by low wages, fewer or no promotion ladders, poor working conditions, and little provision for job security.[102]

Women's work tends to fall in the secondary segment. Clerical work, the largest single occupation for women, has many of the characteristics associated

Reprinted by permission of Field Syndicate.

with the secondary segment. The office provides a good example of segmentation by sex.

> We observe two separate groups of office jobs, divided by sex. Some jobs are clearly "female" (typists, secretaries, key punchers); others are clearly "male" (vice president, product manager, sales manager). Furthermore, groups of jobs are organized into a hierarchy and the "clerical" staff is a largely female hierarchy. Each hierarchy is made up of jobs graded by level representing steps in a career. When a person takes a job she/he occupies not only that particular job, but also a step on a particular career ladder. A person who starts on the clerical career ladder may move up the ranks as she/he gains experience, but she/he rarely is allowed to cross over into a different ladder. Occasionally one hears of a clerk or secretary who becomes an officer in a company. Such stories generate excitement precisely because each is a freak occurrence.[103]

Sex-typing of work can be found even in the professions. In medicine, women are found specializing in pediatrics, anesthesiology, psychiatry, and physical medicine but are underrepresented as surgeons.[104] Women lawyers tend to be concentrated in two areas: trusts/estates and domestic relations. Both are low-prestige specialties with a large proportion of female clients.[105] Although women are increasingly entering managerial and administrative jobs in private industry, they tend to be clustered in areas more traditionally open to females: public relations, personnel, and other staff jobs; consequently, they earn less than men with the same background.[106]

It has long been assumed that women's and men's behavior in work settings is different, that women's behavior accounts for their lack of career advancement. Men are thought to be more ambitious, task oriented, and work involved; women are considered less motivated, less committed, and more oriented to work relationships than to work itself. Recent research, however, has pointed to the importance of the effect of people's location or placement in work settings and its effect on behavior.

Rosabeth Moss Kanter's important research on men and women in the corporate world reveals that structural position can account for what appear to be "sex differences" in organizational behavior (see Panel 12–3). Hierarchical structures of opportunity and power shape women's and men's work behavior. People in low-mobility or blocked situations (regardless of their sex) tend to limit their aspirations, seek satisfactions in activities

PANEL 12–3

Hierarchy and Work Behavior

The structure of organizations plays a powerful role in creating work behavior. Women in low-mobility organizational situations develop attitudes and orientations that are sometimes said to be characteristic of those people as individuals or "women as a group," and the women themselves may even believe that this is so; but those attitudes can be viewed more accurately as universal *human* responses to blocked opportunities. This analysis should lead to a reinterpretation of familiar findings about sex differences in work behavior: that men are more work oriented and aggressive and that women care more about relationships at work. When women seem to lack ambition or commitment, perhaps they are being realistic about the prospects their jobs offer for advancement or improvement.

This structuralist perspective avoids the "blame the victim" approach that explains work behavior in terms of individual dispositions. It also suggests a different kind of social policy for the elimination of sex discrimination than the "sex roles" school of thought. Instead of retraining women (or men) as individuals to acquire work-appropriate behavior, attitudes, and motivation, or providing different models of socialization, change strategies would focus on the structure of the organization as a total system. It is much easier, of course, to approach the individual, the family, or the school with change policies and research programs, as these are relatively small and powerless elements of the society compared to work organizations. But it is those complex organizations that more critically shape the prospects for the work life of adults, and thus it is those systems we must investigate and understand. It is the nature, form, and degree of hierarchy that should bear the burden of change.

Source: *Men and Women of the Corporation* by Rosabeth Moss Kanter. Copyright © 1977 by Rosabeth Moss Kanter. By permission of Basic Books, Inc. Publishers, New York; and "Hierarchy and Work Behavior," *Social Problems* 23 (April, 1976): 427.

outside work, dream of escape, and create sociable peer groups in which interpersonal relationships take over other aspects of work. The jobs held by most women workers tend to be associated with shorter chains of opportunity. What has been considered typical women's behavior can be explained by their structural position.[107]

Just as hierarchical structures track women and men, other processes contribute to sex stratification. In the professions, for example, sponsor-protégé systems and informal interactions among colleagues limit women's mobility. Cynthia Epstein points to the importance of sponsorship in training personnel and assuring leadership continuity. Women are less likely to be acceptable as protégés. Furthermore, their sex status limits or excludes their involvement in the buddy system or the old-boy system.[108] These informal interactions create alliances that can further chances for social mobility, but they are systematically blocked for women. It is clear that the work situations of women are different from those of men.

> The question, Why aren't women more assertive, more ambitious, more career oriented? is essentially a question about why women aren't more like men, and it assumes that they work in the same world as men. We could assume, as suggested above, that women live and work in a different cultural-structural environment from that of men. In this environment they are viewed as outsiders in a place where they are not expected to be. They are also seen as people who are by definition either too passive or too aggressive—people who have a proper place in supportive but not in leadership roles.[109]

Women and Men in Families

Women's status in the family parallels their status in other social institutions. This is readily apparent from the kind of work they do. In the role of wife and mother, a woman earns no money for her household chores of cleaning, ironing, cooking, sewing, and caring for the needs of the household members. Although this work is necessary, it is low in prestige and it is unpaid. Apportioning domestic labor and child rearing to women upholds male privilege by freeing men from such responsibilities.

Although many wife-husband relationships are moving toward equality, men continue to exercise greater marital power. The higher the husband's occupational status, the higher his income, and the higher his overall status, the greater his power.[110] Such resources are acquired outside the family. We have seen that women's opportunities to acquire these resources are much more limited than those of men: American families are still patriarchal. Family life tends to be subordinate to demands of the male-husband role.

THE COSTS AND CONSEQUENCES OF SEXISM

Who Benefits?

Clearly, sex inequality enters all aspects of social life in the United States. This inequality is profitable to certain segments of the economy, and it also gives privileges to individual men.

Capitalists derive extra profits from paying women less than men. Women's segregation in low paying jobs produces higher profits for certain economic sectors; namely, those where most of the labor force is female. In 1969, Hunt and Sherman calculated that the extra profits from employing women at lower rates amounted to about 23 percent of all corporate manufacturing profits.[111] Women who lack the economic support of husbands and who are in the wage labor force on only a temporary basis have always been a source of easily exploitable labor. These women provide a significant proportion of the marginal labor force needed by capitalists to draw upon during upswings in the business cycle and to release during downswings.[112]

Sex inequality and male dominance are suited to the needs of the economy in other ways as well. Capitalism involves not only the accumulation of capital but also the maintenance of labor power. The physical and emotional labor of maintaining wage workers must be done. The unpaid work that women do inside the home keeps capitalism going, servicing its workers both physically and emotionally. Women do domestic labor and child rearing, but they also do the emotional work, building and maintaining interpersonal relationships and ensuring the stability of children and men so they can function in a capitalistic society.[113]

Because domestic work and emotional work are assigned to women, individual men gain leisure and service and the opportunity to pursue their own interests or careers. If women tend to men's "existence needs," such as cooking and taking care of clothing, men gain time at women's expense:

> He reads the evening paper and his wife fixes dinner. He watches the news or an informative television show and she washes the dishes. He retires to his study (or his office or his shop or a soft chair) and she manages the children. Men gain leisure time at the expense of the oppression of women. This is a very fundamental privilege which accrues to the division of labor (or lack of division) in the home.[114]

This domestic division of labor, in turn, can limit women's occupational participation and advancement. Women burdened with domestic duties have less time or energy left over to devote to careers. Thus, the domestic division of labor reinforces the division of labor in the labor force: men's occupational superiority is upheld. The interaction of the two interlocking systems of capitalism and patriarchy has created a vicious cycle of domination and subordination.

The Social and Individual Costs

Sex inequality generates benefits for certain segments of society, but ultimately society and individual women and men pay a high price. Sexism diminishes the quality of life for all Americans. Our society is deprived of half of its resources when women are denied full and equal participation in its institutions. If women are systematically kept from jobs requiring leadership, creativity, and productivity, the economy will obviously suffer. The pool of talent consisting of half the population will continue to be underutilized and underproductive, in effect constituting a massive "brain drain" for the society. This potential for creativity and leadership is lost because of the barriers that keep women "in their place." As Robertson has summarized it:

> Any society that ascribes low status to some of its members on such arbitrary grounds as race, caste, or sex is artificially restricting the economic contribution of part of the population. To be fully efficient, a modern industrial economy must allow social mobility on the grounds of merit, not restrict it on the grounds of an irrational ascribed status.[115]

Sexism also produces suffering for millions. We have seen that individual women pay for economic discrimination. Their children pay as well, especially if employed mothers are unmarried, separated, divorced, or forced by economic circumstances to buttress the earnings of their husbands.[116]

Due to rising divorce rates, women are increasingly likely to carry primary responsibility for supporting themselves and their children. At the same time most women remain in the secondary labor force with wages too low to support themselves, let alone a family. In 1980, the median income of a female head of household was $10,408; for black women it was $7,425, and for Hispanic women it was $7,031.[117] The female-headed household is the fastest-growing household type in this society, and a clear relationship exists between poverty and female-headed households. Most female-headed families are poor. Specifically one in three families headed by women is poor compared to one poor family in every eighteen headed by men. Over half of the children—50 percent of white children and 68 percent of black and Hispanic children—in female-headed households are poor.[118]

The increase in poor female-headed households has been termed "the feminization of poverty."[119] Many women have become part of the "nouveau poor" by losing their middle-class position when they became divorced, separated, or widowed. "This change in their relationship to a male often leaves them with few skills, limited economic resources, and dependent children. As single parents, they come to taste and live the poverty too familiar to many women who never had the benefits of a middle class existence."[120]

Economic discrimination creates poverty especially in families where fathers are absent. A 1977 government study found that if working women were paid what similarly qualified men earn, the number of poor families would decrease by half.[121] A difference between male and female poverty is that male poverty is often the consequence of unemployment and a job is an effective remedy, while female poverty often exists even when a woman works full-time.

The impoverishment of women is costly to society. Households headed by women account for 83 percent of all AFDC (Aid to Families with Dependent Children) recipients, 70 percent of all food stamp households, 60 percent of those using Medicaid, 66 percent of households using subsidized housing, and 67 percent of all legal service clients.[122]

All women pay a psychological price for sexism. The devaluation of women by society can create identity problems, low self-esteem, and a general sense of worthlessness. This is particularly true as women age. Middle-aged and older women in American society face two problems from which men are relatively exempt. The first problem is the loss of sexual attractiveness. The second problem is the loss of their primary role—the bearing and raising of children.

Given the occupational patterns in American society, men generally gain in prestige and power as they age. They therefore tend to retain or even enhance their attractiveness to women. The reverse, however, is not the case.[123] The result is that widowed or divorced men tend to remarry younger women. Widowed or divorced women either remain single or marry older men. Consequently, although the male-female ratio is approximately 1:1 in the forty-five to sixty-four age bracket, there are three times as many single, divorced, and widowed women as there are single, divorced, and widowed men in that age category. Those women who worked inside the home for husbands and children can become "displaced homemakers" through the death, separation, or divorce of a husband.

The second age-related problem for women occurs when their children leave home. This stage is critical for a woman who has been a totally committed "supermother." Her life has been one of self-sacrifice devoted to raising her children. When she is between the ages of forty and fifty-nine, her last child leaves home and she is faced with another thirty years or so of life void of a role that was all-consuming. Menopause thus becomes a special problem for American women, not only because of the hormone changes taking place, but because it represents symbolically their decline into "uselessness" or perhaps their realization of wasted potential. This empty-nest syndrome is a common source of depression among middle-aged women.[124]

Thus, women who have spent their lives carrying out culturally defined tasks (raising and nurturing a family) are now faced with a relative absence of societal expectations.

Sexism also denies men the potential for full human development. "Occupational segregation by sex denies employment opportunities to men who wish to enter such fields as nursing, grade school teaching or secretarial work. Eradication of sexism would benefit such males.[125] It would benefit all males who have been forced into stereotypic male behavioral modes. In learning to be men, boys express their masculinity through physical courage, toughness, competitiveness, and aggression. Expressions typically associated with femininity, such as gentleness, expressiveness, and responsiveness, are seen as undesirable for males. In rigidly adhering to gender expectations, males pay a price for their masculinity.

> The conventional expectations of what it means to be a man are difficult to live up to for all but the lucky few and lead to unnecessarily self-deprivation in the nest when they do not measure up. Even for those who do, there is a price: they may be forced, for example, to inhibit the expression of many emotions.[126]

Male inexpressiveness can hinder communication between husbands and wives, between fathers and children; it has been labeled a "tragedy of American society."[127] Certainly it is a tragedy for such a man himself, crippled by an inability to let out the best part of the human being—his warm and tender feelings for other people.[128] (See Panel 12–4.)

PANEL 12–4

Masculinity and Self-Destructive Behaviors

In the following excerpts Herb Goldberg shows how masculinity is defined in American society to be self-destructive to males.

1. *Emotional expression is feminine.* Women are emotional; men are supposed to control themselves. So men's emotions undergo repression, and they fall victim to stress-induced, psychosomatic illnesses.

2. *Giving in to pain is feminine.* The male learns to equate his masculinity with his ability to take pain. The equation he lives by is a simple one. "The more pain I can take without giving in, the more manly I am." Only after the cumulative symptoms have become so great that they throw him over, does he give in to them and only then because he has to. He can disown personal responsibility and blame the illness.

3. *Asking for help is feminine.* He drives around the neighborhood for a half hour rather than pulling over to ask for help with the directions. When he's hurting, often nobody knows. A recent research study showed that although 65 percent of psychiatrists asked said that they saw more women professionally, 77 percent added that they didn't see more women who actually required psychiatric treatment. According to the researchers, that seemed to indicate that men don't make their first appointment until their symptoms become really severe. Women feel culturally freer to seek help because for a woman it is not viewed as an admission of weakness.

4. *Paying too much attention to diet, especially when you're not sick, is feminine.* He has been taught, and he believes, that because he's a man he needs to eat more heavily, even if, in fact, his work is less physically exerting than a woman's. Therefore, although he sits behind a desk all day in his office, he eats like a warrior embarking on a two-week hunt.

5. *Alcohol abstinence is feminine.* In many small towns across America, the fear of reflecting negatively on one's masculinity by not drinking in the company of one's male friends, almost every evening after work, is far greater than any concern about what the alcohol is doing to the body. Drinking, after all, is *the* primary basis for men relating to each other socially and of proving their masculinity. Again the equation he learns is simple and blatantly self-destructive. "The more liquor I can hold, the more masculine I am."

6. *Self-care is feminine.* Pampering oneself, taking long, leisurely baths, exploring oneself in front of the mirror, going to health spas, and taking "beauty rests" are all "feminine" activities. Men have "more important" things to do, namely, working and being otherwise productive. A man who is unduly involved with his physical well-being is suspect. He is labeled narcissistic, effete, a hypochondriac or worse. Conversely, the man who is the most reckless in attitude to-

(continued)

ward his physical well-being is seen as being most masculine.

7. *Dependency is feminine.* Getting sick often means having to let other people take care of you. Letting other people take care of you, worse still, expecting them to, is feminine. The man who can stand alone, does not rely on others, expresses no dependency and is least needful is the most manly.

8. *Touching is feminine.* The nourishing, healing and comforting roles of touching are well documented in psychological literature. But touching, especially when it is purposeless (meaning it

is not a prelude to sex or a formal greeting), arouses the man's anxiety and makes most men uncomfortable.

In summary, masculinity in the care of the body means:
1) The less sleep I need;
2) The more pain I can take;
3) The more alcohol I can hold;
4) The less I concern myself with what I eat;
5) The less I ask anybody for help or depend on them;
6) The more I control and repress my emotions;
7) The less attention I pay to myself physically, *the more masculine I am.*

Source: Excerpts abridged from pp. 49–52 in *The New Male* by Herb Goldberg. Copyright © 1979 by Herb Goldberg. By permission of William Morrow & Company.

Ideally, men and women should be able to integrate traditionally feminine and traditionally masculine traits. Such flexibility of sex roles, or **androgyny**, would permit all people to be either rational or emotional, either assertive or yielding, depending on what is appropriate to the situation.

FIGHTING THE SYSTEM

Feminist Movements in the United States

Sex inequality in this society has led to feminist social movements. Three stages of feminism have been aimed at overcoming sex discrimination. The first stage grew out of the abolition movement of the 1830s. Working to abolish slavery, women found that they could not function as equals with their male abolitionist friends, and they became convinced that women's freedom was as important as freedom from slavery. In July 1848 the first convention in history devoted to issues of women's position and rights was held at Seneca Falls, New York. Participants in the Seneca Falls convention approved a declaration of independence, asserting that men and women are created equal, and that they are endowed with certain inalienable rights.[129]

During the Civil War, feminists for the most part turned their attention to the emancipation of blacks. After the war and the ratification of the Thirteenth Amendment, abolishing slavery, feminists were divided between those seeking far-ranging economic, religious, and social reforms, and those seeking voting rights for women. The second stage of feminism gave priority to women's suffrage. The women's suffrage amendment, introduced into every session of Congress from 1878 on, was ratified on August 26, 1920, nearly three-quarters of a century after the demand for women's suffrage had been made at the Seneca Falls convention. From 1920 until the 1960s, feminism was dormant. "So much energy had been expended in achieving the right to vote that the woman's movement virtually collapsed from exhaustion."[130]

Feminism was reawakened in the 1960s. Social movements aimed at inequalities gave rise to an important branch of contemporary feminism. The civil rights movement and other protest movements of the 1960s spread the ideology of equality. But, like the early feminists, women involved in political protest movements found that male dominance characterized even movements seeking social equality. Discovering injustice in freedom movements, they broadened their protest to such far-reaching concerns as health care, family life, and relationships between the sexes.

Another strand of contemporary feminism emerged among professional women who discovered sex discrimination in earnings and advancement. Formal organizations, such as the National Organization of Women, evolved seeking legislation to overcome sex discrimination.[131]

These two branches of contemporary feminism gave rise to a feminist consciousness among millions of American women. During the 1960s and 1970s, definite changes occurred in the roles of women and men. Nevertheless, sexism persists and continues to affect the lives of all women and men. (See Panel 12–5).

PANEL 12–5   Social Dilemmas and Critical Choices

The Goals and Tactics of the Women's Movement

What is your position on improving the status of women? If you seek continued change, do you favor something close to an androgynous society where the sex-role differences between men and women would become blurred, or do you prefer leaving some sex-role differences undisturbed but pushing for a real equality between the sexes?

These preferences will somewhat influence the kind of movement for women's rights that you might support. Assuming that you might support some such movement, here are some choices you might have to make: Should the target be the change of people's attitudes or the change of the structure of society? The former requires efforts at "consciousness raising," propaganda, education, and other techniques designed to alter the attitudes of men and women, making them receptive to change. If, however, the choice is a change in laws and customs, the tactics demand political pressure, the election of sympathetic candidates, the passage of appropriate legislation, and court suits. And, if the normal legislative and judicial channels prove too slow or unyielding, one must decide whether the use of nonviolent resistance or even violence is justified.

So, in sum, which goal of the feminist movement do you favor? Just how committed are you to that goal? Can you suggest your own version of tactics that are appropriate to reach that goal?

Social
Structure
and
Equality

An important question is whether sex equality is compatible with present political economic conditions. We have seen that the form of the economy and the distribution of power (capitalist patriarchy) produces sex inequality at all levels of American society. In this regard,

> many serious feminists believe that neither equality nor liberation can emerge within the capitalist economic system—a system in which the primary objective is profit making rather than equality and improvement of the conditions of life for all. They contend that as long as the unequal situation of women does not interfere with production and profits, little will be done to effect real changes.[132]

Since structural problems are largely invisible, it is important that we understand how individual lives are bound up with structural events.

Individual women and men seeking change will continue to discover that, no matter how they struggle for equality, the sexism that is rooted in our culture and our social institutions will continue to affect them. Thus, the insights of sociology have become increasingly significant in the continuing struggle for women's equality.

SUMMARY

This chapter has documented the complex network of social factors in American society that constitute the gender system. Some biological bases may exist for the sexual division of labor and the differences in behavior between the sexes, but the evidence is clear that social factors decidedly channel men and women into those roles and behaviors expected by society.

Both order and conflict theorists agree that sex-role patterns in society are primarily social in origin, not biological. They differ, however, in the interpretation of this arbitrary division. Order-model adherents argue that for men and women to play very different roles has positive consequences for society. One consequence is an efficient division of labor with clear expectations for society's members. Although order theorists would not necessarily claim that child care and housekeeping should be apportioned strictly to women, they would support the notion that someone must do these tasks and that to have them defined by gender makes for an orderly and predictable society.

Conflict theorists criticize the order people for supporting the status quo that is unfair to women. They emphasize how the system keeps women in subordinate roles that translate into dependence, powerlessness, and servitude. In this view men are powerful, and it is in their interests to maintain the unequal distribution of power to continue their political, social, and economic advantages.

The socialization process is a powerful force that influences people to conform to gender-specific expectations; these socially determined differences are detrimental to women. While socialization accounts for differences in women's and men's roles, male dominance is sustained by a complex web of structural forces in society. Women in all social institutions are placed disadvantageously compared to men. Inequality is perpetuated by economic forces in society and by deeply entrenched ideas about women. Men gain privilege from women's subordination. The capitalist economy also benefits from sex inequality.

Ultimately, however, sexism has damaging consequences for women, for men, and for the larger society. It creates poverty among millions, deprives society of the potential contributions of half of the population, and forces women and men into narrow and confining roles.

The pervasive nature of inequality present in a sexist society had led many women to organize and use a variety of tactics, from violent confrontations to court cases, to bring about change. Despite recent gains, women remain subordinate in the society.

CHAPTER REVIEW

1. American society, like other societies, assigns different expectations to women and men, and these expectations are ranked in favor of males. Male dominance refers to the fact that men have greater prestige, power, and privileges than women.

2. The pressures of society are more important than innate biological differences in the formation of sex roles and the ranking of traits associated with the sexes.

3. Conflict and order perspectives provide different explanations of the origin and persistence of the gender system. Order theorists emphasize division of labor and social integration, while conflict theorists emphasize male control of economic resources and women's inequality.

4. Many sociologists have viewed sex inequality as the consequences of behavior learned by individual women and men. More recently sociologists have explained sex inequality as a consequence of the way in which society is structured. The thesis of this chapter is that while socialization accounts for the acquisition

of gender, the systems of capitalism and patriarchy in our society "place" females and males in different and unequal positions.

5. The gender system is reinforced through language, interpersonal behavior, mass communication, religion, the law, and politics.

6. The occupational concentration of women in a few sex-typed occupations contrasts with that of men who are distributed throughout the occupational hierarchy; and women, even with the same amount of education and when doing the same work, earn less than men in all occupations.

7. Labor market segmentation is the basic source of sex inequality in the labor force. Work opportunities for women tend to concentrate in a secondary market that has few advancement opportunities, fewer job benefits, and lower pay.

8. The position of women in families parallels their status in the labor force. Their responsibility for domestic maintenance and child care frees individual

men from such duties and supports the capitalist economy.

9. Sexism deprives society of the potential contributions of half of its members, creates poverty among families headed by women, and limits the capacities of all women and men.

10. Feminist movements aimed at eliminating sex inequality have created significant changes at all levels of society, but because sexism is deeply embedded in the social structure, its elimination will require a fundamental transformation of American society.

FOR FURTHER STUDY

Margaret L. Anderson. *Thinking About Women: Sociological and Feminist Perspectives* (New York: Macmillan Publishing Co., Inc. 1983).

Barbara Sinclair Deckard. *The Woman's Movement, Political, Socioeconomic and Psychological Issues*, 3rd ed. (New York: Harper & Row Publishers, 1983).

James A. Doyle. *The Male Experience* (Dubuque, Iowa: Wm. C. Brown, Co., 1983).

Jo Freeman, ed. *Women: A Feminist Perspective.* 2nd ed. (Palo Alto, Calif.: Mayfield, 1979).

Nona Glazer and Helen Youngelson Wachrer, eds. *Woman in a Man-Made World*, 2nd ed. (Chicago: Rand McNally, 1977).

Rosabeth Moss Kanter. *Men and Women of the Corporation* (New York: Basic Books, 1977).

Julie A. Matthaei. *An Economic History of Women in America* (New York: Schoken Books, 1982).

Margarita B. Melville, ed. *Twice a Minority, Mexican American Women* (St. Louis: The C. V. Mosby Co., 1980).

Marcia Millman and Rosabeth Moss Kanter, eds. *Another Voice: Feminist Perspectives on Social Life and Social Science* (New York: Doubleday/Anchor, 1975).

Charlotte G. O'Kelly. *Women and Men in Society* (New York: Van Nostrand, 1980).

Laurel Walum Richardson. *The Dynamics of Sex and Gender*, 2nd ed. (Boston: Houghton Mifflin, 1981).

Marie Richmond-Abbott. *Masculine and Feminine, Sex Roles Over the Life Cycle* (Reading, Mass.: Addison-Wesley, 1983).

La Frances Rodgers-Rose. *The Black Woman* (Beverly Hills, Calif.: Sage Publications, 1980).

Mary P. Ryan. *Womanhood in America*, 3rd ed, (New York: Franklin Watts, 1983).

Natalie J. Sokoloff. *Between Money and Love, The Dialectics of Women's Home and Market Work* (New York, Praeger Publishers, 1980).

Jean Stockard and Miriam M. Johnson. *Sex Roles* (Englewood Cliffs, N.J.: Prentice-Hall, 1980).

Ann H. Stromberg and Shirley Harkess, eds. *Women Working* (Palo Alto, Calif.: Mayfield, 1978).

Amy Swerdlow and Hanna Lessinger, eds. *Class, Race and Sex: The Dynamics of Control* (Boston: G. K. Hall, 1983).

NOTES AND REFERENCES

1. For an elaboration of the research on sex differences see Arlie Russell Hochschild, "A Review of Sex Role Research," *American Journal of Sociology* 78 (January, 1973), pp. 1011–1029; Eleanor E. Maccoby and Carol Nagy Jacklin, "What We Know and Don't Know about Sex Differences," *Psychology Today* 8 (December, 1974), pp. 109–112 or their book, *The Psychology of Sex Differences* (Palo Alto, Calif.: Stanford University Press, 1974); Nancy Chodorow, "Being and Doing: A Cross Cultural Examination of the So-

cialization of Males and Females," in *Woman in Sexist Society: Studies in Power and Powerlessness*, Vivian Gornick and Barbara K. Moran, eds. (New York: Basic Books, 1971), pp. 259–291; Ernestine Friedl, *Women and Men: An Anthropologist's View* (New York: Holt, Rinehart and Winston, 1975); and "Just How the Sexes Differ," *Newsweek* (May 18, 1981), pp. 72–83.

2. Jane E. Brody, "Genetic Explanations Offered for Women's Health Superiority," *The New York Times* (January 20, 1980), pp. C1, C5.

3. Mary Anne Baker, "How Are We Born Different?" in *Women Today*, Mary Anne Baker, et al., eds., (Monterey, Calif.: Brooks/Cole, 1980), pp. 69–70; and Maccoby and Jacklin, *The Psychology of Sex Differences*.

4. D. M. Quadagno, R. Briscoe, and J. S. Quadagno, "Effect of Perinatal Gonodal Hormones on Selected Nonsexual Behavior Patterns," *Psychological Bulletin* 84 (1977), pp. 62–80.

5. Margaret L. Anderson, *Thinking About Women, Sociological and Feminist Perspectives* (New York: Macmillan, 1983).

6. Charlotte G. O'Kelly, *Women and Men in Society* (New York: Van Nostrand, 1980), p. 41.

7. Quoted in Elsa M. Chaney, *Supermadre: Women in Politics in Latin America* (Austin: University of Texas Press, 1979), p. 19.

8. Jean Stockard and Miriam M. Johnson, *Sex Roles* (Englewood Cliffs, N.J.: Prentice-Hall, 1980), p. 4. Norman Goodman and Gary T. Marx, *Society Today*, 3rd ed. (New York: Random House/CRM, 1978), p. 312.

9. Michelle Zimbalist Rosaldo, "Woman, Culture, and Society: A Theoretical Overview," in *Woman, Culture, and Society*, ed. Michelle Zimbalist Rosaldo and Louise Lamphere (Stanford, Calif.: Stanford University Press, 1974), pp. 17–42.

10. This explanation is most clearly set forth by Rosaldo, "Woman, Culture, and Society," pp. 17–42; Judith Brown, "A Note on the Division of Labor by Sex," *American Anthropologist* 72 (September-October 1970): 1073–1078; and Karen Sacks, "Engels Revisited: Women, the Organization of Production, and Private Property," in *Woman, Culture, and Society*, pp. 207–222.

11. Michele Zimbalist Rosaldo, "The Use and Abuse of Anthropology: Reflections on Feminism and Cross-Cultural Understanding," *Signs: Journal of Women in Culture and Society* 5 (Spring 1980): 389–417.

12. Talcott Parsons, Robert F. Bales, *et al.*, *Family, Socialization and Interaction Process* (New York: Free Press, 1955), pp. 3–9.

13. Randall Collins, "A Conflict Theory of Sexual Stratification," in Hans Peter Dreitzel, ed., *Family, Marriage and the Struggle of the Sexes* (New York: Macmillan, 1972) and *Conflict Sociology* (New York: Academic Press, 1975).

14. *Ibid.*, p. 46. This is a paraphrase of Friedrich Engels' theory of the family in Karl Marx and Friedrich Engels, "The Communist Manifesto," in *Marx and Engels, Selected Works in Two Volumes*, Vol. 1 (Moscow: Foreign Language Publishing House, 1958).

15. See Alice Schlegal, *Sexual Stratification: A Cross Cultural View* (New York: Columbia University Press, 1977); Ernestine Friedel, *Women and Men: An Anthropologists View.* (New York: Holt, Rinehart and Winston, 1975); and Eleanor B. Leacock, "Introduction to the 1972 edition of Engels." *Origin of the Family, Private Property and the State* (New York: International Publishers, 1972).

16. Rosaldo, "The Use and Abuse of Anthropology."

17. Sacks, "Engels Revisited," pp. 219–221.

18. Zillah Eisenstein, "Developing a Theory of Capitalist Patriarchy and Socialist Feminism," in *Capitalist Patriarchy and the Case for Socialist Feminism.* ed. Zillah R. Eisenstein (New York: Monthly Review Press, 1979), pp. 5–40.

19. Joan R. Acker, "Women and Stratification: A Review of Recent Literature," *Contemporary Sociology* 9 (January 1980): 31.

20. Karen Skold, Book Review, *Signs, Journal of Women in Culture and Society* 8 (Winter 1982): 367–372.

21. Nona Glazer, "Introduction, Part Two," in *Woman in a Man-Made World*, ed. Nona Glazer and Helen Youngelson Waehrer, 2nd ed. (Chicago: Rand McNally, 1977), pp. 102–103.

22. Deborah S. David and Robert Brannon, "The Male Sex Role," in *Family in Transition*,

ed. Arlene Skolnick and Jerome H. Skolnick, 3d ed. (Boston: Little, Brown, 1980), p. 117.

23. Anderson, *Thinking About Women*, p. 56.

24. Laurel Walum Richardson, *The Dynamics of Sex and Gender*, 2d ed. (Boston: Houghton Mifflin, 1981), p. 48.

25. Nancy Frazier and Myra Pollack Sadker, *Sexism in School and Society* (New York: Harper & Row, 1973), p. 84. For a guide to non-sexist parenting see Letty Cottin Pogrebin, *Growing Up Free: Raising Your Child in the 80's* (New York: McGraw-Hill, 1980).

26. Michael Lewis, "There's No Unisex in the Nursery," *Psychology Today* 5 (May, 1972), pp. 54–57.

27. See L. M. Lansky, "The Family Structure Also Affects the Model: Sex Role Attitudes in Parents of Preschool Children," *Merrill-Palmer Quarterly* 13 (April, 1967), pp. 139–150; and P. H. Mussen and E. E. Rutherford, "Parent-Child Relations and Parental Personality in Relation to Young Children's Sex Role Preferences," *Child Development* 34 (1963), pp. 589–607.

28. Anne Statham Macke and William R. Morgan, "Maternal Employment, Race, and Work Orientation of High School Girls," *Social Forces* 57 (September, 1978), pp. 187–204.

29. Lenore J. Weitzman, Deborah Eifler, Elizabeth Hokada, and Catherine Ross, "Sex-Role Socialization in Picture Books for Preschool Children," *American Journal of Sociology* 77 (May, 1972), pp. 1125–1150.

30. Dean Walley, *What Boys Can Be* (Kansas City: Hallmark Cards, n.d.).

31. Dean Walley, *What Girls Can Be* (Kansas City: Hallmark Cards, n.d.).

32. Weitzman et al., "Sex-Role Socialization," pp. 1144–1145.

33. Lisa A. Serbin and K. Daniel O'Leary, "How Nursery Schools Teach Girls to Shut Up," *Psychology Today* 9 (December, 1975), p. 57.

34. Reported in Barbara Sinclair Deckard, *The Women's Movement*, 3rd ed. (New York: Harper and Row, 1983), p. 55.

35. Janet Lever, "Sex Differences in the Games Children Play," *Social Problems* 23 (April, 1976), pp. 478–487.

36. Joyce A. Ladner, *Tomorrow's Tomorrow* (New York: Doubleday, 1971).

37. Sarah Goddard Power, "Women, the Economy, and the Future," *Innovator* (University of Michigan, School of Education), 13 (September 1981): 6.

38. See "Guidelines for Creating Positive Images in Educational Materials (New York: Macmillan, 1975); "Guidelines for Equal Treatment of the Sexes in McGraw-Hill Book Company Publications" (New York: McGraw-Hill, 1974).

39. National Organization for Women, *Dick and Jane as Victims: Women on Words and Images* (Princeton, N.J.: National Organization for Women, 1972).

40. Lenore J. Weitzman, "Sex Role Socialization," in *Woman: A Feminist Perspective*, ed. Jo Freeman, 2d ed. (Palo Alto, Calif.: Mayfield, 1979), p. 179.

41. " 'He' Could Stir Women's Lib Nightmare," Associated Press release, November 6, 1971.

42. See Betty Levy, "Do Schools Sell Girls Short," in *And Jill Came Tumbling After: Sexism in American Education*, Judith Stacey, Susan Bereaud, and Joan Daniels, eds. (New York: Dell, 1974), pp. 142–146. See also, Diane McGuinness, "How Schools Discriminate Against Boys," *Human Nature* 2 (February, 1979), pp. 82–88.

43. Robert L. Spaulding, *Achievement, Creativity, and Self-Concept Correlates of Teacher-Pupil Transactions in Elementary Schools*, Cooperative Research Project No. 1352 (Washington, D.C.: U.S. Department of Health, 1963). For a review of similar studies, see Pauline S. Sears and David H. Feldman, "Teacher Interactions wih Boys and with Girls," in Stacey, *et al.*, *And Jill Came Tumbling After*, pp. 147–158.

44. Cited in Bill Gilbert and Nancy Williamson, "Programmed to Be Losers," *Sports Illustrated* (June 11, 1973), p. 73.

45. Marie Richmond-Abbott, *Masculine and Feminine, Sex Roles Over the Life Cycle*. (Reading, Mass.: Addison-Wesley, 1983), p. 169.

46. David Monagan, "The Failure of Coed Sports," *Psychology Today*, March 1983: 58–63.

47. Richardson, *Dynamics of Sex and Gender*, p. 63.

48. Deckard, *The Woman's Movement*.

49. Elayn Bernay, "Affirmative Inaction and Other Facts, Trends, Tactics for Academic Life," *Ms.* November 1978, p. 88.

50. *The Ann Arbor News*, September 8, 1983.

51. *Ibid.*

52. John J. Pietrofesa and Nancy K. Scholossberg, *Counselor Bias and the Female Occupational Role* (Detroit: Wayne State University, 1970).

53. Unpublished study by N. W. Friedersdorf, cited in Nancy K. Schlossberg and John J. Pietrofesa, "Perspectives on Counseling Bias: Implications for Counselor Education," *Counseling Psychologist* 4 (April 1974): 47.

54. Richardson, *Dynamics of Sex and Gender*, p. 63.

55. Simone de Beauvoir, *The Second Sex*, trans. H. M. Parshley (New York: Bantam, 1970).

56. Linda Peterson and Elaine Enarson, "Blaming the Victim in the Sociology of Women: On the Misuse of the Concept of Socialization" (Paper presented at a meeting of the Pacific Sociological Association, San Jose, Calif., March 1974), p. 8.

57. *Ibid.*

58. Karen L. Adams and Norma C. Ware, "Sexism and the English Language: The Linguistic Implications of Being a Woman," in *Women: A Feminist Perspective*, p. 489.

59. Richmond-Abbott, *Masculine and Feminine*, p. 115.

60. Allen Nilson, "Sexism in English: A Feminist View," *Female Studies* 6 (Old Westbury, N.Y.: The Feminist Press, 1972). Quoted in Richmond-Abbott, *Masculine and Feminine*, p. 115.

61. Robin Lakoff, *Language and Woman's Place* (New York: Harper/Colophon, 1975) pp. 14–15.

62. Mary Brown Parlee, "Conversational Politics," *Psychology Today* 12 (May 1979): 48–56.

63. Pamela M. Fishman, "Interaction: The Work Women Do," *Social Problems* 25 (April 1978): 397–406.

64. Nancy M. Henley, *Body Politics: Power, Sex, and Nonverbal Communication* (Englewood Cliffs, N.J.: Prentice-Hall, 1977).

65. See Betty Friedan, *The Feminine Mystique* (New York: Dell, 1963), pp. 28–66; Margaret Lefkowitz, "The Women's Magazine Short-Story Heroine in 1957 and 1967," In *Toward a Sociology of Women*, ed. Constantine Saf-

ilios-Rothschild (Lexington, Mass.: Xerox College Publishers, 1972), pp. 37–40; and Janet Saltzman Chafetz, *Masculine/Feminine or Human?* (Itasca, Ill.: F. E. Peacock, 1974), pp. 41–43.

66. Gaye Tuchman, "Women's Depiction by the Mass Media," *Signs: Journal of Women in Culture and Society* 4 (Spring 1979): 531–532.

67. *Ibid.*, p. 532.

68. *Ibid.*, p. 523.

70. Richmond-Abbott, *Masculine and Feminine*, pp. 123–124.

71. For a summary of the research, see Matilda Butler and William Paisley, *Women and the Mass Media* (New York: Human Sciences Press, 1980), pp. 103–114. See also Cornelia Butler Flora, "Changes in Women's Status in Women's Magazine Fiction," *Social Problems* 26 (June 1979): 558–569; and Carol Caldwell, "You Haven't Come a Long Way, Baby," *New Times*, June 10, 1977, pp. 57–62.

72. Erving Goffman, *Gender Advertisements* (New York: Harper/Colophon, 1979), p. viii, from the introduction by Vivian Gornick.

73. Suzanne Gordon, "The New Corporate Feminism." *The Nation* (February 5, 1983) p. 143.

74. "Perspective: On 'Superwoman'," *University Record* (University of Michigan), May 2, 1981.

75. The following examples are taken largely from Chafetz, *Masculine, Feminine or Human?* pp. 96–98.

76. Leviticus 27:4.

77. Richard Gilman, "Where Did It All Go Wrong?" *Life*, August 13, 1971, p. 51.

78. "Unmanning the Holy Bible," *Time*, December 8, 1980, p. 128; "The God-Language Bind," *Christian Century*, April 16, 1980, pp. 430–431.

79. Kenneth A. Briggs, "Study Documents Growing Impact of Female Clergy." *The Dallas Morning News*. (Sunday, November 15, 1981), p. 28A.

80. See Peg Simpson, "A Victory for Women," *Civil Rights Digest* 11 (Spring 1979): 13–21.

81. Alexandra Lett and Harold Silverman, "Coffee, Tea, and Dignity," *Civil Rights Quarterly Perspectives* 12 (Spring 1980): 4–11.

82. Deckard, *The Woman's Movement*, p. 182.

83. Marilyn Johnson "Women and Elective Office," *Society* 17 (May-June 1980): 64.

84. "Getting a Gender Message," *Time* (July 25, 1983), pp. 12–14.

85. Francine D. Blau, "Women in the Labor Force: An Overview," in *Women: A Feminist Perspective*, p. 272.

86. U.S. Bureau of the Census, "Population Profile of the United States, 1980," *Current Population Reports*, Series P-20, No. 363 (Washington, D. C.: Government Printing Office, 1981), p. 29.

87. Ann H. Stromberg and Shirley Harkess, eds., *Women Working* (Palo Alto, Calif.: Mayfield, 1978), p. xvi.

88. Deckard, *The Woman's Movement*, p. 97.

89. Louise Kapp Howe, *Pink Collar Workers* (New York: Avon, 1977).

90. *The New York Times* (April 24, 1983), p. 1.

91. " 'Male Job' Concept Vanishing," *Denver Post*, (December 13, 1982) C-1.

92. Karin Stallard, Barbara Ehrenreich, and Holly Sklar, *Poverty in the American Dream* (Boston: Institute for New Communications, South End Press, 1983).

93. Deckard, *The Woman's Movement*, p. 18.

94. Louise A. Tilly, "Women's Employment— Past, Present, and Future." A Proposal for a Series of events and projects to be held at the University of Michigan, Fall 1984– Winter 1985." July, 1982.

95. Nancy F. Rytina, "Occupational Segregation and Earnings Difference by Sex," *Research Summaries*.

96. Bob Kuttner, "The Declining Middle," *The Atlantic Monthly* 252 (July 1983), p. 60.

97. Max L. Carey, "Revised Occupational Projections to 1985," *Monthly Labor Review* (November 1976): 15–16.

98. Stallard, Ehrenreich, and Sklar, *Poverty in the American Dream*, p. 9.

99. *The Earnings Gap between Women and Men*, Department of Labor, Women's Bureau, (Washington, D.C.: Government Printing Office, 1979).

100. *A Growing Crisis, Disadvantaged Women and Their Children*, United States Commission on Civil Rights, Clearinghouse Publication, 78, (May 1983):20.

101. Joan Acker, "Issues in the Sociological Study of Women's Work," in *Women Working*, pp. 134–161.

102. Francine D. Blau and Carol L. Jusenius, "Economists' Approaches to Sex Segregation in the Labor Market: An Appraisal," in *Women and the Workplace*, ed., Martha Blaxall and Barbara Regan (Chicago: University of Chicago Press, 1976), pp. 196–197.

103. Evelyn Nakano Glenn and Roslyn L. Feldberg, "Clerical Work: The Female Occupation," *Women: A Feminist Perspective*, p. 314.

104. Jill Quagdagno, "Occupational Sex-Typing and Internal Labor Market Distributions: An Assessment of Medical Specialties," *Social Problems* 23 (April 1976): 442–453.

105. Michelle Patterson, "Sex and Specialization in Academe and the Professions," in *Academic Women on the Move*, ed. Alice S. Rossi and Ann Calderwood (New York: Russell Sage, 1973), pp. 313–331.

106. "Women and the Executive Suite," *Newsweek*, September 14, 1981, pp. 65–68.

107. Rosabeth Moss Kanter, *Men and Women of the Corporation* (New York: Basic Books, 1977), pp. 129–163.

108. Cynthia Fuchs Epstein, *Woman's Place* (Berkeley: University of California Press, 1970), pp. 167–197.

109. Acker, "Issues in the Sociological Study of Women's Work," p. 151.

110. Dair Gillespie, "Who Has the Power? The Marital Struggle," in *Family, Marriage, and the Struggle of the Sexes*, ed. Hans Peter Dreitzel (New York: Macmillan, 1972), p. 133.

111. Quoted in Jan M. Newton. "The Political Economy of Women's Oppression," in *Women on the Move: A Feminist Perspective*, ed. Jean Ramage Lepaluoto (Eugene: University of Oregon Press, 1973), p. 121.

112. Richard C. Edwards, Michael Reich, and Thomas E. Weisskopf, "Sexism," in *The Capitalist System*, 2d ed. (Englewood Cliffs, N.J.: Prentice-Hall, 1978), p 333.

113. *Ibid.*, p. 334.

114. Newton, "The Political Economy of Women's Oppression," p. 121.

115. Ian Robertson, *Sociology* (New York: Worth, 1977), p. 306.

116. Strum, "Pink Collar Blues," p. 34.
117. Stallard, Ehrenreich and Sklar, *Poverty in the American Dream*, p. 9.
118. *Ibid.*, p. 6.
119. Diana Pearce, "The Feminization of Poverty: Women, Work, and Welfare," *The Urban and Social Change Review*. 11 (1978): 28–36.
120. Lynne Weber Cannon and Stella Warren, "Feminization of Poverty." *Newsletter, Center for Research on Women*, Memphis State University. 1 (April 1983): 2–3.
121. Patricia C. Sexton, *Women and Work*, R. and D. Monograph, No 46 (Washington, D.C.: U.S. Department of Labor, Employment and Training Administration, 1977). Cited in Stallard, Ehrenreich and Sklar, *Poverty in the American Dream*, p. 9.
122. Stallard, Ehrenreich and Sklar, *Poverty in the American Dream*, p. 47.
123. Inge Powell Bell, "The Double Standard: Age" in *Women: A Feminist Perspective*, pp. 145–155.
124. Pauline B. Bart, "Depression in Middle-Aged Women," in *Woman in Sexist Society*, pp. 163–186.
125. Barbara B. Regan and Martha Blaxall, "Oc-cupational Segregation in International Women's Year," in *Women and the Workplace*, p. 1.
126. Joseph H. Pleck, "Prisoners of Manliness," *Psychology Today* 15 (September 1981): 69.
127. Jack Balswick and Charles Peck, "The Inexpressive Male: A Tragedy of American Society," *Family Coordinator* 20 (1971): 363–368.
128. Jack O. Balswick with James Lincoln Collier, "Why Husbands Can't Say 'I Love You', " in *The Forty-Nine Percent Majority*, ed. Deborah S. David and Robert Brannon, (Reading, Mass.: Addison-Wesley, 1976), p. 59.
129. Judith Hole and Ellen Levine, "The First Feminists," in *Women: A Feminist Perspective*, pp. 543–555.
130. *Ibid.*, p. 554.
131. Jo Freeman, "The Women's Liberation Movement: Its Origins, Organizations, Activities, and Ideas," *Women: A Feminist Perspective*, pp. 557–574.
132. Acker, "Issues in the Sociological Study of Women's Work," p. 155.

Part 4

Social Institutions

13

The American Economy

Each new affirmation of unemployment renews the pain: the first trip to the employment agency, the first friend you tell, the first interview and, most dreaded of all, the first trip to the unemployment office.

Standing in line at the unemployment office makes you feel very much the same as you did the first time you ever flunked a class or a test—as if you had a big red "F" for "Failure" printed across your forehead. I fantasize myself standing at the end of the line in a crisp and efficient blue suit, chin up, neat and straight as a corporate executive. As I move down the line I start to come unglued and a half hour later, when I finally reach the desk clerk, I am slouching and sallow in torn jeans, tennis shoes and a jacket from the Salvation Army, carrying my worldly belongings in a shopping bag and unable to speak.

You do eventually become accustomed to being unemployed, in the way you might accept a bad limp. And you gradually quit beating yourself for not having been somehow indispensable—or for not having become an accountant. You tire of straining your memory for possible infractions. You recover some of the confidence that always told you how good you were at your job and accept what the supervisor said: "This doesn't reflect on your job performance; sales are down 30 percent this month."

But each time you recover that hallowed self-esteem, you renew a fight to maintain it. Each time you go to a job interview and give them your best and they hire someone else, you go another round with yourself and your self-esteem. Your unemployment seems to drag on beyond all justification. You start to glimpse a stranger in your rearview mirror. The stranger suddenly looks like a bum. You look at her with clinical curiosity. Hmmm. Obviously into the chronic stages. Definitely not employable.

We unemployed share a social stigma similar to that of the rape victim. Whether consciously or subconsciously, much of the work-ethic-driven public feels that you've somehow "asked for it," secretly wanted to lose your job and "flirted" with unemployment through your attitude—probably dressed in a way to invite it (left the vest unbuttoned on your three-piece suit).

But the worst of it isn't society's work-ethic morality; it's your own, which you never knew you had. You find out how much self-satisfaction was gained from even the most simple work-related task: a well-worded letter, a well-handled phone call—even a clean file. Being useful to yourself isn't enough.

But then almost everyone has heard about the need to be a useful member of society. What you didn't know about was the loneliness. You've spent your life almost constantly surrounded by people, in classes, in dorms, and at work. To suddenly find yourself with only your cat to talk to all day distorts your sense of reality. You begin to worry that flights of fancy might become one way.

But you always were, and still are, stronger than that. You maintain balance and perspective, mainly through resorting frequently to sarcasm and irreverence. Although something going wrong in any aspect of your life now seems to push you into temporary despair much more easily than before, you have some very important things to hang on to—people who care, your sense of humor, your talents, your cat and your hopes.

And beyond that, you've gained something—a little more knowledge and a lot more compassion. You've learned the value of the routine you scorned and the importance of the job you took for granted. But most of all, you've learned what a "7.6 percent unemployment rate" really means.

Source: Jan Halvorsen, "How It Feels to Be Out of Work," *Newsweek* (September 22, 1980), p. 17.

The final five chapters of this book describe the fundamental institutions of society. As noted in Chapter 2, institutions are social arrangements that channel behavior in prescribed ways in the important areas of social life. They are interrelated sets of normative elements—norms, values, and role expectations—that the people making up the society have devised and passed on to succeeding generations in order to provide "permanent" solutions to society's perpetually unfinished business.

The institutions of society—family, education, religion, polity, and economy—are interrelated. But while there are reciprocal effects among the institutions, the economy is the most basic institution. The way that society is organized to produce and distribute goods and services is the crucial determinant in the way the other institutions are organized. We begin, then, with a chapter on the economy. The following chapters on the family, education, religion, and polity will show how strongly each is affected by the form of the economy found in the contemporary United States.

The task of this chapter is to describe the American economy. Four areas will be emphasized: the domination of huge corporations, the maldistribution of wealth, the structural transformation of the economy, and the current economic crises. We begin, though, with a brief description of the two fundamental ways societies can organize their economic activities.

CAPITALISM AND SOCIALISM

All the ways that industrialized societies organize their economic activities can be divided into one of two fundamental forms: capitalism and socialism. Each of these types will be examined in its pure form (that is, how it might exist in ideal circumstances). Although no society has a purely capitalist or socialist economy, examining these ideal types provides examples of extremes so that we can assess the American economy more accurately.

Capitalism   Several crucial conditions must be present for pure capitalism to exist. The first is private ownership of property. Individuals are encouraged to own, not only private possessions, but most important, the capital necessary to produce and distribute goods and services. In a purely capitalist society there would be no public ownership of any potentially profitable activity.

The pursuit of personal profit is the second essential ingredient of capitalism. This goal implies that individuals are free to maximize their personal circumstances. Most important, the proponents of capitalism argue that this profit-seeking by individuals has positive consequences for the society. Thus, the act of seeking individual gain through personal profit is considered morally acceptable and socially desirable.

Competition is the mechanism that keeps individual profit-seeking in check. Potential abuses such as fraud, faulty products, and exorbitant prices are negated by the existence of competitors who will soon take business away from those who violate good business judgment. So, too, economic inefficiency is minimized as market forces cause the inept to fail and the efficient to succeed.

These three elements—private property, personal profit, and competition—require a fourth condition if true capitalism is to work. This is a government policy of laissez-faire (literally, to leave alone). The government must allow the marketplace to operate unhindered. This requires a minimum of government interference in economic life. Any government intervention in the marketplace will, argue capitalists, distort the economy by negatively affecting incentives and freedom of individual choice. If left unhindered by government, the profit motive, private ownership, and competition will achieve the greatest good for the greatest number. This "greatest good" is translated into individual self-fulfillment and the general material progress of society.

Socialism

The three goals of socialism are democratism, egalitarianism, and efficiency. True socialism must be democratic. Representatives of a socialist state must be answerable and responsive to the wishes of the public they serve. Nations that claim to be socialistic but are totalitarian counter this fundamental aspect of socialism. The key to differentiating between authentic and spurious socialism is to determine who is making the decisions and whose interests are being served. Thus it is a fallacy to equate true socialism with the politicoeconomic systems found in Russia and China. These societies are socialistic in some respects; that is, their material benefits are more evenly distributed when compared to those in the United States. But the economies and governments of these countries are controlled by a single political party in an inflexible and authoritarian manner. Although they appear to have democratic elections, these countries are far from democratic. The people have no electoral choices but to "rubber stamp" the choices of the ruling party. The people in these repressive societies are denied civil liberties and freedoms that should be the hallmark of a socialist society. In a pure socialist society democratic relations must be found throughout the social structure: in government, at work, at school, and in the community.

The second principle of socialism is egalitarianism. This goal is equality: equality of opportunity for the self-fulfillment of all; equality rather than hierarchy in making decisions; and equality in sharing the benefits of society. Thus, there is a fundamental commitment in socialism to achieving a rough parity by leveling out gross inequities in income, property, and opportunities. The key is a leveling of the advantages so that all citizens receive the necessities (food, clothing, medical care, living wages, sick pay, retirement benefits, and shelter).

The third feature of socialism is efficiency. This refers to the organization of the society to provide, at the least possible individual and collective cost, the best conditions to meet the material needs of its citizens. This means that production of the necessary goods must be assured, as well as the distribution of the goods produced, and services offered must be planned and managed. The key method to accomplishing this economic efficiency for socialism is the substitution of public for private ownership of the means of production. The people own the basic industries, financing institutions, utilities, transportation, and communication companies. The goal is serving the public, not making profit (as is the case in capitalism). Thus the government would plan to achieve societal goals such as protecting the environment, combatting pollution, saving natural resources, and developing new technologies. Socialism, it is argued, is efficient because public policy is decided by rationally assessing the needs of society and how the economy might be organized to best achieve them. This requires, of course, that the economy be regulated by the government, which acts as the agent of the people. Prices and wages are set by the government. Important industries might be run at a loss if necessary. Dislocations such as surpluses or shortages or unemployment are minimized by central planning. The goal is to run the economy for the good of the society.

THE CORPORATION-DOMINATED ECONOMY

The American economy has always been based on the principles of capitalism; however, the present economy is far removed from a free enterprise system. There are two important discrepancies between the ideal system and the real one we operate in. The American economy is no longer based on competition among more or less equal private capitalists. It is now dominated by huge corporations that, contrary to classical economic theory, control demand rather than being responsive to the demands of the market. However well the economic system might once have worked, the increasing size and power of corporations disrupt it. This calls into question just what is the appropriate economic form for a modern industrialized society. We will examine the consequences of concentrated economic power domestically and internationally, for they create many important social problems. The second contradiction of American economic life is the existence of what has been called corporate socialism: the dependence of corporations on governmental largesse, contracts, and regulation of the market for profit. We will examine these developments in turn.

Monopo-
listic
Capitalism

Karl Marx, over 100 years ago when bigness was the exception, predicted that capitalism was doomed by several inherent contradictions that will produce a class of people bent on destroying it. The most significant of these contradictions for our purposes is the inevitability of monopolies.* Marx hypothesized that free enterprise will result in some firms becoming bigger and bigger as they eliminate their opposition or absorb smaller competing firms. The ultimate result of this process is the existence of a monopoly in each of the various sectors of the economy. Monopolies, of course, are antithetical to the free-enterprise system because they, not supply and demand, determine the price and the quality of the product.

*Marx prophesied that capitalism carried the seeds of its own destruction. In addition to resulting in monopolies, capitalism: (1) encourages crises—inflation, slumps, depressions—because the lack of centralized planning will mean overproduction of some goods and underproduction of others; (2) encourages mass production for expansion and profits but in so doing a social class, the proletariat, is created that has the goal of equalizing the distribution of profits; (3) demands the introduction of labor-saving machinery, which forces unemployment and a more hostile proletariat; and (4) will control the state, the effect of which is that the state will pass laws favoring the wealthy, thereby incurring the further wrath of the proletariat. All these factors increase the probability of the proletariat building class consciousness, which is the condition necessary before class conflict and the ushering in of a new economic system.[1]

For the most part, the evidence in American society upholds Marx's prediction. Although there are a few corporations that are virtual monopolies (Xerox, American Telephone and Telegraph, and IBM), most sectors of the American economy are dominated by **shared monopolies.** Instead of a single corporation controlling an industry, the situation is one in which a small number of large firms dominate an industry. When four or fewer firms supply 50 percent or more of a particular market, a shared monopoly results, which performs much as a monopoly or cartel would. Most economists agree that above this level of concentration—a four-firm ratio of 50 percent— the economic costs of shared monopoly are most manifest. Government data from 1977 show that a number of industries are highly concentrated. Some of the industries in which the four largest companies combine to supply more than 50 percent of the market follow:[2]

Percentage of Market

light bulbs	90
breakfast cereals	89
turbines/generators	86
aluminum	76
chocolate/cocoa	73
photography equipment	72
brewing	64
guided missiles	64
roasted coffee	61

Shared monopolies raise the cost to consumers considerably and thus are a major source of inflation. Two examples make this point:

☐ In 1980 the Federal Trade Commission, after an eight-year study, released data showing that consumers had paid more than $1.2 billion in higher prices for ready-to-eat cereals over a fifteen-year period. These overcharges of 15 percent, it was alleged, were the direct result of the monopoly in the cereal industry by Kellogg, General Mills, and General Foods. In one year alone, consumers paid $100 million more than they would have for cereals if there had been a more competitive market.[3]

☐ In April 1979 the sales of American cars declined by 42 percent. Under the principle of supply and demand, auto prices should have fallen under these conditions, yet they were raised an average of $500 per car.[4]

This trend toward ever-greater concentration among the largest American business concerns has accelerated because of two activities—mergers and interlocking directorates.

Megamergers. In 1978 the sale of conglomerate mergers cost approximately $5 billion. Just two years later, the amount had increased to an astonishing $44.3 billion, and the 1981 total approached $70 billion. The Reagan administration encouraged these mergers by relaxing the antitrust law enforcement on the grounds that efficient firms should not be hobbled.

Paradoxically, President Reagan opposed big government on the grounds that it is wasteful, while claiming that the bigger businesses get, the more efficient they become.[5] In 1981 DuPont gained control of Conoco, the ninth-largest oil company, in the biggest corporate takeover in history; Standard Oil of Ohio bought Kennecott, the major copper producer; and Fluor Corporation bought St. Joe Minerals.[6]

This trend has increased the likelihood of monopoly or shared monopolies. Larger firms have more influence over government policy. They have increased leverage to threaten to lay off workers or move jobs abroad if they do not get favorable government treatment such as tax breaks and the relaxation of regulations.[7]

Defenders of a free and competitive enterprise system should attack the existence of monopolies and shared monopolies as un-American. There should be strong support of governmental efforts to break up the largest and most powerful corporations. A decade ago, Mark S. Green offered the following commentary:

> Huey Long once prophesied that fascism would come to the United States first in the form of antifascism. So too with socialism—*corporate* socialism. Under the banner of free enterprise, up to two-thirds of American manufacturing has been metamorphosed into a "closed enterprise system." Although businessmen spoke the language of competitive capitalism, each sought refuge for themselves: price-fixing, parallel pricing, mergers, excessive advertising, quotas, subsidies, and tax favoritism. While defenders of the American dream guarded against socialism from the left, it arrived unannounced from the right.[8]

Interlocking Directorates. Another mechanism for the ever-greater concentration of the size and power of the largest corporations is interlocking directorates, the linkage between corporations that results when an individual serves on the board of directors of two companies (a direct interlock) or when two companies each have a director on the board of a third company (an indirect interlock). Such arrangements have great potential to benefit the interlocked companies by reducing competition through the sharing of information and the coordination of policies. As a Senate report has put it:

> Personal interlocks between business leaders may lead to a concentration of economic or fiscal control in a few hands. There is in this the danger of a business elite, an ingrown group impervious to outside forces, intolerant of dissent, and protective of the status quo, charting the direction of production and investment in one of several industries.[9]

In 1914, passage of the Clayton Act made it illegal for a person to serve simultaneously on corporate boards of two companies that were in direct competition with each other. Financial institutions and indirect interlocks, however, were exempt. Moreover, the government has had difficulty in determining what constitutes "direct competition." The result is that despite the prohibition, interlocking directorates are widespread. For example, there is a direct interlock between AT&T and Citicorp, linking a customer of financial services and a lending institution. Indirect interlocks, even among competitors, are commonplace. IBM and AT&T, for example, are competitors in telecommunications equipment and services, yet in 1976 they were indirectly linked through common memberships on the boards of twenty-two other companies.

Evidence of the proliferation of interlocking directorates is substantial.[10] In 1976, for example, each of the thirteen largest corporations (holding one-eighth of the nation's corporate assets) had an average of 4.5 direct and 122.5 indirect links with the other twelve.[11] Obviously the potential for cohesiveness, common action, and unified power is strong among the directors linked in this tight network.

Instead of functioning as a free enterprise system, then, the American economy is controlled by huge corporations that have political power to guarantee their privileged positions. These companies need not be concerned with sound business principles and quality products, because there is no real threat of competition. In other words, the concentration of industrial wealth means that the principles of free enterprise cannot work.[12] Nevertheless, many large corporations devote considerable efforts to convincing the public that the American economy *is* competitive despite the evidence. Many advertisements depict the economy as an Adam Smith style of free market with competition among innumerable small competitors. This, however, is a dream world. Competition does exist among the mom-and-pop stores, but they control only a minute portion of the nation's assets. The largest assets are located among the very large corporations, and competition there is virtually nonexistent.[13]

Multi-national Corpora-tions

The thesis of the previous section was that there is a trend for corporations to increase in size resulting, eventually, in huge enterprises that join with other large companies to form effective monopolies. This process of economic concentration provides the largest companies with enormous economic and political power. Another trend—the globalization of America's largest corporations—makes their power all the greater. This fact of international economic life has very important implications for social problems, both domestically and abroad.

There has been a tendency of late for American corporations to increase their foreign investments sharply. Why are American corporations shifting more and more of their total assets outside of the U.S.? The obvious answer is that the rate of profit tends to be higher abroad. Resources necessary for manufacture and production tend to be cheaper in many other nations, and labor costs are substantially lower. Wages in general are much lower than in the U.S., and unions are nonexistent.

The consequences of this shift in production from the U.S. to outside are significant. Most important is the drying up of many semi- and unskilled jobs. The effects of the increased unemployment are twofold: increased welfare costs and increased discontent among those in the working class.

We will return to this problem of domestic job losses through overseas capital investments later in this chapter when deindustrialization is discussed.

The problems of domestic unemployment exacerbated by overseas investment are the problems of lost revenues through taxes and a negative balance of payments. Tax revenues are lost because corporations can escape domestic taxes by having goods produced overseas and by undervaluing exports and overvaluing imports. Indirectly, taxes are also lost by increased unemployment. The balance-of-payments problem is aggravated by the flow of investment money overseas and the purchase of goods produced in foreign countries.

Another result of the twin processes of concentration and internationalization of corporations is the enormous power wielded by the gigantic multinational corporation. In essence, the largest corporations control the world economy. Their decisions to build or not to build, to relocate a plant, to start a new product, or to scrap an old one have a tremendous impact on the lives of ordinary citizens in the countries they operate from and invest in.

In their desire to tap low-wage workers the multinational corporations have tended to locate in poor countries. On the surface this would appear to have positive consequences for these nations (e.g., by providing a higher standard of living and access to modern technology). Unfortunately, this has not been the case. One reason is that the profits generated in these countries tend to be expatriated back to the United States in the form of dividends. Second, global companies do not have a great impact in easing the unemployment of the poor nations because they use advanced technology whenever feasible, and this reduces the demand for jobs. Third, the multinational companies tend to exploit the natural resources of the poor countries. An important consequence of this abuse is that exploited countries are beginning to unite in order to curb the abuses of the corporations. The Organization of Petroleum Exporting Countries (OPEC) was formed to demand higher prices in order to compensate for many years of exploitation and to achieve independence from the multinationals. The immediate result was an increase in the price of oil by approximately 500 percent. Organizations are being formed also among the countries exporting copper, tin, bauxite, coffee, and tea. Unfortunately, these efforts, although directed at the multinational companies, are paid for by the American consumer since the U.S. companies merely raise their retail prices accordingly.

Barnet and Muller have summarized the negative impact of global corporations on underdeveloped countries in the following statement:

> It is an unhappy fact that the development policies pursued by international corporations . . . contributed more to the exacerbation of world poverty, world unemployment, and world inequality than to their solution. . . . The unfortunate role of the multinational business in maintaining and increasing worldwide poverty results primarily from the dismal reality that global corporations and poor countries have different—indeed, conflicting—interests, priorities, and needs. The primary interest of the corporation is profit maximization, and

this means that it is often advantageous for the balance sheet if income is diverted from poor countries. Eager as they are to be good corporate citizens, the managers owe their primary allegiance to company shareholders. Their businesses, they like to say, are neither charities nor welfare organizations, although some do devote modest resources to good works. The claims of the global corporations rest instead on a theory of the marketplace which says, in effect, that by enriching themselves they enrich the whole world. This, unfortunately, has not been the reality.[14]

Finally, multinational corporations tend to meddle in the internal affairs of other nations in order to protect their investments and maximize profits. Two examples of this activity are: (1) the active involvement of IT&T in the overthrow of the socialist government in Chile, and (2) the support of various oil companies to keep the Reza Shah in power in Iran.

CAPITALISM AND INEQUALITY

Inequality is endemic to capitalism. In the competition for profits there are winners and losers. We have seen how corporate wealth is concentrated through shared monopolies and interlocking directorates. Individuals, too, are advantaged or disadvantaged by the structure of capitalism. Let's consider four additional manifestations of inequality that occur in the contemporary American version of capitalism—the concentration of private wealth, the concentration of want and misery, the segmented labor market, and the capitalist patriarchy.

Concentration of Private Wealth

The wealth in America is concentrated among the few. "Approximately 1.6 percent of the population own 80 percent of all capital stock, 100 percent of all state and municipal bonds, and 88.5 percent of all corporate bonds."[15] Looked at another way, 0.5 percent of the population own 20 percent of all the wealth. And as Maurice Zeitlin has pointed out, contrary to popular belief, the amount the wealthy own has remained stable over the years.

> Since the end of World War II, there has been no change in their (the wealthy) share of the nation's wealth; it has been constant in every year studied, at roughly five-year intervals, since 1945. The richest 1 percent own a quarter, and the top half of 1 percent own a fifth, of the combined market worth of everything owned by every American. Remarkably, economic historians who have culled manuscript census reports on the past century report that on the eve of the Civil War the rich had the same cut of the total: The top 1 percent owned 24 percent in 1860 and 24.9 percent in 1969 (the latest year thoroughly studied). Through all the tumultuous changes since then—the Civil War and the emancipation of the slaves, the Populist and Progressive movements, the Great Depression, the New Deal, progressive taxation, the mass organization of industrial workers, and World Wars I and II—this class has held on to everything it had. They owned America then and they own it now.[16]

A few families are fabulously wealthy. Michael Parenti describes the holdings of the DuPonts and the Rockefellers in the following passage:

> The DuPont family controls eight of the largest defense contractors and grossed over $15 billion in military contracts during the Vietnam war. The DuPonts control ten corporations that each have over $1 billion in assets, including General Motors, Coca-Cola and United Brands, along with many smaller firms. The DuPonts serve as trustees of scores of colleges. They own about forty manorial estates and private museums in Delaware alone, and, in an attempt to keep the money in the family, have set up thirty-one tax-exempt foundations. The family is frequently the largest contributor to Republican presidential campaigns and has financed right-wing and antilabor organizations such as the proto-fascist American Liberty League and the American Conservative Union. In 1976 Pierre DuPont won the governorship of Delaware.
>
> Another powerful family enterprise, that of the Rockefellers, holds over $300 billion in corporate wealth, extending into just about every industry in every state of the Union and every nation in the non-socialist world. The Rockefellers control five of the twelve largest oil companies and four of the largest banks in the world. They finance universities, churches, "cultural centers," and youth organizations. At one time or another, they or their close associates have occupied the offices of the president, vice-president, secretaries of State, Commerce, Defense, and other cabinet posts, the Federal Reserve Board, the governorships of several states, key positions in the Central Intelligence Agency (CIA), the U.S. Senate and House, and the Council on Foreign Relations.[17]

Concentration of Want and Misery

The inequality generated by a capitalist economy has a dark side. Summarizing the 1982 data on poverty (found in Chapter 11), 15 percent of the population (34.4 million Americans) are below the poverty line—an increase of 2.6 million persons from 1981. According to the National Council on Economic Opportunity, another 30 million are on the edge of poverty.[18] The data indicate that the poor are concentrated among certain social categories, especially people of color and families headed by women.

Again, summarizing from earlier chapters, research strongly substantiates how the "life chances" of the poor are jeopardized by their lack of resources. The fewer the resources available, the greater are the possibilities for any of the following to occur:

- Premature births and babies born mentally retarded because of prenatal malnourishment;
- Below average life expectancy;
- Death from tuberculosis, influenza, pneumonia, cancer of the stomach, lung, bronchus, and trachea, and death from accidents;
- Impaired health because of differences in diet, sanitary facilities, shelter, and medical care;
- More frequent and longer periods of illness;
- An arrest, conviction, and serving of a longer sentence for a given violation;
- A lower than average level of educational attainment;
- Spouse and child abuse, divorce, and desertion.

Thus, the economic position of a family has very telling consequences on the probability of good health, educational attainment, justice, and a stable marriage.

Segmented Labor Market

The capitalist economy is divided into two separate sectors that have different characteristics, different roles, and different rewards for laborers within each.[19] The primary sector is composed of large, bureaucratic organizations with relatively stable production and sales. Jobs within this sector require developed skills, are relatively well paid, occur in good working conditions, and are stable. Within this sector there are two types of jobs. The first type, those in the upper tier, are high status professional and managerial jobs. The pay is very good for the highly educated persons in these jobs. They have a high degree of personal autonomy, and the jobs offer variety, creativity, and initiative. Upward mobility is likely for those who are successful. The second type, the lower-tier jobs within the primary sector, are held by working-class persons. The jobs are either white-collar clerical or blue-collar skilled and semi-skilled. The jobs are repetitive and mobility is limited. The jobs are relatively secure because of unionization, although much more vulnerable than those in the upper tier. When times are difficult, these workers tend to be laid off rather than terminated.

The secondary economic sector is composed of marginal firms where product demand is unstable. Jobs within this sector are characterized by poor working conditions, low wages, few opportunities for advancement, and little job security. Little education or skill is required to perform these tasks. Workers beginning in the secondary sector tend to get locked in because they lack the skills required in the primary sector and they usually have unstable work histories. A common interpretation of this problem is that secondary sector workers are in these dead-end jobs because of their pathology—poor work history, lack of skills, and lack of motivation. Such an explanation, however, blames the victim.[20] Poor work histories tend to be the result of unemployment caused by the production of marginal products and the lack of job security. Similarly, these workers have few, if any, incentives to learn new skills or stay for long periods with an employer because of the structural impediments to upward mobility. And, unlike the primary sector, workers in the secondary sector are more likely to experience harsh and capricious work discipline from supervisors, primarily because there are no unions.

The significance of this dual labor market is twofold. First, placement in one of these sectors corresponds with social class, which tends to be perpetuated from generation to generation. And second, its existence reinforces racial, ethnic, and gender divisions in the labor force. White males, while found in both segments, tend to predominate in the upper tier of the primary sector. White females tend to be clerks in the lower tier of the primary sector, and white ethnics tend to be overrepresented in the production lines of the lower tier of the primary sector. Males and females of color are found disproportionately in the secondary sector. This explains why unemployment rates for blacks and Hispanics are consistently twice as high as that for whites. It explains the persistent wage differences found by race and gender. It also explains the vast overrepresentation of people of color and women living in poverty. Referring to women, Ehrenreich and Stallard have argued that occupational segregation makes a crucial difference:

> For women, employment is not necessarily an antidote to poverty. The jobs that are available to us are part of the problem. The list is familiar—clerical work, sales, light manufacturing, and the catchall category, "service work," which includes nurse's aides and grade-school teachers, waitresses, and welfare caseworkers. Only 20 out of 420 listed occupations account for 80 percent of employed women, and it is this occupational segregation that accounts for women's low average earnings. In general, "women's work" not only pays less than men's but is less inflation proof. . . . The extreme occupational segregation of women in our society makes for a crucial difference between women's poverty and men's. For men, poverty is often a consequence of unemployment, and is curable by getting a job. But for women, concentrated in the low-wage stratum of the work force, a job may not be a solution to poverty. According to the National Advisory Council on Economic Opportunities, "poverty among hundreds of thousands of women already working underlines the failure of the 'job' solution. Of the mothers working outside the house who headed households with children less than 18 years old in 1978, more than one quarter had incomes below the poverty level."[21]

Similarly, people of color are doubly disadvantaged:

> The combination of racial [disadvantage] with the primary-secondary segmentation compounds the immobility, low wages, and poor working conditions of the large number of black workers [and we would add Hispanics, Native Americans, and others of color] who participate in the secondary labor market. On the whole they are considerably worse off than the white poor and the near poor who work in the secondary sector.[22]

Capitalist Patriarchy

Closely tied to segmented labor markets is the phenomenon of capitalist patriarchy. Although male supremacy (patriarchy) existed before capitalism and is found in noncapitalist societies today, a strong relationship between the two helps to explain the present oppression of women in American society.[23] Current sexual inequality results from a long history of patriarchal social relations where men have consciously kept women in subordinate roles at work and in the home. Men as workers consistently have acted in their own interests to retain power and to keep women either out of their occupations or in subordinate and poorly paid work roles. Historically through their unions, males insisted that the higher-status and better-paying jobs be exclusively male. They lobbied legislatures to pass legislation supportive of male exclusiveness in occupations and in opposition to such equalization measures as minimum wages for women. Also, the male unions prevented women from gaining the skills that would lead them to equal paying jobs. The National Typographical Union in 1854, for example, insisted that women not only be refused jobs as compositors but that they not be taught the skills necessary to be a compositor.[24]

Throughout American history, capitalists have used sexual inequality in the workplace to their advantage. Women were hired because they would work for less money than men, which made men all the more fearful of women in the workplace. Capitalists even used the threat of hiring cheaper women to take the place of more expensive men to keep the wages of both sexes down and to lessen labor militancy.

In contemporary American society, capitalism and patriarchy interact to oppress women. Males and females are accorded different, and unequal, positions in church, government, school, work, and family activities. Looking only at work, women and men do different work both in the family and in the labor force. This division of labor between the sexes preserves the differential power, privilege, and prestige of men.[25] In monetary terms, in 1981 the average female employee earned 59 percent of the average male employee's salary. This difference is even more substantial than it appears at first glance. In 1983 the Census Bureau estimated that the gap in lifetime earnings between males and females is approximately $500,000 if they are high school graduates and $1.6 million if they are college graduates.[26] When the type of work is considered, women are vastly overrepresented in non-leadership and limited mobility jobs—figures for women are: 98 percent of secretaries, 97 percent of receptionists, 94 percent of bank tellers, 93 percent of telephone operators, 93 percent of nurses, and 86 percent of cashiers.[27] Both of these examples—percent of income and type of work—give men power over women in the public sphere.

THE STRUCTURAL TRANSFORMATION OF THE ECONOMY: AMERICAN CAPITALISM IN CRISIS

There have been two fundamental turning points in human history.[28] First, the Neolithic Revolution began about 8,000 B.C., marking the transition from nomadic pastoral life (where the animal and vegetable sources of food were hunted and gathered) to life in settlements based on agriculture. During this phase of human existence cities were built, tools were developed and used, language, numbers, and other symbols became more sophisticated, and mining and metal working were developed.

The second fundamental change began in Great Britain in the 1780s—the Industrial Revolution. This revolution was characterized by the following:[29]

□ Small-scale farming declined and was replaced by large-scale commercial agriculture. One indication of when the industrial revolution occurred in a country was when the number of farm workers fell below 50 percent of the labor force: this happened in Great Britain in 1780, in Belgium in 1850, in the eastern United States before 1860, in Australia before 1870, in Germany in 1875, in France about 1890, and in the U.S.S.R. in 1947.[30]
□ Industry (manufacturing and mining) surpassed agriculture as an employer.
□ Employment at home or near home declined and was replaced by work at central locations such as factories and shops.
□ Urban populations grew rapidly.

□ Intensification of the division of labor occurred, which meant the decline of craftsmen and the rise of specialists trained to do repeated tasks.

□ Machines replaced animals as an energy source.

□ Life at work became increasingly coordinated and standardized. Factory life was bureaucratized, the clock dominated, and parts became interchangeable.

□ New forms of transportation and communication developed to increase geographical mobility and to unify previously isolated regions.

□ Wood and animal substances were replaced substantially by iron, coal, petroleum, rubber, and other substitutes.

□ The development of mercantile, materialist, and competitive values had a profound effect on politics, culture, science, philosophy, and religion.

While the first revolution, the Neolithic Agricultural Revolution, took almost 10,000 years to run its course, the second lasted but 200 years. The Industrial Revolution really involved three distinct but related technological revolutions, each of which brought a fundamental change in the relationship of people and work. The first phase lasted about 60 years in Great Britain and involved primarily the application of steam power to textiles, mining, manufacturing, and transportation. The second phase of the industrial revolution occurred largely between 1860 and 1910 in the United States, Great Britain, and Germany. It was marked by a significant cluster of inventions and discoveries—the use of oil and electricity as energy sources for industry and transportation and the invention and development of the telephone, telegraph, the automobile, the airplane, and the first plastics. The final stage of the industrial revolution is still in progress although in decline since about 1970. The major scientific technological breakthroughs of this stage were atomic fission and fusion, supersonic aircraft and missiles, television, computers, and biotechnology. This third industrial revolution has resulted in a major transformation that sets the stage for a new era. Whereas employment throughout the industrial revolution was characterized by ever greater domination by manufacturing, now employment has begun to shift toward service occupations and the collection, storage, and dissemination of information.

This worldwide trend is confirmed by 1980 data showing that more people are employed in service occupations (such as teaching, office work, banking, insurance, accounting, retailing, government, and mail delivery) than in manufacturing and related industries in the United States, Great Britain, Canada, Australia, New Zealand, Japan, Sweden, Norway, Denmark, Finland, France, Austria, Italy, Switzerland, West Germany, East Germany, the Netherlands, Belgium, and Luxembourg.[31]

The present generation is in the midst of social and technological changes that are more far-reaching and are occurring faster than at any other time in human history.[32] Manufacturing, the backbone of the American economy in this century, is no longer the dominant source of employment. Today there are more workers involved in the generating, processing, analyzing, and distributing of information and similar services than are found in agriculture, mining, and manufacturing combined.[33]

TABLE 13–1   Selected Characteristics of the U.S. Labor Force, 1940 and 1980

	1940	1980
Percentage in production of goods (agriculture, mining, construction and manufacturing)	54%	32%
Proportion in white-collar occupations	31	54
Proportion of workforce age 25–29 with college degree	6	25

Source: Table constructed from data found in Eli Ginzberg, "The Mechanization of Work," *Scientific American* 247 (September 1982), pp. 66–75.

Some startling technological advances have been made, especially in the past decade or so. The unraveling of the mysteries of the genetic code has led to genetic engineering. Satellites have permitted instant global communication. Fiber optics and lasers have applications in a wide range of fields. And perhaps most significant, the development of microprocessors has revolutionized computers, the storage and retrieval of information, and the development of robots.

Automation and Employment

Robots are a good example of how the workplace is being transformed by the influx of microprocessors. Robots can be programmed to lift, weld, paint, assemble, package, and inspect products on the assembly line. Presently, robots cost about $4 an hour (amortizing their cost and maintenance over an eight-year life span) while assembly line workers cost about $16 per hour in wages and benefits. Not only are they cost effective but robots do not get bored, get tired, go on strike, require cost of living increases, or bicker among themselves. Not too surprisingly, capitalists are purchasing robots to replace workers at an ever-increasing rate. The already depressed sectors of the economy such as automobile manufacturing are especially vulnerable to robots. General Motors had 1,500 robots at the end of 1982 and expects to have 20,000 by the end of 1993. The result, of course, will be fewer and fewer industrial jobs, and for the workers who remain, less and less leverage in bargaining with management. One estimate is that by 1990 robots and other forms of automation will reduce the number of jobs in American industry by 3 million.[34]

In addition to automation three other factors explain the decline of the number of manufacturing jobs. First, the population growth rate, which has been high from the post-war baby boom, has stabilized at a low rate, significantly reducing the demand for many products. Second, a decline in manufacturing has resulted from foreign competition. The steel industry provides a good example of this. Following World War II, the United States produced 50 percent of the world's steel, but in 1982 it produced only 13 percent, resulting in a 57 percent decline in steel mill jobs since 1957. Other nations, especially Japan and West Germany, were more competitive in the world market because of more efficient plants. The third reason for the decline of manufacturing jobs is that the management in U.S. companies have made a series of miscalculations. For example, they were laggard in modernizing plants, they did not anticipate the consumer demand for fuel-efficient transportation that resulted from high energy costs, and they opted for cosmetic style changes to stimulate demand rather than improving their product.

The result is that the old-line manufacturing industries such as steel, automobiles, rubber, and textiles have faded in importance. Over 1,500 plants in these industries have closed permanently since 1975, and, literally millions of jobs have been lost that will not be replaced. Moreover, all of the data suggest that this trend will continue. Peter Drucker, an esteemed management expert, has predicted that in the next twenty-five years as many as 15 million manufacturing jobs will evaporate and only about 5 to 10 percent of the work force will hold manufacturing jobs—a figure roughly equivalent to the proportion now engaged in agriculture.[35] The dramatic changes of today and in the near future create turmoil in the economy and for individuals and families confronted with the loss of traditional jobs and accelerated change.[36]

Capital Flight and Unemployment

Another force—capitalism—converges with massive technological change to heighten the economic crises confronting us today. The goal of corporate executives is the maximization of profit. Corporate self-interest supersedes all other considerations as corporate leaders make their decisions. When profit motives dominate decision making, it makes good corporate sense to replace workers with robots and especially to move operations to another region or another nation where wages are lower and the work force more docile. Economists Bluestone and Harrison have shown how the capitalist quest for profits has led to much of the current economic crisis.[37] Their thesis is that corporations, in their quest for profits, have deindustrialized America by closing plants and moving them to more profitable geographical and social climates.

This deindustrialization of America occurs because of four actions by profit-maximizing corporations. First, corporations use their excess profits to purchase companies in related or unrelated enterprises rather than to expand and modernize their plants. U.S. Steel, for example, paid $6 billion to acquire Marathon Oil—money it could have spent to rebuild its antiquated plants so that they would be more competitive with the Japanese and German steel companies. This trend toward megamergers has at least two negative consequences: (1) it increases the centralization of capital, which reduces competition and raises prices for consumers; and (2) it diminishes the number of jobs.

A second corporate action that deindustrializes America involves the role of banks. The decision by banks to grant or withhold loans is often the crucial difference in the survival of a business. Bluestone and Harrison cite the example of the shutdown of the Youngstown Sheet and Tube Company in Ohio. Youngstown Sheet and Tube sought loans to finance the modernizing of their plant, but the banks declined. At that very time, however, some major U.S. banks were increasing their loans dramatically to the Japanese steel industry because of greater profit.

Between 1975 and 1977 alone, Citibank increased its loans to Japanese steel from about $59 million to over $230 million. Chase Manhattan's investments in Japanese steel rose from $59 million to over $204. And the loans from the Chemical Bank of New York increased more than five times, from $15 million in 1975 to over $82 million just two years later.[38]

The third action affecting deindustrialization is the decision by U.S. firms to shift their operations overseas. Moving to foreign countries increases profits because labor is so much cheaper, the laborers are not unionized, and the company is not affected by what they consider restrictive laws in the United States. The obvious result is the loss of jobs in the United States. During the 1970s, for example, General Electric expanded its work force by 5,000 by adding 30,000 foreign jobs and reducing its U.S. employment by 25,000.[39] In 1983 Atari, a subsidiary of Warner Communications, closed its plant in Santa Clara, California, laid off 1,700 workers, and moved most of its manufacturing operations to Taiwan and Hong Kong. The decision was based on differences in wages—for example, computer assemblers in California received $8.16 an hour while those in Taiwan were paid less than $2 an hour. Other high-technology giants with plants in the Far East are Hewlett-Packard, Digital Equipment, Hughes Aircraft, General Dynamics, Emerson Electric, RCA, Sylvania, and Zenith.[40] The magnitude of this foreign investment by U.S. firms cannot be overemphasized.

Between 1950 and 1980, direct foreign investment by U.S. businesses increased *sixteen times*, from about $12 billion to $192 billion. . . . The total overseas output of American multinational corporations is now larger than the gross domestic product of every country in the world except the United States and the Soviet Union . . . [And] every $1 billion of direct private U.S. foreign investment seems to eliminate (on balance) about 26,500 domestic jobs.[41]

The fourth and final means by which corporate decisionmakers participate in the deindustrialization of America is through the internal movement of capital within the United States, primarily from the frost-belt states of the industrial northeast and midwest to the sun-belt states. For example, between 1969 and 1976 about 1.4 million jobs were lost in New England (730,000 in Massachusetts) from plant closings, particularly in the textile, apparel, and shoe industries.[42] Or consider Youngstown, Ohio where in 1977 the Youngstown Sheet and Tube Company closed, destroying 4,100 jobs. Since job layoffs have a ripple effect that cause layoffs in suppliers and other allied areas, as well as in retail areas because of reduced consumer demand, it was estimated that the loss of these 4,100 jobs would ultimately cause the loss of 12,000 to 13,000 other jobs.[43] Two years after the layoffs at

Youngstown Sheet and Tube Company, U.S. Steel's mill in Youngstown was shut down, eliminating 3,500 more jobs. Houston, Texas, on the other hand, has experienced rapid growth—from 1971 to 1978 some 99 large firms and thousands of smaller ones moved to Houston. In 1979 alone the Houston economy generated 79,000 new jobs.

This regional job gap caused by a shift in capital results in urban decay in some communities, while others undergo rapid growth. Both kinds of communities, however, experience traumatic dislocations. The decaying communities cannot afford to provide basic services because they have lost their tax base, and boom communities cannot meet the demand for new roads, sewage treatment, schools, hospitals, recreation facilities, housing, and the like.

The new technology and the shift of capital have combined to create special hardships on many workers. We will focus here on the major problem—unemployment. Unlike other historical periods when technological advances created jobs, today's technology such as the computer and other micropro-cessor devices are eliminating jobs. Moreover, many of the jobs in this new era are being exported to others countries. And, as we have seen, the abandonment of many factories in the industrial north has created dislocations. Many workers in blue-collar jobs, especially older workers, lack the training to compete for the new high-tech jobs, and many companies are unwilling to invest in their training because of their age. This generation, once accustomed to high-wage jobs, is now left with little hope. Another category, young minorities, are also highly unemployable in this new technological era because of a combination of employer discrimination and structural discrimination that has left them poorly educated.

The unemployment statistics are grim. In November 1982 the official jobless rate was 10.8 percent (12 million people). This rate, however, minimizes the actual number of unemployed persons. Not counted are those who do not look for work because they believe none is available (1.6 million, double the number since 1972). Another 2.1 million are working part time but would like full-time work. When these additional unemployed or partially employed are counted, the unemployment rate actually exeeds 17 percent.

Also hidden by the official statistics are the differences in unemployment by social category. For example, when the official rate was 10.8 percent, the rate was 9.7 percent for whites, 15.7 percent for Hispanics, and 20.2 percent for blacks.[44] Also, the unemployment rate was six times greater for machine operators than for managers and professionals. And in Flint, Michigan, a city primarily engaged in automobile manufacturing, the unemployment rate was 24.6 percent in early 1983; in Hibbing, Minnesota, where iron ore is mined, the unemployment rate was 28.4 percent.[45]

The personal costs of unemployment are devastating. First, if the unemployed are not hired back by their original employer, those that find jobs elsewhere tend to experience a decline in occupational status and income.[46]

Second, the loss of income and personal assets makes the unemployed vulnerable to unanticipated financial crises such as health problems or an accident. These events may cause them to lose their homes, file for bankruptcy, or to be unable to provide adequate health care for themselves and family members.

Third, a number of physical and mental problems are associated with the trauma of unemployment. Research evidence shows that when workers are involuntarily unemployed, they tend, when compared to the employed, to have hypertension, high cholesterol, ulcers, respiratory diseases, and hyperallergic reactions. Similarly, they are more prone to headaches, upset stomachs, depression, anxiety, and aggression.[47] Harvey Brenner, using national data from 1940–1973, found that each 1 percent increase in the unemployment rate sustained for six years resulted in:[48]

> 37,000 total deaths (including 20,000 cardiovascular deaths)
>> 920 suicides
>> 650 homicides
>> 500 deaths from cirrhosis of the liver
>> 4,000 state mental hospital admissions
>> 3,000 state prison admissions.

These pathologies are the result of the much-reduced standard of living and the wounds to the self-esteem that accompany forced unemployment. And, as

> self-esteem decreases, problems of alcoholism, child and spouse abuse, and aggression increase. . . . moreover, feelings of lost self-esteem, grief, depression, and ill health can lessen the chances of finding reemployment; this failure in turn, can exacerbate the emotional distress, generating a cycle of destruction.[49]

The irony is that what is "in fact a social disease—there simply is not enough work to go around and someone is going to be unemployed—is seen as a personal disease."[50] The unemployed blame themselves—which, given the structural nature of unemployment, is most often a case of blaming the victim.

The implications of unemployment for families are significant. In addition to the consequences of lowered affluence and purchasing power, the family is affected by the unemployed's lowered self-esteem, which may translate into withdrawal from social relationships, problem drinking, and the physical and mental abuse of spouse and children. A study in Wisconsin found, for example, that cases of child abuse increased an average of 123 percent in nine counties where the unemployment rate had increased by at least 3.1 percent. In contrast, those counties where unemployment declined tended to have reduced reports of child abuse.[51] Other negative impacts on the children of unemployed parents include: an increase in infant mortality, a disproportionately high number of infants suffering from anemia due to nutritional deficiencies, and a higher incidence of problems in school with grades and behavior.[52]

OTHER ECONOMIC PROBLEMS

Economic
Cycles

Like other industrial nations, the United States is subject to periodic inflation and deflation (see Panel 13–1). This disequilibrium occurs for two fundamental reasons. First, the American economy is strongly affected by international events. We are part of an interdependent network where decisions in other countries concerning war or peace, monetary policies, price of products, boycotts, strikes, and price increases or decreases can profoundly affect our economy. The availability and price of goods, employment patterns, and expansion or contraction of output in this country are also affected by wars, famine, drought, floods, and other disasters that occur around the world.

The second fundamental cause of economic cycles in the United States is the general governmental policy of noninterference in private business affairs. Of course, the government exerts some control through taxation, control of interest rates, and regulation of utilities and transportation, but for the most part the companies act independently. They decide what to produce, how much to produce, where to locate their plants, what to charge, how many people to employ, and how much to spend on research and development. The traditional assumption by government is that a market governed by the law of supply and demand will work for the greatest good to the greatest number. This leads to a situation where some products are overproduced while others are underproduced, creating problems of distribution, employment, and pricing. Such a system increases the probability of times when too many dollars chase too few goods, a period called inflation.[53] But rather than focus on why these stages occur, let's look at the consequences of each.

The Consequences of Inflation.   Inflation is a time of rapidly rising prices. For example, comparing prices in 1970 with those in 1980, we find the price of haircuts rose 85 percent, a pound of hamburger 110 percent, a semi-private hospital room 188 percent, a gallon of gasoline 250 percent, and a pound of coffee 266 percent.[54]

The evidence is that in 1982 the average American family with one wage-earner was worse off financially than ten years earlier. Income during this period rose by 114 percent but income taxes jumped 155 percent and Social Security taxes soared 242 percent. When the shrinkage in purchasing power is considered, after-tax income in 1972 was $9,702, and in 1982 it was $8,543 (in constant 1972 dollars).[55]

Home ownership has become much more difficult to obtain in the past decade. In 1970 the average home in Colorado, for example, cost $17,300 and required 20.9 percent of the average wage earner's income for the monthly mortgage payments, taxes, utilities, and maintenance. In 1980 the average Colorado home cost $64,100 and took 51 percent of the wage earner's income.[56]

A Marxian Analysis of Economic Depressions

[The Nineteenth Century explanation of the causes of depressions by Karl Marx] seems brilliant when compared to the muddled musings of today's mainstream economists.

Stated in its briefest and necessarily most simplified form, *Marx's labor theory of value holds that depressions occur when workers are unable to buy back all the goods they produce.* Periodically, therefore, capitalists *can't find markets for all of their merchandise.* Warehouses are overstocked, factories are forced to cut back production or shut down entirely, companies go bankrupt, workers are laid off.

Does all that sound familiar? It's exactly what has been happening these last three years.

Economists in and out of government, liberals and conservatives, concede that "things won't get better until the consumer starts buying." Robert Ortner, chief economist for the U.S. Department of Commerce, says, "Everything depends on the consumer." But who are these indispensable consumers? *For the most part, they are America's 100 million workers and their families. They haven't been buying because they can't afford to buy; their earnings don't permit them to purchase all they produce.*

Other factors have also contributed to our economic disarray, of course. An important one is the almost *three trillion dollars in military expenditures since World War II,* which have saddled us with a *trillion-dollar national debt and an annual $100 billion in interest payments.* (The military budget is, in effect, our biggest unemployment compensation program; it subsidizes more than five million workers in the arms industry, as well as three million uniformed and civilian personnel. This huge ex-

penditure, which produces nothing of value, means all of us must work harder and earn less to take up the slack.)

The Vietnam war, in particular, played an important part in bringing our economy to its current sorry state. Its cost, which reached an annual $30 billion at its peak, was met by deficit spending, and the consequences are still being felt. So are the results of the 1973 war in the Middle East, the *Arab oil embargo* and the huge increase in oil prices, the revival of international protectionism and trade wars, and the mounting indebtedness on the part of individuals, businesses, and national governments.

All these, however, are problems of the sort that a capitalist economy ought to be able to deal with. What has kept our capitalist economy from dealing with them is the *deeper sickness identified by Marx—the structural flaw that makes depressions unavoidable. When the wealthier classes have finished siphoning off their profit, rent, and interest, the working class is left short; it can't buy back what it has produced.*

Our mainstream economists begin with the assumption that the system we have is the one we must keep in perpetuity, with minor adjustments at best. Perhaps that is why they refuse to acknowledge Marx's essential contribution—his description of the *inherent defect and inherent injustice of capitalism.* Much else in Marxist doctrine may need to be revised or rejected, but any economic analysis that does not begin by recognizing the validity of that central theme is bound to wallow in confusion, incapable of offering a practical solution to our problems.

Our crisis is enduring and recurrent. Sooner or later we will enjoy a brief respite from the current recession/depression, only to plunge into an even deeper one in a short while. Twenty years ago, an unemployment rate of 3 percent was considered "normal"; now Reagan Administration economists predict a "recovery" by 1987 with a "normal" unemployment rate of 7 percent. Millions of unemployed workers are unlikely ever to return to their jobs.

In that context, to ignore the Marxist formulation is to ignore reality. When we are ready at last to cure the sickness of our economy, we will have to do so by instituting structural change—national decentralized planning, a redistribution of income in favor of the less affluent, social control of the economy and ownership of basic industries, and the introduction of what we have always preached but never practiced—government by the consent of the governed.

Nothing less will do. [Italics added]

Source: Sidney Lens, "Making Marx Respectable," *The Progressive* 47 (February, 1983), p. 16. Reprinted by permission from *The Progressive*, 409 East Main Street, Madison, Wisconsin 53703.

In 1982 the nationwide average price of a home was $82,500. The cost of buying a home for $85,000, assuming a down payment of 10 percent and a 30-year mortgage at 12 percent, is a monthly payment of $787, which does *not* include taxes, insurance, utilities, and maintenance costs. To qualify for such a loan, a person needs an income of $37,776, which eliminates all but about 3 percent of the population. But even if homes are reduced in size, say to 900 square feet of living space with no bathtub, the cost is $70,000 and only 15–20 percent of American families can qualify for such a purchase.[57]

Another cost-of-living problem is debt management. In their zeal to sell products, capitalists encourage consumers to forsake thrift and go into debt to purchase their portion of the good life. Personal debt in 1981 amounted to more than $1.5 trillion, which translates into $6,737 per capita, up from $3,613 in 1975.[58] Personal debt is often necessary but can become a burden especially in a recession or if one becomes unexpectedly ill or unemployed. The result is that many people overreach their means, have their purchases repossessed, and must, in some cases, declare bankruptcy. In 1981 456,914 bankruptcies were filed, up from 179,194 just three years earlier.[59]

The increased cost of living is seen clearly in the cost of raising children. The Department of Agriculture estimated that a child born in 1979 will cost $134,414 to raise to age eighteen. In contrast, a child born in 1960 cost a comparatively modest $37,274 to raise to age eighteen.[60]

Similarly, the cost of a college education has increased dramatically. In 1980–1981 the average annual cost of tuition, room and board, transportation, books and personal expenses averaged $6,082 in a private school and $3,409 in a public school. These costs were 90 percent higher than those in 1970. The average yearly increase in tuition of about 10 percent results in a dropout rate of about 2 percent of students currently enrolled.[61]

Another group especially hard hit during inflationary periods are those people on fixed incomes (e.g., welfare recipients, teachers, nurses, assembly line workers, postal employees, and retired persons on pensions). These persons lose purchasing power during high inflation and therefore must restrict purchases to necessities. But even the necessities may be out of reach for many, as happened with the recent rapid rise in utility, phone, and food prices.

Other victims of inflation are organizations dependent on tax revenues. State agencies, school districts, universities, communities, and states all suffer from the burden of increased expenses (fuel, goods, services, salaries) in inflationary times. Quality education is also a victim of inflation. Inflation forces school districts to allot greater portions of their budgets to non-educational expenditures: fuel, construction, power, and interest costs. Unless these districts raise taxes to cover the increased inflation, the amount spent for actual education (teachers, equipment, special programs) declines. Typically, however, the answer is to reduce special education classes, increase class size, and spend less on teaching materials.

The Consequences of Recession and Deflation.   The most obvious effect of an economic downturn is increased unemployment. As consumers lower

their rates of consumption, companies let employees go. The automobile industry provides a good illustration of this cycle. Because the auto industry uses 65 percent of all the rubber in the United States, 30 percent of the zinc, 24 percent of the steel, 17 percent of the aluminum, and 13 percent of the copper, workers in all of these allied industries are laid off when car sales fall. This affects some 50,000 companies supplying materials, parts, and services to automobile manufacturers. One estimate by the Nobel laureate economist Wassily Leontif is that for every $1 billion in reduced auto sales, 22,900 auto workers are laid off, and an additional 34,100 unemployed in allied industries.[62]

Recessions are hardest on those already disadvantaged. Unemployment rates are always highest for minorities. But unemployment is only one of their special problems. One expert mentioned earlier, Harvey Brenner, studied death statistics in the United States from 1914 to 1970 and concluded that every recession caused increased deaths of unborn and infants, particularly among ethnic minorities and poor whites. He has estimated that a recent two-year recession cost the lives of 10,000 to 15,000. Brenner has listed three reasons for additional deaths during a recession: the inability of lower income women to pay for prenatal care; substandard nutrition; and mental depression. The problem is compounded as poverty and inadequate diets make the subjects more susceptible to infectious diseases and other illnesses.[63]

An obvious consequence of deflationary times is a rise in bankruptcies. In 1982 business failures occurred at an annual rate of 80 per 10,000 companies, the highest rate since the record year of 1933, which was during the Great Depression.[64] Companies owned by blacks are hit especially hard by an economic recession. There are two reasons for this stronger effect: (1) the vast majority of black businesses are small and marginal; and (2) they tend to operate in low-income neighborhoods where unemployment is especially high. These two factors combine to make banks and other financial enterprises wary of loaning money to black businesses to keep them afloat in hard times.

The economic deprivation caused by hard times provides the impetus for many social changes and problems. Family life is directly affected in at least two ways. First, the fertility rate goes down. Marriages and children are postponed, and there is increased use of abortion and contraceptive methods. Second, marriages seem to reflect the tensions caused by economic worries, resulting in raised rates of divorce, separation, and desertion.

There appears to be a direct relationship between bad economic times and mental problems.[65] The stress of losing a job or the fear of losing one can cause anxiety, hypertension, depression, and low self-esteem. One study found that admissions to mental hospitals increased between 1926 and 1968 whenever the economy turned downward, then leveled off as it stabilized.[66] After the 1980 recession in Iowa, for example, researchers found increases over the same six month period in the previous year ranging from 10 to 30 percent in new patients/clients in state mental hospitals, mental health clinics, and alcohol abuse programs.[67] We also know that 1,000 additional suicides can be expected nationally for every increase of one percentage point in the unemployment rate.[68]

Increased crime also appears to be an inevitable consequence of economic hard times. A study done by the Federal Bureau of Prisons documents this trend. Researchers found that the federal prison population tended to increase noticeably roughly fifteen months (accounting for processing criminals) after periods of high unemployment.[69]

These personal and social problems associated with recession raise some serious doubts about governmental policies that actually encourage economic downturns. The Federal Reserve Board, for example, typically fights inflation by raising interest rates. This credit tightening affects the housing industry, slows down new business investment, and dampens consumer spending. Ignored, however, are the human costs of such a policy. Also disregarded are the other sources of inflation such as price fixing through shared monopolies, the increased cost of importing oil, enormous military expenditures, unbalanced government budgets, and corporate socialism.

The National Debt

In response to the demands of various pressure groups, the assumed need to grow, and the problems of the business cycle, in the last forty years government has tended to spend more tax dollars than it has taken in. We have seen how the economy has become dependent on the huge defense industry. These enormous expenditures (in excess of $250 billion annually) are considered sacrosanct by most, and they are increased yearly. These and other subsidies drain the government coffers. Recessions cause the national debt to mount because tax revenues are smaller (because of declining profits by businesses and high unemployment), and welfare costs increase. The result is a staggering budget and a huge national debt. The debt reached the half-trillion point in 1975 and $1.14 trillion by the end of fiscal 1982. This presents the federal government with financial problems of unprecedented magnitude. If the national debt is $1.14 trillion and the government must pay 9 percent interest, the interest alone amounts to $136.8 billion a year, or $372.6 million a day.

Dependence on Foreign Oil

In 1953 the United States imported 648,000 barrels of oil a day at $1.82 a barrel—a daily cost of $1,179,360. In 1980 we imported an average of 6,043,000 barrels of oil a day at approximately $26 a barrel—a daily cost of $157,118,000. This represents a tremendous drain on the United States, a negative balance of payments of many billions of dollars annually. The result is a terrific strain on the American economy that will not lessen until the U.S. becomes self-sufficient in energy resources. This is unlikely in the near term because: (1) the huge demand for energy in this country continues; and (2) the government has not committed sufficient resources to the development of alternative sources of energy (wind, tides, sun, geothermal, methane from waste, coal, and oil shale).

United States dependence on foreign oil means that if the supply were to be cut off or reduced significantly, there would be tremendous dislocations in the economy of the country and the lifestyle of Americans. The probability of a disruption in the flow of international oil is relatively high, because most of the world's oil exports come from politically sensitive areas where war, acts of terrorism, and international blackmail are always possible.

Lack of Economic Planning

The inability of governments to plan adequately for energy shortages indicates a weakness of free enterprise economies. The capitalist philosophy dating back to Adam Smith is that the government should stay out of economic affairs. According to this view, the marketplace will force businesses to make the decisions that will best benefit them, and indirectly, the citizenry. Yet when the government does receive valuable information with which it could make decisions to avert future crises, the strong tendency in the United States is to remain aloof. For example, in 1951 President Harry Truman named a commission to plan what the country should do about the likelihood of scarce resources in 1975. That commission, although underestimating the problems, foresaw the trends accurately. The report called for immediate efforts to conserve energy, for ways to safeguard outside oil sources, and for massive increases in energy output. The report was not implemented.

Ironically, the government is involved in central planning in the areas of space exploration and defense. As one commentator has said:

> The U.S. launched Mariner 10 on Nov. 3, 1973, and it flew to Venus and then to Mercury, which it circled for a total of a billion miles. It performed magnificently and sent back photographs. That took years of planning. But planning for a thing like that is one thing. Social planning and foreseeing energy shortages before they happen, that is different, and to some, slightly sinister.[70]

The issue of central planning revolves around whether the society is able *and* willing to respond to present and future social problems. Is a capitalist society capable of meeting the problems of poverty, unemployment, social neglect, population growth, energy shortages, environmental damage, and monopoly? Robert Heilbroner, a distinguished economist, has argued that we will not prepare for the problems of the future: " . . . the outlook is for what we may call 'convulsive change'—change forced upon us by external events rather than by conscious choice, by catastrophe rather than by calculation."[71]

The lack of central planning points to the undemocratic nature of American society. It is commonly believed that the people, through their economic choices, actually govern business decisions. While this is partially true, it ignores the manipulation of the public by business interests through advertising and other "hypes."[72] Neither the public nor its elected representatives are involved in the economic decisions of the giant corporations—and these decisions often have dire consequences domestically and internationally.

As the historian Andrew Hacker has argued:

> The power to make investment decisions is concentrated in a few hands, and
> it is this power which will decide what kind of a nation America will be.
> Instead of government planning there is boardroom planning that is accounta-
> ble to no outside agency: and these plans set the order of priorities on na-
> tional growth, technological innovation, and ultimately, the values and behav-
> ior of human beings. Investment decisions are sweeping in their
> ramifications—no one is unaffected by their consequences. Yet this is an area
> where neither the public nor its government is able to participate.[73]

The lack of central planning is also a result of the resistance of powerful
interest groups in society. Short-term goals such as employment for labor
groups or profit for corporations lead special interests to block government
efforts to meet future needs. The oil industry, for example, has systematically
fought any plans that would threaten its profits. Thus, the power of the
economic dominants has the effect of superseding the interests of the nation.

Coping with Zero Economic Growth

The strong tendency of capitalism is continual expansion.[74] A kind of boost-
erism has prevailed and continues to dominate which "equates growth with
progress, and finds in the concept of expansion the first principle of the
American Dream."[75] Individuals, corporations, communities, and the society
itself seemingly demand growth in technology, profits, size, and level of
affluence. The history of the United States bears vivid testimony to this
proclivity. But the present situation and the foreseeable future strongly
suggest that the United States (and all advanced technological societies)
will soon be approaching a no-growth state. This situation will result from
the depletion of resources and the drastic ecological dangers of industrial
expansion, especially from pollution and increased heat.

Will capitalism be able to meet the demands of an economic system in
which growth has ceased or been very greatly reduced? The most profound
problem will arise from the maldistribution of income. The efforts of the
lower and middle classes to improve their positions can only be met by
diminishing the absolute incomes of the upper classes. This will present
a classic confrontation between the "haves" and the "have nots." This
problem will pose extreme political and economic difficulties for capitalism.
According to Heilbroner, this situation will likely lead to a more authoritarian
system:

> The struggle for relative position would not only pit one class against another,
> but also each against all, as lower and middle groups engaged in a free-for-all
> for higher incomes. This would bring enormous inflationary pressures of the
> kind that capitalism is already beginning to experience, and would require the
> imposition of much stronger control measures than any that capitalism has yet
> succeeded in introducing—indeed, than any that capitalist governments have
> yet imagined.
>
> In bluntest terms, the question is whether the Hobbesian struggle that is
> likely to arise in such a straight-jacketed economic society would not impose

intolerable strains on the representative democratic political apparatus that has been historically associated with capitalist societies. . . .

It is possible that some capitalist nations, gifted with unusual political leadership and a responsive public, may make the necessary structural changes without surrendering their democratic achievements. At best, our inquiry establishes the approach of certain kinds of challenges, but cannot pretend to judge how individual nations may meet these challenges. For the majority of capitalist nations, however, I do not see how one can avoid the conclusion that the required transformation will be likely to exceed the capabilities of representative democracy.[76]

The Trend toward Reducing the Scope (and Cost) of Government

The current political mood in the United States is toward limiting the role of government at all levels. Inflation and the high cost of government programs have brought about a taxpayers' revolt. The passage of the Jarvis-Gann bill (Proposition 13) in California by a 2 to 1 margin in 1978 showed clearly that the voters wanted to lower their taxes, even at the cost of restricting governmental activities (indeed, for some the goal was the reduction of government because they believed that the larger the role of the government, the fewer the freedoms of the individuals). The Jarvis-Gann plan, although not successful in all states, appears to have set a precedent as legislators in other states and at the federal level have introduced similar legislation with widespread legislative, corporate, and citizen support. The election of Ronald Reagan and a number of conservatives to Congress in 1980 also indicates this trend.

This trend has several important implications. First, it will curtail the ability of the government to reduce unemployment. The rate of employment will be a function of the economy. Conservatives argue that lower taxes will encourage businesses to expand, thereby increasing the demand for workers. Others are concerned, however, that employers will take the increased profits resulting from lower taxes and increase their dividends to stockholders, which will not have the effect of easing the employment problem. Or, if plant expansion is desirable, money will be spent on automated equipment, which actually would reduce the demand for workers.

A second probable consequence of this trend will be reduced government power to plan effectively for the future. Central planning, subsidies for developing new forms of energy or methods to curb pollution, and the like will be ineffectual.

Another result, if the Jarvis-Gann fever spreads appreciably, would be the curtailment of all but essential government services. What is essential depends on "whose ox is being gored," but we can safely predict that social services such as food stamps, rent supplements, aid for dependent children, day care centers, bilingual education programs, and others will be drastically reduced or eliminated. Moreover, legislation to spread benefits to all segments of the population (such as a national health insurance program) will be soundly defeated. If these programs are curtailed, then the gap between the haves and have-nots will continue to widen, increasing the possibility of conflict.

SUMMARY

The economy is an institution. By this, sociologists mean that the economy is a patterned, organized way that has evolved in society to accomplish a key survival need—in this case the way society is organized to insure that the goods and services required for societal and individual survival are produced, distributed, and consumed. But there is a paradox to all institutions that is illustrated by the economy. While the economy is absolutely necessary, it is a source of social problems.

The particular way the American economy is organized—its norms, values, and the distribution of people in economic roles—causes some very important problems. Some of these are economic cycles, unemployment, broad differentials in remuneration by type of work, discrimination in the labor market, a consumption ethic in a time of energy and resource shortages, subsidization of the already advantaged, taking advantage of the powerless in the United States and abroad, the profit motive superseding humanitarian values, and the concentration of economic power among a relatively few huge corporations that minimizes or even destroys competition.

American society must not only cope with these problems but deal with the new ones of the present era: pollution, shortages, worldwide interdependence, stagflation, the extraordinary power of multinational companies, and increased tensions (domestically and internationally). Four fundamental changes appear necessary to this observer if the United States is to be even moderately successful in meeting these problems: (1) central planning to meet societal goals and anticipated problems; (2) a shift away from an economy dependent on defense to one that has productive consequences (mass transit, energy creation, renewal of resources, and other public works); (3) a redistribution of wealth to alleviate material suffering among the impoverished by guaranteeing decent work at an adequate minimum annual wage, and adequate health care; and (4) extension of public ownership to utilities, transportation, and all natural resources.

CHAPTER REVIEW

1. Economic activity involves the production and distribution of goods and services.

2. There are two fundamental ways society can organize its economic activities—capitalism and socialism.

3. Capitalism in its pure form involves: (a) the private ownership of property; (b) the pursuit of personal profit; (c) com-petition; and (d) a government policy of allowing the marketplace to function unhindered.

4. Socialism in its pure form involves: (a) democracy throughout the social structure; (b) equality—equality of opportunity, equality rather than hierarchy in making decisions, and equality in sharing the benefits of society; and (c) efficiency in providing the best conditions to meet the material needs of the citizens.

5. Marx's prediction that capitalism will result in an economy dominated by monopolies has been fulfilled in the United States. But rather than a single corporation dominating a sector of the economy, the United States is characterized by the existence of *shared monopolies*—where four or fewer corporations supply 50 percent or more of a particular market.

6. Economic power is concentrated in a few major corporations and banks. This concentration has been accomplished primarily through mergers and interlocking directorates.

7. The power of America's largest corporations is increased by their international activities. Multinational corporations have important consequences: (a) decline in domestic jobs; (b) crippling of the power of unions; (c) hurting the government through lost revenues in taxes and a negative balance of payments; (d) increased power of corporations over the world economy and world events; and (e) exploitation of workers and natural resources in Third World countries.

8. Inequality is endemic to capitalism. Corporate wealth and private wealth are highly concentrated. Poverty, too, is concentrated disproportionately among people of color and in households headed by women. Two features of contemporary society promote these inequities: (a) the segmented labor market; and (b) capitalist patriarchy.

9. The economy of the United States is in the midst of a major structural transformation—from one based on manufacturing to one based on the collection, storage, and dissemination of information.

10. Deindustrialization refers to the movement of capital by corporations and banks to more profitable geographical and social climates. This occurs in four ways: (a) by corporations using excess profits to purchase other companies rather than modernize their plants; (b) by banks making loans to only the successful companies (foreign or domestic); (c) by firms shifting their operations overseas; and (d) by corporations closing plants in one part of the country and opening them elsewhere.

11. Unemployment is a major economic problem created by automation and deindustrialization. The personal consequences of unemployment involve increased vulnerability to financial crises and increased susceptibility to a number of physical and mental difficulties.

12. A major economic problem facing society is economic cycles. In inflationary times people on fixed incomes are especially hurt, home ownership declines, and organizations dependent on tax revenues suffer. During economic downturns, unemployment and bankruptcies increase, minorities and the poor are especially hard hit, and crime and mental illness increase.

13. Other economic problems facing the United States are: (a) an enormous national debt; (b) dependence on foreign oil; (c) a lack of economic planning; and (d) coping with zero economic growth.

14. Two facts about institutions of society are especially important: (a) although they are interrelated, the economy is the most dominant and shapes each of the other institutions; and (b) the particular way that an institution is organized is at once a source of stability and a source of problems.

FOR FURTHER STUDY

Barry Bluestone and Bennett Harrison, *The Deindustrialization of America* (New York: Basic Books, 1982).

Richard C. Edwards, Michael Reich, and Thomas E. Weisskopf, eds. *The Capitalist System: A Radical Analysis of American Society*, 2nd ed. (Englewood Cliffs, N.J.: Prentice-Hall, 1978).

Stuart Ewen, *Captains of Consciousness: Advertising and the Social Roots of Consumer Culture* (New York: McGraw-Hill, 1976).

David M. Gordon, Richard Edwards, and Michael Reich, *Segmented, Divided Workers* (Cambridge: Cambridge University Press, 1982).

Michael Harrington, *Decade of Decision* (New York: Simon and Schuster, 1980).

Robert Heilbroner and Lester Thurow, *Five Economic Challenges* (Englewood Cliffs, N.J.: Prentice-Hall, 1981).

Barry Jones, *Sleepers Awake! Technology and the Future of Work* (Melbourne: Oxford University Press, 1982).

Robert Lekachman, *Greed is Not Enough: Reaganomics* (New York: Pantheon, 1982).

James O'Connor, *The Fiscal Crisis of the State* (New York: St. Martin's Press, 1973).

Michael Parenti, *Power and the Powerless* (New York: St. Martin's Press, 1978).

William Ryan, *Equality* (New York: Vintage Books, 1982).

Albert Szymanski, *The Capitalist State and the Politics of Class* (Cambridge, Mass.: Winthrop, 1978).

Lester Thurow, *The Zero-Sum Society* (New York: Basic Books, 1980).

Maurice Zeitlin, ed., *American Society, Inc.: Studies of Social Structure and Political Economy of the United States*, 2nd ed. (Chicago: Rand McNally, 1977).

NOTES AND REFERENCES

1. See Robert J. Werlin, "Marxist Political Analysis," *Sociological Inquiry* 42 (No. 3–4, 1972), pp. 157–181; *Karl Marx: Selected Writings in Sociology and Social Philosophy*, T. B. Bottomore, trans. (New York: McGraw-Hill, 1956), pp. 127–212. See also Michael Harrington, *The Twilight of Capitalism* (New York: Simon and Schuster, 1976).

2. "Trend Toward Bigness in Business Speeds Up," *U.S. News and World Report*, (August 24, 1981), p. 69.

3. Associated Press release (October 3, 1980).

4. Sidney Lens, "Blaming the Victims," *The Progressive* 44 (August, 1980), p. 27.

5. Richard Stout, "The Great Concentration," *Rocky Mountain News* (July 28, 1981), p. 41.

6. See, "The New Urge to Merge," *Newsweek* (July 27, 1981), pp. 50–57.

7. "Merger Madness," *The Progressive* 45 (September 1981), pp. 10–11.

8. Mark J. Green, "The High Cost of Monopoly," *The Progressive* 36 (March 1972): 4.

9. U.S. Senate Committee on Governmental Affairs, *Interlocking Directorates among the Major United States Corporations* (Washington, D.C.: Government Printing Office, 1978), p. 6.

10. See, Johannes M. Pennings, *Interlocking Directorates* (San Francisco: Jossey-Bass, 1980); and John A. Sonquist and Thomas Koenig, "Interlocking Directorates in the Top U.S. Corporations," *Insurgent Sociologist* 5 (Spring 1975): pp. 195–229.

11. Maureen Jung, Dean Purdy, and D. Stanley Eitzen, "The Corporate Inner Group," *Sociological Spectrum* 1 (July/September 1981): 317–333.

12. George S. McGovern, "The State of the Union," *Rolling Stone* (March 13, 1975), p. 25.

13. T. R. B., "Why Mobil Isn't Loved," *New Republic* (October 14, 1978), p. 3.

14. Richard Barnet and Ronald Muller, "Global Reach–1," *The New Yorker* (December 2, 1974), p. 80.

15. Michael Parenti, *Democracy for the Few*, 4th ed. (New York: St. Martin's), p. 11.

16. Maurice Zeitlin, "Who Owns America? The Same Old Gang," *The Progressive* 42 (June 1978), p. 15.

17. Parenti, *Democracy for the Few*, pp. 14–15.
18. Cited in Coleman McCarthy, "What Poor? Only 25 Million," *Fort Collins Coloradoan* (October 4, 1981), p. A-10.
19. See, Michael J. Piore, "Notes for a Theory of Labor Market Stratification," in *Labor Market Segmentation*, Richard L. Edwards et al., eds., (Lexington, Mass.: D. C. Heath, 1975), pp. 125–150; Edna Bonacich, "Advanced Capitalism and Black/White Relations in the United States: A Split Labor Market Interpretation," *American Sociological Review* 41 (1976), pp. 34–51; Ivar Berg, ed., *Sociological Perspectives on Labor Markets* (New York: Academic Press, 1981); and David M. Gordon, Richard Edwards, and Michael Reich, *Segmented Work, Divided Workers* (Cambridge: Cambridge University Press, 1982).
20. Richard C. Edwards, "The Social Relations of Production in the Firm and Labor Market Structure," in *Labor Market Segmentation*, Richard C. Edwards et al., eds., (Lexington, Mass.: D. C. Heath, 1975), pp. 3–26.
21. Barbara Ehrenreich and Karin Stallard, "The Nouveau Poor," *Ms.* (August 1982), p. 220.
22. Harold M. Baron, "Racial Domination in Advanced Capitalism," in *Labor Market Segmentation*, Richard C. Edwards et al., eds., (Lexington, Mass.: D. C. Heath, 1975), p. 205.
23. Zillah R. Eisenstein, *Capitalist Patriarchy and the Case for Socialist Feminism* (New York: Monthly Review Press, 1979).
24. Heidi I. Hartmann, "Capitalism, Patriarchy, and Job Segregation by Sex," *Signs* 1 (Spring, 1976), pp. 137–169.
25. Maxine Baca Zinn, "Sex Roles and Sexism," in D. Stanley Eitzen, *Social Problems*, 2nd ed. (Boston: Allyn and Bacon, 1983), p. 137.
26. Kathleen O'Dell, "Lifetime Pay for USA Men Twice Women's" *USA Today* (March 14, 1983), pp. 1A, 3A.
27. "Women in the U.S.—How Their Lives are Changing," *U.S. News and World Report* (November 29, 1982), p. 55.
28. This section is taken primarily from Barry Jones, *Sleepers Awake! Technology and the Future of Work* (Melbourne: Oxford University Press, 1982).
29. Ibid., pp. 2–4.
30. Ibid., p. 2.
31. Ibid., p. 35.
32. Ibid., p. 254.
33. Gary Hart, "Investing in People for the Information Age," *The Futurist* 17 (February 1983), p. 10.
34. Cited in David Halberstam, "Robots Enter Our Lives," *Parade Magazine* (April 10, 1983), p. 22.
35. Cited in Hart, "Investing in People," p. 11.
36. Issac Asimov, "Disassembling the Assembly Line," *American Way* (May 1981), pp. 13–14.
37. Barry Bluestone and Bennett Harrison, *The Deindustrialization of America* (New York: Basic Books, 1982).
38. Ibid., p. 145.
39. Ibid., p. 6.
40. John Hillkirk, "Atari Move: Start of a Tragic Trend?" *USA Today* (February 23, 1983), p. 3B.
41. Bluestone and Harrison, *Deindustrialization of America*, pp. 42, 45.
42. Ibid., p. 34.
43. Ibid., p. 69.
44. "Unemployment Rate," *Rocky Mountain News* (January 3, 1983), p. 63.
45. Peter McGrath, "Left Out," *Newsweek* (March 21, 1983), p. 29.
46. Bluestone and Harrison, *Deindustrialization of America*, p. 55.
47. From a number of studies cited in ibid., pp. 63–64.
48. Cited in ibid., p. 65.
49. Ibid., p. 66.
50. Lester Thurow, "The Cost of Unemployment," *Newsweek* (October 4, 1982), p. 70.
51. Daphne Siev White, "Unemployment's Children: They're Growing Up Old," *On Campus* 2 (April 1983), pp. 1, 8–9.
52. Ibid.
53. For analyses on the causes of inflation, see Robert L. Heilbroner, "The Inflation In Your Future," *The New York Review of Books* (May 1, 1980), pp. 6–10; Robert M. Solow, "All Simple Stories About Inflation Are Wrong," *The Washington Post* (May 18, 1980), pp. G1, G4; and Robert D. Hershey, Jr., "Inflation at 13.3%: What Is This Rapacious Thing?" *The New York Times* (February 3, 1980), Section 3, pp. 1, 8.

54. "What 10 Years Did to the Consumer's Dollar," *U.S. News & World Report* (September 8, 1980), p. 58.

55. David R. Francis, "Study Says Americans on Economic Treadmill," *Rocky Mountain News* (August 15, 1982), p. 57.

56. Bruce Wilkinson, "No Relief in Sight for Home Costs," *Rocky Mountain News* (February 9, 1983), p. F1.

57. Thomas P. Murphy, "Giving Up on the American Dream," *Forbes* (August 29, 1983), p. 166.

58. Otto Friedrich, "The American Way of Debt," *Time* (May 31, 1982), p. 46.

59. Ibid., pp. 46–49.

60. "Cost of Raising a Child Put at $134,414," Associated Press release (November 10, 1981).

61. Peter Adams, "College Crunch," *USA Today* (May 12, 1983), p. 1A.

62. Cited in Edwin McDowell, "Stalled Autos: As Detroit Goes, So Goes Toledo," *The New York Times* (June 22, 1980), Section 3, p. 4.

63. Cited in Don Kirkman, "Two-Year Recession Toll of 10,000 Babies Forecast," *Rocky Mountain News* (October 24, 1974), p. 28.

64. "Bankruptcies: Fiscal, Moral," *The Progressive* (June 1982), p. 1.

65. For a classic examination of this relationship see Emile Durkheim, *Suicide*, John A. Spaulding and George Simpson, translators

(Glencoe, Ill.: The Free Press, 1951). This book first was published in 1897.

66. M. Harvey Brenner, *Mental Illness and the Economy* (Cambridge: Harvard University Press, 1973).

67. Roger Moore, "Suicide Rises as Economy Dips in Iowa," *Des Moines Register and Tribune* (September 28, 1980), pp. 1A, 3B.

68. Cited in ibid., p. 1A.

69. Cited in Nancy Keebler, "Recession Leaves Its Mark on Family Structure," *The National Observer* (March 29, 1975), p. 4.

70. TRB, "The Case for More Planning," *Rocky Mountain News Trend* (March 30, 1975), p. 2.

71. Robert L. Heilbroner, *An Inquiry into the Human Prospect* (New York: W. W. Norton, 1974), p. 132.

72. See Stuart Ewen, *Captains of Consciousness: Advertising and the Social Roots of the Consumer Culture* (New York: McGraw-Hill, 1976).

73. Andrew Hacker, *The End of the American Era* (New York: Atheneum, 1970), p. 52.

74. This section is taken primarily from Heilbroner, *The Human Prospect*, pp. 82–95.

75. Wallace Stegner and Page Stegner, "Rocky Mountain Country," *The Atlantic Monthly* 241 (April, 1978), p. 86.

76. Heilbroner, *The Human Prospect*, pp. 88–90.

14

Families in America

Maxine Baca Zinn

"Diversity" is the word for the present state of the American family. We have more divorces, single-parent families, and mixed families from remarriages than ever before, but the ideal of marrying and having children is still very much a part of the American experience.

□ At current rates, half of all American marriages begun in the early 1980s will end in divorce.
□ The number of unmarried couples living together has more than tripled since 1970.
□ One out of four children is not living with both parents.

The list could go on and on—teenage pregnancies, up; adolescent suicides, up; birthrate, down. Over the past decade, popular and scholarly commentators have cited a seemingly endless wave of grim statistics about the shape of the American family. The

Maxine Baca Zinn is the senior author of this chapter.

trends have caused a number of concerned Americans to wonder if the family as we know it will survive the twentieth century.

And yet, other observers ask us to consider more positive developments:

☐ In a recent national survey, 78 percent of all adults said they get "a great deal" of satisfaction from their family lives; only 3 percent said "a little" or "none."
☐ In the same survey two-thirds of the married adults said they were "very happy" with their marriages; only 3 percent said "not too happy."
☐ In another recent survey of parents of children in their middle years, 88 percent said that if they had to do it over, they would choose to have children again.

☐ The vast majority of the children (71 percent) characterized their family life as "close and intimate."

Family ties are still important and strong, the optimists argue, and the predictions of the demise of the family are greatly exaggerated.

Neither the dire pessimists who believe that the family is falling apart nor the unbridled optimists who claim that the family has never been in better shape provide an accurate picture of family life in the near future. But these trends indicate that what we have come to view as the "traditional" family will no longer predominate.

Adapted from Andrew Cherlin and Frank Furstenburg, Jr., "The Family in the Year 2000," *The Futurist*, 17 (June 1983).

The primary task of this chapter is to provide an understanding of how families are related to the larger society. We risk making errors in attempting to describe any American institution since there is so much variation. The family is especially diverse, with regional, social-class, religious, racial, and ethnic differences. Yet distinct patterns may be found in family life and these patterns reflect the opportunity structure of society.

This chapter will emphasize linkages between the family and other social institutions and the diversity that different linkages produce. The connections between family and society will be revealed as we describe with "broad brushstrokes" family life in past times. This will be compared with family life in contemporary society at both macro- and microlevels. Finally, we discuss families of the future.

THE MYTHICAL AMERICAN FAMILY

Family life is difficult to think about objectively. Our perceptions are clouded by our own family experiences, by cultural ideals about family, and paradoxically, by the very familiarity of family life. Because the family is familiar, we tend to take it for granted, to view it as "natural" (see Panel 14–1). Other obstacles have handicapped the study of the family: "It is

Expectations about the family. Reality or Myth?

No one is neutral about a subject like "the family." We have all been raised in families and have strong feelings about the people we are related to and the institution that binds us to them. Here is where we experienced our first emotions and ambivalences: love and hate, joy and pain, giving and taking. Family is where people touch, physically and in their total being. Here we learned to hope, to suffer disappointment, to trust, and to be wary. Above all, family is where people get their start in life, where they experienced the most sharing and where they expect to be able to return when in need. Expectation is, in fact, the key: People *expect* families to provide "togetherness" for better or for worse, in sickness and in health, etc., as the marriage vow sets it up. And most seemingly objective observations of reality are measured against such expectations to gauge the health of the institution of family. From such expectations, we frame questions like "Is the family falling apart?" and call state and national conferences about the matter. In other words, our feelings about the family strongly affect our thinking about it.

From Renate Bridenthal, "The Family: The View from a Room of Her Own," p. 225 in *Rethinking the Family*, Barrie Thorne and Marilyn Yalom, Eds., Longman (1982).

morally sacred, and it is secret."[1] The family is not merely a social institution, it is associated with a larger societal morality of good and right. It is, at the same time, the most private of all society's institutions. The norm of privacy gives the family a secret quality that exists alongside its familiarity. To a greater extent than ever before, family life goes on behind closed doors.[2] The family is a "backstage" area where people can be relaxed and behave in ways they would not in public.[3] According to Arlene Skolnick, this privacy accounts for the deceptive quality of family life:

> Privacy results in pluralistic ignorance—we have a backstage view of our own families, but can judge others only in terms of public presentation. The gap between public norms and private behavior can be wide; marital relationships tend to be even more private and invisible than those between parents and children.[4]

We have little direct knowledge of what goes on behind closed doors, but we do know what family life *should* be. "Family" in American society is a symbol, a visual image of adults and children living together in mutually satisfying and harmonious ways. Family evokes warmth, caring, physical and psychological nurturance in a setting apart from the troubled world. Tufte and Meyerhoff have described the image of the contemporary family in the following way:

It is quintessentially the private (and some feel the only contemporary private) opportunity for vulnerability, trust, intimacy, and commitment, for lasting, pleasant and peaceful relations, for fullness of being in the human realm. The family thus is located as the physical site for a vast (and repressed) range of human expression, the valid arena (and again perhaps the only arena) where quality of life is a concern. It is in the family that we find the opportunity for psychologically bearable, nonexploitive personal life.[5]

This image characterizes the family as a refuge from an impersonal world, a place of intimacy, love, and trust where individuals may escape the competition of dehumanizing forces in modern society. Lasch named this image a "haven in a heartless world," and described it as a glorification of private life made necessary by the deprivations experienced in the public world.[6] In this image, family and society are set apart. Relations inside the family are idealized as nurturant while those outside the family, especially in business and work, are seen as competitive.

Relationships between husbands and wives and between parents and children are especially idealized in the family image. The ideal states that families are formed in the marriage of one man and one woman who will satisfy each other's emotional and physical needs till death do they part. When children are added to this exclusive dyad, then "parenting" becomes the natural extension of the husband and wife relationship. Parents mold and shape happy children (who will become successful adults) by providing "proper" child care.[7]

This view assumes a division of labor based on sex: "a breadwinner husband, freed for and identified with activities in a separate sphere, and a full-time mother defined as the core of the family."[8] It also assumes a single uniform family experience for all members of society. This image of the family is mythical in many respects. To begin with, full-time homemakers are found in few families. In 1980 only 7 percent of United States households included a father as a sole wage earner, a full-time mother and homemaker, and at least one child living at home.[9] And the "perpetually happy family" set apart from the rest of the world ignores the persistent effects of economic conditions on family life, the social inequalities that prevent some people from acquiring the good things in life, and the inevitable problems that arise as human beings go about the business of living in families.

A striking gap exists between the mythical family model and family life as we actually experience it in this society. New sociological research on the family challenges the myths and offers new perspectives. The following revisionist perspectives on the family will be presented in this chapter:

1. The family is not a natural unit but a social construction that varies according to its socioeconomic context.
2. The family and the economy are interconnected.
3. Family life in past times was different but not more stable or harmonious than in the present.
4. Diversity in American families is associated with social stratification.
5. Women and men experience the family in different ways.

AMERICAN FAMILIES OF THE PAST

Family Life
in Colonial
America

Social historians have gathered evidence that disputes many social science assumptions about the family of past times. For example, we took for granted that "extended" families—grandparents, parents, and children—living together under one roof were the predominant family structure before industrialization, and that the industrial revolution broke families down into "nuclear" families with only parents and children living together. However, historians discovered that the nuclear family has been the norm for the past 200 years, not only in America but in western Europe as well.

The family of the past was commonly assumed to be strong, stable, and happy. This stereotype, "the classical family of Western nostalgia," has often been used as a basis for making judgements about the current state of the family.[10] In reality, family life in past times was quite different from what we commonly assume it was. Setting aside the stereotypes of the past has given us a better understanding of the nature and problems of family life today.

Economy, Family, and Society.   To understand changes in the family, we must examine economic developments. Historians have described three economic periods that will be discussed in this chapter. They are (1) the family-based economy, (2) the family-wage economy, and (3) the family-consumer economy.[11]

In the first period, the household was the basic unit of the colonial economy because production occurred primarily in the home.[12] Each family provided the market with a commodity needed by other families. No sharp distinction was made between economic life and domestic life. Household members were responsible for the production of goods.

Households were nuclear in structure, that is composed of parents and nonadult children living together. Although many households contained servants, boarders, lodgers, apprentices, and other nonrelated workers, the average household did not contain extended kin.[13]

Families were not private as we know them today but were domains of work and living that were closely connected with society. Boundaries between home and society were almost nonexistent. What happened within a family was not "their own business" but was a community affair. The larger community was involved in matters of family living. For example, disobedient children were punished not only with a thrashing at the hands of fathers but also could be liable to action by the courts. Or colonial magistrates might remove a child from the care of "unseemly" parents and place him or her in some other family. Or again, a local court could order the reunion of a husband and wife who had decided to live apart.[14]

Family Roles.   In the early colonial period, marriages were arranged according to the economic needs and prospects of families. Wives and husbands were primarily workers. Women worked in the home plot and in the house, while men worked out of doors and in the fields. Women's work, while vital to the community, was performed within the context of a larger gender system. The social status of women, their power and prestige in the colonies, was inferior to that of men. Communities and families were patriarchal in every respect.

> A woman's vow to obey her spouse was repeatedly underscored by colonial writers and preachers. She owed her mate "reverent subjection" and was obliged to submit to his superior judgement in all things. New England clergymen referred to male authority as a "government" that the female must accept as "law," while Southern husbands such as William Byrd of Virginia, charged assertive wives with "impertinence." Not only were women obliged to scrupulously abide by the lawful commands of patriarchs, but they were "still subject even to those who are sinful and unkind."[15]

Women were subordinate but they were not completely set apart. The division of women's and men's work converged in the family economy.

Children, like spouses, were viewed in economic terms, as workers for the family economy. Colonial society did not recognize childhood as we do today. The prevailing view was that children were miniature adults. Demos has described the world of the colonial child in the following manner:

> His work, much of his recreation, and his closest personal contact were encompassed within the world of adults. From the age of six or seven he was set to a regular round of tasks about the house or farm (or, in the case of a craftsman's family, the shop or store). When the family went to church, or when they went visiting, he went along. In short, from his earliest years he was expected to be—or try to be—a miniature adult.[16]

The Emergence of Modern Family Life

Economy, Family and Society. In the second economic period called the *family-wage economy*, a new family form emerged. Employment at or near the home declined and was replaced by work at central locations such as factories and shops. This change led to the new concept of "going to work."[17] In the family-wage economy workers earned their living outside the home, and the household became dependent upon wages that the workers brought home.[18] As a result, in the years between the American Revolution and 1830, a modern family life emerged with qualities distinctly different from those in colonial society.

The transfer of production out of the household altered family life in two important ways. First, families surrendered functions previously concentrated in the home and took on more highly specialized functions. Second, family units became increasingly private, set apart from society by distinct boundaries.

As family functions were taken over by other institutions, the family assumed a more specialized set of functions for the larger society, specifically those of procreation, consumption, and child rearing.[19]

The separation of work and family created a division of public and private spheres of living. This privatization of family living meant that people's activities in their families were observable to fewer and fewer outsiders. As the "audience" of family behavior changed, individuals were less subject to social control by nonfamily members.

Family Roles.   In the half-century after the American Revolution, romantic love replaced economic considerations in bringing couples together.

The historical processes that were transforming the American economy produced far-reaching changes in women's and men's roles. Women were especially affected by the transformation because they lost their integral position in the economic life of America.[20]

Women in the emerging family of the middle class were not defined as workers. The home acquired a sentimental quality. It became a retreat where meaning and satisfaction were to be found. This family as a retreat altered the gender system and produced a distinguishing feature of the modern family; that is, the sharp division between the roles of husbands and wives.

> Women's activities were increasingly confined to the care of children, the nurturing of husband, and the physical maintenance of the home. Moreover, it was not unusual to refer to women as the "angels of the house" for they were said to be the moral guardians of the family. They were responsible for the ethical and spiritual character as well as the comfort and tranquility of the home.[21]

The family as a retreat was more characteristic of middle-class families than of working-class families. Changes in family life were gradual and they varied significantly from class to class. When female occupations such as carding, spinning and weaving were transferred from home to factory, the poorer women followed their traditional work and became industrial workers. Some families retained their rural economic base and sent daughters to work in factories. These women worked both outside of their homes and continued to do traditional domestic and family tasks.[22] Around the end of the eighteenth century, attitudes toward children and practices in regard to their upbringing underwent dramatic changes. These changes took place at the same time that families began to be cut off from society and that women's and men's roles became segregated. The most notable change in the new conception of children is that they began to be seen as different from adults. They were now considered more innocent. Childhood was perceived much as it is today, as a period of life worth recognizing, cherishing and even extending.[23]

Immigration, Colonization, and Family Diversity

The transformation of the American family as described above does not apply to European immigrants or people of color. As the nation's economy industrialized, wave after wave of immigrants filled the industrial labor force. Through working for wages, they became an integral part of the economy and society. Immigrant families were crucial in assisting their newly arrived kin and other members of their ethnic groups to adapt to the new society. Many immigrants came to America in family groupings or they sent for families once they were established in cities. Kin assisted in locating jobs and housing and providing other forms of support. Contrary to the typical portrayal of immigrants, their transplanted kinship and ethnic bonds did not disintegrate, but rather were maintained and regenerated in the new society.[24]

The developing capitalist economy did not provide equal opportunities for all. People of color were prevented from becoming part of the industrial labor force by a complex web of forces called internal colonialism (see Chapter 11).[25] Blacks and Chicanos were forced to be laborers in nonindustrial sectors of the economy. They were brought to this society to work in unfree, unskilled labor systems that were tightly controlled. Slavery destroyed West African kinship systems and assaulted the families that developed among the slaves by breaking them up when it suited the owners' economic interests. Chicano families, on the other hand, were adversely affected by migratory labor, but they were able to retain considerable strength due to different, less-total forms of control and the proximity to their native land. In both cases, systems of racial control shaped much of family life. In neither case was the family institution destroyed.

In the history of the family in America, the black family undoubtedly has experienced greater stress than any other. First slavery, and then the burdens of urban life with pernicious poverty and discrimination, pressed hard on family life. In the last ten years, historians have begun to revise dramatically our perceptions of the slave family. The general thrust of the revision has been to show how families adapted to adverse conditions and endured with remarkable completeness. Herbert Gutman's book, *The Black Family in Slavery and Freedom*, is the most important work in this revisionist history. Gutman presents an enormous amount of evidence to show that despite the abuses of slavery, the family as a cultural institution remained intact through the creation of kinship networks.[26] The book and television version of *Roots*, with its vivid emphasis on the strength of family bonds among slaves, dramatizes the new scholarship.[27]

Historical and economic conditions have produced variation in the family patterns of people of color. As women of color have worked outside of the home and taken care of their own families, their family roles have developed along different lines from those in the dominant society. Families were crucial to the survival of people of color as distinctive kinship patterns enabled the systematic sharing of limited resources.

FAMILIES IN CONTEMPORARY AMERICAN SOCIETY

The Family in Capitalism   The historical development of the family shows the interrelationship of family life with the economic structure of society. The emergence of capitalism moved the center of production from the domestic unit to the workplace. When the workplace became separated from the home, the family became a private domain and a unit of consumption. The third economic period, the family-consumer economy, is an extension of the family-wage system.[28]

In this period technological changes, increased productivity, and the mass production of goods created households that specialize in consumption. Economic production goes on in the capitalist economy with the labor of family members contributing to their economic standing.[29]

The modern family is characterized by its dependence on the economic market, its privacy, and its sharply divided gender system. Zaretsky has shown how in capitalism the split between work and home is related to another split—one between personal life and public life.[30] The development of subjective and personal realms encourages consumerism. The pursuit of personal life becomes a central purpose of the modern family. It is now an emotional retreat—a specialized institution focusing on the socialization of young children and the stabilization of adult personalities through identity and emotional gratification.

The separation of public and private worlds creates yet another division— division between women's and men's roles and activities. Women are identified with family roles of consumption, emotional support, and childcare while men are identified with "public" activities. This patriarchal ordering is suited to the capitalist economy. Capitalism depends on the maintenance of labor power. The domestic labor and emotional work that women do in families enables male workers to function in a capitalist economy.

The family in contemporary society is an ideal that implies a private, autonomous retreat set apart from society. This image obscures the real relationship between families and the economy. A better way of understanding the interconnection is to distinguish between family and household. While a **family** involves blood ties among husbands, wives, and children, a household is a material or economic unit.[31] **Households** are units in which people pool resources and perform certain tasks. "They are units of production, reproduction, and consumption. They are residential units within which people and resources get distributed and connected."[32] Households vary in membership, composition, and the resources they have for living, a fact not recognized by the concept "family." "Family" implies a single form but the reality of household diversity enables us to see how families exist within an economic system.

The
Changing
Compo-
sition of
Households
and
Families

According to the 1980 census, the nation had a total of 80,376,609 households. These households are defined by the census bureau as taking one of three general forms: family, nonfamily, and single-person households. First, family households consist of two or more persons living together who are related by birth or marriage. The most common family household is a married couple with or without children in the home. A single parent with one or more children also comprises a family household. Second, nonfamily households consist of two or more unrelated individuals who share living quarters. They can be nonmarried couples, of the same or opposite sex. Third, single-person households are individuals who live alone in their own separate residential units.[33]

The average American household is steadily declining in size. Three main reasons can be identified for this: (1) Families now have fewer children; (2) More families now have only one spouse in residence; and (3) An increase in single-person households has increased the overall total and decreased the average size.[34] Panel 14–2 highlights changes in American households during the 1970s. The figures indicate that the family, in its old sense of a breadwinning husband and a homemaking wife, is giving way to a variety of different forms. Two changes deserve special attention: (1) the increase in the number of families with employed wives, and (2) the increase in the number of families headed by women.

PANEL 14–2

What Happened to American Households During the 1970–1980 Decade

□ From 1970 to 1980 the total number of households rose from 63,401,000 to 79,108,000. This amounted to an increase of 24.8 percent, more than double the general population rise of 11.5 percent. During the decade the number of persons in the average household declined from 3.14 to 2.75. This drop was due to fewer children in each family, more single-parent households, and—most important—more people living alone.

□ During the decade family households fell from 81.2 percent of the total to 73.9 percent. By the same token, nonfamily households rose from 18.8 percent of the total to 26.1 percent.

□ Within the family household category, families containing a married couple declined from 86.9 percent of that group to 82.5 percent. Put another, more graphic way, the actual number of married couples increased by only 7.7 percent, one-third less than the general population rise. On the other hand, families with nonmarried heads grew by 52.3 percent.

□ Of the 8,540,000 families headed by women, 5,918,000 (or 69.3 percent) contained at least one child under the age of 18. This represented a 71.7 percent rise from 1970, when 3,447,000 homes with children had women as their heads. (As it happened, the number of solo fathers remained fairly constant, changing from 716,000 in 1970 to 736,000 in 1980.)

□ By 1980 altogether 23.4 percent of all children aged 17 or under were living with one parent, another relative, or some nonrelative. This was the situation for 17.3 percent of white children and 57.8 percent of black children.

□ Between 1970 and 1980, families where the head was a widow dropped by 49.6 percent. So did those headed by separated women, with a drop of 18.7 percent. On the other hand, the proportion of divorced women as family heads rose by 33.2 percent. Even more striking were single women ("never married" in Census terminology) whose share increased by 90.6 percent.

□ Among married couples, the proportion with no children rose by 24.2 percent, while those with 3 or more declined by 39.5 percent. However, the Census counts as "childless" older couples whose children have left home. If we focus on younger couples, we find that in 1970 among those where the husband was under 25, only 44.6 percent did not yet have any children. By 1980 the childless group had grown to 52.0 percent. And where the husband was 30 to 34, the proportion without children rose from 10.2 percent to 17.6 percent.

(continued)

□ Nonfamily households, taken together, increased from 11,919,000 to 20,682,000 between 1970 and 1980, a growth of 73.5 percent, which was more than six times that for the overall population.

□ Altogether, 6,965,000 more people were living by themselves in 1980 compared with 1970. This increase came from several sources, all of them associated with the trend away from family living. First, young people are not only marrying later, but they are living on their own while in the single state. Among those the Census calls the "never married," the number of men with residences of their own grew by 118.3 percent, while the comparable figure for women went up 89.3 percent.

□ Next came persons who were separated or divorced and no longer living with their former mates. The number of men in this category rose by 121.8 percent, with the parallel figure for women 79.4 percent. The sexual discrepancy derives from the fact that when divorced and separated women have children they generally get custody. Given that arrangement, these women fall in the category of "single heads of families" whereas their former husbands are classed as "living alone."

□ For some time, more widowed men and women have been living by themselves rather than with their adult children. The number of widows living alone rose by 31.9 percent during the decade, with the figure for widowers up 16.4 percent. But these growth rates were not as sharp as those for the other groups.

□ A total of 2,866,000 households consisted of unrelated persons sharing quarters. This group broke down as follows: 25.1 percent were 2 men living together; 19.2 percent were 2 women; and 55.8 percent were mixed-sex arrangements. In this third group, 31.5 percent had children on the premises, in most cases from the woman's previous marriage. Indeed, in only 37.2 percent of the mixed-sex households had both partners never been married. (It should be noted that these figures do not include people who spend a lot of time together but keep their own apartments.)

□ Altogether, 1970 to 1980 saw the creation of 15,707,000 new households. Of these, 55.6 percent were of the nonfamily variety. And among the 44.4 percent that were counted as family households, there were 3,518,000 new ones with single heads as opposed to 3,452,000 containing married couples. This means that only 22.0 percent of total household growth came from couples who were married. Moreover, whereas in 1970 couples with 2 or more children accounted for 28.1 percent of all households, by 1980 they were down to 19.0 percent.

Source: Andrew Hacker, ed. *U/S: A Statistical Portrait of the American People*. (New York: The Viking Press, 1983), pp. 90–91. Copyright © 1981 by Andrew Hacker. Reprinted by permission of Viking Penguin, Inc.

Slightly more than half (50.3 percent) of all married women are in the labor force.[35] Almost half of all children in husband-wife families have "working mothers." The increase in women's labor force participation has had major effects on family life. It has lowered birth rates and provided women with economic resources that must often be balanced with traditional domestic responsibilities.

The large increase in the number of families headed by women is one of the most important social developments of the recent past. In 1970, female-headed families were 10 percent of all families. By 1981 female-headed families were 18.8 percent of all families with children under 18 years of age. The number of female-headed families had increased by 2.8 million (97 percent) since 1970. There were proportionately more female-headed families in the black family population than in any other subgroup. By 1981, women headed 47.5 percent of black families with children. Among Hispanics, women headed 21.8 percent of all families in 1981. For whites, the proportion was smallest. Women headed 14.7 percent of white families with children present in 1981. There is a clear relationship between the household composition and its economic well-being. Women with children but no husband lack the economic resources of dual-earner families. The earning gap found in all occupations makes female-headed households especially vulnerable. Table 14–1 depicts the low median income of female householders when compared to husband-wife families and the increasing disparities between the two since 1970.[36]

Stratification and Family Life

The unequal distribution of society's rewards and resources determines patterns of family living. Families are imbedded in a class hierarchy. Furthermore, the family is the principal unit in the social class system. As noted in Chapter 9, most children will have the same "life chances" as their parents. The "haves" will pass on their advantages to their children and likewise, the "have-nots" will transmit their disadvantages to their offspring. A family's placement in the class system is the single most important determinant of family life.

Households in different classes "vary systematically in their ability to hook into, accumulate, and transmit wealth, wages, or welfare."[37] This variation is closely related to the connections that households and families have with other social institutions. The social networks or relationships outside the family—at work, school, church, voluntary associations—produce differential access to society's resources, and they produce class and racial differences in families.

Among the middle class, households are based on a relatively stable and secure resource base. Therefore, the "families that organize such households have boundaries that conform closely to the nuclear family ideal of autonomy and self-support. When exceptional economic resources are called for, non-familial institutions usually are available in the form of better medical coverage, expense accounts, credit at banks, and so on."[38] These links with nonfamily institutions are precisely the ones that distinguish life in middle-class families from families in other economic groups. The strongest links are with the occupations of middle-class family members, especially those of the husband-father.[39] Occupational roles greatly affect family roles and the quality of family life.[40] Occupations are part of the larger opportunity structure of society: those that are highly valued and carry high income rewards are unevenly distributed. The amount of the paycheck determines how well a given household can acquire the resources needed for survival

TABLE 14–1   Median Income by Race and Type of Family

	1970	1981	Increase 1970–1981
Type of family			
Husband-wife families*	$10,516	$25,065	138%
Wife in labor force	12,276	29,247	138
Female householder, no husband present	5,093	10,960	115
Male householder, no wife present	—	19,889	—
White families			
Husband-wife families	10,723	25,474	138
Wife in labor force	12,543	29,713	137
Female householder, no husband present	5,754	12,508	117
Male householder, no wife present	—	20,421	—
Black families			
Husband-wife families	7,816	19,624	151
Wife in labor force	9,721	25,040	158
Female householder, no husband present	3,576	7,506	110
Male householder, no wife present	—	14,489	—

*This item may be read as follows: Median income earnings for female householder families with no husbands present rose from $5,093 to $10,960, an increase of 115 percent, between 1970 and 1981.
Sources: U.S. Department of Commerce, Bureau of the Census, *Consumer Income: Income in 1970 of Families and Persons in the United States*, series P–60, no. 80, pp. 33, 35, and 37; *Money Income and Poverty Status of Families and Persons in the United States, 1981* (Advance Data), series P–60, no. 134, pp. 6, 7, 8, and 10.
Reprinted from "A Growing Crisis, Disadvantaged Women and Their Children," U.S. Commission on Civil Rights, Clearing House Publication 78 (May 1983), p. 6.

and perhaps for luxury. The job or occupation that is the source of the paycheck connects families with the opportunity structure in different ways.

In the working class, resources are dependent on hourly wages acquired in exchange for labor. When such hourly wages are insufficient or unstable, individuals in households must pool their resources with others in the larger family network. Pooling of resources may involve exchanging baby-sitting, sharing meals, or lending money. Pooling represents an attempt to cope with the limitation of resources that are necessary for survival,[41] and it requires that the boundaries of the family be expanded.

At the lower levels of the class hierarchy, survival is especially dependent on pooling resources with a wide network of people that become, in effect, "family." The lower one moves in the class structure, the more uncertain and difficult survival through wage work becomes and the more important the kin network becomes in providing subsistence over time. Much has been written about these networks among poor black families—"extremely flexible, and fluctuating groups of people committed to resource pooling, to sharing, to mutual aid, who move in and out from under one another's roofs."[42] The fluctuating boundaries of families among working-class and poor people should not be considered unstable. Rather they organize and sustain the limited resources that they have available. Even the black single-parent family, which has sometimes been criticized as "disorganized" or even "pathological," is usually embedded in a stable functioning kinship network. These networks should not be romanticized but neither should they be considered deviant.[43] Chicano families also exhibit strong and persistent kinship bonds that provide socioeconomic and emotional support.[44] Looking at these families without racist assumptions, we see that variation in family organization is a way of adapting to harsh conditions.

> The very poor have used their families to cement and patch tenuous relations to survival; out of their belief in "family," they have invented networks capable of making next-to-nothing go a long way. It isn't the family that is deficient, but the relationship between household and productive resources.[45]

What is most important about the differences in family boundaries is that they arise out of different kinds of linkages with institutions that are *consequences* of class position, not causes of that position. Lacking economic resources to purchase services from specialists outside of the family, poor people turn to relatives and exchange these services. This family network then becomes a crucial institution in both the working class and the lower class.

Middle-class families with husbands (and perhaps wives) in careers have both economic resources and built-in ties with supportive institutions such as banks, credit unions, medical facilities, and voluntary associations. These ties are intrinsic to some occupations and to middle-class neighborhoods. They are structurally determined. Such institutional linkages strengthen the autonomy of middle-class families. In contrast, blue-collar jobs lack ties that would link family with work and other institutions. Thus, the boundaries of the middle-class family are more circumscribed because institutional ties support a degree of autonomy from kin. Families lower in the socioeconomic hierarchy display more openness of boundaries simply because kinship resources must be maximized in the absence of other forms of institutional support.

Turning to the upper class, we find that family boundaries are more open than those of the middle class, even though class boundaries are quite closed. Among the elite, family constitutes not only a nuclear family, but the extended family as well. The elite are described as having multiple households.[46] The concerns and much of day-to-day life exist within the larger context of a network of relatives.[47]

The institutional linkages of the elite are national in scope. Families in various sections of the country are connected by such institutions as boarding schools, exclusive colleges, exclusive clubs, and fashionable vacation resorts.

In this way the elite remains intact, and the marriage market is restricted to a small (but national) market.[48]

Family life is privileged in every sense:

> Wealthy families can afford an elaborate support structure to take care of the details of everyday life. Persons can be hired to cook and prepare meals and do laundry and to care for the children.[49]

The vast economic holdings of these families allow them to have a high degree of control over the flow of rewards and resources and to enjoy freedoms and choices not normally available to other families in society. As a result, these families maintain privileged access to life chances and lifestyles.

Kinship ties, obligations, and interests are more extended in classes at the two extremes than they are in the middle.[50] In the upper extreme and toward the lower end of the class structure, kinship networks serve decisively different functions. At both extremes they are institutions of resource management. The kin-based family form of the elite serves to preserve inherited wealth. It is intricately tied to other national institutions that control the wealth of society. The kin-based family form of the working and lower classes is a primary institution through which individuals participate in social life as they pool and exchange their limited resources to insure survival. It is influenced by society's institutions, but it remains separate from them.

Structural Transformation and Family Life

In the past decade both the family and the economy have been viewed as institutions in crisis.[51] Structural transformation of the American economy will undoubtedly place even greater stress on family life. As the need for skilled labor diminishes, many blue-collar families will be confronted with the loss of traditional jobs. Deindustrialization will make millions of workers the victims of economic dislocation. Minority families will be especially affected due to structural discrimination that has left them with a poor education.

The new technology may affect families in other ways. For example, the movement of certain types of work from the office to home computer terminals will have serious consequences. "Electronic homework" combines high-tech with early nineteenth-century working conditions. This work can provide women with young children an opportunity to work part-time on a flexible schedule. At the same time, the dangers of exploitation are great. Most of the people who will be engaged in electronic homework are women. The prospect of being "home-centered" may not be so appealing to a generation of women who have been abandoning the home to enter the labor market in record numbers. Electronic homework could well become dead-end work and deprive women of the social status that working with others provides.[52]

CHANGING FAMILY ROLES

Marriage   Most Americans eventually marry. In 1980, 61.1 percent of the American population were married. Single persons made up 25 percent of the population, of whom 7.4 percent were widowed and 5.8 percent were divorced.[53] Men were more likely to be married than women (69.3 percent compared to 61.7 percent). The median age at first marriage was 24.6 for men and 22.1 for women.[54]

In American society, marriage is idealized as a relationship based on love, a haven of personal fulfillment. Especially when compared with marriages in other societies, American marriages are thought to be characterized by relative equality between the spouses. This idyllic view of marriage fails to take into account the impact of the gender system on the marital relationship. As noted in Chapter 12, women and men are assigned different roles that are unequally ranked. This difference constitutes the foundation on which marriage rests. As a result of the gender system, men and women experience marriage and the family in different ways.

Jessie Bernard's classic work on marriage revealed that every marital union actually contains two marriages—and that the two do not always coincide.[55] When researchers ask husbands and wives identical questions about their marriages, they often get quite different replies even on fairly simple, factual questions. Bernard coined the concept "his" and "her" marriage to describe the differences in women's and men's experiences. Generally, differences reveal that men seem to be happier in marriage than women and that marriage is better for men than for women. This finding will be surprising to many because of the stereotype that women get most of their fulfillment through marriage. Bernard has examined the advantages of marriage and found that they are greater for men. Men gain more than women in marriage. Comparing married and unmarried men of the same background, she found that in psychological, social, health, and labor market characteristics, married men were better off. However, the psychological, social, health, and labor market benefits for married women are not as high as the benefits for married men. Furthermore, married women express more unhappiness than married men. According to Bernard and other social scientists, this problem of unhappiness can be explained by the legal, social, and personal changes that take place in women's lives when they become wives. Taking on the wife role of housewife creates dependency and affects women's self-esteem.[56] Housewives exhibit much higher rates of such dysfunctional mental symptoms as anxiety, paranoia, and phobias than do either married men or single women.

Though couples marry for togetherness, the reality of marriage is such that many activities of the spouses are segregated. Women, whether they work outside of the home or not, are responsible for domestic and childrearing activities while men pursue their work or other interests. Not only are women and men required to fill separate role activities, but the activities are governed by different sets of values.[57] Husbands and wives, though they live in the same physical space, experience differently the social world of the family.

Role segregation makes communication problematic for many couples. As they go about their separate activities, they may find they have less and less to talk about. This is especially true in blue-collar families where roles are traditionally segregated. Lack of economic resources makes it difficult for wives and husbands to go out by themselves, and so they spend time with relatives in sex-segregated activities (the men watch a ballgame on television while the women prepare meals and watch over children). Leisure time spent in the home includes little real interaction. The following excerpt from Lillian Rubin's study of working class families illustrates the separateness of wives and husbands:

> Frank comes home from work; now it's about five, because he's been working overtime every night. We eat right away, right after he comes home. Then, I don't know. The kids play a while before bed, watch t.v., you know, stuff like that. Then, I don't know . . . maybe watch more t.v. or something like that. I don't know what else—nothing, I guess. We just sit, that's all. The husband: I come home at five and we supper right away. Then, I sit down with coffee and a beer and watch t.v. After that, if I'm working on a project I do that for a while. If not, I just watch t.v.[58]

The quality of marital relationships is strongly influenced by class position. The three positive attributes most frequently mentioned by working-class women in Rubin's study were "He's a steady worker, he doesn't drink, he doesn't hit me."[59] Not one woman in the professional middle-class families mentioned these qualities when answering the same question. They tended to focus on such issues as intimacy, sharing, and communication and, while expressed in subtle ways, on the comforts, status, and prestige, that their husbands' occupations afford. Rubin comments on the difference in working class marriages:

> Does this mean that working-class women are unconcerned about the emotional side of the marriage relationship? Emphatically it does not. It says first that when the material aspects of life are problematic, they become dominant as issues acquiring solutions, and second, that even when men are earning a reasonably good living, it is never "taken for granted" when financial insecurity and marginality are woven into the fabric of life.[60]

While marriages in this society differ in many ways, marriage as an institution has remained patriarchal. Marital power is the ability to control the spouse and to influence or control family decisions and activities. Husbands in all social classes have greater power than wives, although we find important differences in the operation of marital power. The classic study of marital power by sociologists Blood and Wolfe found that power was related to the resources that partners bring to the marriage. Resources are anything that a person brings to the marriage that enables the family to satisfy needs: for example, money, education, attractiveness, and social status. They found that the higher the husband's status in occupation, income, and education, the greater decision-making power he had in the family. Husbands with white-collar occupations had greater power than husbands with blue-collar occupations.[61] Still, the stereotype of the egalitarian middle-class marriage persists partly because the middle class has a more egalitarian *ideology*.

Actually, the ideology and the actual distribution of power are at odds. As Goode has commented:

> Lower-class men concede fewer rights ideologically than their women in fact obtain, and the more educated men are more likely to concede more rights ideologically than they in fact grant.[62]

Blood and Wolfe concluded that marriages would eventually become more equal as wives acquired more resources. Other sociologists have argued that marriages will likely remain male dominated because men automatically have greater resources than women. Better job opportunities and earnings are built into the structure of society and then carried into the private family where men can dominate with little outright effort.[63] In order to change the unequal distribution of marital power, women would have to equal their husbands' resources. While this may be occurring in some couples where wives have high-status and high-paying occupations, for most couples, sexism in the larger society contributes to a power imbalance in marriage.

PANEL 14–3

I Want a Wife

I belong to that classification of people known as wives. I am A Wife. And, not altogether incidentally, I am a mother.

Not too long ago a male friend of mine appeared on the scene fresh from a recent divorce. He had one child, who is, of course, with his ex-wife. He is obviously looking for another wife. As I thought about him while I was ironing one evening, it suddenly occurred to me that I, too, would like to have a wife. Why do I want a wife?

I would like to go back to school so that I can become economically independent, support myself, and, if need be, support those dependent upon me. I want a wife who will work and send me to school. And while I am going to school I want a wife to take care of the children. I want a wife to keep track of the children's doctor and dentist appointments. And to keep track of mine too. I want a wife to make sure my children eat properly and are kept clean. I want a wife who will wash the children's clothes and keep them mended. I want a wife who is a good nurturant attendant to my children, who arranges for their schooling, makes sure that they have an adequate social life with their peers, takes them to the park, the zoo, et cetera. I want a wife who takes care of the children when they are sick, a wife who arranges to be around when the children need special care, because, of course, I cannot miss classes at school. My wife must arrange to lose time at work and

(continued)

not lose the job. It may mean a small cut in my wife's income from time to time, but I guess I can tolerate that. Needless to say, my wife will arrange and pay for the care of the children while my wife is working.

I want a wife who will take care of *my* physical needs. I want a wife who will keep my house clean. A wife who will pick up after me. I want a wife who will keep my clothes clean, ironed, mended, replaced when need be, and who will see to it that my personal things are kept in their proper place so that I can find what I need the minute I need it. I want a wife who cooks the meals, a wife who is a *good* cook. I want a wife who will plan the menus, do the necessary grocery shopping, prepare the meals, serve them pleasantly, and then do the cleaning up while I do my studying. I want a wife who will care for me when I am sick and sympathize with my pain and loss of time from school. I want a wife to go along when our family takes a vacation so that someone can continue to care for me and my children when I need a rest and change of scene.

I want a wife who will not bother me with rambling complaints about a wife's duties. But I want a wife who will listen to me when I feel the need to explain a rather difficult point I have come across in my course of studies. And I want a wife who will type my papers for me when I have written them.

I want a wife who will take care of the details of my social life. When my wife and I are invited out by my friends, I want a wife who will take care of the babysitting arrangements. When I meet people at school whom I like and want to entertain, I want a wife

who will have the house clean, will prepare a special meal, serve it to me and my friends, and not interrupt when I talk about the things that interest me and my friends. I want a wife who will have arranged that the children are fed and ready for bed before my guests arrive so that the children do not bother us.

And I want a wife who knows that sometimes I need a night out by myself.

I want a wife who is sensitive to my sexual needs, a wife who makes love passionately and eagerly when I feel like it, a wife who makes sure that I am satisfied. And, of course, I want a wife who will not demand sexual attention when I am not in the mood for it. I want a wife who assumes the complete responsibility for birth control, because I do not want more children. I want a wife who will remain sexually faithful to me so that I do not have to clutter up my intellectual life with jealousies. And I want a wife who understands that *my* sexual needs may entail more than strict adherence to monogamy. I must, after all, be able to relate to people as fully as possible.

If, by chance, I find another person more suitable as a wife than the wife I already have, I want the liberty to replace my present wife with another one. Naturally, I will expect a fresh, new life; my wife will take the children and be solely responsible for them so that I am left free.

When I am through with school and have a job, I want my wife to quit working and remain at home so that my wife can more fully and completely take care of a wife's duties.

My God, who *wouldn't* want a wife?

Source: Judy Syfers, "I Want a Wife," *Ms.* (December 1979), p. 144. Copyright © 1970 by Judy Syfers.

Divorce and Remarriage   While most Americans marry, many marriages are fraught with conflict and eventually they are dissolved. At current rates about half of all marriages will end in divorce. In 1981 a total of 1.21 million divorces were granted, the highest number in the nation's history. The high divorce rate has contributed to the growing number of single-parent families discussed earlier. Three-fifths of all divorces involve couples with children living at home. In at least nine out of ten cases, the wife retains custody of the children after a separation. Although joint custody has received much attention in the press, national data show that it is still uncommon.[64]

Divorce and marital separation are not evenly distributed through the population but vary according to social and economic characteristics. The following are some generalizations about divorce in the United States.[65]

1. Half of all divorces occur during the first seven years of marriage.
2. The divorce rate is related to economic conditions. The rate increases during prosperity. Apparently this is due to unwillingness to break up a marriage when wives and children will need greater economic support.
3. The younger the age at marriage of the partners, the greater the likelihood of divorce. "Women whose first marriage ended in divorce have been, on the average, about two years younger when they entered marriage than married women of the same age who have not been divorced."[66]
4. The higher the income, the less the likelihood of divorce.
5. The higher the education for males, the lower the incidence of divorce. In contrast to males, a more complicated pattern is found for women. The highest rate of divorce is found among the least educated women, followed by those with post-graduate degrees. The lowest rates were found for those women with high school and college educations.
6. About four out of every five of those persons who obtain a divorce will remarry, with men more likely than women to do so.[67]
7. Blacks have a higher incidence of divorce than whites or Hispanics. In 1980 the percentage of males over 15 who were divorced was 6.4 for blacks, 4.7 for whites, and 3.5 for Hispanics. The rate for females by race was 8.7 percent, 6.4 percent, and 6.9 percent respectively. (See Table 14–2.)

There are many reasons for the increased divorce rate. Some of these are: increased independence (social and financial) of women; deindustrialization that eliminates many jobs for men and makes women's employment necessary; women's inequality; greater tolerance of divorce by religious groups; and reform of divorce laws, especially the adoption of no-fault divorce in many states (that is, one spouse no longer has to prove that the other was at fault in order to obtain a divorce). An important reason is the striking change in public attitudes toward divorce. While divorce is a difficult step and one that commands sympathy for the partners and children, "it is no longer considered a violation of public decency. Whether the individual is viewed as the sinner or as sinned against, divorce is generally accepted today as one possible solution for family difficulties."[68]

According to the most recent U.S. Census study, 73 percent of divorced persons remarry. However, the proportion of remarriage is not the same for the sexes—68.8 percent of divorced women remarry, compared to 78.3 percent of divorced men. The imbalance increases with age. Since men die

TABLE 14–2	Marital Status of the Population Over Age 15, 1980 (as a percentage of the population)		

	Total	Men	Women
All persons			
Single	25.7	29.3	22.4
Married, spouse present	58.0	60.8	55.4
Married, spouse absent	3.1	2.6	3.6
Widowed	7.4	2.5	11.9
Divorced	5.8	4.8	6.6
Whites			
Single	24.3	28.0	20.9
Married, spouse present	60.5	63.0	58.1
Married, spouse absent	2.4	2.1	2.7
Widowed	7.3	2.3	11.8
Divorced	5.6	4.7	6.4
Blacks			
Single	36.5	40.2	33.4
Married, spouse present	37.7	42.3	34.0
Married, spouse absent	9.2	7.2	10.9
Widowed	8.9	3.9	13.0
Divorced	7.7	6.4	8.7
Hispanics			
Single	30.1	32.6	27.6
Married, spouse present	55.1	58.2	52.1
Married, spouse absent	5.7	4.4	6.9
Widowed	3.9	1.4	6.4
Divorced	5.2	3.5	6.9

Source: U.S. Department of Commerce, Bureau of the Census, *Current Population Reports: Marital Status and Living Arrangements, March 1980*, Washington, D.C.: U.S. Government Printing Office, October 1981.

earlier, by ages 55 to 64 only 88 men remain for every 100 women, and by ages 65 and over, only 67 men remain for every 100 women. So even though there are fewer older men, they participate in more of the remarriages than do women their own age. The chief reason is that divorced men are more apt to choose younger women, including women who have not been married before, as their second wives.[69]

By adding a male income, remarriage may solve the economic problems many single-parent families face. It may also relieve the many burdens of running a household alone. Remarriage also frequently involves blending together two families into one, a process that is complicated by the absence of clear-cut ground rules for how to accomplish the merger. Families formed by remarriages can become quite complex, with children from either spouse's previous marriage and/or from the new marriage, along with numerous sets of grandparents, stepgrandparents, and other kin and quasi-kin (see Panel 14–4).[70]

Whose Family Is This, Anyway?

Art Buchwald

In trying to deal with the social and economic condition of the modern family, the government always seems to refer to "a married couple with two children" as the norm.

Unfortunately the "norm" is not normal anymore.

And that's why most government figures are haywire.

Taking the place of the family of four is the family of eight or nine, depending on how many marriages have been involved.

This is the more realistic family profile of the '80s: Betsy is the divorced mother of three young children whose former husband, Edward, is married to Ruth, who has four children of her own. Edward gives child support and some alimony to Betsy, but not enough to pay the bills. So Betsy has to work. Ruth also has to work to help Edward pay Betsy and keep her kids in shoes, because her former husband, Ralph, doesn't work and won't contribute to child support.

He is married to Greta, (his third marriage) who has one child by a former marriage to John. Since she left John to marry Ralph, she gets no alimony, and she has to work to support the child and her husband, whom she is thinking of divorcing because he's having an affair with the lady upstairs, Maria, who has no children living with her.

The judge awarded custody of her children to Maria's parents when her husband Kip said he was moving into an apartment that didn't take kids. The grandparents, Bob and Lilly, were retired, but Bob had to find a job to support his grandchildren.

One of the grandchildren, Rona, had a child out of wedlock, and she found a job at a McDonald's. So she leaves her baby with Bob and Lilly when she works the night shift.

The father of Rona's child is Hal, who is happily married to Carla, and they have five children, three by Hal's first marriage to Inez and two by Carla's first marriage to Fred.

Inez left Hal after she fell in love with his best friend, Dick, whose wife had gone to live in a commune with a religious sect.

Since Dick said he would only marry Inez if they had no children, Inez told Hal he could have the kids, though she sees them on weekends when she isn't doing volunteer work for an adoption agency.

Fred's something else again. He is living with Dedra, who has two children, but he told her he doesn't want to get married again because he doesn't trust women. Dedra doesn't mind because the father of her children, Danny, was a cad, and she's not ready to make another commitment. The state does not consider them a family of four for tax purposes, because they aren't legally wed. So although Fred supports the children, he cannot deduct them as dependants.

Danny lives with his sister Ella, who has four children and a husband named Sid. Sid is sore as hell about this arrangement because he can barely support his family, much less Danny, who only works when the spirit moves him.

Ella keeps introducing Danny to her divorced friends in hopes he'll marry one of them. But her friends all seem to have children, and Danny says his first reponsibility is to his own kids.

One of Ella's divorced friends, Caroline,

(continued)

has one child and is living with a man named Arnie. She was collecting welfare when her caseworker paid a surprise visit to her flat and discovered Arnie was living there. "The man in the house" rule prevailed, and her payments stopped. Caroline got a job, the city closed down the daycare center in her neighborhood, and she couldn't work, so she had to move in with her sister who has four children.

I guess I could go on but I might confuse you. The point is that government statisticians keep sticking to their fantasies that every household consists of a family of four—a mother, a father and two children. That's why nothing they plan turns out to be right.

Source: Copyright 1981, Los Angeles Times Syndicate. Reprinted from the *Washington Post*, March 8, 1981, with permission of the author.

The Interdependence of Work and Family Roles

The belief that work and family roles operate independently of each other is referred to by Rosabeth Moss Kanter as "the myth of separate worlds." Many people do not recognize that the institutions of the economy and the family are linked together and dependent on one another in numerous ways.[71] The economy provides jobs with varying amounts of social status and economic resources for the family and in this way sets limits on its standard of living. The family supplies skilled workers to the economy. The segmented labor force imposes different constraints on families such as the amount of time spent working and the scheduling of work, which determine the amount of time workers can spend with their families. In addition, work has psychological costs and benefits that influence family interaction. Family roles, especially the traditional roles of wife and mother, influence labor force participation and commitment to work.[72] Relationships between work and family roles are complex. These relationships vary according to the nature of the work, the sex of the persons performing the roles, and the composition of the family.[73] Single-provider families with only husbands employed outside of the home have given way to the dominant pattern of dual-provider families. We have also seen that a large number of families are headed by single mothers who may or may not be employed.

Women's increased labor force participation has dramatically altered the connections between work and family life, but in many ways women continue to be associated with the family and men with the world of work. The close connections between work and family roles are revealed in Joseph Pleck's analysis of "the work-family role system." He has conceived of this system in terms of male and female work roles in the workplace and male and female work roles in the marriage. According to Pleck, role segregation in the family parallels sex segregation in the workplace. Traditional division of labor is reinforced by different definitions of women's and men's work and family roles. For women, the demand of the family roles are permitted to intrude into their work roles more than vice versa. If an emergency or irregularity arises requiring a choice between family and work, the family of the working woman will often take priority. For example, when there is a crisis for a child in school, it is the child's working mother rather than the working father who will usually be called to take responsibility. For husbands, the relationship is reversed. The work role takes priority over the family role. Many husbands take work home with them or use time at home to recuperate from the stresses they face in their work role. Husbands are expected to manage their families so that family responsibilities do not interfere with their work efficiency and so that their families will make any adjustments necessary to the work role.[74] Family life tends to be subordinate to the demands of the male work role. Miller points to the male involvement in work, success, and striving, and its effect on families:

> This is the pressure that often molds the family. Accommodation to it is frequently the measure of being a "good wife"—moving when the male's "future" requires it, regulating activities so that the male is free to concentrate on work or business. It isn't sexism or prejudice that are at work here—although they are contributing factors—but the compulsive concentration upon the objective of achievement and the relegating of other activities to secondary concerns. Egalitarian relationships cannot survive if people are not somewhat equally involved with each other and if the major commitment is to things outside the relationship that inevitably intrude upon it.[75]

While professional and managerial work may impose demands on husbands that keep them away from their families, blue-collar work often creates frustrations and alienation that is detrimental to family interaction.[76]

The tremendous increase in women's employment has created changes in family living patterns. Employed married women enhance the family's economic resources, contributing on the average about one-fourth of the family's income if working part time, and 40 percent if employed full time.[77] But in other ways the family resources can be strained when women work outside of the home:

> No longer is there a full-time homemaker to attend to housework, child care, and to support the husband's occupational role. The employed wife, of course, also lacks support from a full-time homemaker. Who will keep the children away when both spouses come home feeling stressed and exhausted? When both parents are working, child care is needed for preschool children, and supervision must be found for children after school. Although couples attempt to streamline housekeeping, the needs of children are less tractable, and time for families to spend with one another in leisure activities may radically decline when there are two paid jobs, as well as family work.[78]

Although wives share the provider role, husbands do not often share the family labor. Most recent studies of family work have found that husbands of employed wives contributed little more than husbands of nonemployed wives.[79] The deep-seated notion that housework is women's work has produced a "double day" for many employed women at the expense of leisure, sleep, and time that might be spent on work-related activities away from the job itself. For the single parent, the problems of diminished resources and the added roles are especially severe. Even if husbands in dual-provider families do not contribute much to housework, they do make some home maintenance contributions to the family.

In spite of the stresses of work and family, wives who work outside of the home report that they are happier than are housewives, even though the demands on them are greater.[80] (See Panel 14–5.) Work has a profound affect on a woman's sense of self-worth, her feelings of being in charge of her life, and her chance of avoiding depression and anxiety.[81] Working wives have additional resources that they can use to have a greater say in important family decisions, and in this way they can alter the traditional balance of family power.

Even though these positive consequences can arise from women's employment, one of the most fundamental problems remains unsolved: that of child care. In recent years the increase in women's employment has been greatest among women with very young children. (See Table 14–3.) Sixty-four percent of all children between the age of three and five spend part

TABLE 14–3 Female Labor Force Participation Rates by Marital Status, Children in the Household, and Age: 1950–1980 (in percents)

	1950	1960	1970	1980[a]	Percentage Increase
Single[b]	40.6	41.8	45.6	52.5	29.3
Married, husband present	21.6	30.5	40.8	49.4	128.2
No children in household[c]	30.3	34.7	42.2	46.7	54.1
Children under 6 in household[c]	11.9	18.6	30.3	43.2	263.0
Children 6–17 in household[c]	28.3	39.0	49.2	59.1	108.8
Aged 20–24	46.0	46.1	57.7	67.7	47.2
25–34	34.0	36.0	45.0	65.4	92.4
35–44	39.1	43.4	51.1	65.5	67.5
45–54	37.9	49.8	54.4	59.6	57.3
55–64	27.0	37.2	43.0	41.7	54.4
Percent of women workers who work year-round, full time	—	36.9	40.7	43.7[d]	18.4[e]

[a] For married women and women with children in the household, percentages refer to 1979.
[b] Includes never married, separated, divorced, and widowed.
[c] For women who are married with husband present only.
[d] Data for 1978.
[e] Base year is 1960.
Source: U.S. Department of Labor 1980. Reprinted from Kathleen Gerson, "Changing Family Structure and the Position of Women." Reprinted by permission of *Journal of the American Planning Association* 49:2 (Spring 1983) pp. 138–143.

Happiness Is A Good Job

What contributes to a woman's sense of well-being? Our book, Lifeprints: New Patterns of Love and Work for Today's Women, and the study of women on which it is based, began by trying to answer that one central question. It ended by recognizing that there are two questions that need answering: First, what makes a woman feel good about herself as a valued member of society who is in control of her life? Second, what makes a woman find pleasure and enjoyment in her life? The special message of this book, and of the study, is that for many of today's women these two questions are indeed separate, and the answers to each are different.

Our research, which was funded by a $250,000 grant from the National Science Foundation, is based on in-depth interviews of a sample of some 300 women between the ages of 35 and 55. We chose this age group because these are the years that represent the core of a woman's life. We did not find that the differences according to age were very great, although the oldest women in the group grew up in the years when the feminine mystique was in full sway, while the youngest encountered the women's movement in early adulthood. The women were divided into six groups: never married, employed; married, without children, employed; married, with children, employed; married, without children, at home; married, with children, at home; divorced, with children, employed. The employed women, in roughly equal numbers, were in high-, medium- or low-prestige jobs. The study, which was conducted from 1978 to 1980, was designed specifically to look at women in different job roles and family situations.

In our culture, the sources of what we call a sense of "mastery"—feeling important and worthwhile—and the sources of what we call a sense of "pleasure"—finding life enjoyable—are not always identical. Women often are told, "You can't have it all." Sometimes what

the speaker really is saying is: "You chose a career, so you can't expect to have closer relationships or a happy family life," or "You have a wonderful husband and children—what's all this about wanting a career?" But women need to understand and develop both aspects of well-being, if they are to feel good about themselves.

Our study shows that, for women, well-being has two dimensions. One is mastery, which includes self-esteem, a sense of control over your life, and low levels of anxiety and depression. Mastery is closely related to the "doing" side of life, to work and activity. Pleasure is the other dimension, and it is composed of happiness, satisfaction and optimism. It is tied more closely to the "feeling" side of life. The two are independent of each other. A woman could be high in mastery and low in pleasure, and vice versa. For example, a woman who has a good job, but whose mother has just died, might be feeling very good about herself and in control of her work life, but the pleasure side could be impaired for a time.

The concepts of mastery and pleasure can help us pinpoint the sources of well-being for women, and remedy past oversights. In the past, women were encouraged to look only at the feeling side of life as the source of all well-being. But we know that both mastery and pleasure are critical. And mastery seems to be achieved largely through work.

In our study, all the groups of employed women rated significantly higher in mastery than did women who were not employed.

The theme of achievement and work—jobs, education, career goals—dominated our interviews, especially when we asked women about their joys and regrets, hopes and frustrations. When we asked, "Thinking of your life as a whole, what things are the most rewarding?" nearly half the women in the sample mentioned their achievement in ed-

(continued)

ucation or work. When we asked what major issues the women were dealing with in their lives, 47 percent mentioned career and economic issues, compared to 23 percent who mentioned issues of intimacy. And, when we asked, "If you could live your whole life over, what one thing would you most like to change?" the most frequent response was that they would seek better educational or career preparation. Very few women mentioned marriage or children as things they would change if they could repeat their lives, and a scant 2 percent of women who had never married or were childless said they would marry or have children.

These answers were striking in light of the commonly held belief that women's lives are dominated by issues of marriage and children. To a surprising degree, these daughters of the feminine mystique era are, as adults, concerned with work and achievement. The probability seems very high that today's young women will be even more involved in these pursuits.

A woman's well-being is enhanced when she takes on multiple roles. At least by middle adulthood, the women who were involved in a combination of roles—marriage, motherhood, and employment—were the highest in well-being, despite warnings about stress and strain.

Source: Grace Baruch, Rosalind Barnett, and Carly Rivers. "Happiness Is A Good Job," reprinted by permission of *Working Woman* (February 1983), pp. 75–78.

of their day in facilities outside of the home. Mothers are left to work out their own arrangements for child care, and often they are unsatisfactory.

It is often assumed that maternal employment adversely affects children. However, the separation of mother and child for brief periods is not harmful if adequate substitute care is provided. Kristin A. Moore and Isabell Sawhill have reviewed a number of studies and found that the children of employed mothers compare favorably in intellectual and social development with the children of mothers at home. Furthermore, employed mothers tend to stress independence in their children.[82]

The changing connections between work and family pose new problems for women and men, for work institutions, and for the family. Sex inequality in the workplace and in the home lies at the heart of these problems:

> Reducing workplace inequalities between men and women would improve women's economic position and give them greater leverage to draw men more fully into household and parenting responsibilities, thus allowing both sexes to better integrate work and childrearing. Reducing inequalities in the household would give women greater freedom to pursue outside goals and would also increase the care fathers provide for their children, thus offsetting the loss of time spent with mothers. Neither of these goals is likely to succeed, however, unless the obstacles to integrating work and childrearing are reduced for both sexes.[83]

Children and Adolescents

American society places a high value on children. A primary responsibility of parents is to teach their children the attitudes, values, and behaviors considered appropriate by the parents (and society). This teaching ensures that most children will be reared to take socially acceptable niches in the society when they reach adulthood. Parents, therefore, are important so-cialization agents in the child's formative years.

However, the belief that early family experience is the most powerful influence in a child's life is not supported by evidence. Arlene Skolnick points to two serious flaws in this notion: the assumption that the child is passive, and the assumption that parents exert influence in a vacuum.[84] To begin with, children are not passive. They come into the world with unique temperaments and characteristics. Parents have greater power and authority than children, yet children can also shape parents. Second, the assumption of parental determinism is not well founded. Parents are not simply in-dependent agents who train children, free of outside influences. For example, an employed parent may behave quite differently than an unemployed one, becoming more depressed, defensive, or physically abusive. Indirectly, parents communicate to their children what to worry about. The stresses or supports parents find in the neighborhood, the workplace, and the economy, all influence children.[85]

There are two broad patterns of socialization that can be identified in American society. One stresses punishment for wrong behavior while the others emphasizes rewards for good behavior. The first demands the child's obedience to adults. The second allows the child freedom to explore and to discover things for him- or herself. Thus, one is adult-centered, while the other is child-centered. One pattern is much more strict when it comes to thumb sucking, toilet training, cleanliness, and aggression control, while the other is more tolerant. The more strict, adult-centered mode of socialization is called repressive socialization; the more tolerant, child-centered mode is referred to as participatory socialization. Repressive socialization is based on the premise that children can and should be molded to conform, to be obedient. Participatory socialization, on the other hand, assumes that children should be given freedom to explore and develop their unique potentials.

Although few parents are consistent in the manner in which they interact with their children, there appear to be discernible patterns by social class. The empirical evidence is that working-class parents tend toward repressive socialization while middle-class parents are more likely to practice participatory socialization.

Class differences in socialization result from different conditions of family life experienced by parents at different class levels. The members of the middle class, for example, tend to have a good deal of autonomy in their occupations, while working-class people are more likely to have to take orders under strict supervision—each class passing its experience on to the children. Parents, apparently, use the mode of socialization that they are most familiar and comfortable with and the one that makes adjustment to life the easiest. The socialization patterns continue over time as the behaviors specific to a particular class are reinforced. Children live in relatively class-homogeneous neighborhoods, thereby giving the members of a neigh-borhood the impression that a particular mode is the most natural one because almost everyone follows it.

Persons also tend to marry within their social class. This, too, reinforces one type of socialization practice as the typical one for a particular social class.[86]

Participatory socialization has not always been the primary mode of the middle classes. Child-rearing practices, especially among the middle and upper classes, have vacillated according to the prevailing views of experts. The bulletin *Infant Care*, published by the United States Children's Bureau, has gone through a number of editions and has changed significantly since its inception in 1914. In that year the views of psychologist John B. Watson were enunciated. He believed that the development of the child was shaped entirely by the habits he acquired. Thus, mothers were instructed never to rock their baby, to begin toilet training by the third month, and never to let the child suck his thumb. In the 1930s the philosophy of Sigmund Freud prevailed. The concern then was with the emotional damage that could occur from unfavorable experiences during the first years of life. Parents were enjoined to make the child's environment supportive and loving.[87]

Participatory socialization, so prevalent in the contemporary American middle class, is due in large measure to the persuasive influences of Dr. Benjamin Spock, whose book *Baby and Child Care* sold more than 21 million copies from 1947 to 1970.[88] Most parents—at least middle-class parents—were greatly influenced by the child-rearing philosophy of Spock. He argued that young children should be treated with kindness in a relaxed atmosphere. Babies should not be fed on a rigid time schedule, but when they want to eat. Children should be taught to love rather than fear their parents. In later editions (1957 and 1968), Spock was less permissive but the basic philosophy remained—that children should be raised in a relaxed, loving environment. Although accused by many of advocating wanton permissiveness, Spock, especially in his later editions, placed great emphasis on the child's need for parental control and the importance of not letting the child become a tyrant in the home.

There is another mode of socialization that characterizes a sizable minority of lower-class families and is found in some families in the other social classes as well—and that is excessive freedom. This freedom is different from that found in participatory socialization, because in this case the freedom does not result from adherence to a particular philosophy of child raising, but from either neglect by the parents or rebellion by the children. Either of these may prevail in the lower class as the result of several factors: (1) the chance of two parents being present in the home is reduced because of the conditions of lower-class life; (2) children living in an achievement-oriented society may not have respect for their parents and may therefore disobey their wishes; (3) for the minority-group families that are so predominant in this stratum, there may be a huge "generation gap" because the youngsters consider their parents "uncle toms" for not fighting the system that keeps them in such a lowly state.

About 13 percent of the total population is between the ages of thirteen and nineteen. This is a very significant category in American society for several reasons. First, teenagers are a strong economic force. For example, they account for more than one-fourth of the record sales and more than one-third of the movie audiences. They spend collectively an enormous amount of money on clothes and toiletries. As they shift from fad to fad, fortunes are made and lost in the clothing and entertainment industries. Second, adolescents are a financial burden to society. Most adolescents are in school and not in the labor market. They are furnished with an education that they do not pay for. Within each family, adolescents and the younger children are economic liabilities. They do not earn their way. The United States is probably the first nation to transform children from a family asset as labor to a family liability as student-consumer. A third basis for this category's importance is that many adolescents are disenchanted and alienated. This results in withdrawal, apathy, or rebellion.

Why is the stage of adolescence in American society a period of stress and strain for so many? The most important reason is that it is an age of transition from one social status to another. There is no clear line of demarcation between adolescence and adulthood. Are people considered adult when they can get a full-time job, when they are physically capable of producing children, or when they can be drafted for military service? There is no clear distinction. Most primitive societies, by contrast, have "rites of passage" that often seem cruel and barbaric but do serve the function of clearly identifying the individual as a child or an adult. Adulthood in American society is unclear. As Stephens has said, "The postponement of sociological adulthood produces a social status which is filled, somewhat uncertainly, by millions of our society's members. This is adolescence; the state of being physically mature but not working, sexually mature but not married, 'grown-up' but still dependent on parents."[89] Surely much of the acting out by adolescents in the United States can be at least partially explained by these status ambiguities.

These status ambiguities are probably unavoidable in a society where the state of technological development demands an extended period of education. Full-time schooling for a college degree or beyond tends to defer marriage well beyond the age of full biological maturity. This presents special problems for the adolescent. Young men and women are permitted and encouraged to date without chaperons. They are sexually mature and are members of a society that places a good deal of emphasis on sex (through movies, novels, magazines, and advertising).

Children, too, are away from home a good deal at school activities, club meetings, on dates, and being with their friends. The time children spend with others tends to be more with peers than with adults (especially as the child becomes a teenager). The typical peer group of children tends to be homogeneous. This results from seeking friends who share the same interests. A less obvious reason is that young people are restricted in choice of friends by propinquity. The typical urban or suburban neighborhood is noted for its sameness—in architecture and age of homes, but more importantly in the characteristics of the inhabitants. The individuals tend to be of the same race, socioeconomic level, and even age. Thus, the relationships that children form tend to be limited to persons who are similar in important ways.

The typical American youngster at some point in time turns away from parents to peers for opinion, advice, and companionship. The impact of the peer group on the child is great. A study by James Coleman of youngsters in ten high schools is especially instructive on this point. He found that although approximately three-fourths of the boys' parents wanted their youngsters to be remembered as brilliant students, only 31 percent of the boys wanted to be so remembered (44 percent wanted to be remembered as athletic stars). Apparently, the attitudes of the students were not only anti-intellectual but antithetical to those of their parents.[90]

Adolescents have a tremendous need to be popular, to be acceptable, to belong. They are "other-directed," which means that their peer groups become so important that they are the sources of direction for the individual.[91] Thus, the sources for attitudes, clothing styles, hairstyle, and slang for most teenagers are their close friends.

The Aged

The age distribution of the population has shifted in recent years, with more and more Americans living past the arbitrary dividing line of 65 years of age. In 1940, for example, 9 million persons (6.8 percent) were 65 or older, whereas more than 25 million Americans (11.2 percent) were in that category in 1980. This change in the composition of the population has important effects upon family life and the society in general.

The elderly in American society are somewhat analogous to adolescents in the ambivalence they face, because they are in a transition stage (in this case between work and death). As a category they are neither self-sufficient nor productive. As a category, the elderly in America are accorded low status, unlike in many societies where they are believed to be especially wise and therefore hold the power. In a sense they constitute a minority group, for they are subject to unfavorable treatment (forced retirement, difficulty in finding employment). They are believed by many to be inflexible, cantankerous, and unreliable—all false stereotypes.[92] These negative stereotypes are held by many Americans. They probably stem from the fear of old age that is prevalent in the youth-oriented American society.

Stereotypes of the aged are difficult to dispel, largely because research on aging is a recent development in both the biological and the social sciences, and research findings reach the public at a snail's pace. Many widely held but inaccurate images, inadvertently repeated through the mass media, come from social workers who serve the poor, the lonely, and the isolated, and from physicians and psychiatrists who see the physically ill and the mentally ill. Thus, we base many of our current stereotypes on a picture of the needy rather than on a picture of the typical older person.

Studies of large and representative samples of older persons are now appearing, however, and they go far toward exploding some of our outmoded images. For example, old persons do not become isolated and neglected by

their families, although both generations prefer separate households. Old persons are not dumped into mental hospitals by cruel or indifferent children. They are not necessarily lonely or desolate if they live alone. Few of them ever show overt signs of mental deterioration or senility, and only a small proportion ever become mentally ill. For those who do, psychological and psychiatric treatment is by no means futile.

Retirement and widowhood do not lead to mental illness, nor does social isolation. Retirement is not necessarily bad; some men and women want to keep on working, but more and more choose to retire earlier and earlier. Increasing proportions of the population evidently value leisure more than they value work. Nor do retired persons sicken physically from idleness and feelings of worthlessness. Three-fourths of the persons questioned in a recent national sample reported that they were satisfied or very satisfied with their lives since retirement. This is in line with earlier surveys. Most persons over sixty-five think of themselves as being in good health and they act accordingly, no matter what their physicians think.

But the most insidious stereotype of all, in many ways, puts the old (or, for that matter, the young or the middle-aged) into a distinct category or a distinct group. There is, in truth, no such thing as "the" young, or "the" old. People *do* differ; they also become increasingly different over time, as each person accumulates an idiosyncratic set of experiences and becomes committed to a unique set of people, things, interests, and activities. One has only to recall, for instance, the range of differences among the members of one's high school graduating class and then to see these persons at a class reunion twenty-five years later. They are much more varied as forty-year-olds than they were as eighteen-year-olds.

Another way in which the elderly tend to be isolated from kinship ties is through the death of one's mate—widowhood. There are about 11 million widowed persons with the present ratio of widows to widowers being more than 4 to 1. This dramatic difference results from a variance in life expectancy—a difference of almost eight years—and the tendency for males to marry someone younger than themselves (usually about a two-year differential). Thus, the average married female can expect ten years of widowhood—and, therefore, dependency upon Social Security, insurance, savings, or help from her family.[93]

Isolation of the elderly also occurs from a break in occupational ties. In the past when many persons farmed or owned small businesses, work was a lifetime process. In an industrial, bureaucratized society, however, retirement is usually abrupt. Many firms have established a policy that makes retirement compulsory at a given age (regardless of the individual's expertise, experience, and willingness to continue). Since one's work is the source of income, social status, and identity, to be cut off against one's will may be a traumatic experience from which it is difficult to recover.

A final source of isolation is the breakup of community ties. A relatively recent trend has been the creation of entire communities for the aged in Florida, California, and Arizona. Many old people are enticed to leave their home communities and live in these age-segregated communities. Another way in which the elderly may be separated from community life is by living in nursing homes or being confined in mental hospitals.

Violence in American Families

The family has two faces. On the positive side, it is a haven from an uncaring, impersonal world, a place where love and security prevail. The family members love each other, care for each other, and accept each other under all circumstances. However, there is another side to the family. The presence of tension and discord can be found in all families at various phases in the family life cycle. The intensity that characterizes intimate relationships can give way to conflict. Some families resolve the inevitable tensions that arise in the course of daily living, but in other families, conflict gives way to violence.

The family is a major location of violence in society. One-fourth of all the murders in the United States involve the killing of spouses, parents, and children. The most common request for police help is for "domestic disturbances." More police personnel are killed (22 percent) trying to settle family fights than in any other line of duty. Millions of wives and children are regularly assaulted by husbands and parents. Even the elderly are sometimes physically abused by their adult children. Here we will consider only one form of family violence, husbands physically abusing their wives. Violence by wives directed at husbands, compared to the reverse type, is less likely to occur, is likely to cause less physical damage, and is often the result of self-defense toward an abusive husband. This is not intended to minimize the existence of physical violence by wives, because it does occur,[94] but the frequency and severity are much less than husbands' attacks on wives. Therefore, we will describe wife abuse in some detail.

The actual statistics on battered wives are impossible to obtain. The reasons for this are fairly obvious. Foremost, the events generally take place in private with no witnesses other than family members. Battered women are often attended by physicians who treat their wounds either without asking embarrassing questions or, if they know the cause, without reporting the abuse to the authorities. The victims, most commonly, lie about the causes of their injuries because of shame or fear. Last, many victims do not go to public agencies for help because they have often found them to be unresponsive. This is especially true of the police and the courts because they typically feel that most domestic violence is a private affair and none of their business. Also, the situation often comes down to the wife's word against her husband's, leaving prosecution difficult if not impossible.

Understanding the limitations of the data on spouse abuse, we can examine some estimates of the frequency of its occurrence:

□ From a sample of 2,143 couples representative of the general population, 3.8 percent reported one or more physical attacks by their spouse over the past year, with the average number of assaults being 2.4. Extrapolating these data to the national population, the researchers estimated that 1.8 million wives are beaten by their husbands. Given the underreporting in these data, the true incidence rate is probably closer to 50 or 60 percent of all couples . . .[95]

□ At one point in time in their married lives, 25 to 50 percent of all wives are physically assaulted by their husbands.[96]

□ A psychologist who specializes in helping abuse victims has estimated that 50 percent of all women will be victims of battering at some point in their lives.[97]

□ Wife-beating is estimated by the FBI to be the most frequently occurring crime in the country.[98]

□ Sixteen percent of college students reported their parents had been physically violent toward one another within the previous year.[99]

□ In 3 percent of divorce actions, husbands mentioned the wife's physical abuse as a reason for seeking a divorce; 37 percent of wives involved in divorce actions mentioned physical abuse by their husbands as a reason for the suits.[100]

These statistics, although imprecise, reveal that wife abuse is a fairly common practice. We do know some facts about the conditions under which this phenomenon occurs. Foremost, while battered women are found in all social strata,[101] they tend to be found most often in families threatened by economic hardships. Dibble and Straus found from their study of 2,143 American couples that violence against spouses decreases as income increases. They reason that this occurs because:

> Low-income husbands are less in a position to live up to their role obligations as providers than are middle-class husbands. Their wives are, therefore, less likely to recognize the male as the head of the house than are their middle-class counterparts. When such recognition and other resources are lacking, husbands may, in turn, use force to control their wives. . . . In contrast . . . high-income husbands have economic and prestige resources which let them control their wives without the need to use force.[102]

Pregnancy seems to be a time when wives are most vulnerable to attack. The National Institute of Mental Health has found that a quarter of battered women were victims while pregnant.[103]

Those couples given to verbal aggression are more prone to engage in physical violence than those couples who are not.[104] This is contrary to the catharsis hypothesis, which argues that verbal aggression allows couples to get rid of their pent-up hostilities, thereby reducing the potential for physical violence.

Research on husbands known to be abusers of their wives has tended to find that these men are "underachievers," when compared to their wives. They may be less intelligent, less successful in their jobs or schools, or lower in certain status characteristics compared to their wives. A common pattern is for the husband's occupational status to be lower than that of his father-in-law, implying that a woman, in the eyes of her husband, retains the social status of her father.[105] The inability to be superior to one's wife in a male-dominated society apparently leads to the tendency to prove one's superiority over her in physical ways.

Wife-beating is also generated by a number of problems facing the husband in his marriage, his work, or other situation. These may include financial difficulties, sexual dysfunction, and jealousy.

A major contributing factor to being violent in a family situation is coming from a family that was itself violence prone. Husbands who batter their wives most often come from homes in which they were beaten by their parents or in which they had observed their own fathers beating their mothers. Much less likely, but significant nonetheless, is that women who are victims of wife abuse have tended also to come from homes where they were abused as children and/or their mothers were victims of physical abuse.

There are a number of psychological and interpersonal reasons for wife battering, and each case is in some ways idiosyncratic. For our purposes, though, let's focus on the societal supports for such violence, as argued by Murray Straus:

> The causes of wife-beating are to be found in the very structure of American society and its family system. Demonstrating this, even in principle, is a vast undertaking. All that can be done here is to identify seven of the main factors and to give the general flavor of the argument. . . . They are:
>
> □ the family is a type of social group characterized by a high level of conflict;
> □ the United States is a nation which is fundamentally committed to the use of violence to maintain the status quo or to achieve desirable changes;
> □ the child rearing patterns typically employed by American parents train children to be violent.
>
> This in turn:
>
> □ legitimizes violence within the family and
> □ builds violence into the most fundamental levels of personality and establishes the link between love and violence;
> □ reinforces the male dominant nature of the family system with a . . . tendency to use physical force to maintain that dominance when it is threatened;
> □ while the sexual inequalities inherent in our family system, economic system, social services, and criminal justice system, effectively leave many women locked into a brutal marriage. They literally have no means of redress, or even of leaving such a marriage.
>
> It is the combination of these factors which makes the family the most violent of all civilian institutions, and which accounts for that aspect of family violence which we call wife-beating.[106]

THE MODERN FAMILY FROM THE ORDER AND CONFLICT PERSPECTIVES

From the order perspective, the nuclear family (composed of father, mother, and their children) serves important survival functions for society (e.g., replacement of members, regulation of sexual behavior, socialization of new members, care and protection of members). Many functions that were performed by the family in past times have been taken over by other social institutions. Today, the family's primary functions are to socialize children and provide stabilization for adult family members. According to this view, the family operates most effectively when a division of labor is present in the nuclear family. Women fill the expressive or emotional roles and men fill the instrumental or economic roles. The trend toward greater depersonalization in society (living in densely populated cities and working in bureaucracies) is countered by families serving as havens.[107] Thus, the isolated nuclear family is an important adaptation making an achievement-oriented industrial society workable. In this way, the family "fits" with other social institutions and contributes to the maintenance of social order.

From the conflict perspective, the family is shaped by the demands of capitalism. At the macrolevel, the family is a vital part of the capitalist economy because it produces both workers and consumers to keep the economy going. The family is one of the primary mechanisms for perpetuating social inequality. Wealth is locked up in elite families and then passed down through intergenerational inheritance. This limits the resources and opportunities of those who are lower in the socioeconomic hierarchy. As we have seen, families pass on their advantages and disadvantages to their offspring. While this transmission of social class position promotes stability in society—which the order theorists cherish—it also promotes inequality based on ascription.

The family serves the requirements of capitalism in still another way: by idealizing the realm of the "personal." This serves the economy through heightened consumerism, and it also supports the interests of the dominant class by promoting false consciousness. The family is one of the primary socialization agents of youth, and as such it promotes the status quo by transmitting the culture of society. Children are taught to accept the inequalities of society as "natural," and they are taught to accept the political and economic systems without question. However, these very systems may need reform (or even transformation) to increase the likelihood of their serving the needs of everyone in society.

The family, from the conflict perspective, is not necessarily the haven posited by the order theorists. At the microlevel, conflict is generated by: (1) female resistance to male domination; and (2) the demands of work and economic hardships that work against intimacy and companionship between spouses. Thus, the modern family is not a tranquil institution, but one fraught with potential and actual conflict.

Conflict theorists argue that the isolated nuclear family has positive consequences for capitalism, but it is highly negative for individuals.[108] The economic system benefits when employers are able to move individuals from place to place without great disruption. The economy is served when employers do not have to worry about satisfying the emotional needs of workers. Finally, the system benefits when the family is isolated and therefore cannot affect society.

This has negative consequences for individuals, the conflict theorists maintain, because the family has sole responsibility for maintaining a private refuge from an impersonal society and for providing personal fulfillment, and is thus structured to fail. The demands are too great. The family, alone, cannot provide for all the emotional needs of its members, although its members try to fulfill these needs through consumerism, "the joy of sex," and child-centered activities. Conflict theorists would argue that society should be restructured so that personal fulfillment, identity, and other individual needs are met not only in the family but also in the community, at work, and in the other institutions of society.

FAMILIES OF THE FUTURE

We have examined a number of marriage/family trends of the late 1970s and early 1980s that have interesting implications for the future of families. Some of the most important are:

□ The proportion of couples living together outside of marriage is increasing.
□ Individuals are marrying later.
□ Couples are having fewer children.
□ The number of childless couples is rising.
□ An ever-greater proportion of wives are working outside the home.
□ The divorce rate continues to climb.
□ The proportion of dual-provider families is rising.
□ The fastest-growing family type is the household maintained by a woman with no husband present.

Do these trends indicate the nuclear family is dying? We can safely predict that some form of the nuclear family will characterize American society for the foreseeable future. Still, changes in marital and family life will create different life patterns for children and adults. Cherlin and Furstenburg predict that many children born in the 1980s will follow this sequence of living arrangements: live with both parents for several years, live with their mothers after their parents divorce, live with their mothers and stepfathers, live alone for a time in their early twenties, live with someone of the opposite sex without marrying, get married, get divorced, live alone again, get remarried, and end up living alone once more following the death of their spouses.[109]

Estimates are that about one-half of all young children alive today will spend some time in a single-parent family before they reach eighteen; about nine out of ten will eventually marry and then divorce; and about one out of three will marry, divorce, and then remarry.[110]

Although the nuclear family will continue to exist, there will be increasing diversity in patterns of family living. Such a variety of family forms has come under attack by contemporary conservatives. The "profamily" ideology they espouse is actually a call for a return to the traditional, patriarchal nuclear family with the husband in the labor force and the wife remaining in the home to care for the children.[111] Religious groups such as the Moral Majority are not alone in using emotionally charged family issues to gain support. They claim to champion the family, but by ignoring social and economic changes, their programs actually undermine stable family life.[112]

SUMMARY

The family is one of the most basic of all social institutions. Although the exact form of marriage and family varies by society, families universally provide society not only with a regular input of new members, but also serve as one of society's fundamental agents of socialization. Most significant, the family is the primary place where society's age and sex roles are learned and reinforced. Thus, like all institutions, the family is conservative, preserving the unity and stability of society.

Historical developments of the family are closely connected with economic developments. Contemporary family life is characterized by diversity that results (at least in part) from society's unequal distribution of resources. The family differs by social class, by race, and even by gender.

American families face a number of potential crises, most of them rooted in economic conditions. Changes in the labor force are eliminating jobs for many who support families. On the other hand, the labor market has created a huge increase in the number of women who work and care for families with or without husbands. This has not been accompanied by changes that would ease the demands of women's multiple roles.

The divorce rate is now the highest in history. Remarriage rates are also high. Many individuals now live in different types of families during the course of a lifetime. However, the family will continue because it will be a source of stability, of primary relations, and of emotional irrationality in a shifting, secondary, and overly impersonal and rational social world.

CHAPTER REVIEW

1. The family is one of the most idealized of all of society's institutions. There are disparities between common images of the family and real patterns of family life. New research has given us a better understanding of the American family in the past and present.

2. American families have always been nuclear in structure. In the colonial period, families were the central unit of the larger agriculturally based economic system. The family economy was based on the productive labor of all family members. This gave women an integral part in the colonial economy. Family and community were intertwined as families performed wide-ranging functions for their members. With the development of a wage economy, families became separate from the surrounding communities. As people left the home to work, the family took on a "private" quality, and the natures of women's work and men's work took on new meanings.

3. Family diversity became pronounced as society incorporated European immigrants and racial ethnics. Immigrants used their families to assist them in adapting to industrial work and urban living. Racial minorities were excluded from equal participation in the developing capitalistic economy; their families made survival possible for them.

4. The modern family is characterized by privacy and sharply segregated age and sex roles. Household size has declined and household composition has become increasingly diverse. More families now have only one spouse in residence than ever before.

5. Families are embedded in a class hierarchy. Different social classes have different links with institutions that can provide resources for family support, which creates variation in household and family structure. These variations also produce differences in forms of marital interaction and patterns of socialization.

Class position is the most important determinant of the quality of family life.

6. The changing nature of work has a direct impact on the family. Dual-provider families have increased problems with child care, the allocation of family tasks, and role overload. At the same time, employed wives report high values of their own well-being.

7. Although work and family are interdependent, husbands give priority to jobs over families, and employed wives give priority to families over their jobs. Sexism in the larger society reinforces sex segregation and patriarchy in families. Women and men experience the family in different ways, and men benefit more than women from family arrangements.

8. The family is not a tranquil institution, but one fraught with potential and actual conflict.

9. The divorce rate continues to rise in American society. The reasons for this trend are: increased social and financial independence of women; increased affluence; greater tolerance of divorce by religious groups; passage of no-fault divorce laws; and a change toward leniency in the public attitude toward divorce.

10. A primary responsibility of parents is to teach their children the culture—to teach them to fit into society. There are two basic modes of socialization used by parents. Repressive socialization demands conformity to rigid rules enforced by physical punishment. Participatory socialization allows children the freedom to explore and develop their unique potentials.

11. Adolescence is a difficult time in American society for many young people and their parents. The fundamental reason for this is that these people are in a transitional stage between childhood and adulthood with no clear distinction to indicate when adulthood is reached.

12. The aged also experience ambivalence because they are in a transitional stage between work and death. Moreover, they are the objects of discrimination in a youth-oriented society.

13. The family is a major source of violence in American society. One-fourth of all the murders in the United States involve the killing of spouses, parents, and children. Wife abuse is most common in low-income families.

14. Order theorists view the family as a source of stability for individuals and society. The traditional division of labor by sex contributes to social order.

15. Conflict theorists argue that the traditional family supports capitalism but is detrimental to individuals. The family is a major source of false consciousness, and the primary agent by which the system of social stratification is perpetuated.

16. A number of trends indicate that the American family is changing: for example, higher divorce rate, the rising number of childless marriages, and the fact that the fastest-growing family type is the household with no man present. One possibility for the future is for increased pluralism and social freedom with a wide diversity of acceptable lifestyles. An opposite scenario for the future is for ever-greater societal constraints on the family. Society in this case may demand a narrow range of choices to meet some crises or because the people in power demand conformity to their way.

FOR FURTHER STUDY

Mary Jo Bane, *Here to Stay: American Families in the Twentieth Century* (New York: Basic Books, 1976).

Caroline Bird, *The Two-Paycheck Marriage* (New York: Pocket Books, 1979).

Carl Degler, *At Odds, Women and the Family in America From the Revolution to the Present* (Oxford: Oxford University Press, 1980).

Michael Gordon, ed., *The American Family in Social-Historical Perspective*, 3rd ed. (New York: St. Martin's, 1983).

Kenneth Kenniston, *All Our Children: The American Family Under Pressure* (New York: Harcourt Brace Jovanovich, 1977).

Sar A. Levitan and Richard S. Belous, *What's Happening to the American Family?* (Baltimore: The Johns Hopkins University Press, 1981).

George Masnick and Mary Jo Bane, *The Nation's Families: 1960–1990* (Cambridge, Mass.: The Joint Center for Urban Studies of MIT and Harvard University, 1980).

Charles H. Mindel and Robert W. Habenstein, *Ethnic Families In America*, 2nd ed. (New York: Elsevier, 1981).

Harriet Pipes McAdoo, ed., *Black Families* (Beverly Hills, Calif.: Sage Publications, 1981).

Lillian Breslow Rubin, *Worlds of Pain: Life in the Working-Class Family* (New York: Basic Books, 1976).

Arlene S. Skolnick and Jerome H. Skolnick, eds., *Family in Transition* (Boston: Little Brown and Co., 1983).

Barrie Thorne and Marilyn Yalom, eds., *Rethinking the Family* (New York: Longman, 1982).

Patricia Voydanoff, ed., *Work and Family* (Palo Alto, Calif.: Mayfield Publishing Company, 1984).

Betty Yorburg, *Families and Societies, Survival or Extinction* (New York: Columbia University Press, 1983).

Eli Zaretsky, *Capitalism, the Family, & Personal Life* (New York: Harper Colophon, 1976).

NOTES AND REFERENCES

1. Arlene S. Skolnick, *The Intimate Environment*, 3rd ed. (Boston: Little Brown and Company, 1983), p. 33.

2. Barbara Laslett, "The Family as a Private and Public Institution: An Historical Perspective," pp. 44–59 in *The Family: Functions, Conflicts, and Symbols*, Peter Stein, Judith Richman and Natalie Hannon, eds. (Reading, Mass.: Addison-Wesley Publishing Co., 1977).

3. Erving Goffman, *The Presentation of Self in Everyday Life* (Garden City, N.Y.: Doubleday, 1959).

4. Arlene Skolnick, "Public Images, Private Realities: The American Family in Popular Culture and Social Science," pp. 297–315 in *Changing Images of the Family*, Virginia Tufte and Barbara Meyerhoff, eds. (New Haven: Yale University Press, 1979).

   Virginia Tufte and Barbara Meyerhoff, eds., *Changing Images of the Family* (New Haven: Yale University Press, 1979), pp. 17–18.

6. Christopher Lasch, *Haven in a Heartless World* (New York: Basic Books, Inc., 1977).

7. Ray L. Birdwhistell, "The Idealized Model of the American Family," pp. 462–467 in *Marriage and Family in a Changing Society*, James M. Henslin, ed. (New York: The Free Press, 1980), p. 496.

8. Barrie Thorne, "Feminist Rethinking of the Family: An Overview," in *Rethinking the Family: Some Feminist Questions*, Barrie Thorne and Marilyn Yalom, eds. (New York: Longman, 1982), p. 4.

9. Patricia Voydanoff, ed., *Work and Family*, "Introduction" (Palo Alto, Calif.: Mayfield Publishing Company, 1984), p. 3.

10. William J. Goode, "Idealization of the Recent Past: The United States," pp. 43–53 in *Family in Transition*, 4th ed., Arlene S. Skolnick

and Jerome H. Skolnick, eds. (Boston: Little Brown and Company, 1984).

11. Louise A. Tilly and Joan W. Scott, *Women, Work, and Family* (New York: Holt, Rinehart and Winston, 1978).

12. Much of this discussion is based on pp. 103–106 of Margaret L. Anderson, *Thinking About Women* (New York: Macmillan Publishing Co., 1983).

13. Barbara Laslett, "Family Membership, Past and Present," pp. 53–72 in *Family in Transition*, 4th ed., Arlene S. Skolnick and Jerome H. Skolnick, eds. (Boston: Little Brown and Company, 1984).

14. John Demos, "The American Family of Past Time," pp. 59–77 in *Family in Transition*, 2nd ed., Arlene S. Skolnick and Jerome H. Skolnick, eds. (Boston: Little Brown and Company, 1977).

15. Mary P. Ryan, *Womanhood in America: From Colonial Times to the Present*, 3rd ed. (New York: Franklin Watts, 1983), p. 35.

16. Demos, "The American Family of Past Time," p. 64.

17. Barry Jones, *Sleepers Awake! Technology and the Future of Work* (Melbourne: Oxford University Press, 1982), p. 2.

18. Anderson, *Thinking About Women*, p. 105.

19. Tamara K. Hareven, "Modernization and Family History: Perspectives on Social Change," *Signs, Journal of Women in Culture and Society* 2(1976): pp. 190–206.

20. Ryan, *Womanhood in America*, p. 81.

21. Carl Degler, *At Odds, Women and the Family in America from the Revolution to the Present* (Ithaca: Oxford University Press, 1980), p. 261.

22. Tamara K. Hareven, "Women and Men: Changing Roles," pp. 93–118 in *Women and Men: Changing Roles, Relationships and Perceptions*, Libby A. Carter, Anne Firor Scott and Wendy Martyna, eds. (Aspen Institute for Humanistic Studies, 1976).

23. Degler, *At Odds*, p. 66.

24. See the following critiques of the traditional portrayal of immigrant families: Rudolph J. Vecoli, "Contadini in Chicago: A Critique of the Uprooted," *Journal of American History* 51:405–417 and Frances H. Early, "The French-Canadian Family Economy and Standard of Living in Lowell, Massachusetts,

1870, pp. 482–503 in *The American Family in Social Historical Perspective*, 3rd ed., Michael Gordon, ed. (New York: St. Martin's Press, 1983).

25. Robert Blauner, *Racial Oppression in America* (New York: Harper and Row, 1972).

26. Herbert G. Gutman, *The Black Family in Slavery and Freedom, 1750–1925* (New York: Pantheon, 1976).

27. Skolnick, *The Intimate Environment*, p. 168.

28. Tilly and Scott, *Women, Work, and Family*.

29. Anderson, *Thinking About Women*, p. 106.

30. Eli Zaretsky, *Capitalism, The Family, and Personal Life* (New York: Harper Colophon Books, 1976).

31. Anderson, *Thinking About Women*, p. 114.

32. Rayna Rapp, "Family and Class in Contemporary America: Notes Toward an Understanding of Ideology," in *Rethinking the Family: Some Feminist Questions*, Barrie Thorne and Marilyn Yalom, eds. (New York: Longman, 1982), p. 170.

33. Andrew Hacker, ed., *U/S: A Statistical Portrait of the American People* (New York: The Viking Press, 1983), p. 93.

34. Ibid., p. 89.

35. Ibid., p. 93.

36. *A Growing Crisis, Disadvantaged Women and their Children*, United States Commission on Civil Rights, Clearinghouse Publication, 78 (May 1983), p. 5.

37. Rapp, "Family and Class in Contemporary America," p. 170.

38. Ibid., p. 181.

39. Donald Gilbert McKinley, *Social Class and Family Life* (Glencoe, Ill.: The Free Press, 1964), p. 4.

40. David M. Schneider and Raymond T. Smith, *Class Differences and Sex Roles in American Family and Kinship Structure* (Englewood Cliffs, N.J.: Prentice-Hall, 1973).

41. Rapp, *Family and Class in Contemporary America*, p. 176.

42. Ibid., p. 177.

43. Andrew Cherlin and Frank F. Furstenburg, Jr., "The American Family in the Year 2000," *The Futurist* 17 (June 1983), p. 10.

44. Maxine Baca Zinn, "Familism Among Chicanos: A Theoretical Review," *Humboldt Journal of Social Relations* 10 (Spring 1983), pp. 224–238.

45. Rapp, *Family and Class in Contemporary America*, p. 180.

46. Ibid., p. 182.

47. Everett D. Dyer, *The American Family, Variety and Change* (New York: McGraw-Hill, 1979), p. 209.

48. Paul M. Blumberg and P. W. Paul, "Continuities and Discontinuities in Upper-Class Marriage." *Journal of Marriage and the Family* 37 (February 1975), p. 69.

49. Peter J. Stein, Judith Richman, and Natalie Hannon, *The Family: Functions, Conflicts, and Symbols* (Reading, Mass.: Addison-Wesley, 1977), p. 9.

50. McKinley, *Social Class and Family Life*, p. 22.

51. Betty Yorburg, *Families and Societies, Survival or Extinction?* (New York: Columbia University Press, 1983), p. 186.

52. Philip Mattera, "Home Computer Sweatshops," *The Nation* (April 2, 1983), p. 390.

53. Anderson, *Thinking About Women*, p. 115.

54. Hacker, *U/S, A Statistical Portrait of the American People*, p. 101.

55. Jessie Bernard, *The Future of Marriage* (New York: Bantam, 1973).

56. Ibid., p. 192.

57. Martha Baum, "Love, Marriage, and the Division of Labor," in *Family, Marriage, and the Struggle of the Sexes*, Hans Peter Dreitzel, ed. (New York: The Macmillan Co., 1972), p. 102.

58. Lillian B. Rubin, *Worlds of Pain* (New York: Basic Books, 1973), p. 124.

59. Ibid., p. 93.

60. Ibid., p. 94.

61. Robert O. Blood and Donald Wolfe, *Husbands and Wives* (New York: The Free Press, 1960).

62. William J. Goode, *World Revolution and Family Patterns* (New York: The Free Press, 1963), p. 21.

63. Dair L. Gillespie, "Who Has the Power?" The Marital Struggle," pp. 105–157 in *Family, Marriage, and the Struggle of the Sexes*, Hans Peter Dreitzel, ed. (New York: The Macmillan Company 1972).

64. Cherlin and Furstenburg, "The American Family in the Year 2,000," p. 8.

65. Unless otherwise noted, the source used for the information below is Reiss, *The Family System in America*, Chap. 17.

66. Paul C. Glick, "Some Recent Changes in American Families," *Current Population Reports*, Series P–23, No. 52 (Washington, D.C.: U.S. Government Printing Office, 1975), p. 9.

67. Hugh Carter and Paul C. Glick, *Marriage and Divorce: A Social and Economic Study*, rev. ed. (Cambridge, Mass.: Harvard University Press, 1976), p. 403; and U.S. Bureau of the Census, *Current Population Reports*, Series P–20, No. 312 (Washington, D.C.: U.S. Government Printing Office, 1977), Tables 3 and F.

68. William J. Goode, "Family Disorganization," in *Contemporary Social Problems*, 4th ed., Robert K. Merton and Robert Nisbet, eds. (New York: Harcourt Brace Jovanovich, 1976), p. 529.

69. Hacker, *U/S A Statistical Portrait of the American People*, p. 113.

70. Cherlin and Furstenburg, "The American Family in the Year 2,000," p. 8.

71. Rosabeth Moss Kanter, *Work and Family in the United States: A Critical Review and Agenda for Research and Policy* (New York: Russell Sage Foundation, 1977).

72. Jeylan T. Mortimer and Jayne London, "The Varying Linkages of Work and Family," in *Work and Family*, Patricia Voydanoff, ed.

73. Patricia Voydanoff, ed., *Work and Family*, p. 7.

74. Joseph Pleck, "The Work-Family Role System," *Social Problems* 24 (April 1977), pp. 417–427.

75. S. M. Miller, "Confusions of a Middle-Class Husband," in the *Future of the Family*, Louise Kapp Howe, ed. (New York: Touchstone, 1972), p. 106.

76. M. P. Farrell and S. Rosenberg, *Men at Midlife* (Boston: Auburn House, 1981).

77. H. Hayghe, "Working Wives' Contributions to Family Income in 1977," *Monthly Labor Review* 39 (1979), pp. 62–64.

78. Mortimer and London, "The Varying Links of Work and Family," p. 27.

79. Joseph L. Pleck, G. L. Staines, and L. Laing, "Conflicts between Work and Family Life," *Monthly Labor Review* 40 (March 1980), pp. 29–32.

80. Marie Richmond-Abbot, *Masculine and Feminine, Sex Roles Over the Life Cycle*

(Reading, Mass.: Addison-Wesley, 1983), p. 275.

81. Grace Baruch, Rosalind Barnett, and Caryl Rivers, "Happiness is a Good Job," *Working Woman* (February 1983), pp. 75–78.

82. Kristin A. Moore and Isabell V. Sawhill, "Implications of Women's Employment for Home and Family Life," pp. 153–171 in *Work and Family*, Patricia Voydanoff, ed.

83. Kathleen Gerson, "Changing Family Structure," *Journal of the American Planning Association* 49 (Spring 1983), p. 145.

84. Arlene S. Skolnick and Jerome H. Skolnick, eds., "Introduction," *Family in Transition* (Boston: Little Brown and Company, 1983), p. 11.

85. Ibid.

86. There are a number of sources that document the differences in mode of socialization by social class. Especially important is the article that summarizes twenty-five years of studies of parent-child relationships by Urie Bronfenbrenner, "Socialization and Social Class through Time and Space," in E. E. Maccoby, T. M. Newcomb, and E. L. Hartley, eds., *Readings in Social Psychology* (New York: Holt, Rinehart and Winston, 1958), pp. 400–425. See also Melvin L. Kohn, "Social Class and Parental Values," *American Journal of Sociology* 64 (January, 1959), pp. 337–351; and James D. Wright and Sonia R. Wright, "Social Class and Parental Values for Children: A Partial Replication and Extension of the Kohn Thesis," *American Sociological Review* 41 (June, 1976), pp. 527–537.

87. For a historical review of child-rearing patterns, see Robert R. Sears, Eleanor E. Maccoby, Harry Levin, *et al.*, *Patterns of Child Rearing* (Evanston, Ill.: Row, Peterson, 1957).

88. Benjamin Spock, *Baby and Child Care* (New York: Simon and Schuster (Pocket Books), 1947).

89. William N. Stephens, "Family and Kinships," in *Sociology: An Introduction*, Neil J. Smelser, ed. (New York: John Wiley, 1967), p. 542.

90. James S. Coleman, *The Adolescent Society* (New York: Free Press, 1961).

91. For a discussion of "other-directness" in American society, see David Riesman, *The Lonely Crowd* (New Haven, Conn.: Yale University Press, 1950).

92. Milton L. Barron, *The Aging American* (New York: Thomas Y. Crowell, 1961), Chap. 4, "The Aged as a Quasi-Minority Group."

93. Felix Berardo, "Widowhood Status in the United States: Perspective on a Neglected Aspect of the Family Life Cycle," *The Family Coordinator* 17 (July, 1968), pp. 191–203.

94. For discussions of battered husbands, see Suzanne K. Steinmetz, "The Battered Husband Syndrome," *Victimology* 2, Numbers 3–4 (1977–78), pp. 449–509; Richard J. Gelles, "The Myth of Battered Husbands," *Ms.* 8 (October, 1979), pp. 65–66, 71–74; and "The Battered Husbands," *Time* (March 20, 1978), p. 69.

95. Murray A. Straus, "Wife Beating: How Common and Why?" *Victimology* 2, Numbers 3–4 (1977–78), pp. 449–451.

96. ABC News, October 18, 1979.

97. Lenore E. Walker, *The Battered Woman* (New York: Harper & Row, 1979), p. 1.

98. Reported in Laura Shapiro, "Violence: The Most Obscene Fantasy," *Mother Jones* 2 (December, 1977), p. 11.

99. Murray A. Strauss, "Leveling, Civility, and Violence in the Family." *Journal of Marriage and the Family* 36 (1974), pp. 13–27.

100. Suzanne K. Steinmetz, "Wifebeating, Husbandbeating—A Comparison of the Use of Violence between Spouses to Resolve Marital Conflicts," in *Battered Women: A Psychological Study of Domestic Violence*, Marina Roy, ed. (New York: Van Nostrand, 1977), p. 65.

101. Leonore E. Walker, *The Battered Woman* (New York: Harper and Row, 1979), p. 16.

102. Ursula Dibble and Murray S. Straus, "Some Social Structure Determinants of Inconsistency Between Attitudes and Behavior: The Case of Family Violence," *Journal of Marriage and Family* 42 (February 1980), p. 79.

103. Reported in William Steif, "U.S. Government, Slowly Aiding Battered Wives," *Rocky Mountain News* (October 27, 1979), p. 76.

104. Richard J. Gelles, "No Place to Go: The

Social Dynamics of Marital Violence," in *Battered Women*, pp. 57–58; see also, Murray A. Straus, "Sexual Inequality, Cultural Norms, and Wife Beating," *Journal of Marriage and the Family* 36 (February, 1974), pp. 13–30.

105. John E. O'Brien, "Violence in Divorce Prone Families," *Journal of Marriage and the Family* 33 (November, 1971), pp. 692–698.

106. Straus, "Wife Beating," pp. 449–451. See also Murray A. Straus, "A Sociological Perspective on the Prevention and Treatment of Wifebeating," in *Battered Women: A Psychosociological Study of Domestic Violence*, Maria Roy, ed. (New York: Van Nostrand, 1977), pp. 232–233.

107. Talcott Parsons and Robert F. Bales, *Family Socialization and Interaction Process* (Glencoe, Ill.: The Free Press, 1955).

108. The following argument is from Eli Zaretsky, *Capitalism, The Family & Personal Life* (New York: Harper Colophon, 1976).

109. Cherlin and Furstenberg, Jr., "The American Family in the Year 2,000," pp. 8–9.

110. Ibid., p. 9.

111. Zillah R. Eisentein, "The Sexual Politics of the New Right: Understanding the 'Crisis of Liberalism' for the 1980's," *Signs, Journal of Women in Culture and Society* 7 (Spring 1982), pp. 567–588.

112. Michael Lerner, "Recapturing the 'Family Issue,'" *The Nation* (February 6, 1982), p. 141.

15

Education in America

In the spring of 1983, after eighteen months of study, The National Commission on Excellence in Education issued its report simultaneously to the Secretary of Education and as an open letter to the American people. The introduction to this scathing indictment of America's public schools follows:

> Our nation is at risk. Our once unchallenged preeminence in commerce, industry, science, and technological innovation is being overtaken by competitors throughout the world.

This report is concerned with only one of the many causes and dimensions of the problem, but it is the one that undergirds American prosperity, security, and civility. We report to the American people that while we can take justifiable pride in what our schools and colleges have historically accomplished and contributed to the United States and the well-being of its people, the educational foundations of our society are presently being eroded by a rising tide of mediocrity that threatens our very future as a nation and a people. What was unimaginable a generation ago has begun to occur—others are matching and surpassing our educational attainments.

If an unfriendly foreign power had attempted to impose on America the mediocre educational performance that exists today, we might well have viewed it as an act of war. As it stands, we have allowed this to happen to ourselves. We have even squandered the gains in student achievement made in the wake of the Sputnik challenge. Moreover, we have dismantled essential support systems which helped make those gains possible. We have, in effect, been committing an act of unthinking, unilateral educational disarmament.

Our society and its educational institutions seem to have lost sight of the basic purposes of schooling, and of the high expectations and disciplined effort needed to attain them.

Source: Excerpt from National Commission on Excellence in Education, *A Nation at Risk*, reprinted in *The Chronicle of Higher Education* (May 4, 1983), pp. 1–16.

This chapter is divided into five sections. The first describes the characteristics of American education. The second focuses on how corporate society reproduces itself through education—in particular, how the schools socialize youth in accordance with their class position and point them toward factory, bureaucratic, or leadership roles in the economy. The third section describes the current role of education in perpetuating inequality in society. Next, we examine alternatives to eliminate the class bias in education. The final section summarizes the chapter by looking at education from the order and conflict perspectives.

THE CHARACTERISTICS OF AMERICAN EDUCATION

Education as a Conserving Force

The formal system of education in American society (and in all societies) is conservative, since the avowed function of the schools is to teach newcomers the attitudes, values, roles, specialties, and training necessary to the maintenance of society. In other words, the special task of the schools is to preserve the culture, not to transform it. Thus, the schools indoctrinate their pupils in the culturally prescribed ways. Children are taught to be patriotic. They learn the myths, the superiority of their nation's heritage, who are the heroes and who are the villains. Jules Henry has put it this way:

> Since education is always against some things and for others, it bears the burden of the cultural obsessions. While the Old Testament extols without cease the glory of the One God, it speaks with equal emphasis against the gods of the Philistines; while the children of the Dakota Indians learned loyalty to their own tribe, they learned to hate the Crow; and while our children are taught to love American democracy, they are taught contempt for the totalitarian regimes.[1]

There is always an explicit or implicit assumption in American schools that the American way is the only really right way. When this assumption

"CLASS WILL CONFINE ITS STYLE OF CLASSROOM PRAYER TO THE NORMAL, PROPER, ACCEPTED, CONSERVATIVE, ALL-AMERICAN, RIGHT-WING CHRISTIAN VARIETY!"

is violated on the primary and secondary school level by the rare teacher who asks students to consider the viability of world government, or who proposes a class on the life and teachings of Karl Marx or about world religions, then strong enough pressures usually occur from within the school (administrators, school board) or from without (parents, the American Legion, Daughters of the American Revolution) to quell the disturbance. As a consequence, creativity and a questioning attitude are curtailed in school, as Parenti points out forcefully in Panel 15–1.

PANEL 15–1

"The Politics of the Classroom"

Only recently have I come to realize how intensive was the political indoctrination I underwent while a grade school pupil some thirty years ago. Persons who insist that we "keep politics out of the classroom" fail to realize that the grade school's first commitment is to the propagation of values and practices that sustain the sociopolitical status quo. I observe that these things remain much the same, and the observation has made me extremely conscious of the politics of my 1942

grade school classroom. There was then, and there is now, more political socialization going on in the average public school than in the average local political club.

My recollections go back to the autumn of 1942, to the grade school in New York's East Harlem where I was taught the religion of nationalism, complete with its hymns (Star Spangled Banner), its sacred symbols (Old

(continued)

Glory), its rituals (flag drill, salutes), its holy scriptures (Declaration of Independence, Constitution, Gettysburg Address), its litany and incantations (pledge of allegiance, patriotic slogans), its Early Church Fathers (Washington, Adams, Jefferson), its harbingers and prophets (Paul Revere, Patrick Henry), its martyrs (Nathan Hale, Abraham Lincoln), its Judases and apostates (Benedict Arnold, John Wilkes Booth), and its myths of divine origin (Plymouth Rock, Constitution Hall).

My classmates and I were treated to stories of America's territorial and commercial expansion that suffered from few of the cumbersome distractions normally caused by historical fact. . . . Our understanding of slavery probably owed more to the perspective of the plantation owners than to that of the abolitionists, the latter being portrayed by our teachers as unattractive troublemakers. We believed that slaves, although occasionally treated cruelly, were generally well taken care of, a view confirmed in our minds by the appearance of the movie *Gone with the Wind.* . . . But our best hatred was reserved for the Japanese and Germans with whom we were locked in mortal combat. . . . The Japanese, we knew, were the wartime equivalent of the Indians, unspeakably cruel, inhuman and subhuman, yellow skin being little different from red skin—which may have explained why cowboys were enlisted to do the killing. The Germans, in our minds, were somewhat more human. True, they were capable of showing unmistakable signs of enmity such as goose-stepping, speaking in harsh accents,

and shooting people, but it did not escape us that they were represented as being of the same species as we, indeed of the same race. (None of us had heard of Auschwitz.)

This, then, was my political education by the end of grade school: my mind was a repository of simple lies and monstrous caricatures taken from the movie screen and fortified by the school, there being much congruity between the fantasies of Hollywood and the preachments of P.S. 85. At the age of ten I was a flag-waving, gut-responding nation-state chauvinist who shrieked with delight when rows of enemy soldiers were machine-gunned in their tracks and who experienced the death of each American soldier (complete with plaintive background music) and the downing of each American plane as a personal loss.

With Hiroshima, apocalyptic fantasy found its reality. The forces of the righteous had prevailed; the sheer display of our power was confirmation of our virtue. America emerged supreme and God showed he had sense enough to be on our side. It was my unexamined faith that the United States was the greatest and finest of all countries, the guardian of freedom, the nation that acted only with benevolent intent and beneficial effect, the shining light and hope of all mankind. This was the conviction of a grade school child but also the one I carried into my years of college teaching. Nor was that so remarkable: it is still the faith held by most Americans, certainly by those men who rule even now as I write.

Mass
Education

Americans have a basic faith in education. This faith is based on the assumption that a democratic society requires an educated citizenry so that individuals may participate in the decisions of public policy. It is for this reason that they not only provide education for all citizens, but also compel children to go at least to the eighth grade or until age sixteen (although this varies somewhat from state to state).

It is hard to quarrel with the belief that all children should be compelled to attend school, since it should be for their own good. After all, the greater the educational attainment, the greater the likelihood of larger economic rewards and upward social mobility. However, to compel a child to attend school for six hours a day, five days a week, forty weeks a year, for at least ten years, is quite a demand. The result is that many students are in school for the wrong reason. The motivation is compulsion, not interest in acquiring skills or curiosity about their world. This involuntary feature of American schools is unfortunate since so many school problems are related to the lack of student interest.

As a result of the goal of and commitment to mass education, an increasing proportion of persons have received a formal education. In 1940, for example, 38 percent of Americans age twenty-five to twenty-nine had completed high school. This proportion increased to 75 percent in 1970 and 85.7 percent in 1980.[2]

Local Control of Education

Although the state and federal governments finance and control education in part, the bulk of the money and control for education comes from local communities. There is a general fear of centralization of education—into a statewide educational system or, even worse, federal control. Local school boards (and the communities themselves) jealously guard their autonomy. Since, as it is commonly argued, local people know best the special needs of their children, local boards control allocation of monies, curricular content, and the rules for running the schools, as well as the hiring and firing of personnel.

There are several problems with this emphasis on local control. First, tax money from the local area traditionally finances the schools. Whether the tax base is strong or weak has a pronounced effect on the quality of education received (a point I shall return to later in this chapter). Second, local taxes are almost the only outlet for a taxpayers' revolt. Dissatisfaction with high taxes (federal, state, and local) on income, property, and purchases is often expressed at the local level in defeated school bonds and school tax levies. Third, since the democratic ideal requires that schools be locally controlled, the ruling body (school board) should represent all segments of that community. Typically, however, the composition of school boards has overrepresented the business and professional sectors and overwhelmingly underrepresented blue-collar workers and various minority groups. The result is a governing body that is typically conservative in outlook and unresponsive to the wishes of people unlike themselves. A final problem with local control is the lack of curriculum standardization across school districts. Families move on the average of once every five years (and the rate is probably higher for families with school-age children), and the large number of children moving from district to district often find a wide variation in curriculum and graduation requirements.

The Competitive Nature of American Education

It is not surprising that the schools in a highly competitive society are competitive. Competition extends to virtually all school activities. The compositions of athletic teams, cheerleading squads, "pompon squads," debate teams, choruses, drill teams, bands, and dramatic play casts are almost always determined by competition between classmates. Grading in courses, too, is often based on the comparison of individuals ("grading on a curve") rather than on measurement against a standard. To relieve boredom in the classroom, teachers often invent competitive games such as "spelling baseball," or "hangman." In all these cases, the individual learns at least two lessons: (1) your classmates are "enemies," for if they succeed, they do so at your expense; and (2) fear of failure is the great motivator, not intellectual curiosity or love of knowledge.

The "Sifting and Sorting" Function of Schools

Schools play a considerable part in choosing the youth who come to occupy the higher-status positions in society. Conversely, school performance also sorts out those who will occupy the lower rungs in the occupational prestige ladder. Education is, therefore, a selection process. The sorting is done with respect to two different criteria: a child's ability and his or her social class background. Although the goal of education is to select on ability alone, ascribed social status (the status of one's family, race, and religion) has a pronounced effect on the degree of success in the educational system. The school is analogous to a conveyor belt, with people of all social classes getting on at the same time but leaving the belt in accordance with social class—the lower the class, the shorter the ride. (See Panel 15–2.)

PANEL 15–2

Cooling Out the Failures

Although our schools can be a golden avenue of opportunity for those who succeed in them, they are also the arena in which many confront failure that condemns them to the more subservient positions in our society. How are those who "fail" handled so they do not become bitter revolutionaries intent on overthrowing the system that so brutally used them?

"Cooling out" is the process of adjusting victims to their loss. When someone has lost something that is valuable to him, it leads to intense frustration. This frustration and its accompanying anger are dangerous to society because they can be directed against the social system if the social system is identified as being responsible for the loss. But our educational system is insidiously effective, and many who fail within it (perhaps most), never even need to be cooled out. They learn early in grade school that they are stupid and that higher education is meant for others. They suffer miserably in school as they continue to be confronted year after year with more evidence of their failure, and they can hardly wait until they turn sixteen so they can leave for greener pastures. Such persons are relieved to end their educational miseries and need no cooling out.

For those who do need to be cooled out, however, a variety of techniques is used. The primary one makes use of the ideology of individualism. To socialize students into major cultural values means to teach them more values than conformity and competition. . . . Two other major values students consistently confront in our educational system are the ideologies of individualism and equal opportunity. They are taught that people make their own way to the top in a land of equal opportunity. Those who make it do so because of their own abilities, while those who do not make it do so because of a lack of ability or drive on their own part. They consequently learn to blame themselves for failure, rather than the system. It was not the educational system that was at fault, for it was freely offered. But it was the fault of the individual who failed to make proper use of that which society offered him. Individualism provides amazing stabilization for the maintenance of our social system, for it results in the system going unquestioned as the blame is put squarely on the individual who was himself conned by the system.

If this technique of cooling out fails to work, as it does only in a minority of cases, other techniques are put into effect. Counselors and teachers may point out to the person that he is really "better suited" for other tasks in life. He may be told that he will "be happier" doing something else. He might be "gradually disengaged" from the educational system, perhaps be directed to alternate sources of education, such as vocational training.

The individual may also be encouraged to blame his lack of success on tough luck, fate, and bad breaks. In one way or another, as he is cooled out, he is directed away from questioning the educational system itself, much less its relationship to maintaining the present class system and his subservient position within it. . . .

Finally, the malcontent-failure has the example before him of those from similar social class circumstances as his own who did "make it." This becomes incontrovertible evidence that the fault does lie with himself and not the system, for if they could make it, so could he. This evidence of those who "made it" is a powerful cooling out device, as it directly removes any accusatory finger that might point to the educational and social systems.

Having our educational system set up in such a way that some lower class youngsters do manage to be successful and are able to enter upper middle class positions serves as a pressure valve for our social system. In the final analysis, it may well be this pressure valve which has prevented revolutions in our country—as the most able, the most persistent, and the most conforming are able to rise above their social class circumstances. And in such instances, the educational system is pointed to with pride as representing the gateway to golden opportunity, freely open to all.

Source: James M. Henslin, Linda K. Henslin, and Steven D. Keiser, "Schooling for Social Stability: Education in the Corporate Society," in *Social Problems in American Society*, James M. Henslin and Larry T. Reynolds, eds., 2nd ed. (Boston: Allyn and Bacon, 1976), pp. 311–312.

The Preoccupation with Order and Control

Most administrators and teachers share a fundamental assumption that school is a collective experience requiring subordination of individual needs to those of the school.[3] American schools are characterized, then, by constraints on individual freedom. The school day is regimented by the dictates of the clock. Activities begin and cease on a timetable, not in accordance with the degree of interest shown or whether students have mastered the subject. Silberman characterizes this as the "tyranny of the lesson plan," meaning that teachers too often see the lesson plan as the end rather than as a means to an end. Another indicator of order is the preoccupation with discipline (that is, absence of unwarranted noise and movement, and concern with the following of orders).

In their quest for order schools also demand conformity in clothing and hair styles. Dress codes are infamous for their contraints upon the freedom to dress as one pleases. School athletic teams also restrict freedom, and these restrictions are condoned by the school authorities. Conformity is also demanded in what to read, where to set the margins on the typewriter, and how to give the answers the teacher wants.

The many rules and regulations found in schools meet a number of expressed and implicit goals. The school authorities' belief in order is one reason for this dedication to rules: teachers are rated not on their ability to get pupils to learn but rather on the degree to which their classroom is quiet and orderly. The community also wants order. A survey of high school students' parents found that nearly two-thirds believe that "maintaining discipline is more important than student self-inquiry."[4] An important reason is that schools operate on the assumption of distrust. As Christopher Jencks has observed, "The school board has no faith in the central administration, the central administration has no faith in the principals, the principals have no faith in the teachers, and the teachers have no faith in the students."[5] The consequence of this distrust is a self-fulfilling prophecy. When teachers are not treated as professionals (not consulted on matters that concern them most, required to punch time clocks), they do not act as professionals. When students are treated as slaves, they do not develop into self-reliant, self-motivated individuals. An excerpt from a famous (or infamous) book entitled *The Student as Nigger* dramatizes the demands for order in American schools.

[Students] haven't gone through twelve years of public school for nothing. They've learned one thing and perhaps only one thing during those twelve years. They've forgotten their algebra. They've grown to fear and resent litera-ture. They write like they've been lobotomized. But Jesus, can they follow or-ders! . . . . Students don't ask that orders make sense. They give up expecting things to make sense long before they leave elementary school. Things are true because the teacher says they're true. At a very early age we all learn to ac-cept "two truths," as did certain medieval churchmen. Outside of class, things are true to your tongue, your fingers, your stomach, your heart. Inside class things are true by reason of authority. And that's just fine because you don't care anyway. Miss Wiedemeyer tells you a noun is a person, place or thing. So let it be. You don't give a rat's ass; she doesn't give a rat's ass. The impor-tant thing is to please her. Back in kindergarten, you found out that teachers only love children who stand in nice straight lines. And that's where it's been at ever since.[6]

The paradoxes listed below indicate the many profound dilemmas in American education. They set the foundation for the remaining sections of this chapter, which deal with the crises facing education and with some alternative modes.

☐ Formal education encourages creativity but curbs the truly creative in-dividual from being too disruptive to society.

▢ Formal education encourages the open mind but teaches dogma.

▢ Formal education has the goal of turning out mature students but does not give them the freedom essential to foster maturity.

▢ Formal education pays lip service to meeting individual needs of the students but in actuality encourages conformity at every turn.

▢ Formal education has the goal of allowing all students to reach their potential, yet it fosters kinds of competition that continually cause some people to be labeled as failures.

▢ Formal education is designed to allow people of the greatest talent to reach the top, but it systematically benefits certain categories of people regardless of their talent: the middle- and upper-class students who are white.

THE POLITICAL ECONOMY OF EDUCATION IN CORPORATE SOCIETY

Americans want to believe that their society is a meritocratic one in which the most intelligent and talented people rise to the top. Since public schools are free and available to everyone, individuals can go as high as their ability and drive will take them. In this view education is the great equalizer, providing opportunities for everyone to develop his or her full potential. This section and the next argue that this belief is a myth. The truth is that schools reinforce inequality in society.[7] This belief, besides being a myth, has an especially negative outcome: it tends to blame or credit individuals for their level of failure or success without considering the aspects of the social structure that impel or impede their progress (another instance of blaming the victim). Thus, it results in praise of the system and condemnation of individuals who are defined as losers.

The Role of Education in Corporate Society

The schools perform several vital functions for the maintenance of the prevailing social, political, and economic order. Education, along with the institutions of the family and religion, has a primary responsibility for socializing newcomers to the society. A second function of education is the shaping of personalities so that they are in basic congruence with the demands of the society. In other words, one goal of the educational system of any society is to produce people with desired personality traits (such as competitiveness, altruism, bravery, conformity, or industriousness, depending upon the culture and organization of the society). A third function is preparing individuals for their adult roles. In American society this means preparing individuals for the specialized roles of a highly complex division of labor. It also means preparing youngsters for life in a rapidly changing world. Early in American history the primary aims of schooling were teaching the basics of reading, writing, spelling, and arithmetic, so that adults in an agrarian society could read the Bible, write letters, and do simple accounting. Modern society, on the other hand, demands people with specialized occupational skills, with expertise in narrow areas. The educational system is saddled with providing these skills in addition to the basics. Moreover, the schools have taken over the teaching of citizenship skills, cooking, sewing, and even sex education—skills and knowledge that were once the explicit duty of each family to transmit to its offspring.

Contemporary schools go beyond these functions, however. They exist to meet the needs of the economy by providing employers with a disciplined and skilled labor force and a means to control individuals in order to maintain political stability. A review of the changing role of the school in American history will make this role clear.[8]

When most Americans were farmers and artisans, the schools had a relatively simple task because the skills society required were essentially unchanged from generation to generation and were generally learned at home. As the economy changed to a factory system in urban settings, the family became less important as an agent of economic socialization, and the school grew in importance. Work became specialized, technology changed rapidly, and work was done in large organizations with rigid authority structures. The workers were no longer in control of their own labor but were controlled by the owners of the factories. Thus, workers were placed in potentially oppressive and alienating work situations. This was a concern to capitalists because the workers might unite to challenge the existing system. Stability was also threatened by the rising numbers of immigrants who entered the United States to live in urban centers and work in factories.

According to radical educational historians, mass public education was perceived by those in power as the answer to these problems in a changing society, for the church and family were no longer effective in teaching the skills and uniformity in belief necessary for an effective and tractable work force.

> An ideal preparation for factory work was found in the social relations of the school: specifically, in its emphasis on discipline, punctuality, acceptance of authority outside the family, and individual accountability for one's work. The social relations of the school would replicate the social relations of the work-place, and thus help young people adapt to the social division of labor. Schools would further lead people to accept the authority of the state and its agents—the teachers—at a young age, in part by fostering the illusion of the benevolence of the government in its relations with citizens. Moreover, because schooling would ostensibly be open to all, one's position in the social division of labor could be portrayed as the result not of birth, but of one's own efforts and talents.[9]

Social Class Biases of the Educational System

Through their curricula, testing, bureaucratic control, and emphasis on competition, the schools reflect the social class structure of society by processing youth to fit into economic slots quite similar to those of their parents. As the educational system rapidly expanded during the nineteenth and early twentieth centuries, a system of class stratification emerged within the schools.[10] As the high schools opened to youth of all social classes, the older curriculum, which provided a standard education for all, was supplanted by the "progressive" notion that school should be tailored to meet the individual needs of each child. While this makes obvious sense, the effects of the new curriculum tended to provide vocational school tracks for children of working-class families and preparation for college for children of professionals. Such a division was not blatant, because "objective" tests were used to decide the program for each child. Though seemingly fair, these tests were biased. The IQ test, for example, is clearly biased to reward children who have had middle-class experiences.[11] Thus, they unfairly legitimate a hierarchical division of labor by separating individuals into different curricula, with different expectations, which in turn then fulfill the prophecy of the original test scores. Moreover, they serve to reconcile people to their eventual placement in the economic system.[12]

The amount of schooling one has is directly correlated with economic success in society. Thus, schools act as society's gatekeepers. But the way in which the schools work biases the outcome, as we have seen. Two "rules-of-the-school" games serve to buttress this further. The first is that

> excellence in schooling should be rewarded. Given the capacity of the upper class to define excellence in terms on which upper class children tend to excel (for example, scholastic achievement), adherence to this principle yields inegalitarian outcomes (for example, unequal access to higher education) while maintaining the appearance of fair treatment. Thus the principle of rewarding excellence serves to legitimize the unequal consequences of schooling by associating success with competence. At the same time, the institution of objectively administered tests of performance serves to allow a limited amount of upward mobility among exceptional children of the lower class, thus providing further legitimation of the operations of the social system by giving some credence to the myth of widespread mobility.[13]

The second "rule of the game" is the principle that elementary and secondary schooling should be financed largely from local revenues. This principle is supported on the seemingly logical grounds that the local people know what is best for their children. The effect, however, is to perpetuate educational inequalities. The next section catalogs the reasons for this and the many other ways in which education reinforces inequality.

EDUCATION AND INEQUALITY

Education is presumed by many to be the great equalizer in American society—the process by which the disadvantaged get their chance to be upwardly mobile. The data in Table 15–1 show, for example, that the higher the educational attainment, the higher the income. But these data do not in any way demonstrate equality of opportunity through education. On the contrary, the schools have helped perpetuate social and economic differences.

As we have seen, a fundamental function of the schools is to "sift and sort" their products. Those who succeed in school will occupy the higher-status positions in society. Conversely, school performance also sorts out those who will occupy the lower rungs in the occupational prestige ladder.

TABLE 15–1   Median Income of Men and Women (full-time year-round workers) by Education, 1980

Years of School Completed	Males	Females
Less than high school	$13,117	$ 8,216
One to three years of high school	16,101	9,676
High school graduate	19,469	11,537
One to three years of college	20,909	12,954
College graduate	24,311	15,143
Five or more years of college	27,690	18,100

Source: U.S. Bureau of the Census, "Money, Income and Poverty Status of Families and Persons in the United States, 1981," *Current Population Reports*, P–60, No. 134 (July 1982).

Education is therefore a selection process. The sorting is done with respect to two different criteria: the child's ability and his or her social class background. Although the goal of education is to select on ability alone, ascribed social status (the status of one's family, race, and religion) has a pronounced effect on the degree of an individual's success in the educational system.

To document this assertion and analyze its consequences, this section examines two factors: (1) the comparison of school performances by socioeconomic background, and (2) how the educational system tends to reinforce the socioeconomic status differentials in performance.

The Relation Between School Success and Socioeconomic Status

The evidence that educational performance is linked to socioeconomic background is clear and irrefutable. The advantages of the children of the relatively affluent over those of the poor are enormous, as seen in the following illustration from a study by the Carnegie Council on Children:

Jimmy is a second grader. He pays attention in school, and enjoys it. School records show he is reading slightly above grade level and has a slightly better than average I.Q. Bobby is a second grader in a school across town. He also . . . . enjoys school and his test scores are quite similar to Jimmy's. Bobby is a safe bet to enter college (more than four times as likely as Jimmy) and a good bet to complete it—at least twelve times as likely as Jimmy.

Bobby will probably have at least four years more schooling than Jimmy. He is twenty-seven times as likely as Jimmy to land a job which by his late forties will pay him an income in the top tenth of all incomes. Jimmy has one chance in eight of earning a median income.

These odds are the arithmetic of inequality in America. . . . Bobby is the son of a successful lawyer whose annual salary of $35,000 puts him well within the top 10 percent of the United States income distribution in 1976. Jimmy's father, who did not complete high school, works from time to time as a messenger and a custodial assistant. His earnings, some $4,800, put him in the bottom 10 percent.[14]

The research of Bowles and Gintis also makes the point that socioeconomic background determines how much education one receives. They found that those in the lowest 10 percent in socioeconomic background *with the same average IQ scores* as those in the highest 10 percent will receive an average of 4.9 fewer years of education.[15]

Christopher Jencks and his associates have added to the work of Bowles and Gintis, providing the most current and methodologically sophisticated analysis of the determinants of upward mobility in their book *Who Gets Ahead?*[16] Among their findings is that educational attainment, especially graduation from college, is very important to later success; but it is not so much what one learns in school, as the obtaining of the credentials that counts. Most important, the probability of high educational attainment is closely tied to family background.

Inequality in education occurs also along racial lines (which is closely related to socioeconomic status). In 1980, for example, 82.5 percent of adult whites were high school graduates, compared to only 69.7 percent of adult blacks. The Coleman report, an analysis of all third-, sixth-, ninth-, and twelfth-grade pupils in 4,000 schools, noted that whites surpass blacks in various achievement areas and that the gaps increase the longer they remain in school.[17] Clearly, the school is to blame, for in no instance is the initial gap narrowed. Moreover, the increasing gaps are *understated*, since there is a greater tendency for the people of lowest aptitude among the minority groups to drop out of school.

William Ryan has summarized the situation as follows:

> The school is better prepared for the middle-class child than for the lower-class child. Indeed, we could be tempted to say further that the school experience is tailored for, and stacked in favor of, the middle-class child. The cause-and-effect relationship between the lack of skills and experiences found among lower-class children and the conditions of lower-class life has yet to be delineated. So far, explanations of this relationship have been, at best, sketchy, and have been based on casual observation. We know poor and middle-class children exhibit certain differences in styles of talking and thinking, but we do not know yet why or how these differences occur.
>
> We do know, however, that these differences—really differences in *style* rather than ability—are not handicaps or disabilities (unlike barriers to learning such as poor vision, mild brain damage, emotional disturbance or orthopedic handicap). They do represent inadequate *preparation* for the reality of the modern urban school. They are, in no sense, cultural or intellectual defects.[18]

How is the educational system stacked in favor of middle- and upper-class child and against children from the lowest classes?* At least four

---

*I have phrased the question so as to focus on the system, not the victims, contrary to the typical response, which is to focus on the "cultural deprivation" of the poor. That approach attacks the home and culture of poor people. It assumes that these people perform inadequately because they are handicapped by their culture. Observers cannot, however, make the value judgment that a culture is "deprived." They can only note that their milieu does not prepare children to perform in schools geared for the middle class. In other words, children of the poor and/or minority groups are not nonverbal—they are very verbal, but not in the language of the middle class.

interrelated factors explain why the educational system tends to reinforce the socioeconomic status differentials in the United States: finances, curriculum, segregation, and personnel.

Finances   Though not a guarantee of educational equality, if schools spent approximately the same amount of money per pupil, this would be a significant step toward meeting that goal. This has not been accomplished nationwide, because wealthier states are able to pay much more per pupil than are poorer states. Table 15–2 provides a state-by-state comparison in per-pupil expenditures for 1982–1983. These data show that each New York student, for example, is supported by a subsidy of $4,303 while the average student in Alabama is funded at only a $1,546 level. Since the federal government provides only about 8 percent of the money for schools, equalization across state lines is impossible as long as the states vary in wealth and commitment to public education.

The disparities in per-pupil expenditures within a given state are also great, largely because of the tradition of funding public schools through property taxes. This procedure is discriminatory because rich school districts can spend more money than poor ones on each student, and at a *lower* taxing rate. Thus suburban students are more advantaged than students from the inner city; districts with business enterprises are favored over

TABLE 15–2   Public School Per-Pupil Expenditures by State, 1982–1983

State	Expenditure	State	Expenditure	State	Expenditure
Ala.	$1,546	Ky.	$2,291	N.D.	$3,055
Alaska	6,301	La.	2,718	Ohio	2,087
Ariz.	2,342	Maine	2,651	Okla.	3,030
Ark.	2,035	Md.	3,486	Ore.	3,502
Calif.	2,727	Mass.	2,958	Pa.	3,290
Colo.	2,989	Mich.	3,684	R.I.	3,792
Conn.	3,746	Minn.	3,157	S.C.	2,016
Del.	3,799	Miss.	1,919	S.D.	2,386
D.C.	3,767	Mo.	2,512	Tenn.	2,124
Fla.	2,970	Mont.	2,981	Texas	2,557
Ga.	2,217	Neb.	2,747	Utah	1,969
Hawaii	3,213	Nev.	2,311	Vt.	2,992
Idaho	2,110	N.H.	2,341	Va.	2,740
Ill.	3,209	N.J.	4,190	Wash.	2,887
Ind.	2,650	N.M.	2,904	W.Va.	2,480
Iowa	2,917	N.Y.	4,303	Wis.	3,429
Kan.	3,094	N.C.	2,680	Wyo.	3,992

Source: National Education Association, reported in *USA Today* (September 21, 1983), p. 4A. Reprinted with permission, *USA Today*.

agricultural districts; and those districts blessed with natural resources are better able to provide for their children than are districts with few resources. In Colorado, for example, in 1982 property owners in the Rangely school district were taxed 5 mills, and this raised $547 per student per mill, while in Center school, taxes were more than 9 times that rate—45 mills—yet that raised only $20 per student per mill.[19]

In a major setback to equal funding within each state, the U.S. Supreme Court ruled 5–4 in the 1973 case of *San Antonio Independent School District* v. *Rodriguez* that the Texas school finance system, based on local property tax, did *not* violate the equal protection clause of the Fourteenth Amendment. This judgment had two major consequences: (1) It sanctioned the long-standing discriminatory practice of financing education on the basis of the wealth of the local district; and (2) it said, in effect, that school finance is a matter left to each individual state. The state courts have grappled with this problem of equity funding for schools with mixed results. The most progressive state has been California: Its program is based on the 1971 decision by its Supreme Court in *Serrano* v. *Priest*. The ruling in this case stated that to tie the quality of schools to a community's ability to raise taxes discriminates against the poor, because it makes the quality of a child's education a function of the wealth of his or her parents and neighbors. This landmark ruling has led the way for other states to rule against the traditional methods for funding education. There remain a number of states that continue to have discriminatory school finance systems. Others are striving to achieve reasonable financial equality.[20] In most cases disparities remain because of generous minimal guarantees of state aid to districts regardless of need, which is added to the amount collected from the traditional property taxes. In Colorado, for example, a 1973 law mandated that the state move toward equity, but implementation of the formula in 1982 meant that the per-pupil expenditure in the poorest district was $1,800, and $3,204 in the wealthiest.[21] The Colorado Supreme Court ruled in 1982 that the state's school financing was legal since the state constitution did not require equality in per-pupil spending.

The role of the federal government in providing funds for education shifted significantly during the Reagan administration in two ways. First, the amount allocated to federal aid to education was cut by 25 percent. Since federal monies have almost exclusively been used for compensatory programs to help the disadvantaged, the poor suffer disproportionately from such cuts. In the 1981–1982 school year, for example, $111 million was cut from programs to help low-income children with basic skills in reading and mathematics. These cutbacks will reverse some significant gains by the disadvantaged. From 1970 to 1980 the overall reading performance of nine-year-olds rose by 3.9 percent, while blacks raised their average by 9.9 percent, providing some strong evidence that Title I funds for elementary students from disadvantaged backgrounds were working. Also, research in 1978 on Head Start concluded that the participants in this program "were less likely to require remedial education, less likely to be left back, and scored higher in math achievement tests. A cost/benefit analysis found that the benefits of Head Start outweighed costs by 236 percent."[22] Obviously, any reduction in the financial support of such programs will have detrimental effects on the success of economically disadvantaged students.

A second significant move by the Reagan administration was to disburse the federal monies to the states rather than to the local school districts as had been the case. The probable result is that the monies will be less likely than before to reach the disadvantaged.[23] The state legislatures will decide how the money will be spent. Given that many legislatures are controlled by rural elements, it is likely that less money than before will go to urban schools, where the largest number of financially disadvantaged students is found. The commitment of many state legislatures to provide adequate funds for racial minorities is questionable. In fact, the aim of much federal aid to schools since 1965 was to achieve equity for the poor and minorities who had suffered under the previous system of states' rights. Finally, some legislatures may be inclined to reduce state aid by the amount that the federal government provides, as a way to cut their costs while appearing to keep state funds for education at the same level.

Current budget cuts at the state level, federal cutbacks, and property tax reductions such as those resulting from California's Proposition 13 have put unusual financial strains on many local districts. One solution has been for local school boards to start charging fees for children wishing to participate in so-called frills such as music, athletics, and drama. This approach is discriminatory because poor children are less likely to participate or, if they do, to do so at a sacrifice by their parents. If these activities have educational value, then any strategy that makes participation the result of the ability of parents to pay is clearly discriminatory.

Obtaining a college diploma is a most important avenue to later success. The poor are severely disadvantaged by the U.S. system of higher education in two ways. First, their taxes help subsidize public higher education (typically at least one-third of the average college student's costs are subsidized by states); yet—and this is the second way in which the poor are disadvantaged—their children are likely to find the costs of higher education prohibitive. These costs are rising rapidly, making college attendance by children of the poor even less likely in the future.[24]

Curriculum American schools are essentially middle or upper class. The written and spoken language in the schools, for example, is expected to be middle class. For children of the poor, however, English (at least middle-class English) may be a second language.

In these and other matters, the curriculum of the schools does not accommodate the special needs of the poor. To the contrary, the schools assume that the language and behaviors of the poor are not only alien but wrong—things to be changed. This assumption denigrates the ways of the poor and leads to loss of ego strength (a trait already in short supply for the poor in a middle-class world).

The curriculum also is not very germane to the poor child's world. What is the relevance of conjugating a verb when you are hungry? What is the relevance of being able to trace the path of how a bill becomes a law when your family and neighbors are powerless? Irrelevancy for the poor is also seen in the traditional children's primers, which picture middle-class surroundings and well-behaved blond children. There is little effort at any educational level to incorporate the experience of slum children in relation to realistic life situations of any kind. Schools also have a way of ignoring real-life problems and controversial issues. Schools are irrelevant if they disregard topics such as race relations, poverty, and the distribution of community power.

The typical teaching methods, placement tests, and curricula are inappropriate to children from poor families. This factor, along with the others mentioned earlier, results in failure for a large proportion of these youngsters. They perceive themselves (as do others in the system) as incompetents. As Silberman has put it:

> Students are not likely to develop self-respect if they are unable to master the reading, verbal, and computational skills that the schools are trying to teach. Children must have a sense of competence if they are to regard themselves as people of worth; the failure that minority-group children, in particular, experience from the beginning can only reinforce the sense of worthlessness that the dominant culture conveys in an almost infinite variety of ways, and so feed the self-hatred that prejudice and discrimination produce. Chronic failure makes self-discipline equally hard to come by; it is these children's failure to learn that produces the behavior problems of the slum school . . . and not the behavior problems that produce the failure to learn.[25]

Silberman's discussion of the problems of minority-group children can be broadened to include all poor children (who are, after all, also a minority group). The poor of all races experience prejudice and discrimination. They quickly learn that they are considered misfits by the middle class (teacher, administrator, citizen).

Segregation American schools tend to be segregated by social class, both by neighborhood and, within schools, by ability grouping. Schools are based in neighborhoods that tend to be relatively homogeneous by socioeconomic status. Racial and economic segregation is especially prevalent at the elementary school level, carrying over to a lesser degree in the secondary schools. Colleges and universities, as we have seen, are peopled by a middle- and upper-class clientele. Thus, at every level, children tend to attend a school with others like themselves in socioeconomic status and race. This results most often in unequal facilities, since rich districts provide more than poor districts do for their pupils. Moreover, within districts, the schools labeled "lower class" tend to get a disproportionately smaller slice of the economic pie than "middle-class" schools.

Although segregation according to the socioeconomic composition of neigh-borhoods is by no means complete, the tracking system within the schools achieves almost total segregation by socioeconomic status. Tracking, employed by about half the high schools in the United States, divides the entire student body into two or more distinct career lines such as college preparatory, vocational, business, general, or remedial. The rationale for tracking is that it provides a better fit between the needs and capabilities of the student and the demands and opportunities of the curriculum. Slower students do not retard the progress of brighter ones, and teachers can adapt their teaching to the level of the class. The special problems of the different ability groups, from "gifted" to "retarded," can be dealt with more efficiently when groups of students share the same or similar problems.

Although these benefits may be real, tracking is open to some serious criticisms. First, those in lower tracks are discouraged from producing up to their potential. Second, college-bound students develop feelings of su-periority while others may define themselves as inferior. Third, and most important, the tracking system is closely linked to the stratification system— that is, students from low-income families are disproportionately placed in the lowest track, resulting in a reinforcement of the social class structure. If this criticism is correct, the tracking system so prevalent in American schools denies equality of educational opportunity and thus is contrary to the ideal of the school system as open and democratic.

Why does the tracking system have such a strong effect? There are four principal reasons why this system stunts success.

Stigma. Assignment to a lower track carries a strong stigma. Such students are labeled as intellectual inferiors. Their self-esteem wanes as they see how others perceive them and behave toward them. Thus, individuals assigned to a track other than college prep perceive themselves as "second class," as unworthy, stupid, and in the way. Clearly, assignment to a low track is destructive to a student's self-concept.

The Self-fulfilling Prophecy. This effect is closely related to stigma. If placed in the college-prep track, students are likely to receive better instruction, have access to better facilities, and be pushed more nearly to their capacity than those assigned to other tracks. The reason is clear: the teachers and administration *expect* great things from the one group and lesser things from the other. Moreover, these expectations are fulfilled. Those in the higher track do better and those in the lower track do not. These behaviors justify the greater expenditures of time, faculties, and experimental curricula for those in the higher track—thus perpetuating what Merton has called a "reign of error."[26]

An example comes from the controversial study by Rosenthal and Jacobson. Although this study has been criticized for a number of methodological shortcomings, the findings are consistent with theories of interpersonal influence and with the labeling view of deviant behavior. In the spring of 1964, all students in an elementary school in San Francisco were given an

IQ test. The following fall the teachers were given the names of children identified by the test as potential academic spurters, and five of these were assigned to each classroom. The "spurters" were chosen by means of a table of random numbers. The only difference between the "experimental group" (those labeled as "spurters") and the "control group" (the rest of the class) was in the imaginations of the teachers. At the end of the year all the children were again tested, and the children from whom the teachers expected greater intellectual gains showed such gains (in IQ and grades). Moreover, they were rated by their teachers as being more curious, interesting, happy, and more likely to succeed than the children in the control group.[27]

The implications of this example are clear. Teachers' expectations have a profound effect on students' performance. When students are overrated, they tend to overproduce; when they are underrated, they underachieve. The tracking system is a labeling process that affects the expectations of teachers (and fellow students and parents). The limits of these expectations are crucial in the educational process. Yet the self-fulfilling prophecy can work in a positive direction if teachers have an unshakable conviction that their students *can* learn. Concomitant with this belief, teachers should hold *themselves,* not the students, accountable if the latter should fail.[28] Employed in this manner, the self-fufilling prophecy can work to the benefit of *all* students.

Future Payoff.   School is perceived as relevant for those students going to college. Grades are a means of qualifying for college. For the non-college-bound student, however, school and grades are far less important for entry into a job. At most they need a high school diploma, and grades really do not matter as long as one does not flunk out. Thus, non-college-bound students often develop negative attitudes toward school, grades, and teachers. These attitudes for students in the lower tracks are summed up by sociologist Arthur Stinchcombe:

> Rebellious behavior is largely a reaction to the school itself and to its prom-
> ises, not a failure of the family or community. High school students can be
> motivated to conform by paying them in the realistic coin of future advantage.
> Except perhaps for pathological cases, any student can be motivated to con-
> form if the school can realistically promise something valuable to him as a
> reward for working hard. But for a large part of the population, especially the
> adolescent who will enter the male working class or the female candidates for
> early marriage, the school has nothing to offer. . . . In order to secure conform-
> ity from students, a high school must articulate academic work with careers of
> students.[29]

As we have seen, being on the lower track has negative consequences. These students are more rebellious both in school and out and do not participate as much in school activities. Finally, what is being taught is often not relevant to their world. Thus, we are led to conclude that many of these students tend to feel that they are not only second-class citizens but perhaps even pariahs. What other interpretation is plausible in a system that disadvantages them, shuns them, and makes demands of them that are irrelevant?

The Student Subculture. The reasons given above suggest that a natural reaction of persons in the lower track would be to band together in a subculture that is antagonistic toward school. This subculture would quite naturally develop its own system of rewards, since those of the school are inaccessible. David Hargreaves, in *Social Relations in a Secondary School*, showed this to be the case in an English secondary school that incorporated tracks (or "streams," as they are called in England): boys in the high stream were drawn to the values of the teachers, while lower-stream boys accorded each other high status for doing the opposite of what the teacher wanted.

These factors show how the tracking system is at least partly responsible for that fact that those in the lower tracks are relatively low achievers, unmotivated, uninvolved in school activities, more prone to drop out of school, and to break school or community rules. To segregate students either by ability or by future plans is detrimental to the students labeled as inferior. It is an elitist system that needs to be reevaluated and changed. Tracking is a barrier to equal educational opportunity for lower-income and other minority students who are disproportionately assigned to the lowest track. It is an elitist system that for the most part takes the children of the elite and educates them to take the elite positions of society. Conversely, children of the nonelite are trained to recapitulate the experiences of their parents. In a presumably democratic system that prides itself on providing avenues of upward social mobility, such a system borders on immorality.

In conclusion, inequality in the educational system causes many people to fail in American schools. This phenomenon is the fault of the schools, not of the children who fail. To focus on these victims is to divert attention from the inadequacies of the schools. The blame needs to be shifted.

> We are dealing, it would seem, not so much with culturally deprived children as with culturally depriving schools. And the task to be accomplished is not to revise, and amend, and repair deficient children but to alter and transform the atmosphere and operations of the schools to which we commit these children. Only by changing the nature of the educational experience can we change its product.[30]

POSSIBLE WAYS TO PROMOTE EQUALITY OF OPPORTUNITY

A fundamental tenet of American society is that each individual, regardless of sex, race, ethnicity, religion, age, and social class, has the opportunity to be unequal on her or his own merits. In other words, the system must not impede individuals from reaching their potential and from gaining the unequal rewards of an unequal society.[31] The data presented in this chapter have shown that American schools block the chances of minority and poor children in their quest to be successful in society. This section outlines several programs that schools could adopt to promote equality of opportunity for all children. These programs are directed at the inequalities resulting from poverty, race, and geographic locality.

Reforming the Financing of Education

First, there must be a commitment to a free education for all. Presumably, public education at the elementary and secondary levels is free, but this is a fallacy. Although circumstances vary by district, typically children must pay for their supplies, textbooks, locker rental, towels, admission to plays and athletic events, insurance, transportation, meals, and the like. Some districts waive these costs for poor families, but this does not occur uniformly across the United States, and the procedures for granting these waivers are often degrading (that is, done in such a way that others know who receives the handouts). These costs are regressive because they take a larger proportion of the poor family's budget, thereby increasing the pressure to withdraw the child from school, where he or she drains the family resources. By making education absolutely free to all children, communities could reduce dropout rates among the poor. As mentioned in the chapter on poverty, a program of greater scope would also provide a living allowance for each child from a poor family who stayed in school beyond the eighth grade. This program would be analogous to the GI bill, which provided similar benefits to returning servicemen.[32]

These reforms require additional sources of money, and this brings us to the second financial reform: equalization of allocations across districts. As noted earlier, the traditional reliance on property taxes within a school district has created many inequities. Equalizing educational opportunities for all American children entails changing the system by which residents in property-rich communities can support lavish schools at low tax rates while those in poorer districts have to sacrifice more for lesser educational benefits. Obviously, this notion meets resistance on two fronts: from residents of the wealthier districts and from those who fear the loss of local autonomy in making school policies.

Currently, a number of states are attempting to equalize school expenditures per pupil by minimizing local property tax dependence and increasing state aid. Connecticut has instituted an equalization plan that shows promise of achieving equity in educational opportunity. The four key elements of this progressive plan are:

1. All towns, regardless of wealth, are guaranteed supplemental funds from the state so that their budgets equal that generated by the ninth wealthiest town in the state. Local wealth is determined by a formula combining an equalized property valuation and personal federal income tax.

2. To compensate for the additional costs of educating students from economically disadvantaged families, children from needy families are counted as 1.5 for purposes of per-pupil expenditures.
3. Each school district must spend at a baseline level, thus ensuring that certain minimum expenditures are found uniformly throughout the state. Districts may spend beyond this limit, but if they do not meet the minimum expenditure, the state withholds money on a dollar-for-dollar basis.
4. Each school district must offer a program of instruction that includes a full range of course offerings as specified by the state department of education.[33]

This plan's requirement that individual districts give up some autonomy to the centralizing authority of the state is a problem for many who value highly local control of the schools. Supporters, however, argue that this worry is offset because the plan is structured to achieve financial equity across districts. The fiscal and educational reforms of Connecticut are significant departures from the old system of school finance, where the advantaged increase their advantages. The Connecticut plan is being closely monitored by other states to see how effective it is in achieving the important goal of financial parity on a per-pupil basis statewide.

Busing for Racial Balance

Ever since the landmark desegregation case *Brown* v. *Board of Education* in 1954, the federal courts have upheld the right of black children to attend a nondiscriminatory school system. The court-ordered busing of students across school boundaries for the purpose of achieving racial balance in schools is in this tradition. The basic assumption of the courts in desegregating the schools is that segregated schools are inherently unequal even if the cost per pupil is equal (although it rarely is). Busing has been and continues to be an important and highly emotional issue dividing parents, educators, and politicians. Generally, research findings disclose four positive effects of school desegregation:[34]

1. Racial isolation in public schools has been significantly reduced by busing. Court-ordered desegregation decreased segregation between minority students and whites by 50 percent from 1968 to 1976.
2. Racial prejudice, especially among black students, is reduced.
3. The school performance of white children is unaffected while minorities benefit academically from desegregated schools. The earlier minority children experience desegregation, the more likely they will be positively affected academically.
4. Minority students from desegregated elementary and secondary schools are more likely to attend and remain in predominantly white colleges.

Although the evidence supports the importance of integrated schools for improving the education of the disadvantaged, the merit of forced busing to accomplish this goal is questionable. First is the irony that busing for integration actually promotes segregation. Sociologist James Coleman has noted that the fear of busing has increased "white flight" to residential areas or to private schools where white inhabitants are not threatened.[35] The result is that major urban areas are becoming increasingly black.

Second, busing attacks the symptom rather than the sources of the problem. Blacks are disproportionately unemployed. They live in segregated neighborhoods. Norman Cousins has argued that we must attack these problems rather than the limited one of the schools.

> What is happening is that we are bypassing the fundamentals in the search for an answer. It is the condition of the black in America that continues to be the central, overriding, and saturating issue. Everything involved in lifting a people out of their low estate in society—housing, health, economic opportunity, nutrition, access to justice under the law—fits into this total challenge.[36]

A third problem with busing is that it creates an emotional climate detrimental to education. There are numerous reasons why busing is such an explosive issue. Parents object to their children's attending a school far away from home when neighborhood schools exist. Attending schools at a distance is not only inconvenient, it also signifies a loss of control over their children's schools. Busing is also a highly charged issue because white parents fear their children's education will be negatively affected by the intrusion of blacks. White parents typically believe that blacks possess a deviant value system (violence, immorality, lack of ambition, and instant gratification). They fear that from exposure to such a life style their own children might acquire these traits. Related to this is the fear that blacks in white schools will become disruptive and create a situation in which teachers must emphasize discipline rather than education. Coleman has described this logic:

> The theory is that children who themselves may be undisciplined, coming into classrooms that are highly disciplined would take on the characteristics of their classmates, and be governed by the norms of the classrooms, so that the middle-class values would come to govern the integrated classrooms. In that situation, both white and black children would learn. What sometimes happens, however, is that characteristics of the lower-class black classroom, namely a high degree of disorder, come to take over and constitute the values and characteristics of the classroom in the integrated school. It's very much a function of the proportion of lower-class pupils in the classroom. . . . The proportion that creates a basically antischool atmosphere differs from school to school. But you can see if 70 or 80 percent of the children are undisciplined in their ordinary behavior pattern, then the values of the classroom are going to be undisciplined. If 70 or 80 percent are disciplined, then you're all right, unless you have a situation in which white teachers are afraid to discipline lower-class black children, which sometimes happens too.[37]

Finally, busing sometimes creates an atmosphere of hatred, tension, and violence that clearly is disruptive to the educational process. The presence of demonstrating adults heaping abuse on children, other forms of violence by adults and students, the presence and behavior of the police, the surveillance by the media, and the efforts of the school at social control all create a situation in which formal education cannot occur.[38] Moreover, white and black parents, even those supporting busing, are reluctant to allow their children to participate because they realistically fear for their safety.

Accounts from the media give the impression that desegregated schools are always imbued with tension, violence, and an atmosphere not conducive to learning. The process of desegregating schools, however, can be structured to minimize problems and maximize the positive results. Research shows that race relations will be improved, achievement enhanced, self-esteem increased, and the life chances of students improved if schools have the following characteristics:

▢ Students are desegregated early, in kindergarten if possible.
▢ Students are assigned so that schools and classrooms are neither predominantly white nor predominantly black.
▢ A sizable number of children who are high achievers are assigned to each classroom.
▢ Substantial interaction is encouraged among the races in academic and extracurricular activities. Most important, this contact must be deliberately structured to maximize equal-status contact.
▢ Instruction is individualized so that students work to achieve personal goals and are not competing on a personal basis in academic subjects.
▢ Texts and curricula include multicultural themes in depth.
▢ The principal fulfills the crucial role of fostering a social climate supportive of integration and academic goals.
▢ The teachers recruited are nonracist, prointegration, fair, and insistent on high performance; are trained to handle diversity in the classroom; and understand the power of their expectations for students so that expectations may be used positively.
▢ The student body remains relatively stable over time.[39]

Alternatives to Busing

There are two types of alternatives to busing. One encourages school integration by increasing the attraction of special-purpose schools to both races. The other reverts to the segregated neighborhood school but attempts to provide compensatory programs for the disadvantaged.

Because integrated schools encourage equality of educational opportunity, schools within a district should be so desirable that students of both races *want* to attend because of the superior program offered. In this plan, in addition to its basic curriculum each school would have a special emphasis that would act as an "educational magnet" to attract pupils.[40] One school could emphasize the performing arts and music, while another could stress biology and botany, or foreign languages, or the open-classroom approach, to name a few. The emphasis would be on offering programs that members of both races would want. Students would attend a particular school because of its program, not because of a court order. This would achieve integration without discontent and incidentally create programs to fit the needs of students.

The other alternative to forced busing is to allow children to attend their neighborhood school regardless of its racial composition. Going back to the neighborhood school would allow parents to regain control over their children's education. Because neighborhood schools are likely to be racially unbalanced, and because this imbalance has been proved to be detrimental to blacks, school districts could allocate more money per student to schools more than 50 percent black.[41] This money could reduce class sizes, attract outstanding teachers, finance special programs, provide tutors, and the like.

Special Programs for the Disadvantaged of All Races

The most important variable affecting school performance is not race but socioeconomic status. Regardless of race, children from poor families tend to do less well in school than children from families who are better off. Compensatory programs such as Head Start and Follow Through are predicated on the assumption that if children from lower-class homes are to succeed in middle-class schools, they must have special help to equalize their chances. California has initiated an innovative program to eliminate the learning gap between middle-class and lower-class children. This program is for all youngsters from kindergarten through the third grade and aims at having "every youngster reading and writing, computing, and excited about school by the time he or she is eight years old."[42] This goal is accomplished through parent involvement and individualized instruction. Using parent volunteers, paid aides, and teachers reduces the adult-pupil ratio to 1:10. Early results show that although all students benefit from this plan, children from schools in lower-class areas are gaining faster than those in other schools. Although the plan is expensive, administrators hope that the costs will be offset by great reductions in expenditures for remedial work for older students. The payoff for the children is enormous: the program allows them to be "normal" participants in school and to avoid the stigma of failure.[43]

The problem with compensatory programs is that they "blame the victim." The effort is to change the individual so that he or she will adapt to society. As noted in this and earlier chapters, these programs are based on the assumption that the individual is culturally deprived and needs extra help. By blaming the individual, well-meaning people direct attention away from the schools and society—the real sources of the problem. The two types of programs described below focus on the reformation of the school and the society.

Reforming Schools to Allow Realization of Individual Potential

The California experiment mentioned above is an attempt to change the schools to minimize the differences between the children of the advantaged and disadvantaged. But this plan, like most, does not question the structure and philosophy of the educational system, which opponents argue essentially stifles children in attaining their potential. In the view of the critics, the system itself is wrong and the generator of many profound problems. These critics want to reconstruct the entire educational enterprise along very different lines. This demand for change is based on three related assumptions. The first is that the school is a microcosm of the larger society. Since society is sick (competitive, repressive, inhumane, materialistic, racist, and imperialist) so, too, are the schools. Changing society entails changing the schools.

The second assumption of the radical critics of education is that the process of public education as it presently exists damages, thwarts, and stifles children. The schools somehow manage to suppress the natural curiosity of children. They begin with inquisitive children and mold them into acquisitive children with little desire to learn.

Third, the educational system is a product of society and hence shapes its products to meet the requirements of society. The present system is predicated on the needs of an industrial society in which citizens must follow orders, do assigned tasks in the appropriate order and time span, and not challenge the status quo. But these behaviors will not be appropriate for life in the near future or perhaps even the present. The future will likely require people who can cope with rapid turnover—changes in occupations, human relationships, and community ties. Moreover, the citizens of the future (present?) must be able to cope with a complex of choices. Does an educational system that is built on order, on a rigid time schedule, and on the lecture method adequately prepare youngsters for life as it is and will be?

The proponents of these and other alternatives are critical of American education. They conclude that American schools are failing not only children from the ghettos of large cities, but also suburban and small-town youngsters. The schools fail because they treat children as miniature adults; because they treat children as a group rather than as individuals; because they stifle creativity; because they are repressive; and because they fail to allow children to reach their potential. It is important to recognize that this is not a new situation.

As Peter Drucker has stated:

> Today's school does no poorer a job than it did yesterday; the school has simply done a terribly poor job all along. But what we tolerated in the past we no longer can tolerate. . . . The school has suddenly assumed such importance for the individual, for the community, for the economy and for society, that we cannot suffer the traditional, time-honored incompetence of the educational system.[44]

This approach makes the revolutionary assumption that the success or failure of the child lies with the school, not the child. The child is innately curious. If he or she is apathetic, then, it must be the fault of the school. Because the self-fulfilling prophecy is such a powerful factor, teachers should hold *themselves*, not their students, responsible if the students do not learn. Middle-class bias in all its forms (teacher expectations for behavior/class bias tests, materials) must be eradicated from schools because it ensures the failure of the lower-class child.

Restruc-
turing
Society

The approaches to equality described above focus on changing either individual students or the schools. But if equality of opportunity is truly the goal, education cannot accomplish it alone. The problem is not in the individual or in the school, but in the structure of society. As Bowles has argued:

> The burden of achieving equality of educational opportunity. . . . cannot be borne by the educational system alone. The achievement of some degree of equality of opportunity depends in part on what we do in the educational system but also, to a very large degree, in what we do elsewhere in the economy, in the polity, and in the society as a whole.[45]

Closing the achievement gap between advantaged and disadvantaged students cannot be accomplished without a society-wide assault on racism and poverty. Christopher Jencks and his associates maintain that this requires fundamental changes in the system of societal rewards: a redistribution of wealth through equalizing occupational rewards, a minimum income for all members of society, and a reduction in the ability of parents to transmit their economic advantages and disadvantages to their offspring.[46] After a thorough investigation of inequality in American society, they concluded that inequality in the schools is not the major cause of economic stratification among adults. Poverty can only be eliminated through fundamental revisions in the economic and familial institutions. This is not to say that reform of the schools should be ignored. Efforts to improve American schools should parallel attempts to restructure the other institutions of society.[47]

EDUCATION FROM THE ORDER AND CONFLICT PERSPECTIVES

From the order perspective, schools are of crucial importance in maintaining societal integration. They are a vital link between the individual and society, deliberately indoctrinating youth with the values of society, and teaching the skills necessary to fit into society. Most important, the schools sift and sort children so that they will find and accept their appropriate niche in the societal division of labor.

The conflict perspective emphasizes that the educational system reinforces the existing inequalities in society by giving the advantaged the much greater probability of success (in grades, in achievement tests, in IQ tests, in getting an advanced education; all of which translate into economic and social success outside school). Conflict adherents also object to the "hidden curriculum" in schools—that is, learning to follow orders, to be quiet, to please persons in authority regardless of the situation. In short, students learn to fit in, to conform. This may be functional for society and for students who will act out their lives in large bureaucracies, but it is not conducive to personal integrity and to acting out against situations that ought to be changed.

CHAPTER REVIEW

1. The American system of education is characterized by: (a) conservatism—the preservation of culture, roles, values, and training necessary for the maintenance of society; (b) belief in mass education; (c) local control; (d) competition; (e) reinforcement of the stratification system; and (f) preoccupation with order and control.

2. The belief that American society is meritocratic, with the most intelligent and talented at the top, is a myth. Education, instead of being the great equalizer, reinforces social inequality.

3. Schools perform a number of functions that maintain the prevailing social, political, and economic order: (a) socializing the young; (b) shaping personality traits to conform with the demands of the culture; (c) preparing youngsters for adult roles; and (d) providing employers with a disciplined and skilled labor force.

4. The curricula, testing, bureaucratic control, and emphasis on competition in schools reflect the social class structure of society by processing youth to fit into economic slots similar to those of their parents.

5. The schools are structured to aid in the perpetuation of social and economic differences in several ways: (a) by being financed principally through property taxes; (b) by providing curricula that are irrelevant to the poor; and (c) by tracking according to presumed level of ability.

6. The tracking system is closely correlated with social class; students from low-income families are disproportion-

ately placed in the lowest track. Tracking thwarts the equality of educational opportunity for the poor by generating four effects: (a) stigma, which lowers self-esteem; (b) self-fulfilling prophecy; (c) a perception of school as having no future payoff; and (c) a negative student subculture.

7. Equality of educational opportunity must begin with the reform of education finance in order to equalize the budgets of schools regardless of the wealth of individual districts.

8. Racial desegregation of schools has positive effects for pupils, particularly those belonging to minorities. Many programs of forced integration have failed because they have created tensions and violence. Research has shown, however, that with proper organization, desegregation of schools can be successful.

9. Compensatory programs have achieved some success in narrowing the gap between children of the poor and of the affluent. The problem with these programs is that they blame the children for not measuring up to society's standards. Thus, this approach diverts attention from the schools and society—the real sources of the problem.

10. Radical critics of the educational system argue that the schools fail all children, whether they are from the ghettos or suburbs. Schools, as they are presently structured, damage, thwart, and stifle children. Inquisitive children become acquisitive children with little desire to learn. Schools shape children to fit into a society where citizens follow orders and do assigned tasks without questioning.

11. The restructuring of schools will not meet the goal of equality of educational opportunity, radical critics argue, unless the society is also restructured. This change requires a society-wide assault on racism and poverty and a redistribution of wealth to reduce the inequities that result from economic advantage.

FOR FURTHER STUDY

Education: General

Samuel Bowles and Herbert Gintis, *Schooling in Capitalist America: Educational Reform and the Contradictions of Economic Life* (New York: Basic Books, 1976).

Martin Carnoy, ed., *Schooling in a Corporate Society: The Political Economy of Education in America*, 2nd ed. (New York: David McKay, 1975).

John I. Goodlad, *A Place Called School* (New York: McGraw-Hill, 1983).

Jules Henry, *Culture against Man* (New York: Random House (Vintage Books), 1963).

John Holt, *The Underachieving School* (New York: Dell Publishing, 1972).

Frank Musgrove, *School and the Social Order* (New York: John Wiley & Sons, 1979).

Joseph A. Scimecca, *Education and Society* (New York: Holt, 1980).

Charles E. Silberman, *Crisis in the Classroom* (New York: Random House, 1970).

Education and Inequality

Randall Collins, *The Credential Society: A Historical Sociology of Education and Stratification* (New York: Academic Press, 1979).

Paula Freire, *Pedagogy of the Oppressed*, Myra Bergman Ramos, trans. (New York: Seabury Press, 1970).

Robert J. Havighurst and Daniel U. Levine, *Society and Education*, 5th ed. (Boston: Allyn and Bacon, 1979).

Institute for the Study of Educational Policy, *Equal Educational Opportunity: More Promise than Progress* (Washington, D.C.: Howard University Press, 1978).

Christopher Jencks et al., *Who Gets Ahead? The Determinants of Economic Success in America* (New York: Basic Books, 1979).

Jerome Karabel and A. H. Halsey, eds., *Power and Ideology in Education* (New York: Oxford University Press, 1977).

Caroline Hodges Persell, *Education and Inequality* (New York: Free Press, 1977).

Ray C. Rist, *The Invisible Children: School Integration in American Society* (Cambridge, Mass.: Harvard University Press, 1978).

James E. Rasenbaum, *Making Inequality: The Hidden Curriculum of High School Tracking* (New York: Wiley/Interscience, 1976).

Joel Spring, *The Sorting Machine* (New York: Longman, 1976).

Adam Yarmolinsky, Lance Liebman, and Corinne S. Schelling, eds., *Race and Schooling in the City* (Cambridge, Mass.: Harvard University Press, 1981).

NOTES AND REFERENCES

1. Jules Henry, *Culture against Man* (New York: Random House/Vintage, 1963), pp. 285–286.
2. Andrew Hacker, ed., *U/S: A Statistical Portrait of the American People* (New York: Viking, 1983), p. 251.
3. The following discussion depends largely on Charles E. Silberman, *Crisis in the Classroom* (New York: Random House, 1970), pp. 122–157. Excerpts from this work are reprinted by permission of Random House,

Inc.; copyright © 1970 by Charles E. Silberman.

4. Silberman, *Crisis in the Classroom*, p. 145.

5. Quoted in ibid., p. 133. As a former high school teacher, I can attest to the validity of Jencks's statement.

6. Jerry Farber, *The Student as Nigger* (New York: Pocket Books, 1970), p. 92.

7. This section is based on the work of several authors who have written on the political economy of education: Samuel Bowles, "Unequal Education and the Reproduction of the Social Division of Labor," in *Power and Ideology in Education*, Jerome Karabel and A. H. Halsey, eds. (New York: Oxford University Press, 1977), pp. 137–153; Samuel Bowles, "Schooling and Inequality from Generation to Generation," *Journal of Political Economy* (May-June 1972); Samuel Bowles and Herbert Gintis, "I.Q. and the U.S. Class Structure," *Social Policy* 3 (January-February 1973): 65–96; Joel H. Spring, *Education and the Rise of the Corporate State* (Boston: Beacon Press, 1972); Michael B. Katz, *The Irony of Early School Reform: Educational Innovation in Mid-Nineteenth Century Massachusetts* (Cambridge, Mass.: Harvard University Press, 1968); Michael B. Katz, *Class, Bureaucracy, and Schools: The Illusion of Educational Change in America* (New York: Praeger, 1971); and the writers in Martin Carnoy, ed., *Schooling in a Corporate Society: The Political Economy of Education in America*, 2d ed. (New York: David McKay, 1975).

8. This passage is based primarily on Bowles, "Unequal Education," pp. 137–153. See also Katz, *Class, Bureaucracy, and Schools*.

9. Bowles, "Unequal Education," p. 139.

10. Katz, *The Irony of Early School Reform* and *Class, Bureaucracy, and Schools*. See also, Robert J. Antonio, "The Political Economy of Education," in *Political Economy: A Critique of American Society*, Scott G. McNall, ed. (Glenview, Ill.: Scott, Foresman, 1981), pp. 46–72.

11. See Jerome Kagan, "What Is Intelligence?" *Social Policy* 4 (July-August, 1973): 88–94.

12. Bowles and Gintis, "I.Q. and U.S. Class Structure," p. 74. See also Richard Sennett and Jonathan Cobb, *The Hidden Injuries of Class* (New York: Random House/Vintage, 1973).

13. Bowles, "Unequal Education," p. 148.

14. Richard H. DeLone, *Small Futures; Children, Inequality, and the Limits of Liberal Reform* (New York: Harcourt Brace Jovanovich, 1979), cited in Murray Kempton, "Arithmetic of Inequality," *The Progressive* 43 (November 1979): 8–9.

15. Samuel Bowles and Herbert Gintis, *Schooling in Capitalist America: Educational Reform and the Contradictions of Economic Life* (New York: Basic Books, 1976), p. 31.

16. Christopher Jencks et. al., *Who Gets Ahead? The Determinants of Economic Success in America* (New York: Basic Books, 1979).

17. James S. Coleman et. al., *Equality of Educational Opportunity* (Washington, D.C.: Government Printing Office, 1966).

18. William Ryan, *Blaming the Victim* (New York: Pantheon Books, 1971), pp. 35–36.

19. Carol Hunt, "Inequities Continued in School Finance Act," *The Denver Post* (May 11, 1982), p. 3B.

20. David C. Long, "Rodriguez: The State Courts Respond," *Phi Delta Kappan* 63 (March 1983), pp. 481–484. For a description of one plan, see Leo L. Mann, "School Finance Reform in Connecticut," *Phi Delta Kappan* 62 (December 1980): 250–251.

21. Art Branscombe, "Court Upholds School Finance Law," *The Denver Post* (May 25, 1982), pp. 1A, 8A.

22. Cited in Marilyn Gittell, "Localizing Democracy out of the Schools," *Social Policy* 12 (September-October 1981): 11. See also Albert Shanker, "Bleak Days Ahead for Schools," *American Teacher* 4 (May 1980): 4.

23. Gittell, "Localizing Democracy out of Schools," pp. 4–11; and Kevin Roderick, "Blacks Narrow Gap in Reading," *Los Angeles Times* (April 29, 1981), pt. 1, p. 24.

24. "College Costs Up 13 Percent, Double 1972," *Chicago Sun-Times* (September 1, 1981), p. 26.

25. Silberman, *Crisis in the Classroom*, p. 67.

26. For an extensive treatment of this phenomenon in other contexts, see Robert K. Merton, *Social Theory and Social Structure* (Glencoe, Ill.: Free Press, 1957), pp. 421–436.

27. Robert Rosenthal and Lenore Jacobson, *Pygmalion in the Classroom: Teacher Expectations and Pupils' Intellectual Development* (New York: Holt, Rinehart and Winston, 1968). See also Nancy Dworkin and Yehoash Dworkin, "The Legacy of Pygmalion in the Classroom," *Phi Delta Kappan* 60 (June 1979): 712–715; and Sam Kerman, "Teacher Expectations and Student Achievement," *Phi Delta Kappan* 60 (June 1979): 716–718.

28. Silberman, *Crisis in the Classroom*, p. 98.

29. Quoted in Schafer, Olexa, and Polk, "Programmed for Social Class," in *Schools and Delinquency*, Kenneth Polk and Walter E. Schafer, eds. (Englewood Cliffs, N.J.: Prentice-Hall, 1972), p. 49.

30. Ryan, *Blaming the Victim*, p. 60.

31. Eugene M. Labovitz, "Education as a Social Problem; A Critical Evaluation" (paper presented at the annual meeting of the Society for the Study of Social Problems, San Francisco, (August 1975), p. 7.

32. See Michael Harrington, Introduction to *Poverty in America: A Book of Readings*, Louis A. Ferman, Joyce L. Kornbluh, and Alan Haber, eds. (Ann Arbor: University of Michigan Press, 1965), pp. xii–xiii.

33. The following list is based on Mann, "School Finance Reform in Connecticut," pp. 250–251.

34. Willis D. Hawley, "Increasing the Effectiveness of School Desegregation: Lessons from the Research," in *Race and Schooling in the City*, Adam Yarmolinsky, Lance Liebman, and Corinne S. Schelling, eds. (Cambridge, Mass.: Harvard University Press, 1981), pp. 145–162.

35. See "Second Thoughts," *Newsweek* (June 23, 1975), p. 56; "Busing Backfired," *National Observer* (June 7, 1975), pp. 1, 18. For critiques of Coleman's arguments, see the entire issue of *Social Policy* 6 (January-February 1976).

36. Norman Cousins, "Busing Reconsidered," *Saturday Review* (January 24, 1976), p. 4. See also Marvin Caplan, "Truth—and Shame—about Busing," *Dissent* 23 (Fall 1976): 383–391.

37. Quoted in "Busing Backfired," p. 18.

38. There is evidence that experience in such an acrimonious climate significantly lowers the achievement performance of the bused minority students. See Lawrence G. Felice, "Mandatory Busing and Minority Student Achievement: New Evidence and Negative Results" (Report to the U.S. Office of Education, n.d.).

39. These ideas are taken from Hawley, "Increasing the Effectiveness of School Desegregation," pp. 145–162, and Nancy H. St. John, "The Effects of School Desegregation on Children: A New Look at the Research Evidence," in *Race and Schooling in the City*, pp. 84–103. For additional suggestions for improving desegregation plans, see Ronald G. Schnee, "Improving Desegregation Plans," *Phi Delta Kappan* 62 (February 1981): 429–433.

40. Doug McInnis, "Magnet Programming–A Concept Worth Keeping," *Christian Science Monitor* (December 13, 1976), p. 30.

41. See Edwin T. Roberts, Jr., " . . . Dangerous Distraction of Forced Busing," *National Observer* (February 22, 1975), p. 12.

42. "What U.S. Education Needs: Interview with Wilson Riles, California State Superintendent of Public Instruction," *U.S. News & World Report* (September 1, 1975), p. 57.

43. Ibid., pp. 57–59.

44. Peter F. Drucker, "School around the Bend," *Psychology Today* 6 (June 1972): 49.

45. Samuel Bowles, "Toward Equality of Educational Opportunity," in *Equal Educational Opportunity*, an expansion of the winter 1968 special issue of the *Harvard Educational Review*, prepared by the editorial board of the *Harvard Educational Review* (Cambridge, Mass.: Harvard University Press, 1969), p. 121.

46. Christopher Jencks et al., *Inequality: A Reassessment of the Effect of Family and Schooling in America* (New York: Basic Books, 1972).

47. Christopher Jencks, "Adding Up Our School Days, Getting—What?" *New York Times* (December 1, 1972).

16

Religion

in

America

"All human beings have an innate need to tell and hear stories and to have a story to live by. Religion, whatever else it has done, has provided one of the main ways of meeting this abiding need. Most religions begin as clusters of stories, embedded in song and saga, rite and rehearsal. Go back as far as the bloody Babylonian epic of Gilgamesh or to Homer's accounts of the gods and heroes of Hellas. Or read the tales told by Bantu priests, Cheyenne holy men or Eskimo shamans. They are all, in their own way, stories.

The Hebrew Scriptures are largely stories; so is the New Testament. Rabbis, saints, Zen masters and gurus of every persuasion convey their holy teachings by jokes, kōans, parables, allegories, anecdotes and fables. There has never been a better raconteur than Jesus of Nazareth himself."

Source: Harvey Cox, *The Seduction of the Spirit: The Use and Misuse of People's Religion* (New York: A Touchstone Book, Simon and Schuster, 1973), p. 9.

Religion is a ubiquitous phenomenon that has a tremendous impact on any society and its members. It is part of a large social system, affected by and affecting the other institutions of the society—that is, patterns of the family, the economy, education, and the polity. Since religious trends may be responses to fundamental changes in society, and some religious ideas may constrain social behaviors in a narrowly prescribed manner, the understanding of any society is incomplete unless one comprehends the religion of that society.

But, what is religion? The variety of activities and belief systems that have fallen under this rubric is almost infinite. (See Panel 16–1.) There are some elements essential to religion, however, that allow us to distinguish it from other phenomena.[1] A starting point is that religion is created by people (that is, it is a part of culture). It is an integrated set of ideas by which a group attempts to explain the meaning of life and death. Religion is also a normative system, defining immorality and sin as well as morality and righteousness. Let us amplify some of these statements further.

□ Religion deals with the ultimate of human concerns—the meaning of life and death. It provides answers as to the individual's place in society and in the universe.[2]

□ There is an emphasis on human conduct. There are prescriptions for what one ought to do as well as the consequences for one's misconduct.

□ There is a distinction between the sacred and the secular. Some objects and entities are believed to have supernatural powers and are therefore

---

PANEL 16–1   Cross-Cultural Panel

The Cargo Cult of Melanesia

Some religions prophesy a radical change in the future (the end of the world, the 1,000 year reign of Christ, or a return to some golden age). One such "millenarian movement" is the cargo cult of Melanesia. The islands in Melanesia have been visited throughout history by foreigners in sailing ships, steamships, and airplanes. Each time the visitors brought riches unknown to the island people. The natives were greatly impressed by these goods, which they believed were being manufactured and sent to them by their ancestors.

The natives were most impressed with the cargo brought to the islands by plane during World War II (canned food, clothing, tools, radios, watches, guns, and motorcycles). When the War ended, however, the supplies were used up and not replaced by new shipments.

The island prophets proclaimed that if airstrips were built, these would entice back the planes with their fabulous cargo. As a result, the natives have built airstrips in the jungle, complete with hangars, radio shacks, beacon towers, and airplanes (all made out of bamboo sticks and leaves). The airports are manned 24 hours a day, with bonfires set at night to serve as beacons for the expected cargo planes.

Thus, 40 years or so after World War II, the natives await the phantom cargo that will hail the beginning of a new age. When the planes finally arrive their lives will be filled with riches and plenty. They will be reunited with their deceased ancestors, heralding the beginning of heaven on earth.

treated with respect, reverence, and awe. What is sacred and what is not is a matter of belief. The range of items believed to be sacred is limitless. They may be objects (idols, altars, or amulets), animals or animal totems, parts of the natural world (mountains, volcanos, or rivers), transcendental beings (gods, angels, devils), or persons (living or dead, such as prophets, messiahs, or saints). (See Panel 16–2.)

PANEL 16–2

Holy Tortilla

Lake Arthur, N.M.—The woman crawled on her knees from the railroad tracks in this tiny southern New Mexico town down the dirt road to the house of Maria and Eduardo Rubio.

She came in to worship, then crawled out beyond the tracks and disappeared.

The Rubios were not surprised. They have accepted that the Lord works in mysterious ways. And so have the 10,190 pilgrims who since Oct. 5, 1977, have made their way to the modest Rubio home in the middle of southeastern New Mexico's beanfields.

Mrs. Rubio was making lunch for her husband, a farmhand, on that October afternoon. That's when the face of Jesus appeared on a tortilla frying in her skillet.

She called her sister to witness the "miracle," and awakened Eduardo, who was taking a nap.

"She was crying," recalled Blanca Rubio, 21, one of the family's six children. "He told her to go to the church and the priest blessed it."

Word of the event spread. The Rubios erected a wall in their living room to separate the television and the couch from a shrine to the holy object. A family from a town about 50 miles away donated a specially built altar topped by a hollow square about 10 inches deep.

Inside that square rests a spray of lavender and white plastic flowers, which Mrs. Rubio changes occasionally, a wad of cotton simulating a cloud, and the tortilla. In a square-inch of burn marks on it, some see the profile of a long-haired man with a likeness to some depictions of Jesus.

On the wall above the altar, and beside a velvet painting of a weeping Jesus, are a string of *milagros*—small metal emblems depicting arms, legs, hearts, eyes and other ailing body parts believers want hung for healing near the tortilla.

Sometimes it works, Mrs. Rubio said in Spanish. "A lady about 55 years old came here a couple of years ago in a wheelchair. She was paralyzed and promised to walk here all the way from Artesia once a year if she was cured.

"She was, and made her first walk last year," Mrs. Rubio claimed.

The oil refineries of Artesia are about 11 miles south of Lake Arthur.

Each weekend, someone prays for a sick relative or expresses gratitude for a recovery at the shrine of the tortilla. "Just yesterday, a neighbor's son pulled out of a coma, and she came by to offer thanks," said Mrs. Rubio.

More than a hundred letters have come to Lake Arthur, a few from as far as Europe, asking the Rubios' prayers to remedy a hundred kinds of suffering.

Source: Steve Chawkins, "Holy Tortilla: Burden or Blessing?" *Rocky Mountain News* (June 6, 1982), p. 10. Reprinted by permission.

□ Because the sacred is held in awe, there are beliefs (theologies, cosmologies) and practices (rituals) to express and reinforce proper attitudes among believers about the sacred. The set of beliefs attempts to explain the meaning of life. Moreover, these beliefs present a set of guidelines for action toward the sacred, and toward one's fellows. Ritual, with its symbolism and action, evokes common feelings among the believers (awe, reverence, ecstasy, fear) which lead to group unity.

□ An essential ingredient of religion is the existence of a community of believers. There must be a social group that shares a set of beliefs and practices, moral values, and a sense of community (a unique identity).

One important consequence of a group of persons having the same religious heritage and beliefs is unity. All believers, whether of high or low status, young or old, are united through the sharing of religious beliefs. Thus, religion, through the holding of common values to be cherished, sins to be avoided, rules to be followed, and symbols to be revered, integrates. Group unity is also accomplished through the universal feeling that God or the gods look upon this particular group with special favor (the ethnocentric notion that "God is on our side"). An example of this is found in a verse of the national anthem of Great Britain:

> O lord our God, arise
> Scatter our enemies
> And make them fall.
> Confound their politics,
> Frustrate their knavish tricks,
> On thee our hopes we fix,
> God save us all.

Another consequence of religion is that it constrains the behavior of the community of believers, thus providing a social control function. This is accomplished in two ways. First, there are explicit rules to obey which if violated will be punished. Second, in the process of socialization, children internalize the religious beliefs and rules. In other words, they each develop a conscience which keeps them in line through guilt and fear.

A final positive consequence of religion—positive in the sense that it aids in uniting persons—is the legitimation of social structures that have profane origins.[3] There is a strong tendency for religious beliefs to become intertwined with secular beliefs, thereby providing religious blessings to the values and institutions of society. In American society, for example, private property and free enterprise have become almost sacred. Democracy, too, is believed to be ordained by God.

The very same religious bases that promote group integration also divide. Religious groups tend to emphasize separateness and superiority, thereby defining others as inferior ("infidels," "heathens," "heretics," or "nonbelievers"). This occurs because each religious group tends to feel it has the way (and perhaps the only way) to achieve salvation or reach nirvana or whatever the goal.

Religious differences accentuate the differences among societies, denominations, and even within local churches. Since religious groups have feelings of superiority, there may be conflict brought about by discrimination, competition for converts, or feelings of hatred. Also, because religious ideas tend to be strongly held, groups may split rather than compromise. Liberals and fundamentalists, even within the same religion, denomination, or local church, will, doubtless, disagree on numerous issues. A common result, of course, is division.

A major divisive characteristic of religion is its tendency, through established churches, to accept the acts of the state. American churches, for example, have condoned such things as slavery, segregation, white supremacy, and war.* Within the church, there have always been those who spoke out against the church's cohabitation with the secular. This ability of the church to rationalize the activities of the state no matter how onerous has split many churches and denominations. The slavery issue, for example, split Baptists into American Baptists and Southern Baptists.

Conflict itself can occur between religious groups (with the sanction of each religion). Recent world history gives bloody evidence of this occurrence (for example, Moslems versus Hindus in India and Pakistan, Moslems versus Jews in the Middle East, Catholics versus Protestants in Northern Ireland). Religious conflict has also occurred within the United States at various times. Confrontations between Catholics and Protestants, between warring sects of Muslims (Black Muslims versus Sunni Muslims), as well as Protestants and Jews, have been fairly commonplace.[5] Clearly, religious values are reason enough for individuals and groups to clash.

RELIGION FROM THE ORDER PERSPECTIVE OF EMILE DURKHEIM

Durkheim, the French sociologist, wrote *The Elementary Forms of Religious Life* in 1912. This classic work explored the question of why religion is universal in human societies. He reasoned that religion must help to maintain society. Durkheim studied the religion of the Australian aborigines to understand the possible role of religion in societal survival.

Durkheim found that each aborigine clan had its own totem, an object it considered sacred. The totem—a kangaroo, lizard, tree, river, or rock formation—was sacred because the clan believed that it symbolized the unique qualities of the clan. Two of Durkheim's interpretations are important in this regard. First, people bestow the notion of the sacred onto something, rather than that object being intrinsically sacred. Second, what the group

---

*Actually, the church has sometimes actively pursued some of these policies. The Puritan Church of the early settlers condoned witch hunts. The defeat of the Indians was justified by most Christian groups on the grounds that they were heathens and in need of white man's religion. Finally, most religious denominations sought Biblical rationalizations for slavery.[4]

worships is really society itself. Thus, people "create" religion.* Because the members of a society share religious beliefs, they are a moral community and as such the solidarity of the society is enhanced.

The society is held together by religious rituals and festivals in which the group's values and beliefs are reaffirmed. Each new generation is socialized to accept these beliefs, ensuring consensus on what is right and wrong. Religion, then, whether it be among the pre-industrial Australian aborigines, the Muslims of the Middle East, the Buddhists of Asia, or the Christians of North America, serves the same functions of promoting order and unity.

RELIGION FROM THE CONFLICT PERSPECTIVE OF KARL MARX

Whereas Durkheim interpreted the unity achieved through religion as positive, Marx viewed it as negative. Religion inhibits societal change by making existing social arrangements seem right and inevitable. The dominant form of economics in society, the type of government, the law, and other social creations are given religious sanction. Thus, the system remains stable, which the order theorists see as good, when it perhaps should be transformed to meet the needs of all of the people.

Religion promotes the status quo in other ways. The powerless are taught to accept religious beliefs that are against their own interests. The Hindus, for example, believe that it is the person's duty to accept his or her caste. Failure to do so will result in being reincarnated to a lower caste or even as an animal. Christianity proclaims that the poor should accept their lot in this life for they will be rewarded in Heaven. In short, somehow oppression and poverty are reinterpreted by religion to be a special form of righteousness. Thus, religion is the ultimate tool to promote false consciousness.

SOME DISTINCTIVE FEATURES OF AMERICAN RELIGION

Civil
Religion

One feature of American religion, traditionally, has been the separation of Church and State (established by the First Amendment to the Constitution). This is both a consequence and the cause of the religious diversity found in the United States. There is a relationship between religion and the state in America, but it differs from the usual conception of one dominant church that is inseparable from the state. In many respects, God and Country are conceived by most Americans as one. This has been labeled the civil religion of the United States.[7]

---

*This raises an important question: Do we create God or is there a supernatural somewhere that human beings grope to find? Durkheim is correct in stating that religion is a social product. This universal response, however, does not prove or disprove the existence of a God or Gods. Sociologists as individuals may have strong religious beliefs, but as sociologists they focus on the complex interrelationship between religion and society.[6]

America's **civil religion** is seemingly antithetical to the constitutional demand for separation of Church and State. The paradox is that on the one hand the government sanctions God (the Pledge of Allegiance has the phrase, "one nation, under God"; the phrase, "In God We Trust," is stamped on all money; every Presidential inaugural address except Washington's second has mentioned God; and present-day Presidents have regularly scheduled prayer breakfasts), while at the same time declaring it illegal to have prayer and/or religious instruction in the public schools. The basis for the paradox is that the civil religion is not a specific creed. It is a set of beliefs, symbols, and rituals that is broad enough for all citizens to accept. The God of the civil religion is all things to all people. One thing is certain—politicians, if they want to be successful, must show some semblance of piety by occasionally invoking the blessings of this nondenominational, nonsectarian God.

There are several central themes of the civil religion that are important for the understanding of American society. First, there is the belief that God has a special destiny for the United States. This implies that God is actively involved in history and, most important, that America has a holy mission to carry out God's will on earth. John F. Kennedy phrased this message well in the conclusion to his inauguration address: "With a good conscience our only sure reward, with history the final judge of our deeds, let us go forth to lead the land we love, asking His blessing and His help, but knowing that here on earth God's work must truly be our own."[8] This belief has been the source of self-righteousness in foreign relations. It has allowed Americans to subdue the "pagan" Indians, win the frontier, follow a policy of manifest destiny, and defeat fascism. Currently, the defeat of communism is seen as a holy crusade.

A second aspect of the civil religion is maintenance of the status quo. The God of civil religion is more closely allied to law and order than to changing the system. Thus, civil religion tends strongly toward uncritical endorsement of American values and the system of stratification. Order and unity are the traditional ways of God, not change and dissent. Thus, public policy tends to receive religious sanction.

At the same time, however, the civil religion enjoins Americans to stand up for certain principles—freedom, individualism, equal opportunity. Consequently, there are occasions when current governmental policy or the policy of some group is criticized because it does not measure up to certain ideals. The civil religion of America, then, accomplishes both the priestly (acceptance of what is) and the prophetic (challenging the existing system) roles of traditional religion, with emphasis, however, on the former.

The Variety of Religious Belief

Some societies are unified by religion. All persons in such societies believe the same religious ideas, worship the same deities, obey the same moral commandments, and identify strongly with each other. Superficially, through its civil religion, the United States appears to be homogeneous along religious lines. Moreover, 87 percent of Americans in 1981 were Christians.[9] But the range of attitudes and beliefs among Christians in American society is fantastically wide. Among Roman Catholics, for example, there are radical priests who disobey the instructions of bishops, cardinals, and even the Pope. At the same time, however, there are priests who rigidly adhere to all the rules set down by the church authorities. If anything, the range within Protestantism is even greater. In 1981, a Gallup poll reported that 37 percent of Protestants (down, by the way, from 65 percent in 1963) believed that the Bible is to be taken literally, word for word;[10] for others, the Bible is purely allegorical. This difference has led to a schism in the Missouri Lutheran Synod.[11] Some religious groups have so much faith in the healing power of religion that their members refuse to see physicians under any circumstances. Within Protestantism are Amish, Quakers, high-church Episcopalians, Pentecostal Holiness groups, Congregationalists, and even snake handlers.

Further evidence for the diversity of religious expression in the United States is found in the variance of beliefs concerning basic tenets of Christianity. Glock and Stark have demonstrated in their study of a random sample of church members in four metropolitan counties in northern California the wide disagreement among the various denominations, Protestant and Catholic, on a number of presumably central tenets of Christianity. They found, moreover, that with few exceptions there is considerable within-denomination variation on each of these articles of faith.[12]

Religious Organization

Very broadly, American religious organizations can be divided according to their secular commitments into two categories—churches and sects.[13]

Religious groups have a choice—to reject and withdraw from the secular society, or to accommodate to it. The basis for a decision to reject the social environment is maintenance of spiritual and ethical purity. Such a choice, by definition, entails withdrawal from the world, thereby consciously avoiding any chance to change it. The opposite choice—accommodation—requires compromise and the loss of distinctive ideals but it also means that the group can influence the larger society. The accommodation or resistance to the secular world is the fundamental difference between a church and a sect.

The **church,** as an ideal type, has the following attributes:

□ The tendency to compromise with the larger society and its values and institutions.
□ Membership tends to occur by being born to parents who belong. Membership, moreover, takes place through infant baptism, which implies that all members are "saved."
□ A hierarchy of authority, with those at the top being trained for their vocation.
□ Acceptance of a diversity of beliefs, since the membership is large, and for many the scriptures are interpreted metaphorically rather than literally.
□ There is a tolerance of the popular vices.

A **sect** in its perfect form is exactly opposite a church in every way.

- There is a fundamental withdrawal from and rejection of the world. A sect is a moral community separate from and in many ways hostile toward the secular world.[14]
- Membership is only through a "conversion" experience. Membership is therefore voluntary and limited to adults. Hence, adult baptism is the only accepted form of baptism.
- Organization is informal and unstructured. Ministers are untrained. They became ministers by being "called" from the group.
- The belief system is rigid. The Bible is the source and it is interpreted literally. The goal of the membership is spiritual purity as found in the early Christian Church.
- There are rigid ethical requirements restraining the members from the popular vices of drinking, smoking, card playing, dancing, and cursing.

The church-sect dichotomy does not exhaust all the possibilities. Some religious groups would fit somewhere in between—as institutionalized sects. These groups (for example, Mormons, Disciples of Christ, and Southern Baptists) incorporate features of both a church (trained leadership, some accommodation to the larger society) with the sectlike attributes of adult baptism, and an unwillingness to compromise on some theological questions.

For our purposes, however, the church-sect dichotomy, while oversimplifying the situation, is useful in two ways: to depict a form of social change, and to show why certain categories of persons are attracted to one type and not the other.

The church-sect dichotomy illustrates an important sociological phenomenon—the very process of organization deflects away from the original goal of the group. A group may form to pursue a goal such as religious purity, but in so doing it creates a new organization, which means that some of the group's energies will be spent in organizational maintenance. Consequently, a sect may form with the explicit intention of eliminating a hierarchy and a codification of beliefs. Patterns of behavior emerge, however, as certain practices are found to be more effective. In particular, the selection of ministers tends to become routinized, and a system of religious instruction for children is developed so that they will learn the catechism in the proper sequence. Sects, then, tend to become churches. This is illustrated by the type of leader found in each. Often a sect is formed by a charismatic person and his followers. This person is followed because he is believed to possess extraordinary qualities of leadership, saintliness, gifts of prophecy, or ability to heal. What happens to such an organization when this leadership is gone? The organization is faced with a crisis of succession. Groups typically find ways to pass on the **charisma** ("routinization of charisma") by either: (1) selection of the successor by the original charismatic leader, (2) designation of a successor by the group closest to the original leader ("disciples"), (3) hereditary transmission, or (4) transmission of charisma by ritual ("laying on of hands").[15] In this last instance there is the recognition of a charisma of office—that is, whoever holds the position possesses charisma. When this occurs, the organizational machinery is advanced enough to move the group away from its sectlike qualities toward a church. The important sociological point here is that organizations seldom remain the same. The simple tends to become complex. But the process does not stop at complexity; as the original goal of the sect (religious purity with the necessity of separation from the world) is superseded when the organization gets larger and more bureaucratic, some persons will become dissatisfied enough to break away and form a new sect. Thus, the process tends to be cyclical.

Increased bureaucratization (and subsequent splintering) is characteristic of modern urban society. This leads us to a final consideration relative to the church-sect dichotomy—the motivation to join sects. At the risk of oversimplification, we can identify two important features of sects that help explain why some categories of persons are especially prone to join sects rather than churches. The first is that a sect (more so than a church) may provide a total world of meaning and social identity, and a close circle of persons to whom members can turn when troubled. The sect provides precisely those things missing in the lives of many urban dwellers. They find meaning in a meaningless world. They find friends in a sea of strangers. They find stability in a setting that is rapidly undergoing change. Thus, the alienated are especially attracted to sects. So, too, are new migrants to the city. In the city, they are confronted with a variety of new and difficult problems—industrialized work, work insecurity, loss of kinship ties, and disruption of other primary group ties. The sects, unlike the established city churches, appeal to such persons by their form of worship, emphasis on individual attention, and lack of formal organization appeal.[16]

A second variable affecting attraction to a sect or church is social class. Generally, low-status persons tend to be attracted to sects rather than churches because religious status is substituted for social status (or as the Bible puts it, "and the last shall be first"). It makes sense for persons of low social or economic status to reject this world and the religious bodies that accommodate to it. Such persons would be especially attracted to a religious group that rejects this world and assures its followers that in the next world "true believers"—those who are religiously pure—will have the highest status. The sect represents to its followers a reaction against or escape from the dominant religious and economic systems in society. It is a protest against the failure of established churches to meet the needs of marginal groups.[17] The sect, moreover, rejects the social class as irrelevant and, in fact, a system of rewards that is in exact reverse order from God's will.*

Churches, on the other hand, attract the middle and upper classes. Since these persons are successful, they obviously would not turn to a religious organization that rejects their world. As Max Weber said over fifty years ago:

> Other things being equal, classes with high social and economic privilege will scarcely be prone to evolve the ideas of salvation. Rather, they assign to religion the primary function of legitimizing their own life pattern and situation in this world.[18]

Both the sect and the church, consequently, have well developed theodicies.[19] A **theodicy** is a religious legitimation for a situation that otherwise might cause guilt or anger (such as defeat in a war or the existence of poverty among affluence). Sects tend to have a theodicy of suffering—i.e., a religious explanation for their lack of power and privilege. Churches must explain the inequalities of society, too, but their emphasis is on legitimation of possessing power and privilege. This tendency to develop theodicies has the important social function of preserving the status quo. Churches convince their adherents that all is well, that one should accept one's fate as God-given. This makes people's situations less intolerable and the possibility

---

* It is incorrect to say, however, that all lower-class persons who are alienated will join religious sects in order to attack the establishment. Their estrangement may lead them to join other kinds of social movements (e.g., labor or political) or toward social isolation.

of revolution remote—the suffering know they will be rewarded, while the guilt of the well-off is assuaged. Consequently, there is no reason to change the system.

<table>
<tr><td>

The
Relation-
ship
between
Socio-
economic
Status and
Religion

</td><td>

The dominant religion in the United States, Christianity, stresses the equality of all men in the sight of God. All persons, regardless of socioeconomic status, are welcomed in Christianity. We might expect, therefore, that the distribution of members by socioeconomic status within any denomination would be randomly distributed. We might also assume that the organization of any local congregation would ignore status distinctions. Although these two assumptions seem to have surface validity, the empirical situation refutes them.

</td></tr>
</table>

We have seen that sects and churches tend to have a social class bias— the lower the socioeconomic status, the greater the probability of belonging to a sect. There also seems to be a ranking of denominations in terms of the socioeconomic status of their members. Although there is always a range of the social classes within any one denomination, there is a modal status that characterizes each. The reasons for this are varied: the proportion of members living in rural or urban areas, which immigrant groups brought the religion to the United States and during what historical period, the appeal of the religious experience (ritual, evangelism, close personal ties, salvation, legitimation of the social system, or attacks on the establishment). This last point is especially important because "life conditions affect men's religious propensities, and life conditions are significantly correlated with the facts of stratification in all societies."[20]

There is a relationship between socioeconomic status and denominational affiliation. Figure 16–1 presents data from a national sample that orders the major Protestant denominations by decreasing status.

Even though Figure 16–1 shows that the denominations can be ranked by socioeconomic status, it is clear that each denomination includes persons of high, middle, and lower status. As Demerath has stated, "Episcopalians may be *relatively* upper class, but more than 40 percent are from the lower class. Baptists may be *relatively* lower class, but they claim their Rockefellers as well."[21]

Local churches, even more so than denominations, tend to be homogeneous in socioeconomic status. This is partly the result of residential patterns— that is, neighborhoods are relatively homogeneous by socioeconomic status and the local churches are attended mostly by persons living nearby. Another reason, and perhaps just as important, is the tendency for persons to want to belong to organizations composed of persons like themselves. They do not want to feel out of place, so they are attracted to churches where the members have the same lifestyle (for example, speech patterns, clothing tastes, and educational background). The result, then, is that persons belonging to a particular denomination will often seek out the local congregation in the city where they feel most comfortable. To paraphrase Broom and Selznick,

FIGURE 16–1   Religious Preference and Socioeconomic Status

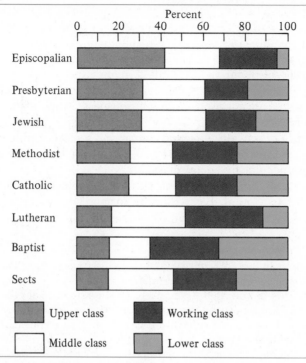

Source: National Opinion Research Center, General Social Surveys, 1974–1978, reprinted in H. Paul Chalfant, R. E. Beckley, and L. E. Palmer, *Religion in Contemporary Society* (Palo Alto, Calif.: Mayfield, 1981), p. 386.

"although rich and poor, educated and uneducated are members of one denomination, they tend to worship under different roofs."[22]

There is some range, however, in every local church. Probably no one congregation is comprised totally of persons from exactly the same status niche. Although the status differentials may be minimal within a local congregation, they are evidently important to the parishioners. The rule is that the higher the socioeconomic status of the member, the greater his or her influence in the running of the local church. There is greater likelihood that such persons will be elected or appointed to office (elder, deacon, trustee, Sunday school superintendent) and that their opinions will carry greater weight than persons of lower social status. This may be partly a function of the disproportionately large financial contributions by the more well-to-do, but the important point here is that the secular world intrudes in the organization of each local congregation.

The common indicators of religious involvement—church membership, attendance at church services, and participation in the church's activities—

all demonstrate a relationship to socioeconomic status. On each of these measures, persons of high status are more involved than those of low status.[23] Unfortunately, these are not very good measures of religiosity, although often assumed to be. The problem is that upper-class persons are much more likely to join and actively participate in all sorts of organizations. The joining of churches and attending services are but the manifestations of a more general phenomenon—the tendency for middle- and upper-class persons to be "joiners" while lower-class individuals tend to isolate themselves from all types of organizations. The spuriousness of the relationship between socioeconomic status and "religiosity" is more clearly seen when we analyze the importance of religion to persons of varying socioeconomic circumstances, as well as differences in religious beliefs and the degree to which church activities are secular by social class.

Goode, after comparing white-collar church members with working-class church members, found that while the former were more likely to belong and participate in formal activities of the church, the latter were in fact more religious.

> They participate less in formal church activities, but their religious activity does not appear to be nearly so secularized. It is more specifically religious in character. This is indicated by the fact that on a number of other religious dimensions, dimensions not dependent on extraneous nonreligious variables, individuals of manual-status levels appear to display a considerably higher level of religious response. This is true particularly of psychological variables, such as religious "salience," the greater feeling that the church and religion are great forces in the lives of respondents. It is also true for "religiosity" as measured by a higher level of religious concern, and for religious "involvement," the extent to which the individual is psychologically dependent on some sort of specifically religious association in his life.[24]

Table 16–1 presents evidence for the "secularization of religion" by the upper classes and the difference by level of education on religious beliefs. Examination of Table 16–1 reveals that the higher the educational status of the respondent, the more likely to hold liberal religious beliefs. This means, in effect, that the middle- and upper-status categories have tended to abandon the bases of Christianity.

In summary, there is a rather complex relationship between socioeconomic status and religion. Although the relatively poor and uneducated are more likely to be indifferent to religion than the better educated and financially well-off, those who are religious tend to make religion a more integral part of their lives than better-off persons. They go to church more for religious than secular reasons. They believe much more strongly than the well-to-do in the fundamental beliefs as expressed in the Bible. Thus, we have the paradox that on many objective measures of religious involvement—church attendance and participation in formal church activities—the middle- and upper-status persons exceed those of lesser status, whereas if importance of religion in the lives of the individual is considered, the poor who go to church outstrip their more economically favored brethren.

	Level of Education		
	College	High School	Grade School
Percent responding true to "My religious faith is the most important influence in my life."	56	72	81
Percent responding true to "I believe in the divinity of Jesus Christ."	74	87	94
Percent believing the Bible is the literal word of God.	21	40	56
Percent responding true to "I constantly seek God's will through prayer."	51	69	86

Source: The Gallup Report, *Religion in America*, Report Nos. 201–202 (June–July 1982), adapted from a number of tables, pp. 112, 114, 122, and 174. Reprinted by permission.

RELIGIOUS TRENDS

Religion in American society is a paradox. On the one hand, religion seems to be losing its vitality. The data show that in the past 25 years or so there has been a downward trend and recently a leveling off in regular church attendance (see Table 16–2). Protestants during this period have stayed near the 40 percent attendance level while the percentage of Catholics attending church at least once a week has fallen from 72 percent in 1954 to 52 percent in 1981. The data also show that the percentage of young adults attending church regularly has fallen and that the largest denominations—Episcopal, Methodist, and Presbyterian—are falling in both attendance and membership.[25]

On the other hand, however, there are indications that Americans are just as religious as ever and in some areas there is even dramatic growth. On the first point, Americans have consistently and overwhelmingly believed in God. Gallup has reported that 94 percent of adult Americans believe in God or a universal spirit, which is the highest rate found in the nations of North America and Europe. Similarly, more Americans (71 percent) believe in life after death than do these other nations. (Canada is the next highest at 54 percent and West Germany the lowest with only one-third of adults accepting this belief.)[26]

Contrary to the experience of the mainline churches, some religious groups are growing rapidly in members and interest. The fastest growing in percentage gain is the Mormon Church with a national growth of 83,000 new members annually. More significant because of their growing numbers

TABLE 16–2   Percentage Attending Church During Average Week

1954	46	1968	43
1955	49	1969	42
1956	46	1970	42
1957	47	1971	40
1958	49	1972	40
1959	47	1973	40
1960	47	1974	40
1961	47	1975	40
1962	46	1976	41
1963	46	1977	41
1964	45	1978	41
1965	44	1979	40
1966	44	1980	40
1967	43	1981	41

Source: *The Gallup Report*, Report Nos. 201–202 (June–July, 1982), p. 44.

nationwide and their political leverage, are the evangelical denominations and sects.

In this section we will highlight four major trends of American religion: (1) the decline of the mainline churches; (2) the rise of the evangelicals; (3) the new political activism of the evangelicals and the decline of religious pluralism; and (4) the consciousness movement. Since social conditions have led to these shifts, the focus will be on the societal conditions that have given impetus to these trends.

Decline of the Mainline Denominations

The major churches have been experiencing declining membership, attendance, and revenues. The reasons for this are not altogether clear, but the following appear plausible. These denominations have lost their vitality as they have become more and more churchlike (and have moved away from the qualities characterizing sects). The beliefs within these churches have become so pluralistic that to many the faith seems "watered down." Many churchgoers want authority but they too often receive only more ambiguity.

Since other parts of society emphasize rationality, efficiency, and bureaucracy, many persons seek a religion that will emphasize feelings and fellowship. However, the mainline churches, for the most part, are just as impersonal and ossified as the other bureaucracies found in society.

The Catholic Church has been especially vulnerable to losses in attendance. In this case, the rigidity of the Catholic hierarchy is partly responsible. The Church has taken strong stances against contraception, abortion, and divorce. Many Catholics feel that the Church authorities are out of step with contemporary life. The Catholic and some other traditional churches have also lost credence with some for their refusal to accept women in leadership roles. This patriarchal emphasis by some churches, however, is a positive attraction for some individuals as we will see later.

Rise of the Evangelicals

The most obvious reason why the evangelicals are increasing in number is their great emphasis on saving souls. They stress this activity because Christ commanded "Go ye into all the world and preach the gospel to every creature."

The evangelicals provide for many the ingredients they find missing in the mainline churches. They offer friendship, emotional release, a personal relationship with Christ, and rigid guidelines for beliefs and behaviors. This last point is an important one. Modern life in American society is characterized by rapid change and a plurality of ideas and choices. Although many are comfortable with change, many others seek authority, a foundation to provide consistency and constancy in their lives. The evangelicals provide a rigid set of beliefs based on the infallibility of the Bible as the word of God. This desire for authority has increased in the populace through a number of societal factors roughly dating back to the assassination of President John Kennedy.

> We lost our leaders. We lost a war, which tore us apart at home. We lost confidence in business and government. A president once admired by millions left office in disgrace. Inflation soars. Energy is scarce. International tensions mount one upon another. And for many who were over 30 during the '60s, the radical changes in young people's values and life styles underscored the loss of a taken-for-granted morality that was once as integral to American culture as baseball, popcorn and Chevrolet.[27]

The evangelicals have increased their popularity with a tremendous emphasis on the use of direct mail advertising, radio, and television. This type of ministry began with the advent of radio in the 1920s, and expanded greatly with the growth of television in the '50s and '60s and cable television in the late 1970s. The enormity of this impact is in the number of people affected and the amounts of money generated. Hadden and Swann have estimated that the number of people watching religious broadcasts rose from about 10 million in 1970 to 20 million in 1980.[28] The top five electronic preachers in 1979 together received $205 million in contributions. The largest amount was the $51 million collected by Reverend Jim Bakker of the PTL (Praise the Lord) Club, which surpasses the national budgets of many entire denominations in the United States.[29]

The success of this electronic church has been enhanced by the use of sophisticated methods such as professional production of programs, computerized mailing lists, and personalized letters written by computers. The successful evangelical preachers have adapted the communication technologies used by business and politicians to reach and manipulate their audience with the greatest effectiveness.

A final reason for the growth of the evangelical movement has to do with its base in the South and Southwest. The Bible Belt happens to correspond with the Sun Belt, the region of fastest population growth. As business enterprises and individuals leave the Northeast and Midwest for the warm South, they are entering a religious climate that is evangelical in tone and substance. In time, these migrants will be likely candidates for membership in the evangelical churches.

Political Activism and the Decline of Religious Pluralism

The traditional emphasis of evangelicals on saving souls, while undiminished, has added a new dimension—saving the morals of society through political activism.[30] This concern has risen as the result of recent court decisions and legislative acts legalizing abortion, defining the rights of homosexuals, permitting pornography, liberalizing divorce through "no fault" laws, and prohibiting prayer in the schools. These acts, and others such as affirmative action and the possibility of an Equal Rights Amendment to the Constitution are viewed as undercutting the traditional family and promoting immorality. The foes, in this view, are liberal politicians who are allowing the nation's moral foundations to crumble. Deserving of support are those politicians who are conservative Christians and are opposed to the ERA, gay rights, abortion, Communist expansion, and disarmament. In the 1980 election, for example, the evangelicals (led by Reverend Jerry Falwell's Moral Majority) worked for the election of Ronald Reagan as President and focused their attention on the defeat of key liberals in the Senate. They were successful on both counts. The Moral Majority is a misnomer, however, because it has never been a majority. While there are areas where it is a strong political force, on the national level the unfavorable attitudes toward it by Americans outweigh favorable views by more than a 2–1 ratio.[31]

One consequence of the political efforts by the Christian right wing is an upsurge in religious bigotry. The evangelicals assume that their position is the only correct one. They have the only answer for women's rights (against), capital punishment (for), and national defense (increased spending), and so on. As a result, there can be no compromise. Some Christians are good and others are bad. The conservative churches are right and the liberal ones wrong. The commonalities among Christians are forgotten as the issues divide.

Finally, the political activism of the evangelicals is spawned by and directed at moral concerns, narrowly defined. Their political efforts are not concerned with racial injustice, poverty, or other problems of inequity. In short, the moral outrage of the evangelicals is selective. This issue of political activism is a topic we will return to shortly.

The "Consciousness Revolution"

A recent trend has been toward eastern religions such as Zen, Yoga, and Hare Krishna or toward quasi-religion (Transcendental Meditation),[32] personal awareness, and mysticism. Although there are obvious differences between these groups, there are some commonalities that may explain their appeal. The key words used in all of these diverse belief systems are "consciousness," "inner awareness," "peace," "authenticity," "natural," and "self." The assumptions that are shared by these philosophies are:[33]

1. We are at the beginning of a New Age. The past focused on conquering the external world, but the new frontiers are inner.
2. Changes in society will not occur until people are changed.
3. There are forces within us that are immensely powerful yet remain untapped (these forces are "supernatural," even "divine").
4. The goal, then, is to develop the "you that could be."

Tom Wolfe has termed this movement "The Age of Me." "The old alchemical dream was changing base metals into gold. The new alchemical dream is: Changing one's personality—remaking, remodeling, elevating, and polishing one's very self. . . ."[34]

There are some major differences between the eastern religions and the non-religious personality development movements. Harvey Cox, the esteemed theologian, has studied the converts to the eastern religions such as Zen Buddhism, Hare Krishna, and the Unification Church, and found that they have rejected western religions in search for:[35] (1) a supportive community; (2) experiential religion; and (3) strong authority.

These reasons are not too different from those given by converts to evangelical Christianity. They, too, are responding to society, and a malaise they feel keenly from impersonal bureaucracies. There is a major difference, however, in society's response to the converts to Oriental religions. There have been legal attempts to close their temples, make their religions subject to taxes, and to disallow them from purchasing property. Parents have had their children kidnapped and "deprogrammed" because they are so appalled by their actions.[36] (See Panel 16–3.) Ironically, their children are living a life of peace, sharing, and self discipline—traits that parents typically encourage in their children.[37] In this context, however, these traits are interpreted negatively because they reject Christianity, competition, materialistic consumption, and status striving—all so very much part of American society.

PANEL 16–3   Social Dilemmas and Critical Choices

The Freedom of Youth to Differ from Their Parents

A commonly held assumption is that parents have the right to transmit their religious and moral views to their children. At what point are children free to shift away from their parents' views if they wish? Are we a free society? Do we adhere to the principle of religious freedom?

These questions have come to national attention as some parents have hired persons to "abduct" their adult children from religious cults such as Hare Krishna or Sun Myung Moon's Unification Church, and "deprogram" them from beliefs which they believe to be sinister (that is, different, very different from their religious views).[38]

Perhaps it is ironic that they seek to release their children from groups that control the behavior of children in a manner consonant

(continued)

with what most parents would want of their children. As Nicholas Von Hoffman has put it:

> The real baffler is why the Moonies' parents object so vehemently to their children being members of the sect. The parents should be rejoicing. They ought to be sending the Moon Man contributions. He gets people to do what parents want their children to do. Moonies are always clean, neat and conservatively dressed; they abstain from sex, alcohol and other drugs of pleasure; they get up early and they work hard all the live-long day; they go to church frequently and pray incessantly; they espouse no radical causes, and they uphold established authority no matter how barbaric. The wonder is that parents aren't insisting their children join the sect. This Korean reverend is so successful at getting Americans to live up to what are popularly regarded as Christian norms the guy should rent himself out to school boards as a consultant.[39]

Back to our original question, however: At what point should these young people be free to defy their parents' views, and do they have an unconditional right to be defiant? Do the parents have any rights in this situation, and

if so, on what grounds? If you were able to influence a city mayor or state senator on enforcing the law on this issue, which way would you argue?

In fact, however, many state and local authorities have already decided the issue without consulting you; they have sided with the parents on this issue. Many judges and other government officials have disregarded the First Amendment and attacked these religious groups that are so different (for example, taking away tax-exempt status, placing adults under the guardianship of their parents in order to be deprogrammed). The system, from the government to parents, not to our surprise, supports orthodoxy and persecutes nonconformity. Americans have a difficult time accepting groups with foreign ideas (groups that oppose values like individual competition, personal ambition, and materialism/consumerism upon which traditional American society rests). Some might say the actions of the authorities resemble the Inquisition prevalent in medieval Europe.[40]

What is your opinion? Do parents have the right to continue their control over the minds of their children beyond adolescence—and by force? When are the rights of the individual violated—for youth? For parents? What is the role of society in demanding ideological conformity?

THE ROLE OF THE CHURCH: COMFORT OR CHALLENGE?

The contemporary Christian church is faced with a basic dilemma brought about by its two contradictory roles (analogous to order and conflict approaches to the social order)—to comfort the afflicted and to afflict the comforted (or to comfort and to challenge). It is the church's commitment to both of these functions that has generated much of the trouble in the contemporary church.[41] The comforting role is one of aiding individuals in surmounting trials and tribulations of sickness, the death of loved ones, financial woes, social interaction with family, neighbors, colleagues, or enemies. The church aids by such means as pastoral counseling and collecting and distributing food and clothing to the needy. Another way the church comforts the afflicted is through providing a rationale for suffering (theodicy), the consequence of which is sanctification of the status quo.

Three related criticisms of the comforting function are immediately apparent. First, some would say that the church (and the clergy) have allowed this function to supersede the other role of challenger. Second, if the church would do more challenging and less comforting, evils such as poverty would be reduced. By helping people to accept an imperfect society, the church preserves the status quo—that is, the injustice and inequality that caused the problems in the first place. In this way, religion *is* an opiate of the masses because it convinces them to accept an unjust situation rather than working to change it from below. Third, the comfortable will not feel guilty, thereby preventing them from working to change the system from above.

The other function of the church—to challenge—is the injunction to be an agent of social protest and social reform. The church, through its pronouncements and leadership, seeks to lead in the fight to right the inequities of the society. A fundamental problem is in winning the support of the members. Change is almost by definition controversial, since some persons benefit under the existing social arrangements. When the church takes a stand against racial segregation, abortion, war, the abuses of business or labor, some members will become alienated. They may withdraw their financial support or even leave the church. The church, of course, has a commitment to its members. Since it cannot afford to lose its membership, the church may compromise its principles. Such an action, however, may make others angry at the church because of its hypocrisy. Consequently, the church is in the unenviable position of trying to keep a very precarious balance between compromise and purity.

The evidence is that, in general, the contemporary Christian church has opted in favor of the comforting function. The most popular preacher of the 1960s and 1970s was Billy Graham. His theology is an excellent example of the prevailing "comforting" view. He has said, for example: "We should work for peace but all we can really do is patch things up, because the real war is in man's *own* heart. Only when Christ comes again will the lion lie down with the lamb and the little white children of Alabama walk hand in hand with the little black children."[42] This philosophy is anti-interventionist. One does not attack society. One either waits until the Second Coming or one changes the hearts and minds of individuals. Social problems, by this philosophy, are a result of the sinful nature of human beings and are to be dealt with on that level rather than on the level of changing the law or the social structure. Religion in this light is essentially a private transaction between an individual and God, and not a force for overcoming social ills. But this refusal to become involved in social issues supports the status quo, which is a form of involvement. As the Reverend Malcolm Boyd has argued:

> There is a brand of Christianity which tells the rest of the world that it awaits the Second Coming of Christ to solve pressing "social problems" such as hunger, starvation, war, racism, sexism, colonialism, grinding poverty, and the ab-

sence of equal opportunity. This brand of Christianity explains that it renders unto God what belongs to God, and renders unto Caesar what belongs to Caesar, and it remains uninvolved in the arena of social issues. It lies.

For it is, in fact, cohesively involved in social issues by its support of the status quo on which it is dependent. It is rewarded by privilege, tax exemptions, and deductible financial benefits, and that ineffable sort of prestige bestowed traditionally upon docile religion by seasoned manipulators of caesaropapism—which means to say, the state using religion for its own purposes.[43]

Of course, the clergy vary in their interpretation of the role of the church. They are truly people in conflict. There are conflicting expectations of the clergy from all sides (resulting in role conflict). The church hierarchy expects the clergy to behave in a particular way (consider the rules issued by the Catholic hierarchy, for example). Most parishioners will doubtless favor the comforting role. Most joined the church to be comforted (if poor, to know they will be rewarded later; if rich, to have their wealth and power legitimized). In a survey 5,000 persons were asked what qualities of leadership they looked for in their religious leaders. The findings were clear—regardless of denomination people favored clergy who behave responsibly, counsel well in personal crisis, present a decorous appearance, and preach the Bible with competence. An awareness of social problems was far down the list of priorities, but even then the response was tempered with the qualifier that while clergy should be aware of social problems, they should not be actively engaged in solutions to them.[44] Although they are a minority in most congregations, some parishioners wish the clergy to take stands on controversial issues and work for social change. A final source of the clergy's role conflict arises from their own definition of the role. These various expectations, and the resulting role conflict on the clergy, amount to one reason why they may drop out. Another is that if they take a stand (or do not), they may automatically alienate a segment of the parish and perhaps the church hierarchy. They may, consequently, be forced to resign.

Those who do not resign may solve their dilemma by being noncontroversial. This non-boat-rocking stance is all too familiar and results in another problem—irrelevancy. By not talking about social problems, one in fact legitimates the status quo. Hence, the inequities of the society continue, since the moral force of the churches is mainly quiet.

The evidence is that the majority of clergy are opting for the "comforting" function over the "challenging" function. A 1980 Gallup Poll of clergy found that:[45] (1) 65 percent thought their churches should concentrate more on personal renewal than social renewal (the percentage agreeing with this was significantly higher among clergy from evangelical, Southern Baptist, and Baptist churches); (2) only 6 percent of the clergy would like to see religious periodicals address themselves more effectively to "social dimensions of faith and ministry;" and (3) only 45 percent had tried to persuade church, religious, and government organizations to aid the poor.

Not all clergy are content with the emphasis on comfort. As noted in the previous section, increasing numbers of clergy have become politically active on the "moral" issues of abortion, homosexuality, pornography, and the like. Typically, though, this view of morality ignores the social problems of inequalities and injustices. Other clergy are not content to let the church continue to perpetuate injustice by not speaking and acting out. They are committed to a socially relevant church, one that seeks social solutions to social problems.

A trend in the 1980s appears to be a resurgence in religious activism on social issues, not only by religious fundamentalist groups opposed to such things as sex education in the schools, gay rights, and the Equal Rights Amendment, but also by the leadership in the mainline churches. The leaders in almost every mainline religious organization have gone on record as opposing the government's budget cuts to the disadvantaged, U.S. military aid to dictatorships, and the arms race. For example, the bishops of the Catholic Church in the United States have formally challenged the fundamental assumptions and strategies of the U.S. defense system (such as the deployment of the MX missile, the doctrine of nuclear deterrence, and increased expenditures for the military). Justifying this new wave of social concern by the church, Joseph Bernardin, the Archbishop of Chicago, has said:

> Some people say we shouldn't talk politics and that we should address ourselves to truly religious issues. Well, it's not as simple as all that. It's our responsibility to address the moral dimension of the social issues we face.
> These issues, of course, do have a political dimension as well as a moral dimension. I don't deny that, but that doesn't mean we're not permitted to talk about them. But our perspective must always be from the moral or ethical dimension. I reject out of hand that we have taken a leftward swing. What we are trying to do is focus on the teaching of the Gospel as we understand it, and to apply that teaching to the various social issues of the day. Our central theme is our respect for God's gift of life, our insistence that the human person has inherent value and dignity.[46]

But political stands from the general leadership of a denomination are viewed quite differently from political activism by local ministers or priests. When local ministers or priests speak out, participate in marches, work for integrated housing, and demonstrate against excessive militarism, most of their parishioners become upset. As a result, the socially active clergy often become the objects of discrimination by their parishioners. Another consequence is that the laity trust their clergy less and less. As behavior in one area is questioned—e.g., social activism—church members are likely to withdraw confidence in others as well. Finally, churches have divided on this issue. Some want social action instead of just pious talk. Others want to preserve the status quo. The hypocrisy found in many churches forces splits, the formation of underground churches, or total rejection of Christianity as the source of social action. Others may leave because they feel that the church has wandered too far from the beliefs upon which the faith was founded. (See Panel 16–4.) This dilemma accelerates the current dropout problem—by parishioners and clergy alike.[47] The problem (if the author may here interject his bias) seems to be that for the most part those

The Church and the Establishment

The theme of this essay is that it is *normal* for the Church *not* to effectively protest or to actively seek solutions on behalf of those being victimized by the social order. I am not referring to the innocuous pap the Church routinely hands out in muted and safe tones on quiet Sunday mornings to yawning and bored parishioners. This it does with the regularity of ritual—and is regularly ineffectual. I am, rather, referring to the Church, with its millions of members and its potential power, not protesting the Established Order on behalf of the downtrodden of society, not taking a stand for those persons who are being systematically brutalized by a discriminatory social system.

Why, for example, is the Church largely silent when it exists in the midst of a white supremacist society which selected its most physically fit and able youth (primarily from the ranks of its lower income groups—those groups which didn't have the privileged protection of deferments—its blacks, Indians, and Appalachian whites) and sent them thousands of miles in a genocidal onslaught against a yellow peasant population? Where was the voice of the Church when our corporate warlords spouted their democratic ideology as the basis for napalming women and children, with never a word about the profits being raked off the war industries based on the production of wholesale death and destruction? Why didn't the Church protest when the military dehumanized our youth by teaching them to slaughter *groups* of yellow peasants as regular policy and ordered them by direct command to cold-bloodedly shoot *individual* peasants whose only "guilt" was that of being *suspected* of having collaborated with the Viet Cong? Where was the voice of the Church when those youth, who learned their lesson so well, applied it to a village such as My Lai? Why was the Church mostly silent when a dehumanized American public initially reacted with a "That's war" philos-

ophy or a "We-don't-know-enough-about-it-to-make-a-judgment" attitude? Where is the Church when it is surrounded by a populace so brainwashed that it cannot see that the My Lai massacre was the logical extension of an inhuman, demoralizing policy being systematically and cruelly followed by the United States Government for the sake of profit and power?

Even when the social malaise came to the point where the poverty-stricken and our students began to riot and government troops, tanks, and helicopters were brought into play in order to hold down the masses, it was only a small part of the Church which responded in protest. When our corrupting and corrupted leaders dehumanize large numbers of our citizens by placing profits before human values, and when, through inadequate diets, the minds of our poor are blunted, their bodies debilitated, while at the same time others stuff themselves to the point that concern with too much fat on the figure becomes a major preoccupation, the Church is strangely silent.

One wonders where the Church is when more money is annually spent in the United States on alcohol . . . than the combined amount spent on public aid by federal, state, and local governments. . . . Or when more than *eight* times as much is spent on tobacco . . . than on funding the Job Corps. . . . Or when more money is spent annually on cat and dog food . . . than the total amount spent by all our federal, state, and local governments on meals for public school children. . . .

The reason the Church seldom joins social protest is because the Church itself typically sides with the Established Order of society. It does not view discriminatory and victimizing social arrangements as evil so much as it does the disturbances arising from these social arrangements. For example, the Church does not protest the conditions which lead

(continued)

to riots as much as it does rioting. It gives out insipid statements about deploring conditions which lead men to riot but then comes down firmly and with no hesitation solidly against those who riot, pointing to the evils of destroying that which is so sacred in American society—property. In this way the Church defends the propertied, those in control (and, not incidentally, its own larger contributors), and comes down hard with its predictable lines about "respect" for "law and order."

Can we really expect anything different from the Church? If we take the lessons of history seriously instead of paying attention to ecclesiastical ideology, we would find that it is normal for the Church *not* to speak out,

not to take the side of the impoverished, the weak, and defenseless, or when it does speak out, to do so in such a muted and weak way that it affects no one. Historically, it is only rarely that the privileged classes of a society have effectively worked to change the conditions of the less fortunate of their society: This is because those very conditions serve to maintain the privileged in their exalted positions. Those who protest run the risk of bringing into play forces which lead to their own destruction. If members of the privileged classes were to protest, they would run the risk of losing their positions of privilege. And . . . the Church is part of the privileged sector of American society.

Source: Excerpted from James M. Henslin, "From Prophets to Profits: The Church and the Establishment," in *Social Problems in American Society*, 2nd ed., James M. Henslin and Larry T. Reynolds, eds. (Boston: Allyn and Bacon (Holbrook Press), 1976), pp. 270–272.

who drop out are the social activists who leave the church with a residue of "comforters." If this is the case, the future of the church is bleak unless there is a reversal and prophets of social action ascend—an unlikely possibility given the propensity of most parishioners for the message of "comfort" over the message of "challenge."

SUMMARY

As usual, order and conflict theorists view this social phenomenon—religion— very differently. Also, as usual, the unity and diversity found within this institution suggest that both models of society are partially correct.

Adherents of the order model emphasize the solidarity functions of religion. Religion helps individuals through times of stress and it benefits society by binding people together through a common set of beliefs, reaffirmed through regularly scheduled ceremonial rituals.

Conflict theorists acknowledge that religion may unify in small societies but in diverse societies religious differences divide. Religious conflict occurs commonly at all levels, however, from intersocietal religious warfare, to schisms in local congregations. From the conflict perspective, religious unity within a society, if it does occur, has negative consequences. Such unity is used to legitimate the interests of the powerful (for example, slavery, racial segregation, conquest of "pagans," and war). Similarly, the interests of the powerful are served if the poor believe that they will be rewarded in the next life. Such a "theodicy" prevents revolutions by the oppressed and serves, as Marx suggested, as "an opiate of the masses."

There are some contemporary trends in American religion that will be interesting to observe in the coming decade. Will the fundamentalist boomlet become the dominant mode of religious expression? Will religion become increasingly emotional? Will the "consciousness movement" gain momentum or be a passing fad? Will the rejection of social action by many religious persons encourage or discourage membership growth and with what other consequences for the mission of religion and the solutions to the pressing problems of society? What will be the effects of the politics of the evangelicals on American society?

CHAPTER REVIEW

1. Religion is socially created and has a tremendous impact on society. It is an integrated set of beliefs by which a group attempts to explain the meaning of life and death. Religion defines immorality and sin as well as morality and righteousness.

2. The consequences of religion are unity among the believers, conformity in behavior, and the legitimation of social structures. Religion also divides. It separates believers from non-believers, denominations, religions, and even the members of local religious groups.

3. Emile Durkheim, an order theorist, explored the question of why religion is universal. He reasoned that what any group worships is really society itself. The society is held together by religious rituals and festivals in which the group's values and beliefs are reaffirmed.

4. Karl Marx, a conflict theorist, saw religion as inhibiting social change by making existing social arrangements seem right and inevitable. Religion further promotes the status quo by teaching the faithful to accept their condition—thus religion is the ultimate tool to promote false consciousness.

5. Civil religion is the belief that God and Country are one. God is believed to have a special destiny for the United States. Order and unity are thus given religious sanction.

6. Although most Americans identify with Christianity, there is a wide variety of religious belief in American society.

7. American religious organizations can be divided according to their secular commitment into two categories. A *church* tends to compromise with the larger society, tolerates popular vices, and accepts a diversity of beliefs. A *sect*, in sharp contrast, rejects the world. It is a moral community with rigid ethical requirements and a narrow belief system.

8. A *theodicy* is a religious legitimation for a situation that otherwise might cause guilt or anger. Sects tend to have a theodicy of suffering, explaining their lack of power and privilege. Churches have theodicies that legitimate the possession of power and privilege.

9. There is a relationship between socioeconomic status (SES) and religion: (a) the lower the SES, the greater the probability of belonging to a sect; (b) there is a relationship between SES and denominational affiliation; (c) the higher the SES of the member, the greater his or her involvement and influence in the local church.

10. One trend is the decline in the mainline denominations. These churches are often bureaucratic and impersonal. Their beliefs are pluralistic. The Catholic Church is losing members because its stands against contraception and divorce are out of tune with contemporary life.

11. Another trend is the rise of the evangelicals. These groups offer what many find missing in the mainline churches—friendship, emotional release, a personal relationship with Christ, and strong beliefs. The narrow view of the evangelicals has led to a decline of religious pluralism.

12. A third trend is the increased political activism of the evangelicals and the mainline churches.

13. A final trend has been the upsurge toward eastern religions as a means to explore new levels of consciousness.

14. The contemporary Christian church is faced with a basic dilemma brought about by its two contradictory roles—to comfort the afflicted and to afflict the comforted. The comforting function is criticized because it focuses on helping the individual but ignores the problems of society. The challenging function—the injunction to be an agent of social protest and social reform—is criticized because it is divisive, alienating some members who disagree with the position taken. The evidence is clear that the majority of clergy are opting for the "comforting" function over the "challenging" function.

FOR FURTHER STUDY

Robert N. Bellah, *The Broken Covenant: American Civil Religion in Time of Trial* (New York: Seabury Press, 1975).

Peter L. Berger, *A Rumor of Angels: Modern Society and the Rediscovery of the Supernatural* (Garden City, N.Y.: Doubleday (Anchor Books), 1970).

Daniel Cohen, *The New Believers: Young Religion in America* (New York: Ballantine Books, 1975).

Harvey Cox, *The Seduction of the Spirit: The Use and Misuse of People's Religion* (New York: Simon and Schuster, 1973).

Alan Crawford, *Thunder on the Right: The "New Right" and the Politics of Resentment* (New York: Pantheon, 1980).

Emile Durkheim, *The Elementary Forms of Religious Life* (New York: The Free Press, 1965).

Donald B. Kraybill, *Our Star-Spangled Faith* (Scottdale, Pa.: Herald Press, 1976).

Max Weber, *The Protestant Ethic and the Spirit of Capitalism* (London: Allen and Unwin, 1930).

Bryan Wilson, *Religion in Sociological Perspective* (New York: Oxford University Press, 1982).

NOTES AND REFERENCES

1. These elements are taken primarily from Elizabeth K. Nottingham, *Religion and Society* (New York: Random House, 1954), pp. 1–11.

2. See especially Peter L. Berger, *The Sacred Canopy* (New York: Doubleday, 1967).

3. Peter L. Berger, "Religious Institutions," in *Sociology*, Neil J. Smelser, ed. (New York: John Wiley, 1967), pp. 343–344.

4. Pierre L. van den Berghe, *Race and Racism: A Comparative Perspective* (New York: John Wiley, 1967), p. 82.

5. Earl Raab, ed., *Religious Conflict in America* (Garden City, N.Y.: Doubleday (Anchor

Books), 1964); see also Robert Lee and Martin E. Marty, *Religion and Social Conflict* (New York: Oxford University Press, 1964).

6. Emile Durkheim, *The Elementary Forms of Religious Life* (New York: The Free Press, 1965). Originally published in 1912.

7. The following is taken largely from Robert N. Bellah, "Civil Religion in America," *Daedalus* 96 (Winter, 1967), pp. 1–21; and Conrad Cherry, "American Sacred Ceremonies," in *American Mosaic: Social Patterns of Religion in the United States*, Philip E. Hammond and Benton Johnson, eds. (New York: Random House, 1970), pp. 303–316. For other scholarly treatises on the sources and measurement of civil religion, see William A. Cole and Philip E. Hammond, "Religious Pluralism, Legal Development, and Societal Complexity: Rudimentary Forms of Civil Religion," *Journal for the Scientific Study of Religion* 13 (June, 1974), pp. 177–189; Robert E. Stauffer, "Civil Religion, Technocracy and the Private Sphere: Further Comments on Cultural Integration in Advanced Societies," *Journal for the Scientific Study of Religion* 12 (December, 1973), pp. 415–425; and Ronald C. Wimberley, Donald A. Clelland, Thomas C. Hood, and C. M. Lipsey, "Measuring Civil Religion," paper read at the annual meeting of the American Sociological Association, Montreal, August, 1974. See also, Robert N. Bellah, *The Broken Covenant: American Civil Religion in Time of Trial* (New York: Seabury, 1975); and the entire issue of *Journal of Church and State* 22 (Winter, 1980).

8. Bellah, "Civil Religion in America," pp. 1–2. For other examples of civil religion in American society, see especially: "God-Language in the Inaugural," *The Christian Century* 94 (January 5–12, 1977), pp. 3–7; Leo Sandon, Jr., "James Reston: Prophet of American Civil Religion," *The Christian Century* 94 (January 5–12, 1977), pp. 15–18; and Donald B. Kraybill, *Our Star-Spangled Faith* (Scottdale, Pa.: Herald Press, 1976).

9. *The Gallup Report*, Nos. 201–202 (June-July, 1982), p. 23.

10. Ibid., p. 32.

11. See Richard J. Cattani, "Missouri Lutheran Synod Makes Schism Official," *Christian Science Monitor* (December 8, 1976), p. 7.

12. Charles Y. Glock and Rodney Stark, *Religion and Society in Tension* (Chicago: Rand McNally, 1965).

13. Ernst Troeltsch, *The Social Teaching of the Christian Churches*, Olive Wyon, trans. (New York: Macmillan, 1931); and Liston Pope, *Millhands and Preachers* (New Haven, Conn.: Yale University Press, 1942), pp. 117–140.

14. For a contemporary analysis of the sect-church division, see John Scanzoni, "Resurgent Fundamentalism: Marching Backward into the '80s?" *The Christian Century* (September 10–17, 1980), pp. 847–849.

15. Max Weber, *The Theory of Social and Economic Organization*, A. M. Henderson and Talcott Parsons, trans. (Glencoe, Ill.: Free Press, 1947), pp. 358–366.

16. J. Milton Yinger, *Sociology Looks at Religion* (New York: Macmillan, 1961), pp. 21–25.

17. This is the conclusion of Liston Pope after his study of the rise of sects in a small town in North Carolina: Pope, *Millhands and Preachers*, p. 140.

18. Max Weber, *The Sociology of Religion*, Ephraim Fischoff, trans. (Boston: Beacon Press, 1963), p. 107.

19. Peter L. Berger, *The Sacred Canopy: Elements of a Sociological Theory of Religion* (Garden City, N.Y.: Doubleday, 1967), pp. 53–80.

20. Thomas O'Dea, *The Sociology of Religion* (Englewood Cliffs, N.J.: Prentice-Hall, 1966), p. 60. For an elaboration of this point, see the insightful discussion by Weber in *The Sociology of Religion*.

21. N. J. Demerath, III, *Social Class in American Protestantism* (Chicago: Rand McNally, 1965), p. 3.

22. Leonard Broom and Philip Selznick, *Sociology*, 4th ed. (New York: Harper & Row, 1968), p. 321.

23. This relationship does not always hold, however, if other dimensions of religious involvement are examined. See especially Demerath, *Social Class in American Protestantism*, pp. 1–124.

24. Erich Goode, "Social Class and Church Participation," *American Journal of Sociology* 72 (July, 1966), p. 111.

25. *The New York Times* (December 30, 1979), p. 13.
26. Gallup Poll, cited in *Public Opinion* 2 (March/May 1979), p. 37.
27. Jeffrey K. Hadden, "Soul-Saving Via Video," *The Christian Century* (May 28, 1980), p. 611.
28. Jeffrey K. Hadden and Charles E. Swann, *Prime Time Preachers* (Reading, Mass.: Addison-Wesley, 1981), p. 6.
29. Cited in "Stars of the Cathode Church," *Time* (February 4, 1980), pp. 64–65.
30. See George F. Will, "Who Put Morality in Politics?" *Newsweek* (September 15, 1980), p. 108; and Martin E. Marty, "Fundamentalism Reborn," *Saturday Review* (May 1980), pp. 37–42.
31. *The Gallup Report*, p. 72.
32. A Gallup Poll found that approximately 10 million Americans are involved in eastern religions, reported in *Public Opinion* 2 (March/May, 1979), p. 27.
33. Melvin Maddocks, "America's Therapy Industry," *Christian Science Monitor* (January 10, 1977), pp. 16–17.
34. Tom Wolfe, "The Me Decade and the Third Great Awakening," *New West* (August 30, 1976), p. 36.
35. Harvey G. Cox, "Why Young Americans are Buying Oriental Religions," *Psychology Today* (July, 1977), pp. 36–42.
36. See Frederick Bunt, "Deprogramming and Religious Liberty," *The Humanist* (September/October, 1979), pp. 48–49.
37. Harvey G. Cox, "Four Big Ones," *Journal of Current Social Issues* 14 (Spring 1977), p. 28.
38. For a defense of "deprogramming" by its leading practitioner, see Ted Patrick, *Let Our Children Go!* (New York: E. P. Dutton, 1976).
39. Nicholas Von Hoffman, "Moonies, Hare Krishnas Are Ideal American Kids, Right?" *Rocky Mountain News* (April 8, 1977), p. 51.
40. See Garry Wills, "The Secular Inquisition against Moonies," *Rocky Mountain News* (April 17, 1977) and "The Freedom to Be Strange," *Time* (March 28, 1977), p. 81.
41. Much of the following discussion is taken from Charles Y. Glock, Benjamin B. Ringer, and Earl R. Babbie, *To Comfort and to Challenge: A Dilemma of the Contemporary Church* (Berkeley, Calif.: University of California Press, 1967), especially Chap. 9; and Jeffrey K. Hadden, *The Gathering Storm in the Churches* (Garden City, N.Y.: Doubleday, 1969).
42. "The Preaching and the Power," *Newsweek* (July 20, 1970), p. 52.
43. Malcolm Boyd, "Does God Have a Candidate?" *The Progressive* 41 (November, 1976), p. 27.
44. David S. Schuller, Merton P. Strommen, and Milo L. Brekke eds., *Ministry in America* (New York: Harper & Row, 1981).
45. Cited in Robert T. Henderson, "Ministering to the Poor: Our Embarrassment of Riches," *Christianity Today* (August 8, 1980), p. 18.
46. Quoted in "Bishops and the Bomb," *Time* (November 29, 1982), p. 77.
47. Harold E. Quinley, "The Dilemma of the Activist Church: Protestant Religion in the Sixties and Seventies," *Journal for the Scientific Study of Religion* 13 (March 1974), pp. 1–21.

17

The Structure of Power
in
American Society

In Washington, D.C. there are about 15,000 lawyers, association executives, public relations experts, and technical workers who are lobbyists. These lobbyists work on behalf of interest groups to influence legislators and regulatory agencies. Lobbyists' tactics include supplying information, doing favors, providing entertainment, giving campaign contributions, flooding Congress with telegrams, and furnishing transportation.

The phenomenon of lobbying can be interpreted in two opposite ways—*each of which illustrates a fundamental view of the distribution of power for the whole society*. The first view is that lobbying is the essence of democracy, as competing pressure groups each present their best case to the decision-makers. These officials, faced with these countervailing forces, tend to compromise and make decisions most beneficial to the public.

In contrast, others view lobbying as another instance of the privileged few consistently getting their way. Interest groups are not equal in power. Some have enormous power and are not challenged by effective opposition. For example, the American Petroleum Institute speaks for 350 corporations and has an annual lobbying budget of $30 million. Also, the United States Chamber of Commerce has a $20 million budget and represents 89,500 corporations and 2,500 local communities. These and other business-oriented lobbies are extremely well organized and financed. Their opposition is negligible. Clearly, from this perspective, power in Washington is centralized and represents the powerful few.

The compelling question of this chapter is: Who are the real power wielders in American society? Is it an elite, or are the people sovereign? The location and exercise of power is difficult to determine, especially in a large and complex society such as the United States. Decisions are necessarily made by a few people, but in a democracy these few are to be representatives of the masses and therefore subject to their influence. But what of nonrepresentatives who aid in shaping policy? What about the pressure on the decision makers by powerful groups? What about those pressures on the decision maker which are so diffuse that the leaders may not even know who is applying the pressure?

MODELS OF THE NATIONAL POWER STRUCTURE

There are two basic views of the power structure—**elitist** and **pluralist.** The elitist view of power is that there is a pyramid of power. Those persons at the apex control the rest of the pyramid. The pluralists, on the other hand, see power as dispersed rather than concentrated. Power is broadly distributed among a number of organizations, special interests, and the voters. This chapter is devoted to the examination of different elitist and pluralist conceptions of power in the United States. As we survey each, the fundamental question we should ask ourselves is: How does this model mesh with the facts of contemporary America? Does the model portray things as they are or as they should be?

Pluralist
Models

Pluralism I: Representative Democracy. Many Americans accept the notion promoted in high school civics books that the United States is a "government of the people, by the people, for the people." Democracy is the form of government in which the people have the ultimate power. In a complex society of over 235 million persons, the people cannot make all decisions; they must elect representatives to make most decisions. So, decision making is concentrated at the top, but it is to be controlled by the people who elect the decision makers. This model is shown in Figure 17–1.

The most important component of a democratic model is that the representatives, because they are elected by the people, are responsive to the wishes of the people.

FIGURE 17–1   Representative Democracy

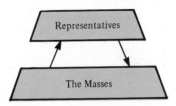

This model, however, does *not* conform to reality. The United States is undemocratic in many important ways. The people, although they do vote for their representatives every few years, are really quite powerless. For example, who makes the really important decisions about war and peace, economic policies, and foreign policy? The people certainly do not. And in the light of the Pentagon Papers, which concerned the conduct of American leaders in the Indochina War, it is clear that the American people have been deliberately misinformed by the leadership. The record shows that many times the American people have been deceived when the object was to conceal clandestine illegal operations, mistakes, undemocratic practices, and the like. The following events are instances of official U.S. deceit during our involvement in Southeast Asia.[1]

□ *Item:* In 1963, the U.S. supported—but officially denied its involvement in—the coup against South Vietnam's President Ngo Dinh Diem.
□ *Item:* In 1964, President Johnson used an incident in which American ships were allegedly shot at in the Tonkin Gulf to give him a free hand to escalate the war in Vietnam. Congress was deliberately misled by the official representation of the facts.
□ *Item:* President Johnson praised our Asian allies for sending "volunteers" to fight in Vietnam when in fact our government had paid Thailand and the Philippines $200 million each if they would make this gesture.
□ *Item:* President Nixon and his advisors told the American public that the neutrality of Cambodia had not been violated when U.S. pilots had already conducted 3,600 bombing missions in a five-year period in that country. To carry out this deception, the death certificates of Americans who died in Cambodia were falsified by our government.

These examples could be multiplied many times over with cover-ups of the CIA involvement in the takeover of the Allende government in Chile; the U.S.-sponsored invasion of Cuba in 1961; the attempted whitewashing of sheep deaths in Utah because of an unintended release of chemicals used in biological warfare; the denial by Attorney General Mitchell that ITT had offered $400,000 to underwrite the 1972 Republican National Convention, and so on.

Not only have the American people been misinformed, but the basic democratic tenet that the public be informed has been defied. On the one hand, Congress has shown its contempt for the electorate by the use of secret meetings. The executive branch, too, has acted in secret. Recent presidents have gone months without a press conference, have used "executive privilege" to keep presidential advisors from testifying before congressional committees, and have refused to debate opponents in election campaigns.

By permission of Johnny Hart and News Group Chicago, Inc.

Many persons who are appointed rather than elected wield tremendous power. Technical experts, for example, evaluate extremely complicated issues; they can virtually dictate to the president and Congress what is needed for defense, shoring up the economy, or winning friends abroad, because they are the experts. The coterie of advisors may convince the president to act in particular ways. The members appointed to the regulatory agencies have tremendous power to shape various aspects of the economy.

Perhaps one of the most undemocratic features (at least in its consequences) of the American political system is a result of the manner in which campaigns are financed. Political campaigns are expensive, with statewide campaigns sometimes costing hundreds of thousands of dollars while a national campaign runs into the millions (excluding primaries, President Nixon spent more than $36 million and McGovern spent in excess of $18 million in the 1972 election campaign). This money is raised from contributions. Nixon, for example, received over $14 million from 100 persons for his 1972 campaign. Such contributions are given for a number of reasons, including the hope of future favors or payoffs for past benefits. Thus, the passage of favorable laws, beneficial governmental rulings, maintenance of tax loopholes, or appointment to prestigious government posts such as ambassador may be the reward for financing candidates. Some individuals and interest groups even donate to the candidate of both parties to ensure that their interests are served regardless of the election outcome. The result is that the wealthy have power while the less well-to-do and certainly the poor have no hold on office holders.[2]

To counter the potential and real abuses of large contributions, the Presidential campaigns of 1976 and 1980 were financed from public funds. Congressional candidates, however, were allowed to accept contributions from individuals and special interest groups. Most of the money has come from special interest groups through Political Action Committees (PACs). In 1974 PACs gave $12.4 million to Congressional candidates. In 1976 they gave $22.6 million, which increased to $35 million in 1978. PACs contributed another $450 million to Congressional races in 1980, and $80 million in 1982, leading some cynics to comment that we have "the best Congress money can buy."[3] These PACs are formed to represent interests such as labor unions, doctors, realtors, auto dealers, teachers, and corporations. Each PAC may give up to $5,000 to any candidate in a primary and another $5,000 in a general election. As U.S. News & World Report editorialized, "PACs of every ilk have a way of contributing their allowed $5,000 chunks to candidates who either have voted 'right' or had better do so shortly."[4]

Although no one can prove conclusively that receiving a PAC contribution buys a vote, evidence leads to such a conclusion. In 1982, for example, the National Automobile Dealers' Association opposed a proposed law suggested by the Federal Trade Commission that would require used-car dealers to disclose known defects to potential buyers. The dealers' association, through various PACs, distributed campaign contributions of more than $840,000 to more than 300 senators and representatives, 85 percent of whom voted against the used-car rule, killing it by a greater than two-to-one margin.[5]

Another example concerns a congressional vote on whether to fund the Clinch River nuclear breeder reactor in 1981. Ralph Nader's Public Citizen's Congress Watch noted that the five companies involved in designing and building the reactor contributed about $280,000 to members of Congress. Of eleven representatives receiving more than $3,000, ten voted to build the reactor (the other was absent at the time of the vote); of those representatives who received $1,500 to $3,000, 76 percent voted for the project; and of those representatives who did not receive any money, 71 percent voted to kill it.[6]

Money presents a fundamental obstacle to democracy because only the interests of the wealthy tend to be served. Elections are very expensive. In 1980, for example, five Senators spent over $2 million each to wage their campaigns. One governor—Jay Rockefeller of West Virginia—spent $11.6 million ($28.92 per vote received) to win. Moreover, the data show consistently that the winners outspend the losers. In the 1978 Senate races candidates who outspent their opponents won 28 of the 33 contested races. Thus, it takes money and lots of it to be a successful politician. The candidate must either be rich or be willing to accept contributions from others.[7] In either case, the political leaders will be part of or beholden to the wealthy.

There are a number of other undemocratic features that belie the validity of this model. The "seniority system" in Congress gives extraordinary power to those individuals with longevity of service. The electoral college system is undemocratic. So is the party nomination system; the people choose from among the nominees for President, but they have little voice in their selection as nominees. The establishment of voting district boundaries is often "gerrymandered" by the party in power to keep themselves in power. Minority groups of all kinds may have little if any representation because of the many "winner-take-all" electoral systems.

Another objection, and a most telling one, is that the majority of citizens are relatively uninformed and apathetic about politics—thereby giving power to those already in office by default. Surveys show that 65 percent of the eligible voters do not regularly vote, half cannot name their congressperson, 68 percent cannot identify anything their representative has ever done, 96 percent cannot identify any policy the representative stands for—all rather minimal tests of political activity, and the figures are worse for state and municipal levels.[8]

This model of democracy also neglects the vast power of the various interest groups on specific issues. Organized labor, the American Medical Association, environmentalists, farmers, and other interest groups often mobilize and get beneficial legislation involving tariffs, taxes, contracts, subsidies, or whatever.

Closely related to the financing of campaigns is the process by which political candidates are nominated. Being wealthy or having access to wealth is essential for victory because of the enormous cost (it costs up to $3 million to elect a senator and as much as $600,000 for a representative). This means that the candidates tend to represent a limited constituency—

the wealthy. "Recruitment of elective elites remains closely associated, especially for the most important offices in the larger states, with the candidates' wealth or access to large campaign contributions."[9]

The two-party system also works to limit choices among candidates to a rather narrow range. Each of the parties is financed by the special interests—especially business.

> When all of these direct and indirect gifts (donations provided directly to candidates or through numerous political action committees of specific corporations and general business organizations) are combined, the power elite can be seen to provide the great bulk of the financial support to both parties at the national level, far outspending the unions and middle status liberals within the Democrats, and the melange of physicians, dentists, engineers, real-estate operators and other white-collar conservatives within the right wing of the Republican Party.[10]

Affluent individuals and the largest corporations influence candidate selection by giving financial aid to those sympathetic with their views and withholding support from those who differ. The parties, then, are constrained to choose candidates with views congruent with the monied interests.

Pluralism II: Veto Groups.   Although some groups have more power than others and some individuals have more power than others, the power structure in the United States is viewed according to the "veto groups" model as a plurality of interest groups.[11] Each interest group (for example, the military, labor, business, farmers, education, medicine, law, veterans, the aged, blacks, and consumers) is primarily concerned with protecting its own interests. The group that primarily exercises power varies with the issue at stake. There is a balance of power, since each "veto group" mobilizes to prevent the others from actions threatening its interests. Thus, these groups tend to neutralize each other.

The masses are sought as an ally (rather than dominated, as is the case in the various elitist models) by the interest groups in their attempts to exert power over issues in their jurisdiction. Figure 17–2 shows the relationship between the various levels in this model.

This pluralist model assumes that there are a number of sectors of power. The most powerful persons in each are usually wealthy—probably upper class. But, the pluralist view is that the upper class is not a unified group—there is considerable disagreement within the upper-class category because of differing interests. Power is not concentrated, but is viewed as a shifting coalition depending upon the issue. The basic difference between pluralists and elitists is on the question of whether there is a basic unity or disagreement among the powerful from different sectors (basically, those who are wealthy enough to be upper class).

There are several criticisms of this pluralistic model. They stem from the knowledge that it, like the other pluralistic model (for representative

FIGURE 17–2   Veto-Groups Model

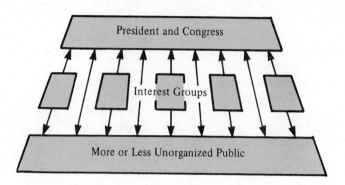

democracy), is an idealized conception of the distribution of power—as such, it does not conform with reality and is subject to question on several grounds. First, is the power structure so amorphous that power shifts constantly from one power source to another? Second, are the interest groups so equal in power that they neutralize each other? The special bias of this view is that it does not give attention to the power differentials among the various interest groups. It is absurd to claim that the power of big business is neutralized by the countervailing power of farmers. A more probable occurrence is that there is a hierarchy of power among these "veto groups."

A final criticism is that the leaders in each sector come disproportionately from the upper economic strata. If this assertion is correct, the possibility of a power elite that transcends narrow interest groups is present, since they may know each other, tend to intermarry, and have similar economic interests (as we will see later).

The pluralist models are not altogether faulty. There are a number of possible power centers that often compete for advantage. Shifting coalitions are possible. There are instances when selected officials are responsive to public opinion. See Panel 17–1 for varied attempts to change the behavior of the powerful. However, it seems to this observer that most of the evidence supports an elitist view, although each of the three types described below also has its faults.

Elitist Models   The elitist views of societal power are usually structured quite similarly to those of Karl Marx. For Marx, economics was the basis for the stratification system (that is, unequal distribution of rewards including power). The economic elite, because of similar interests (that is, keeping the status quo) and limited social interaction patterns, is a unified group. The economic elite controls the state and its inhabitants.

Implicit in the Marxian conception of the powerful is the notion of conspiracy. The elite manipulate the masses through religion, nationalism, control of the media, and control of the visible governmental leaders.[12]

The Antinuclear Movement

Some extraordinary events occurred in 1982: (1) resolutions calling for a nuclear arms freeze were passed in nine state legislatures, in 81 city councils, and in more than 300 New England town meetings; (2) the largest political rally in American history took place—750,000 marchers in New York City united to demonstrate their concern over the escalating arms race; and (3) numerous polls revealed that about three-fourths of Americans supported a mutual nuclear arms freeze.

We can trace a number of roots for this gathering of momentum against established government policy. One major element was (and continues to be) the use of organized civil disobedience—the deliberate breaking of the law—to dramatize the widespread support of present trends and to galvanize public opinion. The acts of the Plowshares Eight on September 9, 1980 taken collectively comprised one such event. In this celebrated case demonstrators broke into a General Electric plant and damaged nuclear warhead cones. What follows is the description and rationale of this highly symbolic act by one of the activists, Philip Berrigan:

They will hammer their swords into plowshares.

—*Isaiah 2:4*

The instrument we employed at General Electric's Re-entry Division Plant in King of Prussia, Pennsylvania, was traditionally a peaceful tool for building—fabricating homes, making toys, shaping metal, repairing, and mending. Isaiah and Micah used it as a metaphor for the authority of God—for spiritual rebirth, for conversion to compassion and justice, for a new face toward God, sister and brother, above all for the outlawing of war.

So at 6:50 A.M. on September 9, 1980, we strode into GE's squat, cost-efficient matrix of the Mark 12A (a first-strike re-entry vehicle deployed currently on Minuteman III, and planned for Trident II and MX); slipped by security; went unerringly to a huge room marked "nondestructible testing"; found nose cones and components, and began their conversion. And, perhaps, our own.

Hammers and blood. The blood a reminder of common parenthood, common nature, purpose, destiny. No more genocide in our name, no suicide by Mark 12A, Trident, MX, cruise.

The logic of nuclear weaponry is nihilistic and despairing—if one can conceive a weapon, it must be built; if one can build it, it must be used. The logic of hope runs counter—what is made can be unmade; only then is the murderous intention destroyed.

Our action defined us as conservatives—obviously not Tories or Reaganites, but modest custodians of a tradition that honors life and defends the wretched of the Earth—poor people, the weak, victims. The keepers of that vision are too many to enumerate here, for America can claim more than its share—native Americans, slaves, indentured servants, poor artisans, radical farmers, women, labor organizers, students, people of the "cloth," political prisoners, philosophers, and poets. From those times when the first European colonizers claimed the continent's land, the oppressed have produced the justice fighters, whereas the privileged were, at best, interpreters of the vision and, at worst, parasites.

The American experience reveals in almost cyclic fashion—Jefferson thought a revolution every twenty-five years necessary to check the plutocrats—a widespread outcry from the downtrodden, and from the few who stood with them.

(continued)

Such a time was the Vietnam era, the genocidal adventure in Indochina—the "undeclared" war, the war by proxy (especially at the end); the laboratory war; the war of human beings against overwhelming technology; the war that turned the empire downhill from its apex—on greased skids, as we've discovered since.

That war was a Church-State boot camp for my wife, Elizabeth McAlister, and for Dan and myself. We lost our milk teeth in civil rights classrooms—in the black ghettos, at Selma, New Orleans, Atlanta, Washington, Harlem—and cut our molars at Fort Myer, Virginia (1966), the March on the Pentagon (1967), Baltimore's Customs House (1967), Catonsville (1968), and Harrisburg (1971). The Church greeted our voices and non-violent resistance with silencing, exile, and ostracism; the State with arrest, interminable trials, conviction, imprisonment.

When the Paris Peace Accords were signed in 1973, some of us encountered a vision grown tired. No more political agitation on campuses; no more huge marches on Washington; no more disruption of war-making bureaucracy or technology; not many resisters in prison to keep consciences honest and minds re-minded. A few hung in there in 1973, 1974, and early 1975, stubbornly insisting that our blunders—infighting, egotism, and sexism—had not obviated the vision, nor relieved us of the responsibility of opposing the bloody plague of imperial, corporate America.

One question nagged at us: How does one survive sanely, nonviolently, faithfully in a society mobilized against such survival? To put it another way, given corporate capitalism's appetite for war, given the Bomb as diplomatic bargaining chip, what is the meaning and price of discipleship?

Our answer—it is by no means the only one—was to form the nonviolent community of resistance. The Community for Creative Nonviolence began in Washington in 1972, and Jonah House in Baltimore in 1973. With little notice and less media coverage, we took up resistance to the war again—tons of rubble dumped on Pentagon approaches, civil disobedience at the White House over violations of the Paris Peace Accords, two raids on the Vietnamese Overseas Procurement Office, several sit-ins against President Ford's "amnesty" program, arrests at the National Security Agency, a whole summer (1974) of tiger cages outside the Rotunda of the Capitol. Small actions, but something during a disillusioned and jaded time.

Resistance communities sprouted and slowly grew—out of vision, pain, and necessity. Friends formed the Pacific Life Community (an anti-Trident coalition) in Washington, and it spread to California and Oregon. Others collected East Coast resisters into the Atlantic Life Community, concentrating on the Pentagon, Electric Boat in Groton, Connecticut (producer of the new Trident), United Technologies in Hartford, GE in the Philadelphia area, Rockwell in Pittsburgh, and assorted war-making think tanks. At the Pentagon, we sustained a five-year campaign—thousands of arrests (a thousand in 1980 alone).

A student wrote recently, "Your protest was futile! It hasn't changed public opinion; it hasn't reduced nuclear arms." He attends a Catholic high school and studies justice and peace in one of his classes. In answering him I wrote, "Why do you say 'futile'? Our action is making you think, isn't it?"

Perhaps that's a key, however imperfect. The struggle to prevent nuclear war is, in an altogether unprecedented way, a struggle for spirit, heart, and mind.

The intention to use the Bomb—most Americans would use it, in one circumstance or another—evidences a moral paralysis, a militarization of soul, a submission to violence as necessity, a bankruptcy of ethical option that amounts to slavishness.

Official propaganda peddles the Bomb as guarantor of our freedoms. That is a stupefying lie: It is, to the contrary, a symbol of moral and physical slavery, of mass suicide, and, perhaps, of omnicide (the killing of all things).

Will Americans—we led the lockstep to the nuclear precipice; we must lead the retreat from it—settle for a "freedom" defined by declining life expectancy, by a questionable future for our children, and by a right to life eroded by technicians, war profiteers, generals, and politicians? If overlords, with a terrible ease, can deprive a whole people of their "inalienable" right to life, what does "freedom" mean?

Civil disobedience offers the hope of liberation, the hope of survival. In his classic essay, Thoreau called civil disobedience a "duty"—personal and political. Personal duty because enslavement of blacks and exploitation of Mexicans enslaved and exploited every American. Political duty because government, then as now, was unrepresentative, *was* the slaveholders, the exploiters, the devious and ruthless enemy of the people.

Thoreau's grasp of the law was incisive: "It is not desirable to cultivate a respect for the law, so much as for the right. ... Law never made men a whit more just; and by means of their respect for it, even the well-disposed are daily made the agents of injustice."

Two convictions support our civilly disobedient attitude toward the law: First, the State has perverted law to the point of legalizing its nuclear psychosis. Second, the State is invincible unless such legalizing is rendered null and void by non-violent civil disobedience. We cannot leave the State invincible in its determination to initiate (or provoke) nuclear war.

Who expects politicians, generals, and bomb makers to disarm? People must disarm the bombs. That's the only way it will happen.

Source: Philip Berrigan, "Why We Seized the Hammer," *The Progressive* 45 (May 1981), pp. 50–51. Reprinted by permission from *The Progressive*, 409 East Main Street, Madison, Wisconsin 53703. Copyright © 1981, The Progressive Inc.

Power Elite I: Communist Conspiracy. The "communist conspiracy" view is not taken seriously by social scientists, and most citizens would see little reality in its assumptions. However, G. William Domhoff has estimated that it is shared by 5 to 15 million adult Americans.[13] In this ultraconservative view of the power structure, the United States is led by a small, cohesive group of ideologues. This group is thought to be a "conspiracy" which shares an ideology that is collectivist (anti-capitalism and pro-welfare) and internationalist (one-world government), ridiculing the traditional virtues of rugged individualism and blind patriotism. As evidence of this "conspiracy," there is the existence of a bipartisan group called the Trilateral Commission. This is a group of 275 prominent businessmen, scholars, and politicians from North America, Western Europe, and Japan. It was formed in 1973 under the initial leadership of David Rockefeller, head of Chase Manhattan Bank. Its proponents argue that this organization strengthens the ties among the United States and its allies. Its conservative opponents see the Trilateral Commission as an international elite, whose interests transcend national loyalties. They see it as the forerunner of world government. They also fear its influence on domestic politics. President Carter, a former member, had on his administration team other Trilateralists— Zbigniew Brzezinski, Walter Mondale, Cyrus Vance, and Harold Brown. The Reagan Administration is also represented by Trilateral members in high places—George Bush and Caspar Weinberger.

An important component of this view is that the leaders act together, and secretly, to manipulate the masses so that certain agreed-upon goals are accomplished. They are motivated by an ideology that is antithetical to all that America has stood for in the past.

Within the ultra-right-wing literature, some variations are found as to who comprises the conspiracy. For some, it is composed of Jews. For others, it is the "Eastern Establishment" of bankers and industrialists who control the Republican Party. Another variation is that the leaders are either card-carrying communists or the dupes of the communists. The founder of the John Birch Society, Robert Welch, has written, for example, that President Dwight D. Eisenhower was a Communist. He said, "My firm belief that Dwight Eisenhower is a dedicated, conscious agent of the Communist conspiracy is based on an accumulation of detailed evidence so extensive and so palpable that it seems to me to put this conviction beyond any reasonable doubt."[14]

Although there is a tendency by academics not to take this model seriously, there are at least two aspects of this view that make sense. First, the ultra-right-wingers are convinced that the big money interests (heads of major banks, industrial giants, and insurance companies) actually run the country. This can make a good deal of sense, as we will see later, although the degree to which they are unified in trying to run the country is debatable. Second, both political parties are dominated largely by the same kinds of people—the wealthy. From that viewpoint it really does not make very much difference which party is in power or who is appointed to the highest government posts—the interests of the wealthy tend to be served.

There are some notable points of this model that do not fit the facts. The government is not dominated by Jews or Communists who work for the overthrow of the government. As Domhoff has asked: Is David Rockefeller a communist? Is he against capitalism?—not likely. There is no "conspiracy." The leaders tend to have similar economic interests, and they work for what they consider best for the country and its economy; this means a strong defense, protected industry, prosperity, and economic growth. They are not a tightly knit organization that works secretly for the goal of America's downfall. This is a paranoid view of the world that is just plain false.

Power Elite II: The Thesis of C. Wright Mills. C. Wright Mills' view of the American structure of power posits that the key persons in three sectors— the corporate rich, the executive branch of the government, and the military— all combine to form a **power elite** that makes all important decisions.[15]

The elite is a small group of persons who routinely interact together. They also, as Mills assumed, have similar interests and goals. The elite is the power elite because the members have key institutional positions—that is, they command great authority and resources in a specific and important sector, and each sector is dependent upon the other sectors.

There are three levels in Mills' pyramid of power. The uppermost is the power elite—composed of the leaders of three sectors. Mills implied that of the three, the corporate rich are perhaps the most powerful (first among "equals"). The middle level of power is comprised of local opinion leaders, the legislative branch of government, and the plurality of interest groups. These bodies, according to Mills, do the bidding of the power elite. The third level is the powerless mass of unorganized people who are controlled from above. They are exploited economically and politically. The three levels of power are depicted in Figure 17–3.

Mills believed that the power elite was a relatively new phenomenon resulting from a number of historical and social forces that have enlarged and centralized the facilities of power, making the decisions of small groups much more consequential than in any other age.[16]

The two important and related factors giving rise to the recent emergence of the power elite are: (1) the means of power and violence are now infinitely greater than they were in the past, and (2) they are also increasingly centralized. The decisions of a few become ultimately crucial when they have the power to activate a system that has the capabilities of destroying hundreds of cities within minutes. Transportation, communication, the economy, the instruments of warfare are examples of several areas that have become centralized— making a power elite possible. The federal government taxes, regulates, and passes laws so that the lives of almost all Americans are affected. This

---

FIGURE 17–3   Mills's Pyramid of Power

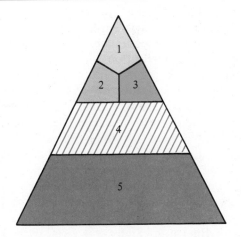

Legend: 1, corporate rich; 2, executive branch; 3, military leaders; 4, leaders of interest groups, legislative branch, local opinion leaders; 5, unorganized masses.

same bureaucratic process is evident in the military, where decisions are more and more centralized. The Pentagon, which oversees the largest and most expensive feature of the government, is a relatively new phenomenon. The economy in the United States was once composed of many, many small productive units that were more or less autonomous. But over time the number of semiautonomous economic units has dwindled through mergers, interlocking directorates, and chainstores, putting the financial squeeze on the small businessperson. The result is that the economy has become dominated by less than 200 giant corporations.

The tremendous advances in transportation and communication have made it much more likely that the persons holding key positions in the political, economic, and military hierarchies can be in contact with each other if they wish to do so. If, as Mills assumed, they have similar interests, then they must be in contact so that their activities can be coordinated to the best mutual advantage.

The key decision makers also have instruments to influence the masses, such as television, public relations firms, and techniques of propaganda that are unsurpassed in the history of mankind. Hence, if there is a power elite and they want to manipulate the masses to accept their decisions, they have the instruments of mass persuasion at their disposal.

Mills also contended that the importance of institutions has shifted. Whereas the family and religion were once the most important American institutions, they (along with education) have become subordinate to the three power institutions of the economy, polity, and military—thus making the leaders of these three domains the power elite. Mills said, "Families and churches and schools adapt to modern life; governments and armies and corporations shape it; and, as they do so, they turn these lesser institutions into means for their ends."[17] For example, religious institutions supply chaplains to the armed forces, where they increase the effectiveness of the combat units by raising morale. Schools train persons for their places in the giant corporations. Fathers and sons are sometimes taken from their homes to fight and die for their country. And, Mills said, the symbols of these lesser institutions are used to legitimate the decisions of the power elite who dominate the powerful institutions.

A most important impetus for the formation of the power elite was World War II. American participation in a war worldwide in scope and where the possibility of defeat was very real meant, among other things, that a reorganization of various sectors had to be accomplished. The national government, particularly the executive department, had to be granted dictatorial powers so that the war could be conducted. Decisions had to be made quickly and in secret, two qualities not compatible with a democracy. The nation's corporations had to be mobilized for war. They made huge profits. Finally, the military became very prominent in decision making. Their expertise was essential to the making of wartime strategy.

Following World War II, the United States was faced with another threat, the spread of communism. This meant, in effect, that the executive department, the corporations, and the military did not shift back to their peacetime ways. The military remained in the decision-making process, the corporations remained dependent upon lucrative defense contracts, and the executive branch continued to exercise its autonomous or at least semiautonomous powers.

All these factors, according to Mills, ensured that the domains of the polity, economy, and military were enlarged and centralized. Decisions made in each of these domains became increasingly crucial to all citizens, but particularly to the leaders of the other key domains. The result had to be a linkage between the key persons in each domain. It was in their interests to cooperate. Since each sector affected the others, the persons at the top of each hierarchy had to interact with the leaders from the other sectors, so that the actions and decisions would benefit all. Thus, they have come to form a triangle of power, an interlocking directorate of persons in the three key domains making coordinated decisions—a power elite.

An important ingredient in Mills' view is that the elite is a self-conscious cohesive unit. This unity is based on three factors: psychological similarity, social interaction, and coinciding interests.

1. *Psychological similarity.* The institutional positions men and women occupy throughout their lifetimes determine the values they will hold. For example, career military men hold certain values by virtue of being socialized into the military subculture. The famous quote that "What's good for General Motors is good for the country" by Secretary of Defense (under President Eisenhower) Charles Wilson is also indicative of this probability. Thus, for Mills, the psychology of these leaders is largely shaped by the values they develop in their institutional roles. Additionally, the psychological similarity among the members of the elite is derived from their similar social origins and style of life.

2. *Social interaction.* Mills stated that the ruling elite are involved in a set of overlapping groups and intricately connected cliques.

> The people of the higher circles may also be conceived as members of a top social stratum, as a set of groups whose members know one another, see one another socially and at business, and so, in making decisions, take one another into account. The elite, according to this conception, feel themselves to be, and are felt by others to be, the inner circle of "the upper social classes." They form a more or less compact social and psychological entity; they have become self-conscious members of a social class. People are either accepted into this class or they are not, and there is a qualitative split, rather than merely a numerical scale, separating them from those who are not elite. They are more or less aware of themselves as a social class and they behave toward one another differently from the way they do toward members of other classes. They accept one another, understand one another, marry one another, tend to work and to think if not together at least alike.[18]

3. *Coinciding interests.* A third unifying condition hypothesized by Mills is the existence of similar interests among the elite. The interest of the elite

is, among other things, maintenance of the capitalist system with themselves at the top. Additionally, the government needs adequate defense systems, to which the military agree and which the corporations gladly sell for a profit. The huge corporations have large holdings in foreign countries. They therefore expect the government to make policy decisions that will be beneficial (profitable) for American interests. These similar interests result in a unity and a need for planning and coordination of their efforts. Since each sector affects the other, the persons at the top of each hierarchy must interact with leaders of the other sectors so that their actions will benefit all. Top decisions, Mills argued, thus become coordinated decisions.

Empirical Evidence for the Existence of a Military-industrial Power Elite. Mills postulated that there was an interlocking directorate uniting key persons in the business, military, and economic sectors. The relationships among the three are therefore:

There is much evidence supporting the linkages for each of the three relationships pictured above.

On the surface the federal government appears to have great power over business—through taxation, the power of the regulatory agencies (for example, Federal Trade Commission, Interstate Commerce Commission, and Securities and Exchange Commission), the power to determine interest rates and the flow of money, and so on. But who are the people who wield power in the executive branch of the government? The evidence is that they tend to be wealthy businesspeople.[19] The leaders either are rich or they are dependent upon contributions from the wealthy. The important appointees of the president (cabinet members, members of regulatory agencies, Supreme Court justices, ambassadors) most often are executives in the large corporations, corporation lawyers, or bankers. The implication is clear, if Mills was correct, that the linkage between the executive branch and business is very strong and that the leaders in both areas are alike in attitudes and actions because of similar interests.

The Defense Department is dependent upon Congress for money, including the appropriations for new programs. The Defense Department, according to the Constitution, must be headed by a civilian appointed by the president and approved by the Senate. The president is also Commander-in-Chief of the Armed Forces, and the final authority for important policy decisions.

The alliance between the government and the military is not a one-way relationship, however, since Congress and the executive department are influenced in many ways by the military. Frequently, they must rely upon the testimony of military experts, and the assessment of America's spy network determines to a significant degree what course of action the government will take. Furthermore, the Pentagon has thousands of public relations personnel around the world. One of their jobs is to convince the public and the government of the importance of its programs and of the need for new weaponry.

Government officials also receive great pressure from state and local governments to keep and/or to increase military expenditures in their local areas. In fiscal 1980, California had $13.9 billion in military contracts, followed by New York with $5.6 billion, Texas with $5.3 billion, Connecticut with $3.9 billion, Massachusetts with $3.7 billion, Virginia with $3.3 billion, and Missouri with $3.2 billion.[20] The military payrolls and other revenues generated locally by military expenditures affect all segments of local communities—businesspeople, teachers, homeowners, blue-collar workers, and professionals. Even universities benefit, some very substantially. In 1982, for example, the top seven university recipients of defense contracts were: Johns Hopkins with $235.5 million, M.I.T. with $216.6 million, Illinois Institute of Technology with $44.4 million, University of California with $35.3 million, Georgia Tech with $26.7 million, Stanford with $22.8 million, and the University of Texas with $15.7 million.[21] Because so many benefit from military spending one critic of the military-industrial complex, Senator William Proxmire from Wisconsin, has suggested that the system should rather be called the "military-industrial-bureaucratic-labor-intellectual-technical-academic complex."[22] Proxmire's label indicates the interconnectedness and extent of military dominance in American life.

But while all of these groups exert pressure on governmental officials to continue huge outlays for defense, the greatest coercion comes from business (hence, the term "military-industrial complex"). In many respects the military cannot be separated from business. The military needs weapons, ammunition, vehicles, clothing, and other materials. Industries gladly supply them for a profit.* The needs of both are apparently rarely satiated. The military continually seeks more sophisticated weaponry and delivery systems, while industry seeks more contracts and profits.

In the United States, the pressure applied to governmental decision makers by the military has reaped great monetary benefits for large military contractors. Business prospers handsomely because, as we have seen, all the risks of military contract business are underwritten by the taxpayers. Profits are higher than in the competitive consumer market. Because weapon systems rapidly become technologically obsolete, there is a constant demand for new generations of such systems, resulting in endless demand and profit. Finally, each new weapon system is more sophisticated than its predecessor, making weapons production profits escalate.[24]

It appears that fear of communism, need for an adequate defense, and pressures from the military, local government officials, businessmen, and corporations have helped to keep military budgets very high since World War II. This raises questions about what constitutes an adequate budget for

---

*In fiscal 1982 the seven largest defense contractors were: General Dynamics ($5.9 billion), McDonnell Douglas ($5.6 billion), United Technologies ($4.2 billion), General Electric ($3.7 billion), Lockheed ($3.5 billion), Boeing ($3.2 billion), and Hughes Aircraft ($3.1 billion).[23]

defense. The current Pentagon budget is bigger than those of the Soviet Union and China combined. Moreover, the American stockpile of weapons is capable of killing all of the earth's beings many times over.

But instead of reducing the budget or at least maintaining it at its present level, Congress increases the budget yearly. This growth is due in part to inflation and the costs of an all-volunteer army, but it also results from the Pentagon and its corporate friends seeking larger expenditures for more sophisticated weaponry and delivery systems. For example, the military budget following the U.S. withdrawal from Vietnam *increased*. When President Reagan was faced with the twin problems of rampant inflation and a severely unbalanced budget, his solution was to reduce the budget while *increasing* the military budget. Moreover, his commitment was to a tremendous increase in military spending—to spend $1 trillion from 1981 to 1985.[25] This program requires that government programs in other areas, most notably social programs for the disadvantaged, be curtailed severely.

The greatest impetus for huge outlays for defense comes from business. The military continually seeks more sophisticated weaponry and delivery systems, while industry seeks more contracts and profit. But why is industry so interested in obtaining governmental contracts? Kaufman has pointed out that producing goods for the military is more profitable, less competitive, and more susceptible to control through lobbying in Washington than commercial work.[26]

Kaufman stressed first that there is much less competition for defense contracts. The general rule for government procurement is that purchases shall be made through written competitive bids obtained by advertising for the items needed. In World War II this rule was suspended. After the war the rule was put back into force, but with seventeen exceptions. According to Kaufman, about 90 percent of the Pentagon's contracts are negotiated under these seventeen exceptions. The meaning is clear that in all but 10 percent of the cases, contracts are made on a basis other than competitive bids.

What does it take to get a contract, if it is not being the lowest bidder? The answer is not easy, for there are many possibilities, including superior design, more efficient programs, performance on schedule, and better quality control. Perhaps more important is convincing a few key men in the Pentagon. A good deal of time and money is spent in trying to influence these men. Not the least of these methods is the practice in industry of hiring former military officers. As Jack Anderson has put it:

> The giant contractors, such as Northrop Corporation and Rockwell International, court Pentagon officials assiduously. The way to many a defense contract has been greased by a mixture of booze, blondes and barbeques. The brass hats and the industrialists shoot together in duck blinds. They ski together on the Colorado slopes. They drink together and play poker together. And invariably, the tab is picked up by some smiling corporate executive. The relationship is so cozy that many Pentagon officials, upon retirement, go to work for the companies that had come to them for contracts. The last time we counted them, we found 715 former Pentagon bigwigs scattered over the pay-

rolls of the top defense contractors. It's a rare contractor that doesn't employ a few retired generals and admirals who are on a first-name basis with the Pentagon's big brass. Northrop Corporation, for example, has 64 ex-Pentagon officials on the payroll. This may help to explain how Northrop has managed to wangle a whopping $620.3 million in military contracts. Boeing Corporation, which is doing a $1.56 billion business with the Pentagon, has 48 former Pentagon bigwigs on the staff. And Rockwell International, with $732.3 million in defense contracts, has 36 ex-officials in key jobs.[27]

In addition to reduced competition, defense contractors receive other benefits from the government. The Pentagon generously provides capital (land, buildings, and equipment) to its contractors. Since 1976 all money spent to buy or lease plant and equipment has been charged to the government. Moreover, all development expenses are now paid for by the Pentagon. Congress may even "bail out" a contractor facing bankruptcy, but only, it would seem, if the corporation is very large and a prime supplier of defense material. The Lockheed Corporation in 1971, for example, received a government loan of $250 million. Moreover, if a defense contractor has been inefficient or careless in its cost estimates, resulting in cost overruns, the government may absorb some of the additional cost. This is done under a 1958 law authorizing modification of defense contracts whenever such action is necessary to "facilitate the national defense" in times of declared national emergency. Thus, when Lockheed had cost overruns of approximately $1.1 billion on its C-5A jet transport and other procurement disasters, the government ruled that Lockheed's liability would be for only $200 million.

The gist of these assertions is that there are tremendous profits to be made in defense contracting, and many, if not most, of the risks are borne by the government. The irony is that this is in opposition to the free-enterprise system. Apparently, American capitalism is, in fact, a form of corporate socialism where very large corporations receive government aid while smaller business ventures must operate on the principle of "survival of the fittest."

Much of Mills' argument seems to fit with the realities of American politics. Certainly the men at the top of the key sectors wield enormous power. The last several decades have seen shifts in this power with the decline of the role of Congress and the rise in military clout.

There are some elements in Mills' thesis, however, that are not consistent with the facts. First, Mills believed that the three subelites that comprise the power elite are more or less equal, with the corporate rich probably having the most power. The equality of these groups is not proved. Certainly, the military seems second-rate compared to the executive branch, Congress, and the large corporations. Military leaders are influential only in their advisory capacities and their ability to convince the executive branch and Congress. What looks like military power is often actually the power of the corporations and/or the executive branch carried out in military terms. In the view of many observers (especially Domhoff, as we will see in the next section), the business leaders comprise the real power elite. While this is debatable, the fact is that they far surpass the military in power, and since the executive branch is composed of ex-businesspeople, the logical conclusion is that business interests prevail in that sector as well.

Conflict occurs among the three sectors. There is often bitter disagreement between corporations and the government, between the military and the executive branch, and between the military and some elements in the business community. How is this conflict to be explained if, as Mills contended, the power elite is a group that acts in concert, with joint efforts planned and coordinated to accomplish the agreed-upon goals? There is a good deal of empirical evidence that the heads of the three major sectors do *not* comprise a group.

Mills relegates a number of powerful (or potentially powerful) forces to the middle ranges of power. What about the power of pressure groups that represent interests other than business or the military? Certainly organized labor, farmers, professional organizations such as the American Medical Association, and consumers exert power over particular issues. Sometimes business interests even lose. How is this to be explained?

Finally, is Congress only in the "middle level" of the power structure? In Mills' view, Congress is a rubber stamp for the interests of business, the executive branch, and the military. Congress is apparently not composed of "puppets" for these interests, although the laws most often seem to favor these interests. But Congress does have its mavericks, and some of these persons, by virtue of seniority, exert tremendous power (for either the blockage or passage of legislation). Should not the key congressional leaders be included in the power elite? The problem is that they often have interests that do not coincide with those of the presumed "elite."

Power Elite III: Domhoff's "Governing Class" Theory. While in the Mills view, power is concentrated in a relatively small, cohesive elite, G. William Domhoff's model of power is more broadly based in a "governing class."[28] Domhoff defined this "governing class" as the uppermost social group (approximately 0.5 percent of the population), which owns a disproportionate amount of the country's wealth and contributes a disproportionate number of its members to the controlling institutions and key decision-making groups of the country. This status group is composed mainly of rich businessmen and their families, many of whom are, according to Domhoff's convincing evidence, closely knit through stock ownership, trust funds, intermarriages, private schools, exclusive social clubs, exclusive summer resorts, and corporation boards (see Chapter 9).

The "governing class" in Domhoff's analysis controls the executive branch of the federal government, the major corporations, the mass media, foundations, universities, and the important councils for domestic and foreign affairs (for example, the Council on Foreign Relations, Committee for Economic Development, National Security Council, National Industrial Conference Board, the Twentieth Century Fund). (See Panel 17–2.) If they can control the executive branch, this governing class can probably also control the very important regulatory agencies, the federal judiciary, the military, the Central Intelligence Agency, and the Federal Bureau of Investigation.

Reagan's Ruling Class

Ronald Brownstein and Nina Easton have investigated the top 100 appointees of President Reagan to the executive branch. The following excerpts are from Ralph Nader's introduction to their work.

[Presidential] inaugurals always attract their share of the super-rich, coming to see and be seen. However, in [the case of President Reagan's inauguration] some came to stay. They were part of the new government whose leaders were invested by an electoral college landslide produced, in turn, by securing half of the half of the voters who bothered to come to the polls on November 4, 1980. This is, unabashedly, a government of the wealthy. Its top six members—President Reagan, Vice-President George Bush, Attorney General William French Smith, Secretary of Defense Caspar Weinberger, Secretary of State Alexander Haig, and Secretary of the Treasury Donald Regan are all multimillionaires. Mr. Regan, fresh from heading the world's largest brokerage company, Merrill Lynch, suggested in a *New York Times* interview that his material worth is $35 million. The Midas touch does not stop with these gentlemen. Over a fourth of the top one hundred Reagan Administration officials have net worths of seven figures, or more. In 1981, public financial reports indicated that Secretary of Commerce Malcolm Baldrige received income just that year between $1.5 and $2.5 million, on top of his government salary. Secretary of Transportation Drew Lewis received nearly one million dollars in the same period.

Ronald Reagan knew only a small fraction of the one hundred men and very few women whom he appointed to his government's top positions. But, his recruiters knew how to find his mirror images. Our studies and interviews of the officials in this book demonstrate a remarkable sameness among them—of attitudes, ideologies, and even styles of thinking and explaining. It was difficult to find a maverick, apart from a few to the extreme right of Mr. Regan.

The recruitment drive was directed by the "Kitchen Cabinet," a group of close-knit, wealthy friends of Mr. Reagan who groomed him for the California governorship and the Presidency. The hard core of this Kitchen Cabinet included Attorney General William French Smith, Justin W. Dart, industrialist and drug store chain mogul, Holmes P. Tuttle, a Los Angeles automobile dealer, William A. Wilson, a California rancher and real estate developer, Henry Salvatori, an oil producer, and Earle M. Jorgenson, president of a steel company. Joseph Coors of Coors Brewing Company and Walter H. Annenberg, publisher, were active in the post-election, pre-inaugural period. Meeting regularly in California and Washington as an executive advisory committee to recommend prospective nominees for high level appointments in the new Administration, the group left little to chance. As described by Henry Salvatori, three criteria guided their selection procedure: "One, was he a Reagan man? Two, a Republican? and three, a conservative?" Salvatori told the *National Journal* that the committee members agreed with one another 99 percent of the time on the final decisions, and Reagan accepted almost all their recommendations.

White House Chief of Staff James A. Baker III was engaging in understatement when he said: "Anytime the President's friends—members of the kitchen cabinet—want to see him we put them on the schedule."

(continued)

Reaganites lend their presence to gatherings of the Eagles, a rarified club established by the Republican National Committee (RNC). Membership is assured by a $10,000 contribution to RNC. An admiring President Reagan attended their annual dinner at the Washington Hilton Hotel on January 20, 1982. "This is a very impressive gathering," he said. "When I walked in I thought I was back in the studio on the set of 'High Society'." Donnie Radcliffe spotted a guest in flowing pink chiffon offering a discordant note: "Actually, I think this whole thing is rather ridiculous," she said. "I mean the country's in a recession and on the first anniversary we're all here throwing away thouands of dollars."

Corporate executives in the audience might have disagreed with this evaluation. Their thousands of dollars were an investment in Congress and the White House with a rate of return which, historically, has been well worth the effort. Politicians, indeed, have much to offer to these high bidders—shunting aside regulations, preserving subsidies and monopolistic licenses, going soft on corporate crime prosecutions, expanding profitable government contracts and

keeping other excluded American publics from challenging the consolidation of the corporate state.

The regime is foremost a homogenized government by elites. Even organized labor leaders are out; also gone are the minorities, the poor, the elderly, consumers and environmentalists. Their clientele agencies have either disappeared or become moribund. Most of the laws respecting their rights are, of course, still intact. But their interpretation, implementation and enforcement reflect heavily corporatist or elitist mentalities. Top officials, while they would not use such words, are quite forthright in expressing their meaning. Their logic runs this way. They truly believe that the rich are simply more talented and skilled people. If unleashed and assisted, corporations can bring economic progress. If the U.S. is equipped with more awesome weaponry, war can be deterred. Washington lawyer Fred Dutton's description of Attorney General William French Smith's view typifies this perspective: "Smith's philosophy is that a small central establishment of a few people who have proven successful should run the rest of our lives."

Source: Ralph Nader, "Introduction," Ronald Brownstein and Nina Easton, *Reagan's Ruling Class: Portraits of the President's Top One Hundred Officials* (New York: Pantheon, 1983), excerpts from pp. xv–xviii, xx. Copyright © 1982, 1983, by Ralph Nader. Reprinted by permission of Pantheon Books, a Division of Random House, Inc.

The "governing class" has greater influence (but not control) than any other group upon Congress and state and local governments. These parts of the formal power structure are not directly controlled by the "governing class" in Domhoff's analysis, but since he claims that such a class controls the executive and judicial branches, the Congress is effectively blocked by two of the three divisions of government. Thus, American foreign and domestic policies are initiated, planned, and carried out by members and organizations of a power elite that serves the interests of an upper class of rich businesspeople.[29] Decisions are made that are considered appropriate for the interests of the United States—a strong economy, an adequate defense, and social stability. While perhaps beneficial to all Americans, policies designed to accomplish these goals especially favor the rich. Consequently, American corporations overseas are protected, foreign trade agreements are made that benefit American corporations, and the tax structure benefits corporations or the very wealthy (by means of allowances for oil depletion, for capital gains and capital losses, for depreciation of equipment, and for other business expenses).

Domhoff has demonstrated in detail the manner in which the governing class interacts (which we have already examined in Chapter 9). Once he established the interlocking ties brought about by common interests and through interaction, he cited circumstances that show the impact of individuals and subgroups within the elite upon the decision-making structure of the United States. To mention a few:

□ Control of presidential nominations through the financing of political campaigns: The evidence is clear that unless candidates have large financial reserves or the backing of wealthy persons, they cannot hope to develop a national following or compete in party primaries.

□ Control of both major political parties: Even though the Democratic Party is usually considered the party of the common man, Domhoff shows that it, like the Republican Party, is controlled by aristocrats.[30]

□ Almost total staffing of important appointive governmental positions (cabinet members, members of regulatory agencies, judges, diplomats, and presidential advisors): These appointees are either members of the upper class or persons who have held positions in the major corporations, and are thereby persons who accord with the wishes of the upper class.

As a result of the circumstances above (and others), all the important foreign and domestic decisions are seen as made by the governing class. Domhoff's view of the power structure is reconstructed graphically in Figure 17–4.

In many ways, Domhoff's model of the American power structure was a refinement of the one posited earlier by Mills. Domhoff's assessment of the power structure was similar to Mills' in that they both: (1) view the power structure as a single pyramid; (2) see the corporate rich as the most powerful interest group; (3) relegate Congress to a relatively minor role and place the executive branch in an important role in the decision-making process; and (4) view the masses as being dominated by powerful forces rather than having much grass-roots power.

The major difference between the views of Mills and Domhoff is that Domhoff has asserted the complete ascendancy of the upper class to the apex of power. The executive branch is controlled by upper-class business-people, industrialists, and financiers rather than the two groups being more or less equal partners in the power elite, as Mills saw it. Moreover, the placement of the military in the pyramid of power is quite different. Mills

FIGURE 17–4   Domhoff's View of the Structure of Power

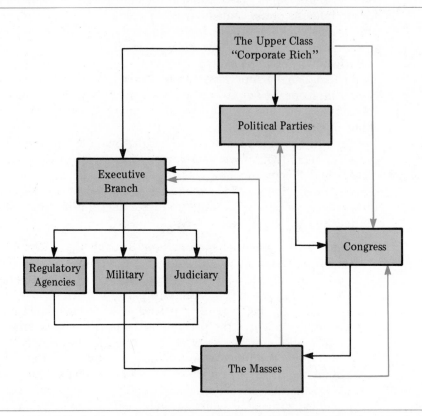

Legend: black line, control; color line, influence. This model is based on my interpretation of Domhoff and is therefore subject to minor errors in emphasis.

saw the military as part of the alliance of the "troika," while Domhoff saw the military as having much less power and being dominated by the corporate rich through the executive branch.

Domhoff's book is quite persuasive, but there are several criticisms that should be mentioned. First, much of Domhoff's proof is in the form of listing the upper-class pedigrees of presidential advisors, cabinet members, ambassadors, regulatory agency members, and so on. While persons in these positions are disproportionately from upper-class backgrounds (as evidenced by their attendance at prestige schools, their membership in exclusive social clubs, and their placement in the various social registries), we are given no proof that these persons actually promote the interests of the corporate rich. This is an assumption by Domhoff that appears reasonable, but it is an oversimplification. There is always the possibility of wealthy persons making decisions on bases other than economics, such as religious or moral altruism or civil rights or human rights. Thus, Domhoff's assumption is one of Marxian economic determinism, and as such is subject to the criticism of oversimplification of a complex process. While an economic motive of some kind may explain a great deal of social behavior, its operation with other prestige factors may be very complex, and it will not explain all of human behavior.

Although Domhoff has denied his belief in an upper-class conspiracy, his books strongly suggest that he does hold this view, at least implicitly. The upper class is shown to get its way either by force or fraud. His chapter on social legislation showed, for example, that workmen's compensation, social security, and collective bargaining were accomplished not by pressure from working people, but because the upper class felt it was in their long-range economic interest to pass such seemingly socialistic legislation. Domhoff, therefore, viewed the efforts of the upper class (assuming that they indeed form an elite) as only self-seeking, never altruistic. Moreover, the power of labor and other pressure groups in the forming of social legislation was virtually ignored.[31]

Power Elite IV: Parenti's "Bias of the System" Theory.[32]   Commonly we think of the machinery of government as a beneficial force promoting the common good. While the government can be organized for the benefit of the majority, it is never neutral.[33] The state regulates; it stifles opposition; it makes and enforces the law; it funnels information; it makes war on "enemies" (foreign and domestic); and its policies determine how resources are apportioned. And in all of these areas, the government is generally biased toward policies that benefit the wealthy, especially the business community.

Power in America is concentrated among those who control the government and the largest corporations.[34] This assertion is based on the assumption that power is not an attribute of individuals but rather of social organizations.[35] The elite in American society is composed of those persons who occupy the power roles in society. The great political decisions are made by the president, the president's advisors, cabinet members, the members of regulatory agencies, the Federal Reserve Board, key members of Congress, and the Supreme Court. The individuals in these government command posts have the authority to make war, raise or lower interest rates, levy taxes, dam rivers, and institute or withhold national health insurance.

Once economic activity was the result of many decisions made by individual entrepreneurs and the heads of small businesses. Now a handful of companies have virtual control over the market place. The decisions by the boards of directors and the management personnel of these huge corporations determine employment and production, consumption patterns, wages and prices, the extent of foreign trade, the rate at which natural resources are depleted, and the like.

The few thousand persons who comprise this power elite tend to come from backgrounds of privilege and wealth. It would be a mistake, however, to equate personal wealth with power. Great power is only manifested through decision making in the very large corporations or in government.

We have seen that this elite exercises great power. Decisions are made by the powerful and these decisions tend to benefit the wealthy disproportionately. But the power elite is not organized and conspiratorial.

The interests of the powerful (and the wealthy) are served, nevertheless, because of the way society is organized. This bias occurs in three ways— by their influence over elected and appointed governmental officials at all levels; through systemic imperatives; and through the ideological control of the masses.

As we saw in an earlier section, the wealthy are able to receive favorable treatment by actually occupying positions of power or by having direct influence over those who do. The laws, court decisions, and administrative decisions tend to give the advantage.

More subtly, the power elite can get its way without actually being mobilized at all. The choices of decision makers are often limited by various **systemic imperatives.** Whoever is in power is constrained in their decision making by tradition and by economic imperatives. There are pressures on the government to do certain things and not to do others. Inevitably, this bias favors the status quo, allowing those with power to continue. For example, no change is always easier than change. The current political and economic systems have worked and generally are not subject to question, let alone change. In this way the laws, customs, and institutions of society resist change. Thus the propertied and the wealthy benefit while the propertyless and the poor continue to be disadvantaged.

In addition to the inertia of institutions, there are other systemic imperatives that benefit the power elite and the wealthy. One such imperative is for the government to strive to provide an adequate defense against our enemies, which stifles any external threat to the status quo. Moreover, this means that Congress, the president, and the masses tend to support large appropriations for defense, which provides extraordinary profit to many corporations. In addition, the government will protect our multinational companies in their overseas operations, which, of course, promotes a healthy and profitable business climate for them. Domestically, government policy is also shaped by the systemic imperative for stability. The government promotes domestic tranquility by squelching dissidence.

Power is the ability to get what one wants from someone else. This can be achieved by force or by getting that someone to think and believe in accordance with your interests. "The ability to control the definition of interests is the ability to define the agenda of issues, a capacity tantamount to winning battles without having to fight them."[36] This is accomplished by the schools, churches, and families in society. The schools, for instance, consciously teach youth that capitalism is the only correct economic system. This is indoctrination with conservative values that achieves a consensus among the citizenry concerning the status quo. In other words, the people tend to accept the system, even though it may work against their interests (false consciousness). Through the very powerful socialization process each of us comes to accept the system, obey the law, favor military solutions, and accept the present arrangements in society because they seem the only options that make sense. Thus, there is a general consensus on what is right—and wrong. In sum, the dominance of the wealthy is legitimized. "The interests of an economically dominant class never stand naked. They are enshrouded in the flag, fortified by the law, protected by the police, nurtured by the media, taught by the schools, and blessed by the church."[37]

Finally, the belief in democracy works to the advantage of the power elite, as Parenti has noted in the following passage:

> As now constituted, elections serve as a great asset in consolidating the existing social order by propagating the appearances of popular rule. History demonstrates that the people might be moved to overthrow a tyrant who shows himself provocatively indifferent to their woes, but they are far less inclined to make war upon a state, even one dominated by the propertied class, if it preserves what Madison called "the spirit and form of popular government." Elections legitimate the rule of the propertied class by investing it with the moral authority of popular consent. By the magic of the ballot, class dominance becomes "democratic" governance. According to the classical theory of democracy, the purpose of suffrage is to make the rulers more responsive to the will of the people. But history suggests the contrary: more often the effect and even the intent of suffrage has been to make the enfranchised group more responsive to the rulers, or at least committed to the ongoing system of rule. In the classical theory, the vote is an exercise of sovereign power, a popular command over the rulers, but it might just as easily be thought of as an act of support extended by the electorate to those above them. Hence, an election is more a *surrender* than an *assertion* of popular power, a gathering up of empowering responses by the elites who have the resources for such periodic harvestings, an institutionalized mechanism providing for the regulated flow of power from the many to the few in order to legitimate the rule of the few in the name of the many.[38]

THE CONSEQUENCES OF THE NATIONAL POWER STRUCTURE

The way power is concentrated in American society raises the question—who benefits? At times most everyone does, but for the most part, the decisions made tend to benefit the wealthy. Whenever the interests of the wealthy clash with those of other groups or even the majority, the interests of the wealthy are served. As examples, examine carefully how the president and Congress deal with the problems of energy shortages, inflation, or deflation. Who is asked to make the sacrifices? Where is the budget cut—are expenditures for the military reduced or are funds for food stamps slashed? When the Congress considers tax reform, after the roar of rhetoric recedes, which groups benefit by the new legislation or by the laws that are left alone? When a corporation is found guilty of fraud, violation of antitrust laws, bribery, or whatever, what are the penalties? How do they compare with the penalties for crimes committed by poor individuals such as "welfare chiselers," and thieves? When there is an oil spill or other ecological disaster caused by huge enterprise, what are the penalties? Who pays for the cleanup and the restoration of nature? The answers to these questions are obvious—the wealthy benefit at the expense of the less well-to-do. In short, the government is an institution made up of people—the rich and powerful or their agents—who seek to maintain their advantageous positions in society.

Before we examine the bias of the system in the contemporary scene, let's briefly describe its continuation throughout American history.[39] The government's policy has primarily, although not exclusively, favored the needs of the corporate system.

PANEL 17-3

The Framers of the Constitution: Plotters or Patriots?

The question of whether the framers of the Constitution were motivated by financial or national interest has been debated ever since Charles Beard published *An Economic Interpretation of the Constitution* in 1913. Beard believed that the "founding fathers" were guided by their class interests. Arguing against Beard are those who say that the framers were concerned with higher things than just lining their purses. True, they were moneyed men who profited directly from policies initiated under the new Constitution, but they were motivated by a concern for nation building that went beyond their particular class interests, the argument goes. To paraphrase Justice Holmes, these men invested their belief to make a nation; they did not make a nation because they had invested. "High-mindedness is not impossible to man," Holmes reminds us.

That is exactly the point: high-mindedness is a common attribute among people even when, or especially when, they are pursuing their personal and class interests. The fallacy is to presume that there is a dichotomy between the desire to build a strong nation and the desire to protect wealth and that the framers could not have been motivated by both. In fact, like most other people, they believed that what was good for themselves was ultimately good for the entire society. Their universal values and their class interests went hand in hand, and to discover the existence of the "higher" sentiment does not eliminate the self-interested one.

Most persons believe in their own virtue. The founders never doubted the nobility of their effort and its importance for the generations to come. Just as many of them could feel dedicated to the principle of "liberty for all" and at the same time own slaves, so could they serve both their nation and their estates. The point is not that they were devoid of the grander sentiments of nation building but that *there was nothing in their concept of nation that worked against their class interest and a great deal that worked for it.*

People tend to perceive issues in accordance with the position they occupy in the social structure; that position is largely—although not exclusively—determined by their class status. Even if we deny that the framers were motivated by the desire for personal gain that moves others, we cannot dismiss the existence of their class interest. They may not have been solely concerned with getting their own hands in the till, although enough of them did, but they were admittedly preoccupied with defending the wealthy few from the laboring many—for the ultimate benefit of all, as they understood it. "The Constitution," as Staughton Lynd noted, "was the settlement of a revolution. What was at stake for Hamilton, Livingston, and their opponents, was more than speculative windfalls in securities; it was the question, what kind of society would emerge from the revolution when the dust had settled, and on which class the political center of gravity would come to rest."

The small farmers and debtors who opposed a central government have been described as motivated by self-serving, parochial interests—unlike the supposedly higher-minded statesmen who journeyed to Philadelphia and others of their class who supported ratification. How or why the wealthy became visionary nation builders is never explained. In truth, it was not their minds that were so much broader but their economic interests. Their motives were neither higher nor lower than those of any other social group struggling for place and power in the United States of 1787. They pursued their material interests as single-mindedly as any small freeholder—if not more so. Possessing more time, money, information, and organization, they enjoyed superior results. How could they have acted otherwise? For them to have ignored the conditions of governance necessary for the maintenance of their enterprises would have amounted to committing class suicide— and they were not about to do that. They were a rising bourgeoisie rallying around a central power in order to protect their class interests. Some of us are quite willing to accept the existence of such a material-based nationalism in the history of other countries, but not in our own.

Finally, those who argue that the founders were motivated primarily by high-minded objectives consistently overlook the fact that the delegates repeatedly stated their intention to erect a government strong enough to protect the haves from the have-nots. They gave voice to the crassest class prejudices and never found it necessary to disguise the fact—as have latter-day apologists—that their uppermost concern was to diminish popular control and resist all tendencies toward class equalization (or "leveling," as it was called). Their opposition to democracy and their dedication to moneyed interests were unabashedly and openly avowed. Their preoccupation with their class interests was so pronounced that one delegate, James Wilson of Pennsylvania, did finally complain of hearing too much about how the sole or primary object of government was property. The cultivation and improvement of the human mind, he maintained, was the most noble object—a fine sentiment that evoked no opposition from his colleagues as they continued about their business.

If the founders sought to "check power with power," they seemed chiefly concerned with restraining mass power, while assuring the perpetuation of their own class power. They supposedly had a "realistic" opinion of the rapacious nature of human beings— readily evidenced when they talked about the common people—yet they held a remarkably sanguine view of the self-interested impulses of their own class, which they saw as inhabited largely by virtuous men of "principle and property." According to Madison, wealthy men (the "minority faction") would be unable to sacrifice "the rights of other citizens" or mask their "violence under the forms of the Constitution." They would never jeopardize the institution of property and wealth and the untrammeled uses thereof, which in the eyes of the framers constituted the essence of "liberty." Recall Hamilton's facile reassurance that the rich will "check the unsteadiness" of the poor and will themselves "ever maintain good government" by being given a "distinct permanent share" in it. Power corrupts others but somehow has the opposite effect on the rich and the well-born—so believed many of the rich and wellborn.

Source: Michael Parenti, *Democracy for the Few*, 4th ed. (New York: St. Martin's Press, 1983), pp. 69–72.

The Founding Fathers were wealthy members of the upper class. The Constitution they wrote gave the power to people like themselves—property owners. (See Panel 17–3.) This bias continued throughout the nineteenth century as bankers, railroad entrepreneurs, and manufacturers joined the landed gentry to make the power elite. The shift from local business to large-scale manufacturing during the last half of the nineteenth century saw a concomitant increase in governmental activity in the economy. Business was protected from competition by protective tariffs, public subsidies, price regulation, patents, and trademarks. Throughout that century when there was unrest by troubled miners, farmers, and laborers, the government inevitably took the side of the strong against the weak. The militia and federal troops were used to crush the railroad strikes. Antitrust laws, which were not used to stop the monopolistic practices of business, were invoked against labor unions. President Cleveland's Attorney General, Richard Olney, a millionaire owner of railroad stocks,

> used antitrust laws, court injunctions, mass arrests, labor spies, deputy marshals and federal troops against workers and their unions. From the local sheriff and magistrate to the President and the Supreme Court, the forces of "law and order" were utilized to suppress the "conspiracy" of labor unions and serve "the defensive needs of large capitalist enterprises."[40]

During this time approximately 1 billion acres of land in the public domain (almost one-half the present size of the United States) were given to private individuals and corporations. The railroads in particular were given huge tracts of land as a subsidy. These lands were and continue to be very rich in timber and natural resources.

This active intervention of the government in the nation's economy during the nineteenth century was almost solely on the behalf of business. "The federal government did exercise a kind of laissez-faire in certain other areas: little attention was given to unemployment, work conditions, the spoliation of natural resources, and the living conditions of millions of destitute Americans."[41]

The early 20th century was a time of great governmental activity in the economy, which gave the appearance of restraining big business. However, the actual result of federal regulation of business was to increase the power of the largest corporations. The Interstate Commerce Commission, for instance, helped the railroads by establishing common rates to replace ruinous competition.[42] The federal regulations in meat packing, drugs, banking, and mining weeded out the weaker cost-cutting competitors, leaving a few to control the markets at higher prices and higher profits.[43] Even the actions of that great "trust-buster," Teddy Roosevelt, were largely ceremonial.[44]

World War I intensified the governmental bias toward business. Industry was converted to war production. Corporate interests became more actively involved in the councils of government. Governmental actions clearly favored business in labor disputes. The police and military were used against rebellious workers because strikes were treated as efforts to weaken the war effort and therefore treasonous.

The New Deal is typically assumed to be a time when the needs of those impoverished by the Great Depression were paramount in government policies. But the central dedication of the Franklin Roosevelt administration was to *business recovery* rather than *social reform*.[45] Business was subsidized by credits, price supports, bank guarantees, stimulation of the housing industry,

and the like. Welfare programs were instituted to prevent widespread star-
vation, but even these humanitarian programs also worked to the benefit
of the big business community. The government provided jobs, minimum
wages, unemployment compensation, and retirement benefits, which obviously aided those in dire economic straits. But these programs were actually
promoted by the business community because of benefits to them. The
government and business favored social programs at this time not because
millions were in misery but because of the threat of violent political and
social unrest. Two social scientists, Piven and Cloward, after an historical
assessment of government welfare programs, have determined that the government institutes massive aid to the poor *only* when the poor constitute
a threat.[46] When large numbers of people are suddenly barred from their
traditional occupations, the legitimacy of the system itself may be questioned.
Crime, riots, looting, and social movements bent on changing the existing
social, political, and economic arrangements become more widespread. Under
this threat, relief programs are initiated or expanded by the government to
diffuse the social unrest. During the Great Depression, Piven and Cloward
contend, the government remained aloof from the needs of the unemployed
until there was a surge of political disorder. Added proof for Piven and
Cloward's thesis is the contraction or even abolishment of public assistance
programs when stability is restored.

The historical trend for government to favor business over less powerful
interests continues in current public policy. Let's look at some examples.

Subsidies
to Big
Business

There is a general principle that applies to the government's relationship
to big business—business can conduct its affairs either undisturbed by or
encouraged by government, whichever is of greater benefit to the business
community. The following are some illustrative cases in which governmental
decisions benefitted business:

□ *Item:* In 1979 the Chrysler Corporation, after sustaining losses of $207
million in the previous year, appealed to the government and received
$1.5 billion in loan guarantees.[47] The government's aid to Chrysler is
typical—if the company is big enough. Earlier in the 1970s Penn Central
received $125 million when it faced bankruptcy, and the government
guaranteed Lockheed $250 million in new bank loans. Thus, the big
companies receive emergency help while the government does very little
to aid the approximately 25,000 small businesses and 300,000 individuals
going bankrupt annually (1982 rate).
□ *Item:* Quotas are placed on imports of beef, wheat, oil, and other products
to protect the profits of American industry.
□ *Item:* Although the House voted 293 to 94 in 1974 to create a federal
consumer protection agency, the bill was defeated in the Senate by a
filibuster. The legislation was opposed by the National Association of
Manufacturers, the National Association of Food Chains, and some 300
other companies and trade associations.[48]

□ *Item:* The automobile industry got the Justice Department to sign a consent decree that blocked any attempt by public or private means to sue it for damages occurring from air pollution.

□ *Item:* A number of major U.S. corporations such as DuPont, General Motors, Ford, Exxon, and ITT owned factories in enemy countries during World War II. These factories produced products for the Axis war effort. "After the war, rather than being prosecuted for trading with the enemy, ITT collected $27 million from the U.S. government for war damages inflicted on its German plants by Allied bombings. GM and Ford subsidiaries built the bulk of Nazi Germany's heavy trucks which served as 'the backbone of the German Army transportation system.' GM collected more than $33 million in compensation for damages to its war plants in enemy territories. Ford and other multinational corporations collected lesser sums."[49]

□ *Item:* The federal government directly subsidizes the shipping industry, railroads, airlines, and exporters of iron, steel, textiles, paper, and other products.

□ *Item:* Government-regulated industries such as trucking and railroads result in excess prices and profits. The federal government maintains "prices at noncompetitive, monopolistic levels in 'regulated' areas of the economy at an estimated annual cost of $80 billion to American consumers."[50]

□ *Item:* From 1965 to 1967 several major petroleum companies leased acreage in Alaska for oil exploration, paying $12 million for leases worth at least $2 billion. In another oil lease auction, the companies paid the government $900 million for lands that are expected to be worth some $50 billion within a decade.[51] In 1979 during the midst of an oil shortage crisis, the government leased 33,749 acres of land surrounding an area of active wells *without competitive bids* for $1 dollar per acre. The value of the leases has been estimated at $10 million.[52]

□ *Item:* The government develops new technologies at public expense and then turns them over to private corporations for their profit. Using the case of nuclear energy, Ralph Nader has said: "Nuclear power would never have existed if it weren't for the government. The government funded the basic research, funded the technology, gave the designs to the utilities gratis, enriched the uranium, protected the utilities from liability under the Price-Anderson Act, and has now decided to pay the costs for nuclear wastes. From start to finish, it's a classic case of an industry that has been sponsored, shielded, and protected by the government."[53]

Perhaps the best illustration of how business benefits under current governmental policies is the system of legal loopholes allowed on federal income taxes. Although the maximum statutory tax rate on corporate profits is 46 percent, corporations (including the most profitable) can usually escape with a very much lower rate. Some corporations may even escape federal income taxes altogether. In 1980, for example, although Chase Manhattan Bank had domestic profits of $200 million it did not pay any federal taxes *and received a refund of $46 million.* American Telephone and Telegraph had profits of $8 billion in that year, yet paid a federal tax of 8 percent (by paying 8 percent instead of the 46 percent legal maximum rate, AT&T received tax welfare of nearly $3 billion).[54] These tax subsidies are legal tax handouts recovered through such loopholes as accelerated depreciation of plants and equipment, sales of leases, and energy depletion allowances. The estimated total tax loss to the government for fiscal 1984 (from tax breaks to all U.S. corporations) was estimated to be $67.9 billion.[55]

Foreign Policy for Corporate Benefit

The operant principle here is that "foreign policy seems to be carried on in the light of the needs of the munitions makers, the Pentagon, the CIA, and the multinational corporations."[56] Several examples make this point. First, military goods are sold overseas for the profit of the arms merchants. Sometimes arms are sold to both sides in a potential conflict, the argument being that if we did not sell them the arms, then the Russians would, so we might as well make the profits.[57]

The government has supported foreign governments that are supportive of American multinational companies regardless of how tyrannical these governments might be. The Reza Shah's government in Iran, Chiang's regime in China, Chung Hee Park's dictatorship in South Korea, and Ferdinand Marcos' rule in the Philippines are four examples of this tendency.

Our government has directly intervened in the domestic affairs of foreign governments to protect American corporate interests. The most blatant example occurred when ITT encouraged the government (through the CIA) in 1970 to depose the Allende government in Chile because Allende favored policies that threatened ITT's presence in Chile.[58]

The Powerless Pay the Burden

Robert Hutchens, in his critique of American governmental policy, characterized the basic principle guiding internal affairs as: "Domestic policy is conducted according to one infallible rule: the costs and burdens of whatever is done must be borne by those least able to bear them."[59] Let's review several examples of this.

When threatened by war the government institutes a military draft. A careful analysis of the draft reveals that it is really a "tax on the poor."[60] During the height of the Vietnam War, for instance, only 10 percent of men in college were drafted, although 40 percent of draft-age men were in college. Even for those educated young men who ended up in the armed services, there was a greater likelihood of their serving in noncombat jobs than for the non-college-educated. Thus, the chances for getting killed while in the service were about three times greater for the less educated than for the college educated.[61] Even more blatant was the practice that occurred legally during the Civil War. The law at that time allowed the affluent who were drafted to hire someone to take their place in the service.

The poor, being powerless, can be made to absorb the costs of societal changes. In the nineteenth century the poor did the back-breaking work that built the railroads and the cities. Today they are the ones pushed out of their homes by urban renewal, the building of expressways, parks, and stadia.[62]

The government's attempts to solve economic problems generally obey the principle that the poor must bear the burden. A common "solution" for runaway inflation, for example, is to increase the amount of unemployment. Of course the poor, especially minorities (whose rate of unemployment is consistently twice the rate for whites), are the ones who make the sacrifice for the economy. This "solution," aside from being socially cruel, is economically ineffective because it ignores the real sources of inflation—excessive military spending, excessive profits by energy companies (foreign and domestic), and administered prices set by shared monopolies, which, contrary to classical economic theory, do not decline during economic downturns.[63]

More fundamentally a certain level of unemployment is maintained continuously, not just during economic downturns. Genuine full employment for all job seekers is a myth. But why, since all political candidates extol the work ethic and it is declared national policy to have full employment? Economist Robert Lekachman has argued that it is no accident that we tolerate millions of unemployed persons. The reason is that a "moderate" unemployment rate is beneficial to the affluent. Among these benefits are:[64] (1) people are willing to work at humble tasks for low wages; (2) the children of the middle and upper classes avoid the draft as the unemployed join the volunteer army; (3) the unions are less demanding; (4) workers are less likely to demand costly safety equipment; (5) corporations do not have to pay their share of taxes because local and state governments give them concessions to lure them to their area; and (6) the existing wide differentials between white males and the various powerless categories such as females, teenagers, Hispanics, and blacks are retained.

"Trickle Down" Solutions

Periodically the government is faced with the problem of finding a way to stimulate the economy during an economic downturn. One way to accomplish this goal is to spend federal monies through unemployment insurance, government jobs, and housing subsidies. In this way the funds go directly to those most hurt by shortages, unemployment, inadequate housing, and the like. Opponents of such plans advocate that the subsidies should go directly to business, which would help the economy by encouraging companies to hire more workers, add to their inventories, and build new plants. Thus, by subsidizing business in this way, the advocates argue, everyone benefits. To provide subsidies to businesses rather than directly to needy individuals is based on the assumption that private profit maximizes the public good.

There are two possible reasons why government officials tend to opt for these "trickle down" solutions. First, because they tend to come from the business class, government officials believe in the conservative ideology that says what is good for business is good for America. The second reason for the pro-business choice is that government officials are more likely to hear arguments from the powerful. Since the weak, by definition, are not organized, their voice is not heard or, if heard, not taken seriously in decision-making circles.

Although the government most often opts for "trickle down" solutions, such plans are not very effective in fulfilling the promise that benefits will trickle down to the poor. The higher corporate profits generated by tax credits and other tax incentives do not necessarily mean that companies will increase wages or hire more workers. What is more likely is that corporations will increase dividends to the stockholders, which further exacerbates the existing problem of the maldistribution of resources. Job creation is also not guaranteed because companies may use their newly acquired wealth to purchase labor-saving devices. If so, then the government programs will actually have widened the gulf between the "haves" and the "have-nots."

In summary, this view of power argues that the power of wealthy individuals and the largest corporations is translated into public policy that disproportionately benefits the power elite. Throughout American history there has been a bias that pervades government and its policies. This bias is perhaps best seen in the aphorism once enunciated by President Calvin Coolidge and repeated in 1981 by President Reagan: "The business of America is business."

CONCLUSION

Power is unequally distributed in all social organizations. In our examination of the structure of power at the societal level, two basic views were presented—the pluralist and the elitist. The former is consistent with the world view of order theorists, while the latter is congruent with the way conflict theorists perceive reality (see Table 17–1).

One glaring weakness of many pluralists and elitists is that they are not objective. Their writings tend often to be polemics because so much effort is spent attempting to prove what they believe is the nature of the power structure. The evidence is presented so as to ensure the absolute negation of the opposite stance. This points to a fundamental research problem. Are the data reliable? Are our observations distorted by bias? Sociologists or political scientists are forced in the study of power to rely on either the perceptions of others (who are presumed to be knowledgeable) or their own observations, which are distorted by not being present during all aspects of the decision-making process. Unfortunately, one's perceptions are also affected by one's model (conflict or order; Marxian or democratic). Ideological concerns often cause either faulty perceptions or a rigidity of thought that automatically rejects conflicting evidence.

The task for sociologists is to determine the real distribution of power without ideological distortion. Given these problems with objectivity, we must ask ourselves: (1) What is the power structure really like? (2) What

TABLE 17–1   Assumptions of the Order and Conflict Models about Politics

Order Model	Conflict Model
1. People in positions of power occupy bureaucratic roles necessary for the rational accomplishment of society's objectives.	1. People in positions of power are motivated largely by their own selfish interests.
2. The state works for the benefit of all. Laws reflect the customs of society and ensure order, stability, and justice—in short, the common good.	2. The state exists for the benefit of the ruling class (law, police, and courts protect the interests of the wealthy).
3. Pluralism: (1) competing interest groups; (2) majority rule; (3) power is diffused.	3. Power is concentrated (power elite).

facts are consonant with the pluralist model and what facts fit the elitist model? With these questions in mind, let us enumerate some conditions of societies that affect the distribution of power.

All societies are composed of different segments. The bases for segmentation may be sex, age, race, religion, physical prowess, social class, occupational specialty, or special interest. The extent of segmentation and the degree of competition among such groups are variables. It is safe to assume that most segmented parts of a society would hope for and work toward greater power (and therefore advantage) in that society (although some may not if they have been socialized to accept their role and to accept that attempts to change it would bring serious religious or other sanctions).

The second basic condition of societies is that they all require some coordination among the various segments. The more complex the society, the greater the problem of coordination. Complex societies also require rapid decision making. Both of these requirements—rapid decision making and coordination—mean that decision making *must* be concentrated in a few persons. It is an empirical question as to whether power is concentrated in one or several elites or whether the "people" retain power while not actually making most decisions.

Finally, the degree of power centralization is a variable. The logical range is from absolute equality of all individuals and groups on the one hand to total power in one person or group on the other. All societies are found somewhere between these two extremes. Various factors affect change in the degree of power centralization. As Mills noted, World War II and the Cold War were important factors giving increased power to the executive branch and the military sector of American society. Force and fraud may also be used by certain individuals and groups to increase their power.

These conditions are accepted by elitists and pluralists. Where both of these theorists go wrong is in their distorted interpretations of the real world. Let us examine the *real* situation which, hopefully, will aid in the formulation of a more realistic view of the power structure. First, what is there about the elitist position that fits reality?

- A contemporary trend has been for federal government to assume more and more power, thereby lessening the power of the state and local governments.
- The executive branch has a tremendous amount of power, particularly in foreign affairs. Congress has tried to reassert its historic role, but the executive branch continues to have great power in this area. Some examples are: sending the military forces to various places, fighting undeclared wars, diplomatic decisions, and CIA activities.
- There is no question but that the wealthy in America have great influence in Congress and in the executive branch. This influence is accomplished through campaign contributions, control of the political parties, occasional bribes, and through being either elected or appointed to high offices. It is also fair to say that American foreign and domestic policy is, for the most part, based on the assumption that if business interests benefit, all Americans benefit.
- Even if there are a number of different sectors of power present (the pluralist position), the leaders of each are almost universally wealthy, members of the establishment who more or less favor the status quo. This is true, for example, in industry, in banking, for labor, and for the farm bloc. Because of great wealth they probably have some interests in common (the economic status quo, an adequate defense system, protecting American interests abroad, and an expanding economy).

What is there about the pluralist position that fits reality?

- There are many separate power structures. Each operates generally within its own sphere of influence—the AFL-CIO in labor, the AMA in medicine, the NEA in public education, the NAM for large business concerns, and so forth. Each tries to influence Congress and the executive branch on issues affecting it. Within each of these domains there is a hierarchy of power. A powerful elite then makes decisions and in other ways influences its public (and this influence is often reciprocal).
- The various power structures are unequal in power. The economic elite is the most powerful. But there are shifting coalitions that may at times effectively counterbalance the unequal power of the corporate rich. Or one group may band with the corporate rich against some other coalition.
- Pressure groups exert a tremendous influence on decision making. They may be organized or diffuse, but they can and do bring change. Blacks, migrant workers, young people, the aged, consumers, have by individual and collective efforts caused a shift in policy on occasion.

A realistic view of the power structure must incorporate the valid points mentioned above from both pluralistic and elitist views. The resulting model of power hinges on the empirical answer to the basic question: how democratic is the political process in American society?

CHAPTER REVIEW

1. In answering the question: Who are the real power wielders in American society? there are two contrasting answers from pluralists and elitists.

2. The "representative democracy" version of pluralism emphasizes that the people have the ultimate power. The people elect representatives who are responsive to the people's wishes. This version ignores the many instances in which the people have been deliberately misled by their leaders, secrecy, and the undemocratic manner in which election campaigns are funded.

3. The "veto groups" version of pluralism recognizes the existence of a number of organizations and special interest groups that vie for power. There is a balance of power, however, with no one sector getting its way. The groups tend to neutralize each other resulting in compromise. Critics of this view of power argue that it is an idealized version that ignores reality. The interest groups are not equal in power. Power does not shift from issue to issue. Also, at the apex of each of the competing groups are members of the upper class, suggesting the possibility of a power elite.

4. One version of the elitist view of power is the belief in a communist conspiracy. This view holds that the power structure in the United States is led by a conspiratorial elite that share an anti-capitalist and internationalist ideology. The placement of members of the Trilateral Commission in high government places regardless of whether there is a Democrat or Republican president is evidence of such a conspiracy. This view of power is not taken seriously by social scientists but it is held by millions of Americans.

5. C. Wright Mills' view of power is that there is a power elite composed of the top people in the executive branch of the federal government, the military, and the corporate sector. Although these persons represent different interests they tend to perceive the world alike because of their similar social class backgrounds and similar role expectations; because they interact socially; because their children go to the same schools and intermarry; and because they share similar interests. There is considerable evidence for the linkages among these three sectors. There are some problems with this view, however. The equality of these three groups is not a fact. There is conflict among the three sectors. There are other sectors of power that are ignored.

6. G. William Domhoff's view of power is that there is a governing class—the uppermost social class. The very rich control the nation's assets, control the corporations, are overrepresented in the key decision-making groups in society, and through contributions and activities they control both major political parties. The major criticism of this view is that while the people in key positions tend to have upper-class pedigrees, there is no evidence that these people actually promote the interests of the corporate rich.

7. Michael Parenti's "bias of the system" view is another elitist theory. The powerful in society (those who control the government and the largest corporations) tend to come from backgrounds of privilege and wealth. Their decisions tend to benefit the wealthy disproportionately, but the power elite is not organized and conspiratorial. The interests of the wealthy are served, nevertheless, by the way society is organized. This bias occurs by their influence over elected and appointed officials, systemic imperatives, and through the ideological control of the masses.

FOR FURTHER STUDY

Paul A. Baran and Paul M. Sweezy, *Monopoly Capital* (New York: Monthly Review Press, 1968).

Ronald Brownstein and Nina Easton, *Reagan's Ruling Class* (New York: Pantheon, 1983).

G. William Domhoff, *The Powers That Be: Processes of Ruling Class Domination in America* (New York: Random House (Vintage Books), 1979).

Thomas R. Dye, *Who's Running America*, 2nd ed. (Englewood Cliffs, N.J.: Prentice-Hall, 1979).

Martin N. Marger, *Elites and Masses: An Introduction to Political Sociology* (New York: Van Nostrand, 1981).

C. Wright Mills, *The Power Elite* (New York: Oxford University Press, 1956).

Marvin E. Olsen, ed., *Power in Societies* (New York: Macmillan, 1970).

Michael Parenti, *Power and the Powerless* (New York: St. Martin's, 1978).

David Reisman, *The Lonely Crowd* (New Haven, Conn.: Yale University Press, 1951).

Leonard Silk and Mark Silk, *The American Establishment* (New York: Basic Books, 1980).

NOTES AND REFERENCES

1. The following examples are summarized from David Wise, *The Politics of Lying: Government Deception, Secrecy, and Power* (New York: Random House (Vintage Books), 1973).

2. See Warren Weaver, Jr., "What Is a Campaign Contributor Buying?," *The New York Times* (March 13, 1977), p. E2.

3. Barbara Haddad Ryan, "Common Cause: Special Interests Won on Nov. 4," *Rocky Mountain News* (November 16, 1980), p. 4. See also, Jack Bass, "For Regulating Corporate Political Action Committees," *The New York Times* (May 30, 1979), p. A23.

4. Marvin Stone, "Political Spending: Running Wild," *U.S. News & World Report* (October 23, 1978), p. 112; and Walter Isaacson, "Running with the PACs," *Time* (October 25, 1982), pp. 20–26.

5. "The Death Lobby," *The Nation* (September 11, 1982), pp. 196–197.

6. Cited in Otis Pike, "The Cancer of Congressmen and Campaign Funds," *Denver Post* (August 31, 1982), p. 2B.

7. See Marlys Harris, "The Candidates' Family Finances," *Money* 9 (March 1980), pp. 82–90.

8. John Walton, "Economic Order," *Society Today Resource Letters* (Del Mar, Calif.: CRM Books, 1971), p. 2.

9. Walter D. Burnham, "Party System and the Political Process," in *The American Party*

System, William N. Chambers and Walter D. Burnham, eds. 2nd ed. (New York: Oxford University Press, 1975), p. 277.

10. G. William Domhoff, *The Powers That Be: Processes of Ruling Class Domination in America* (New York: Random House, 1979), p. 148.

11. The fullest description of this pluralistic model is found in the classic by David Riesman with Nathan Glazer and Reuel Denney, *The Lonely Crowd* (New Haven, Conn.: Yale University Press, 1951), pp. 213–217.

12. Karl Marx and Friedrich Engels, *The German Ideology* (New York: International Publishers, 1947), p. 39. For a review of other classical elitist theorists, see Marvin E. Olsen, "Elitist Theory as a Response to Marx," in *Power in Societies*, Marvin E. Olsen, ed. (New York: Macmillan, 1970), p. 106–113.

13. This model of the American power structure is described in G. William Domhoff, *The Higher Circles: The Governing Class in America* (New York: Random House (Vintage Books), 1971), Chap. 8. Three ultraconservative books provide the bases for Domhoff's description: Dan Smoot, *The Invisible Government* (Dallas: Dan Smoot Report, 1962); Phyllis Schlafly, *A Choice Not an Echo* (Alton, Ill.: Pere Marquette Press, 1964); and William S. McBirnie, *Who Really Rules America: A Study of the Power Elite* (Glendale, Calif.: Center for American Research and Education, 1968).

14. Associated Press story in the *Christian Science Monitor*, April 1, 1961.

15. The model described here was first put forth in the classic book by C. Wright Mills, *The Power Elite* (New York: Oxford University Press, 1956). It contains the first assertion of the existence and threat of a military-industrial complex in the United States.

16. The following is taken from C. Wright Mills, "The Power Elite," in *Reader in Political Sociology*, Frank Lindenfeld, ed. (New York: Funk & Wagnalls, 1968), pp. 263–276.

17. Ibid., p. 267.

18. Mills, *The Power Elite*, p. 11. See also G. William Domhoff, "How Fat Cats Keep in Touch," *Psychology Today* 9 (August, 1975), pp. 44–48.

19. Mills, *The Power Elite*, Chap. 10, gives the evidence up to 1954. More recent evidence is found in G. William Domhoff, *Who Rules America?* (Englewood Cliffs, N.J.: Prentice-Hall, 1967), Chap. 4.

20. "Businesses That Gain Most in Defense Boom," *U.S. News & World Report* (March 23, 1981), p. 43.

21. *U.S. News & World Report* (April 4, 1983), p. 46.

22. William Proxmire, *America's Military-Industrial Complex* (New York: Praeger, 1970).

23. *U.S. News & World Report* (April 4, 1983), p. 46.

24. Michael Parenti, *Power and the Powerless* (New York: St. Martin's, 1978), p. 86.

25. Although this policy for ever increased military budgets is very popular, some observers have raised serious questions. See Emma Rothschild, "Boom and Bust," *New York Review of Books* (April 3, 1980), pp. 31–33; *The Progressive* 44 (July, 1980), entire issue.

26. The following account is taken largely from Richard F. Kaufman, "The Military-Industrial Complex," in *Crisis in American Institutions*, Jerome H. Skolnick and Elliott Currie, eds. (Boston: Little, Brown, 1970), pp. 178–192. See also Paul Lewis, "All Systems Are Go for the Arms Makers," *The New York Times* (May 23, 1976), Sec. 3, pp. 1, 4; "The New Face of the Defense Industry," *Business Week* (January 10, 1977), pp. 52–58; and "A 'Cheerful' Military-Industrial Complex," *The Washington Spectator* (July 15, 1976), pp. 1–3.

27. Jack Anderson, "Weapons Makers and Pentagon Brass Are Happy Family," *Rocky Mountain News* (February 1, 1976), p. 51.

28. The discussion below is taken from Domhoff's books: *Who Rules America?* and *The Higher Circles: The Governing Class in America*.

29. See Chapter 5 of Domhoff's *The Higher Circles* for "how the power elite makes foreign policy," and Chapter 6 for "how the power elite shapes social legislation." Both of these chapters are persuasive in showing empirically the power of the upper class in the making of key decisions.

30. See Michael Parenti, "The Left," *The Progressive* 46 (October 1982), pp. 23–26.

31. Domhoff, *The Higher Circles*, Chapter 6.

32. See Parenti, *Power and the Powerless;* and Parenti, *Democracy for the Few*, 4th ed. (New York: St. Martin's, 1983).

33. See John C. Leggett, "The Political Institution," in Larry T. Reynolds and James M. Henslin, *American Society: A Critical Analysis* (New York: David McKay, 1973), pp. 66–108; and Parenti, *Power and the Powerless.*

34. This position is supported by the arguments and the empirical evidence found in: Thomas R. Dye, *Who's Running America? Institutional Leadership in the United States* (Englewood Cliffs, N.J.: Prentice-Hall, 1976); Adolph A. Berle, Jr. and Gardiner C. Means, *The Modern Corporation and Private Property*, rev. ed. (New York: Harcourt, Brace and World, 1968); Paul A. Baran and Paul M. Sweezy, *Monopoly Capital: An Essay on the American Economic and Social Order* (New York: Monthly Review Press, 1968); and C. Wright Mills, *The Power Elite* (New York: Oxford University Press, 1959).

35. Dye, *Who's Running America?*, pp. 5–8.

36. Parenti, *Power and the Powerless*, p. 41.

37. Ibid., p. 84.

38. Ibid., p. 201.

39. The following is taken largely from Parenti, *Democracy for the Few*, pp. 60–75. See also, Alan Wolfe, *The Seamy Side of Democracy*, 2nd ed. (New York: Longman, 1978), pp. 21–50.

40. Ibid., p. 78. See also, Matthew Josephson, *The Politicos, 1865–1896* (New York: Harcourt, Brace, 1938).

41. Parenti, *Democracy for the Few*, p. 80.

42. See Samuel P. Huntington, "The Marasmus of the ICC," *Bureaucratic Power in National Politics*, Francis Rourke, ed. (Boston: Little, Brown, 1965), pp. 73–86.

43. Ibid., p. 67.

44. See Patrick Renshaw, *The Wobblies* (Garden City, N.Y.: Doubleday, 1968), p. 24. See also, Parenti, *Democracy for the Few*, p. 81.

45. Ibid., p. 85.

46. Frances Fox Piven and Richard A. Cloward, *Regulating the Poor* (New York: Pantheon, 1971).

47. For arguments on both sides of the corporate bail-out issue, see "Should Taxpayers Bail Out Chrysler?" *U.S. News & World Report* (November 26, 1979), pp. 99–100; and Michael Schwartz and Glenn Yago, "What's Good for Chrysler Is Bad for Us," *The Nation* (September 12, 1981), pp. 200–203.

48. Morton C. Paulson, "What Is Business Afraid Of?" *National Observer* (October 5, 1974), p. 14.

49. Bradford Snell, "GM and the Nazis," *Ramparts* (June 1974), pp. 14–16; Thomas Di Baggio, "The Unholy Alliance," *Penthouse* (May 1976): 74–91; and Joseph Borkin, *The Crime and Punishment of I. G. Farben* (New York: Free Press, 1978).

50. Parenti, *Democracy for the Few*, p. 92.

51. Ibid., p. 79. See also James Ridgeway, *The Politics of Ecology* (New York: Dutton, 1970), and Barry Weisberg, "Ecology of Oil: Raping Alaska," *Eco-Catastrophe* (San Francisco: Canfield, 1970), pp. 107–109.

52. Associated Press release, September 13, 1979.

53. Quoted in "Alternatives for American Growth," *Public Opinion* 2 (August/September 1979): 12–13.

54. Philip Stern, "How AT&T Got $3 Billion in Tax Welfare," *Des Moines Register* (March 29, 1982), p. 7A.

55. *U.S. News & World Report* (March 21, 1983), p. 75.

56. Hutchins, "Is Democracy Possible?," p. 4.

57. Anthony Sampson, *The Arms Bazaar: From Lebanon to Lockheed* (New York: Viking, 1977).

58. See Anthony Sampson, *The Sovereign State of ITT* (Greenwich, Conn.: Fawcett, 1974).

59. Hutchens, "Is Democracy Possible?," p. 4.

60. See Peter Ognibene, "The Politics of the Draft," *Saturday Review* (June 23, 1979), p. 12.

61. See Maurice Zeitlin, Kenneth G. Lutterman, and James W. Russell, "Death in Vietnam: Class, Poverty, and the Risks of War," *American Society, Inc.*, 2nd ed., Maurice Zeitlin, ed. (Chicago: Rand McNally, 1977), pp. 143–155; and Lawrence M. Baskier and William A. Strauss, *The Draft, The War, and the Vietnam Generation* (New York: Knopf, 1978).

62. See Herbert J. Gans, "The Uses of Power:

The Poor Pay All," *Social Policy* 2 (July-
August, 1971), pp. 20–24.

63. Michael Harrington, "Social Retreat and
Economic Stagnation," *Dissent* 26 (Spring,
1979), pp. 131–134.

64. Robert Lekachman, "The Specter of Full
Employment," in Jerome H. Skolnick and
Elliot Currie, eds., *Crisis in American Institutions*, 4th ed. (Boston: Little, Brown,
1979), pp. 50–58.

Epilogue

Any analyst of American society has the option of emphasizing either the social system as a smoothly functioning unit or the disunity and lack of harmony within it. American society for the most part does work rather smoothly. If we examine the whole of history, we must conclude that the system has improved in many respects. But this society has severe problems—the persistence of poverty, racial discrimination, injustice, violence, and the intransigence of the institutions to change, to name but a few. We must recognize that American society has many paradoxical dichotomies—unity and disunity, affluence and poverty, freedom and oppression, stability and change.

The topics selected for this book, the order in which they were presented, and the emphases have tended to focus on the problems, faults, and weaknesses of American society. This strategy was employed because these aspects of society are often minimized, but more important, because the society needs reform. Since institutions are made by people, they can be changed by people. As long as there are problems, we cannot be content with the status quo. A full understanding of the complex nature of society must, however, precede the implementation of social change. That has been one goal of this book.

The primary purpose of any sociology book is to make the reader more perceptive and more analytical regarding social life. I hope that you have gained new perspectives and new insights about our society from the reading and thinking required for analyzing American society. I hope that you will build upon this knowledge in a lifelong quest to understand better this complex system called American society and to work for its improvement.

Glossary

Accommodation. Acceptance of one's position in a situation without struggle.

Achieved status. A position in a social organization attained through personal effort.

Ageism. Discrimination against the elderly.

Aggregate. A collection of individuals who happen to be at the same place at the same time.

Alienation. An individual's feeling of separation from the surrounding society.

Altruistic suicide. The sacrificing of one's life for the good of the group.

Androgyny. Having the characteristics of both males and females.

Anomie. Durkheim's term that indicates a social condition characterized by the absence of norms or conflicting norms. At the individual level, the person is not sure what the norms are, which leads to a relatively high probability of suicide.

Anticipatory socialization. Learning and acting out the beliefs, norms, and values of a group before joining it.

Argot. The specialized or secret language peculiar to a group.

Ascribed status. Social position based on such factors as age, race, and family over which the individual has no control.

Assimilation. The process by which individuals or groups voluntarily or involuntarily adopt the culture of another group, losing their original identity.

Baby Boom. A term referring to a 15-year-period in American history following World War II when an extraordinary number of babies were born.

Blaming the victim. The belief that some individuals are poor, criminals, or school dropouts because they have a flaw within them.

Bourgeoisie. Marx's term for the class of persons that own the means of production in a capitalist society.

Bureaucracy. A system of administration that is characterized by specialized roles, explicit rules, and a hierarchy of authority.

Bureaucratization. The trend toward greater use of the bureaucratic mode of organization administration within society.

Capitalism. The economic system based on private ownership of property, guided by the seeking of maximum profits.

Capitalist Patriarchy. A condition of capitalism where male supremacy keeps women in subordinate roles at work and in the home.

Case study. The research strategy that involves the detailed and thorough analysis of a single event, community, or organization.

Caste system. The closed system of social stratification. Membership is fixed at birth and is permanent.

Caveat emptor. The Latin phrase that means "let the buyer beware."

Charisma. The extraordinary attributes of an individual that enable the possessor to lead and inspire without the legal authority to do so.

Church. The highly organized, bureaucratic form of religious organization that accommodates itself to the larger society.

Civil religion. The set of religious beliefs, rituals, and symbols outside the church that legitimates the status quo.

Class consciousness. Karl Marx's term that refers to the recognition by persons in a similar economic situation of a common interest.

Class segregation. Barriers that restrict social interaction to the members of a particular social class.

Cloning. The artificial production of genetically identical offspring.

Cohabitation. The practice of living together as a couple without being married.

Commune. A small, voluntary community characterized by cooperation and a common ideology.

Conflict perspective. A view of society that posits conflict as a normal feature of social life, influencing the distribution of power and the direction and magnitude of social change.

Consensus. Widely held agreement on the norms and values of society.

Conspicuous consumption. The purchase and obvious display of material goods to impress others with one's wealth and assumed status.

Constraint. The state of being controlled by some force.

Contraculture. A culturally homogeneous group that has developed values and norms that differ from the larger society because the group opposes the larger society.

Control group. A group of subjects in an experiment who are not exposed to the independent variable but are similar in all other respects to the group exposed to the independent variable.

Correlation. The degree of relationship between two variables.

Counterculture. A subculture that fundamentally opposes the dominant culture.

Crime. An act that is prohibited by the law.

Cultural deprivation. An ethnocentric term implying that the culture of another group is not only deficient but also inferior.

Cultural relativity. Customs of another society must be viewed and evaluated by their standards, not by an outsider's.

Cultural tyranny. The socialization process forces narrow behavioral and attitudinal traits on persons.

Culture. The knowledge that the members of a social organization share.

Culture of poverty. The view that the poor are qualitatively different in values and life styles from the rest of society and that these cultural differences explain continued poverty.

Deferred gratification. The willingness to sacrifice in the present for expected future rewards.

Deflation. The part of the economic cycle when the amount of money in circulation is down, resulting in low prices and unemployment.

Deindustrialization. The widespread, systematic diversion of capital (finance, plant, and equipment) from productive investment in the nation's basic industries into unproductive speculation, mergers, acquisitions, and foreign investment.

Democracy. The form of government where the citizens participate in government, characterized by competition for office, public officials being responsive to public opinion, and the citizenry having access to reliable information upon which to make their electoral choices.

Demography. The scientific study of the size, composition, and changes in human populations.

Dependent variable. A variable that is influenced by the effect of another variable (the independent variable).

Deprogramming. The process where persons believed to be "brainwashed" by cults are abducted and retrained against their will.

Derogation. Discrimination in the form of words that put a minority "down."

Deviance. Behavior that violates the expectations of society.

Differential association. The theory that a person becomes deviant because of an excess of definitions favorable to the violation of societal expectations over definitions supporting the norms and values.

Direct social control. Direct intervention by the agents of society to control the behavior of individuals and groups.

Discrimination. To act toward a person or group with partiality, typically because they belong to a minority.

Division of labor. The specialization of economic roles resulting in an interdependent and efficient system.

Dual career marriage. A marriage in which a husband and wife both are employed outside the home.

Dysfunction. A consequence that is disruptive for the stability and cohesion of the social organization.

Economy. The institution that ensures the maintenance of society by producing and distributing the necessary goods and services.

Ego. According to Freud, the conscious, rational part of the self.

Egoistic suicide. Persons lacking ties to social groups are, Durkheim found, more susceptible to suicide than those with strong group attachments.

Elitist view of power. The assumption that power is concentrated in a few rather than dispersed (the pluralist view).

Epistemology. The philosophical position that all reality is socially constructed.

Ethnic group. A social group with a common culture distinct from the culture of the majority because of race, religion, or national origin.

Ethnocentrism. The universal tendency to deprecate the ways of persons from other societies as wrong, old-fashioned, or immoral and to think of the ways of one's own group as superior (as the only right way).

Ethnomethodology. The subdiscipline in sociology that studies the everyday living practices of people to discover the underlying bases for social behavior.

Eugenics. The attempt to improve the human race through the control of hereditary factors.

Experimental group. A group of subjects in an experiment who are exposed to the independent variable, in contrast to the control group, which is not.

False consciousness. In Marxian theory, the idea that the oppressed may hold beliefs damaging to their interests.

Family. A particular societal arrangement whereby persons related by ancestry, marriage, or adoption live together, form an economic unit, and raise children.

Feminization of poverty. This refers to the rapid rise of female headed households living in poverty.

Feral children. Children reputedly raised by animals, who have the characteristics of their peers (animals) rather than human beings.

Fertility. The frequency of actual births in a population.

Folkways. Relatively unimportant rules that if violated are not severely punished.

Function. Any consequence of a social arrangement that contributes to the overall stability of the system.

Functional integration. Unity among divergent elements of society resulting from a specialized division of labor.

Functionalism (the order perspective). The theoretical perspective that emphasizes the order, harmony, and stability of social systems.

Gender. Refers to the cultural and social definition of feminine and masculine. Differs from sex, which is the biological fact of femaleness or maleness.

Generalized other. Mead's concept that refers to the internalization of the expectations of the society.

Genetic engineering. The scientific effort to manipulate DNA molecules in plants and animals.

Glossolalia. The emotional religious experience involving the incoherent "speaking in tongues."

Group. A collection of people (two or more) who, because of sustained interaction, have evolved a common culture.

Hedonism. The pursuit of pleasure and self-indulgence.

Hidden curriculum. That part of the school experience that has nothing to do with formal subjects but refers to the behaviors that schools expect of children (obedience to authority, remaining quiet and orderly, etc.).

Hierarchy. The arrangement of people or objects in order of importance.

Horizontal mobility. Change in occupations or other situations without moving from one social class to another.

Household. A residential unit of unrelated individuals who pool resources and perform common tasks of production and consumption.

Id. Freud's term for the collection of urges and drives persons have for pleasure and aggression.

Ideal type. An abstraction constructed to show how some phenomenon would be characterized in its pure form.

Ideological social control. The efforts by social organizations to control members by controlling their minds. Societies accomplish this, typically, through the socialization process.

Ideology. The shared beliefs about the physical, social, or metaphysical world.

Independent variable. A variable that affects another variable (the dependent variable).

Inflation. The situation when too much money purchases too few goods, resulting in rising prices.

Institution. Social arrangements that channel behavior in presented ways in the important areas of societal life.

Institutional derogation. This occurs when the normal arrangements of society act to reinforce the negative stereotypes of minority groups.

Institutional discrimination. When the social arrangements and accepted ways of doing things in society disadvantage minority groups.

Institutional racism. When the social arrangements and accepted ways of doing things in society disadvantage a racial group.

Institutional sexism. When the social arrangements and accepted ways of doing things in society disadvantage females.

Institutional violence. When the normal workings of the society do harm to a social category.

Interest group. A group of like-minded persons who organize to influence public policy.

Intergenerational mobility. The difference in social class position between a son and his father.

Internalization. In the process of socialization society's demands become part of the individual, acting to control his or her behavior.

Intragenerational mobility. The movement by an individual from one social class to another.

Labeling theory (societal reactions). The explanation of deviant behavior that stresses the importance of the society in defining what is illegal and in assigning a deviant status to particular individuals, which in turn dominates their identities and behaviors.

Latent function. An unintended consequence of a social arrangement or social action.

Life chances. Weber's term that refers to the chances throughout one's life cycle to live and experience the good things in life.

Looking-glass self. Cooley's concept that refers to the importance of how others influence the way we see ourselves.

Machismo (macho). An exaggerated masculinity, evidenced by male dominance, posturing, physical daring, and an exploitative attitude toward women.

Macro level. The large-scale structures and processes of society, including the institutions and the system of stratification.

Majority group. The social category in society holding superordinate power and who successfully impose their will on less-powerful groups (minority groups).

Male chauvinism. Exaggerated beliefs about the superiority of the male and the resulting discrimination.

Manifest function. An intended consequence of a social arrangement or social action.

Marginality. The condition resulting from taking part in two distinct ways of life without belonging fully to either.

Material technology. Refers to the technical knowledge needed to use and make things.

Matriarchal family. A family structure in which the mother is dominant.

Meritocracy. A system of stratification in which rank is based purely on achievement.

Micro level. The social organization and processes of small-scale social groups.

Military-industrial complex. The term that refers to the direct and indirect relationships between the military establishment (the Pentagon) and corporations.

Minority. A social category composed of persons that differ from the majority, are relatively powerless, and are the objects of discrimination.

Modal personality type. A distinct type of personality considered to be characteristic of the members of a particular society.

Model. The mental image a scientist has of the structure of society. This influences what the scientists look for, what they see, and how phenomena are explained.

Monogamy. The form of marriage in which an individual may not be married to more than one person at a time.

Monopolistic capitalism. The form of capitalism prevalent in the contemporary United States, where a few large corporations control the key industries, destroying competition and the market mechanisms that would ordinarily keep prices low and help consumers.

Monopoly. When a single firm dominates an industry.

Mores. Important norms, the violation of which results in severe punishment.

Mortality rate. The frequency of actual deaths in a population.

Multinational corporation. A corporation that operates in more than one country.

Myth of peaceful progress. The incorrect belief that throughout American history disadvantaged groups have gained their share of power, prosperity, and respectability without violence.

Nominalist. A philosophical position that a group is nothing more than the sum of its parts.

Nomos. Literally, meaningful order. The opposite of anomie.

Norm. This part of culture refers to rules that specify appropriate and inappropriate behavior (in other words, the shared expectations for behavior).

Nuclear family. A kinship unit composed of husband, wife, and children.

Nuptiality. The proportion of married persons.

Ontology. The philosophical position that accepts the reality of things because their nature cannot be denied.

Order model. The conception of society as a social system characterized by cohesion, consensus, cooperation, reciprocity, stability, and persistence.

Paradigm. The basic assumptions a scientist has of the structure of society (see **Model**).

Participatory socialization. The mode of socialization in which parents encourage their children to explore, experiment, and question.

Patriarchal family. A family structure in which the father is dominant.

Peer group. Friends usually of the same age and socioeconomic status.

Peter Principle. The view that most people in an organization will be promoted until they eventually reach their level of incompetence.

Pluralism. A situation in which different groups live in mutual respect but retain their racial, religious, or ethnic identities.

Pluralist view of power. The diffuse distribution of power among various groups and interests.

Polity. The societal institution especially concerned with maintaining order.

Population implosion. The trend for people to live in ever-denser localities (the movement of people from rural areas to the urban regions).

Poverty. A standard of living below the minimum needed for the maintenance of adequate diet, health, and shelter.

Power. The ability of A to get B to do its wishes whether B agrees to or not.

Power elite. Mills' term for the coalition of the top echelon of military, executive branch of the federal government, and business.

Prestige. The respect of an individual or social category as a result of their social status.

Primary deviance. The original illegal act preceding the successful application of the "deviant" label.

Primary group. A small group characterized by intimate, face-to-face interaction.

Progressive tax. A tax rate that escalates with the amount of income.

Proletariat. Marx's term for the industrial workers in a capitalistic society.

Protestant ethic (Puritan work ethic). The religious beliefs, traced back to Martin Luther and John Calvin, which emphasize hard work and continual striving in order to prove that one is "saved" by material success.

Psychosurgery. A form of brain surgery used to change the behavior of the patient.

Pygmalion effect. Students placed in a track are treated by teachers in a way which ensures that the prophecy is fulfilled.

Racial group. A group socially defined on the basis of a presumed common genetic heritage resulting in distinguishing physical characteristics.

Racism. The domination and discrimination of one racial group by the majority.

Radical nonintervention. Schur's term referring to the strategy of leaving juvenile delinquents alone as much as possible rather than processing (and labeling) them through the criminal justice system.

Random sample. The selection of a subset from a population so that every person has an equal chance of being selected.

Realist. The philosophical position that a group is more than the sum of its parts (referring to the emergence of culture and mechanisms of social control that affect the behavior of members regardless of their personalities).

Recidivism. Reinvolvement in crime.

Reference group. A group to which one would like to belong and toward which one therefore orients his or her behavior.

Reform movement. A social movement that seeks to alter a specific part of society.

Regressive tax. A tax rate that remains the same for all persons, rich or poor. The result is that poor persons pay a larger proportion of their wealth than affluent persons.

Reliability. The degree to which a study yields the same results when repeated.

Religion. The social institution that encompasses beliefs and practices regarding the sacred.

Repressive socialization. The mode of socialization in which parents demand rigid conformity in their children, enforced by physical punishment.

Resistance movement. The organized attempt to reinforce the traditional system by preventing change.

Revolutionary movement. The collective attempt to bring about a radical transformation of society.

Rites of passage. The ritual whereby the society recognizes the adult status of a young member.

Role. The behavioral expectations and requirements attached to a position in a social organization.

Role performance (role behavior). The actual behavior of persons occupying particular positions in a social organization.

Routinization of charisma. The process by which an organization attempts to transmit the special attributes of the former leader to a new one. This is done by various means, for example, "laying on of hands" and the old leader choosing a successor.

Sacred. That which inspires awe because of its supernatural qualities.

Secondary deviance. Deviant behavior that is a consequence of the successful application of the deviant label.

Secondary group. A large, impersonal, and formally organized group.

Sect. A religious organization, in contrast to a church, that tends to be dogmatic, fundamentalistic, and in opposition to "the world."

Secular. Of or pertaining to the world; the opposite of sacred.

Segmented labor market. The capitalist economy is divided into two distinct sectors, one where production and working conditions are relatively stable and secure; the other is composed of marginal firms where working conditions, wages, and job security are low.

Segregation. The separation of one group from another.

Self-esteem. The opinion of oneself.

Self-fulfilling prophecy. An event that occurs because it was predicted. The prophecy is confirmed because people alter their behavior to conform with the prediction.

Sexism. The individual actions and institutional arrangements that discriminate against women.

Sex role. The learned patterns of behavior expected of males and females by society.

Sexual stratification. A hierarchal arrangement based on gender.

Shared monopoly. When four or fewer companies control 50 percent or more of an industry.

Sibling. A brother or sister.

Significant others. Mead's term referring to those persons most important in the determining of a child's behavior.

Social class. A number of persons who occupy the same relative economic rank in the stratification system.

Social control. The regulation of human behavior in any social group.

Social Darwinism. The belief that the principle of the "survival of the fittest" applies to human societies, especially the system of stratification.

Social differentiation. The process of categorizing persons by some personal attribute.

Social inequality. The ranking of persons by wealth, family background, race, ethnicity, or sex.

Social interaction. When individuals act toward or respond to each other.

Social technology. The knowledge necessary to establish, maintain, and operate the technical aspects of social organization.

Socialism. The economic system where the means of production are owned by the people for their collective benefit.

Socialization. The process of learning the culture.

Socialization agents. Those individuals, groups, and institutions responsible for transmitting the culture of society to newcomers.

Social location. One's position in society based on family background, race, socioeconomic status, religion, and other relevant social characteristics.

Social mobility. The movement by an individual from one social class or status group to another.

Social movement. A collective attempt to promote or resist change.

Social organization. The order of a social group as evidenced by the positions, roles, norms, and other constraints that control behavior and ensure predictability.

Social problem. There are two types of social problems: (1) societally induced conditions that cause psychic and material suffering for any segment of the population; and (2) those acts and conditions that violate the norms and values of society.

Social relationship. When two or more persons engage in enduring social interaction.

Social stratification. When people are ranked in a hierarchy that differentiates them as superior or inferior.

Social structure. The patterned and recurrent relationships among people and parts in a social organization.

Social system. A differentiated group whose parts are interrelated in an orderly arrangement, bounded in geographical space or membership.

Society. The largest social organization to which individuals owe their allegiance. The entity is located geographically, has a common culture, and is relatively self-sufficient.

Socioeconomic status (SES). The measure of social status that takes into account several prestige factors, such as income, education, and occupation.

Sociology. The scholarly discipline concerned with the systematic study of social organizations.

Stagflation. The contemporary economic phenomenon that combines the problems of inflation and deflation—high prices, high unemployment, wage-price spiral, and a profits squeeze.

Status. A socially defined position in a social organization.

Status group. Persons of similar status. They view each other as social equals.

Status inconsistency. The situation in which a person ranks high on one status dimension and low on another.

Stereotype. An exaggerated generalization about some social category.

Stigma. A label of social disgrace.

Structured social inequality. This refers to the patterns of superiority and inferiority, the distribution of rewards, and the belief systems that reinforce the inequities of society.

Subculture. A relatively cohesive cultural system that varies in form and substance from the dominant culture.

Subsidy. Financial aid in the form of tax breaks or gifts granted by the government to an individual or commercial enterprise.

Suburb. A community adjacent to a city.

Superego. Freud's term that refers to the internalization of society's morals within the self.

Survey research. The research technique that selects a sample from a larger population in order to learn how they think, feel, or act.

Symbol. A thing that represents something else, such as a word, gesture, or physical object (cross, flag).

Synthesis. The blending of the parts into a new form.

Systemic imperatives. The economic and social constraints on the decision makers in an organization, which promote the status quo.

Technology. The application of science to meet the needs of society.

Theodicy. The religious legitimation for a situation that might otherwise cause guilt or anger (such as defeat in a war or the existence of poverty among affluence).

Tracking. A practice of schools of grouping children according to their scores on IQ and other tests.

Transcience. Toffler's term that refers to the rapid turnover in things, places, and people characteristic of a technological society.

Underemployment. Being employed at a job below one's level of training and expertise.

Undocumented immigrant. Immigrants who have entered the United States illegally.

Urbanism. The ways in which city life characteristically affect how people feel, think, and interact with one another.

Urbanization. The trend referring to the movement of people from rural to urban areas.

Urban region (AKA megalopolis, conurbation, strip city). The extensive urban area that results when two or more large cities grow together until they are contiguous.

Validity. The degree to which a scientific study measures what it attempts to measure.

Value neutrality. The attempt by scientists to be absolutely free of bias in their research.

Values. The shared criteria used in evaluating objects, ideas, acts, feelings, or events as to their relative desirability, merit, or correctness.

Variable. An attitude, behavior, or condition that can vary in magnitude from case to case (the opposite of a constant).

Voluntary association. Organizations that people join because they approve of their goals.

White flight. Whites leaving the central cities for the suburbs to avoid interaction with blacks, especially the busing of children.

Index

Abortion, 79, 373
Achieved characteristics, 237
Achieved status, 114, 237
Achievement, means to, 123–124
ACTION, 183
Adams, James, 185
Adolescents, 465–467
Advertising, 172–173
Aged:
  abuse of, 470
  central cities and, 83
  family and, 467–469
  isolation of, 469
  political power of, 83
  poverty and, 280
  retirement and, 468
  stereotypes of, 151, 467–469
  women, 469
Aggregate, 20
Agnew, Spiro, 169–170
Aid to Families with Dependent
  Children, 292, 385
Aimore tribe, 114
Altruistic suicide, 28–29
American society. See United
  States
American Sociological Associa-
  tion, 14
American values, 117–135
  behavior and, 126–131
  competition, 122–123
  individual freedom, 125–126
  material progress, 125
  means to achieve, 123–124
  progress, 124–125
  success, 121
  work, 120, 130
Amish, 26, 53, 166–167
Amman, Jacob, 166, 167
Anderson, Jack, 562–563
Anectine, 175
Annenberg, Walter H., 565
Anomic suicide, 29
Anthony, Susan B., 373
Antinuclear movement, 553–555
Antonovsky, Aaron, 263
Apomorphine, 175
Arabs, 176–177
Arapesh, 112
Asch, Solomon, 29–30

Ascribed characteristics, 237
Ascribed status, 114, 237
Asians, 54, 60
Automation, 416–417

Babbie, Earl R., 375
Baby boom, 89–93
  social mobility and, 259
Baker, James A., III, 565
Bakker, Jim, 531
Baldridge, Malcolm, 565
Balinese, 115
Banfield, Edward C., 203, 205,
  285–287, 322, 323
Bankruptcy, 423
Barnet, Richard, 409–410
Barnett, Rosalind, 463
Barrera, Mario, 316
Baruch, Grace, 463
Beach, Frank, 112
Bear, Robert, 26
Beauvoir, Simone de, 368
Becker, Howard S., 10–11
Behavior:
  explanations of, 11–13
  groups and, 31–32
  Type A, 103–104
  Type B, 104
  values and, 126–131
Bell, Daniel, 89
Benedict, Ruth, 156
Benokraitis, Nijole, 328
Berger, Peter L., 5, 7, 106, 145
Bernard, Jessie, 452
Berrigan, Philip, 555
Bias:
  minimizing, 14
  in sociology, 10–11
Bias theories, of discrimination,
  324–326
Bierstedt, Robert, 145
Big business. See Corporations
Biological deficiency theories:
  of deviance, 199–200
  of discrimination, 320–321
  of poverty, 282–285
Birth rate, 86
Blackballing, 250
Black Panthers, 183
Blacks, 313–315

busing of, 504–506
capital punishment and, 212
in cities, 83–84
Civil Rights Movement and, 94
crime and, 324–325
criminal justice system and,
  211–213
cultural deficiency theory and,
  323
discrimination and, 313–315
divorce among, 456
education of, 240, 335–337
employment, types of, 339, 341–
  342
family structure of, 321–322
health of, 342–343
income of, 333–335, 338
IQ tests and, 283
legal bias against, 219
in Los Angeles, 54, 55
political power of, 83
poverty of, 134, 279
prejudice and, 150–151
segregation of, 83, 499, 504–507
sport and, 4
subculture of, 134
supremacy of, 109
unemployment among, 337–
  339
violence and, 43–44, 59, 60
women, 380
Blaming-the-victim and deviance,
  48, 205–210
Blau, Peter M., 22, 77, 260
Blauner, Robert, 332
Blood, Robert O., 453–454
Bouvier, Leon F., 90–91
Bowles, Samuel, 262, 494–495,
  509
Boyd, Malcolm, 535–536
Bradley, Tom, 55
Brenner, Harvey, 425
Bridenthal, Renate, 439
Bronfenbrenner, Urie, 156
Bronowski, J., 114–115
Broom, Leonard, 526–527
Brown, George, 24
Brown, Harold, 556
Brown v. Board of Education, 94,
  504

Brownstein, Ronald, 565–566
Brzezinski, Zbigniew, 556
Buchwald, Art, 458–459
Bureaucracy:
    characteristics of, 75–77
    irrationality of, 75, 78
    power and, 76
    stability and, 75–77
Bureaucratization, 75
Bureau of Indian Affairs, 59, 319
Burns, Haywood, 219
Burt, Cyril, 283
Bush, George, 556, 565
Busing, 504–506

Calvin, John, 120–121
Capitalism, 403–404
    crisis of, 414–420
    family in, 444–445
    inequality and, 410–414
    monopolistic, 405–408
    poverty and, 288–289
    sex stratification and, 359–360
Capitalist patriarchy, 359–360,
    413–414
Caplan, Nathan, 208
Carmichael, Stokely, 44, 326
Carnegie Council on Children,
    260, 494
Carter, Jimmy, 556
Castro, Fidel, 94
Catholics, 53
    attitudes among, 522, 530–531,
    537
    suicide and, 28
    violence and, 59, 60
    See also Religion
Caveat emptor, 125–126
CBS Evening News, 149
Centers, Richard, 246–247, 248
Chambliss, William J., 211
Change, forces for and against,
    73–95
Charisma, 524
Chawkins, Steve, 517
Cherlin, Andrew, 438, 474
Cherokee Indians, 319
Chicanos, 315–317
    cultural deficiency theory and,
    322–323
    families, 444
    See also Hispanics
Children
    cost of raising, 423
    family and, 463–467
    feral, 142–143

poverty and, 280
sex roles and, 360–368
television and, 151, 170–171
welfare for, 297, 298–299
Chinese, 54
Chromosomes, 199, 201
Church, Frank, 185
Church(es):
    attendance, 527–528, 530
    attributes of, 522
    decline of, 529, 530–531
    sect vs., 524–525
    See also Religion
CIA, 183
Cities:
    crime in, 202
    racial transformation of, 83–84
Civil religion, 520–521
Civil Rights Movement, 94
Civil Service Reform Act of 1978,
    223
Civil War, 59
Class consciousness, 245–250,
    252–253
Class segregation, 245, 250
Clayton Act, 407
Cloning, 178, 186
Cloward, Richard A., 174, 575
Cohen, Albert K., 134–135
Colby, William, 183
Cole, Stephen, 215
Coleman, James, 467, 505
Coles, Robert, 278
Collins, Randall, 359
Colonial theory of discrimination,
    332–333
Colonists, revolutionary, 58–59
Commission on Population
    Growth and the American Fu-
    ture, 84, 86, 92
Competition, as American value,
    122–123
Conflict model, 46–47
    assumptions of, 47
    of deviance, 219–224
    education, 509
    family, 473
    poverty, 302
    power, 580
    religion, 520
    sex roles, 359–360
    social control, 181
    socialization, 158
    stratification, 238–239, 270
    synthesis with order, 49–65
    values, 135

Conservatism, political, 269
Conspicuous consumption, 243
Contraculture, 134–135
Control group, 14–15
Convictions, and groups, 30
Cooley, Charles H., 145–146, 148
Coors, Joseph, 565
Corporations, 405–410
    foreign policy and, 577
    monopolies, 405–408
    multinational, 408–410
    subsidies to, 575–577
Cousins, Norman, 505
Couvade, 111
Cox, Harvey, 515
Crime:
    in cities, 202
    functions of, 198
    juvenile, 267–268
    punishment of, 45, 211–214
    social class and, 204–205
    social control of, 175, 177–178
    white-collar, 266–267
    See also Deviance
Criminal justice, 211–213, 266–
    268
Cub Scouts, 122
Cults, 532–534
Cultural deficiency theories:
    of discrimination, 322–324
    of poverty, 285–287
Cultural deprivation, 206
Cultural relativity, 116–117
Culture, 21–22, 102–138
    characteristics of, 105–108
    as constraining force, 106–107
    defined, 20, 104–105
    diversity of, 131–135
    shifts in, 127–129
    of society, 33–34
Currie, Elliott, 37

Dahrendorf, Ralf, 46
Darrow, Clarence, 212
Dart, Justin W., 565
Data:
    collection problems of, 8–13
    sources of, 13–15
Davis, Kingsley, 143, 238
Davis, Ossie, 331
Death, causes of, 264
Death penalty, 212
Debt:
    national, 426
    personal, 423

Deficiency theories:
  of discrimination, 320–324
  of poverty, 282–287
Demerath, N. J., III, 526
Democracy, 546–551
Democratic socialism, 269
Demos, John, 442
Department of Health, Education
    and Welfare, 178
Dependent variable, 15
Depo-Provera, 179
Depressions, economic, 422–423,
    424–426
Desegregation, 504–507
Deviance, 194–231
  blaming the victim for, 205–210
  cultural transmission of, 202
  defined, 196–199
  drugs and, 175
  primary, 214
  psychiatry and, 175–177
  psychosurgery and, 177–178, 179
  secondary, 214
  social class and, 203–204
  societal goals and, 202–203
  urbanism and, 202
Deviance theories, 199–224
  biological, 199–200
  conflict, 219–224
  labeling, 210–218
  psychological, 200–201
  society as sources, 210–224
  sociological, 201–204
Dibble, Ursula, 471
Dickson, Paul, 78
Direct social control, 174–187
  defined, 174
  government and, 180–187
  medicine and, 174–180
  science and, 174–180
  welfare and, 174
Discrimination:
  basis theories of, 324–326
  deficiency theories of, 320–324
  education, 332, 335–337
  income, 333–335
  institutional, 327–329
  jobs, 337–342
  prejudice as cause of, 326
  reverse, 340–341
  structural theories of, 326–333
  themes of, 327–328
  See also Sex discrimination
Divorce, 455–459
Domhoff, G. William, 172, 173,
    251, 253, 555–556, 564–569

Donner, Frank, 187
Doyle, Jack, 203
Draft, and social status, 266
Drucker, Peter, 417, 508
Drugs:
  politics of, 220–221
  used for social control, 175, 187
Duncan, Otis Dudley, 260
Durkheim, Emile, 21, 27–28, 45,
    47, 198, 519–520
Dutton, Fred, 566
Dysfunctions, 65
Dyslexia, 200

Easterlin, Richard A., 259
Easton, Nina, 565–566
Eccles, Jacqueline S., 358
Economic cycles, 421–426
Economy, 401–434
  corporation-dominated, 405–410
  depression, 422–423, 424–426
  family and, 441, 442, 444–445,
    451
  inflation, 421–424
  planning, 427–428
  recession, 424–426
  as social institution, 36
  zero growth in, 428–429
Edison, Thomas, 200
Education, 482–513
  baby boom and, 92
  characteristics of, 484–491
  competitive nature of, 122, 488
  from conflict perspective, 509
  conformity, 165–166, 489–491
  control in, 489–491
  corporate society and, 491–493
  counseling, 368
  criminal justice and, 212–213
  differences, 239–240
  dogma, teaching of, 152, 491
  drop outs, 145, 200, 288, 488–
    489
  equal opportunity in, 502–509
  female role models in, 365–367
  functions of, 149
  ideological social control, 165–
    166
  inequality, 240, 493–502
  income and, 243, 494
  local control of, 487
  MACOS, 152–153
  mass, 486–487
  of minority groups, 332, 335–
    337
  from order perspective, 509

political preferences, 247
politics and, 485–486
purpose of, 152–153
sex roles, 363–368
social class and, 240, 268, 492–
    493
social mobility and, 260, 261–
    262
socioeconomic status and, 494–
    502
sport, 364–365
teacher expectations in, 500–502
textbook bias in, 393–394
tracking in, 268, 500–502
voting preferences and, 247
See also Schools
Education Amendments Act, 363
Egerton, John, 309
Ego, 148
Egoistic suicide, 28
Ehrenreich, Barbara, 413
Elitism. See Power elite
Employment:
  automation and, 416–417
  women and, 376–383
  See also Occupations
Enarson, Elaine, 368
Engels, Friedric, 359
Epistemology, 116
Epstein, Cynthia, 383
Equal Employment Opportunity
    Commission, 333
Equal Rights Amendment, 79, 353,
    375, 532
Erikson, Kai T., 198
Eskimos, 152
Ethnic groups, 53
  differences among, 312–313
  violence and, 60
  See also Minority groups
Ethnicity, 311
Ethnocentrism, 107–108
Ethnomethodology, 109
Etzioni, Amitai, 122–123
Eugenics, 178
Evangelicals, 531–532
Experimental group, 14–15
Experiments, 13–15

Fagot, Beverly, 362
False consciousness, 64–65, 238–
    239
Falwell, Jerry, 532
Family, 436–481
  aged in, 467–469

background and social class,
   251–255, 453, 465
black, 321–322
in capitalism, 444–445
children in, 463–467
composition of, 445–448
conflict model, 473
differences among, 155
division of labor in, 440, 441–
   442, 443, 452–463
divorce and, 455–459
economy and, 441, 442, 444–
   445
expectations about, 439
female-headed, 280, 385, 448
functions of, 372–373
future of, 474
history of, 441–444
household vs., 445
ideological social control and,
   165
income of, 449
instability of, 266
order model, 472–473
sex roles in, 383, 441–442, 443,
   452–463
single-parent, 437
size of, 87–88, 446–447
as socialization agent, 148–149,
   155
statuses, 113
stratification and, 448–451
structural transformation and,
   451
violence in, 469–472
Family-wage economy, 442
Farley, Reynolds, 335, 342
Farmers, and violence, 59
FBI, 182–186
Feagin, Joe R., 328
Federal Reserve Board, 426
Felony, 211
Feminism. See Women's
   movement
Feminization of poverty, 280,
   385
Feral children, 142–143
Festinger, Leon, 30
Folkways, 22, 110
Ford, Clellan, 112
Forensic psychiatrists, 175–177
Freedom, as American value, 125–
   126
Freud, Sigmund, 106, 147–148,
   200
Friday, Paul C., 212, 213

Friedman, Meyer, 104
Fries's Rebellion, 59
Functional integration, 62
Furstenburg, Frank, Jr., 438, 474

Gangs, 134–135
Gans, Herbert, 149, 291
Garfinkel, Harold, 109–110
Gay liberation, 25, 222–223
Gender, 354
   See also Sex roles
Generalized other, 146–147
Gene splicing, 71–72
Genetic engineering, 178–186
Gintis, Herbert, 262, 494–495
Gitlin, Todd, 173
Glantz, Oscar, 248
Glock, Charles Y., 522
Goffman, Erving, 370–371
Goldberg, Herb, 388
Goode, Erich, 528
Goode, William J., 454
Gorman, Benjamin L., 77
Gouldner, Alvin W., 9
Government:
   abuses by, 183–186
   direct social control and, 180–
     187
   ideological social control and,
     171
   reduced scope of, 429
   as source of change, 93–94
   as source of stability, 74
Graham, Billy, 535
Green, Mark S., 407
Greenberg, Benjamin, 173
Gross, Neal, 247–248
Group(s), 20–40
   change and, 77, 79
   control, 14–15
   defined, 26
   experimental, 14–15
   membership as source of order,
     63
   power of, 27–32
   primary, 26–27
   reference, 106
   secondary, 27
Group marriage, 35
Gutman, Herbert, 322, 444

Hacker, Andrew, 447
Hadden, Jeffrey K., 531
Haig, Alexander, 565
Halperin, Morton H., 185
Halvorsen, Jan, 402

Hamer, Fannie Lou, 307–309
Hamilton, Charles V., 44, 326
Hargreaves, David, 502
Harrington, Michael, 79, 287, 295,
   296, 300
Harris, Marvin, 116–117
Hartjen, Clayton A., 202, 216
Hartley, Shirley Foster, 88
Hatt, Paul K., 241
Hauser, Philip M., 263, 264
Hayakawa, S. I., 310–311
Hayden, F. Gregory, 115
Head Start, 497–498, 507
Health:
   groups and, 30–31
   low birth rate and, 88
   poverty and, 264–266, 282–285,
     288
   race and, 342–343
   sex and, 355
   status and, 264–266
Heilbroner, Robert, 427, 428–429
Henry, Jules, 484
Henslin, James M., 489, 539
Henslin, Linda K., 489
Herrnstein, Richard, 178, 283–285,
   320
Hirschi, Travis, 210
Hispanics, 315–317
   cultural deficiency theory and,
     322–323
   education of, 240, 335–337
   health of, 342–343
   income of, 333–335, 338
   in Los Angeles, 54, 55
   occupations of, 339, 341–342
   population in United States, 52–
     53
   poverty and, 280
   unemployment among, 337–339
Hollingshead, A. B., 244, 245,
   265–266, 268
Holmes, Oliver Wendell, 179
Homans, George, 21
Homestead Act of 1862, 94
Homosexuals. See Gay liberation
Hoover, J. Edgar, 182, 184
Hopi Indians, 114, 115, 154
Horizontal mobility, 258
Hormones, 355
Household, 455
   See also Family
Hutchens, Robert, 577
Hyde Amendment, 373

Id, 147, 200

Ideological social control, 164–174
  defined, 164
  family and, 165
  goals of, 164–165
  government and, 171
  media and, 170–171
  religion and, 166–168
  schools and, 165–166
  sport and, 168–170
Ideology:
  and change, 77
  as shared beliefs, 109
Ila, 196
Illegal immigrants, 316–317
Immigration:
  population growth and, 85
  problems in Los Angeles, 54–55
Income:
  education and, 243, 494
  extremes of, 235–236
  health and, 265
  male vs. female, 243, 378–380
  race and, 239, 333–335, 338
Independent variable, 15
India, 116–117
Indians. See Native Americans
Individualism, as American Value,
    125–126
Industrial Revolution, 414–415
Inflation, 421–424
Institutions, 35–37
  defined, 35
  dysfunctions of, 65
  reinforcement of sex roles by,
    369–376
  social control and, 162–193
  stability and, 73–75
Integrative forces, 61–65
Interest groups, 551–552
Intergenerational mobility, 258,
    260
Interlocking directorates, 407–408
Internalization, 106
Internal Revenue Service, 183,
    195, 196
Intragenerational mobility, 258
IQ tests, 88, 283–285
Isensee, Warren, 299

Jacobson, Lenore, 500–501
Japanese, 54, 60, 112–113
Jefferson, Thomas, 187
Jencks, Christopher, 262, 290, 495,
    509
Jensen, Arthur, 283–285, 320
Jews, 53, 60

Jim Crow laws, 108, 219, 314
Johnson, Michael P., 335
Jorgenson, Earle M., 565
Judeo-Christian ethic, 119–120
Justice, 211–213, 266–268

Kagan, Spencer, 156
Kanter, Rosabeth Moss, 382, 459
Kaufman, Richard F., 562
Keiser, Steve D., 489
Keller, Helen, 143
Kennedy, John F., 521
Kennedy, Robert, 184
Kephart, William M., 167
Kerbo, Harold, 237
Keyserling, Leon, 301
Kiesler, Sarah, 358
King, Martin Luther, Jr., 94, 179,
    184–185, 344
Kissing customs, 112–113
Kitagawa, Evelyn M., 263, 264
Kluckholn, Florence, 132
Knowles, Louis L., 327
Koreans, 54
Kwakiutl, 240

Labeling theory, 210–218
  consequences of, 214–216
  critique of, 210–214
  solutions for deviance, 216–218
Labor disputes, 60–61
Labor force:
  characteristics of, 416
  technology and, 416–417
  women in, 376–383
Labor market, segmented, 412–413
Ladner, Joyce, 363
Laissez-faire, 403
Language:
  male dominance and, 369
  social construction of reality
    and, 114–116
  socialization and, 143–144
Larson, Richard F., 77
Lasch, Christopher, 440
Lastrucci, Carlo L., 325
Latent consequences, 45, 124
Law, 181–182
  sex roles and, 373–375
Law and order, 130
Leff, Laurel, 55
Lekachman, Robert, 578
Lemert, Edwin M., 215
Lens, Sidney, 423
Lenski, Gerhard, 244–245
Leslie, Gerald R., 77

Lever, Janet, 363
Lewis, John, 308
Liazos, Alexander, 218
Liberalism, political, 269
Liebow, Elliot, 134, 285, 287
Life chances, 263
Life expectancy, 263–264
Lipset, S. M., 256
Lobbying, 545–546
Lombardi, Vince, 122
Looking-glass shelf, 145–146
Los Angeles, immigrants in, 54–55
Luther, Martin, 120, 121
Lynd, Helen, 129
Lynd, Robert, 129

McCaghy, Charles H., 217, 218
McGee, Reece, 6, 146, 203
Mack, John, 55
MACOS programs, 152–153
Male dominance, reinforcement of,
    369–376
  See also Sexism; Sex roles; Sex
    stratification
Mangaians, 112
Manifest consequences, 45, 124
Manifest destiny, 108
Marcel, Joe, 54
Marginality, 95
Marijuana, 196, 202–221
Marital status, 457
Marriage, 452–463
  divorce and, 455–459
  interracial, 95
  remarriage, 456–459
  sex roles in, 383, 452–455
  social class and, 453
  as social institution, 35
  violence in, 470–472
  work and, 459–463
Marshall, Donald S., 112
Martin, Carl, 54
Marx, Karl, 46, 47, 94, 171, 245–
    246, 248, 249, 250, 252, 253,
    359, 405, 422–423, 520, 552
Material technology, 109
Maya, 115
Mayer, Martin, 93
Mazta, David, 170
Mead, George Herbert, 146–147,
    148, 362
Mead, Margaret, 112, 357
Meals on Wheels, 292
Media:
  as ideological social control,
    170–171

reinforcement of sex roles by, 370–372
as socialization agent, 149–153
source of authority, 12
unifying functions of, 64
Medicaid, 291, 292, 385
Medicine, and social control, 174–180
Meidung, 166–167
Melanesia, 516
Mennonites, 26, 166
Mental health, 265–266
Mergers, corporate, 406–407
Merton, Robert, 202–203
Messenger, John C., 112
Methadone, 175
Mewshaw, Michael, 198
Mexican Americans. *See* Chicanos
Meyer, Marshall W., 77
Meyerhoff, Barbara, 439–440
Michels, Robert, 51
Migration:
    frost belt to sun belt, 84–85
    rural to urban, 82
    urban to suburban, 82–83
Military-industrial power elite, 560–564
Miller, Daniel R., 257
Miller, S. M., 460
Mills, C. Wright, 556–564, 567
Minority groups, 306–350
    American society and, 52–53
    bias theories of, 324–326
    categories of, 311
    characteristics of, 310–312
    criminal justice system and, 211–213
    deficiency theories of, 324–326
    education of, 332, 335–337
    health of, 342–343
    incomes of, 333–335
    jobs of, 339–342
    poverty and, 279
    structural discrimination theories of, 326–333
    unemployment rates for, 337–339
    violence and, 43–44, 59–60
    See also names of specific minority groups
Minor v. Happerset, 373
Mississippi Freedom Democratic Party, 308
Mitchell, John, 123
Modal personality type, 154
Model, 44

Mondale, Walter, 556
Monopolistic capitalism, 405–408
Moore, Joan, 331
Moore, Kristin A., 463
Moore, Wilbert E., 32, 238
Moral Majority, 532
Mores, 22, 110
Mormon Church, 529–530
Morrill Act of 1862, 94
Moynihan, Daniel, 321–322
Muller, Ronald, 409–410
Multinational corporations, 408–410
Murdock, George P., 356
Murray, Jim, 144
Myrdal, Gunnar, 324
Myth of peaceful progress, 57–58, 61

Nader, Ralph, 565–566
National Advisory Council on Economic Opportunity, 292
National Commission on Excellence in Education, 483–484
National Council of Churches, 372
National Council on Economic Opportunity, 411
National debt, 426
National Organization of Women, 389
National Origins Act, 313
National Science Foundation, 152
National Security Agency, 183
Native Americans, 317–319
    Alcatraz takeover by, 59
    Cherokees, 319
    Eskimos, 152
    Hopi, 114, 115, 154
    Kwakuitl, 240
    Navajo, 114, 144
    Passamaquoddy, 59
    Pawnee, 115
    Penobscot, 59, 318
    Plains, 154
    poverty of, 319–320
    Pueblo, 154
    Tepoztlan, 196
    at Wounded Knee, 59
    Zuñi, 154
Navajo Indians, 114, 144
NBC Nightly News, 149
Nelson, Linden L., 156
Nelson, Stephen D., 208
Neolithic Agriculture Revolution, 415
Neuroleptics, 175

New populism, 269
Newspapers, 64
    See also Media
Newsweek, 149
Nixon, Richard, 8, 122, 123, 184, 206, 549
Nominalists, 21
Nomos, 153
Norms, 22, 109–113
North, C. C., 241
Nouveaux riches, 255–256
Nuclear freeze, 553–555
Nuclear power, 71, 79

Observation, 15
Occupations:
    income from, 243
    of minority groups, 339–342
    ranking of, 241–242
    sex inequality and, 376–383
Oil dependence, 409, 422, 426–427
Olney, Richard, 574
Olsen, Marvin E., 21, 32
Olympic games, 168
Ontology, 116
OPEC, 409
Order model, 45–46
    American sociology, 47
    assumptions of, 47
    deviance, 224–225
    education, 509
    family, 472–473
    poverty, 302
    power, 580
    religion, 519–520
    sex roles, 357–358, 360
    social control, 181
    socialization, 158
    social problems and, 48
    social stratification, 238–239, 269–270
    synthesis with conflict model, 49–65
    values, 135
Organization for Economic Cooperation and Development, 81
Oriental Exclusion Act, 108

Parenti, Michael, 74, 149, 411, 486, 569–571, 573
Parks, Rosa, 94
Parole, 212
Parsons, Talcott, 358
Passamaquoddy Indians, 59
Patai, Raphael, 177

Patriarchy, 357
  capitalist, 359–360, 413–414
Peaceful progress, myth of, 57–58,
  61
Peck, Keenen, 173
Penobscot Indians, 59, 318
Perception, and groups, 29–30
Perrow, Charles, 76
Personality (self):
  modal type, 153–154
  as a social product, 145–148
Peter Principle, 76–77, 78
Petersen, David M., 212, 213
Peterson, Linda, 368
Piven, Frances Fox, 174, 575
Plains Indians, 154
Pleck, Joseph, 459
Pluralism, 546–555
Political Action Committees
  (PACs), 549
Political ideologies, and inequal-
  ity, 269
Political parties, 55, 74–75
Political prisoners, 213
Polity, 36
Poor:
  in central cities, 83
  characteristics of, 279–280, 281
  death penalty and, 212
  eugenics and, 178
  societal arrangements and, 207
  urban, 286–287
  See also Poverty
Population, 81–93
  birth rate and, 86–93
  growth of, 81–82, 85–93
  mortality and, 86
  suburban, 82–83
  urban, 83–84
Poverty, 276–305
  abortion policies and, 373
  aged and, 280
  biological theories of, 282–285
  blacks and, 134, 279
  blame for, 286–287
  capitalism and, 288–289
  causes of, 282–292
  children of, 277–278, 280, 287–
    288, 298–299
  conflict model, 302
  costs of, 280–282
  cultural deficiency theories of,
    285–287
  culture of, 285–287
  divorce and, 266
  elimination of, 292–301

  extent of, 279–280
  feminization of, 280, 385
  functions of, 290–291
  health and, 264–266, 282–285,
    288
  Hispanics and, 280
  invisibility of, 279
  kinds of, 296–297
  order model and, 302
  social control and, 26, 178
  social movements and, 95
  structural theories of, 287–292
  traps, 278, 287–288, 296
  war on, 131, 287
Poverty line, 279
Power, 309, 544–586
  consequences of power struc-
    ture, 571–579
  defined, 570
  distribution of, 7, 55
  elitists models of, 555–571
  pluralist models of, 546–555
  violence and, 44
Power elite:
  Domhoff on, 555–556, 564–569
  Mills on, 556–564, 567
  Parenti on, 569–571
Prejudice:
  discrimination and, 325–326
  teaching of, 150–151
Prewitt, Kenneth, 327
Primary deviance, 214
Primary groups, 26–27
Prison(s):
  guards in, 25
  social control in, 175, 177–178
  study of, 10
Progress, as American value, 124–125
Prolixin, 175
Protest, forms of, 55
Protestants, 53
  differences among, 522
  suicide and, 28
  See also Religion
Protestant work ethic, 120
Provost, Caterina, 356
Proxmire, William, 561
Psychiatry, and social control, 175
Psychoanalytic view, 147–148
Psychological theories of deviance,
  200–201
Psychosurgery, 177–178, 179
Public service advertising (PSA),
  172–173
Pueblo Indians, 154
Punishment, consequences of, 45

Quinney, Richard, 181, 223–224

Race:
  American society and, 52–53
  in cities, 83–84
  defined, 311
  distribution, 52–53
  education and, 336, 338
  poverty and, 279
  See also Blacks; Minority groups
Racism, 309–310
  in English language, 330–331
  institutional, 44
  in sports, 4, 7
Radical nonintervention, 216–217
Random sample, 375
Reagan, Ronald, 172, 179, 289,
    291, 293, 294, 407, 497–498,
    562, 565–566
Reaganomics, 289, 291–292,
    497–498, 562
Realists, 21
Reality, social construction of,
    114–116
Recession, economic, 424–426
Recidivism rate, 213
Reference groups, 106
Reform movements, 94
Regan, Donald, 565
Regionalism, 51–52
Reliability, 14
Religion, 514–543
  in American society, 53, 56,
    520–539
  civil, 520–521
  conflict model, 520
  cults, 532–534
  defined, 516–518
  diversity of, 155–156, 521–522
  divisive force, 53, 518–519
  evangelicals in, 531–532
  functions of, 534–536
  fundamentalist, 8
  health and, 30–31
  ministers in, 23
  order model, 519–520
  organization of, 522–526
  political activism and, 532, 537–
    539
  reinforcement of sex roles by,
    372–373
  role of, 534–539
  snake handlers, 31
  social control and, 26, 166–168
  as socialization agent, 155–156
  societal stability and, 73

socioeconomic status and, 526–
529
suicide and, 28
trends in, 529–534
universality of, 45
Religious preferences, 56
Remarriage, 456–459
Representative democracy, 546–551
Research, 13–15
Resistance movement, 77
Retirement, 468
Retirement communities, 469
Reverse discrimination, 340–341
Revolutionary colonists, 58–59
Revolutionary movements, 94
Rivers, Carly, 463
Robots, 416
Rockefeller, David, 555, 556
Rockefeller, Jay, 550
Rockwell, George Lincoln, 55
Role(s):
    conflicts in definition of, 157
    defined, 23, 113
    of family members, 113
    power of, 24–25
    sex (see Sex roles)
    social, 22
    status and, 23–26, 113–114
    variations in performance of, 24
Roosevelt, Franklin D., 574
Roosevelt, Theodore, 574
Rosenman, Ray H., 104
Rosenthal, Robert, 500–501
Ross, Muriel, 367
Rubin, Lillian, 453
Rubington, Earl, 199
Ryan, Joanna, 284
Ryan, William, 205, 284, 295

Salvatori, Henry, 565
Sampling, 375
San Antonio Independent School
    District v. Rodriguez, 497
Sanders, Thomas G., 168
Sapir, Edward, 114
Sawhill, Isabell, 463
Schindler, Paul T., 203
Schools:
    control in, 489–491
    curriculum, 498–499
    desegregation of, 504–507
    differences among, 155
    failures in, 488–489
    finances, 496–498, 503–504
    ideological social control and,
        165–166

magnet, 506–507
politics and, 485–486
segregation in, 499
sexism in, 94, 368, 393
social class biases in, 492–493
as socialization agents, 149
socioeconomic status and, 494–
502
tracking in, 500–502
    See also Education
Schur, Edwin, 199, 216–217
Schwartzman, Andrew, 172
Science, and social control, 174–
180
Scientific reasoning, 324–325
Scott, W. Richard, 22
Seberg, Jean, 183
Secondary deviance, 214
Secondary groups, 27
Sect, 523–524
Segregation, in schools, 499, 504–
507
Sell, Ralph R., 335
Selznick, Philip, 526–527
Serrano v. Priest, 497
Sex discrimination:
    employment, 376–383
    income, 378–380
    law and, 373–375
Sexism:
    consequences of, 383–388
    defined, 354
    in schools, 94, 363–368
    in sport, 4, 364–365
Sex roles, 353–357
    children and, 360–368
    consequences of, 383–388
    in family, 383, 441–442, 443,
        452–463
    institutional reinforcement of,
        369–376
    language and, 370
    law and, 373–375
    learning of, 360–368
    male, 386–388
    media and, 151, 370–372
    physiology and, 354–355
    politics and, 376
    religion and, 372–373
    social bases for, 355–356
    stereotypes of, 369–376
Sex stratification, 353–397
    from conflict perspective, 359–360
    defined, 354
    income and, 378–380
    in occupations, 376–378

from order perspective, 357–
358, 360
Sexual behavior, control of, 176–
177
Shared monopolies, 406
Shaw, George Bernard, 329
Shays's Rebellion, 59
Sherif, Muzafer, 30
Significant others, 147
Silberman, Charles, 79–80, 489,
499
Singsen, Michael, 173
Skolnick, Arlene, 439, 464
Skolnick, Jerome H., 37, 43, 44,
329
Slater, Philip, 80, 131
Slaveholders, 59
Slums, 286
Smith, Adam, 427
Smith, Gerald L. K., 55
Smith, Lillian, 151
Smith, William French, 565, 566
Social change:
    forces against, 73–79
    forces for, 79–95
Social class, 34–35, 239–258
    in American society, 52
    cause of death and, 264
    child rearing patterns and, 257
    class consciousness and, 245–
        250, 252–253
    conflict, 245
    crime and, 203–205
    criteria for upper class, 253
    defined, 237
    divisiveness of, 52
    draft and, 266
    education and, 268, 492–493
    family instability and, 266
    health and, 264–266
    hierarchy of, 251–258
    justice and, 211–213, 266–268
    life chances and, 263
    life expectancy and, 263–264
    lower-lower, 258
    lower-middle, 257
    mental health and, 265–266
    methods to delineate, 244
    middle, 256–257
    occupational prestige and, 241–
        242
    political preferences of, 247, 256
    reality of, 244–250
    religion and, 526–529
    segregation and, 245, 250
    upper, 251–256

Social class (continued)
  upper-lower, 257
  upper-middle, 256
Social control, 25–26, 162–192
  direct, agents of, 174–187
  ideological, agents of, 164–174
  mechanisms of, 164
  power of groups, 27–32
  in traditional societies, 164,
    166–167
Social Darwinism, 282–283
Social determinism, 6
Social differentiation, 236
Social group. See Group
Social institutions. See Institutions
Social interaction, 20
Socialism, 404–405
Socialist Workers Party (SWP),
  185–186
Socialization, 140–160
  agents of, 148–153
  defined, 105, 142
  deviance and, 48
  in future, 156
  power of, 166
  prejudice and, 150–151
  sex roles and, 368
  social control, 164–174
Social mobility, 258–262
  baby boomers and, 259
  defined, 238, 258
  education and, 260, 261–262
  societal factors and, 258–259
  types of, 258
  vertical, 258, 260–261
Social movements:
  change and, 94–95
  defined, 77
Social order, 63
Social organization:
  conflict and, 49
  defined, 20
  process of, 20–22, 32
  See also Group
Social problems:
  American values as source of,
    119–126
  conflict perspective on, 48
  defined, 48
  institutions and, 36
  order perspective on, 48
  society as source of, 48
Social programs, 291–292
Social rank, 237
Social relationship, 20–21
Social roles, 22

Social Security, 93, 293
Social Security Administration
  (SSA), 279
Social stratification, 234–274
  conflict perspective and, 52, 56,
    238–239, 270
  consequences of, 263–268
  defined, 236–237
  family life and, 448–451
  order perspective and, 238–239,
    269–270
Social structure, 20–21, 104
Social systems, 33
  changes in, 73
  implications of, 49–50
  order and conflict in, 44–47
Social technology, 109
Society:
  as blame for poverty, 282, 287–
    288
  culture of, 33–34
  defined, 33
  divisive forces in, 50–57
  integrative forces in, 61–65
  paradoxes of, 40–50
  social structure of, 32–37
  as social system, 33
Sociological perspective:
  assumptions of, 4–7
  general, 3–8
  problems of, 7–8
Sociological theories of deviance,
  201–204
Sociology:
  defined, 20
  discipline of, 3–8, 20, 48
  methods of, 8–15
  radical, 47
Sommer, Barbara B., 375
Sommer, Robert, 375
Southern Christian Leadership
  Conference, 184
Sowell, Thomas, 323–324
Spencer, Herbert, 282–283
Spock, Benjamin, 465
Sport:
  deviance in, 123
  sexism in, 4, 364–365
  social control and, 168–170
Sproul, Lee, 358
Stability, forces for, 73–79
Stallard, Karin, 413
Stark, Rodney, 522
Status:
  achieved, 114, 237
  ascribed, 114, 237

  cause of death and, 264
  consequences of, 263–268
  defined, 22, 113, 237
  draft and, 266
  education and, 268
  family instability and, 266
  health and, 264–266
  justice and, 211–213, 266–268
  life expectancy and, 263–264
  political ideologies and, 269
  religion and, 526–529
  role and, 22–26
Status anguish, 95
Status group, 237
status inconsistency, 92, 95
Status withdrawal, 95
Steadman, Henry, 177
Stephens, William N., 466
Stereotypes:
  aged, 151, 467–469
  minorities, 107, 151, 310
  sex, 107, 151
Sterilization, 127, 178, 179
Stinchcombe, Arthur, 501
Stohr, Oscar, 141–142
Stratified sample, 375
Straus, Murray S., 471, 472
Strodtbeck, Fred L., 132
Structural theories:
  of discrimination, 332–333
  of poverty, 287–292
Subculture, 133–134
  deviance and, 203–204
Suburban population explosion,
  82–83
Success, as American value, 121
Suicide, 28–29
Sullivan, Anne, 143
Superego, 148, 200
Survey research, 13
Sutherland, Edwin H., 202
Swann, Charles E., 531
Swanson, Guy E., 257
Syfers, Judy, 455
Sykes, Gresham M., 79, 221
Symbols, 108–109
Systemic imperatives, 74, 570
Szymanski, Albert, 167–168

Tax(es):
  declining urban base of, 83, 84
  poor and, 291
  subsidies, 269, 297
Teachers, expectations of, 500–502
  See also Education; Schools

Technology, 71–72, 79–81
    employment and, 416–417
    material, 109
    social, 109
Telemetric control system, 177–178
Television:
    change and, 81
    children and, 151, 170–171
    sex roles and, 151
    social control and, 64, 170–171
Temiar people, 114
Tepoztlan Indians, 196
Textbooks, sexism in, 363–364
Theodicy, 525
Tiefer, Lenore, 113
Time, 149
Title IX, of Education Amendments Act, 363
Tiv, 115
Totem, 519
Tracking, in schools, 500–502
Treaty of Guadalupe Hidalgo, 315
Trilateral Commission, 555–556
Trobrianders, 115
Truman, Harry, 427
Tufte, Virginia, 439–440
Tuttle, Holmes P., 565
Type A behavior, 103–104
Type B behavior, 104

Underemployment, 92
Unemployment, 337–339, 419–420
Unions, 60–61
United States:
    economic and status differences in, 239–243
    ethnic groups in, 53
    integrative forces in, 61–65
    population growth in, 81–82, 85–93
    race in, 52–53
    regionalism in, 51–52
    size of, 51–52
    social classes in, 52, 244–258
    social mobility in, 258–262
    violence in, 57–61
Urbanization, 81–84, 202
Urban region, 84
U.S. Public Health Service, 264–265

Validity, 14

Value neutrality, 9–11
Values:
    American, 117–135
    behavior and, 126–131
    consensus on, 62
    defined, 22
    health and, 103–104
    observation of, 118
    as shared beliefs, 113
    sources of, 119–121
Vance, Cyrus, 556
Variables, 15
Vertical mobility, 258, 260–261
Veto groups, 551–552
Victim, blaming, 48, 205–210, 368
Vietnamese, 54
Vigilantism, 60
Violence:
    in American Society, 57–61
    defined, 43–44
    family, 469–472
    institutional, 44, 218
    minority groups and, 43–44, 59–60
    myth of peaceful progress and, 57–58, 61
    official, 44
    political nature of, 44
Von Hoffman, Nicholas, 534
Voting preferences, 247
Voting Rights Act of 1965, 333

Warriner, Charles, 21
WASP supremacists, 59–60
Watergate, 122–123
Watson, John B., 465
Wealth, concentration of, 410–411
Weber, Max, 525
Weinberg, Martin S., 199
Weinberger, Caspar, 556, 565
Weitzman, Lenore J., 362
Welch, Robert, 556
Welfare:
    mothers on, 248
    for needy children, 297, 298–299
    social control and, 174
Wellman, David, 325–326
Wheelis, Allen, 49
Whiskey Rebellion, 59
White-collar crime, 266–267
"White flight," 83
White man's burden, 108

Whorf, Benjamin, 114, 144
Whyte, William H., Jr., 129–130
Wicker, Tom, 207
Wilkins, Roger, 323–324
Williams, Robin M., Jr., 45, 118, 121
Wilson, Charles, 559
Wilson, Everett, 148–149
Wilson, William A., 565
Wilson, Woodrow, 200
Wolfe, Alan, 170
Wolfe, Donald, 453–454
Women:
    black, 380
    in education, 366–367
    education vs. income, 243
    as head of family, 280, 385, 448
    health of, 355
    income of, 243, 366–367, 378–380
    as minority, 311
    occupations of, 366–367, 376–383
    politics and, 376
    poverty and, 280
    role of in family, 441–442, 443, 452–463
    status of, 358, 374–375
    See also Sexism; Sex roles; Sex stratification
Women's movement, 25, 249, 388–389
Work, as American value, 120, 130
    See also Employment; Labor force; Occupations
Workplace, changes in, 128
Wrong, Dennis, 154

Yancos, 114
Yankelovich, Daniel, 129
Yinger, Milton, 133–134
Young, Andrew, 308
Yufe, Jack, 141

Zaretsky, Eli, 445
Zeitlin, Maurice, 410
Zero population growth (ZPG), 86–87
Zimbardo, Philip, 25
Zinn, Maxine Baca, 353, 437
Zuñi Indians, 154